WRONGFUL CONVICTIONS AND THE DNA REVOLUTION

For centuries, most people believed the criminal justice system worked – that only guilty defendants were convicted. DNA technology shattered that belief. DNA has now freed more than 300 innocent prisoners in the United States. This book examines the lessons learned from twenty-five years of DNA exonerations and identifies lingering challenges.

By studying the dataset of DNA exonerations, we know that precise factors lead to wrongful convictions. These include eyewitness misidentifications, false confessions, dishonest informants, poor defense lawyering, weak forensic evidence, and prosecutorial misconduct. In Part I, scholars discuss the efforts of the Innocence Movement over the past quarter-century to expose the phenomenon of wrongful convictions and to implement lasting reforms. In Part II, another set of researchers looks ahead and evaluates what still needs to be done to realize the ideal of a more accurate system.

Daniel S. Medwed's research revolves around the topic of wrongful convictions. His book, *Prosecution Complex: America's Race to Convict and Its Impact on the Innocent* (2012), explores how even well-meaning prosecutors may contribute to wrongful convictions because of cognitive biases and an overly deferential regime of legal and ethical rules. In 2013, he received the Robert D. Klein University Lectureship, which is awarded to a member of the faculty across Northeastern University who has obtained distinction in his or her field of study. He is also a Legal Analyst for WGBH News, Boston's local NPR and PBS affiliate.

Wrongful Convictions and the DNA Revolution

TWENTY-FIVE YEARS OF FREEING THE INNOCENT

DANIEL S. MEDWED

Northeastern University School of Law

CAMBRIDGE
UNIVERSITY PRESS

CAMBRIDGE
UNIVERSITY PRESS

University Printing House, Cambridge CB2 8BS, United Kingdom

One Liberty Plaza, 20th Floor, New York, NY 10006, USA

477 Williamstown Road, Port Melbourne, VIC 3207, Australia

4843/24, 2nd Floor, Ansari Road, Daryaganj, Delhi – 110002, India

79 Anson Road, #06–04/06, Singapore 079906

Cambridge University Press is part of the University of Cambridge.

It furthers the University's mission by disseminating knowledge in the pursuit of education, learning, and research at the highest international levels of excellence.

www.cambridge.org
Information on this title: www.cambridge.org/9781107129962
10.1017/9781316417119

© Cambridge University Press 2017

First published 2017

A catalogue record for this publication is available from the British Library.

Library of Congress Cataloging-in-Publication Data
NAMES: Medwed, Daniel S., editor.
TITLE: Wrongful convictions and the DNA revolution : twenty-five years of freeing the innocent /
edited by Daniel S. Medwed, Northeastern University School of Law.
DESCRIPTION: Cambrdige, United Kingdom ; New York, NY, USA : Cambridge
University Press, 2017.
IDENTIFIERS: LCCN 2016044945 | ISBN 9781107129962 (hardback)
SUBJECTS: LCSH: Judicial error–United States. | Criminal justice,
Administration of–United States. | DNA fingerprinting–Law and legislation–U nited States. |
BISAC: LAW / Criminal Law / General.
CLASSIFICATION: LCC KF9756 .W76 2017 | DDC 345.73/077–DC23 LC record available at
https://lccn.loc.gov/2016044945

ISBN 978-1-107-12996-2 Hardback

For my brilliant wife Sharissa Jones, and our two darling daughters, Clementine and Mili, who will always be actually innocent in my eyes

Daniel S. Medwed

Contents

Contributors

Adele Bernhard
Adjunct Professor of Law, New York Law School

Margaret Burnham
Professor of Law, Northeastern University School of Law; Founder, Civil Rights and Restorative Justice Project

Paul G. Cassell
Ronald N. Boyce Presidential Professor of Criminal Law, S.J. Quinney College of Law at the University of Utah

G. Ben Cohen
Of Counsel, Capital Appeals Project and The Promise of Justice Initiative

Keith A. Findley
Associate Professor, University of Wisconsin Law School, and Co-Director, Wisconsin Innocence Project

Brandon L. Garrett
Justice Thurgood Marshall Distinguished Professor of Law, University of Virginia School of Law

Mark Godsey
Daniel P. and Judith L. Carmichael Professor of Law and Director, Lois and Richard Rosenthal Institute for Justice/Ohio Innocence Project, University of Cincinnati College of Law

Stephanie Roberts Hartung
Teaching Professor, Northeastern University School of Law

Richard A. Leo
Hamill Family Professor of Law and Psychology, University of San Francisco

Erik Luna
Amelia D. Lewis Professor of Constitutional and Criminal Law, Arizona State University

Justin F. Marceau
Professor and Animal Legal Defense Fund Professor of Law, University of Denver Sturm College of Law

Jacqueline McMurtrie
Professor of Law, University of Washington School of Law; Founder, Innocence Project Northwest

Daniel S. Medwed
Professor of Law and Criminal Justice, Northeastern University School of Law

Michael Meltsner
Matthews Distinguished University Professor of Law Northeastern University School of Law

Alexandra Natapoff
Associate Dean for Research, Rains Senior Research Fellow & Professor of Law, Loyola Law School, Los Angeles

Michael L. Radelet
Professor, Department of Sociology and Institute of Behavioral Science, University of Colorado-Boulder

Zoë Robinson
Professor of Law, DePaul University College of Law

Robert J. Smith
Visiting Scholar, University of Texas School of Law and Senior Fellow, Charles Hamilton Houston Institute for Race and Justice, Harvard Law School

George C. Thomas III
Rutgers University Board of Governors Professor of Law and Judge Alexander P. Waugh, Sr. Distinguished Scholar

Sandra Guerra Thompson
Alumnae College Professor of Law and Director of the Criminal Justice Institute at the University of Houston Law Center

Rob Warden
Executive Director Emeritus, Center on Wrongful Convictions, Bluhm Legal Clinic, Northwestern University School of Law

Robert Wicoff
Chief, Appellate Division, Harris County Public Defender's Office (Houston, Texas)

Steven M. Wise
President, Nonhuman Rights Project, Inc.

Acknowledgments

This book has its origins in conversations that I had with Rashmi Dyal Chand, my friend and colleague at Northeastern University School of Law. Several years ago, in her role as research director for our faculty, Rashmi encouraged me to organize a conference on a topic related to my scholarship. With gentle prodding from Rashmi, my idea for the topic took shape, and the concept of turning the conference papers into a book emerged. For that reason, among others, I am in Rashmi's debt. My dean, Jeremy Paul, deserves credit too. I feel fortunate to have a dean who is committed to research and willing to subsidize it even in an era of unrelenting pressures on legal education.

Needless to say, this book would not exist without the sterling chapters provided by the contributors to this volume, almost all of whom are long-standing friends and comrades in the effort to free the innocent. Words are inadequate to express my appreciation.

I am also grateful to John Berger of Cambridge University Press for shepherding the book proposal through the selection process and for his sage editorial advice as it wended its way toward publication. John and I shared many cups of coffee in the "other" Cambridge (Massachusetts), and those conversations, coupled with the caffeine, helped fuel this book on the road to completion. Debbie Gershenowitz of Cambridge University Press introduced me to John, an act of kindness that meant the world to me.

Finally, my wonderful family encouraged me to pursue this project and endured my grumblings about the effort involved in finishing it. So, truly, thank you Sharissa, Mili, and Clementine. Thanks as well to my parents Howard and Mameve Medwed, my brother Jono Medwed, his wife Marnie Davidoff, their children Mirabelle and Gabriel.

Foreword

As public defenders toiling in New York City's criminal courts well before the emergence of deoxyribonucleic acid (DNA) technology, we knew the system was deeply flawed: that eyewitnesses made mistakes, that some suspects confessed to crimes they did not commit, that forensic science all too often rested on dubious scientific principles. We soon realized that DNA could offer a window into the magnitude of those flaws. What we did not know at the time, let alone dare to imagine, was that we were part of a new civil rights movement that would transform the traditional understanding of criminal justice and launch worldwide reform efforts.

A few strategic decisions early on proved vital to the growth and success of our work. First, our choice to focus on credible claims of actual innocence (the "wrong man" cases) through law school clinics inspired a sense of idealism and optimism in budding lawyers not yet rendered cynical by the slings and arrows of the adversary system. This passion for justice was infectious – and the legal establishment caught the bug. We often wonder whether our efforts would have succeeded as much had we established a large non-profit organization at the outset and worked exclusively with veteran defense lawyers.

Second, we began to think broadly about the capacity of DNA to expose problems within the criminal justice system. We learned that DNA's value lay not just in showing singular error in a particular case (e.g., that a serology test failed to identify the actual perpetrator in a rape case) but also in revealing that the rest of the evidence used in that prosecution should be reconsidered as well (e.g., the procedures that led the eyewitness to misidentify the suspect in the rape case to begin with). This allowed for a more holistic attack on the numerous ways in which faulty evidence can produce a wrongful conviction. Indeed, as we accumulated DNA exonerations, we set our sights on several canonical Supreme Court doctrines that had long held sway in the criminal courts and that, we felt, DNA could prove unreliable. These included doctrines related to eyewitness identifications,[1] police interrogations,[2] ineffective assistance of defense counsel,[3] and the admissibility of forensic evidence.[4] In these challenges, we argued for increased reliability in the procedures used in the criminal justice system. A calculated goal of this approach was to undermine the institutional emphasis placed on finality; through litigating the DNA cases we aimed to improve post-conviction access to courts for any and all criminal defendants whose cases rested on shaky, if not outright unreliable, evidentiary grounds. Simply put, we wanted to eliminate restrictions on the post-conviction right to prove "actual innocence" in the courts.[5]

We have encountered some surprises along the way. As seasoned progressive lawyers, we expected resistance from established quarters of the bar: political conservatives, prosecutors, and judges. But we were shocked by the intensity and vitriol of the initial reaction. During those first few years, we had to go to court almost every time we wanted access to biological evidence in order to undergo post-conviction DNA testing. And judges allowed those proceedings to linger for ages. Over time, however, the resistance faded and we experienced a much more pleasant surprise. The phenomena of truth broke down walls. Prosecutors started consenting to DNA tests in some cases, then half the cases, and now virtually all of them. Judges, in turn, began facilitating access to biological evidence and expressing openness to the idea of actual innocence. The notion of a proactive chief prosecutor taking the initiative to investigate potential wrongful convictions in his office was a pipe dream twenty-five years ago. Now it is a reality in the very neighborhood in which we both live, where the late District Attorney Kenneth Thompson spearheaded a vibrant Conviction Integrity Unit in Brooklyn, New York.

We are grateful that Daniel Medwed, our longtime colleague in the movement, has organized this book, and we appreciate the many insightful chapters contained within it. As we think about the next quarter-century of innocence litigation and activism, we must look beyond DNA and reinforce the duty of the system to (1) correct errors by providing ample post-conviction access to the courts and (2) remedy the root causes of those errors through judicial, legislative, and executive action. Error correction should occur at the micro level (rectifying an individual miscarriage of justice) and at the macro level (conducting mass audits and reviews of convictions tainted by a specific kind of flawed evidence). As for potential remedies, we advocate empirically based reforms proven to have high indicia of reliability. We also endorse reforms designed at tackling overt and covert forms of racial discrimination that pervade the criminal justice system.

The criminal justice system is fallible, and inevitably so. But that is no excuse. We should never stop striving to make it as close to perfect as possible – and we will not.

Barry Scheck, co-director
Peter Neufeld, co-director
The Innocence Project

NOTES

1 Manson v. Braithwaite, 432 U.S. 98 (1977).
2 Colorado v. Connelly, 479 U.S. 157 (1986).
3 Strickland v. Washington, 466 U.S. 668 (1984).
4 Frye v. U.S., 293 F. 1013 (D.C. Cir. 1923); Daubert v. Merrell Dow Pharmaceuticals, Inc., 509 U.S. 579 (1993).
5 Herrera v. Collins, 506 U.S. 390 (1993).

Introduction

1

Talking about a Revolution

A *Quarter Century of* DNA *Exonerations*

DANIEL S. MEDWED

Deoxyribonucleic acid (DNA) testing enables scientists to determine the genetic source of biological material with unparalleled accuracy. Since its development in the 1980s, this technology has affected our society in countless ways; it has helped answer questions of paternity, pinpoint hereditary diseases, and create novel biological products. It has also altered the course of criminal law through its capacity to identify biological evidence left by a culprit at a crime scene. DNA is a tool to catch the "bad guy" and free the "wrong guy."

That second attribute of DNA in the criminal justice context – the potential to vindicate the innocent – is the focus of this book. The first use of DNA technology to free an innocent defendant in the United States occurred in 1989, yet scholars are split on which of two cases best deserves to be called the nation's inaugural DNA exoneration. On August 14, 1989, an Illinois state court overturned Gary Dotson's 1979 rape conviction after DNA tests performed on the biological evidence retained from the rape kit excluded him as the perpetrator. This event marked the first time that a court relied directly on DNA results to free a wrongfully convicted defendant.[1] Earlier that year, DNA played a key, if indirect, role in reversing David Vasquez's 1985 rape-murder conviction in Virginia. The results of DNA tests on hairs preserved from the crime scene in that case proved inconclusive. But tests conducted on biological evidence related to other, strikingly similar crimes identified a different man as the perpetrator in those incidents. Law enforcement authorities became convinced the same man had committed all of these acts and that Vasquez did not commit the crime for which he was convicted. The prosecution then joined the defense in asking the Governor of Virginia to pardon Vasquez. That request was granted on January 4, 1989.[2]

Part of the debate over whether the Dotson or Vasquez case counts as the first DNA exoneration involves terminology. What is a post-conviction "DNA exoneration"? It could be construed broadly: any case in which DNA results somehow assist a criminal defendant in overturning their conviction (e.g., Vasquez) and clearing their name. Or one could interpret the phrase more stringently: cases where exculpatory DNA test results directly convince a court or executive branch official to reverse a defendant's conviction on the basis of innocence (e.g., Dotson). The definition could even fall in the middle, say, when DNA significantly helps in toppling a conviction.

This book takes no universal stance on the most appropriate and precise definition of exoneration. It is fair to say that when the contributors to this volume use the term "exoneration," they are referring to a criminal conviction overturned to a large extent on the grounds of actual innocence, namely evidence the defendant did not commit the crime. Yet scholars differ in their views about *how much* evidence is required to claim a particular case is one of actual innocence, *how emphatic* a court or executive official must be in declaring the reversal as one predicated on innocence, and even *how official* the declaration must be.[3] Some cases leave no doubt they qualify as exonerations; the paradigmatic example is a judicial decision formally proclaiming the defendant's innocence. Others are more difficult to classify. Does a judge's decision to order a new trial because there is newly discovered DNA evidence that calls into question the original result, followed by a prosecutor's decision not to pursue a retrial, constitute an exoneration? What if the prosecutor and the defense team disagree over how to characterize the case?[4]

Likewise, what about the phrase "wrongful conviction"? The plain meaning and common usage of the term cover the conviction of actually innocent defendants. But what about other flawed convictions, including those secured because of grave procedural or constitutional errors where the defendant might be factually guilty? Are they not wrongful too? And how should we categorize cases of so-called "legal innocence" where guilt remains uncertain and insufficient evidence exists to prove it beyond a reasonable doubt? For the most part, the contributors to this volume use the phrase "wrongful conviction" narrowly as a synonym for the conviction of the actually innocent. Both the spirit and vision of the book are consistent with this treatment. Some contributors offer slightly different interpretations; others neglect to define it at all.

The ambiguity and uncertainty of the terms "exoneration" and "wrongful conviction" in the ensuing chapters mirror the ambiguity and uncertainty of those terms throughout the literature. Questions about how to classify a case as an exoneration, or to brand a conviction as wrongful, could comprise an entire book. This is not that book.

Instead, this is a book about what we have learned from the use of DNA technology to remedy individual cases and reform the criminal justice system over the past twenty-five years. Putting aside the debate over definitions, it seems clear that 1989 is the year of birth for the DNA revolution in the United States. Before the emergence of DNA testing, the issue of wrongful convictions was largely a matter of speculation. Without scientific proof of a defendant's innocence, even notorious miscarriages of justice could be subject to second-guessing by skeptics. But DNA added scientific certainty to the scholar's theoretical claim; for the first time scholars could point definitively to cases where actually innocent defendants had been convicted.[5] According to the Innocence Project in New York City, DNA evidence contributed to the reversal of more than 300 wrongful convictions in the United States between 1989 and 2014.[6] Because biological evidence is seldom available in criminal cases, DNA exonerations were soon perceived as the tip of the iceberg: a smattering of errors now exposed that suggested the presence of a much bigger problem beneath the surface.

The twenty-fifth anniversary of the Dotson and Vasquez cases provided the ideal opportunity to take stock of the DNA era, and prompted me to host a conference on this topic at my home institution of Northeastern University School of Law in Boston. This book, which has its origins in papers that I solicited for that conference, homes in on two critical questions: (1) what have we learned from a quarter century of documented DNA exonerations, and (2) given what we have learned, how can we prevent wrongful convictions in the years ahead? It addresses those two questions through the lens of a series of essays authored by more than a dozen of the nation's leading scholars and advocates in the field.

At the outset, an introductory chapter (Chapter 2) by Michael Meltsner offers the perspective of a leading civil rights lawyer who engaged in test litigation to reform the criminal justice system in the mid-twentieth century. With emphasis on the efforts of the NAACP Legal Defense Fund, Meltsner canvasses the conventional ways that claims of innocence were recognized (or not recognized), asserted, and resolved. In the process, Meltsner touches on the question of whether the DNA era is more evolution than revolution. With this background in place, the volume then turns to the two vital questions that lie at its heart.

PART I: A LOOK BACK: WHAT HAVE WE LEARNED FROM TWENTY-FIVE YEARS OF DNA EXONERATIONS?

The Big Picture

Part I of the book evaluates what we have discovered over the past quarter century. The opening chapter (Chapter 3), by Brandon L. Garrett, examines the dataset of DNA exonerations as a whole, including updated information reflecting the more than sixty DNA exonerations accumulated since Garrett wrote his renowned book *Convicting the Innocent* in 2011. In many respects, the patterns remain the same. Similarly high percentages of cases contain eyewitness misidentifications and faulty forensics. More of the recent cases involve DNA test results that were either downplayed (although they excluded the defendant) or botched. But a second wave of false confessions raised somewhat distinct issues from the earlier exonerations involving false confessions. New death row exonerations highlight the role of false confessions as well, and the judicial and prosecutorial reluctance to revisit a case with a confession. All of these data show that, although DNA exonerations may fade with time, the underlying sources of error remain.

Next, Richard A. Leo discusses the history of innocence scholarship from the 1930s to the present (Chapter 4). Most scholars and advocates – including DNA pioneers Barry Scheck and Peter Neufeld – have constructed a narrow definition of innocence, framing it in terms of "actual" or "factual" innocence. This construction was crucial to the DNA revolution. As Leo notes, however, conceptions of wrongful conviction have changed in recent years, as some innocence scholars and critics alike have sought to expand the meaning of wrongful conviction to include erasures of convictions, due process errors, and other types of injustice more broadly. Leo reviews these debates, highlighting the analytic costs, benefits, and trade-offs involved with different visions of wrongful conviction. Ultimately, in Leo's view, if innocence scholars' vision of wrongful conviction becomes too expansive, imprecise, or removed from factual innocence, they run the risk of being perceived as engaging in what sociologists have called "domain expansion" – trying to enlarge the domain of a social problem in order to attract more resources or attention – and thus undermining the source of their unique moral claims in academic and policy debates. But if the vision of wrongful conviction is too limited, then many legitimate cases fall outside its net and deprive scholars of a prime opportunity to evaluate the full extent of the problem.

A Closer Look at Specific Lessons

The next three chapters all look at how the lessons learned from the DNA era have affected our understanding of specific areas of criminal justice. The nation's foremost scholar on the topic of criminal informants, Alexandra Natapoff, explores what the DNA revolution has taught us – or not taught us – about the dangers inherent in plea bargaining (Chapter 5). Natapoff acknowledges that the advent of DNA testing and other forensic advances have blown the criminal justice system wide open, demonstrating that on occasion we wrongfully convict the innocent based on evidentiary inaccuracies: weak science, mistaken eyewitness identification, and false confessions. And yet at the same time, the focus on DNA (and forensics more generally) has obscured another massive source of wrongful conviction: the plea bargaining process itself. More than 90 percent of all U.S. convictions are the result of a deal, not a trial, in which accuracy is a commodity that often gets lost in negotiation. At some point, Natapoff insists, the master list of wrongful conviction sources should include the criminal deal – whether it is the deal cut by a jailhouse snitch or an innocent defendant who pleads guilty to avoid a longer sentence. Only then will the true scope of the wrongful conviction problem be apparent.

Following Natapoff's offering, journalist and innocence advocate Rob Warden examines how the DNA revolution has illuminated the roles played by false trial testimony in producing wrongful convictions and by recantations of those statements in overturning them (Chapter 6). The dataset of DNA exonerations has shattered many of the myths surrounding recantations, specifically, that someone who claims to have lied at trial should not be trusted in coming forward now. Largely for that reason, courts and observers historically dismissed recantations as unreliable. But the DNA cases prove that many recantations are credible and should be taken seriously. In fact, the effort to exonerate Gary Dotson in Illinois gained traction after the alleged victim recanted her trial testimony. After showing the significance of recantation evidence in wrongful conviction cases, Warden addresses a disturbing development from Chicago where prosecutors have pursued perjury charges against recanting witnesses based on their original lies. This icy blast of prosecutorial wind could have a chilling effect on the willingness of recalcitrant witnesses to ever come clean, and Warden offers some suggestions about how to prevent it from sweeping across the nation.

Next, Jacqueline McMurtrie looks at a key lesson learned by the litigation of DNA exoneration cases since 1989: that law school clinics are vital to the Innocence Movement. Most innocence organizations focus upon providing direct *pro bono* litigation and investigation services to individuals seeking to prove their innocence of crimes for which they have been convicted. A substantial majority of those organizations are housed within, or affiliated with, law schools. As McMurtrie shows, students have helped reverse wrongful convictions by investigating and litigating cases under the supervision of faculty as part of "innocence clinics" at law schools. This direct client representation model has numerous benefits, as reflected by McMurtrie's own experience running the Innocence Project Northwest (IPNW) at the

University of Washington. Her clinic has freed fourteen innocent people through the use of DNA and non-DNA evidence. But McMurtrie contends this model does not go far enough. The innocence agenda also includes working to redress the causes of wrongful conviction, thereby preventing future miscarriages of justice. In order to promote criminal justice reform measures, McMurtrie touts the virtues of "legislative advocacy" clinics to complement the traditional direct representation innocence clinic and to push for statewide policy reforms. IPNW formed just such a clinic in 2011. It is the only project in the country with two separate clinics; one devoted to client representation and the other committed to accomplishing innocence-related policy reforms. In Chapter 7, McMurtrie discusses how the legislative advocacy clinic has worked symbiotically, and effectively, as a companion to the original, client-based course.

The DNA Era and Changing Views of the Death Penalty

In the next two chapters, some of the nation's leading capital punishment researchers set their keen sights on the contemporary death penalty debate and its relationship to the DNA revolution. In Chapter 8, Michael L. Radelet acknowledges that the publicity surrounding the exoneration of many death row inmates through post-conviction DNA testing over the past twenty-five years has contributed to the decline in support for capital punishment in the United States. But he notes that the "innocence card" is just one among many being played by activists in the complex, multifaceted deck of the current death penalty discourse. Concerns about racial discrimination and financial costs, in Radelet's view, may be equally (if not more) powerful pressure points in the discussion about whether to abandon the ultimate penalty.

In a chapter that nicely complements Radelet's piece, a trio of top-notch scholars – Robert J. Smith, G. Ben Cohen, and Zoë Robinson – appraise the impact of the DNA revolution on the Supreme Court's Eighth Amendment jurisprudence in regard to the death penalty. They tackle the foundational question: should innocence *matter* in determining whether capital punishment violates the prohibition against "cruel and unusual punishment"? Even more, does it matter to the Court? After canvassing recent cases with compelling evidence that states have executed innocent people, Chapter 9 traces the development of the Court's doctrine in this area, showing a link between the rising attention on innocence and Justice Breyer's bold call for abolition in his 2015 dissent in *Glossip* v. *Gross*.[7] They conclude that innocence has emerged as an increasingly key factor in how the Supreme Court views the penalty phase of capital cases.

PART II: A GLANCE AHEAD: WHAT CAN BE DONE TO AVOID
WRONGFUL CONVICTIONS IN THE FUTURE?

The goal of Part I of the book is retrospective: to reflect on a quarter century of
DNA exonerations and gauge what we have discovered. Part II takes a
prospective approach. Considering what we know, how can we change the
criminal justice system to safeguard against future errors?

Substantive Reform

The first three chapters in Part II explore substantive areas of the criminal
justice system that remain problematic – and that are worthy of reform.
Keith A. Findley leads off with a chapter that looks at the "next wave" of actual
innocence cases now that DNA has landed ashore and brought wrongful
convictions to the surface. In his view, DNA exonerations will decline over
time as pretrial testing becomes commonplace and old cases with unexamined
biological evidence become fewer and farther between. Even more, DNA
simply does not exist in most cases; focusing only on clear DNA exonerations
overlooks and hides the vast majority of false convictions. The next generation
of innocence cases, then, will have to embrace a broader definition of innocence: one that recognizes innocence where the bases for prosecution have
been undermined, but ground truth is fundamentally ambiguous or inaccessible. Science-dependent prosecutions – most notably, arson and Shaken Baby
Syndrome cases – exemplify this new claim of innocence. In both types of
cases, the prosecution rests almost entirely upon scientific or expert opinions.
But the science that the system has relied upon has subsequently been either
disproved or undermined in significant ways. Chapter 10 analyzes both
examples (1) to demonstrate the ways that law can depend only uncomfortably
and perilously on science for proof of guilt and (2) to show that when the law
does depend on science so extensively, it must expand its notion of innocence
to incorporate shifting understandings of the underlying science.

George C. Thomas III then scrutinizes an institutional barrier to the
correction of wrongful convictions: prosecutors themselves. As Thomas points
out, many prosecutors view "winning" cases as more important than
unmasking fundamental errors, and therefore provide a meager last line of
defense to prevent injustices. Nowhere is this phenomenon more visible than
in the failure to turn over potentially exculpatory evidence pursuant to the
seminal Supreme Court case of *Brady* v. *Maryland*.[8] Indeed, Thomas analyzes a random sample of cases from the National Registry of Exonerations and

concludes that prosecutorial misconduct, especially *Brady* missteps, comprises a major factor in the conviction of the innocent in non-DNA as well as DNA cases. According to Thomas, part of the failure is our system for appointing or electing prosecutors. When political variables drive selection of these ministers of justice, we should not be surprised that they view winning cases as extremely important. Many European countries, by contrast, impose merit-based requirements on which individuals can be candidates for jobs as prosecutors and then require rigorous training of at least two years before candidates become full-fledged prosecutors. Chapter 11 contends that American jurisdictions should follow the Europeans and, by statute, impose training requirements for prosecutors. The training could be broad-based, making them more effective prosecutors in general, but a large component would seek to enhance their awareness of the risks to innocent defendants. That would improve the last line of defense for innocent persons caught up in the American criminal justice system.

While Thomas looks at the future of the prosecutorial function, Chapter 12 by Adele Bernhard considers the role played by defense counsel in causing wrongful convictions and how courts might boost defense attorney performance. Bernhard discusses how the publicity surrounding DNA exonerations has influenced the willingness of appellate courts to overturn cases on ineffective assistance of defense counsel (IAC) grounds, but not to the extent that is warranted. Bernhard's empirical research reveals that, as the Innocence Movement has matured, courts have reversed cases on the basis of IAC with greater frequency when it comes to failures during the sentencing phase, especially in capital cases. This trend, however, has not surfaced with respect to IAC claims stemming from the investigative or trial phase of the case – precisely the stage where woeful lawyering is most likely to contribute to a miscarriage of justice. In Bernhard's eyes, even if judges become more circumspect in assessing IAC claims, the doctrinal test for ineffectiveness under *Strickland* v. *Washington*[9] remains too subjective and too hard to satisfy; it allows even egregious pretrial and trial missteps to go uncorrected if an appellate court believes the deficient performance did not affect the outcome. Bernhard urges jurisdictions to adopt a standards-based approach in gauging how an attorney fared in a particular case, replete with concrete checklists that would allow for a more objective evaluation.

Procedural Changes

Changing particular substantive aspects of the American criminal justice system could reduce wrongful convictions in the future. But without allowing for procedural opportunities to take aim at those substantive concerns – at Shaken Baby Syndrome cases, at prosecutorial misconduct, at IAC claims – then successes will be infrequent in the post-DNA era. With that in mind, the next five chapters try to harness the power of procedure and offer ideas about how to improve the mechanisms through which innocence claims are litigated.

In Chapter 13, Stephanie Roberts Hartung makes the case for the creation of a distinct "innocence track" in our federal courts to litigate matters where the ground truth about guilt is called into question. Just 14 percent of the first 250 DNA exonerations involved defendants who succeeded in reversing their convictions through appellate or post-conviction procedures. This figure is nearly identical to the reversal rate in a control group of (presumably guilty) convicted prisoners. While innocence advocates have made great strides in altering pretrial and trial procedures to minimize the impact of the underlying causes of wrongful convictions, including modifying eyewitness identification and police interrogation procedures, these reforms offer cold comfort to the innocent prisoners whose trials occurred long before these reforms took effect. According to Hartung, the time has come to implement similar reforms in the post-conviction context, most notably by recalibrating the balance between finality and farness to produce a mechanism to pursue freestanding innocence claims in the federal system.

Paul G. Cassell's chapter is a fine companion to that of Hartung. Cassell also believes that innocence claims should be privileged in the post-conviction context. But he takes his argument much further, contending that scholars must acknowledge the trade-offs inherent in any reform measures and account for their impact on prosecuting factually guilty defendants. In Cassell's eyes, preventing wrongful conviction of the innocent is a fundamental priority of our criminal justice system, yet not the system's only goal. Efforts to minimize conviction of the innocent should not undermine the overarching need to convict the guilty, keep dangerous criminals behind bars, and avoid the suffering of future crime victims. Cassell asserts that some reforms are true "win-win" measures that simultaneously reduce the number of innocents wrongfully convicted while increasing (or at least not decreasing) the number of violent criminals sent to prison. Chapter 14 lays out a few such possibilities, including (1) confining habeas relief to those with claims of factual innocence, (2) replacing the exclusionary rule with a civil damage remedy, (3) moving confession law away from *Miranda* procedures, and (4) requiring defense attorneys to explore their clients' guilt or innocence.

In Chapter 15, Margaret Burnham advocates for a particular type of procedural mechanism to exonerate wrongfully convicted defendants posthumously, especially in racially charged cases from the Deep South. The dataset of DNA exonerations contains just one case of a person cleared of a crime after his death – Timothy Cole, who died in a Texas prison ten years before DNA testing established his innocence of rape. The paltry number of posthumous exonerations is tragic given mounting evidence of pervasive historical injustices in the United States. Recent studies have examined the failures of the criminal justice systems operating in the states of the Deep South during the Jim Crow years between 1930 and 1965. Numerous African-Americans were wrongfully convicted and sentenced to severe terms of incarceration; many were executed by the state based on flimsy evidence. Under current legal norms there is no adequate judicial or executive remedy to redress this history, and undoubtedly no remaining biological material suitable for DNA testing. Posthumous exonerations are disfavored by courts and rarely available in executive pardon proceedings. Chapter 15 looks abroad to countries that have confronted past miscarriages of justice and contemplates possible avenues for relief in the United States for long-past wrongful convictions, particularly those that resulted in execution.

Sandra Guerra Thompson and Robert Wicoff focus not on procedures aimed at correcting individual injustices, but rather on creating procedures to address the problems caused by *systemic* irregularities that affect scores of convicted people. Such irregularities often involve widespread crime lab fraud or flaws in certain forensic scientific tests. As Thompson and Wicoff point out, there are usually no established procedures to ensure that affected defendants have the resources to adequately investigate cases in which possible error is detected on a large scale. Convicted persons may receive notices from the prosecuting authority about the potential problem in their cases, but they do not have a right to counsel to investigate whether the error affected their case and could form the basis of a post-conviction habeas application. Nor is it true that most lawyers can effectively perform the review function. Ideally, the review should be undertaken by a defense attorney familiar with habeas law, assisted by an investigator. The law of habeas corpus is beyond the experience of most criminal defense attorneys, much less that of *pro se* applicants. Chapter 16 explores these issues in detail, and proposes that states pass laws providing for the assignment of post-conviction counsel in such instances. In particular, Thompson and Wicoff recommend the assignment of a centralized organization to handle many of these cases and develop expertise on the topic.

Justin Marceau and Steven Wise examine another glaring hole in the criminal justice system's post-conviction regime: the absence of a clear mechanism to free nonhuman animals. In Chapter 17, Marceau and Wise discuss how animal control statutes not infrequently punish, and sometimes execute, dangerous animals without proper procedures to overturn those penalties.

In their view, the cruelty of punishing innocents is not limited to the incarceration of human animals. They urge that some nonhuman animals deserve liberation from the most horrible confinement. These animals are unquestionably innocent; their conditions of confinement uniquely depraved; and their cognitive functioning, not to mention their ability to suffer, rivals that of humans. Marceau and Wise suggest we should seriously consider habeas-type remedies for nonhuman beings.

The International Arena

The final two chapters gaze beyond the borders of the United States and toward the status of the Innocence Movement in the international arena. In Chapter 18, Mark Godsey discusses the global history of the Movement, tracing it from developments in the United Kingdom in the 1970s through the DNA revolution in the United States to the modern expansion in Africa, Asia, and Europe. As Godsey chronicles, innocence projects are surfacing across the globe and now operate on every inhabited continent. Although the nature of these organizations varies considerably, they share a focus on overturning cases involving egregious miscarriages of justice. Another common theme is that most countries lack procedures that provide adequate access to biological evidence for DNA testing after conviction as well as norms for disclosing police records. Godsey and his international colleagues are working tirelessly to establish innocence groups abroad and implement lasting reforms.

Erik Luna, in turn, examines the issue of actual innocence in the context of war on the global stage (Chapter 19). In Luna's estimation, the "Fog of War" may exacerbate many of the flaws found in domestic wrongful convictions, including a rush to judgment and a reliance on dubious evidence in convicting military officials as well as foot soldiers for war crimes. Luna also dissects the special issues posed by the "war on terrorism" where the line between friend and foe is less clear than in traditional forms of international conflict. Collective punishments and prolonged pretrial detentions mark many government efforts to thwart terrorism, among them, American interventions in the aftermath of the attacks of September 11, 2001. Luna artfully notes that "[t]hough truth and innocence have always taken a beating on the battlefield, the better angels of our nature would seek to prevent miscarriages of justice in wartime, just as they do in times of peace."

* *

As the contributions to this volume demonstrate, we have witnessed a veritable revolution in criminal justice over the past quarter century due to the emergence of DNA technology. DNA testing is now ubiquitous at the front end of criminal cases, weeding out innocent suspects before cases even go to trial. But the lessons learned from DNA extend far beyond the cases in which biological evidence is available for post-conviction testing; they reveal universal truths about the failings in eyewitness identifications, interrogation practices, strategic decisions by prosecutors, the practices of defense lawyers, and so on. These revelations have provided the impetus for concrete reforms.

Much work remains to be done. For this revolution to produce genuine evolution in American criminal justice policy – enlightened changes that exalt accuracy over expediency – innocence advocates must stay vigilant. They must continue to litigate individual miscarriages of injustice and lobby for large-scale reforms. As with any revolution, one wonders whether its lessons will be heeded over time. It is far too early to tell. Perhaps we will have more to say in another twenty-five years.

NOTES

1 *See* Innocence Project, *Profile of Gary Dotson*, available at www.innocenceproject.org/cases-false-imprisonment/gary-dotson.

2 *See* Innocence Project, *Profile of David Vasquez*, available at www.innocenceproject.org/cases-false-imprisonment/david-vasquez.

3 The National Registry of Exonerations is a project spearheaded by the University of Michigan Law School that provides information about all documented exonerations, not just those involving DNA, since 1989. For the definition used by this organization, see National Registry of Exonerations, *Glossary*, available at www.law.umich.edu/special/exoneration/Pages/glossary.aspx.

4 It is not uncommon for prosecutors and innocence project lawyers to battle over terminology, with prosecutors rejecting the notion that the dismissal is premised on "actual innocence." Consider, for instance, the high-profile debate surrounding the release of the "Fairbanks Four" in Alaska in December 2015. *See Attorney: Fairbanks 4 Exonerated, Contrary to State Claim*, ABC NEWS, available at http://abcnews.go.com/US/wireStory/judge-frees-men-convicted-fairbanks-case-35836884.

5 *See* Daniel S. Medwed, *Looking Foreword: Wrongful Convictions and Systemic Reform*, 42 AM. CRIM. L. REV. 1117 (2005).

6 For a current tally of DNA exonerations, see Innocence Project, *Homepage*, available at www.innocenceproject.org.

7 *See generally* Glossip v. Gross, 135 S. Ct. 2726 (2015).

8 373 U.S. 83 (1963).

9 466 U.S. 668 (1984).

2

Innocence before DNA

MICHAEL MELTSNER

INTRODUCTION

The legal status of, and attitude toward, wrongful conviction in the decades before DNA began to impact the criminal law is in marked contrast to what we find today. Professional audiences are generally aware of the shift, in part due to an explosion of relevant scholarship; much will also be known by the laity due to the significant interest shown by the media in covering application of DNA to criminal cases and the Innocence Movement that arose in its wake.[1]

Aspects of the following pre-DNA story will be personal because from the early sixties on I have been dealing with wrongful conviction as a litigator, teacher, writer and activist, though for most of these years I used only the language of legal error, rather than words like "innocence" or "wrongful conviction." The pivot to DNA is perhaps the most important criminal law event to happen in my lifetime but, of course, like any technological fix – think of chemotherapy treatment for cancer – DNA is both wonderful and limited, full of unintended consequences and, indeed, capable of mischief should some use it as an excuse to slacken our pace trying to undo the ills of our criminal justice system.[2]

Writing in 1970, two years before he would argue and win *Furman* v. *Georgia*[3] and six before the case would be sent to assisted living, if not buried,[4] Anthony Amsterdam wrote of the widespread impression "that the decisions of the Supreme Court" during the 1960s "have vastly enlarged the rights of criminal suspects and defendants." The driving force behind this view was the series of decisions incorporating most of the guarantees of the Bill of Rights into the due process clause of the Fourteenth Amendment "so as to make

Frances Hutto provided exceptional research and editorial support for this essay.

these guarantees, originally written to govern only federal criminal proceedings, applicable to state proceedings as well."[5]

The impression, of course, was just that. While Court decisions changed how police, prosecution, defense counsel and judges operated, they left the basic arrangements between law enforcement and civilians unreformed. The Court acted consequentially when it broadened access to post-conviction remedies, required counsel and announced principles that afforded greater protection for due process, but plea bargains continued to dominate conviction and sentencing patterns, especially if one chose to go to trial, and they were largely untouched. The exclusionary rule only applies to situations where evidence is introduced; the *Miranda* warning became a cultural artifact but police adjusted to its constraints quickly. Given the complicated, interconnected and yet decentralized institutions of our criminal justice system, the Court could speak but not often lead. Amsterdam compared the voice of the Justices to the Oracle of Delphi, whose utterances were thought to be of supreme importance but "from the practical point of view, what she said didn't matter much."[6] "To a mind-staggering extent," he wrote, "an extent that conservatives and liberals alike who are not criminal trial lawyers cannot conceive – the entire system of criminal justice below the level of the Supreme Court of the United States is solidly massed against the criminal suspect."[7]

DNA has demonstrated the power to change outcomes, to silence doubters and to inject a modicum of fairness in the worldview of previously closed minds. But, of course, prevention of wrongful conviction transcends DNA testing. The flaws in the criminal process it exposed are still with us. These not only include the list of specific errors that emerged from the cases of the exonerated – tainted confessions, misidentifications, prosecutorial overreaching, incompetent counsel, overvalued forensics — but the structural flaws that were not seriously touched and which govern the day-in, day-out process of our criminal courts and shape the adversary system. These existed before the arrival of DNA; while the Innocence Movement has exposed them to harsh light and growing criticism, they still abide.

INNOCENCE IGNORED: THE AGE BEFORE DNA

Before the age of DNA the conventional wisdom went something like this: No human system is perfect, but our criminal process misfires rarely because procedural rules such as reasonable doubt, the right to counsel, freedom not to testify and the availability of trial by jury all ensure against wrongful conviction. In the years before exonerations became a frequent news event, judges and prosecutors often weighed in with versions of Judge Learned Hand's 1923 bromide – "the ghost of the innocent man convicted" was an "unreal dream."[8] Some, like the late Justice Antonin Scalia, adhered to this view despite it appearing more and more like a legal version of climate change denial. Scalia believed that several hundred exonerations are insignificant when viewed against the number of *all* felony convictions, assuming all these reflect actual guilt.[9] More significant than statistical malfeasance is the unseemliness of a Justice showing indifference, even hostility, to hundreds of (cumulative) years of wrongful imprisonment, some of it spent on death row. Scalia displayed his taste for sarcasm when he used the case of decades-long death row inmate Henry Lee McCollum to assail Justice Harry Blackmun's change of heart about the death penalty.[10] McCollum was subsequently exonerated by DNA testing.[11] When Brandon Garrett writes in a definitive 2011 study that "[w]e now know that the 'ghost of the innocent man' spoken by Judge Hand is no 'unreal dream,' but a nightmare reality," I take it he is referring not only to the horror of the numbers and the loss of confidence in the criminal process, but also to judicial deniers and disbelieving prosecuting attorneys.[12]

One difficulty in describing the way wrongful convictions were viewed in the past was their limited visibility.[13] Then and now, dismissal of charges, acquittal of the innocent, soul searching and the innocence narrative itself was largely opaque, aside from the extraordinary case – the still unclear Sacco and Vanzetti, the Scottsboro boys, the Ohio circus trial of Samuel Sheppard. Talk of factual innocence was usually lodged in the specific, a brilliant lawyer performance or a tangled local story of jealousy, money, prejudice or scandal. When fairness triumphed it had more to do with vindicating constitutional rights than innocence, though often belief in innocence was an essential, if muted, reason for the result. Otherwise, there was very little questioning of the repeated argument that defendants were protected by a prosecutor's goal of only convicting the guilty, and the procedures mandated by the Bill of Rights or state law. It's not that such ideas have left us, but rather that DNA has led to a systemic view of wrongful conviction that rarely surfaced before. In an *ad hoc*, fragmented, politically and geographically diffuse criminal justice system, apparently only reports of technological certainty can shift ingrained habits of mind.

After conviction, on direct appeal, innocence was a stepchild. We treat jury verdicts with deference; motions for new trials face a high threshold and are often time limited. Appellate courts sit to review legal error, not new evidence. Until *Brown* v. *Allen*,[14] followed by the 1963 troika of *Fay*,[15] *Townsend*[16] and *Sanders*,[17] post-conviction relief for state prisoners raising federal constitutional claims in federal courts was extraordinarily constrained. The few cases where it was available overwhelmingly were concerned with legal error. Even when habeas was more accessible, hearings were granted in something like one in twenty cases, with the writ granted in less than half that number.[18]

In the mid-sixties, when the NAACP Legal Defense Fund (LDF) received a grant from the Ford Foundation to set up one of the first criminal law reform programs funded by a major foundation, the National Office for the Rights of the Indigent (NORI) agenda included bail reform, establishing a right to counsel, making legal services available to the poor, arguing for better identification processes, narrowing police discretion, challenging capital punishment and fighting racial discrimination in decision-making at all levels of the criminal process. I was first assistant counsel to LDF at the time, in charge of the NORI criminal law reform program.[19] Some of the issues at stake in NORI cases had an impact on the reliability of trial court verdicts. Certainly many of the doctrines arising in Southern racial cases that were LDF's priority could only have been understood as surrogates for protecting the potentially innocent from criminal conviction.

Still "innocence" was not on the program docket *In Hace Verba*. And when it arose in unmistakable fashion, as it did in cases like Florida's 1963 prosecution of Freddie Pitts and Wilbert Lee, the litigation was still fought on procedural and sentencing turf, not on actual innocence. When another man admitted the killing that sent the two men to death row, their lawyers (with whom LDF collaborated) proceeded primarily with claims of jury discrimination, prosecutorial tampering with evidence, ineffective assistance of counsel and coerced confessions.[20]

Warren Holmes, who had taken the true killer's confession at a lie detector test, told his friend, *Miami Herald* journalist Gene Miller, that he believed Pitts and Lee were innocent. The book Miller wrote, *Invitation to a Lynching* (1975), demonstrated that the men were wrongfully convicted. Even though they had pled guilty (after a beating), the book convinced Florida Attorney General Robert Shevin to tell the Florida Supreme Court that he believed the state had withheld evidence, and that the men were innocent. Shevin later said this confession of error likely cost him his chance at being elected governor, "But it was right and I had to do it."[21] At a new trial, Pitts and Lee were again convicted, but the jury was not told of the prosecution's earlier suppression of evidence. The Supreme Court's 1972 decision in *Furman* meant their death sentences were commuted to life but they were appealing the underlying *convictions* when Governor Reuben Askew pardoned them. With the exception of the pardon (fewer would be granted as the century grew older), the case illuminates the typical treatment of wrongful conviction claims: (1) rarely did an appellate court process supplement its limited review of jury "findings of fact" by considering new evidence; (2) retrial was no assurance of exoneration; and (3) rarer still were cases where a court reviewed a claim on innocence grounds after a guilty plea. While the men remained incarcerated, Charles L. Black Jr. would write a powerful argument against the death penalty, emphasizing that it was enforced in a standardless and arbitrary fashion.[22] The book was called *Capital Punishment, The Inevitability of Caprice and Mistake,* but the "Mistake" in the title is primarily legal, not factual in nature, focusing on the presence of discretion in the capital case system. Luck and outside intervention freed Pitts and Lee despite the state's "mistake," much as in many of the cases reported by Edwin Borchard and others.

Cases of actual innocence could surface at any time but few would lead to soul searching by the authorities or serious efforts to adopt reforms that might prevent them from happening again. One exception was that of George Whitmore Jr., which arose in the midst of efforts to prompt New York to abolish the death penalty.

On August 28, 1963, 21-year-old Janice Wylie, a *Newsweek* researcher, and 23-year-old Emily Hoffert, a schoolteacher, were found stabbed to death in their Manhattan apartment. Wylie had also been raped. The double murders garnered a huge amount of media attention because the victims were young, professional white women from prominent families. The crime soon became known as the "Career Girls Murders." Despite the hundreds of detectives on the case, and the media coverage, eight months went by before the police identified an alleged killer.

In April 1964, Officer Frank Isola picked up George Whitmore Jr., a 19-year-old black man who worked intermittently as a day laborer, for questioning. The day before, a woman named Elba Borrero was attacked by an attempted rapist. Whitmore was seized due to an unlucky confluence of circumstances: he happened to be hanging around near the crime scene in Brooklyn when Isola returned to the area the next day; he was seen as a "drifter" by the police because he lacked stable employment and alternated living with different family members; he had a picture of a blonde, white woman, who police believed was Janice Wylie, in his pocket; and, perhaps most importantly, he was black.

Once in custody, Whitmore was subjected to a 24-hour interrogation, during which he confessed not only to the attempted rape of Borrero, but also to the murders of Wylie and Hoffert and the rape and murder of another woman. Although the police announced that Whitmore had confessed to all the murders and the attempted rape, had supplied information about the Wylie–Hoffert murders that would have been known only by the killer and had stolen a picture of Wylie from the apartment, lawyers and investigators soon began to doubt Whitmore's guilt, especially as more details emerged about his supposed confession. During his arraignment Whitmore recanted, claiming that he had been threatened and beaten during questioning and had signed the confession without knowing what it was or what it said. Although his claims about being beaten were disputed, it was difficult to deny that racial prejudice played a significant role in his confession. Journalist Selwyn Raab reported: "There was one detective who was essentially responsible for coercing George and manufacturing that confession ... and it turned out later that ... he [claimed he] could tell when a black lied, because he could see his stomach churn. So there was no question that the confessions and the arrest and the interrogation of George were racially inspired."[23]

Whitmore also had a solid alibi for the time when the murders of Wylie and Hoffert took place in Manhattan.[24] Investigators following up on the photo of the woman determined that she was alive and lived near where Whitmore claimed to have found the picture. He had kept it so he could brag to his friends about having a white girlfriend.[25] Manhattan prosecutors also realized that Whitmore's confession did not provide any information about the Wylie–Hoffert murders not already known to police.

Despite doubts about the confession and the identification of a new suspect, district attorney Frank Hogan refused to dismiss the indictment. He postponed the double murder trial and instead moved ahead on the attempted rape of Borrero. She had identified Whitmore but he was the only "suspect" whose picture police had shown her. At the trial, the prosecutor presented a button to the jury, arguing it was a match to Whitmore's raincoat and had been torn off by Borrero when he attacked her. It was later discovered that the prosecutor's office had suppressed a report in its possession proving that the button was not in fact a match for Whitmore's coat.[26] While he was convicted of the attempted rape, the verdict was overturned due to racial prejudice demonstrated by members of the jury and discovery that jurors had been reading newspaper articles about the Wylie–Hoffert murders.[27] Whitmore would later face a second trial for the assault on Borrero, and a trial for the murder and rape of another woman that ended with a hung jury. Finally Hogan dismissed the indictment in the Wylie–Hoffert case after the police identified a new suspect who admitted the murder to a friend.

Despite being cleared of the Wylie–Hoffert murders, the unjust treatment Whitmore suffered at the hands of police and prosecutors was far from over. Subsequent efforts to convict him of the assault and murder continued until he was finally exonerated. It took nine years, most of which he spent in prison before he was released. As one journalist observed at the time of Whitmore's death in 2012, "[h]is ordeal was a key factor in the abolition of the death penalty (except for cases involving the killing of a police officer) by the State Legislature and Gov. Nelson A. Rockefeller, in 1965."[28]

The Whitmore case was of importance to LDF lawyers while engaged in shaping a national litigation campaign to restrict and ultimately eliminate the death penalty,[29] but the front page prosecution of a man who turned out to be innocent was more motivational than a directive to mount an attack on the grounds of systemic flaws leading to conviction or execution of the innocent. At LDF, we were first drawn to abolition because of race and would craft arguments against arbitrary and prejudicial procedures and Eighth Amendment cruelty, not innocence.[30] LDF lawyers knew well there were wrongful convictions for legal and factual reasons as well as death sentences that were, as the Supreme Court would be told, without "rhyme or reason unless the reason was race,"[31] but there were few openings for constitutionalizing innocence.

The issue was then seen, as in the Whitmore case, as a matter for dispute at trial in specific cases rather than the product of systemic factors that could be remedied by legal arguments claiming innocence. Or it was an argument for activists dealing with legislators or public opinion, again as in Whitmore, but not for courts of last resort. In Supreme Court litigation, innocence traveled under different terms. I thought that the defendant in my first Supreme Court death case might be innocent. Johnny Coleman was convicted of killing a white man in a scuffle, but I had insufficient facts to contest a jury verdict that had rejected his claim of self-defense for such a foray; he was saved first by two Supreme Court decisions dealing with racial exclusion from the jury and then by an acquittal.[32]

In the aftermath of *Furman*, statutory procedures in capital cases were extensively revised but the focus was on sentencing, not conviction.[33] In short, if any of these changes may have worked to increase the reliability of convictions they would have been welcome but unintended consequences. As far as the life–death decision was concerned, the newly mandated aggravating-mitigating balancing inquiry by the jury had no innocence-related dimension.

In the following sections I examine three areas of law that were relevant to the discovery and avoidance of wrongful conviction in the pre-DNA era – witness identification, disclosure of exculpatory information and access to post-conviction relief. In the pre-DNA era the law in all three failed to offer significant protection against wrongful conviction; developments since have, with the exception of eyewitness identification procedures, shown only modest sensitivity to questions of innocence.

WITNESS IDENTIFICATION

On a January night in 1965, an intruder entered the modest Nashville, Tennessee home of a black woman, Mrs. Margaret Beamer, grabbed her from behind in an unlit hallway and, brandishing a butcher knife, forced her to a nearby patch of woods where he raped her. Mrs. Beamer promptly reported the crime to the police, telling them the culprit had a youthful voice, soft skin and "sort of bushy hair." During the following seven months she was occasionally shown photographs of various men but failed to identify any. In August 1965, the police arrested 16-year-old Archie Nathaniel Biggers on an attempted rape charge arising out of an incident in another Nashville neighborhood. They brought Mrs. Beamer to police headquarters, telling her she would "look at a suspect." In a room where Mrs. Beamer was seated, Biggers, surrounded by four or five officers, was brought to the doorway. At her request, he was told to speak words used by the rapist–"Shut up or I'll kill you" – and she identified him as the rapist.[34]

Biggers was tried, convicted and sentenced to twenty years' incarceration. The only evidence connecting him to the rape was the identification by Mrs. Beamer. Her 13-year-old daughter, who had briefly viewed the intruder, could not identify Biggers. The prosecution also put forward the testimony of four police officers that Mrs. Beamer had in fact identified Biggers at the police station, a matter not in dispute. The defendant testified and denied the rape. In closing argument, the prosecuting attorney characterized the issue in the case as one of identification and related the story of a case he had tried where "violence and terror" had resulted in an accurate identification.[35]

Biggers's appeal was twice heard by the United States Supreme Court. The first led to an affirmance of the conviction by an equally divided Court;[36] the second resulted in a 1972 reversal of a Sixth Circuit decision affirming a district court grant of a writ of habeas corpus on the ground that the show-up identification was so suggestive as to violate due process.[37] Justice Powell, writing for a majority of five, conceded that the stationhouse identification may have been suggestive but it was nevertheless constitutional because there were indicia of Mrs. Beamer's reliability. The Court's approach would soon characterize the manner in which eyewitness identification was treated in the decades prior to the arrival of DNA and the Innocence Movement:

> We turn, then, to the central question, whether under the "totality of the circumstances" the identification was reliable even though the confrontation procedure was suggestive. As indicated by our cases, the factors to be considered in evaluating the likelihood of misidentification include the opportunity of the witness to view the criminal at the time of the crime, the witness'

degree of attention, the accuracy of the witness' prior description of the criminal, the level of certainty demonstrated by the witness at the confrontation, and the length of time between the crime and the confrontation. . . . Weighing all the factors, we find no substantial likelihood of misidentification.[38]

Justice Brennan's dissent criticized the majority for an essentially *de novo* inquiry into such "elemental facts" as the victim's opportunity to observe the assailant and the type of description she gave. This was "an unjustified departure from our long-established practice not to reverse findings of fact concurred in by two lower courts unless shown to be clearly erroneous."[39]

I have no idea whether my client Archie Biggers was guilty of the rape. Such uncertainty is the plight of many lawyers when faced with those who maintain their innocence. And in pondering the outcome in his case I can certainly imagine situations where the police have good reason to show a suspect to a victim individually, without engaging in a formal lineup or photo array. But what I do know is that we run an enormous risk of misidentification when we use a (1) show-up; (2) seven months after a terror-filled crime; (3) after a witness is told she will view a suspect; (4) where he is presented surrounded by police; and finally (5) when the only evidence pointing to guilt is the identification.

There was a hint in Justice Powell's opinion that the result might be different in the future – that a suggestive procedure alone might itself constitute a due process violation in a case (unlike Biggers) that arose *after* the 1967 decision in *Stovall* v. *Denno*,[40] where the Court indicated a defendant could claim "the confrontation conducted . . . was so unnecessarily suggestive and conducive to irreparable mistaken identification" as to deny due process of law. Nevertheless in *Manson* v. *Braithwaite*,[41] the suggestion was ignored. Using the *Biggers* approach, the Court decided that if there is sufficient evidence of reliability even a show-up made noncontemporaneous with the crime would be upheld. *Manson* also followed the end of the Court's brief attempt to increase the reliability of police lineups by granting a right to counsel in *United States* v. *Wade*,[42] and *Gilbert* v. *California*.[43] Within a few years this advance in reducing the frequency of mistaken identification was rendered practically useless by *Kirby* v. *Illinois*,[44] where the right to counsel was restricted to post-indictment lineups.

Despite this about-face, the Court had highlighted doubts about eyewitness identification, leading to increased efforts to fashion new rules that would "minimize the danger of convicting the innocent."[45] Justice Stevens called for states to experiment in devising such rules, probably accomplished "more effectively by the legislative process than by a somewhat clumsy judicial fiat."[46] However, little reform occurred before the DNA-facilitated Innocence Movement made clear that a majority of wrongful convictions involved misidentification, making it the leading cause of wrongful conviction.

Today there is evidence of a massive change in identification procedures and practices in many, but certainly not all, jurisdictions. Defective approaches to identification were known well before the DNA era but its arrival changed the equation. According to one expert in the field,

> DNA exonerations ... after about 2000 sparked reform by establishing three things. First, the undeniability that significant numbers of innocent persons have been convicted throughout the US; Second, that in 75% of exonerations proven by DNA evidence mistaken eyewitness identification had been a contributing factor; third, a body of experimental eyewitness identification science, produced in recent decades, showed why popularly used eyewitness identification procedures were unreliable, and how those procedures could be modified to reduce the risk of mistaken identifications, without significant loss of accurate identifications.[47]

By 2011, "about 25 percent of police departments nationwide ... [had] reformed their photo lineup procedures," a vast improvement from 2002 "when that number was basically zero."[48]

One example of reform among many: The New Jersey Supreme Court announced guidelines making it easier for criminal defendants to challenge such evidence. In *State* v. *Henderson*, the court found a "vast body of scientific research about human memory" that "calls into question the vitality of the current legal framework for analyzing the reliability of eyewitness identifications."[49] Similarly, the National Institute of Justice Guide recommends that witnesses be instructed that (1) the perpetrator may or may not be in the lineup; (2) it is just as important to eliminate innocent persons from suspicion as it is to identify guilty parties; (3) the appearance of the perpetrator may have changed since the incident; and (4) the investigation will continue whether or not an identification is made. A wide range of initiatives have adopted such approaches.[50]

DISCLOSURE OF EVIDENCE: THE PROMISE OF *BRADY V. MARYLAND*

No Warren Court innovation held more promise to improve the reliability of criminal process decision-making than the rule of *Brady* v. *Maryland*,[51] imposing a duty on the prosecution to provide an accused with favorable information material to guilt or punishment "irrespective of the good faith

or bad faith of the prosecution."[52] If taken seriously, *Brady* told the prosecution its dual roles – convicting the guilty and ensuring fairness and justice –
were coequal. While animated by a traditional adversary system concern with
prosecution–defense balance rather than by remedying wrongful convictions,
more than any other 1960s reformist decision (with the exception of *Gideon* v.
Wainwright)[53] the case raised the possibility of reducing wrongful conviction
and increasing the frequency of pretrial dismissal of the innocent. *Brady*
evoked hope, according to one seasoned observer, that "the adversary system
henceforth would be transformed from a 'sporting contest' to a genuine search
for truth."[54]

Brady deals with facts known to the prosecution, police or investigative
agencies that may be unknown to an accused. Therefore, to the extent those
facts bolster a defendant's case they are obviously critically relevant to a claim
of factual innocence. You get a measure of the importance of *Brady* (*if* it
had been given a robust interpretation and then rigorously followed) from
Brandon Garrett's important study, *Judging Innocence*, of several hundred
DNA exonerations. He concludes: "these exonerees could not effectively
litigate their factual innocence likely due to a combination of unfavorable
legal standards, unreceptive courts, faulty criminal investigation by law
enforcement, inadequate representation at trial and afterwards, and a lack of
resources for factual investigation that might have uncovered miscarriages."[55]
Jon Gould reached consistent results in a study of 460 cases from 1980 to 2012:
Defendants in states with more executions per population were at increased
risk of wrongful conviction perhaps due in part to greater numbers of *Brady*
violations. According to Gould, "[i]n several of the erroneous convictions,
a prosecutor convinced of the defendants' guilt despite a lack of conclusive
proof failed to turn over exculpatory evidence or enlisted a non-eyewitness
(such as a jailhouse snitch) to provide corroborating testimony."[56]

Neither a generous interpretation nor strict enforcement of the *Brady* rule
was to be – it went from being a potential giant among Supreme Court
decisions to, with few exceptions, another closely confined, narrowly viewed
precedent. The Court eventually dispensed with the requirement that the
defense request *Brady* material but otherwise the preconditions for disclosure
were tightened. In 2002, the Court ruled prosecutors had no duty to reveal
Brady material during plea negotiations,[57] even though it had previously
found plea bargaining a critical stage of the criminal process.[58] By declining
to extend *Brady* to plea bargaining, the Court shut off a dialogue that might
have been the predicate for pretrial findings of innocence in the pool that
makes up the vast majority of criminal cases. The Court simply failed to deter
the state from suppressing relevant information at the stage where most

criminal cases were decided.[59] While *Brady* commands disclosure of evidence favorable to an accused, it is not always clear from the cases whether the information covered can just be helpful or whether it must be admissible evidence. In *United States* v. *Agurs*,[60] the Court ruled there must be a "substantial basis" for holding the evidence favorable before it need be disclosed. Under *Brady*, the prosecution cannot suppress evidence *material* to guilt *or* punishment, and in *United States* v. *Bagley*,[61] the Court placed the heavy burden on the defense of proving materiality, requiring a showing that there was "a reasonable probability that had the evidence been disclosed to the defense, the result of the proceeding would have been different."[62] Framing the burden this way implies that *even in the case of a willful suppression* by a prosecutor, the defense has to prove the evidence would have led to a different result.

The unfortunate consequence of so hedging the *Brady* rule is to encourage prosecutors, already imbued with the sporting theory of criminal litigation, to at best err in close cases on the side of suppression and at worst game the system by suppressing material that might never be discovered, or if discovered might be ruled immaterial. Bennett Gershman describes other tactics used to avoid *Brady* disclosure, noting that judicial or bar condemnation of prosecutorial abuse of *Brady* is rare. He concludes that instead of transforming the adversary trial into a search for truth we still have a "trial by ambush."[63]

For our purposes, the conclusion is clear: Before DNA, both law and practice treated innocence as a business for juries or, in bench trials, judges implementing reasonable doubt standards and commonplace procedures of presenting, cross-examining and weighing evidence that the parties were able to produce. Inequality of resources and ineffectiveness of counsel were treated with relative indifference or as matters not requiring special concern save in exceptional circumstances. Despite its initial promise, *Brady* fails to inspire confidence that it may protect the innocent.[64]

POST-CONVICTION RELIEF

Whether claims of innocence are framed directly, in their "naked" form[65] or lurk behind constitutional claims on the only basis that offered the possibility of success, access to post-conviction relief is essential. In the pre-DNA era, the Warren Court endorsed a broad vision of habeas corpus, making applications for the writ available to raise federal constitutional claims so long as state courts had been given an opportunity to rule on the question. Efforts to persuade Congress to pass legislation to preclude federal review of state criminal case decisions had actually been launched in earlier decades in

reaction to Supreme Court decisions broadening the "jurisdictional" conception of the reach of habeas,[66] but the push to restrict the availability of the
writ grew more forceful after the Supreme Court's 1953 decision in *Brown* v.
Allen,[67] holding that federal courts were not required to defer to state adjudication of federal rights, that a habeas petitioner is able to relitigate issues
previously presented to the state courts. Justice Robert Jackson dissented in
Brown, complaining that the few meritorious petitions filed by state prisoners
would be lost in the flood of new filings that could be expected. It is probably
no accident that Jackson's clerk, William Rehnquist, would become one of
the key players in restricting the availability of the writ over the course of the
next fifty years.

In 1963, the same year that the Court broadened habeas in *Fay* v. *Noia*,[68]
holding a state prisoner not precluded from raising a constitutional
objection because of a nondeliberate state procedural default, Paul Bator
published an influential law review article. Bator argued that, based on the
need for finality and economy of resources, the federal role should be
limited to cases of a state's total failure to provide basic due process.[69]
Justice Brennan in *Fay* rejected the Bator approach but while resistance to
cluttering habeas with procedural hurdles prevailed during the Warren
Court era and played a critical role in creating the *de facto* capital punishment moratorium that preceded *Furman* v. *Georgia*, shortly thereafter
Court decisions and legislative activity heralded a steady decline in the
notion that state prisoners were entitled to an easily accessible federal
forum to assert federal rights.

Leading habeas scholars Larry Yackle and Joseph Hoffman have set out
the details[70] but briefly put, when Rehnquist was at the Department of
Justice, he became the Nixon administration point man, lobbying Congress
intensely but unsuccessfully to amend the habeas statute to block the
Warren Court decisions.[71] Soon Supreme Court decisions, first during the
Burger Court and then intensifying when Rehnquist became Chief Justice,
produced the restrictions that Congress had declined to enact. When in
1996 Congress did act, after the murderous attack on a federal building in
Oklahoma City, the legislation showed the marks of the Chief Justice's
earlier quest to narrow federal supervision of state criminal convictions.
As one federal judge put it, between "the 1970s through the 1990s, the
Supreme Court made it more difficult for state prisoners to obtain habeas
relief in two ways: by narrowing the grounds on which the courts can
grant relief and by barring petitioners who fail to follow somewhat complicated rules from obtaining review of their claims."[72] The Antiterrorism and
Effective Death Penalty Act, which Rehnquist and Justice Powell supported,

went even beyond Bator's proposal and previous Court decisions by imposing filing time limits and a variety of new procedural hurdles.[73]

Ironically, the number of habeas decisions granting new trials was
infinitesimal. Judge Lynn Adelman cited a study of 2,384 randomly selected
noncapital cases filed in district courts. Relief was granted in seven. The judge
reported her own experience granting relief in 11 out of approximately 300 petitions, arguing that state courts wrongly decide federal claims even more often
than the study reflected and that substantially more than "one out of
284 habeas petitions warrant relief."[74]

In its most important particulars, therefore, the liberalization of habeas was
stalled and then reversed as a result of Supreme Court decisions, ex cathedra
lobbying by Justices, and finally by congressional action.[75] As a result,
an adequate state law ground of decision, including a procedural default,
barred a habeas petition. This replaced *Fay*'s deliberate bypass rule and in
effect shifted the burden from a state need to show the petitioner was gaming
the system to a much stricter requirement that he show state laws were
complied with before federal claims could be vindicated. In *Ross* v. *Moffitt*,[76]
a Rehnquist opinion denied a right to counsel to an indigent seeking discretionary review such as petitioning the Supreme Court itself. The Court
reached the same result with respect to habeas in a capital case.[77] Earlier,
the Court – with narrow exceptions – refused to let habeas petitioners take
advantage of decisions making new law.[78] As Joseph Hoffman put it, after
these decisions, "federal habeas courts are not allowed to reverse state court
adjudications unless the state court's legal ruling was 'unreasonable.'"[79]

These developments serve as a backdrop for understanding the unavail-
ability of a process to examine claims of innocence in the decades even before
DNA evidence became commonplace. In a notable 1970 article, Judge Henry
Friendly proposed his own theory narrowing habeas to state failures to provide
a reliable trial process.[80] Though Friendly supported Bator-like restrictions
on the writ, he excluded cases where a state prisoner offered a colorable
showing of innocence. The privileging of innocence by a highly respected
federal judge might have been seen as a positive change providing a decent
chance to upset wrongful convictions, but this is not the way matters worked
out. The Friendly approach has had limited influence and much of it has
served to increase rather than reduce the precondition demands placed on
the habeas petitioner. In *Brecht* v. *Abrahamson*,[81] the Court used language
alluding to Friendly's innocence exception (habeas restricted to guard against
"extreme malfunctions") to *reduce*, not enhance, opportunities to challenge
the reliability of a state court conviction by increasing preconditions before
federal habeas could overrule a finding of harmless error.[82]

In a 1995 case, *Schlup* v. *Delo*,[83] a petitioner claiming actual innocence had
to show the claimed constitutional violations "probably" led to conviction of
an innocent, a standard less strict than the one Rehnquist had fashioned in
Sawyer v. *Whitley*.[84] More recently, the Court extended the gateway to permit
habeas despite 28 U.S.C. §2244(d)(1), the statute of limitations on federal
habeas, in the *"rare"* case where a "petitioner ... persuades the district court
that, in light of the new evidence, no juror, acting reasonably, would have
voted to find him guilty beyond a reasonable doubt."[85]

The Friendly position had its admirers but when the Justices adopted rules
that required extreme malfunction or cause and prejudice-type proof just to
consider a wrongful conviction challenge, the only result could be a haphaz-
ard, case-by-case fix. Explicit pleading requirements and the need to connect
procedural failings with verdicts become the elements necessary to avoid
dismissal of a petition seeking a hearing on innocence. In such a legal regime,
a DNA claim is pure gold: technology intimidates and it implies certainty.

THE PRESUMPTION OF GUILT

Before DNA, belief in actual innocence was almost always resisted by criminal
justice officialdom. A striking finding by scholars is the skepticism that greets
"not guilty" determinations. Acquittals are generally not taken as meaning
innocence, either in law or in perception. As Dan Givelber and Amy Farrell
conclude,[86] acquittals are commonly used to sanction defendants in later
cases depending on a judge's understanding of the underlying facts; they are
treated by the legal system as almost always a technical reversal of prosecutorial fortunes – certainly not presumed to signify factual, as opposed to legal,
innocence.

Though the universe of cases that goes to trial is small, the evidence
suggests a portion turn on defense claims of innocence.[87] Trials "are focused
on whether the state's evidence is thoroughly persuasive."[88] The reasonable
doubt standard means that "questions of innocence" do not arise or at least
are submerged under the litigation focus on guilty or not guilty verdicts.
While innocence may certainly be on the minds of jurors or judges, their
formal role is to weigh the state's evidence, not probe the defendant's claim
of factual innocence. Of the innocent acquitted, the burden of proof
focus masks the verdict's meaning. It is generally unknown whether defendants have been found factually innocent or are simply the beneficiaries of
a failure of proof. The estimate is that defendants whose cases ultimately
result in acquittals are likely to be actually innocent in one in five cases.[89]
If these innocence cases, whatever their number, are ever identified it is only

because DNA has sensitized officials and the general public to the reality of criminal process fallibility. Rob Warden has pointed out that there would be "no public constituency" for the Innocence Movement without media exposure of errors and official misconduct and that, "until quite late in the 20th century, the mainstream media by and large were deaf to defendants' protestations of innocence and oblivious to any need to reform what was widely regarded as a fair, accurate and, above all, well intentioned criminal justice system."[90]

Finally, we need not determine the oft-contested meaning and function of the presumption of innocence to conclude that it also offered little comfort to the innocent accused in the pre-DNA era. Rather than ensuring that system actors operate as if the defendant is factually innocent before a conviction, "In case after case, the legal term 'innocence' stands in for the idea that the state has not met its burden of proof beyond a reasonable doubt and that the accused, therefore, lacks criminal culpability or responsibility."[91] William Laufer suggests that to make the presumption more than an empty maxim, jurors should be instructed to assume the accused is factually innocent. But nothing has come of such a proposal, even after the general acceptance of DNA and growth of the Innocence Movement. It is easy to see why, given the signals emanating from the proof standards applied to the pretrial process such as those governing arrest, bail, detention decisions, search, seizure and indictment. It is no secret that many jurors begin their service with a sense that there is a reason why a defendant has been charged. Little is done to dispel it, perhaps because of the general perception that defendants are likely guilty. Jurors go through a socialization process and are thought to come out impartial but they are not deaf, dumb and blind. Prosecuting attorneys are privy to the specific evidence that has brought the defendant to the court. We can assume that despite even the best intentions, their disbelief in actual innocence will be conveyed to other system actors.

CONCLUSION

After canvassing an area (witness identification) where reform has begun to take hold and another where there is far to go (sharing exculpatory information), it may be well to remember that there are different ways to think about the impact of DNA, each with different emphasis and prospect. The first is as scientific evidence in cases where DNA is germane to guilt and available. Here DNA has proved to be a remarkable success when measured by the number of laws it has changed, cases it has diverted and exonerations produced.

Another way to see DNA is as creating a new attitude toward justice issues, replacing the previously denied vulnerability of the criminal process to error. DNA testing is not the only force behind current reform proposals but it has played a major role. Significant numbers of Americans have turned against the death penalty; critiques of the pernicious effects of the justice system abound; mass incarceration, mandatory minimums and practices identified with wrongful conviction are under attack. These reform promises are not yet realized but many of them would not have gained ground without the DNA revolution.

DNA also has a capacity to stir transformative, even Utopian, dreams of a truly different system of criminal justice, a world where prosecutors care as much as defense attorneys about removing error from the process, where they really are minsters of justice, where our coercive plea bargaining system and enhanced sentencing after trial universe is replaced, where open files are the norm, and in sum where the presumption of innocence is more than a rhetorical flourish. These are specks on the horizon but we would hardly know they were there at all without the work of the tenacious and resilient advocates who are the movers and shakers of the Innocence Movement.

NOTES

1 The story of Edwin Borchard and those who followed his lead in identifying wrongful convictions has been reported extensively elsewhere. To avoid repetition, I offer a few generalizations about their pre-DNA approaches. I read Borchard's 1932 work, *Convicting the Innocent*, when I was studying at Yale Law School in the late 1950s. I was interested in the views another Yale professor, Judge Jerome Frank, held about legal education, came across his book on innocence (not what I was looking for at all), written with his daughter Barbara in 1957 and learned about Borchard. I must have relished the flaws in the criminal justice system that both books exposed because over 50 years later my work still includes efforts to find more of them. Borchard identified many of the systemic factors that we associate with wrongful conviction. He also found that almost all the wrongfully convicted had few resources and faced enormous odds in clearing their names. It usually took initiative by outsiders, rather than judges or prosecutors, to take the critical action that led to exoneration. These could include the real culprit continuing to commit crimes and ultimately being caught, or the person thought to have been murdered being found alive. On occasion an influential person in the community would push for an investigation. Habeas corpus and writs of error coram nobis are barely mentioned in his text. The Franks also took a case study approach and found similar explanations for system failure. They introduced issues not previously examined by Borchard such as the inequality of resources available to the prosecution and the

defense: even "with the ablest lawyer in the world, an innocent man may be found guilty – solely because of his poverty." JEROME FRANK & BARBARA FRANK, NOT GUILTY 84 (1957). The Franks also highlight that jurors are subject to the same errors of perception and memory as eyewitnesses and victims. They may misinterpret, misunderstand, misremember or even forget testimony given at trial and hold "undetected prejudices" that lead them to find an innocent defendant guilty. *Id.* at 223–24. In their view, a criminal trial staged as a "fight" or "competition" between lawyers is wholly inconsistent with uncovering truth.

2 *See, e.g.*, Katie Worth, *The Surprisingly Imperfect Science of DNA Testing: How a Proven Tool May Be Anything But*, FRONTLINE (PBS), June 2015, available at http://stories.frontline.org/dna. As I write, the serious side effects of technological change are being debated: robots may replace assembly line workers and even jobs that center on judgment and creativity; corporations pay billions for modest startups that offer to collect online data and monetize previously private information; Congress struggles with reigning in National Security Agency data collection. The introduction of DNA into the world of law enforcement is of a piece with these developments. Some fear that DNA will serve to distract from the serious gaps in the fairness and accuracy of institutional practices that are not reachable by the new technology.

3 408 U.S. 238 (1972).

4 *See, e.g.*, Gregg v. Georgia, 428 U.S. 153 (1976).

5 Anthony G. Amsterdam, *The Supreme Court and the Rights of Suspects in Criminal Cases*, 45 N.Y.U. L. REV. 785, 795 (1970).

6 *Id.* at 786.

7 *Id.* at 792.

8 United States v. Garsson, 291 F. 646, 649 (S. D. N.Y. 1923).

9 Debra Cassens Weiss, *Study: Scalia Was Wrong; About 1 in 25 People Sentenced to Death Are Likely Innocent*, ABA JOURNAL, Apr. 29, 2014, available at www.abajournal.com/news/article/study_scalia_was_wrong_about_1_in_25_people_ sentenced_to_death_are_likely_i/ (In this article, Samuel Gross calls Scalia's claim "silly").

10 Kansas v. Marsh, 548 U.S. 163, 194–95 (2006) (Scalia, J., concurring).

11 Jonathan M. Katz & Erik Eckholm, *DNA Evidence Clears Two Men in 1983 Murder*, N.Y. TIMES, Sept. 3, 2014, at A1.

12 BRANDON L. GARRETT, CONVICTING THE INNOCENT: WHERE CRIMINAL PROSECUTIONS GO WRONG 345–46 n. 82 (2011).

13 The *least* visible innocents are the numerous black men and women brutally hung, burned and beaten to death by mobs during the nineteenth and early twentieth centuries. These atrocities were not "wrongful *convictions*" they were "wrongful" *murders* of those who the historical record suggests were overwhelmingly innocent. *See* JAMES ALLEN ET AL, WITHOUT SANCTUARY (2000).

14 344 U.S. 443 (1953).

15 Fay v. Noia, 372 U.S. 391 (1963).

16 Townsend v. Sain, 372 U.S. 293 (1963).

17 Sanders v. United States, 373 U.S. 1 (1963).

18 KARIM H. VELLANI & JOEL D. NAHOUN, APPLIED CRIME ANALYSIS 11 (2001) (observing that "the overall success rate for all habeas petitioners [writ granted] has been very low — around 2 percent — but the rate is much higher for capital defendants."); Nancy J. King, *Enforcing Effective Assistance after Martinez*, 122 YALE L.J. 2428 (2013).

19 *See* MICHAEL MELTSNER, THE MAKING OF A CIVIL RIGHTS LAWYER 156–57 (2006).

20 State v. Pitts, 241 So.2d 399 (Fla. 1970).

21 Karen Branch & Tom Fiedler, *Nightmare Ends for 2 Wrongly Accused*, MIAMI HERALD, May 1, 1998, at A1.

22 CHARLES L. BLACK JR., CAPITAL PUNISHMENT: THE INEVITABILITY OF CAPRICE AND MISTAKE (1974).

23 Robert Siegel, *March on Washington, Coinciding Murders Redefined Liberties*, NATIONAL PUBLIC RADIO, Aug. 26, 2013, www.npr.org/sections/codeswitch/2013/08/27/215838758/march-on-washington-coinciding-murders-redefined-liberties.

24 Paul Vitello, *George Whitmore Jr., Who Falsely Confessed to 3 Murders in 1964, Dies*, N. Y. TIMES, Oct. 15, 2012, at A29, available at www.nytimes.com/2012/10/16/nyregion/george-whitmore-jr-68-dies-falsely-confessed-to-3-murders-in-1964.html.

25 *See* Siegel, *supra* note 23.

26 People v. Whitmore, 257 N.Y.S. 2d 787 (Sup. Ct. Kings Co. 1965).

27 *Id.*

28 T. J. English, *Who Will Mourn George Whitmore*, N.Y. TIMES, Oct. 13, 2012, at A21, available at www.nytimes.com/2012/10/13/opinion/who-will-mourn-george-whitmore.html.

29 MICHAEL MELTSNER, CRUEL AND UNUSUAL: THE SUPREME COURT AND CAPITAL PUNISHMENT (1973, 2011).

30 EVAN MANDERY, A WILD JUSTICE 36 (2013).

31 MELTSNER, *supra* note 29, at 296.

32 Coleman v. Alabama, 368 U.S. 129 (1964); Coleman v. Alabama, 389 U.S. 22 (1967). *See* MELTSNER, *supra* note 29, at 16–17.

33 Bedau & Radelet, *Miscarriages of Justice in Potentially Capital Cases*, 40 STAN. L. REV. 21, 89 (1987) ("So far as we know, none of these post-Furman procedural changes has been introduced with reducing the risk of executing the innocent as the paramount motive.").

34 Biggers v. Tennessee, 390 U.S. 404 (1968).

35 Brief of Petitioner 17, 18, Biggers v. Tennessee, No. 237, October Term 1967.

36 Biggers, 390 U.S. at 404.

37 Neil v. Biggers, 409 U.S. 188 (1972).

38 *Id.* at 199–201.

39 *Id.* at 204.

40 388 U.S. 293, 301–302 (1967).

41 432 U.S. 98 (1977).

42 388 U.S. 218 (1967).

43 388 U.S. 263 (1967).

44 406 U.S. 682 (1972). *See also* Simmons v. United States, 390 U.S. 377 (1968) (photo array).

45 *See* Manson v. Braithwaite, 432 U.S. 98, 117 (1977) (Stevens, J. concurring).

46 *Id.* at 118.

47 Letter from Professor Stanley Z. Fisher on file with the author.

48 Alix Spiegel, *To Prevent False IDs, Police Lineups Get Revamped*, NATIONAL PUBLIC RADIO, July 6, 2011, available at www.npr.org/2011/07/06/137652142/to-prevent-false-ids-police-lineups-get-revamped.

49 27 A.3d 872, 877 (N.J. 2011).

50 Marvin Zalman & Julia Carrano, *Sustainability of Innocence Reform*, 77 ALB. L. REV. 955, 962–964 (2013–14) (summary of initiatives that adopted the National Institute of Justice Guide) and sources cited. *See also* Innocence Project, *Eyewitness Misidentification*, available at www.innocenceproject.org/causes-wrongful-conviction/eyewitness-misidentification (listing ten states where reform such as sequential and blind lineup administration has taken place); Gary I. Wells, *Eyewitness Identification: Systemic Reforms*, 2006 WIS. L. REV 615, 623–31 (2006); NATIONAL INSTITUTE OF JUSTICE, EYEWITNESS EVIDENCE: A GUIDE FOR LAW ENFORCEMENT 1 (1999).

51 373 U.S. 83 (1963).

52 *Id.* at 87.

53 372 U.S. 335 (1963).

54 Bennett L. Gershman, *Reflections on Brady v. Maryland*, 47 S. TEX. L. REV. 685, 727 (2006).

55 Brandon L. Garrett, *Judging Innocence*, 108 COLUM. L. REV. 55, 131 (2008).

56 Jon Gould, *Wrongful Convictions in the United States: An Overview*, OXFORD HANDBOOKS ONLINE 11–14, (2014).

57 United States v. Ruiz, 536 U.S. 622 (2002).

58 Boykin v. Alabama, 395 U.S. 238 (1969).

59 Corinna Barrett Lain, *Accuracy Where It Matters: Brady v. Maryland in the Plea Bargaining Context*, 80 WASH. U. L. REV. 1, 21 (2002).

60 427 U.S. 97 (1976).

61 473 U.S. 667 (1985).

62 *Id.* at 682.

63 Daniel S. Medwed, *The Prosecutor As a Minister of Justice: Preaching to the Unconverted from the Post-Conviction Pulpit*, 84 WASH. L. REV. 35, 46–56 (2009); *Cf.* Fred C. Zacharias, *The Professional Discipline of Prosecutors*, 79 N.C. L. REV. 721, 744 (2001); Richard A. Rosen, *Disciplinary Sanctions against Prosecutors for Brady violations: A Paper Tiger*, 65 N.C. L. REV. 693, 697 (1987).

64 Daniel S. Medwed, *The Zeal Deal: Prosecutorial Resistance to Post-Conviction Claims of Innocence*, 84 B.U. L. REV. 125, 173 n. 249 (2004). *See also* Connick

v. Thompson, 563 U.S. 51 (2011) (denying damages for *Brady* violation leading to wrongful conviction).

65 Herrera v. Collins, 506 U.S. 390 (1993); In Re Troy Davis, 557 U.S. 952 (2009) (Scalia, J. and Thomas, J., dissenting) (Court has never held actual innocence a bar to execution).

66 Judge John J. Parker, *Report of the Committee on Habeas Corpus Procedure submitted to the Judicial Conference of the United States*, June 7, 1943.

67 344 U.S. 443 (1953).

68 372 U.S. 391 (1963).

69 Paul M. Bator, *Finality in Criminal Law and Federal Habeas Corpus for State Prisoners*, 76 HARV. L. REV. 441 (1963).

70 Larry W. Yackle, *The Habeas Hagioscope*, 66 S. CAL. L. REV. 2331 (1993); Joseph L. Hoffmann, *Narrowing Habeas Corpus*, in THE REHNQUIST LEGACY 156 (Craig Bradley, ed., 2006).

71 In the early 1970s, the Department of Justice argued unsuccessfully to restrict habeas by requiring that the constitutional rights considered must relate to the "reliability" of fact finding and claims should not be entertained unless a different result would probably be obtained if the violation had not occurred (H.R. 13722, 92d Cong. (1972) and S. 3833, 92d Cong. (1972)).

72 Lynn Adelman, *The Great Writ Diminished*, 35 NEW ENG. J. CRIM. & CIV. CONFINEMENT 3, 12 (2009).

73 *See* 28 U.S.C. § 2244(d) (1) (providing for a one-year statute of limitations for filing federal habeas corpus petitions).

74 Adelman, *supra* note 72, at 5, 9.

75 Early on, *Fay*, *Townsend* and *Sanders*, as well as their implications supporting a generous review policy, were shelved. Wainwright v Sykes, 433 U.S. 72 (1977). *See also* Coleman v. Thompson, 501 U.S. 722 (1991).

76 417 U.S. 600 (1974).

77 Murray v. Giarratano, 492 U.S. 1 (1989).

78 Teague v. Lane, 489 U.S. 288, 311 (1989); Butler v. McKellar, 494 U.S. 407, 412 (1990).

79 Hoffmann, *supra* note 70, at 179–80.

80 Henry Friendly, *Is Innocent Irrelevant? Collateral Attack on Criminal Judgments*, 38 U. CHI. L. REV. 142 (1970). For proposals for a separate innocence post-conviction track, see Stephanie Roberts Hartung, *Habeas Corpus for the Innocent*, March 2015 (Suffolk University Law School Legal Studies Research Paper No. 15–14, publication forthcoming), available at http://papers.ssrn.com/sol3/papers.cfm?abstract_id=2579351##.

81 507 U.S. 619 (1993).

82 Justice O'Connor dissented, arguing that "the possibility that an error may have caused the conviction of an actually innocent person – is sufficient by itself to permit plenary review of the prisoner's federal claim," Brecht v. Abrahamson, 507 U.S. 619, 652 (1993) (O'Connor, J., dissenting); *cf.* Withrow v. Williams, 507

U.S. 680 (1993) (holding that *Miranda* protects a trial right and protects against the admission of unreliable statements).

83 513 U.S. 298 (1995).

84 505 U.S. 333 (1992) (clear and convincing evidence is required when claiming actual innocence of the death penalty).

85 *McQuiggin v. Perkins*, 133 S. Ct. 1924 (2013).

86 DANIEL GIVELBER & AMY FARRELL, NOT GUILTY: ARE THE ACQUITTED INNOCENT (2012).

87 *Id.* at 52.

88 *Id.* at 61.

89 *Id.* at 142.

90 Rob Warden, *Role of the Media & Public Opinion on Innocence Reform: Past and Future*, in WRONGFUL CONVICTION AND CRIMINAL JUSTICE REFORM: MAKING JUSTICE, 39–56 (Marvin Zalman & Julia Carrano, eds., 2014). *See also* JAMES S. LIEBMAN, SHAWN CROWLEY, ANDREW MARKQUART, LAUREN ROSENBERG, LAUREN GALLO WHITE & DANIEL ZHARKOVSKY, THE WRONG CARLOS: ANATOMY OF A WRONGFUL EXECUTION (2014); FRANK R. BAUMGARTNER, SUZANNA DE BOEF & AMBER BOYDSTUN, THE DECLINE OF THE DEATH PENALTY AND THE DISCOVERY OF INNOCENCE (2008).

91 William S. Laufer, *The Rhetoric of Innocence*, 70 WASH. L. REV. 329, 347–48 (1995) ("The vast difference between the actual operation and the rhetorical commitment of the presumption is nothing short of remarkable"); *cf.* Bell v. Wolfish, 441 U.S. 520 (1979) (noting that the presumption merely allocates the burden of proof).

PART I

A Look Back

*What Have We Learned from Twenty-Five Years
of DNA Exonerations?*

The Big Picture

3

Convicting the Innocent Redux

BRANDON L. GARRETT

INTRODUCTION

I want to say I feel bad about what happened to this woman, but the people who really did this, they are laughing at her, and I hope they will never find her because the day that they do find her, she is really going to be afraid of what she has done to me because I am also a victim of what she has done. If she believes in God, she's going to pay for everything. That is all.[1]

Those were the words of Angel Gonzalez, a 22-year-old man with no prior criminal record, at his sentencing in the summer of 1995 for the rape of an elderly woman in Lake County, Illinois. The prosecutors responded, "There are cases, Judge, which never go away, and this is one of those cases."[2] The case revolved around a confession statement. Angel Gonzalez had been arrested parking his car near the apartment building where the victim lived. He was Hispanic, but did not particularly match the victim's description. She identified him in a highly suggestive procedure, while in the backseat of a patrol car, with Gonzalez placed in front of her in handcuffs. Gonzalez was then kept in police custody all night long, and after having been awake for twenty-six hours, he agreed to answer questions, and he maintained his innocence and described a powerful alibi.

Yet the police claimed that he had confessed in detail. The defense tried to argue the police had put those words in his mouth. The statement that Gonzalez wrote in Spanish did not resemble the statement that was translated into English and which he was asked to sign. But at trial, the prosecutor

This chapter updates data first presented in my book, CONVICTING THE INNOCENT: WHERE CRIMINAL PROSECUTIONS GO WRONG (2011). For their excellent research assistance in updating these data, I thank Kate Naseef, Angela Porter, and Jack Shirley, and for invaluable assistance sharing data, I thank Vanessa Meterko of the Innocence Project.

angrily responded that the confession statement had "numerous consisten-cies," including where and how the assault occurred in "the area of Belvidere Park," with the assault beginning in a car, and then on the ground near "these evergreen trees," matching what the victim had described.[3] And the prosecutor emphasized that there was a videotape just of Gonzalez being given the *Miranda* warnings, and he was "calm, cool, cooperative," since "that's the type of person he is, a black-hearted, vicious rapist. A rapist."[4] There was no video of the actual interrogation that could document who actually said what to the police, although the police admitted they had the capability and could have videotaped the entire conversation.[5]

At the brief sentencing hearing, the defense responded: "He stands before you on his 22nd birthday, an individual who never once prior to the date of this offense, to the date he was stopped by the police, had any problems whatsoever; an individual who led an exemplary life." Gonzalez "went through school. Worked." "So what is an appropriate sentence? To say 55 years is to say let's throw away Angel Gonzalez, let's stomp him into the ground . . . "

And that is what the judge did, sentencing Gonzalez to the "term of 55 years that the State recommended," commenting from the bench, "I suppose in 13 years on the bench, I've seen a lot of indignities that one human being forces upon another, but I can't recall one as great as this."[6]

In March 2015, Gonzalez finally walked free, after almost twenty-one years in prison. Compare his recent DNA exoneration case with another case from a decade before.

"No. No. No. Can't take this. O, Lord. Jesus. No . . . It's wrong. It's wrong. No. No," said one of the five teenagers at his criminal trial. Five youths had reportedly confessed to brutally assaulting and raping a woman who had been jogging in New York City's Central Park in 1989. Our attitudes toward criminal justice have shifted so much in the decades since the height of tough-on-crime and mass incarceration that it is harder to remember now what it was like when the "Central Park Jogger" case became the focus of a national media frenzy, the emblem for heightened fears that a crime wave was out of control. The press labeled the teenagers a "wolf pack," "wilding" in the park that night. In 1990, all five were convicted. The victim had been in a coma and when she recovered, she could not remember anything about the attack. However, police and prosecutors questioned four of the five youths, who had confessed on videotape. Those videotapes were played at the crim-inal trials and formed the center of the government's case. The prosecutor emphasized that the youths knew information that only the culprits could have known. For example, the prosecutor told the jury:

You heard in that video Antron McCray was asked about what [the victim] was wearing and he describes she was wearing a white shirt ... You saw the photograph of what that shirt looked like. There is no way that he knew that that shirt was white unless he saw it before it became soaked with blood and mud. I submit to you that Antron McCray describes details and describes them in a way that makes you know ... beyond reasonable doubt that he was present, that he helped other people rape her, and that he helped other people beat her and that he left her there to die.

The videotaped confession statements did not tell the entire story. The videotaped portions had followed lengthy interrogations that were not recorded. The youths each said they were innocent and that police coerced them into confessing. Even during the portions that were videotaped, officers described facts concerning the crime scene to the youths. There was no evidence that the youths could volunteer information about the crime that had *not* already been told to them by the police. And the confession statements contradicted each other; none of the youths admitted to having raped the victim, but they all pointed to others. There was little evidence in the case aside from their confessions. The crime scene evidence was not consistent with an entire group of individuals attacking the victim. And DNA testing was first being used in criminal cases by 1990. None of the five youth's DNA matched the unknown male DNA profile recovered from the victim. The only other forensic evidence consisted of hair and soil comparisons, which were not very reliable links. Still, they were each convicted.

Meanwhile, a man named Matias Reyes was convicted for another brutal attack that occurred very close to Central Park a few days before the attack on the jogger. Police knew about Reyes at the time, but never made the connection. In 2002, Reyes came forward and confessed to the Central Park Jogger assault. Unlike the teenagers who had been convicted, Reyes could describe in chilling detail how the crime happened. In fact, his account answered unsolved questions about the evidence in the case. And Reyes's DNA matched multiple pieces of crime scene evidence.

Based on those further DNA tests, the Central Park Five were exonerated in 2002, when a judge vacated the convictions and prosecutors declined to bring new charges. Times have changed. In 2012, Ken Burns, Sarah Burns, and David McMahon made a powerful video documentary about the case. And in 2014, the City of New York paid the five men $40 million in compensation for the years that they spent in prison, or about $1 million for each year that they spent in prison. This was the most money the City had ever paid in a wrongful conviction case. It took over twenty years for some justice to be done, and yet the five men were lucky. In most criminal cases, DNA testing cannot be done, because there is no evidence from the crime scene that can be tested. If there had been no DNA to test, and if there had been no match to Reyes, New Yorkers would have remained convinced that five guilty teenagers had confessed to a terrible crime.[7]

The word "exoneration" refers to an official decision to reverse a conviction based on new evidence of innocence. Some exonerations make national news and some do not. Unlike the Gonzalez case, the Central Park exonerations were particularly high profile, in part because of the way that the case had exemplified the 1980s concern about rising crime rates, race, and calls to ratchet up punishment in criminal justice. Other DNA exoneration cases have called into question similarly emblematic tough-on-crime era convictions. Take the case of Michael Blair. Blair was exonerated after spending fourteen years in prison in Texas, having been convicted of the murder of a 7-year-old girl, a crime that had led to the passage of "Ashley's Laws," which created lifetime sex offender registration requirements and enhanced penalties for sex crimes.[8] Henry McCollum, sentenced to death in North Carolina, had his case, which involved a gruesome murder of an 11-year-old girl, used in statewide political campaigns as the poster-case for why the death penalty was necessary and why North Carolina should not enact a Racial Justice Act to protect against race discrimination in the use of the death penalty – except in 2014, DNA tests proved that he was innocent all along.[9] Other cases were high profile locally. Thomas E. Haynesworth was convicted of several sexual assaults in the early 1980s in Richmond, all attributed to a serial rapist dubbed the "Black Ninja." After twenty-seven years in prison, DNA tests exonerated him.[10]

CONVICTING THE INNOCENT

My 2011 book, *Convicting the Innocent: Where Criminal Prosecutions Go Wrong*, tells the story of the first 250 DNA exonerations in the United States. My interest is in the patterns that reach across these cases, from the recent exonerations like that of Angel Gonzalez, to the first DNA exonerations in 1989, of Gary Dotson and David Vasquez. In the United States, as of this writing in Fall 2015, 330 people have been exonerated by post-conviction DNA testing.[11] In just under one-half of those cases, the post-conviction DNA testing also identified the actual culprits. There is no other country in the world in which such a large group of people had their innocence so clearly proven by DNA evidence. The criminal justice system in the United States embraced DNA testing early on, and the first innocence projects – groups dedicated to investigating and litigating cases to free the innocent – were established in the

United States. The data and the stories from these cases show wrongful convictions happen and how to prevent them.

Since I published *Convicting the Innocent*, there have been eighty additional DNA exonerations in the United States. Having now updated data that I collected when researching the book, in many respects, the patterns remain the same. Ten percent of these 330 exonerees, or 34 individuals, were juveniles at the time of arrest.

Twenty of these exonerees had been sentenced to death. Others faced the death penalty, but negotiated plea bargains to avoid the death penalty, or received life sentences at trial. For example, Byron Halsey, a severely mentally ill young man in New Jersey, avoided a death sentence only because of a holdout juror; years later DNA testing showed that his confession statements were false and implicated the actual culprit.[12] Larry Ruffin and two codefendants, Phillip Bivens and Bobby Ray Dixon, were all charged with capital murder, and Givens and Dixon testified against Ruffin to avoid the death penalty (although Dixon recanted and said they were all innocent). Ruffin was sentenced to life in prison, and only eight years after Ruffin died in prison did DNA tests exonerate all three men.[13] In general, many faced quite severe sentences. They spent an average of fourteen years in prison. Ninety-two of these DNA exonerees were sentenced to life in prison, twelve of whom were sentenced to life without parole.

The vast majority of these DNA exonerees were racial minorities. Of the 330 exonerees, 31 percent were white (101), while 62 percent were black (203), 7 percent were Hispanic (24) and 1 percent were Asian (2). While our prisons are disproportionately filled with minority convicts, these figures are starkly disproportionate, even as compared with the already large minority populations of rape and murder convicts in the United States.

Of the 330 individuals, 8 percent or 27 had pleaded guilty while the others were convicted at a criminal trial (four additional individuals had trials on some charges but pleaded guilty to additional charges). This is a modest increase in the DNA exonerations involving guilty pleas; there were 6 percent (16 of 250) in the earlier set of cases. Not only do DNA exonerees disproportionately consist of individuals who had trials, and perhaps as a result received long sentences, during which they had years to pursue post-conviction DNA testing, but some DNA exonerees endured multiple trials, after receiving reversals on appeal or post-conviction, before eventually being exonerated. Of these 330 exonerees, 63 percent were convicted of rape (209), 22 percent were convicted of a rape and a murder (72), 12 percent were convicted of murder (41), and 2 percent were convicted of other crimes like robbery (8). DNA exoneration cases have long

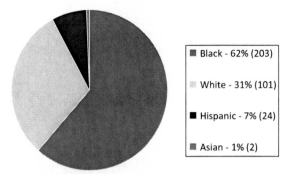

FIGURE 3.1. Race of DNA Exonerees

FIGURE 3.2. Crime of DNA Exoneree Conviction

consisted mostly of cases involving sexual assaults, since DNA testing can be particularly probative in such cases.

There have been some notable changes in the composition of the most recent set of eighty DNA exonerations. They include far more murder convictions than the first 250 DNA exonerations. The most recent eighty cases added twenty additional rape and murder cases, and twenty-one additional murder cases – adding 40 percent more cases with a conviction for a rape and murder, which just about doubled the number of murder cases among DNA exonerations.

These changes have impacted the types of evidence prominent in the DNA exonerees' criminal investigations and trials. Similarly high percentages of cases involve eyewitness misidentifications (72 percent) and forensics (74 percent) as in the previous dataset. Notably, the most recent eighty cases include a far greater proportion of false confessions and informant testimony, which appear to be more commonly relied upon in murder investigations. Twenty-one percent, or 68 of the 330 people, had falsely confessed, and 22 percent, or 74 of the 330 exonerees, had informants testify in their cases. In general, more of the eighty newly exonerated individuals involve relatively recent convictions, as one would expect, and therefore they include cases

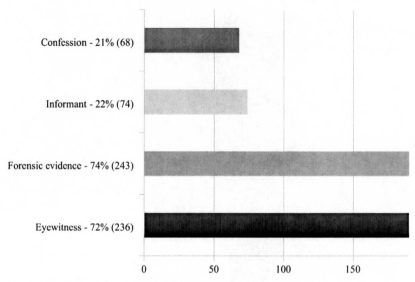

FIGURE 3.3. Evidence Supporting DNA Exoneree Convictions

where DNA testing was available at the time of trial and even excluded the defendant, who was nevertheless still convicted.

Many of the most recent exonerations were particularly hard fought along the path to eventual exoneration. Often because prosecutors were swayed by the confession evidence they continued to litigate the cases for years, despite DNA test results pointing to a wrongful conviction. These most recent exonerations, then, are particularly troubling, because they suggest that absent DNA testing, the underlying problems are still with us today, even if hard-line attitudes toward criminal justice are slowly shifting.

FALSE CONFESSIONS

In the first twenty-one years of post-conviction DNA testing, 250 innocent people were exonerated, 40 of whom had falsely confessed. In just the last five years, there has been a surge in revelations of false confessions – a set of twenty-eight false confessions among eighty recent DNA exonerations since 2010. There have now been sixty-eight DNA exoneration cases involving false confessions. Illustrating the power of contaminated false confessions, defendants in nine of the recent cases were convicted despite DNA tests that excluded them at the time. Sixteen of the new cases involved groups of false confessions by individuals inculpating each other, in which false confessions had cascading effects encouraging police to aggressively pursue more false leads. Of these twenty-eight new false confessions among the DNA exonerees, eleven were juveniles, at least two had an intellectual disability, and two were mentally ill.

Over one-third of all sixty-eight false confessions involved juveniles, and similarly, one-third involved individuals who were mentally ill or had an intellectual disability. These false confession cases have been concentrated in cases involving a murder. Four of the twenty-eight post-2010 false confession cases involved a rape, and the twenty-four others involved a murder, seventeen of which involved both a rape and a murder. Three exonerees had been sentenced to death.

All of these most recent interrogations were lengthy and lasted for more than three hours, with one exception, the case of William Avery, exonerated in 2010, and who was interrogated for eighty minutes and refused to sign the statement the detectives prepared, because it was not true.[14] All of these individuals waived their *Miranda* rights when asked to do so by the police. Only one of these individuals had an interrogation statement recorded in its entirety, apparently, and that exoneree, Johnny Williams, was only able to say about the crime that "I guess I did it," without being able to say what he did.[15]

All but two of these most recent confession statements included details corroborated by crime scene information. In general, sixty-four of these sixty-eight false confessions among DNA exonerees were contaminated with inside information. As a result, this second wave of false confessions should cause real alarm. These confessions, almost without exception, were said to have included detailed facts that only the culprit could have known. And yet we now know these innocent individuals could not have known such supposedly "inside" information. The incredible weight that prosecutors, judges, jurors, and the public may place on confession evidence may explain why these false confession cases are so hard fought, and why it has taken so long for these DNA exonerees to finally obtain their freedom. Nineteen of the entire group of sixty-eight exonerees had DNA tests exclude them at the time they were convicted. Yet the DNA test results were somehow "trumped" by the confession evidence.[16]

Perhaps attitudes toward confession evidence are changing. More jurisdictions are adopting important improvements to interrogation procedures, including videotaping entire interrogations. When Christopher Abernathy was exonerated, after spending nearly thirty years in prison after falsely confessing to a rape and murder, the prosecutors had themselves investigated the case using a Conviction Integrity Unit and joined the motion to free him. The prosecutor noted, "Today, would we be able to try a case on that? I don't think so," she said. "I cannot, I will not let a wrongful conviction stand."[17]

EYEWITNESS MISIDENTIFICATIONS

Of these 330 DNA exonerations, 236 involved an eyewitness misidentification, or 72 percent. Since more of the recent cases involved confessions and informant evidence, the percentage involving eyewitness misidentifications has modestly dropped from the 76 percent reflected in the first 250 DNA exonerations (190 of 250 cases). Of those 236 cases that had eyewitnesses, 218 included eyewitnesses who were victims of the crime.

Almost half, or 117 of the 236 cases, involved cross-racial identifications, 103 of which were cases in which the cross-racial identifications were by victims of the crime. Social scientists have long identified what they term an "other race" effect, in which eyewitnesses have a greater difficulty accurately recalling the faces of individuals of another race (and another age as well).[18] Many of the cases involved multiple misidentifications by multiple eyewitnesses. Of the 236 cases, at least 82 cases involved multiple eyewitnesses; there were two eyewitnesses in 44 cases, three eyewitnesses in 21 cases, four eyewitnesses in 10 cases, and five eyewitnesses in 5 cases. At least 28 of the cases had juvenile eyewitnesses.

Fortunately, the problem of suggestive eyewitness identification procedures has begun to receive more attention. The National Academy of Sciences issued a landmark report in 2014 recommending best practices for law enforcement, and a series of state courts have adopted new rules and jury instructions concerning eyewitness evidence, while courts generally have become more receptive to expert evidence on the topic.[19] Ideally, new research and existing procedures will continue to improve the use of eyewitness evidence in criminal cases.

FLAWED FORENSICS

Of these 330 DNA exonerations, 74 percent or 243 cases involve forensic testimony. Comparatively more of the recent cases involved DNA exclusions at the time of trial, since they involved, as a group, comparatively more recent trials. Twenty-two of the most recent eighty exoneration cases involved DNA analysis. Twenty of those cases involved DNA exclusions of individuals who were nevertheless convicted, three of which involved DNA exclusions that were concealed from the defense; in addition, one case involved inconclusive DNA results presented at trial, and one more case, that of Dwayne Jackson, involved a sample mix-up leading to an error in DNA analysis.[20] That is a large group of cases involving DNA exclusions. In the first 250 DNA exonerations,

22 exonerees had DNA testing at the time of their conviction, 16 of whom had DNA tests that showed innocence, while 4 had flawed DNA tests that incorrectly appeared to show their guilt.[21] Thus, far more of these recent cases involve the situation where DNA testing was done at trial, and either the DNA evidence of innocence was discounted or ignored, or the DNA tests themselves were botched. Half of the forty-four cases among all of the exonerees involving DNA testing at the time of conviction came from these most recent eighty exonerations.

Still other recent cases were ones in which DNA testing was simply not conducted, despite its availability at trial. For example, in the case of Damon Thibodeaux, who was sentenced to death in Louisiana and spent fifteen years in prison before DNA tests exonerated him in 2012, no DNA testing was conducted despite its availability in 1997. At his trial, the prosecution emphasized that if you have a "known perpetrator" and if "someone confesses," then you do not "need DNA to tell you who he is."[22] The appellate courts emphasized that "there is no due process requirement that a statement given to the police must be recorded" and found his confession statements voluntary and reliable "in the absence of proof to the contrary."[23] In response to this litany of cases in which police contaminated undocumented confessions, courts will hopefully insist that entire interrogations be carefully recorded, and review those interrogation statements for their reliability before permitting their use in criminal courtrooms.[24]

The bulk of these DNA exonerees' trials included traditional forensics, not DNA testing, and much of that evidence was presented in an outright erroneous, overstated or vague manner. I was able to locate trial transcripts for 194 of the cases. An additional 16 cases involved guilty pleas and no trial (although some of these pleas were accompanied by trials of co-defendants). There were 95 cases that involved microscopic hair comparisons, 150 cases involved serology or blood typing, 28 cases involved fingerprint evidence, 9 cases involved bite mark comparisons, 7 cases involved shoe print comparisons, and 3 cases involved fiber comparisons. Some of these exonerees had forensics exclude them at trial; 81 of the cases instead involved forensic evidence that excluded the defendant. Of those cases, thirty-four were DNA exclusions, but others involved hair, fingerprint, or serology evidence, which was presented as excluding the defendants. In twenty-three of the cases all of the forensic evidence was presented as having been inconclusive.

Although DNA set these people free, at the time of their convictions, the bulk of the forensics was flawed. Of the 243 cases, 53 percent or 129 cases involved flawed forensics. Those flaws ranged from unscientific testimony at trial that overstated the evidence, to blatantly erroneous testimony that

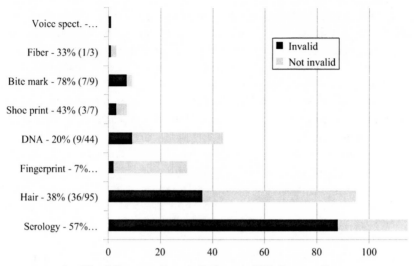

FIGURE 3.4. Invalid and Erroneous Forensic Evidence in DNA Exoneree Cases

provided incorrect statistics, to errors in the lab, to concealed forensic evidence that would have excluded the defendant.[25] The largest group involved overstated and unscientific testimony at criminal trials. In addition, twenty-eight cases involved exculpatory forensic evidence that could have supported a claim of innocence at trial but the existence of this evidence was not disclosed to the defense at the time. Twenty-nine of the cases involved analysis that was erroneous, including some due to lab errors. Some cases involved more than one type of error. The table below displays the cases involving flawed analysis that presented erroneous or overstated conclusions.

Of the remaining cases, those not involving invalid or erroneous or concealed evidence, an additional twenty-one cases involved vague conclusions that evidence like hairs or fibers or bite marks were "similar" or "consistent" with the defendant. That testimony was not overstated, but it was also not particularly probative. For a wide range of traditional forensics, basic research has not been done to validate the reliability of the technique; it is unclear to this day what it means to declare evidence to be "similar" or a "match."

Either flawed or vague forensics were presented in well over half of these cases; at least 62 percent (or 150 of the 243 cases), involved overstated, erroneous, concealed, unreliable, or vague presentation of forensics. Most of the cases that remained are either cases where no transcripts have yet been obtained, or where the forensics outright excluded the defendants at trial. The results suggest that far more must be done to overhaul the use of forensics inside and outside the courtroom.

INFORMANTS

Just as there has been a surge in recent cases involving confessions, there has been a surge in cases involving informant testimony, including jailhouse informant testimony. Of these 330 DNA exonerations, 22 percent or 74 cases involved informants, 35 of which were jailhouse informants, 33 of which were co-defendants testifying against exonerees, and 21 of which were other incentivized witnesses (some cases had more than one type). In the first 250 DNA exonerations, 52 cases involved informants, the largest group of which, 28 cases, involved jailhouse informants, while 23 had co-defendants testify against them and others had different types of incentivized witnesses or confidential informants. The increased numbers of murder cases have brought with them more cases with informants, including jailhouse informants. It is unsettling that the most serious criminal cases, particularly murder cases, can be so jailhouse-informant-driven. Few jurisdictions across the country have adopted any rules to better safeguard the reliability of informant testimony in response to these wrongful convictions, although some have required that informant testimony be corroborated or evaluated at pretrial hearings, and some prosecuting offices have adopted screening of such testimony. This problem of unreliable and contaminated informant testimony is one that still requires urgent attention.

JUDGING INNOCENCE

These innocent prisoners typically litigated challenges to their convictions for many years along the path to their eventual exoneration.[26] Few had any success along the way. Twenty-nine inmates received vacaturs of their convictions during appeals or post-conviction proceedings, representing 14 percent of the 203 that had written decisions published by judges. This is similar to the 13 percent reversal rate observed among the first 250 DNA exonerations. The group of the eighty most recent DNA exonerations included nine individuals who received reversals and had multiple trials before ultimately being exonerated. David Camm, Thomas Haynesworth, and Juan Rivera had three trials and Ted Bradford, Leon Brown, Donya Davis, Henry McCollum, Joseph Sledge, and Cathy Woods each had two trials.

Most of these exonerees litigated appeals; 123 had reported decisions during their appeals, and eighteen of the twenty-nine individuals that received reversals of their convictions received them during the direct appeals. Fewer, or forty-three exonerees, had reported decisions during state post-conviction proceedings; many state courts do not have strong norms of commonly publishing decisions during such proceedings. Only thirty-eight of these exonerees had reported decisions reflecting federal habeas corpus litigation. The U.S. Supreme Court denied certiorari in forty-three of these exonerees' cases. Best known is the case of Henry McCollum where Justice Blackmun dissented in the denial of certiorari, arguing that the case was flawed and captured the reasons why he had come to view the death penalty as unconstitutional.[27] In Larry Youngblood's case, the Court did more, hearing oral arguments and issuing a written opinion making new law defining a highly restrictive claim for which one could only challenge law enforcement destruction of evidence if it was shown to be intentional. Police had failed to adequately preserve serology evidence from the rape case, so it degraded and could not be blood-typed, but twelve years later, DNA technology had improved and the evidence was now testable. The DNA test results exonerated Youngblood.[28]

The claims litigated on appeal and post-conviction were dominated by state evidentiary claims, particularly since so many cases involved appeals, with over one-half of the exonerees litigating one of the multitude of such claims. Commonly litigated federal constitutional claims included *Jackson* claims regarding sufficiency of the trial evidence, which seventy-six exonerees litigated; ineffective assistance of counsel, which fifty-seven litigated; challenges to suggestive eyewitness identifications, which thirty-six litigated; and *Brady* v. *Maryland* claims concerning suppression of exculpatory evidence, which thirty-one litigated. In addition, fifty-two raised other claims of prosecutorial misconduct. As with the prior examination of these data, few exonerees raised actual innocence or newly discovered evidence of innocence claims during their appeals or post-conviction, prior to their exoneration itself (at that stage they often did seek an exoneration using a statute permitting relief based on DNA test results or evidence of innocence).

Few of those who asserted a claim of innocence prior to obtaining DNA testing had any success in doing so. One of the recent exonerees, Richard Gagnon, did prevail on a newly discovered evidence of innocence claim in South Carolina, prior to his exoneration; at his original trial the evidence largely consisted of a jailhouse informant, and DNA tests at the time of trial excluded him.[29] The others typically obtained relief more indirectly, like Anthony Chaparro, whose verdict was reversed for a claim of ineffective assistance of counsel, concerning the eyewitness identification evidence and evidence of a third party's guilt.[30] David Camm had his convictions reversed three separate times, concerning improperly admitted evidence, but the reason the appellate courts kept finding the errors prejudicial was in part that the evidence against him was so weak.[31]

Judicial opinions, however, typically did not reflect any sense that these were weak cases. For example, Leon Brown and Henry McCollum, both sentenced to death in North Carolina, had their convictions reversed due to the jury instructions in the case. But that outcome had nothing to do with the challenges to their false confessions and the complete lack of evidence of their guilt, apart from their coercive interrogations.[32] Indeed, of these 330 exonerees, 31 received reported decisions in cases seeking DNA testing, in which they were denied DNA tests; ultimately they did prevail and the test results supported their showing of innocence.

EPILOGUE

Although DNA exonerations may fade with time, many of the same under-lying sources of error in criminal cases still remain. And yet, while there have been modest successes in a range of states since 2011, with new legislation concerning recording interrogations and lineup improvements, as well as new scientific efforts, much of the law and procedures remains the same. Lengthy and coercive interrogations produced false confessions in sixty-eight DNA exoneration cases to date in the United States. Cases like those of Angel Gonzalez, Damon Thibodeaux, and the Central Park Five all show how if an *entire* interrogation is not videotaped, there can be no way to know whether police used coercive tactics or improper threats, or whether police contamin-ated the confession by feeding details concerning the crime. Moreover, even today, some prosecutors still resist even the most powerful showings of inno-cence and continue to seek retrials despite DNA evidence of innocence.

Other types of errors in criminal investigations are the product of shoddy techniques, poor documentation, and a rush to judgment. An eyewitness may fall prey to the same suggestive identification procedures long used around the world. As noted above, a 2014 report by the National Academy of Sciences set out a scientific framework for improving eyewitness identification procedures, based on decades of research, but most police departments in the United States and around the world do not use those procedures.[33] A 2009 report by the National Academy of Sciences set out flaws in the forensic testing so commonly used in criminal cases, but improvements have been very slow in the years since. Contaminated informant testimony, flawed forensic science, poor police investigation, inadequate defense lawyering, and prosecutorial misconduct may cause wrongful convictions in very different criminal justice systems and legal cultures.

The growing global conversation about wrongful convictions provides reason for hope. In recent years, scholars around the world have increasingly documented wrongful convictions and suggested ways to prevent them, including in conferences, books, and articles. There is also far more discussion and sharing of best practices around the globe. From the United States, the model of having nonprofit innocence projects has spread rapidly, particularly in the past decade, to Australia, Canada, Ireland, the Netherlands, New Zealand, the UK, and Taiwan. There is now an Innocence Network of such projects. The UK uses far less coercive interrogation techniques in criminal cases that provide a model for other countries to consider. The UK created an administrative agency, a Criminal Cases Review Commission, to remedy wrongful convictions, an approach since adopted in North Carolina, Scotland, and Norway.[34] A range of jurisdictions, from a growing group of states in the United States to the Netherlands, now routinely videotape at least some entire police interrogations. New research is being done around the world to place forensic techniques on a more reliable scientific foundation, and crime laboratories are beginning to adopt important quality control safeguards and procedures to help limit cognitive bias. Still other countries have adopted new standards for reviewing claims of newly discovered evidence of innocence.

What is most haunting about the wrongful convictions that come to light is that we can never know how many innocent people are convicted. The cases that I describe often surfaced because of sheer luck. Judges, jurors, and lawyers were all convinced of the person's guilt, and they were wrong. It was only because biological evidence was preserved, and lawyers were able to obtain DNA tests, that so many people were ultimately freed using DNA. But most criminal cases have no DNA to test. In other countries, there have been far fewer DNA exonerations or other types of exonerations. That does not mean that each of those criminal justice systems is less error-prone. Instead, it may mean that the countries need to examine their convictions far more carefully. Today, we know quite a bit about how 330 innocent people were convicted of serious crimes in the United States, what went wrong, and how they eventually won their freedom. We can never give them back the lost years of their lives spent in prison for crimes that they did not commit, but we can learn from what went wrong.

NOTES

1 Gonzalez Trial Transcript at 41–42, State of Illinois v. Angel Gonzalez, No. 94 CF 1365 (Cir. Ct. Lake County, Illinois, June 12, 1995).
2 *Id.* at 42.
3 *Id.* at 132–33, 991–92.
4 *Id.* at 133.
5 *Id.* at 928–29.

6 *Id.* at 49, 55.

7 For further reading on the Central Park cases, *see* GARRETT, CONVICTING THE INNOCENT: WHERE CRIMINAL PROSECUTIONS GO WRONG (2011), at 31, 162; *see also* Ken Burns, David McMahon & Sarah Burns, *The Central Park Five*, available at www.pbs.org/kenburns/centralparkfive.

8 *See* Innocence Project, *Michael Blair*, available at www.innocenceproject.org/cases-false-imprisonment/michael-blair.

9 For discussion of the McCollum exoneration, see Brandon L. Garrett, *Confession Contamination Revisited*, 101 VA. L. REV. 395, 397 (2015).

10 Maria Glod & Anita Kumar, *Thomas Haynesworth Exonerated in Rape Case after 27 Years in Prison*, WASH. POST, Dec. 6, 2011.

11 For a current list, see Innocence Project, *Cases: DNA Exoneree Profiles*, available at www.innocenceproject.org/cases-false-imprisonment/front-page#c10=published&b_start=0&c4=Exonerated+by+DNA.

12 Bob Braun, *He's Got a Right to Say the Death Penalty Is Wrong*, N.J. STAR-LEDGER, Nov.19, 2007.

13 Campbell Robertson, *30 Years Later, Freedom in a Case with Tragedy for All Involved*, N.Y. TIMES, Sept. 16, 2010.

14 *See* Garrett, *supra* note 9, at 402 n. 25.

15 *Id.* at 400, 409.

16 *See* Saul M. Kassin, *Why Confessions Trump Innocence*, 67 AM. PSYCHOLOGIST 431, 440–41 (2012).

17 Dan Hinkel, Matthew Walbert & Patrick M. O'Connell, *Tribune Exclusive: Man Free after 30 Years Says 'It's Just Scary To Be Out,'* CHI. TRIB., Feb. 11, 2015.

18 *See, e.g.,* Gary L. Wells & Elizabeth Olson, *The Other-Race Effect in Eyewitness Identification: What Do We Do about It?*, 7 PSYCHOL. PUB. POL'Y & L. 230 (2001).

19 NAT'L RESEARCH COUNCIL, IDENTIFYING THE CULPRIT: ASSESSING EYEWITNESS IDENTIFICATION (2014).

20 The twenty cases among the eighty most recent DNA exonerations in which the DNA testing excluded at the time of trial are those of: Jonathan Barr, Patrick Brown, David Camm, Donya Davis, Jeramie Davis, James Edwards, Joseph Frey, Richard Gagnon, James Harden, Kenneth Kagonyera, Jamie Lee Peterson, Harold Richardson, Juan Rivera, Michael Saunders, Shainne Sharp, Terril Swift, Robert Taylor, Vincent Thames, Robert Lee Veal, and Robert Wilcoxen. In addition, DNA testing in the Uriah Courtney case was inconclusive at the time of trial. On the Dwayne Jackson case, see Jackie Valley, *Man Wrongly Convicted After a DNA Mixup Awarded $1.5 Million*, LAS VEGAS SUN, July 25, 2011.

21 In addition, James Ochoa pleaded guilty despite a DNA test that had excluded him, and Richard Alexander was excluded by a DNA test from an additional sexual assault that prosecutors had said was part of a series of attacks by the same culprit. *See* GARRETT, *supra* note 7, at 315 n. 43.

22 Thidobeaux Trial Transcript at 185, 2025, State v. Thibodeaux, No. 96–4522 (Jefferson Parish Dist. Ct. Sept. 30, 1997, Oct. 2, 1997).

23 State v. Lefevre, 419 So.2d 862, 867 (La. 1982); State v. Thibodeaux, 98–1673 (La. 9/8/99), 750 So. 2d 916, 923–24 (La. 1999).

24 Garrett, *supra* note 9.

25 Each of those categories of flawed forensics is detailed in a law review article. Brandon L. Garrett & Peter J. Neufeld, *Invalid Forensic Science Testimony and Wrongful Convictions*, 95 VA. L. REV. 1 (2009).

26 I first explored these data in an article examining the first 200 DNA exonerations. Brandon L. Garrett, *Judging Innocence*, 108 COLUM. L. REV. 55 (2008).

27 McCollum v. North Carolina, 512 U.S. 1254, 1255 (1994) (Blackmun, J., dissenting).

28 Arizona v. Youngblood, 488 U.S. 51 (1988); GARRETT, *supra* note 7, at 226.

29 *See* National Registry of Exonerations, *Richard Gagnon*, available at www.law.umich.edu/special/exoneration/Pages/casedetail.aspx?caseid=4698.

30 *See* National Registry of Exonerations, *Anthony Chaparro*, available at www.law.umich.edu/special/exoneration/pages/casedetail.aspx?caseid=4558.

31 Camm v. State, 812 N.E.2d 1127 (Ind. Ct. App. Aug. 10, 2004); Camm v. State, 908 N.E.2d 215 (Ind. 2009).

32 State v. McCollum, 364 S.E.2d 112 (N.C. 1988).

33 *See* IDENTIFYING THE CULPRIT, *supra* note 19, at 1–4.

34 Lissa Griffin, *International Perspectives on Correcting Wrongful Convictions: The Scottish Criminal Cases Review Commission*, 21 WM. & MARY BILL RTS. J. 1153 (2013); Criminal Procedure (Scotland) Act, 1995, c. 46, § 194B (1), available at www.legislation.gov.uk/ukpga/1995/46/contents; Scottish Criminal Cases Review Commission, available at www.sccrc.org.uk/home.aspx; Introduction, Norwegian Criminal Cases Review Commission, at www.gjenopptakelse.no/index.php?id=163; Comm'n, Information, available at www.sccrc.org.uk/ViewFile.aspx?id=429.

4

Has the Innocence Movement Become an Exoneration Movement?

The Risks and Rewards of Redefining Innocence

RICHARD A. LEO

Innocence, it turns out, is a complex concept. Yet the Innocence Movement has
drawn power from the simplicity of the wrong-person story of innocence, as
told most effectively by the DNA cases. The purity of that story continues to have
power, but that story alone cannot sustain the innocence movement. It is too narrow.
It fails to accommodate the vast majority of innocent people in our justice system.
– Keith Findley[1]

INTRODUCTION

The history of wrongful conviction in America is often said to begin with
Yale law professor Edwin Borchard's 1932 book, *Convicting the Innocent*.[2]
Borchard catalogued sixty-five cases of actual innocence, described their legal
causes, and recommended possible solutions. Because Borchard's empirical
agenda was to refute assertions that the innocent were never convicted, he
studied only "erroneous criminal convictions of innocent people."[3]
Subsequent compilations of wrongful convictions – in Erle Stanley Gardner's
The Court of Last Resort (1952, 18 cases),[4] Barbara and Jerome Frank's *Not
Guilty* (1957, 34 cases),[5] Edward Radin's *The Innocents* (1964, 80 cases),[6] Hugo
Bedau's chapter in *The Death Penalty in America* (1964, 74 cases),[7] and
Hugo Bedau and Michael Radelet's 1987 *Stanford Law Review* article (350 cap-
ital and potentially capital cases, the largest compilation of wrongful convic-
tions in the pre-DNA era)[8] – also focused on people who were completely

Hamill Family Professor of Law and Psychology, University of San Francisco. I thank Sam Gross,
Daniel Medwed, Peter Neufeld, Jeannie Suk Gersen and Marvin Zalman for helpful comments.
For superb research and library assistance, I thank Jodi Collova, Janelle Hayes, Jenny Lentz,
Salvador Reynoso and Amy Wright.

factually innocent. Like Borchard, these authors focused on "wrong man" errors rather than "due process" errors or other legal mistakes.[9]

With the publication of *Convicting the Innocent* in 1932, Borchard shifted the debate from whether wrongful convictions occurred to *why* they occurred, and what could be done to prevent them. It might be said that Borchard invented a subfield: the empirical study of wrongful convictions. As a result, he has been hailed as a pioneer[10] and his book as a classic.[11] Borchard, in effect, created the template for all the "big picture" books on wrongful conviction cases that followed,[12] from Erle Stanley Gardner's *Court of Last Resort* to Barry Scheck, Peter Neufeld and Jim Dwyer's *Actual Innocence* (2000)[13] to Brandon Garrett's 2011 book bearing the same title as Borchard's.[14] If there were an annual book or career achievement award in the academic study of wrongful conviction, surely it would be named after Edwin Borchard.

But another way to look at the history of the study of wrongful conviction is not through its successes, but through its failures – an irony, to be sure, since wrongful conviction is itself the study of failure – and specifically through the responses of its critics. There is a long history of skepticism about the phenomenon and frequency of wrongful conviction in America, even though more wrongful convictions have been documented in America than in all other First World nations combined. Prior to the publication of Borchard's book, a district attorney in Worcester County, Massachusetts, was reported to have said, "Innocent men are never convicted. Don't worry about it, it never happens in the world. It is a physical impossibility."[15] More famously, Judge Learned Hand declared in 1923, "Our dangers do not lie in too little tenderness to the accused. Our procedure has always been haunted by the ghost of the innocent man convicted. It is an unreal dream."[16] Even after the publication of Borchard's book, Edmund Pearson wrote in *The New Yorker* in 1935 that "the vision of American criminal law as a ravening monster, forever hounding innocent people into the electric chair, is one with which emotional persons like to chill their blood. It is a substitute for tales of ghosts and goblins."[17] Lest one think these views belong to a different era, one need look no further than the views of former Attorney General Edwin Meese[18] or the late Supreme Court Justice Antonin Scalia.[19] Modern critics of the study of wrongful conviction in America no longer characterize it as the stuff of ghosts and goblins, but they nevertheless argue that the problem of "innocence" or "factual innocence" is a "myth,"[20] and that the risk of executing an innocent person "is too small to be a significant factor in the debate over the death penalty."[21]

In this chapter, I argue that the DNA revolution and its ripple effects in American criminal justice during the last 25 years have refuted such views by demonstrating that the problem of wrongful conviction in America is structural and persistent. Barry Scheck and Peter Neufeld, the visionaries who founded the Innocence Project in the early 1990s and became the faces of the American "Innocence Movement," strategically created the term "DNA exoneration," carefully making it synonymous with actual innocence, the title of their best-selling book.[22] As of December 2016, 347 people convicted of crimes in the United States had been exculpated by post-conviction DNA testing, including almost two dozen from death row.[23] More so than any other development in American history, the steady drumbeat of post-conviction DNA exonerations and the media attention they received in the 1990s and 2000s convinced policy makers, journalists, and the American public that the problem of wrongful conviction in America was a reality for hundreds, perhaps tens of thousands,[24] of innocent people. With DNA, the age of innocence arrived, and the ghost of Learned Hand had, finally, been laid to rest.

What distinguished Scheck and Neufeld from earlier innocence pioneers such as Edwin Borchard, Erle Stanley Gardner, and Jim McCloskey was their strategic commitment to innocence-based policy reforms and ultimately their vision for an innocence network and movement.[25] Individually, the DNA exonerations were compelling narratives of deep injustice; collectively, they were an indictment of the American criminal justice system's inability to perform its most basic function – separating the innocent from the guilty. The ever-expanding list of post-conviction DNA exonerations became the foundation of the Innocence Movement and its many "best practices" criminal justice policy reform proposals. For approximately two decades (1992 – 2012), the DNA exonerations posted on the Innocence Project's website were the definitive source of information about wrongful convictions in our era.

That changed in May 2012, when Sam Gross and Rob Warden founded the National Registry of Exonerations, an online repository of both DNA and non-DNA exonerations from 1989 to the present. Housed at the University of Michigan, it listed almost 900 exonerations at that time. As of December 2016, the Registry listed more than 1,900 exonerations, a figure that dwarfed the number of DNA exonerations by more than fivefold, and which continues to grow at a much higher rate than the DNA exonerations. In less than five years, the Registry's compilation of exonerations had not only eclipsed the Innocence Project's list of DNA exonerations numerically but, for many, replaced it as the definitive go-to source on wrongful convictions in America.

Drawing on earlier terminology and definitions used by the Death Penalty Information Center starting in the 1990s, the Registry subtly changed how scholars and journalists classify and count innocence, or its proxy. The Registry moved away from actual or factual innocence (what used to be called "wrong man errors")[26] to a more legalistic idea of an "exoneration" that, as defined by the Registry, is essentially an erasure of a preexisting conviction by a governor, prosecutor, judge, or jury based on some new evidence of factual innocence. In this chapter, I describe the conceptual move away from factual innocence to legal exonerations based on new evidence of innocence as the emerging intellectual foundation of the Innocence Movement, and analyze the costs and benefits of this paradigm shift in how we count, classify, talk, and think about the problem of innocence in America.

1 *The History and Transformation of Wrongful Conviction Scholarship and Activism*

Hundreds of cases of wrongful conviction were documented, aggregated, and described by scholars, journalists, lawyers, and others in the pre-DNA era. Yet, prior to the use of post-conviction forensic DNA testing to free the wrongly imprisoned, the kinds of cases discussed by Borchard, Gardner, Frank, Radin, Bedau, Radelet, and others were typically treated as individual tragedies, no more than one-offs, rather than illustrations of a criminal justice system structurally prone to factual error. Prior to 1989, most observers assumed that factually erroneous convictions were so rare as to be anomalous, if not freakish, especially in serious felony and capital cases.[27] At that time, the conviction of the innocent "was never more than a fleeting issue for most criminal justice practitioners, policy makers, the media and the public," as Robert Norris has written.[28] Across the spectrum, legal officials, academics, the media, and the public perceived the justice system to be virtually infallible.

The DNA exonerations of the innocent – beginning in 1989 with David Vasquez and Gary Dotson[29] – would, of course, change this perception. As the DNA exonerations began to accumulate in the 1990s, they attracted substantial and sustained media coverage, and shattered the "myth of infallibility." The rising number of DNA exonerations produced what Marvin Zalman has called "innocence consciousness," which, he argues, "replace[d] a belief that the justice system almost never convicts an innocent person."[30] In the 1990s and 2000s, the problem of the wrongfully convicted was part of virtually any serious conversation about American criminal justice, and entered popular consciousness as well,[31] as the public became more cognizant of the problem of wrongful conviction than at any time in American history.[32] The innocent but erroneously convicted and incarcerated criminal defendant was no longer perceived as an isolated tragedy, but by many as a regular feature of the landscape of American criminal justice. This awareness gave birth to a number of major systemic reforms for improving the accuracy of evidence gathering in the trial process to prevent wrongful convictions,[33] and contributed, perhaps more than any other factor, to declining support for the death penalty in America.[34]

The introduction of DNA into the criminal justice system meant that it was now possible to reveal innocence or guilt to a scientific certainty (at least in a small percentage of cases with biological evidence that had been preserved), rather than having to rely on contestable judgments about innocence. Unlike pre-1989 exonerations – which some believe were "always controversial"[35] – DNA exonerations of the innocent cast aside any residual doubt about whether the wrongly convicted defendant actually committed the crime.[36] Scheck and Neufeld made the strategic decision early on to focus solely on DNA exonerations for this very reason. As Neufeld commented in 2001: "What we have been trying to do, with the advent of forensic DNA testing, is replace ... speculation, supposition, and subjectivity with hard science."[37] Whereas the wrongful conviction of the innocent was once seen as aberrational, it is now – after more than twenty-five years of forensic DNA testing – seen as so commonplace that most DNA exonerations no longer receive much notice from the American media or public.

2 From DNA-Based Innocence to DNA and Non-DNA Based Exonerations

When Barry Scheck and Peter Neufeld conceived the Innocence Project and the use of post-conviction DNA testing to free the wrongly convicted, they were, of course, part of a tradition of innocence activism and scholarship that can be traced back to Edwin Borchard. That tradition focused on "wrong man" errors or actual innocence, not procedural unfairness, legal erasures of existing convictions, or other types of mistakes and injustices of the system. To this end, Scheck and Neufeld introduced into the American lexicon the concept of a "DNA exoneration," making it synonymous with proof of actual innocence. As Keith Findley has pointed out: "The Innocence Project's list of DNA exonerees is a carefully guarded list that does not admit everyone whose conviction has been erased, even if the case includes favorable DNA evidence. Rather that list ... admits only those whose convictions have been overturned *primarily* on the basis of DNA evidence, and where the DNA *conclusively* proves innocence."[38] The Innocence Project only counts a case as a DNA exoneration if it believes DNA testing conclusively established that the convicted defendant did not commit the crime, and it maintains that all 347 post-conviction DNA exonerees listed on the Innocence Project's website are factually innocent. Scheck and Neufeld have, in effect, succeeded in making a DNA exoneration synonymous with actual innocence.

But while an exoneration ordinarily is not proof of factual innocence, the term "exoneration" appears to have become synonymous with factual innocence even in cases not involving DNA testing. In the remainder of this chapter, I will argue that at least since the publication of the 2005 article "Exonerations in the United States, 1989 through 2003," by Sam Gross and his colleagues, and especially since the founding of the National Registry of Exonerations in 2012, innocence scholars, lawyers, and activists have essentially equated the idea of an exoneration, narrowly defined, with factual innocence. I will analyze whether the Innocence Movement has, in effect, become an exoneration movement, conceptually breaking with the longstanding tradition of wrongful conviction scholarship and activism.[39] I will then seek to evaluate the risks and rewards – for innocence scholarship and activism – of replacing factual innocence (i.e., "wrong man" errors) as the criteria for whose case counts as a wrongful conviction with the idea of a legal exoneration (i.e., erasures of preexisting convictions accompanied by some new evidence of innocence).

The term "exonerate," at least according to dictionary definitions, means "to clear from accusation or blame,"[40] or "to free from a charge; declare blameless."[41] I believe this roughly corresponds to the meaning our culture attributes to the concept of an exoneration, which is thus a broad term that does not necessarily correspond to actual innocence. In fact, the concepts are quite different. Under the above definitions, one can be exonerated and not be factually innocent. That would be the case for an individual against whom charges are dismissed before proceeding to trial, but who, in fact, committed the *actus reus* of the crime. Perhaps even more problematic, as Marvin Zalman has noted, "the term exoneration generally applies to all defendants who are acquitted at trial."[42] Yet, in the American legal system, a "not guilty" verdict only means that the prosecution failed to meet its burden of proving the defendant's guilt beyond a reasonable doubt, not that the defendant is necessarily innocent of the charged crime(s). Jury verdicts, at least by themselves, are flawed indicators of actual innocence in the American system of adjudication.[43] Similarly, a criminal defendant may be factually innocent but never exonerated. Exoneration is *not* an official or unofficial declaration or recognition of factual innocence. It is merely a release from charges, whether or not an individual has been convicted or imprisoned.

How, then, has the concept of exoneration come to be equated with factual innocence? The answer may harken back to the debate in the late 1980s between Hugo Bedau/Michael Radelet and Stephen Markman/Paul Cassell about the risks of executing the innocent in the American criminal justice system. In their landmark 1987 article, Bedau and Radelet relied on official judgments of innocence in almost 90 percent of their miscarriages of justice in capital or potentially capital cases, but only included cases of innocence where they believed "a majority of neutral observers, given the evidence at our disposal, would judge the defendant in question to be innocent."[44] Markman and Cassell, lawyers with no training in social science, criticized Bedau and Radelet's methodology for determining innocence as "subjective," and attacked Bedau and Radelet's conclusions in a few cases by using a similar (i.e., "subjective") methodology in arguing for guilt. Bedau and Radelet had asserted that 23 of their 350 miscarriages of justice resulted in wrongful executions of the innocent, but Markman and Cassell pointed out that in none of these 23 cases had there been an official acknowledgement of innocence by state authorities. Although Markman and Cassell only select-ively reviewed a few of the 350 cases, from which they attempted to generalize to the entirety of Bedau and Radelet's study,[45] they sought to undermine the legitimacy of Bedau and Radelet's conclusions about the risks of executing the innocent.[46]

Less than five years after Markman and Cassell's attack, Congressman Don Edwards contacted the Death Penalty Information Center (DPIC), an information and advocacy organization in Washington, D.C., that opposes capital punishment.[47] Edwards, the chair of the House Judiciary Committee's Subcommittee on Civil and Constitutional Rights, asked the DPIC to prepare a report on the risks of executing the innocent, including a compilation of cases from the prior twenty years in which death row inmates had been released from prison following an acknowledgement of their innocence. DPIC turned to the research of Bedau and Radelet, whose collection of wrongful convictions in capital or potentially capital cases had now grown to more than 400, and who had just published a book on the subject.[48] Yet DPIC replaced Bedau and Radelet's standard for inclusion with a new one. DPIC's "Innocence List" includes:[49]

> Defendants must have been convicted, sentenced to death and subse-quently either
> a. Been acquitted of all charges related to the crime that placed them on death row, or
> b. Had all charges related to the crime that placed them on death row dismissed by the prosecution, or
> c. Been granted a complete pardon based on evidence of innocence.[50]

DPIC defined a case fitting these facts as an "exoneration" because the prisoner's presumption of innocence was effectively restored by the erasure of his initial capital conviction, which it argued had been wrongful. According to DPIC, the defendant was innocent because the legal system had cleared him or her of the crime that had sent him or her to death row.[51]

It was at this moment, in 1993, that the idea of an exoneration absent DNA was first equated with a wrongful conviction. However, DPIC's list of exonerations was based not on factual innocence but on an erasure of a preexisting conviction that restored the defendant's *legal* presumption of innocence. In redefining innocence, DPIC believed it was replacing "subjective judgments" with "objective criteria,"[52] even though its definition of a death penalty exoneration reflected its own value choices and judgments. With this definition of "exoneration," it was no longer necessary to demonstrate factual innocence, a much higher bar.[53] The list of DNA exonerations maintained by the Innocence Project since 1992 and the list of death penalty exonerations maintained by the DPIC since 1993 have been, "for most of the last twenty years, the most oft-cited and 'official' of exoneration lists," as Robert Norris observed.[54] In 2005, Sam Gross and his colleagues effectively merged these two lists,[55] analyzing 340 exonerations in the DNA era. But Gross's criteria for an exoneration more closely tracked the DPIC's criteria:

> As we use the term, "exoneration" is an official act declaring a defendant not guilty of a crime for which he or she had previously been convicted. The exonerations we have studied occurred in four ways: (1) in forty-two cases governors (or other appropriate executive officers) issued pardons based on evidence of the defendant's innocence. (2) In 263 cases criminal charges were dismissed by courts after new evidence of innocence emerged, such as DNA. (3) In thirty-one cases the defendants were acquitted at a retrial on the basis of evidence that they had no role in the crimes for which they were originally convicted. (4) In four cases, states posthumously acknowledge the innocence of defendants who had already died in prison.[56]

Like the list maintained by the DPIC, the Gross team's catalogue was based on the idea of a *legal* exoneration – an erasure of a conviction, thereby restoring a *legal* presumption of innocence – rather than a demonstration of factual innocence. Gross thereby departed from the Borchardian tradition of including only "wrong man" errors. Indeed, Gross and his colleagues noted: "Needless to say, we are in no position to reach an independent judgment on the factual innocence of each defendant in our data,"[57] though they only counted among their exonerations legal erasures of preexisting convictions that were accompanied by some new evidence of innocence.

Building on that 2005 study, Gross and Rob Warden launched the National Registry of Exonerations in May 2012.[58] The mission of the Registry is "to provide comprehensive information on exonerations of innocent criminal defendants in order to prevent future false convictions by learning from past errors." It studies "false convictions – their frequency, distribution, causes, costs and consequences – in order to educate policy makers and the general public about convictions of innocent defendants. We focus on exonerations because the only false convictions that we know about are those that end in exoneration." Relying entirely on public documents, the editors of the Registry do not "make our own judgments about the guilt or innocence of convicted defendants," they point out. "Our criteria for classifying cases as exonerations are based on official actions by courts and other government agencies." Its goal is reforming "the criminal justice system to reduce if not eliminate these tragic errors in the future."[59]

The Registry's definition of an exoneration resembles the classification provided in the 2005 article by Gross and his coauthors, but is slightly more expansive. According to the Registry's website, "In general, an exoneration occurs when a person who has been convicted of a crime is officially cleared based on new evidence of innocence."[60] More specifically:

> A person has been exonerated if he or she was convicted of a crime and later was either: (1) declared to be factually innocent by a government official or agency with the authority to make that declaration; or (2) relieved of all the consequences of the criminal conviction by a government official or body with the authority to take that action. The official action may be: (i) a complete pardon by a governor or other competent authority, whether or not the pardon is designated as based on innocence; (ii) an acquittal of all charges factually related to the crime for which the person was originally convicted; or (iii) a dismissal of all charges related to the crime for which the person was originally convicted, by a court or by a prosecutor with the authority to enter that dismissal. The pardon, acquittal, or dismissal must have been the result, at least in part, of evidence of innocence that either (i) was not presented at the trial at which the person was convicted; or (ii) if the person pled guilty, was not known to the defendant, the defense attorney and the court at the time the plea was entered. The evidence of innocence need not be an explicit basis for the official action that exonerated the person.[61]

The Registry has defined an exoneration, at its core, as an erasure of a preexisting conviction, but its definition differs from the DPIC's by adding that it must be based on some new evidence of innocence. For the DPIC, the theory behind its definition of an exoneration appears to be that the legal erasure of the prisoner's conviction restores a presumption of innocence.

As Keith Findley puts it, "Without proof of guilt, determined by a court, the presumption of innocence defines innocence."[62] The theory underlying the Registry's definition seems to be that an exoneration, as defined by the Registry, is the best proxy and least biased approach for classifying wrongful convictions of the innocent that are otherwise mostly invisible. The Registry's definition significantly improves upon the DPIC's insofar as it requires some new evidence of innocence, providing an additional, if not fully specified,[63] standard for factual innocence.

3 *The Risks and Rewards of Redefining Innocence*

The term "exoneration" has no meaning in criminal law. It is a concept whose popular or everyday meaning – to declare blameless or relieve of a burden – largely corresponds to its dictionary definition.[64] As Hans Sherrer notes, "the historical and modern definition of exoneration makes it clear that it broadly describes relief or discharge from an imposition by a governmental authority."[65] Though it may not have been the intention of the Registry, lawyers, scholars, and innocence activists have appropriated the term "exoneration" and equated it with innocence. But it bears reemphasizing that the concept of an exoneration is much broader than factual innocence and encompasses (1) a criminal suspect against whom charges have been dismissed prior to trial; (2) a criminal defendant who was acquitted at trial; as well as (3) a prisoner whose conviction has been erased, *whether or not the erasure is based on any evidence of factual innocence.* These are all correct usages of the term because in each case the person's presumption of innocence has been restored.[66] Properly understood, an exoneration is logically independent of factual guilt or innocence, as many exonerees may be factually guilty. An exoneration is therefore a procedural judgment of legal error, not a substantive judgment of factual innocence.

But the Registry has defined "exoneration" more narrowly as a proxy for factual innocence, and like all proxies it is an imperfect measure. Moreover, innocence scholars have often treated the Registry's innocence-based definition of an exoneration as if it were interchangeable with factual innocence. It may be that the Registry's definition is the best, or among the best, available proxies for factual innocence, a notoriously hard concept to establish because of the difficulty of proving a negative. But this issue has not been closely examined by innocence scholars.[67]

The Innocence Movement has become an exoneration movement. The currency of the realm is no longer factual innocence per se. Instead, what counts – literally and figuratively – is whether a defendant has been exonerated according to the Registry's partially innocence-based definition. And as innocence has been redefined by many scholars to fit the broader concept of an exoneration, it is worth considering the empirical and normative advantages and disadvantages of this conceptual move for innocence scholarship and the Innocence Movement.

3.1 The Risks of Redefining Innocence

There are at least four risks to substituting the Registry's definition of exoneration – or just about any non-DNA based definition of exoneration, for that matter – for factual innocence. First, critics may accuse innocence scholars and activists of measuring something other than what they say they are measuring. In social science, this is called the problem of validity. More specifically, critics may charge that exonerations, however defined, are not always accurate measures of, or proxies for, factual innocence. They may further charge that the Registry includes some cases of factually guilty individuals, as Sam Gross concedes,[68] perhaps even many, and that in some or even many of the Registry's cases a reasonable inference of factual innocence simply cannot be made from the known facts. If exonerations, as defined by the Registry, are not a good proxy or measure of factual innocence, then critics may suggest that the Registry only generalizes to the type of known exonerations that meet its specialized legal definition, not to known cases of factual innocence. Of course, the editors of the Registry would presumably reject this critique and argue that their definition of an exoneration is the best proxy and least biased direct measure of factual innocence available, not something different from factual innocence.

But there remains an open question: how good of a proxy or measure of factual innocence is the Registry's partially innocence-based definition of an exoneration? Is it a direct measure of factual innocence, as the Registry suggests, or is it more of an indirect measure? How often does the Registry get it right and get it wrong? Is there a way to verify Sam Gross's statement that the Registry's error rate is likely very small?[69] These questions cannot be easily answered but beg an even more fundamental question: Is there a better filter or definition than the Registry's for factual innocence in order to identify true wrongful conviction cases?

One possibility would be to only classify as wrongful convictions those cases in which factual innocence can be proven to a near or absolute certainty, as Borchard did. Updating Borchard's vision in the empirical study of false confessions, my coauthors and I have long used the term *proven false confession* to connote only those false confessions that can be proven to a near or absolute factual certainty.[70] By analogy, one could also speak of *proven* false convictions to connote only those cases of wrongful conviction that can be proven to a near or absolute certainty. Following the definition laid out by me and my coauthors, a *proven false conviction* would include four categories of cases: 1) where it can be objectively established that the conviction is false, such as where it was physically impossible for the convicted defendant to have committed the crime; 2) where it can be objectively established that the defendant was convicted of a crime that did not occur, as when a murder victim subsequently shows up alive; 3) where the true perpetrator is identified and his guilt can be objectively demonstrated; and 4) where scientific evidence dispositively establishes the falsely convicted defendant's innocence. Of course, there would be an inevitable trade-off involved in using this purely (rather than partially) innocence-based definition to identify and study false convictions: it would yield far fewer wrongful convictions than the Registry's list. But it would also have a lower error rate and abandon any necessary reliance on the judgments of prosecutors, judges, executive officials, or juries.[71]

A second risk of substituting the Registry's definition of an exoneration for factual innocence is that critics may charge that the Registry's definition is not "objective" in any meaningful sense, contrary to the claim of some scholars.[72] Instead, critics may assert that it obviously relies on value choices – such as the choice to include jury acquittals following a retrial, even though a jury is only charged with determining whether the prosecution proved its case beyond a reasonable doubt, not with whether the defendant did or did not commit the crime.[73] Ironically, to the extent the Registry emphasizes exonerations as the best proxy for factual innocence, it necessarily relies on official judgments by the legal system – the same system responsible for causing the error in the first place. The judgments of the legal system are human judgments, and they – the opinions of prosecutors, judges, executive officials, and juries – often appear to be wrong.

In addition to relying on these judgments, the editors of the Registry, because of how they defined an exoneration, must also make their own judgments about which cases to include in their data set of exonerations. Unlike the DPIC, the Registry does not assert that it aspires to "objective" or value-free analysis. Although the editors of the Registry state that they "are in no position to reach an independent judgment on the factual innocence of each defendant" in their compilation of exonerees,[74] they must nevertheless make their own independent judgments of the existence and significance of factual innocence. Not all erasures of preexisting convictions are included in the Registry, only those accompanied by some new evidence of innocence, which inevitably involves judgment calls in some of their cases.

Perhaps more important, the Registry does not specify the criteria it utilizes for its case-by-case judgments of inclusion/exclusion. What constitutes evidence of innocence? How much is necessary? How strong does it have to be? What if it is contradicted by other evidence, but that evidence is weak, ambiguous, or inconclusive? The editors of the Registry appear to make conservative judgments about what constitutes new evidence of innocence (evidence that could have made a difference in the outcome at trial) in order to minimize any potential bias introduced by their own judgments. It is important to recognize here one of the outstanding virtues of the Registry: that it is transparent about how it collects, codes, analyzes and disseminates it data; that it is accessible to all, and provides explanations for its conclusions to anyone who asks; and that it invites others to provide any additional information on existing exonerations, thus providing a mechanism for correcting inadvertent errors and further diminishing the likelihood of bias.[75]

A third possible critique of the substitution of the Registry's specialized definition of post-conviction exoneration for factual innocence as the conceptual foundation for the Innocence Movement may be that the Registry, like DPIC, has engaged in what sociologists call "domain expansion."[76] As Peter Conrad and Deborah Potter discuss, "'domain expansion' describes a process by which definitions of social problems expand and become more inclusive. Domain expansion ... extends the definitional boundaries of an established social problem to include similar or related conditions."[77] Domain expansion is not necessarily a problem in and of itself. But it can be when an individual, organization, or social movement expands its definitional categories to include more cases for political or ideological reasons, typically to make a problem appear larger than it otherwise would, more important than other social problems, or to garner more recognition and scarce political or material resources. As Joel Best, who coined the term, writes:

> Claims-makers find themselves in competition, bidding for public awareness, official recognition, program funding, and other scarce resources. Successful claimants capture attention: their problems become the subjects of congressional hearings, *Time* cover stories, Oprah Winfrey programs, and Ann Landers columns. These successes have consequences. Because only a limited number of problems can receive attention, each successful campaign means that other, competing claims will fail to gain recognition. Moreover, successful claims-makers find themselves at a competitive advantage for the future. They are now insiders with experience, visibility, certified expertise, contacts with reporters and policymakers – resources that can make future campaigns easier. Claims-making's competitive nature accounts for the frequency of domain expansion. Domain expansion occurs in the natural history of many social problems.[78]

On the one hand, I believe that the editors of the Registry would strongly dispute any suggestion that they are expanding the domain of innocence, but argue instead that they are using a highly accurate but admittedly imperfect proxy for the same domain. I also suspect they would argue that there is no better way of identifying false convictions than through their partially innocence-based definition of exoneration, which, as a surrogate for a phenomenon that is largely invisible, operates much like the best medical instrument for diagnosing an illness or disease. The editors of the Registry might further point out that their conservative definition minimizes the bias of human judgment when classifying wrongful convictions and is underinclusive, thus excluding numerous wrongful convictions in which people were almost certainly factually innocent but received no official recognition of their innocence. On the other hand, if the Registry's definition of exoneration is not always a good proxy for factual innocence, then it may be picking up a high number of false positives, inadvertently expanding the domain to include something other than false convictions (e.g., due process errors in cases where the state had the right person).[79]

I am not arguing that a "domain expansion" critique has merit as a factual matter – for the most part, I do not believe it does – but, rather, only that the Registry's specialized post-conviction definition of an exoneration and the Innocence Movement's embrace of it opens the door to this critique. Some may even characterize the debates about the significance and frequency of wrongful convictions in America between innocence critics (e.g., Morris Hoffman, Joshua Marquis, Antonin Scalia) and innocence scholars (e.g., Sam Gross, Dan Simon, Keith Findley) as more about domain expansion and domain contraction than about the incidence of wrongful convictions of the innocent. The latter, of course, is presently unknowable despite the human desire to quantify and oversimplify complex social problems.[80]

Finally, a fourth possible critique of substituting the Registry's concept of exoneration for factual innocence is that it may dilute the emotional and moral valence of what animated the Innocence Movement in the first place: the pure tragedy of wrong person errors and their terrible consequences. Scholars have long argued that the wrongful conviction of an innocent person is the worst error that the criminal justice system can make.[81] This American truism dates back at least to Blackstone's famous statement that "it is better that ten guilty persons escape than that one innocent suffer."[82] Blackstone did *not* write that "it is better that ten guilty persons escape than that one exonerated suffer," because the suffering of an exonerated person is not the same as the suffering of an innocent one. There is a difference between an exoneration, which is a legal concept, and actual innocence, which is a factual concept.

To most people, wrong person errors are far more morally troubling than legal exonerations and therefore merit greater concern and more significant consequences.[83] Provable actual innocence, not legal exonerations, is the lifeblood of the Innocence Movement; treating the two concepts as if they are one and the same, as some innocence scholars have argued for,[84] may undermine the movement's moral legitimacy and the extraordinary power of innocence to effect meaningful criminal justice policy reform. To be sure, this has not yet happened. In fact, the ever-expanding count of exonerations collected by the Registry may have a more profound impact on criminal justice reform than a comparatively smaller data set of more provable and pure wrong person errors.

3.2 The Rewards of Redefining Innocence

The recasting of wrongful convictions as evidenced by exonerations rather than proven factual innocence offers several academic, intellectual, and policy advantages. First, and perhaps foremost, innocence advocates believe that they will thereby avoid indeterminate disputes about whether a convicted individual was, in fact, innocent or guilty, as some believe occurred in the Bedau/Radelet-Markman/Cassell debate in the late 1980s and in the Leo/Ofshe-Cassell debate in the late 1990s and early 2000s. Keith Findley has called these "subjective assessments of guilt or innocence" and advocates "relying instead on the only objective measure we have: judgments of the legal system itself."[85] While I disagree with the meaning that Findley attributes to the words "subjective" and "objective" here – the legal system's judgments are hardly "objective" and one set of scholars' analysis of the case evidence supporting innocence may be far more accurate, reasonable and persuasive than another's[2] – Findley's point may be more of a politically pragmatic one. If the innocence community relies on judgments by the legal system rather than on scholarly assessments of guilt or innocence, then some innocence critics, however mistakenly, will be less likely to challenge the accuracy of the data on which innocence scholars rely in their analyses and policy proposals. And, free from such attacks, these analyses and policy proposals are therefore likely to garner more favorable attention both inside and outside the academy. After all, this is one of the lessons of the DNA revolution – that cases of actual innocence demonstrated through post-conviction forensic DNA testing could no longer be meaningfully contested by innocence critics. As Keith Findley has written in this volume:

> DNA produced cases in which no one could seriously debate the claim of innocence. For the first time, we had a pool of cases in which we knew with

as much certainty as science could generate that we had gotten it wrong. The cases forced innocence skeptics to swallow their certainty (and their pride).[87]

A second and related advantage of relying on exonerations as a proxy for factual innocence is that this sidesteps an inherent epistemic problem in the study of wrongful convictions: that we often lack sufficient knowledge or evidence of what occurred to determine with absolute certainty whether someone is innocent. Given the inherent difficulty of proving a negative, it is almost impossible to demonstrate a person's factual innocence in many cases. For this reason, the number of conclusively proven wrongful convictions is undoubtedly much smaller than the number of actual wrongful convictions.[88] While innocence-based exonerations are neither a perfect measure of actual innocence, as Sam Gross has long maintained, nor the only or most conservative one, they still offer a valuable measure of a phenomenon whose underlying data points are largely unknown and unknowable. Put differently, non-DNA exonerations allow us to study a problem that otherwise might remain even more invisible than it already is. Given our investigative resource constraints, as well as our imperfect access to ground truth, innocence-based exonerations may be among the best available surrogates for actual innocence.

Third, studying exonerations as a proxy for factual innocence has advanced the social scientific study of wrongful convictions. The primary advantage of the Registry's definition of an exoneration is that it allows researchers access to more valuable information and data – about the regularity, distribution, causes, correlates, and consequences of many near certain wrongful convictions – than would be available if we limited ourselves solely to those fewer cases in which we can prove factual innocence to an absolute certainty. By relying on an innocence-based definition of exoneration, researchers are able to empirically study patterns and variation in the wrongful conviction of the innocent more quantitatively and thus more systematically, moving away from the qualitatively based explanations that have dominated much of the research literature on wrongful convictions to date and inevitably present problems of generalizability.[89]

Finally, studying innocence-based exonerations has created an important learning moment for the criminal justice system by enabling empirical scholars to more systematically measure innocence and count innocents than ever before. As the ever-expanding list of DNA exonerations in the 1990s and 2000s demonstrated, the problem of convictions of the innocent is persistent and systemic, not merely episodic and aberrational, as some critics claimed.[90] And the more than 1,900 exonerations catalogued by the Registry to date has allowed us to better identify and understand patterns and variation in the many sources of error that lead to wrongful convictions. To be sure, there is a justifiable trade-off here between marginally greater confidence in our judgment of actual innocence on the one hand and substantially more information about the multifaceted phenomenon of the wrongful conviction of the innocent on the other. But by accumulating more systematic and generalizable knowledge about these sources of error, researchers can gain a better understanding of the nature and scope of wrongful convictions. We can thereby provide more empirically informed policy analyses about the best error-reduction strategies, and help improve the ability of American criminal justice to perform its most basic function: separating the innocent from the guilty.

CONCLUSION: MOVING FORWARD

The Innocence Movement in the second decade of the twenty-first century is becoming an exoneration movement, at least conceptually, and this development carries both risks and rewards. The DNA exonerations that began in 1989 shattered the myth of infallibility in the American criminal justice system by demonstrating that it routinely convicts innocent men and women. The use of post-conviction forensic DNA testing created the opportunity for an Innocence Movement to emerge, and the DNA exonerations of the last 25 years have transformed lay and official perceptions about the problem and prevalence of wrongful conviction in America. This has occurred in large part because these cases have established factual innocence beyond dispute. At least since 1996,[91] the list of DNA exonerations maintained, publicized, and continually expanded by the Innocence Project has been the gold standard for researching and writing about innocence, wrongful conviction, and error-reducing policy reforms.

But the DNA exoneration cases have always been the tip of a much larger phenomenon. And, as many have pointed out, the era of DNA exonerations will inevitably come to an end, even as DNA technology improves and the number of innocence-based organizations searching for DNA innocence cases grows.[92] An estimated 80–90 percent of felony cases do not involve biological evidence,[93] and eventually forensic DNA testing will be commonplace across the country prior to trial. The closing of the window of post-conviction DNA testing has not happened as quickly as many observers expected, but it will eventually start to happen. DNA technology may have created the conditions necessary to shatter the myth of infallibility and launch the Innocence Movement, but "post-conviction DNA testing is a contemporary phenomenon, a fleeting moment in history,"[94] as Daniel Medwed has noted. The empirical study of innocence, as well as the Innocence Movement itself, will continue to become increasingly independent of the DNA cases that inspired a generation of wrongful conviction scholarship and activism and changed the landscape of American criminal justice.

With the National Registry of Exonerations' more legalistic and less direct measure of factual innocence than DNA exonerations, its cases will never replace the Innocence Project's DNA cases as the gold standard for scholars. Nevertheless, the Registry may be the most important development in the empirical study of wrongful conviction in the twenty-first century. To be sure, the Innocence Project's database of (DNA) exonerations and the Registry's database of (DNA and non-DNA) exonerations serve different purposes; in a historical sense the Innocence Project made the Registry possible. While the Innocence Project exposed wrongful convictions at a rate never previously imagined, and its work, and that of the broader Innocence Network,[95] has led to strategic litigation and important policy reforms, the Registry has collected substantially more data on wrongful conviction cases. And it has gathered this data on a greater number and variety of them. Despite its higher likely rate of misclassification of wrongful convictions (though very few of those listed on its website have been contested to date), the Registry offers the possibility of gaining more substantial (qualitative and quantitative) insight into the causes, correlates, and consequences of wrongful convictions than any other current database. Even though it has shifted the innocence community's focus from factual innocence to exonerations based on some new evidence of innocence,[96] the Registry has, by sheer virtue of the number of cases it has exposed and the amount of information it has collected, created a treasure trove of data for scholars.

Yet, as the Innocence Movement becomes an exoneration movement, it will do well to remember the historical significance of DNA in the evolution of American consciousness of wrongful convictions. Most wrongful convictions are accidents,[97] and many are discovered by luck[98] and cannot be proven conclusively. For more than half a century prior to the advent of postconviction DNA testing, journalists, lawyers, activists, and academics documented and wrote about hundreds of these "wrong man" cases. The cases rarely received much attention and were typically either contested or dismissed as mere anomalies in an otherwise well-functioning criminal justice system until advances in DNA technology in the last quarter century allowed innocence lawyers and activists to prove factual innocence to a virtual certainty in a significant number of them. This change in "innocence consciousness" would not have occurred but for the Innocence Movement's exclusive focus on factual innocence. But the Registry has dispensed with provable factual innocence as the touchstone for wrongful convictions, and replaced it with a legal, if conservative, definition of exoneration plus some new, but unspecified, evidence of innocence.[99] This conceptual move, if successful in the long run, offers the possibility of greater empirical insight and understanding into the problem of wrongful conviction and its solutions than ever before. But if the Registry's more legalistic criteria for case inclusion return us to an era of contested judgments about the factual guilt and innocence of its subjects, critics may seek once again to dismiss the problem of wrongful conviction as too aberrational to merit serious scholarly or policy concern. The challenge of the Innocence Movement going forward is to build on the gains of the last twenty-five years of DNA testing while not creating opportunities for frivolous critiques from right-wing or left-wing innocence skeptics.[100]

NOTES

1 Keith A. Findley, *Defining Innocence*, 74 ALB. L. REV. 1157, 1207 (2010–11).

2 EDWIN M. BORCHARD, CONVICTING THE INNOCENT: SIXTY-FIVE ACTUAL ERRORS OF CRIMINAL JUSTICE (1932).

3 *Id.* at v. As Marvin Zalman notes, Borchard "wrote *Convicting the Innocent* in 1932 with the express desire of promoting legislation to compensate the wrongly convicted." Marvin Zalman, *Qualitatively Estimating the Incidence of Wrongful Convictions*, 48 CRIM. L. BULL. 221, 247 (2012) (hereinafter *Qualitatively Estimating*). *See also* Marvin Zalman, *Edwin Borchard and the Limits of Innocence Reform*, in WRONGFUL CONVICTION AND MISCARRIAGES OF JUSTICE: CAUSES AND REMEDIES IN NORTH AMERICAN AND EUROPEAN CRIMINAL JUSTICE SYSTEMS 329, 329–55 (C. Ronald Huff & Martin Killias, eds., 2013) (hereinafter *Borchard and Innocence Reform*).

4 ERLE STANLEY GARDNER, THE COURT OF LAST RESORT (1952).

5 JEROME FRANK & BARBARA FRANK, NOT GUILTY (1957).

6 EDWARD RADIN, THE INNOCENTS (1964).

7 Hugo Adam Bedau, *Murder, Errors of Justice, and Capital Punishment*, in THE DEATH PENALTY IN AMERICA 434, 434 (Hugo Adam Bedau, ed., 1964).

8 Hugo Adam Bedau & Michael L. Radelet, *Miscarriages of Justice in Potentially Capital Cases*, 40 STAN. L. REV. 21 (1987).

9 *Id.* at 42.

10 Marvin Zalman, *An Integrated Justice Model of Wrongful Convictions*, 74 ALB. L. REV. 1465, 1478 (2010–2011) (describing Borchard as "a one-man policy juggernaut").

11 Robert Norris, *The "New Civil Rights": The Innocence Movement and American Criminal Justice* 8 (May 2, 2015) (unpublished Ph.D. dissertation, University of Albany, SUNY; Marvin Zalman has called Borchard "the patron saint of the

American innocence movement." *See also* Zalman, *Borchard and Innocence Reform, supra* note 3, at 329.

12 Richard A. Leo, *Rethinking the Study of Miscarriages of Justice: Developing a Criminology of Wrongful Conviction*, 21 J. CONTEMP. CRIM. JUST. 201 (2005).

13 BARRY SCHECK, PETER NEUFELD & JIM DWYER, ACTUAL INNOCENCE: FIVE DAYS TO EXECUTION, AND OTHER DISPATCHES FROM THE WRONGLY CONVICTED (2000).

14 BRANDON L. GARRETT, CONVICTING THE INNOCENT (2011). Garrett's book is far and away the best of the "big picture" books because it is more comprehensive, data-driven and analytical than the others.

15 BORCHARD, *supra* note 2, at v. Borchard described his book as "a refutation of this supposition."

16 United States v. Garsson, 291 F. 646, 649 (S.D.N.Y. 1923).

17 Edmund Pearson, *A Reporter at Large: Hauptmann and Circumstantial Evidence*, NEW YORKER, Mar. 9, 1935, at 41.

18 According to Edwin Meese, "The thing is, you don't have many suspects who are innocent of a crime. That's contradictory. If a person is innocent of crime, then he is not a suspect." Daniel Givelber, *Meaningless Acquittals, Meaningful Convictions: Do We Reliably Acquit the Innocent?*, 49 RUTGERS L. REV. 1317, 1328 n. 34 (1997) (quoting *Reagan Seeks Judges with "Traditional Approach*," U.S. NEWS & WORLD REP., Oct 14, 1985, at 67).

19 Justice Scalia claimed that American criminal convictions have an "error rate of .027 percent – or, to put it another way, a success rate of 99.973 percent." Kansas v. Marsh, 548 U.S. 163, 197 (2006) (Scalia, J., concurring). Many have criticized Justice Scalia for this observation. *See, e.g.*, D. Michael Risinger, *Innocents Convicted: An Empirically Justified Wrongful Conviction Rate*, 97 J. CRIM. L. & CRIMINOLOGY 761, 767 (2007).

20 *See, e.g.*, Joshua Marquis, *The Myth of Innocence*, 95 J. CRIM. L. & CRIMINOLOGY 501 (2005), and Morris Hoffman, *The Myth of Actual Innocence*, 82 CHI-KENT L. REV. 663 (2007).

21 Stephen J. Markman & Paul G. Cassell, *Comment: Protecting the Innocent: A Response to the Bedau-Radelet Study*, 41 STAN. L. REV. 121, 121 (1988). *But see* Samuel R. Gross, Barbara O'Brien, Chen Hu & Edward H. Kennedy, *Rate of False Conviction of Criminal Defendants Who Are Sentenced to Death*, 111 PROC. NAT'L ACAD. SCIS. (PNAS) 7230, 7230 (2014). Gross and his coauthors used survival analysis to estimate that if all death-sentenced defendants remained under sentence of death indefinitely at least 4.1 percent would be exonerated. They concluded that this is a conservative estimate of the proportion of erroneous convictions among death sentences in the United States.

22 SCHECK ET AL., *supra* note 13.

23 *See* Innocence Project, *Homepage*, available at www.innocenceproject.org.

24 Samuel R. Gross, Kristen Jacoby, Daniel J. Matheson., Nicholas Montgomery & Sujata Patil, *Exonerations in the United States, 1989 Through 2003*, 95 J. CRIM. L. & CRIMINOLOGY 523 (2005).

25 *See* Susan A. Bandes, *Framing Wrongful Convictions*, 2008 UTAH L. REV. 5 (2008).

26 *See* Bedau & Radelet, *supra* note 8, at 46–47; Givelber, *supra* note 18, at 1327 n. 32.

27 Zalman, *supra* note 10, at 1479 ("In 1990, very few Americans thought of wrongful convictions as a problem. Most would have said that criminal justice was deficient in not catching, convicting, imprisoning, and executing enough criminals.").

28 Norris, *supra* note 11.

29 For a discussion of the Vasquez and Dotson cases, and their competing claims to the title of "first DNA exoneration in the United States," see Daniel S. Medwed, *Talking about a Revolution: A Quarter Century of DNA Exonerations*, *supra*, in this volume.

30 Marvin Zalman has defined "innocence consciousness" as "the idea that innocent people are convicted in sufficiently large numbers as a result of systemic justice system problems to require efforts to exonerate them, and to advance structural reforms to reduce such errors in the first place. Innocence consciousness replaces a belief that the justice system almost never convicts an innocent person. When translated into public opinion, innocence consciousness becomes one of the forces generating policy change." *See* Zalman, *supra* note 10, at 1468.

31 DNA exonerations were not only extensively covered in national and local print media, but featured in documentaries, television programs, plays, movies, popular true crime books and novels. *See* Norris, *supra* note 11, at 12.

32 *Id.* at 1.

33 In 2004, Congress passed the Innocence Protection Act, which increased prisoners' access to post-conviction DNA testing, improved legal representation in capital cases, and increased federal compensation for prisoners who were wrongfully convicted and subsequently exonerated. All states now provide access to post-conviction DNA testing, and many have established commissions, proposed reforms, or passed laws to decrease the wrongful conviction of the innocent. Approximately thirty states now also provide some form of statutory (monetary and nonmonetary) compensation for the wrongly convicted. *See* Innocence Project, *Compensating the Wrongly Convicted*, June 4, 2015, available at www.innocenceproject.org/free-innocent/improve-the-law/fact-sheets/compensating-the-wrongly-convicted. And, at the local level, numerous agencies have adopted "best practice" reforms, such as voluntarily recording interrogations, improving forensic laboratory accreditation, establishing testing and expert witness standards, and changing eyewitness line-up procedures to reduce false positive identifications, thereby improving the quality and accuracy of evidence that law enforcement collects and that prosecutors, judges, and juries rely on in their various capacities in the pretrial and trial processes.

34 *See* FRANK R. BAUMGARTNER, SUZANNA DE BOEF & AMBER BOYDSTUN, THE DECLINE OF THE DEATH PENALTY AND THE DISCOVERY OF INNOCENCE (2008). For a contrary opinion, see Michael L. Radelet, *How DNA Has Changed Contemporary Death Penalty Debates*, *infra*, in this volume.

35 Bedau & Radelet, *supra* note 8. *See also* SCHECK ET AL., *supra* note 13, at xiii ("Not long ago, to claim that an innocent person had been imprisoned was audacious, even risky, a proposition that was close to unprovable.").

36 Sometimes, DNA testing can produce errors. *See, e.g.,* Katie Worth, *The Surprisingly Imperfect Science of DNA Testing,* THE MARSHALL PROJECT, June 24, 2015, available at www.themarshallproject.org/2015/06/24/the-surprisingly-imperfect-science-of-dna-testing#.

37 Peter Neufeld, *Legal and Ethical Implications of Post-Conviction DNA Exonerations,* 35 NEW ENG. L. REV. 639, 639 (2001).

38 Findley, *supra* note 1, at 1187.

39 I believe Sam Gross would disagree with this characterization, and argue that exonerations, as the Registry defines the term, are the best proxy for wrongful convictions of the innocent, and thus that studying them is not breaking with this tradition of wrongful conviction scholarship. Gross et al., *supra* note 21, at 7230 ("We study exonerations to learn about false convictions. Exonerations and the processes that produce them are ... the best source of the information we have about the accuracy of our system of criminal adjudication, and the only source of direct evidence about the error we most want to avoid: convicting the innocent.").

40 *Exonerate,* MERRIAM-WEBSTER DICTIONARY, available at www.merriam-webster.com/dictionary/exonerate (last accessed on Jan. 17, 2016).

41 AMERICAN HERITAGE DICTIONARY OF THE ENGLISH LANGUAGE 251 (Paperback Ed., 1976).

42 Zalman, *supra* note 10, at 1471.

43 Givelber, *supra* note 18. However, Dan Givelber and Amy Farrell argue that acquittals can indeed sometimes indicate actual innocence. *See* DANIEL GIVELBER & AMY FARRELL, NOT GUILTY: ARE THE ACQUITTED INNOCENT? 142 (2012) (suggesting "that when juries acquit those who refuse to plead because they insist they are innocent, those defendants are likely individuals who did not commit the crimes with which they were charged").

44 Bedau & Radelet, *supra* note 8, at 47.

45 Markman & Cassell, *supra* note 21.

46 Zalman, *Qualitatively Estimating, supra* note 3, at 248 n. 104 ("Markman and Cassell's approach was less scholarship than partisan advocacy, the core technique of trial lawyers.").

47 The Death Penalty Information Center does not state on its website that it opposes capital punishment, but it would be disingenuous for anyone to claim otherwise.

48 Bedau & Radelet, *supra* note 8.

49 Death Penalty Information Center, *Innocence: List of Those Freed from Death Row,* available at www.deathpenaltyinfo.org/innocence-list-those-freed-death-row.

50 This is the definition as of February 2016. *Id.*

51 Marvin Zalman has criticized DPIC's reasoning here "as a skillful polemic that elides rather than meets the point that a person can have a conviction reversed on appeal and yet be guilty in the factual sense ... The DPIC tries to have it both ways, heavily implying factual innocence but retreating to a legal innocence high ground when challenged." *See* Zalman, *Qualitatively Estimating, supra* note 3, at 256–57.

52 *See* Death Penalty Information Center, *Innocence and the Crisis in the American Death Penalty*, available at www.deathpenaltyinfo.org/innocence-and-crisis-ameri can-death-penalty#Seco5a ("Cases are included in DPIC's list based on objective criteria. These criteria differ markedly from subjective judgments about who is actually innocent.").

53 In its 1993 report to Congress, the Death Penalty Information Center listed 48 cases of death row exonerees, and it has continued to maintain and publicize a list of post-1973 death row exonerees on its website. As of this writing in February 2016, the number stands at 156. *See supra* note 49 and accompanying text.

54 Norris, *supra* note 11, at 135.

55 Gross et al., *supra* note 24.

56 *Id.* at 524.

57 *Id.* at 526. Gross and his coauthors go on to write that "that is not our purpose in this report. Instead, we look at overall patterns in the exonerations that have accumulated in the past fifteen years and hope to learn something about the causes of false convictions, and about the operation of the criminal justice system in general. It is possible that a few of the hundreds of exonerated defendants we have studied were involved in the crimes for which they were convicted, despite our efforts to exclude such cases. On the other hand, it is certain – this is the clearest implication of our study – that many defendants who are not on this list, no doubt thousands, have been falsely convicted of serious crimes but have not been exonerated."

58 In addition, Hans Sherrer maintains a searchable database of the wrongly convicted from 117 countries that as of January 26, 2016, listed 6,184 cases. He writes: "The Innocents Database includes persons whose presumption of innocence was restored after their conviction was overturned on direct appeal or post-conviction appeal and they were not retried, persons acquitted after a retrial, and persons granted an executive or legislative pardon based on evidence of their innocence. The sources of information include official court reports, books, and newspaper and magazine articles. Each person's record in the database includes one or more sources for the information about the person's case." *See Innocents Database*, available at http://forejustice.org/search_idb.htm. Marvin Zalman notes that "the listed cases are legal exonerations that include miscarriages of justice that cannot be classified as cases of factual innocence." Marvin Zalman, *Measuring Wrongful Convictions*, in Encyclopedia of Criminology and Criminal Justice 8 (Gerben Bruinsma & David Weisburd, eds., 2014).

59 *See* National Registry of Exonerations, *Our Mission*, available at www.law.umich.edu/ special/exoneration/Pages/mission.aspx.

60 *See* National Registry of Exonerations, *Glossary*, available at www.law.umich.edu/ special/exoneration/Pages/glossary.aspx.

61 *Id.*

62 Findley, *supra* note 1, at 1208.

63 The Registry's standard for factual innocence appears to be whether the new evidence of innocence, if known at trial, might have made a difference at trial.

64 5 J.A. SIMPSON & E.S.C. WEINER, THE OXFORD ENGLISH DICTIONARY 548 (2nd ed. 1989) ("The action of disburdening or relieving ... from blame or reproach; in instance of this a formal discharge").

65 Hans Sherrer, *An Exoneration Can Be Judicial or By Executive or Legislative Clemency*, JUSTICE DENIED, Oct. 28, 2014, available at http://justicedenied.org/wordpress/archives/2811.

66 *See* Findley, *supra* note 1, at 1208. *See also* Elizabeth Joh, *'If It Suffices to Accuse'*: United States v. Watts *and the Reassessment of Acquittals*, 74 N.Y.U. L. REV. 887, 903 n. 87 (1999) (quoting Peter Neufeld, "In our system, not only are you presumed innocent, but when a jury returns a verdict of not-guilty you are, in fact, innocent.").

67 An exception is Keith Findley. *See* Findley *supra* note 1. Sam Gross has put much thought into the Registry's definition of an exoneration for its purposes, so I do not mean to suggest here that he has overlooked these important distinctions.

68 Samuel R. Gross, *Convicting the Innocent*, 4 ANN. REV. L. SOC. SCI. 173, 175 (2008) ("'Exoneration' in this context is a legal concept. It means that a defendant who was convicted of a crime was later relieved of all legal consequences of that conviction because of new evidence of innocence. Some exonerated defendants are no doubt guilty of the crimes for which they were convicted, in whole or in part, but the number is likely very small.").

69 *See* Gross et al., *supra* note 24.

70 Richard A. Leo & Richard J. Ofshe, *The Consequences of False Confessions: Deprivations of Liberty and Miscarriages of Justice in the Age of Psychological Interrogation*, 88 J. CRIM. L. & CRIMINOLOGY 429 (1998); and Steven A. Drizin & Richard A. Leo, *The Problem of False Confessions in the Post-DNA World*, 82 N.C. L. REV. 891 (2004).

71 Sam Gross has stated that "the only wrongful convictions we do know about are those that end up as exonerations: cases in which sufficiently strong evidence has been assembled to persuade a prosecutor, a court or a governor that a convicted defendant is not guilty." *See* Gross, *supra* note 68, at 175. I disagree, as there are proven false convictions based on dispositive evidence of innocence where the legal system never exonerated the defendants. *See, e.g.,* TOM WELLS & RICHARD A. LEO, THE WRONG GUYS: MURDER, FALSE CONFESSIONS, AND THE NORFOLK FOUR (2008).

72 Findley, *supra* note 1, at 1,187 ("Thus, in the end, for policy and research purposes, the only really useful definition of both 'exoneration' and 'innocence' is one that attempts no subjective assessment of guilt or innocence beyond looking to determine whether a conviction has been erased.").

73 Fessenden v. State, 52 So.3d 1, 5–6 (Fla. Dist. Ct. App. 2010) ("When an appellate court reverses a judgment and sentence for lack of evidence, it does not make any determination that the defendant is actually innocent; it merely determines that the State did not provide evidence that could support a verdict of guilt beyond a reasonable doubt. There is a substantial difference in our system of justice between the concept of 'not guilty' and that of 'actual innocence.'").

74 Samuel R. Gross & Michael Shaffer, *Exonerations in the United States, 1989–2012: Report by the National Registry of Exonerations*, June 2012, at 12, available at www.law.umich.edu/special/exoneration/Documents/exonerations_us_1989_2012_full_report.pdf.

75 National Registry of Exonerations, *The First 1,600 Exonerations* 1 (2015), available at www.law.umich.edu/special/exoneration/Documents/1600_Exonerations.pdf ("The Registry changes constantly. We add exonerations every week. We have removed a few cases after learning that they do not in fact meet our criteria. And we constantly update summaries of cases that are already listed to add missing data and correct errors, based on our own research and on information from others.").

76 The notion that some innocence scholars have expanded the domain of the innocent is not an entirely new suggestion, either from right- or left-wing critics. *See, e.g.*, Risinger, *supra* note 19, at 768 n. 11 ("Some of the most active Romillists compiling lists of the factually innocent have sometimes used criteria that were open to charges of being too soft or overinclusive ... For instance, it might have been better if some cases in the compilation by Gross et al. ... had been excluded.... By including weak non-DNA cases as cases of exoneration, Romillists may expose their enterprise to the charge of inflating their numerator through mischaracterization.").

77 Peter Conrad & Deborah Potter, *From Hyperactive Children to ADHD Adults: Observations on the Expansion of Medical Categories*, 47 SOCIAL PROBLEMS No. 4 559 (2000).

78 JOEL BEST, THREATENED CHILDREN: RHETORIC AND CONCERN ABOUT CHILD VICTIMS 78–79 (1990).

79 Daniel S. Medwed, *Innocentrism*, 2008 U. ILL. L. REV. 1549, 1552 (2008) (noting that "a handful of well-known scholars, judges and lawyers have accused the innocence movement of inflating the actual number of wrongful convictions by including factually ambiguous cases in the innocence ledger").

80 *But see* Gross et al., *supra* note 21 (using survival analysis to estimate that if all death-sentenced defendants remained under sentence of death indefinitely at least 4.1 percent would be exonerated and concluding that this is a conservative estimate of the proportion of erroneous convictions among death sentences in the United States).

81 Richard A. Leo, *False Confessions: Causes, Consequences and Solutions*, in WRONGLY CONVICTED: PERSPECTIVES ON FAILED JUSTICE 47 (Saundra D. Westervelt & John A. Humphrey, eds., 2001).

82 4 William Blackstone, COMMENTARIES 358.

83 Zalman, *Qualitatively Estimating, supra* note 3, at 247 ("The conventional, layperson's view focuses on wrongful convictions only in the factual sense.").

84 *See* Findley, *supra* note 1, at 1208 ("Without proof of guilt, determined by a court, the presumption of innocence defines innocence").

85 *Id.* at 1184.

86 *See, e.g.*, Richard A. Leo & Richard J. Ofshe, *The Truth About False Confessions and Advocacy Scholarship*, 37 CRIM. L. BULL. 293 (2001) (decisively refuting nine

failed case challenges and numerous false and misleading factual assertions). *See also* Zalman, *Qualitatively Estimating, supra* note 3, at 249:

> [A]ssessing whether a conviction was erroneous requires the application of human judgment to facts, a process that can be labeled pejoratively as "subject-ive." The word "subjective" carries the connotation of a decision being idiosyn-cratic or even illusory or fanciful. In another sense however, it means that judgment follows from an individual's process of observation and reasoning. In this sense, not only are assessments of wrongful convictions subjective, but so too are the original convictions themselves ... The question is not so much whether such judgments are subjective, but whether they are supported by a sufficient amount of verifiable data and cogent reasoning applicable to the task at hand.

87 Keith A. Findley, *Flawed Science and the New Wave of Innocents, infra*, in this volume.

88 Sam Gross and his coauthors have argued, "Any plausible guess at the total number of miscarriages of justice in America in the last fifteen years must be in the thousands, perhaps tens of thousands." Gross et al., *supra* note 24, at 551. More recently, Gross and Shaffer wrote: "The most important conclusion of this report is that there are far more false convictions than exonerations. That should come as no surprise ... Why would anyone suppose that the small number of miscarriages of justice that we learn about years later – like the handful of fossils of early hominids that we have discovered – is anything more than an insignificant fraction of the total?" Gross & Shaffer, *supra* note 74, at 3.

89 *See* Richard A. Leo & Jon B. Gould, *Studying Wrongful Convictions: Learning from Social Science*, 7 Ohio St. J. Crim. L. 7 (2009).

90 *See, e.g.*, Joshua Marquis, *The Myth of Innocence*, 95 J. Crim. L. & Crimin-ology 501 (2005).

91 Edward Connors, Thomas Lundregan, Neal Miller & Tom McEwen, Convicted by Juries, Exonerated by Science: Case Studies in the Use of DNA Evidence to Establish Innocence after Trial (1996).

92 Findley, *supra* note 1.

93 Daniel S. Medwed, *Introduction: Beyond Biology: Wrongful Convictions in the Post-DNA World*, 2008 Utah L. Rev. 1, 6–8 (2008).

94 Medwed, *supra* note 79, at 1570.

95 Innocence Network, *Homepage*, available at www.innocencenetwork.org.

96 I believe Sam Gross would argue that the Registry's definition of an exoneration is also factual, but that it is a different method of determining facts than DNA testing.

97 Samuel R. Gross & Barbara O'Brien, *Frequency and Predictors of False Conviction: Why We Know So Little and New Data on Capital Cases*, 5 J. Empirical Legal Stud. 927, 929 (2008) ("False convictions are accidents: a system we rely on daily goes wrong, with tragic results. Like other accidents, most false convictions are probably unintended").

98 Gross & Shaffer, *supra* note 74, at 5 ("Many of the exonerated defendants we know about are the beneficiaries of equally improbable chains of happenstance.").

99 As noted above, I believe Sam Gross would dispute this characterization and argue that the Registry's definition of an exoneration is also factual, but that it is a different method of determining facts than, for example, my definition of proven false convictions in this paper. *See supra* note 96 and accompanying text.

100 To be sure, very few of the cases listed on the National Registry of Exonerations' website have been contested to date.

A Closer Look at Specific Lessons

5

Negotiating Accuracy
DNA in the Age of Plea Bargaining

ALEXANDRA NATAPOFF

INTRODUCTION

The Innocence Movement has profoundly rattled our faith in the accuracy and integrity of the criminal process. In many ways, the DNA revolution enabled this upset. Twenty-five years ago, its rigorous certainty set DNA testing apart from other kinds of evidence and forensic tests which, even at their best, often left room for doubt about any particular individual's innocence. Hundreds of exonerations later, DNA testing has conclusively demonstrated that we often convict the innocent in the most serious cases. Today, its tantalizing offer of certainty has made DNA a kind of poster child for the Innocence Movement. All fifty states now have post-conviction DNA testing statutes.[1] Half a dozen innocence projects – including the flagship Innocence Project in New York – only accept cases involving DNA.[2] The Supreme Court recently invoked DNA's celebrated potential for protecting the innocent to uphold the constitutionality of DNA databases.[3]

But DNA's high profile is a double-edged sword. Most wrongful convictions will not involve DNA, since over 80 percent of all criminal cases do not generate biological evidence containing DNA at all, or cannot be resolved through DNA testing.[4] As the website for the Innocence Project explains, "Only a fraction of criminal cases involve biological evidence that can be subjected to DNA testing, and even when such evidence exists, it is often lost or destroyed after a conviction."[5] Yet the clarity of DNA exonerations casts a shadow over other kinds of innocence claims. It is hard to achieve DNA-style certainty in cases involving evidence with larger margins of error and a greater role for human evaluation. We may never know for certain what the eyewitness actually saw, whether the informant actually lied, or whether the fire was

Many thanks to Daniel Medwed for putting together this important collection.

an accident. Instead, such cases call upon us to make inferences and judgments about the likelihood of innocence. DNA's rigor makes such common innocence claims look shaky by comparison, even though ironically we rely on precisely such inferences and judgments to establish guilt in the first place.[6]

More fundamentally, the excitement over DNA's hyper-accuracy promotes a narrow theoretical framework for understanding why we convict innocent people in the first place.[7] It suggests that evidentiary inaccuracy is the primary reason for wrongful conviction, and that conversely, if we could get more accurate evidence we could solve the wrongful conviction problem. This sounds like an obvious truth. But it is at best partial and at worst misleading. The vast bulk of the U.S. criminal system is not engaged in a quest for accuracy based on evidence in the first instance. Instead, it is engaged in bargaining. The plea bargaining process has turned evidence and accuracy into commodities that are traded and negotiated along with all the other inputs into the bargaining process. This does not make evidentiary accuracy irrelevant, but it competes with many other potential deal breakers such as attorney time and skill, a defendant's cooperation, a defendant's criminal record, whether the defendant is out on bail, and local bargaining habits, to name just a few. The systemic power of evidentiary accuracy – and therefore the importance of forensics generally and DNA in particular – ultimately turns on its actual role in producing convictions along with all these other inputs. Because approximately 95 percent of criminal convictions are the result of pleas, not trials,[8] the role of evidentiary accuracy turns out to be contingent on many other factors.

To put it another way, the quest for DNA-like accuracy tempts us to forget that most criminal guilt is negotiated, not "discovered." This is a standard insight in the plea bargaining literature,[9] but it creates some tension with an innocence culture that has traditionally focused on poor investigative techniques and evidentiary accuracy rather than the mechanics of a criminal justice marketplace in which evidence and guilt are negotiable commodities.

That marketplace, however, may be on a collision course with the Innocence Movement. Fourteen percent of the wrongful convictions listed in the National Registry of Exonerations are the result of a plea.[10] The Innocence Project has taken on a number of DNA-related wrongful plea cases.[11] Scholars are increasingly scrutinizing the systemic pressures on innocent people to plead guilty.[12] In a scathing article entitled "Why Innocent People Plead Guilty," U.S. District Court Judge Jed Rakoff recently took public aim at what he called "the prosecutor-dictated plea bargain system [which] creat[es] such inordinate pressures to enter plea bargains [that it] appears to have led a significant number of defendants to plead guilty to crimes they never actually committed."[13]

Plea bargaining pressures all kinds of defendants. Thirty-one of the first 330 post-conviction DNA exonerees pled guilty to serious crimes – including homicide and rape – typically in order to escape the death penalty or a life sentence.[14] But the problem is different, and more widespread, in connection with minor crimes where a guilty plea can permit an innocent defendant to go home with a relatively light sentence of probation or time-served. Minor crimes are typically handled in bulk, rushed through assembly-line plea processes and court proceedings, in which lawyers and judges lack the time and incentives to check whether misdemeanants are actually guilty.[15] In this world, thousands of people routinely plead guilty to misdemeanors of which they are demonstrably innocent.[16] It is here in the quick-and-dirty misdemeanor context – in which there is little evidence, let alone DNA – that the plea bargaining marketplace has truly relinquished its commitment to accuracy.[17]

The extremes of the misdemeanor context teach us something profound about our entire system: more than 90 percent of U.S. convictions are generated by a process that is structurally tolerant of inaccuracy. The bargained nature of the criminal conviction means that evidence is just one piece – and not always the most important piece – of the larger negotiation process that establishes guilt. More accurate facts may shift the bargaining environment in certain kinds of cases, and felony defendants are less likely to succumb to wrongful pleas than misdemeanants, but accurate facts are not enough to ensure accurate convictions across the board. Twenty-five years of DNA-based exonerations have taught us, ironically, that more accurate evidence alone cannot fix the wrongful conviction problem.

Although plea bargaining *per se* is a relatively new concern for the Innocence Movement, the innocence discourse has long grappled with a closely related problem: the dangers of the negotiated convictions available to criminal informants. Informant deals are, in effect, a special kind of plea, in which suspects trade evidence in exchange for leniency.[18] That bargained-for evidence, in turn, famously generates wrongful convictions. Indeed, in its 2004 study, the Center on Wrongful Convictions concluded that "snitches [are] the leading cause of wrongful conviction in U.S. capital cases."[19] Informants are thus a special and familiar example of the larger threat that the criminal deal poses to accurate convictions. This chapter argues that we should understand the criminal deal itself as a primary source of wrongful conviction, precisely because it commodifies and trades away accuracy – even DNA's – in exchange for other institutional values. What Sam Gross calls the "canonical list of wrongful conviction sources" – eyewitness identifications, informants, false confessions, sloppy forensics – should be amended to include the plea bargain, especially the misdemeanor plea.[20] This will not only provide a more accurate picture of the scope of the wrongful conviction problem, but new analytic tools for discerning why we convict the innocent as often as we do.

The chapter proceeds as follows. First, it traces the variable role and influence of evidentiary accuracy itself. In the world of trials and formal adjudication, accuracy matters a lot. In the plea bargaining universe, accuracy is negotiable and thus matters less. This latter point is on display in two bargaining arrangements that routinely lead to wrongful convictions: informants, where *evidence* is obtained by bargaining, and the misdemeanor assembly-line process where *convictions* are obtained by bargaining. These insights are reinforced by new innocence scholarship that goes beyond the traditional evidence/accuracy model to offer more expansive explanations – including psychological and institutional – for why we wrongfully convict. These expansive approaches suggest new ways of thinking about innocence reform, most importantly the need to add plea bargaining to the master list of wrongful conviction sources.

1 *Evidence, Accuracy, and the Trial Model*

A fundamental ideal behind the adversary system is the proverbial quest for truth. The Supreme Court often invokes the "truth-seeking function of the trial"[21] in justifying various rules about evidence, disclosure, and process. To be sure, practice often diverges from this ideal. Trials are infrequent. Legal rules serve multiple purposes, which may or may not promote accuracy.[22] Post-conviction rules severely limit the extent to which factual error – as opposed to legal error – will ever be reviewed.[23] But the adversarial truth-seeking model still dominates important criminal justice stories about what the system does and how we convict people.[24]

Evidentiary accuracy, in turn, drives important aspects of the trial model. Much – although not all – of trial procedure and evidence law is motivated by the understanding that parties are fighting precisely over evidentiary relevance, inferences, and burdens of proof, all driven by the actual evidence in the case.[25] Trials are largely designed around the parties' presentation of evidence and the fact-finders' interpretation of that evidence. Accordingly, in such a world, it makes sense to think that more accurate evidence will generally lead to more accurate results.[26]

Most current innocence reform is aimed at this trial-centric model and the wrongful convictions produced by it.[27] This is due in part to history and mechanics. The vast majority of exonerations occur after a defendant has gone to trial and lost. Out of 1,700 exonerations in the National Registry, 85 percent were the result of a failed trial.[28] This is no accident – it is easier to revisit a conviction where the defendant has maintained his or her innocence and there is a factual record that can be reinvestigated and legally challenged. The classic exoneration story typically involves a lawyer and investigator going back with a fine-toothed comb over a faulty trial record, dismantling and disproving the evidence presented at trial.[29] It is also a model consonant with the (increasingly outdated) notion that a truly innocent defendant will resist pleading guilty. Indeed, some states' post-conviction DNA testing statutes expressly exclude defendants who have pled.[30] As a result, the bulk of the Innocence Movement's proposed reforms are designed with the trial-oriented evidentiary model in mind. Double-blind line-ups, corroboration requirements for jailhouse informants, and recorded interrogations and confessions are all ways of ensuring that evidence itself is produced in more reliable ways.[31] The focus on evidentiary accuracy – and the excitement over DNA's hyper-accuracy – flows from this implicit structural understanding about how we generate convictions and what makes them inaccurate.

2 Plea Bargaining

By contrast, few mistake plea bargaining for a quest for the truth.[32] It is by definition a negotiation in lieu of the trial-based truth-seeking process, and it openly sacrifices factual accuracy on all sorts of issues – from the nature of the crime committed to the amount of money or drugs at stake – in exchange for agreement.[33]

Of course, such convictions must still defend their legitimacy: they must be sufficiently accurate and fair to substitute for trial outcomes.[34] When it upheld plea bargaining's constitutionality, the Supreme Court dismissed concerns about wrongful pleas on the theory that innocent defendants are unlikely to accede to their own wrongful conviction and that courts can and do check the accuracy of guilty pleas.[35] As the Court explained in *Brady* v. *United States*:

> We would have serious doubts about this case if the encouragement of guilty pleas by offers of leniency substantially increased the likelihood that defendants, advised by competent counsel, would falsely condemn themselves. But our view is to the contrary and is based on our expectations that courts will satisfy themselves that pleas of guilty are voluntarily and intelligently made by competent defendants with adequate advice of

counsel and that there is nothing to question the accuracy and reliability of the defendants' admissions that they committed the crimes with which they are charged.[36]

More theoretically, plea dynamics are often conceptualized – and rationalized – as contracts negotiated "in the shadow of trial."[37] The idea is that plea outcomes will not diverge too greatly from what the evidence would show, because if they do, the defendant can simply exercise his trial rights. More subtly, if the defendant has a strong chance of prevailing at trial, this will affect the "price" of the bargain. Perhaps the prosecutor will reduce the charges, or recommend a lower sentence. If the defendant is unsatisfied with the deal, again, he can opt for trial and try to uncover the "truth."[38]

It is important to recognize that this scenario does not preclude wrongful pleas, it merely describes how they take place. An innocent defendant may still face substantial risks of conviction at trial because his or her likelihood of success depends on all sorts of factors unrelated to guilt, most famously whether the defendant has a prior record[39] or is represented by an overwhelmed public defender who lacks investigative and other trial resources.[40] For many defendants, those risks – and the much longer sentences associated with going to trial – are enough to make pleas "a good deal," even for innocent defendants.

But even with these caveats, the "shadow of trial" model overstates the protections against wrongful pleas. A decade ago, William Stuntz and Stephanos Bibas showed that trials – and the strength of the evidence – do not cast a particularly strong shadow over bargained outcomes at all.[41] Instead, the peculiarities of the market and the psychological characteristics of the players largely determine bargains. As Bibas put it, plea bargains are a function of, *inter alia*, "[a]gency costs; attorney competence, compensation, and work-loads; resources; sentencing and bail rules; and information deficits; ... psychological biases and heuristics []: overconfidence, denial, discounting, risk preferences, loss aversion, framing, and anchoring."[42] As a result, "plea bargaining effectively bases sentences in part on wealth, sex, age, education, intelligence, and confidence."[43]

Because plea bargaining is driven only partially by accuracy, the role of evidence recedes.[44] Evidence is one of many inputs, and its value will depend on the nature of the case, the interests of the parties, and myriad other factors. To be clear, this does not make innocence irrelevant. Presumably most prosecutors do not intend to convict the wrong person.[45] Some studies indicate, moreover, that innocent defendants are more likely to resist pleading. For example, in one academic experiment, guilty participants pled at a rate of 89 percent, while innocent participants pled at a lower 56 percent rate.[46] In the Rampart mass exoneration, guilty defendants pled 88 percent of the time while actually innocent defendants pled 77 percent of the time.[47] Such percentages show that while innocence may affect the likelihood of a deal, it is far from enough – notwithstanding the Supreme Court's opinion to the contrary – to prevent a wrongful plea. Instead, we should understand innocence and accuracy as ingredients in the bargain that compete with all the other pressures and inputs that the plea bargaining process involves.

Of course sometimes inaccuracy is good for defendants.[48] Indeed, if the deal is too accurate, that is, no better than an accurate trial outcome, a rational defendant should theoretically proceed to trial. Accordingly, the paradigmatic favorable plea bargain is often inaccurate in the defendant's favor: it will be one in which a defendant is convicted of a lesser crime and/or punished less than an accurate evaluation of the facts would warrant.[49] In practice, this model is heavily distorted by the trial penalty,[50] especially under the U.S. Sentencing Guidelines,[51] but it nevertheless captures some of the basic plea bargaining dynamics.

Other kinds of inaccurate bargains also help defendants. For example, it is common in federal drug cases to negotiate the amount of drugs that will be attributed to the defendant for sentencing purposes.[52] A defendant caught with ten kilograms of cocaine could, as part of a plea, negotiate that amount down and substantially reduce the sentence.[53] Likewise, in minor cases, defendants may plead to crimes they have not committed at all so as to avoid convictions that have more serious collateral consequences. A drug possession charge with immigration implications, for example, can be bargained into a disorderly conduct charge, even though factual speaking there is no evidence of that latter crime whatsoever.[54]

To put it another way, plea bargaining is often inaccurate for complex, even sound reasons, and accuracy is not the system's only foundational value.[55] But accuracy still matters, and the innocence discourse is an important reminder not to let the cost-benefit instrumentalism of plea bargaining obscure the injustices of wrongful conviction. The pressures on innocent defendants to plead are well known. Because overwhelmed public defenders typically lack the resources to investigate innocence claims, factual records remain lopsided in the government's favor. The threat of the death penalty – and the chance to avoid it – may induce innocent defendants to plead.[56] Defendants with prior convictions are famously leery of going to trial because jurors are more likely to convict once they learn of the defendant's priors.[57] Misdemeanor defendants held without bail, or on bail they cannot afford to pay, often plead guilty to time-served rather than remain incarcerated pending trial.[58]

Even with respect to DNA itself, we are already seeing how its vaunted accuracy is being bargained away. Faced with exonerating DNA evidence, the prosecutors who convicted Bruce Goodman of murder did not change their minds. Instead, they revised their original theory of Goodman's guilt and then negotiated a post-conviction deal that would release but not exonerate him.[59] Some prosecutors now demand that defendants waive their rights to post-conviction DNA testing as a condition of a plea.[60]

In all these ways, factual accuracy can fade or even disappear into the crucible of the bargaining process. Accordingly, improving the accuracy of evidence remains a partial response to the wrongful conviction problem.

3 The Informant Deal – Negotiated Evidence

The Innocence Movement has long grappled with one infamous way that bargaining distorts accuracy. Criminal informants – sometimes referred to as "snitches"– generate a large percentage of known wrongful convictions by fabricating false evidence.[61] But the underlying reason that most informants lie is because of the deal: the promise that in exchange for evidence or cooperation the informant will escape liability or punishment for his or her own crimes. Without the incentive of a deal, an informant would be just another witness with no particular reason to lie or fabricate and therefore no more or less reliable than an uncompensated lay witness.[62] The source of informant unreliability thus lies not in the individual person but in the bargaining market.[63]

Informants pervade the U.S. criminal system. While the proverbial "jailhouse snitch" has received the lion's share of attention,[64] informant deals are routinely cut in connection with every type of defendant and every type of crime. In particular, drug enforcement relies heavily on informant deals to produce arrests; it is sometimes quipped that "every drug case involves a snitch." Since drug cases make up approximately one-third of federal and state criminal dockets, the potential for fabricated evidence and wrongful conviction is far-reaching.[65]

For example, in Hearne, Texas, a federally funded drug task force relied on a single drug informant to generate dozens of arrests in a local housing project. Some arrestees pled guilty immediately in order to obtain release.[66] It turned out that the informant – a drug dealer with mental health problems facing a new burglary charge – had lied across the board, a debacle that resulted in dozens of exonerations, an ACLU lawsuit, and a movie.[67] But Hearne was not unusual: drug task forces commonly rely on unreliable compensated criminal informants. In other words, built into the war on drugs is a mechanism likely to produce wrongful convictions based on informant-generated, bargained-for evidence.

Despite the prevalence of informant use and a number of high-profile exonerations, informants are not commonly at the top of the wrongful conviction list. One reason is that snitch-based wrongful convictions can be difficult to prove. Rife with uncertainty, they often lack physical evidence, while human reliability is difficult to "test." Courts have been staunchly skeptical of informant recantations, even when the original informant testimony was the sole evidence on which the defendant was convicted.[68] Because post-conviction burdens of proof are reversed, a shaky informant may be enough for the government to get a conviction but that same informant's recantation will not be enough for a defendant to prove actual innocence. For example, in a recent case in Washington State, three young men were wrongfully convicted based solely on the trial testimony of a highly compensated informant.[69] A week after trial, another codefendant came forward and admitted that he and the informant had fabricated the evidence against the three innocent young men. This recantation explained in detail how the informant had gotten his information and his incentives for doing so, including the extraordinarily lenient deal that he received, and the fact that one of the real perpetrators was his own brother.

Nevertheless, the court held that the codefendant recantation was not enough for a new trial. Years later, the convictions were vacated based on ineffective assistance of counsel, and the three men sought damages for wrongful conviction and their four years of incarceration. The court again denied their claims, finding that the recantation was insufficient to show actual innocence and concluding that so many people had lied in connection with the case that actual innocence could not be shown.[70]

Informant cases and the deals that generate them may also command less attention because they make up a smaller percentage of the highly scrutinized set of DNA exonerations that constitute the basis for so much innocence scholarship.[71] This trend is likely to continue. Drug cases are not typical candidates for DNA exonerations. Moreover, the kinds of high-profile cases most likely to turn on informant testimony – the jailhouse snitch who comes forward to solve a homicide, for example – will often lack other solid evidence that could provide definitive proof of innocence. Perhaps the most infamous example is the Cameron Todd Willingham execution, a case that ostensibly rested on faulty arson expertise but that was bolstered when a jailhouse informant came forward alleging a confession.[72] Indeed, this is why informant testimony is so risky in the first place – it often comes into being precisely in order to shore up weak cases in which other evidence is not dispositive. But from an exoneration perspective, the lack of additional evidence makes it more difficult to prove innocence after the fact.

These are the sorts of hurdles that such non-DNA exonerations confront. The lingering uncertainty about whether an informant lied, even though we know an enormous amount about their incentives and opportunities to do so, can never be conclusively resolved through a test or a lab. The more we grow accustomed to DNA-type certainty, the harder it will be to exonerate based on the run-of-the-mill certainty of human judgment and common sense.

4 Misdemeanor Wrongful Convictions – Negotiated Guilt

One of the greatest underappreciated sources of wrongful conviction occurs in the misdemeanor context. These wrongful convictions are largely plea bargains, not trials, and offer a different way of understanding the sources of wrongful conviction than the evidence-oriented analysis typical of serious cases. The basic dynamic is captured by Sam Gross:

> The [wrongful conviction] problem may be worst at the low end of the spectrum, in misdemeanor courts where almost everybody pleads guilty. . . . In the past year, 45 defendants were exonerated after pleading guilty to low-level drug crimes in Harris County, Tex[as]. They were cleared months or years after conviction by lab tests that found no illegal drugs in the materials seized from them. Why then did they plead guilty? As best we can tell, most were held in jail because they couldn't make bail. When they were brought to court for the first time, they were given a take-it-or-leave-it, for-today-only offer: Plead guilty and get probation or weeks to months in jail. If they refused, they'd wait in jail for months, if not a year or more, before they got to trial, and risk additional years in prison if they were convicted. That's a high price to pay for a chance to prove one's innocence.[73]

Similarly, for many years New York police pursued an order-maintenance policy of arresting young black men in public housing projects and charging them with trespassing, regardless of their right to be on the premises. Because most of those arrested pled out to avoid pretrial detention, that police policy resulted in numerous wrongful convictions. One Bronx public defender – who now works for the Innocence Project – explained the phenomenon back in 2007:

> In the Bronx, well over half of my cases are misdemeanors, and I have had a disgraceful number of innocent clients, many of whom plead guilty to a trespassing charge. . . . Trespassing arrests are up a staggering 25 percent since 2002 and this is no crime wave, no trespassing epidemic. The Clean Halls program is a major component of "Operation Impact," which was launched by the NYPD in 2003 and targets [low income African-American]

neighborhoods [] by flooding them with rookie police officers trying to make as many arrests as possible. In the 28-month period following the launch of the operation, 72,000 arrests were made in the targeted areas. I have handled more trespassing cases than any other single criminal charge, and I've never had one actually go to trial.[74]

In Baltimore, police use loitering and other low-level arrests to maintain authority and order in low-income, high-crime African-American neighborhoods. As former police officer and now-sociology professor Peter Moskos described it, "[t]hough any minor charge will suffice, loitering is the most widely used minor criminal charge in Baltimore. Loitering is defined, in part, as 'interfering, impeding, or hindering the free passage of pedestrian or vehicular traffic after receiving a warning.' In practice, loitering is failing to move when ordered to move by a police officer."[75] Prosecutors dismiss approximately one-third of Baltimore loitering arrests.[76] Given high plea rates, the remaining two-thirds likely result in convictions even though the underlying conduct will rarely meet the legal standard for loitering.[77]

Innocent misdemeanants like these do not plead guilty because the evidence in their cases is inaccurate. They plead because accuracy and evidence do not matter much at all. The pressures to plead are structural and often divorced from the evidence. They flow instead from police arrest practices, the threat of pretrial incarceration, overburdened public defenders, cookie-cutter prosecutorial charging policies, and the legislative decision to authorize incarceration for the most minor offenses.[78]

Pressure to plead also flows from assembly-line courts' institutional need to clear massive caseloads. Many lower court judges are reluctant to permit substantive litigation over minor cases because it holds up their dockets. Litigators in lower courts report that judges are often openly hostile to defense counsel who attempt to litigate rather than plead. Now a law professor, Eve Brensike Primus recalls attempting to raise substantive issues before misdemeanor judges who told her, when she was a public defender, to "save it for appeal."[79] Such judicial hostility to the truth-seeking process thus forces bargains even in the face of meritorious innocence claims.

For all these reasons, the fact that misdemeanor defendants are innocent does not, as the traditional model assumes, give them sufficient leverage to avoid conviction. In New York, it took several lawsuits to persuade the Bronx District Attorney's office to stop prosecuting those trespassing cases.[80] In Maryland, an appellate court has already explained that defendants who are arrested for sitting or standing on street corners, or failing to move when police order them to do so, are factually innocent of loitering.[81] None of these defendants are being wrongfully convicted because the evidence is unreliable, or inaccurate, or should have been tested by a different lab. It is an entirely different problem, one that is missed when we focus solely on evidentiary accuracy.

Focusing on felonies also skews our understanding of the scope of the wrongful conviction problem. The United States files approximately two to three million felony cases a year, of which 1 or 2 percent are homicide and rape cases – the kinds of cases that dominate DNA exonerations, innocence project caseloads, and media attention. By contrast, over ten million misdemeanor cases are filed every year, under low visibility circumstances in which appeals are rare and exonerations even rarer.[82] If wrongful misdemeanor pleas are anywhere near as common as the examples above suggest, that means that hundreds of thousands of low-level arrestees are pleading guilty every year to crimes they did not commit. While some will avoid going to jail, the criminal records, fines, and collateral consequences of those wrongful convictions can nevertheless burden those defendants for a lifetime.[83]

As these examples show, there is an underappreciated racial dimension to wrongful convictions. The kinds of baseless minor arrests highly likely to result in wrongful convictions are also those most likely to be visited upon African Americans: urban order offenses like loitering, trespassing, and disorderly conduct. Because we overpolice and overarrest young black men in place like Baltimore and the Bronx for precisely these types of offenses, and because the misdemeanor process then exerts enormous pressure on them to plead guilty, many of these young African Americans are probably actually innocent.[84]

Such racially skewed wrongful convictions will remain unaffected by the availability of DNA testing, more accurate forensic labs, and double-blind line-ups. They *might* be affected by bail reform to permit minor offenders to stay out of jail pending trial.[85] They *might* be affected by reduced public defender caseloads.[86] They *might* be affected by judicial resistance to massive assembly-line dockets, or community resistance to racial profiling. But as of yet, such reforms are not conventionally understood as innocence reforms. Someday they will.

5 *Expanding the Wrongful Conviction Model*

The innocence conversation is expanding. While evidentiary inaccuracy remains the touchstone, scholars are rapidly adding new dimensions to the wrongful conviction model. From prosecutorial tunnel vision[87] to police misconduct[88] to human cognitive failure more generally,[89] we are seeing a variety of institutional and structural critiques of the criminal process that go beyond claims about evidentiary inaccuracy. Scholars are starting to ask about the independent roles of race, class, unconscious biases, and plea bargaining that lead to wrongful conviction.[90] These efforts ask us to "'step[] back' from the traditional focus on the direct or immediate causes and consequences of wrongful convictions and examin[e] criminal justice systems, the actors in them, and the sociopolitical environments in which they operate to help explain how and why justice miscarries in the form of wrongful conviction."[91]

These new critiques further illuminate the risks inherent in the plea bargaining marketplace. They tell us that the criminal process should be understood as a diverse collection of fallible human actors – from police to prosecutors to defense attorneys and judges – laboring under cognitive and psychological limitations, driven by professional incentives and implicit biases. Plea bargaining empowers those very same cognitively constrained actors to negotiate convictions through a highly subjective unregulated bargaining process. Or, as Albert Alschuler recently described it, "a nearly perfect system for convicting the innocent."[92] In sum, these conceptual expansions all point to the need for more attention to plea bargaining as a primary source of wrongful conviction.

CONCLUSION

In many ways, DNA exonerations enabled the entire innocence revolution. They showed conclusively, without room for speculation, that the evidence and processes that we use to convict serious offenders are deeply flawed.[93] To the extent that DNA continues to destabilize our faith in the accuracy of other forms of evidence and the conviction process more generally, it helps all types of innocence cases – a rising tide that lifts all boats.

But the structural lessons of DNA are limited.[94] DNA's hyper-accuracy not only overshadows more common, less "testable" innocence claims, it banks on the notion that our criminal system is primarily committed to accuracy in the first instance. Since it is not, innocence advocacy should take aim at the plea bargaining market that produces more than 90 percent of our nation's criminal convictions and that reduces accuracy, evidence, and guilt to negotiable commodities.

This, of course, is easier said than done. Regulating the plea environment is an enormous undertaking, in part because it strikes at the heart of police and prosecutorial discretion, a defining characteristic of American law enforcement and our justice process.[95] Were the innocence revolution to challenge plea bargaining's tolerance of inaccuracy, it would pose a significant threat to business-as-usual in nearly every case and for every official player.

Despite these far-reaching implications, a few states are already toying with the idea of constraining the plea bargaining market in order to avoid wrongful convictions. In the Texas legislature, for example, a bill introduced in 2015 would ban the use of compensated informants in death penalty cases. H.B. 564 bill reads in part:

> [T]estimony of an informant or of an alleged accomplice of the defendant is not admissible if the testimony is given in exchange for a grant or promise by the attorney representing the state or by another of immunity from prosecution, reduction of sentence, or any other form of leniency or special treatment.[96]

In effect, the bill concludes that informant evidence procured by deal is inherently too unreliable to be used in capital cases at all. Not only would this be a major change in the informant law landscape, it could open the door to flat restrictions on other forms of highly unreliable evidence.

Similarly in New York, an informant regulation bill would prohibit prosecutors from striking cooperation deals with defendants chargeable with homicide, rape, or kidnapping.[97] Part of the motivation is the classic innocence concern over evidentiary reliability: the prospect of avoiding punishment for such crimes is a massive incentive to fabricate. But it may also reflect an even deeper impulse to regulate plea bargaining more generally, on the notion that some crimes should not be negotiable at all.

Informant reform is a promising start, but it represents just one part of the bargaining landscape. Even if we banned compensated informant-generated evidence altogether,[98] it would not protect defendants from agreeing to their own wrongful conviction. As long as defendants retain the right to waive the factual bases for their own guilty pleas and the government retains the power to pressure them into doing so,[99] we invite wrongful convictions as a routine matter. No amount of DNA testing can fix this structural challenge. Instead, we should amend the master list of wrongful conviction causes to include the phenomenon of plea bargaining in its own right. Then we can better bring the powerful tools of innocence advocacy and scholarship to bear on this troubling source of miscarried justice.

NOTES

1 Innocence Project, *Access to Post-Conviction Testing*, available at www.innocence project.org/free-innocent/improve-the-law/fact-sheets/access-to-post-conviction-dna-testing.

2 *See* Innocence Network, *Innocence Network Member Organizations*, available at www.InnocenceNetwork.org/members.

3 Maryland v. King, 133 S. Ct. 1958 (2013).

4 Daniel S. Medwed, *Introduction: Beyond Biology: Wrongful Convictions in the Post-DNA World*, 2008 UTAH L. REV. 1, 1–2 & nn. 6–8 (2008).

5 Innocence Project, *The Causes of Wrongful Conviction*, available at www.innocen ceproject.org/causes-wrongful-conviction/the-causes.

6 *See* Margaret Raymond, *The Problem with Innocence*, 49 CLEV. ST. L. REV. 449, 455 (2001) (worrying that DNA-based exonerations "ha[ve] the potential to send an enduring and unrealistic message: that criminal defendants can and, perhaps, should offer substantial, convincing, and irrefutable proof of their own innocence, ideally, evidence that is as substantial, convincing, and irrefutable as DNA evidence."); *see also* Jennifer E. Laurin, *Book Review: Still Convicting the Innocent*, 90 TEX. L. REV. 1473, 1492–95 (2012) (reviewing BRANDON GARRETT, CONVICTING THE INNOCENT: WHERE CRIMINAL PROSECUTIONS GO WRONG (2011)).

7 *See generally* EXAMINING WRONGFUL CONVICTIONS: STEPPING BACK, MOVING FORWARD (Allison Redlich, James R. Acker, Robert J. Norris & Catherine L. Bonventre, eds., 2014).

8 *See, e.g.*, Lindsey Devers, *Plea and Charge Bargaining*, BUREAU OF JUSTICE ASSIST-ANCE (2011), available at www.bja.gov/Publications/PleaBargainingResearchSum mary.pdf.

9 *See* Part II, *infra*.

10 The Registry lists 224 exonerations out of 1,634 as resulting from a plea. National Registry of Exonerations, *Homepage*, available at www.law.umich.edu/special/exon eration/Pages/about.aspx.

11 *See, e.g.*, Innocence Project, *Press Release*, available at www.innocenceproject.org/ news-events-exonerations/press-releases/innocence-project-will-appeal-decision-of-west-virginia-court-which-refuses-to-reverse-guilty-plea-of-man-who-has-served-over-a-decade-for-a-rape-dna-evidence-proves-he-didnt-commit.

12 *See, e.g.*, John H. Blume & Rebecca Helm, *The Unexonerated: Factually Innocent Defendants Who Plead Guilty*, 100 CORNELL L. REV. 157 (2014); Stephanos Bibas, *Plea Bargaining's Role in Wrongful Convictions*, in Redlich et al., EXAMINING WRONGFUL CONVICTIONS, *supra* note 7; Lucian E. Dervan & Vanessa A. Edkins, *The Innocent Defendant's Dilemma: An Innovative Empirical Study of Plea Bargaining's Innocence Problem*, 103 J. CRIM. L. & CRIMINOLOGY 1 (2013); Russell Covey, *Police Misconduct as a Cause of Wrongful Convictions*, 90 WASH. U. L. REV. 1133 (2013); BRANDON GARRETT, CONVICTING THE INNOCENT: WHERE CRIMINAL PROSECUTIONS GO WRONG (2011) (identifying wrongful guilty pleas); Samuel Gross, *Pretrial Incentives, Post-Conviction Review, and Sorting Criminal Prosecutions by Guilt or Innocence*, 56 N.Y.L. SCH. L. REV. 1009, 1014–21 (2012); Laurin, *Still Convicting the Innocent*, *supra* note 7, at 1495; DANIEL S. MEDWED, PROSECUTION COMPLEX: AMERICA'S RACE TO CONVICT AND ITS IMPACT ON THE INNOCENT 52–60 (2012) (on prosecutorial decision-making and its impact on plea bargaining); DAN SIMON, IN DOUBT: THE PSYCHOLOGY OF THE CRIMINAL JUSTICE PROCESS 10 (2012).

13 Jed S. Rakoff, *Why Innocent People Plead Guilty*, N.Y. REV. OF BOOKS, Nov. 20, 2014.

14 Innocence Project, *When the Innocent Plead Guilty*, available at www.innocence project.org/news-events-exonerations/when-the-innocent-plead-guilty.

15 Alexandra Natapoff, *Misdemeanors*, 85 S. CAL. L. REV. 1313 (2012).

16 *See* Part 4. *infra*.

17 *Compare* Josh Bowers, *Punishing the Innocent*, 156 U. PA. L. REV.1117 (2008) (arguing that pleading guilty can be beneficial for innocent petty offenders) with Stephanos Bibas, *Exacerbating Injustice*, 157 U. PA. L. REV. PENNUMBRA 53 (2008) (arguing that the instrumental benefit of pleading guilty does not outweigh the injustice of the wrongful minor conviction).

18 ALEXANDRA NATAPOFF, SNITCHING: CRIMINAL INFORMANTS AND THE EROSION OF AMERICAN JUSTICE 69–81 (2009).

19 ROB WARDEN, THE SNITCH SYSTEM: HOW SNITCH TESTIMONY SENT RANDY STEIDL AND OTHER INNOCENT AMERICANS TO DEATH ROW (2005). The study catalogued 111 capital exonerations, of which 51 were based on incentivized testimony. The oft-quoted statistic that false eyewitness identification is the largest source of wrongful conviction derives from an evaluation of DNA-based exonerations. GARRETT, *supra* note 12, at 9; *see also* Innocence Project, *Eyewitness Misidentification*, available at www.innocenceproject.org/causes-wrongful-convic tion/eyewitness-misidentification.

20 Samuel R. Gross, *Convicting the Innocent*, 4 ANN. REV. L. & SOC. SCI. 173, 186 (2008).

21 Portuondo v. Agard, 529 U.S. 61, 69 (2000); James v. Illinois, 493 U.S. 307, 311–12 (1990); United States v. Agurs, 427 U.S. 97, 120 (1976).

22 *See* Darryl Brown, *The Decline of Defense Counsel and the Rise of Accuracy in Criminal Adjudication*, 93 CAL. L. REV. 1585, 1587 (2005) ("Accurate fact-finding is only one goal [of adjudication]; dispute resolution is another, and in American criminal justice, constraint of government power is a third. Those purposes sometimes conflict."). *See also* Illinois v. Gates, 462 U.S. 213, 257 (1983) (White, J., concurring) (noting that "[t]he primary cost [] of [] the exclusionary rule [is that it] interferes with the truthseeking function of a criminal trial by barring relevant and trustworthy evidence").

23 I am indebted to Jennifer Laurin for this point.

24 Jennifer E. Laurin, *Criminal Law's Science Lag: How Criminal Justice Meets Changed Scientific Understanding*, 93 TEXAS L. REV. 1751, 1757 (2015) (describing the tension between the "criminal justice system's enduring concern for accuracy and, relatedly, legitimacy" on the one hand, and the evolution of scientific knowledge on the other); Alexandra Natapoff, *Deregulating Guilt: The Information Culture of the Criminal System*, 30 CARDOZO L. REV. 965 (2008) (describing tension between the trial sphere's truth commitments and the loose informational rules that govern plea bargaining and investigative decisions).

25 Ronald J. Allen & Brian Leiter, *Naturalized Epistemology and the Law of Evidence*, 87 VA. L. REV. 1491, 1501 (2001) ("[I]t is striking and important that the vast majority

of the rules of evidence have as their primary rationale their (alleged) truth-conducive virtues.").

26 *But see* Andrea Roth, *Defying DNA: Rethinking the Role of the Jury in an Age of Scientific Proof of Innocence*, 93 B.U. L. REV. 1643, 1681–84 (2013) (documenting cases in which juries issued guilty verdicts notwithstanding DNA-based proof of defendants' innocence).

27 SIMON, *supra* note 12, at 10; James R. Acker, Allison D. Redlich, Robert J. Norris & Catherine L. Bonventre, *Stepping Back – Moving Beyond Immediate Causes: Criminal Justice and Wrongful Convictions in Social Context* 5–8, in Redlich et al., EXAMINING WRONGFUL CONVICTIONS, *supra* note 7.

28 As of November 5, 2015, the Registry lists 261 exonerations out of 1,700 as resulting from a plea. National Registry of Exonerations Homepage, available at www.law .umich.edu/special/exoneration/Pages/about.aspx.

29 BARRY SCHECK, PETER NEUFELD & JIM DWYER, ACTUAL INNOCENCE: WHEN JUSTICE GOES WRONG AND HOW TO MAKE IT RIGHT (2003).

30 MEDWED, *supra* note 12, at 150; Samuel R. Wiseman, *Waiving Innocence*, 96 MINN. L. REV. 952, 955 & n. 14 (2012) (approximately one-third of states with DNA testing statutes exclude defendants who pled).

31 *See* Brown, *supra* note 22, at 1591 (arguing that the adversarial process is becoming less important because its evidentiary inputs are becoming more accurate).

32 *See* Alison Orr Larsen, *Bargaining Inside the Black Box*, 99 GEO. L.J. 1567, 1611 (2011) ("Plea bargaining is perhaps the most prominent example of the criminal justice system operating collateral to a quest for truth."). *See also* Poventud v. City of New York, 750 F.3d 121, 143 (2d Cir. 2014) (Lynch, J., concurring) (noting that defendant's guilty plea does not permit us to "know" whether he committed the crime, referring to the guilt resulting from a plea as a "legal convention"). *But see Id.* at 157 (Jacobs, J., dissenting) (guilty plea establishes factual truth of defendant's underlying admissions).

33 William J. Stuntz, *Plea Bargaining and Criminal Law's Disappearing Shadow*, 117 HARV. L. REV. 2548 (2004); Brown, *supra* note 22, at 1610–11.

34 Lafler v. Cooper, 132 S. Ct. 1376, 1388 (2012) (the right to competent counsel must encompass competent plea bargaining because "criminal justice today is for the most part a system of pleas, not a system of trials"); *see also* Missouri v. Frye, 132 S. Ct. 1399, 1407 (2012) (same).

35 Brady v. United States, 397 U.S. 742, 758 (1970); *see also* North Carolina v. Alford, 400 U.S. 25, 38 (1970) (court was empowered to accept the defendant plea in part because the "evidence against him … substantially negated his claim of innocence," notwithstanding defendant's claim that he was actually innocent).

36 397 U.S. at 758.

37 Robert Scott & William Stuntz, *Plea Bargaining as Contract*, 101 YALE L.J. 1909, 1937, 1948 (1992).

38 *Id.* at 1949.

39 *See* Covey, *supra* note 12.

40 *See* Scott & Stuntz, *supra* note 37, at 1947–48. Trial and sentencing outcomes can also be affected by such nonevidentiary matters as whether a defendant is African-American or dark-skinned, see David S. Abrams, Marianne Bertrand & Sendhil Mullainathan, *Do Judges Vary in Their Treatment of Race?*, 41 J. Leg. Stud. 347, 350 (2012); Jennifer L. Eberhardt, Paul G. Davies, Valerie J. Purdie-Vaughns & Sheri Lynn Johnson, *Looking Deathworthy: Perceived Stereotypicality of Black Defendants Predicts Capital-Sentencing Outcomes*, 17 Psychological Sci., No. 5, 383–86 (2006); the racial composition of the jury pool, Shamena Anwar, Patrick Bayer & Randi Hjalmarsson, *The Impact of Jury Race on Criminal Trials*, 10 Q.J. Econ. 1093 (2012); and judicial election cycles, Carlos Berdejo & Noam M. Yuchtman, *Crime, Punishment and Politics: An Analysis of Political Cycles in Criminal* Sentencing, 95 Rev. Econ. Stats. 741 (2013).

41 Stuntz, *supra* note 33; Stephanos Bibas, *Plea Bargaining Outside the Shadow of Trial*, 117 Harv. L. Rev. 2463 (2004).

42 Bibas, *supra* note 41, at 2464.

43 *Id.* at 2469. *See also* Sherod Thaxton, *Leveraging Death*, 103 J. Crim. L. & Criminology 475, 483 (2013) (empirical study concluding that threat of death penalty increased likelihood that defendants would plead guilty by approximately 20 percent).

44 *See also* Natapoff, *Deregulating Guilt*, *supra* note 24 (describing how the trial, plea, and investigative spheres all have different relationships to rules and evidence).

45 Medwed, *supra* note 12, at 5.

46 Dervan & Edkins, *supra* note 12, at 34–35 (psychological study).

47 Covey, *supra* note 12, at 1173. *See also* Oren Gazal-Ayal & Avishalom Tor, *The Innocence Effect*, 62 Duke L.J. 339, 352–62 (2012).

48 *See* Simon, *supra* note 12, at 4 (on false acquittals).

49 Scott & Stuntz, *supra* note 37, at 1949.

50 Covey, *supra* note 12, at 1166–70.

51 U.S.S.G. § 3E1.1 (providing automatic 3-point offense level reduction for defendants who plead guilty).

52 Rakoff, *supra* note 13 ("For example, the prosecutor can agree with the defense counsel in a federal narcotics case that, if there is a plea bargain, the defendant will only have to plead guilty to the personal sale of a few ounces of heroin [] but if the defendant does not plead guilty, he will be charged with the drug conspiracy [] involving many kilograms of heroin.").

53 *See* U.S.S.G. § 2D1.1(c) (drug table).

54 Jason Cade, *The Plea-Bargain Crisis for Noncitizens in Misdemeanor Court*, 34 Cardozo L. Rev. 1751, 1773 (2013).

55 *See* Brown, *supra* note 22, at 1587 ("Accurate fact-finding is only one goal [of adjudication]."); Raymond, *supra* note 6 (worrying that the innocence paradigm obscures the rights and needs of the guilty). *Compare also* William Blackstone, 4 Commentaries ("Better that ten guilty persons escape, than that one innocent suffer") *with* Ronald J. Allen & Larry Laudan, *Deadly Dilemmas*, 41 Tex. Tech.

L. REV. 65, 75 (2008) ("Imposing an unbridgeable firewall against false convictions is not only impossible but undesirable. It is a project that, if realized, would visit unearned, grievous harm on vast numbers of innocent citizens, victimized by those guilty felons whom the justice system – holding both its nose and its breath – wrongfully acquitted.").

56 *See, e.g.,* The Innocence Project, *The Cases: Christopher Ochoa,* available at www.innocenceproject.org/cases-false-imprisonment/christopher-ochoa (in which Christopher Ochoa pled guilty to a murder he did not commit in order to avoid the death penalty).

57 Russell Covey, *Longitudinal Guilt: Repeat Offenders, Plea Bargaining, and the Variable Standard of Proof,* 63 FLORIDA L. REV. 431, 444–447 (2011) (chronicling numerous reasons why repeat offenders are less likely to prevail at trial and more likely to plead).

58 Nick Pinto, *The Bail Trap,* N.Y. TIMES MAGAZINE, Aug. 13, 2015.

59 MEDWED, *supra* note 12, at 159–61.

60 *See, e.g.,* Perez v. United States, 2015 WL 3413596, Slip Op. at 7 (S.D.N.Y. May 28, 2015) (upholding plea agreement containing DNA testing waiver); *see also* Wiseman, *supra* note 30.

61 WARDEN, *supra* note 19; GARRETT, *supra* note 12, at 124; Alexandra Natapoff, *Beyond Unreliable: How Snitches Contribute to Wrongful Convictions,* 37 GOLDEN GATE U. L. REV. 107 (2006).

62 *Cf.* George Harris, *Testimony for Sale: The Law and Ethics of Snitches and Experts,* 28 PEPP. L. REV. 1 (2000) (comparing expert witnesses and informants).

63 *See* Ian Weinstein, *Regulating the Market for Snitches,* 43 BUFF. L. REV. 563 (1999).

64 *See, e.g.,* Cal. Penal Code § 1111.5 (restricting use of in-custody informants).

65 Tbls. 5.44.2006 & 5.24.2010, SOURCEBOOK ONLINE, available at www.albany.edu/sourcebook/pdf/t5442006.pdf.

66 *The Plea: Erma Faye Stewart and Regina Kelly,* PBS FRONTLINE, June 17, 2004 (documenting wrongful pleas taken in Hearne, Texas sweep).

67 NATAPOFF, *supra* note 18, at 3–4.

68 Adam Heder & Michael Goldsmith, *Recantations Reconsidered: A New Framework for Righting Wrongful Convictions,* 2012 UTAH L. REV. 199 (2012).

69 Innocence Project Northwest, *Our Clients' Stories of Innocence: Tyler Gassman, Robert Larson and Paul Statler,* available at www.law.washington.edu/Clinics/IPNW/Stories.aspx#gassman. Disclosure: I testified as an expert witness on behalf of the original defendants in their subsequent civil compensation case.

70 Larson et al. v. State of Washington, Court's Decision, Case No. 2014-02-00090-6, Feb. 12, 2015.

71 GARRETT, *supra* note 12, at 10 (21 percent of DNA exonerations were informant cases).

72 Maurice Possley, *The Prosecutor and the Snitch,* THE MARSHALL PROJECT, Aug. 3, 2014; David Grann, *Trial By Fire,* THE NEW YORKER, Sept. 7, 2009.

73 Samuel R. Gross, Op-Ed, *The Staggering Number of Wrongful Convictions in America,* WASH. POST, July 24, 2015.

74 M. Chris Fabricant, *Rousting the Cops*, VILLAGE VOICE, Oct. 30, 2007.

75 PETER MOSKOS, COP IN THE HOOD: MY YEAR POLICING BALTIMORE'S EASTERN DISTRICT 114–15 (2008).

76 Complaint, Maryland NAACP et al. v. Baltimore City Police Dep't. et al., Civil Case No. 24-C-06-005088 (Balt. City Cir. Ct., 2006) (challenging illegal order-maintenance arrests); Edward Ericson Jr., *Copping Out: A City Council Report on False Arrests by Baltimore Police Fails to Address the Root of the Problem*, BALT. CITY PAPER, Oct. 5, 2005, available at www2.citypaper.com/film/story.asp?id= 10980 (one third of Baltimore loitering arrests dismissed).

77 *See, e.g.*, Williams v. State, 780 A.2d 1210, 1218 (Md. Ct. Spec. App. 2001) (overturning loitering conviction).

78 *See* Natapoff, *Misdemeanors*, *supra* note 15; Pinto, *supra* note 58.

79 Eve Brensike Primus, *Our Broken Misdemeanor Justice System: Its Problems and Some Potential Solutions*, 85 S. CAL. L. REV. POSTSCRIPT 80 (2012).

80 Joseph Goldstein, *Prosecutor Deals Blow to Stop-and-Frisk Tactic*, N.Y. TIMES, Sept. 25, 2012.

81 Williams, 780 A.2d at 1218.

82 ROBERT C. BORUCHOWITZ, MALIA N. BRINK & MAUREEN DIMINO, MINOR CRIMES, MASSIVE WASTE: THE TERRIBLE TOLL OF AMERICA'S BROKEN MISDEMEANOR COURTS 7 (2009); Eve Brensike Primus, *Structural Reform in Criminal Defense: Relocating Ineffective Assistance of Counsel Claims*, 92 CORNELL L. REV. 679, 694 (2007) (on the infrequency of misdemeanor appeals).

83 Natapoff, *Misdemeanors*, *supra* note 15; Jenny Roberts, *Why Misdemeanors Matter: Defining Effective Advocacy in the Lower Criminal Courts*, 45 U.C. DAVIS L. REV. 277 (2011).

84 Alexandra Natapoff, *Young Black Men Coerced to Plead Guilty*, WASH. POST, Nov. 11, 2015, available at www.washingtonpost.com/news/the-watch/wp/2015/11/11/ the-cost-of-quality-of-life-policing-thousands-of-young-black-men-coerced-to-plead-guilty-to-crimes-they-didnt-commit/.

85 Pinto, *supra* note 58.

86 Alexandra Natapoff, *Gideon Skepticism*, 70 WASH. & LEE L. REV. 1049 (2013); *see also* Roberts, *supra* note 83.

87 MEDWED, *supra* note 12. *See also* Laurie L. Levenson, *Searching for Injustice: The Challenge of Postconviction Discovery, Investigation, and Litigation*, 87 S. CAL. L. REV. 545 (2014) (describing prosecutorial incentives to stymie postconviction proceedings); DAVID A. HARRIS, FAILED EVIDENCE: WHY LAW ENFORCEMENT RESISTS SCIENCE (2012) (focusing on police and prosecutorial decision-making).

88 Covey, *Police Misconduct*, *supra* note 12.

89 SIMON, *supra* note 12, at 3.

90 *See generally* Redlich et al., EXAMINING WRONGFUL CONVICTIONS, *supra* note 7.

91 Acker et al., *supra* note 27.

92 Albert W. Alschuler, *A Nearly Perfect System for Convicting the Innocent*, 79 ALBANY L. REV. (forthcoming 2016) (draft on file with author).

93 SCHECK ET AL., *supra* note 29.

94 *See* Laurin, *supra* note 6, at 1476 (arguing that DNA should be understood as a "conversation starter" rather than a model for innocence reform).

95 William J. Stuntz, *The Pathological Politics of Criminal Law*, 100 MICH. L. REV. 505, 509 (2001).

96 H.B. 564, Leg. Sess. 84(R) (Tex. 2015).

97 A. 02906, 2015 Gen. Assem., Reg. Sess. (N.Y. 2015).

98 A reform I have not advocated. NATAPOFF, *supra* note 18.

99 North Carolina v. Alford, 400 U.S. 25 (1970).

6

Reacting to Recantations

ROB WARDEN

One lesson of the DNA forensic age is that recantations of trial testimony by prosecution witnesses deserve to be taken seriously,[1] notwithstanding time-honored dicta to the contrary.[2] Unfortunately, the lesson seems to have been lost on some prosecutors and judges.[3]

The nation's first DNA exoneration – of Gary Dotson in Cook County, Illinois, in 1989[4] – exemplifies a dichotomy that persists between innocence advocates and law enforcement more than a quarter of a century later. A decade before his exoneration, Dotson was convicted of a crime that had not occurred: the abduction and rape of 16-year-old Cathleen Crowell, who recanted in 1985, by which time she had become a born-again Christian, gotten married, and was known as Cathleen Crowell Webb.[5] She said she had faked the rape out of fear that she was pregnant by her boyfriend, her intent having been to create a cover story for her parents in case her fear came to fruition – which it had not.[6] Her recantation was deemed false by prosecutors, by the judge before whom Dotson had been tried, by the Illinois Prisoner Review Board, by the governor of Illinois, and by reporters covering the story for the state's most influential newspaper, the *Chicago Tribune*.[7] Dotson's conviction stood for another four years, until August 14, 1989, when DNA established his innocence and the validity of Webb's recantation.[8]

As of August 14, 2015, the twenty-sixth anniversary of the Dotson exoneration, the Innocence Project had chronicled 320 DNA exonerations,[9] of which 47 (14.7 percent) involved recantations by prosecution witnesses.[10] During the same period, in cases that the Innocence Project does not attribute to DNA, the National Registry of Exonerations chronicled 1,319 exonerations, of which 383 (29 percent) involved recantations by state witnesses.[11]

If, at first glance, the numbers suggest that the system is open to fair and prompt evaluation of recantations, they actually suggest nothing of the sort. Because post-conviction DNA testing is a statutory right in all states,[12]

the criminal justice system's tacit acknowledgment of the veracity of recantations following DNA exclusions is independent of what prosecutors and
judges may think of them. The non-DNA cases seem more telling. That the
mean time between recantation and exoneration in them is more than
twice that in DNA cases – 5.3 years versus 2.5 years[13] – may well reflect to
some degree the skepticism that law enforcement harbors about recantations.

What the numbers leave no doubt about is that recantations are not
inherently unreliable. Nonetheless, while some prosecutors and judges persist
in assaulting that reality with archaic dicta,[14] a new mode of attack has been
launched on recantations in the birthplace of the DNA exoneration. The
attack is the brainchild of former Cook County State's Attorney Anita Alvarez.
Her weapon is the Illinois perjury statute, which provides that, when materially conflicting statements have been made under oath, the prosecution
"need not establish which statement is false" – no matter how long ago or
under what circumstances the first statement was made.[15]

The case that provoked Alvarez's ire began in 1992, when Willie Johnson, a
drug dealer, was seriously wounded and two of his cohorts were fatally shot on
the front porch of his home in Chicago.[16] As he was being prepped for surgery,
Johnson gave police a description of the shooters – one of whom, he said, was
known as "Duke" and drove a white Oldsmobile.[17] Within hours, police
stopped such a car driven by 17-year-old Albert ("Duke") Kirkman and in
which Cedric Cal, also 17, was a passenger. Police returned to the hospital
with an array of photos, from which Johnson identified Kirkman and Cal as
the killers.[18] In 1994, based solely on Johnson's testimony, a Cook County jury
found the youths guilty of the double murder and aggravated battery with a
firearm.[19] They were sentenced to natural life in prison.[20]

Fifteen years later, in 2009, Johnson recanted his trial testimony, stating in
an affidavit, "I am coming forward now because Duke and Cal don't belong
in prison for shooting me and killing my best friends. They didn't do it. They
weren't there and [had] nothing to do with what went down that night."[21]
Johnson said he had falsely accused the youths to protect himself and his
family from reprisal by one of the actual killers – a drug dealer who knew
Johnson could identify him; Kirkman and Cal were simply scapegoats,
whom Johnson regarded as "enemies" in a rivalry over drug turf.[22] In the
fifteen years since the trial, Johnson said, he had matured, he no longer
feared reprisal from the drug dealer, and he regretted ruining two innocent
men's lives.[23]

Johnson's recantation seemed sincere, if only because it was unlikely
that he would go out of his way to help the men who had killed two of
his best friends and tried to kill him. But there were other reasons to

believe it: A witness who knew Johnson, Kirkman, and Cal testified at the 1994 trial that about a month after the shooting Johnson told him that the youths were not involved.[24] The recantation was corroborated by Johnson's sister and by his then-girlfriend.[25] Moreover, Kirkman and Cal had credible alibis.[26]

In sum, Johnson's recantation was as plausible as Cathleen Crowell Webb's. As the saga played out in the Cook County criminal justice system, however, it was *déjà vu* all over again – only worse. After hearing Johnson's revised rendition of the crime, Circuit Court Judge Michael Brown deemed it "not credible."[27] Based on a brief telephone conversation that Johnson testified he had with a gang leader who told him "to do the right thing," Brown inferred that the recantation must have been coerced, saying, in ruling from the bench, "I have no idea why [the gang] would urge Willie Johnson to come forward. Nonetheless, it does not appear for a desire to see that [justice] is done, but to further their own ends."[28]

A month after Brown ruled, Alvarez obtained Johnson's perjury indictment, which was highly unusual, if not unprecedented, in a post-conviction case.[29] Shortly thereafter, twenty-three former judges and prosecutors sent Alvarez a letter urging her to drop the case, pointing out that, unless she could prove the recantation itself false, prosecuting Johnson stood to chill recantations generally, running counter to sensible public policy, which ought to encourage – not discourage – truthful recantations.[30]

Alvarez responded, "I agree wholeheartedly with your contention that a prosecutor should never engage in tactics or enforce policies that would chill truthful testimony of any kind, at any stage of a criminal proceeding."[31] But she then proceeded to do precisely what she assured the judges and prosecutors she would not do: In response to a motion to dismiss the case, which was pending before Circuit Court Judge Dennis J. Porter,[32] she argued that, "The statute under which defendant is charged does not require proof of which of the two statements is false."[33]

Alvarez had done other things that called her commitment to justice into question, as those in the Innocence Movement who have dealt with her can attest.[34] In 2012, after DNA exonerated four young men of the rape and murder of a 14-year-old girl and linked a known sex criminal to the crime, she asserted in a *Sixty Minutes* interview that, notwithstanding the DNA, the youths might be guilty and justified not charging the sex criminal on the ground that it was "possible that this convicted rapist wandered past an open field and had sex with a fourteen-year-old girl who was dead."[35] In 2013, Alvarez similarly declined to charge a man linked by DNA to a murder for which another man had been wrongly convicted and exonerated,[36] and belatedly acquiesced – after years of stubborn resistance – to the exoneration of a man who had been imprisoned more than twenty years for a home invasion and double murder he could not have committed because he had been in jail when the crime occurred.[37]

Gary Dotson and eleven other exonerated Illinois defendants who had been convicted as a result of perjured prosecution testimony that had been recanted after their trials joined the twenty-three former judges and prosecutors in an amicus brief supporting a motion to dismiss the Johnson indictment, urging Judge Porter to bar the prosecution.[38] *Amici* asserted that Alvarez had "a disabling conflict of interest and clear bias in the application of the perjury law" – using it to punish Johnson for a recantation unfavorable to the prosecution while ignoring perjury by police officers whose lies under oath had been documented by video footage.[39]

Judge Porter denied the motion, after which Johnson – having no defense, it being obvious that both his 1994 testimony or his 2009 recantation could not be true, and facing, in view of his felony record, up to ten years in prison and a $25,000 fine if convicted at trial – pleaded guilty in exchange for a thirty-month prison sentence.[40] To mitigate harm to Kirkman and Cal, Johnson's lawyers emphasized that he remained adamant that they were innocent and had taken the plea deal only "when confronted with the probability that the truth of his 2011 recantation would be considered irrelevant and inadmissible" if he had gone to trial.[41]

Johnson was packed off to prison, the victim of a classic Catch-22 – living proof, perhaps, of the old adage that no good deed goes unpunished. Illinois Governor Pat Quinn grasped the injustice that Alvarez had wrought and, on his final day in office, commuted Johnson's sentence to time served.[42] But Johnson's release after serving only a little more than three months of his thirty-month sentence, left his conviction intact and did nothing to change what Johnson had portrayed as a worse injustice – the wrongful convictions of two innocent teenagers who remain behind bars more than two decades later. Kirkman and Cal are pursuing federal writs of habeas corpus,[43] but even if they are vindicated, the prosecution of Johnson, as his lawyers put it, "will have a palpably chilling effect on the willingness of witnesses to give truthful recantations in the future. ... [E]very witness who gives a sworn recantation of earlier sworn testimony will have created a record upon which a perjury indictment may be obtained."[44]

The Johnson case has ramifications beyond Illinois. Alvarez's handiwork could go viral – spreading to other states where prosecutors disdain actual innocence claims and where the law allows perjury prosecutions based on conflicting statements without regard to when the first statement was made.[45]

Actual prosecutions, however, are unnecessary to chill recantations since the mere specter of perjury prosecutions is sufficient to deter witnesses from repudiating their fraudulent trial testimony.[46]

It may be tempting to dismiss Alvarez as an inconsequential aberration in an age of enlightenment spawned by the DNA revolution. Before she failed in her bid for reelection in 2016, she had developed a national profile and managed to cast herself as an authority on ethics – as one of four keynote speakers at a National District Attorneys' Association Summit on Prosecution Integrity in July 2015.[47] She also indignantly condemned perjury by one of her assistant prosecutors, who had been caught lying under oath to justify what an audio recording indicated had been an illegal search and seizure in connection with the shooting of a Chicago police officer in 2012.[48] Alvarez thus has positioned herself as a no-nonsense, let-the-chips-fall-where-they-may defender of truth and justice, and it is conceivable that she could still emerge as a national role model in a movement to undermine the advances of the DNA revolution. Because the threat of perjury prosecutions is real, it is of paramount importance to stop them. But how?

For starters, when perjury charges are brought based on conflicting statements, innocence advocates should enlist local legal luminaries and mainstream news media to expose the wrongheadedness of discouraging truthful recantations[49] – the goal being to persuade prosecutors to adhere to Alvarez's claim "that a prosecutor should never engage in tactics or enforce policies that would chill truthful testimony of any kind, at any stage of a criminal proceeding."[50]

On the legislative front, it would be useful if innocence advocates in states where perjury prosecutions are not expressly precluded worked to bring those states' statutes into conformity with those barring prosecutions unless the earlier statement is made within a statutory limitation period.[51] Even in the unlikely event of success, however, imposing limitations would not solve the problem, which primarily affects pretrial recantation cases. In light of the coercive nature of perjury prosecutions,[52] one way to confront the issue would be to move to recuse prosecutors' offices in all cases in which recanting witnesses are charged with perjury. There is authority, albeit scant, for recusal of entire prosecutors' offices when conflicts of interest create appearances of unfairness[53] – as they do in inherently coercive perjury prosecutions of recanting witnesses.

But, in the final analysis, the overarching goal of innocence advocates should be to establish statutory and case law providing that convictions should not be allowed to rest solely on the testimony of liars – which, except under rare circumstances,[54] recanting witnesses are.

NOTES

1 Adam Heder & Michael Goldsmith, *Recantations Reconsidered: A New Framework for Righting Wrongful Convictions*, 2012 UTAH L. REV. 99 (2012); Shawn Armbrust, *Reevaluating Recanting Witnesses: Why the Red-Headed Stepchild of New Evidence Deserves Another Look*, 28 B.C. THIRD WORLD L.J. 75 (2008).

2 People v. Shilitano, 218 N.Y. 161, 170 (1916) ("There is no form of proof so unreliable as recanting testimony. . . . Those experienced in the administration of the criminal law know well its untrustworthy character"); People v. Marquis, 176 N.E. 314, 315 (Ill. 1931) ("Recanting testimony is regarded as very unreliable"); Dobbert v. Wainwright, 468 U.S. 1231, 1233–34 (1984) ("Recantation testimony is properly viewed with great suspicion. It . . . is very often unreliable and given for suspect motives").

3 *See, e.g.*, State v. Worthington, 2015-Ohio-3173 (Ohio App. 12th. Dist, Aug, 10, 2015) (slip copy) (affirming trial court's denial of motion to withdraw guilty plea to multiple counts of rape in light of affidavits from eight witnesses stating that the purported child victims in the case had recanted their allegations); People v. Jones, 45 Misc.3d 1201(A) (N.Y. Sup. 2014) (citing Shilitano, 218 N.Y. 161 [1916], in affirming murder conviction despite recantations of all three witnesses who identified defendant at trial); People v. Newkirk, 2012 IL App.2d 111226-U (Ill.App.2d. Dist. 2012) (citing Marquis, 176 N.E. 314 [Ill. 1931], in affirming aggravated criminal sexual assault conviction despite recantations by both alleged victims); Brown v. State, 334 S.W 3d 789 (Tex.App.2010) (affirming aggravated robbery conviction despite recantation of the sole witness who linked defendant to the crime); Heath v. State, 3 So.3d 1017, 1024 (Fla. 2009) (citing dicta that recanted testimony is "exceedingly unreliable," in affirming murder conviction and death sentence despite recantation of state's key witness).

4 Dolores Kennedy, *Gary Dotson*, National Registry of Exonerations [hereinafter "NRE"], available at www.law.umich.edu/special/exoneration/Pages/casedetail.aspx?caseid=3186. As Daniel Medwed discusses in his introductory chapter to this volume, it might be argued that Dotson was not first. Daniel S. Medwed, *Talking about a Revolution: A Quarter Century of DNA Exonerations, supra*, in this volume. A few months before DNA established Dotson's innocence, David Vasquez, who was serving life for a rape-murder in Virginia, received a gubernatorial pardon after DNA linked a serial killer to a murder that was strikingly similar to the murder for which Vasquez had been convicted. There was, however, no testable DNA in the Vasquez case itself. *See* Dana Priest, *Va. Man Pardoned after Five Years in Prison*, WASH. POST, Jan. 5, 1989, at 1.

5 Kennedy, *supra* note 4.

6 *Id.*

7 Ann Marie Lipinski & John Kass, *Rape Conviction Stands*, CHI. TRIB., Apr. 12, 1985, at 1; Lipinski & Kass, *"She Looked So Good on TV" / But on Witness Stand, Webb Lost Her Credibility*, CHI. TRIB., Apr. 14, 1985, at C1; Lipinski & Kass, *Dotson "Guilty"-But Set Free*, CHI. TRIB., May 13, 1985, at 1.

8 Larry Green, *12-Year Legal Nightmare at an End: Recanted Testimony, High-Tech Help to Clear Gary Dotson*, L.A. TIMES, Aug. 15, 1989, at 5. Dotson was not in prison during those four years because Governor James R. Thompson commuted his 25-to-50-year sentence to time served in 1985. Ann Marie Lipinski & John Kass, *Dotson "Guilty" – But Set Free*, CHI. TRIB., May 13, 1985, at 1 ("Thompson's decision had the effect of satisfying public opinion on Dotson's behalf without dismissing the mounting inconsistencies in Webb's recantation").

9 Innocence Project, *The Cases: DNA Exoneree Profiles*, available at www.innocen ceproject.org/cases-false-imprisonment.

10 Original research from NRE data. Details available from r-warden@law.northwes tern.edu.

11 *Id.* The NRE defines exoneration as restoration of legal innocence based at least in part on evidence not presented at a defendant's trial, or, if the defendant pleaded guilty, evidence that was unknown to him or her at the time of the plea. NRE, *Glossary*, available at www.law.umich.edu/special/exoneration/Pages/glossary.aspx.

12 Innocence Project, *Access to Post-Conviction DNA Testing*, available at www.inno cenceproject.org/files/imported/dna_innocenceproject_website.pdf.

13 *See supra* note 10 and accompanying text. The comparatively low percentage of recantations in DNA cases may reflect nothing more than that there is little to be gained by pursuing recantations when DNA exclusions are in the offing.

14 *See supra* note 2 and accompanying text.

15 *See* 720 ILL. COMP. STAT. 5/32–2. The perjury statutes of all states authorize prosecutions on conflicting statements, but twenty-one states require that both sworn statements be made within the statute of limitations: Alabama, ALA CODE § 13A-10-104 (a); Arizona, A.R.S. § 13–2705; California, CAL. PENAL CODE § 118 (a); Colorado, COLO. REV. STAT. ANN. § 18–8-505(1); Hawaii, H.R.S § 710-1065; Iowa, I.C.A. § 720.2; Kentucky, K.R.S. § 523.050; Maine, 17-A M.R.S.A. § 451; Massachusetts, MASS. GEN. LAWS Ch. 268 § 1; Minnesota, MINN. STAT. ANN. § 609.48 Subd. 3; Montana, M.C.A. 45–7-201(6); Nebraska, NEB. REV. STAT. § 28–915(6); New Hampshire, N.H. REV. STAT. § 641:1(I)(b); New York, N.Y. PENAL L. § 210.15; North Dakota, N.D.C.C., 12.1–11-01(3); Pennsylvania, 18 PA. C.S.A. § 4902(e); Rhode Island, Gen. Laws 1956, § 11–33-1(b); Tennessee, T. C. A. § 39-16-707; Utah, U.C.A. 1953 § 76–8-502; Vermont, 13 V.S.A. § 2901a; Wisconsin, W.S.A. 946.32(1)(a). The federal perjury statute also bars prosecutions unless the conflicting statements occurred within the statute of limitations. 18 U.S. CODE § 1623(c)(2).

16 People v. Cal, 2013 IL App (1st) 112354-U, at 5. *See also* People v. Kirkman, 2013 IL App (1st) 112362-U, at 5.

17 Chicago Police Dept., Area 4, Violent Crimes Unit, Beat No. 1112, Supplemental Report, Apr. 21, 1992, at 9 (quoting Johnson regarding white Oldsmobile and "Duke").

18 *Id.* at 10.

19 *See supra* note 16, at 2 (in both opinions).

20 *Id.*

21 Affidavit of Willie Johnson, May 8, 2009.

22 *Id.*

23 *Id.*

24 Transcript of Proceedings, testimony of Michael Sylvester, People v. Cal, 92 CR 10385, Circ. Ct. of Cook County, Hon. Daniel Kelley, Feb. 9, 1994, at 37–46.

25 Affidavit of Latonya Johnson, Mar. 23, 2009 ("Willie stated [shortly after his release from the hospital] that the people who shot them were still at large [unlike Kirkman & Cal]. .... Because they were still at large, my family, including Willie, went into hiding"); Affidavit of LaTrese Buford, Apr. 24, 2009 (describing how she also went into hiding in fear of the killers).

26 Transcript of Proceedings, testimony of Secnoba Comb, *supra* note 24, at 53 et seq. (stating that she and her grandchildren were with Cal across the street from the crime scene when they heard the shots and that they crossed the street together and watched police process the scene); Affidavit of Larry Thomas, Jan. 1, 1998 (stating that he had been in the courtroom during the trial, that he had come to testify that he and Kirkman were together at the time of the crime, but that the defense rested without calling him to the stand).

27 Transcript of Proceedings, People v. Cal, 92 CR 10385, Jan. 19, 2011 & July 15, 2011, at 13.

28 *Id.* at 8.

29 True Bill, People v. Johnson, Cook County G.J. No. 320, Aug. 18, 2011 (charging a continuing offense of perjury beginning "on or about February 8, 1994, and continuing on through January 19, 2011"). There are no reported appellate decisions anywhere in the nation in cases involving post-conviction recantations by prosecution witnesses when the earlier statement was outside a statute of limitations. There have been numerous perjury prosecutions in cases involving pretrial recantations. Paula Gray, for instance, was convicted of perjury after her pretrial recantation. People v. Gray, 87 Ill.App.3d 142, 145–146 (Ill.App.1st Dist.1980).

30 Letter re: People v. Johnson, Apr. 24, 2014, signed by former Illinois Appellate Court Justice Warren D. Wolfson on behalf of himself and twenty-two others, including former prosecutors Scott Turow, former U.S. Attorney and Illinois Gov. James R. Thompson, former Illinois Attorney General Tyrone C. Fahner, former U.S. Attorneys Thomas P. Sullivan and Dan K. Webb, and former Judge George N. Leighton, after whom the Cook County Criminal Courts Building is named.

31 Letter to Warren Wolfson re: People v. Johnson, June 5, 2014.

32 Defendant's Motion to Dismiss Indictment, People v. Johnson, 11 CR 13172, before Hon. Dennis J. Porter. Circ. Ct. of Cook County, June 2, 2014 (contending that there is "no Illinois authority for charging perjury as a continuing offense, let alone perjury based on two separate sworn statements so many years apart").

33 People's Response to Defendant's Motion to Dismiss Indictment, People v. Johnson, 11 CR 13172, July 10, 2014.

34 *See, e.g.*, Peter Neufeld, *Alvarez Lacks Insight Into Wrongful Convictions*, Chi. Trib., Dec. 21, 2012, at 37 (criticizing her "utter unwillingness to admit that the convictions of nine teenage boys were tragic failures of the criminal justice system"); Don Rose, *Anita Alvarez and the Office of Self Promotion and Protection*, Chi. Daily Observer, May 13, 2014, available at www.cdobs.com/archive/fea tured/anita-alvarez-and-the-office-of-self-promotion-and-protection/.

35 Byron Pitts (correspondent), *Chicago: The False Confession Capital*, 60 Minutes, CBS-TV, Dec. 9, 2012, available at www.cbsnews.com/news/chicago-the-false-con fession-capital/.

36 Steve Mills, *Suspect in Assault Linked to Homicide*, Chi. Trib., Sept. 4, 2013, at 12 (reporting that the man arrested in a sexual assault case previously had been implicated in a homicide by DNA evidence "but Cook County prosecutors never charged him").

37 Steve Mills, *20 Years to Undo Wrongful Conviction*, Chi. Trib., June 30, 2013, at 1.

38 James I. Kaplan, Lauren Beslow, Daniel B. Lewin, Quarles & Brady LLP *(pro bono)*, Brief of Persons Concerned About the Integrity of the Cook County Criminal Justice System as Amici Curiae in Support of Defendant, People v. Johnson, 11 CR 13172, July 15, 2014. Like Dotson, seven of the eleven exonerated prisoners – Kenneth Adams, Jonathan Barr, Rolando Cruz, James Harden, Dana Holland, Maurice Patterson, and Willie Rainge – were exonerated by DNA. Three of the other exonerations were dependent on virtually irrefutable corroboration of the recantations. James Kuppelberg was exonerated after it was the established that the recanting witness in his case had lied at trial when he testified that from the window of his attic apartment he had seen Kuppelberg set an arson fire; that proved impossible because the view was obstructed by a building. Recanting witnesses originally had linked Daniel Taylor and Deon Patrick to a home invasion and double murder – a crime that they could not have committed because Taylor was in police custody when it occurred. Among the eleven, only one, Jacques Rivera, was exonerated solely on the basis of a recantation. For summaries of all eleven cases, see NRE, *Illinois Cases*, available at www.law .umich.edu/special/exoneration/Pages/browse.aspx?View={B8342AE7-6520-4A32-8A06-4B326208BAF8}&FilterField1=State&FilterValue1=Illinois.

39 *Brief of Persons Concerned, supra* note 38, at 9–10. In a recent case cited in the brief a Chicago police officer testified before a grand jury that he had been assaulted by the manager of a massage parlor who had been arrested in a vice raid. Video footage produced four months later left no doubt that the police had assaulted the manager – not the other way around. *See* Klyzek v. City of Chicago, et al., 14 CV 02547 (N.D. Ill., filed May 14, 2014).

40 Report of Proceedings, People v. Johnson, 11 CR 13172, Oct. 7, 2014.

41 Gabriel A. Fuentes, Andrew W. Vail & Justin C. Steffen, Jenner & Block LLP, *pro bono*, Petition of Willie Johnson for Executive Clemency, Illinois Prisoner Review Board, filed Dec. 3, 2014, at 10.

42 Frank Main, *Quinn Commutes Sentence of Man Who Lied in Murder Case*, Chi. Sun-Times, Jan. 13, 2015, at 6.

43 U.S. ex rel. Cal v. Williams, No. 14–3834 (N.D. Ill., filed May 23, 2014). The proceedings were stayed pending resentencing pursuant to Miller v. Alabama, 132 S. Ct. 2455 (2012) (holding that mandatory life without parole for juvenile offenders violates the Eighth Amendment).

44 Fuentes et al., *supra* note 41, at 14–15.

45 *See supra* note 15 (listing states in which both statements must be within the statute of limitations).

46 Intimidation of witnesses with threats of prosecution for perjury, of course, is improper. *See, e.g.*, Webb v. Texas, 409 U.S. 95, 97 (1972) (reversing a conviction because "[t]he trial judge gratuitously singled out this one witness for a lengthy admonition on the dangers of perjury"); U.S. v. Vavages, 151 F.3d 1185, 1192–93 (9th Cir. 1998) (reversing a conviction due to "the prosecutor's thinly veiled threats to prosecute [an alibi witness] for perjury and to withdraw her plea agreement in the event she testified in support of [defendant's] alibi"). The impropriety of perjury warnings is fact-specific, however. Informing a witness that he or she could be charged with perjury, thus, is not invariably impermissible. *See, e.g.*, U.S. v. Viera, 839 F.2d 1113, 1114–15 (5th Cir. 1988) (affirming a conviction, observing that "[a] prosecutor is always entitled to attempt to avert perjury and to punish criminal conduct"); U.S. v. Davis, 974 F.2d 182, 185 (D.C. Cir. 1992) (affirming conviction of defendant who did not testify in his own defense after the prosecutor warned that he might be charged with perjury).

47 *See* National District Attorneys Association, *Summit on Prosecution Integrity*, available at www.ndaa.org/summit.html. *See also* John Byrne & Hal Dardick, Foxx: *Cook County State's Attorney Win About 'Turning the Page,'* Chi. Trib., May 16, 2016.

48 Steve Schmadeke, *Prosecutor Fired over Alleged Perjury*, Chi. Trib., Sept. 15, 2015, at 1 (quoting Alvarez as describing herself as "appalled … livid … outraged" over prosecutor's alleged perjury).

49 Although their efforts fell short of stopping the Johnson prosecution, Chicago media warned of the danger that the case would chill truthful recantations. *See, e.g.*, Eric Zorn, *What to do about Witnesses Who Lie*, Chi. Trib., Sept. 7, 2011, at 31 (noting that "the system must … encourage genuine recantations … and remove the self-interest of law enforcement officials who reflexively attempt to justify what they've done rather than objectively review it"); Editorial, *Threat of Perjury Can Chill Testimony*, Chi. Sun-Times, Sept. 8, 2011, at 24 (asserting that "it's disturbing … that Cook County prosecutors have charged a man with perjury because he recanted his 2004 testimony that led to life sentences for two other men"); Editorial, *Law Shouldn't Discourage Truth*, Chi. Sun-Times, May 6, 2014, at 19 (contending that "to discourage recantations that might be true … turns the truth-finding mission of the courts upside down").

50 *See supra* note 31 and accompanying text.

51 *See supra* note 15.

52 In Texas, after a witness whose testimony had resulted not only in the conviction but also the execution of a man who may have been innocent recanted to a *Houston Chronicle* reporter, the Bexar County prosecutor threatened to charge the witness

with "murder by perjury" if he repeated the recantation under oath. Rick Casey, *'Murder by Perjury' in Cantu Case?*, HOUS. CHRON., Dec. 5, 2005, at 1.

53 *See, e.g.*, Carrie Leonetti, *When the Emperor Has No Clothes III: Personnel Policies and Conflicts of Interest in Prosecutors' Offices*, 22 CORNELL J. L. & PUB. POL'Y 53 (2012); Rachel Pecker, *Quasi-Judicial Prosecutors and Post-Conviction Claims of Innocence: Granting Recusals to Make Impartiality a Reality*, 34 CARDOZO L. REV. 1609 (2013).

54 A recantation, of course, can be merely a retraction of a mistake. For instance, Jacques Rivera was exonerated in 2011 of a murder for which he had been in prison for twenty-two years, after the only witness who linked him to the crime –a 12-year-old boy – recanted, saying that, after identifying Rivera, he saw the killer on the street and realized that he had made a mistake. People v. Rivera, 88 CR 15436, Hon. Neera Walsh, Cir. Ct. of Cook County, Sept. 12, 2011.

7

A Tale of Two Innocence Clinics

Client Representation and Legislative Advocacy

JACQUELINE MCMURTRIE

INTRODUCTION

The "Innocence Movement"[1] came of age in the 1990s, which was also a decade of growth for clinical legal education.[2] The turn of the century brought further expansion of both causes' mission. Published in 2000, *Actual Innocence*[3] is heralded as the "foundational document of the innocence paradigm."[4] Its gripping narrative of the wrongly convicted was accompanied by an agenda of criminal justice reforms to protect the innocent.[5] Clinical law faculty, whose numbers nearly doubled in the decade preceding *Actual Innocence*,[6] responded to its call to establish clinics "to represent clients in DNA and non-DNA cases."[7] The number of law school clinics providing *pro bono* legal and investigative services to individuals seeking to prove innocence of crimes for which they were convicted grew exponentially in the following years.[8] Since 1992, when the Innocence Project in New York City launched the first innocence clinic at Cardozo Law, thousands of students have either represented or provided legal assistance to prisoners exonerated through DNA testing or other newly discovered evidence.

The partnership between the Innocence Movement and clinical legal education is fitting given the shared benefit to each of involving students in the exoneration of wrongly convicted clients. Doing so furthers the Innocence Movement's primary goal of freeing innocent prisoners. And, client representation innocence clinics address clinical legal education's mission to teach students essential lawyering skills while achieving social justice.[9] However, the Innocence Movement has not expanded the partnership to advance its secondary goal of policy reform. Drawing from lessons learned from DNA exonerations, social scientists, and legal scholars have shaped an agenda of criminal justice reforms to prevent the arrest, prosecution, and conviction of innocent persons.[10] Yet very few innocence organizations, including those based at law schools, employ faculty or staff who focus on policy reform. Only one organization, Innocence Project Northwest (IPNW), offers a clinical law experience devoted to policy advocacy. Since the IPNW Legislative Advocacy Clinic was first offered in 2011, law students have successfully advocated for bills to compensate the wrongly convicted and preserve biological evidence.

This chapter will summarize the Innocence Movement's successes, and describe the challenges it faces moving forward in regard to client and policy advocacy. It will discuss why the Innocence Movement's early focus on client representation was a natural fit for clinical legal education programs. The chapter will explore having the Innocence Movement join forces with a new wave in clinical legal education, which recognizes the advantages of engaging students in policy advocacy and community education to achieve social change.[11] Some law school offerings are "integrated" or "combined" clinics, where students represent clients and participate in broader-scale projects.[12] Others, like the IPNW Legislative Advocacy Clinic, immerse students in an exclusive policy experience. The integrated/combined and project-based clinics expand a student's toolkit of transferable legal skills by engaging students in a wide range of nonlitigation strategies. Most importantly, as the IPNW experience demonstrates, the clinics are effective in achieving social change. This may be the time for the Innocence Movement to issue a new call to law schools: "to establish clinics to redress the causes of wrongful conviction."

1 *The Innocence Movement's Dual Mission: Client Advocacy and Reform*

The Innocence Movement has achieved success in its mission to free innocent prisoners. Still, the need for client representation has not abated even as the number of exonerations has risen and the number of innocence organizations has grown. Projects continue to receive thousands of requests for assistance each year.[13] The Innocence Movement's reform agenda, as discussed later, has proven difficult to implement. Policy reform is complex and multifaceted; it encompasses not only legislative advocacy,[14] but also strategic litigation,[15] administrative rule changes,[16] and community education.[17] Many successful reform efforts were driven by state coalitions[18] or commissions.[19] However, a review of the Innocence Movement's ambitious reform agenda reveals that very few states have undertaken comprehensive reform measures to ameliorate the problem of wrongful conviction.

1.1 Client Advocacy

Few miscarriages of justice compare to imprisoning innocent people for crimes they did not commit. As Barry Scheck and Peter Neufeld discuss in this book's Foreword, the advent of DNA technology sparked a revolution in a criminal justice system that had previously considered wrongful conviction to be a rarity.[20] As of December 2015, the Innocence Movement has exonerated 337 people, after post-conviction DNA testing established to a scientific certainty they were imprisoned for crimes they did not commit.[21] DNA exonerations have also led to an increased acceptance that wrongful convictions occur in cases where there is no biological material to test. The National Registry of Exonerations maintains an up-to-date list of all known exonerations since 1989.[22] The Registry has identified more than 1,700 cases of wrongful convictions overturned through DNA testing and other new exculpatory evidence.[23] The combined years of incarceration served by innocent prisoners freed since 1989 exceeds 15,000 years.[24] The damaging consequences of convicting the innocent reach much further than overall years of wrongful imprisonment. Litigating cases against innocent suspects places a tremendous drain on resources,[25] is devastating to innocent defendants and their families, harms public safety as the actual perpetrator remains free to commit additional crimes,[26] and leads to an erosion of trust in the criminal justice system.[27]

The Innocence Movement's early focus on client representation addressed a pressing need to provide legal services to individuals who had no other access to justice. Before innocence organizations were formed, innocent prisoners had very few resources to help navigate the complex post-conviction process. Because post-conviction proceedings are civil actions, there is no constitutional right to court-appointed counsel.[28] Most prisoners are poor and cannot afford to hire a lawyer.[29] The growth in innocence organizations has corresponded with, if not directly caused, a spike in exonerations. DNA exonerations steadily increased after 1989 and recently plateaued, while non-DNA exonerations increased sixfold.[30]

Each exoneration illustrates the need to remedy the causes of wrongful conviction to prevent future miscarriages of justice and to advocate for compensation for the wrongly convicted. The joy of freedom is tempered by the suffering experienced by persons convicted and imprisoned for crimes they did not commit. Once released, exonerees face an uphill battle to reenter a world that is much more complex than the one they left. Upon reentry, they endure even more significant hardships than properly convicted defendants. These burdens include loss of family ties, the inability to secure employment and housing, difficulties in obtaining health insurance, as well as counseling and other social services.[31] Thus, the Innocence Movement's mission of investigating and litigating cases of wrongful conviction is critical, not only for its impact on the individual, but also because exoneration narratives motivate reform.[32]

1.2 Reform

Actual Innocence's detailed list of reforms has developed and grown in the years since the book's publication. Although this chapter cannot provide a comprehensive summary of the social scientific research supporting key innocence reforms, the agenda can be divided into three broad categories: (1) improving prisoners' ability to establish innocence – through DNA testing, reforms to the post-conviction process, and the formation of commissions to investigate allegations of wrongful conviction; (2) obtaining fair and adequate compensation for the wrongly convicted; and (3) implementing "best practices" to address known sources of error, thereby decreasing future cases of wrongful conviction. As discussed later, much remains to be done to remedy the range of flaws in the criminal justice system: flaws identified through the work of innocence advocates, social scientists, and legal scholars.

1 **Improving Prisoners' Ability to Establish Innocence**. Only one reform, the right to post-conviction DNA testing, is found in every state.[33] This accomplishment is diminished by the fact that many state laws contain restrictions that prevent individuals from accessing scientific evidence to prove their innocence.[34] Some post-conviction DNA testing statutes expressly bar relief to people who confessed or pled guilty,[35] even though data shows 21 percent of the first 330 DNA exonerees confessed, pled guilty, or made incriminating statements.[36] A number of statutes do not allow individuals who are released from prison to request testing, despite the continued stigma and collateral consequences they face due to their criminal convictions.[37] Other statutes limit applications for testing to certain types of felonies,[38] impose a statute of limitations on requests,[39] and do not allow for an appeal of an order denying testing.[40]

Prisoners litigating post-conviction claims on the basis of exculpatory DNA results, or other new evidence, face onerous legal barriers. State courts impose heavy burdens of proof on defendants seeking to prove their innocence through newly discovered evidence.[41] Statutes of limitations may prevent defendants from advancing meritorious claims.[42] In federal court limits on litigating freestanding innocence claims and the procedural barriers to any habeas litigation – especially in the context of successive petitions – force prisoners through an almost impassable procedural gauntlet.[43] The judicial system's inability to adequately address innocence claims has led scholars to recommend formation of permanent criminal justice review commissions for that purpose.[44] The model innocence commission would be comprised of members from throughout the criminal justice system.[45] Its features would include subpoena powers, investigative resources, and political independence.[46] To date, only three states have formed permanent criminal justice reform commissions.[47] Another eight states formed ad-hoc commissions, which convened for a given period of time and disbanded after issuing a report with policy recommendations.[48]

2 **Fair and Adequate Compensation**. Statutes providing for some form of compensation are in place in thirty states, Washington D.C., and the federal system.[49] Laws governing compensation for the wrongfully convicted vary widely. Many provide insufficient monetary compensation or inadequate support for necessary housing, counseling, health, and educational services.[50] Others contain restrictions or disqualifications limiting an exoneree's ability to receive compensation.[51] Twenty states do not publically recognize society's moral obligation to provide assistance to exonerees in cases where wrongful convictions resulted from an honest error, rather than from intentional civil rights violations.

3 **Best Practices**. The factors contributing to wrongful conviction and how to prevent their effects have been studied for more than a century. The body of social scientific research was recently analyzed by Jon B. Gould and Richard A. Leo, who are law professors and social scientists.[52] They identify seven common sources of error: mistaken eyewitness identification, false confessions, tunnel vision, informant testimony, imperfect forensic science, prosecutorial misconduct, and inadequate defense representation.[53] Gould and Leo conclude that the factors producing wrongful convictions on the front end, and prolonging the incarceration of innocent prisoners on the back end, are detectible – and they can, in theory, be remedied.

However, when criminal justice scholar Robert J. Norris and his colleagues surveyed the fifty states to determine what safeguards were in place as of November 2010 to prevent wrongful convictions, the results were disheartening.[54] Although eyewitness identification plays a major role in convicting the innocent, only ten states had some form of eyewitness identification policy.[55] Errors in forensic science are substantial contributors to wrongful conviction, yet only thirteen states had created permanent forensic science oversight entities by statute, and in two additional states, the state attorney general established oversight entities.[56] Although a significant number of people exonerated through DNA testing confessed, only nineteen states had addressed the electronic recording of custodial interrogations.[57] False informant testimony is a leading factor of wrongful capital convictions; nonetheless, only eight states had reformed the use of criminal informants in some way that it would likely increase the accuracy of such evidence.[58] As Gould and Leo conclude: "[w]ith all of the information that has been amassed over the last century of inquiry, it is embarrassing to the point of shameful that criminal justicians, policy makers, and politicians do not follow the example of other professions and seek to learn from and prevent systemic error."[59]

The challenges and difficulties in actualizing policy reforms were analyzed by Professors Keith A. Findley and Larry Golden, who were early leaders in the Innocence Movement.[60] Findley and Golden identify three obstacles to success. First, the fragmented and diffuse nature of the criminal justice system necessarily requires a piecemeal approach to reform.[61] The rules, procedures, policies, and politics vary among counties and municipalities, and local police and prosecutors may resist reform efforts because they believe change will lead to a decreased ability to prosecute guilty suspects.[62] Second, the criminal justice system's preference for finality acts as a barrier to reform.[63] Third, the Innocence Movement's organizational challenges, which include resource disparity among projects, add to the difficulties in making headway on policy initiatives.[64] Findley and Golden describe the challenges in the policy arena as "formidable" and conclude that success will be tied to sufficient funding for individual projects, developing frameworks to accommodate the "varied, locally autonomous organizations" and identifying ways to "cut through the morass of state and local laws, regulations, practices, and interests that compose the nation's criminal justice system."[65]

Despite these challenges, Innocence Movement activists recognize that minimizing wrongful convictions requires combining litigation on behalf of the wrongly convicted with systemic reform.[66] To further this mission, the Innocence Project added a policy department when it transformed from a clinical law program to a national organization.[67] In this regard, the Innocence Movement experience parallels that of other public interest legal organizations. A study of approximately fifty public interest organizations found that "although litigation is still crucial, it is used more selectively in tandem with other approaches."[68] The following sections will explore how the Innocence Movement can partner with clinical legal education to achieve broad social change by complementing litigation with other advocacy tools.

2 The Innocence Movement's Partnership with Clinical Legal Education

The Innocence Movement's initial focus on client representation was par-tially driven by a need to overcome the common perception that wrongful convictions were an anomaly.[69] And the trend toward client representation continued when talented litigators, who were not trained in policy advocacy, were the first to found innocence organizations.[70] Clinical legal education was also founded on a litigation paradigm.[71] Professor Margaret Martin Barry traces this original focus to funding sources.[72] In the 1960s, the Council on Legal Education for Professional Responsibility offered seed funding to establish clinics at law schools to provide legal assistance to indigent persons.[73] The influential American Bar Association's MacCrate Report, published in 1992, "triggered a flurry of activity in the world of legal education" which was also litigation-centric.[74] The Report identified funda-mental lawyering skills and professional values law students ought to possess upon graduation in order to practice law.[75] They included problem solving, legal analysis and reasoning, legal research, factual investigation, communi-cation, counseling, negotiation, litigation and alternative dispute resolution procedures, organization and management of legal work, and resolution of ethical dilemmas.[76] In the same year, the American Association of Law Schools Committee on the Future of the In-House Clinic set forth nine goals of clinical education, which would be met in "In-House, Live-Client Clinics."[77]

Following the client-centric trend of clinical legal education, scholarship on innocence clinics has focused on teaching a client representation clinic. Jan Stiglitz, Justin Brooks, and Tara Shulman drew from their experiences in the California Innocence Project to create a blueprint for a law school innocence litigation clinic.[78] They discuss course content and issues regarding whether to accept non-DNA as well as DNA cases; whether to continually accept cases or have a fixed number of cases; credit hours; grading versus a credit/no-credit course; faculty-student ratio; supervision; student selection; and physical plant needs.[79] They explain that the course content for an innocence clinic will change from year to year because it will be driven by the needs of the clinic's projected casework.[80] They recom-mend the curriculum include classes combining substantive and skills topics needed to effectively work on cases; sessions on the law and procedures governing post-conviction practice; "firm meetings" where students present their cases to their classmates; and experiential learning opportunities pro-vided by videos, guest speakers, and field trips to prisons, crime labs, and courthouses.[81]

Professors Daniel S. Medwed and Keith A. Findley, who taught client-representation innocence clinics, engage in a thoughtful discussion of a question that has long interested clinical legal educators: the comparative advantages and disadvantages of students' participating in small individual representation clinics versus working on institutional larger scale projects.[82] Advocates of clinics with small, individual cases argue the clinics enhance student learning by facilitating ownership and client-centered representation through following a case from start to finish as the "first chair."[83] Innocence clinic cases do not fall into this category. They are complex, can span over many years, and the stakes for the client are tremendous. Medwed describes the challenges to clinical teaching methodology posed by innocence cases' size, complexity, and unpredictability.[84] He argues it is difficult, and perhaps impossible, to allow law students to take ownership of the cases and to gain the benefits of nondirective clinical supervision.[85] Medwed suggests innocence clinic students take a more limited role in a case's trajectory by screening or reviewing, rather than litigating, cases.[86]

Findley suggests Medwed's concerns can be addressed through a teaching methodology developed at the Wisconsin Innocence Project, where students are involved in the initial case screening process, as well as post-conviction litigation, when applicable.[87] The model requires integration of three teaching methodologies (1) immersion (requiring a substantial time commitment from students); (2) strategies for making big cases smaller, such as compartmentalization, connection, collaboration, and continuity; and (3) offering students a variety of cases and problems.[88] Findley provides concrete examples of the Wisconsin Innocence Project's successful implementation of these strategies.[89]

To be sure, students in client advocacy innocence clinics learn valuable skills, including fact development, interviewing, counseling, negotiation, legal research and writing, and oral advocacy. Because innocence cases are so complex, students must learn organization and time management skills. As Findley concludes, innocence clinics also provide an effective means for teaching "about the importance of being thorough and skeptical, about professional ethics and values, about fostering a capacity for critical reflection about doctrine and the criminal justice system, and, ultimately, about judgment."[90] Innocence clinics can bolster a student's awareness of and attachment to social justice. In Findley's words, "[o]ne of the tremendous virtues of innocence projects is that the dominant mission – to free the innocent – is one that engenders passionate commitment by clinical faculty, students and volunteers alike."[91] And Medwed agrees: "Merely participating in an innocence project and striving toward the exoneration of a wrongfully convicted prisoner has a certain intrinsic value: a chance for a student to associate herself with a socially desirable objective and, accordingly, derive some personal fulfillment from that association."[92]

Although innocence clinics have been grounded in litigation, there are other examples of successful social justice legal clinics, where students represent clients while also participating in community projects.[93] Barry, an early champion of such efforts, argues that clinical legal education fails clients and students if it confines itself to litigation-centric models.[94] She contends that clinics and poverty lawyers achieve broad social change only by "complementing litigation with other tools such as transactional services, community organizing and housing development."[95] By engaging in such work, law students learned to collaborate (rather than being ensconced in an adversarial position) and are obliged to educate themselves about the social and political environment of the community in which they operated.[96]

Against this backdrop, clinical legal education programs have expanded beyond the client representation model, by offering integrated/combined clinics, or project-based clinics. The integrated/combined model can take a variety of forms, but all offer students the opportunity to simultaneously immerse themselves in more than one legal advocacy strategy.[97] For example, a clinic may combine individual and organizational representation in litiga-tion with legislative advocacy and community education, or pair transactional work with policy advocacy and community education.[98] The project-based model engages students in a range of nonlitigation advocacy and transactional work, which can take place in any area of substantive law.[99] Professor Anna E. Carpenter discusses the Air Quality Project, at Georgetown Univer-sity Law Center, as one such endeavor.[100] In that clinic, students worked with public health experts to support a community that was concerned about their neighborhood's air quality.[101] The students helped the public health experts understand the legal and policy implications of their research findings and worked with the community members to assist them in advocating for improved air quality.[102]

Clinical law scholars have articulated the pedagogical benefits of teaching multidimensional advocacy skills in a clinical setting.[103] Students learn first-hand about a variety of strategies and legal tools which can be employed to create social change, including individual representation, organizational representation, community education, and policy advocacy.[104] Project-based clinical work, which can encompass legislative and policy reform, has the advantages of teaching many different lawyering skills, such as complex problem-solving, strategic planning, strategic communication, negotiation, collaboration, and project management skills.[105] As Carpenter notes, "through projects, students are challenged to find creative solutions to complex and ill-defined problems that have no clear litigation remedy, to understand how lawyers might have a role in solving such problems (including when lawyers need to collaborate with other professionals or lay experts), and to take into account the textured social and political aspects of complex problems."[106]

By engaging in more than one form of legal advocacy at a time, students can more fully experience, and reflect upon, law's impact on social change.[107] The benefits to students, as well as to the clients they serve, in having a clinical law program that addresses both client representation and policy advocacy have been borne out by the experience of Innocence Project Northwest.

3 *Innocence Project Northwest*

Founded in 1997, Innocence Project Northwest (IPNW) was the third national innocence organization.[108] Originally a volunteer organization, it transitioned to a clinical law offering at the University of Washington School of Law in 2002.[109] For more than a decade, IPNW focused on providing investigative services and legal representation to indigent people imprisoned for crimes they did not commit.[110] Recognizing the need for policy reform, IPNW added a Policy Staff Attorney in 2010, and launched the IPNW Legislative Advocacy Clinic in the fall of 2011.

3.1 Client Representation

Students in the IPNW Clinic investigate and litigate claims of actual innocence on behalf of prisoners under the supervision of law school faculty. The seminar component of the course covers legal issues commonly raised in post-conviction practice, such as ineffective assistance of counsel, prosecutorial misconduct, police misconduct, newly discovered evidence, witness misidentification, the use of unreliable jailhouse snitches and government informants, false confessions, and unreliable forensic evidence. The curriculum shifts each year depending upon the students' anticipated casework.

The IPNW Clinic follows the model described by Findley: students work on cases at every stage of the proceedings. In the practice component of the course, students will review prisoners' applications to the project to identify cases where there may be a viable claim of innocence and where there is evidence, such as post-conviction DNA testing, to support the claim. Students will conduct an investigative review in cases where there is strong evidence of innocence. This includes corresponding and meeting with clients in prison, gathering and reading police reports, trial transcripts, and appellate briefs.

In cases where there is potential for DNA testing, students will investigate whether physical evidence still exists and if so, under what conditions it was stored. They may also conduct a factual investigation, including locating and interviewing fact witnesses (often with an investigator), expert witnesses, and trial and appellate counsel. If the case proceeds to litigation, students conduct research, draft motions and briefs, and advocate in all appropriate forums for the release of clients. IPNW Clinic students have represented clients throughout Washington State and argued motions in the state trial and appellate courts,[111] the Washington Supreme Court,[112] and the United States Court of Appeals for the Ninth Circuit.[113]

This model seems to work. IPNW faculty, staff, volunteers, and students have obtained exonerations for fourteen individuals who collectively served more than 100 years in prison for crimes they did not commit. The factors contributing to their wrongful conviction are ones that have been identified nationwide as causing conviction of the innocent.[114]

3.2 Legislative Advocacy

The decision to create a separate clinic, rather than integrate policy advocacy into the client representation clinic, was driven by several pragmatic circumstances. First, IPNW's Policy Director, Lara Zarowsky, is a "legislative lawyer."[115] She came to law school intending to work as a policy advocate, participated in the IPNW Clinic during law school, and worked for the legislature after graduation. Second, the law school's successful Child and Youth Advocacy Clinic provided a framework and a partnership for legislative advocacy. And finally, the classroom components of the client representation and legislative advocacy clinics focus on different substantive and skills training, and the practice components of each clinic are time intensive.

The IPNW Legislative Advocacy Clinic teaches students a broad array of advocacy skills in order to actively participate in the state legislative process on issues involving the identification, rectification, and prevention of wrongful convictions. In the fall quarter, students participate in class sessions, trainings, and meetings designed to comprehensively understand the Washington State legislative process and develop skills necessary to participate in that process. The course includes guest lecturers from professionals involved in policy making, such as lobbyists, legislators, legislative staff, and state agency representatives. Students also begin to work with stakeholders interested in introducing bills, or preparing to respond to proposed legislation. During the winter quarter, when the legislature is in session, students work to bring about the introduction of bills, draft bill language, work with stakeholders and legislative staff, develop oral and written testimony, identify additional witnesses, shepherd their bills through the committee process, and work to get the bills adopted into law. They may testify on behalf of the bill and craft a media strategy. Students track and analyze bills relevant to their work and formulate a position and strategy for supporting, opposing, or amending legislation proposed by outside organizations.

In 2013, the Clinic worked closely with a broad coalition of supporters to pass a comprehensive wrongful conviction compensation statute.[116] The statute recognizes the tremendous injustice of wrongful conviction and seeks to address the unique challenges exonerees face upon release. The compensation statute, which passed with near unanimous consent, provides $50,000 per year of wrongful incarceration and $25,000 per year spent wrongfully on parole, in community custody, or as a registered sex offender.[117] It also includes payment of child support accrued during wrongful incarceration and provides the wrongly convicted with reentry services[118] as well as tuition waivers to state universities and colleges.[119] When signing the bill into law, Governor Jay Inslee acknowledged, "[w]hile the impact on the person and his or her family cannot be quantified, some measure of compensation will help those wrongly convicted get back on their feet."[120]

The IPNW Legislative Advocacy Clinic has earned wide respect in the Washington State Legislature, as evidenced by the overwhelming bipartisan support for its bills. Building on the relationships formed in prior years, the Clinic had another legislative victory in 2015 when the evidence preservation bill it championed passed into law. Prior to the law's passage, no state law prevented the destruction of crime scene DNA evidence. As a result, IPNW was forced to close many cases after discovering that critical DNA evidence, often the only evidence capable of exonerating an innocent person, had been destroyed without having been subjected to scientific analysis. The new law requires the preservation of biological material collected from a crime scene and prepared for scientific testing throughout the length of the sentence imposed for the crime.[121] In the case of unsolved or "cold" cases, such evidence must be preserved through the statute of limitations for the crime.[122]

Many synergies exist between the IPNW client representation and the legislative advocacy clinics. The two clinics hold joint class sessions on common topics of interest and students attend each other's court and legislative hearings. The legislative advocacy clinic also works closely with IPNW Clinic exonerees, empowering them to become a voice in the statewide and national Innocence Movement. IPNW Clinic clients Alan Northrop, Larry Davis, James Anderson and Ted Bradford's compelling testimony in support of the compensation bill was critical to its passage. Ted Bradford, who was exonerated through post-conviction DNA testing, has testified in the Oregon and Nebraska Legislatures in support of bills to expand the availability of DNA testing. And the culmination of both clinics' work occurred when a client exonerated through the IPNW Clinic's advocacy received compensation through the bill championed by the IPNW Legislative Advocacy Clinic.[123]

CONCLUSION

To be sure, innocence-related policy work can take place in a number of different forums, but there is space for it under the umbrella of clinical legal education. IPNW serves as a model for clinical law programs across the country to engage in both litigation and policy advocacy as a means of implementing systemic reform to improve prisoners' ability to establish innocence, provide for fair and adequate compensation, and implement best practices to minimize wrongful convictions. The two IPNW clinics work symbiotically. The Legislative Advocacy's undertakings are grounded in the compelling stories of the clients exonerated through the work of the IPNW Clinic; students in the IPNW Clinic who provide individual client representation receive a broader perspective from the policy work done by the IPNW Legislative Advocacy Clinic. Students have the opportunity to reflect on lawyering strategies within the context of the other clinic. Doing so not only enhances the Innocence Movement's goals, but it also furthers clinical legal education's goal of developing thoughtful, reflective practitioners.

NOTES

1 This chapter adopts the definition of "innocence movement" coined by Marvin Zalman in *An Integrated Justice Model of Wrongful Convictions*, 74 ALB. L. REV. 1465, 1468 (2010–2011). Zalman describes the "innocence movement" as a "related set of activities by lawyers, cognitive and social psychologists, other social scientists, legal scholars, government personnel, journalists, documentarians, freelance writers who, since the mid-1990s, have worked to free innocent prisoners and rectify perceived cause of miscarriages of justice in the United States."

2 *See id.* at 1487–98 (summarizing the convergence of events in the 1990s laying the foundation for today's Innocence Movement); Margaret Martin Barry, Jon C. Dubin & Peter A. Joy, *Clinical Legal Education for this Millennium: The Third Wave*, 7 CLINICAL L. REV. 1, 30–32 (2000) (reporting the steady increase of clinical law faculty and programs during the 1990s).

3 BARRY SCHECK, PETER NEUFELD & JIM DWYER, ACTUAL INNOCENCE: FIVE DAYS TO EXECUTION AND OTHER DISPATCHES FROM THE WRONGLY CONVICTED (2000).

4 Zalman, *supra* note 1, at, 1492.

5 SCHECK ET AL., *supra* note 4, at 255–60.

6 *See* Margaret Martin Barry et al., *supra* note 3, at 30 ("While precise figures are not available due to less systemic record keeping before 1995, the AALS Directories of Law Teachers for 1989–90 and 1999–2000 reflect an increase from approximately 800 Clinical Legal Education Section members in 1989–90 to 1300 a decade later.").

7 SCHECK ET AL., *supra* note 3, at 260.

8 *See* Stephanie Roberts Hartung, *Legal Education in the Age of Innocence: Integrating Wrongful Conviction Advocacy into the Legal Writing Curriculum*, 22 B.U. PUB. INT. L.J. 129, 139 (2013) (documenting the growth of innocence law school clinics from sixteen in 2002 to sixty-three in 2012). For a discussion of the expansion of innocence organizations over the last thirty years, see Jacqueline McMurtrie, *The Innocence Network: From Beginning to Branding*, in CONTROVERSIES IN INNOCENCE CASES IN AMERICA 22–29 (Sarah Lucy Cooper, ed., 2014).

9 Jayashri Srikantiah & Jennifer Lee Koh, *Teaching Individual Representation Alongside Institutional Advocacy; Pedagogical Implications of a Combined Advocacy Clinic*, 16 CLINICAL L. REV. 451, 452 (2010) (observing that "clinical legal education's bedrock goals [are] simultaneously effecting social justice and training law students in fundamental lawyering skills").

10 *See e.g.*, Marvin Zalman & Julia Carrano, eds., WRONGFUL CONVICTION AND CRIMINAL JUSTICE REFORM: MAKING JUSTICE (2014); Jon B. Gould & Richard A. Leo, *One Hundred Years Later: Wrongful Convictions after a Century of Research*, 100 J. CRIM. L. & CRIMINOLOGY 825 (2010).

11 *See e.g.*, Marcy L. Karin & Robin R. Runge, *Toward Integrated Law Clinics that Train Social Justice Advocates*, 17 CLINICAL L. REV. 563 (2011).

12 *Id.*; Srikantiah & Koh, *supra* note 9, at 456–57.

13 For example, the Innocence Project receives over 3,000 new requests per year, and is evaluating between 6,000 and 8,000 cases at any given moment. *See* Innocence Project, *Homepage*, available at www.innocenceproject.org.

14 *See, e.g.*, 725 ILL. COMP. STAT. ANN. 5/103–2.1 (requiring electronic recording of custodial interrogations for cases of homicide and eight other violent felonies).

15 Rebecca Brown & Stephen Saloom, *The Imperative of Eyewitness Identification Reform and the Role of Police Leadership*, 42 U. BALT. L. REV. 535, 551–52 (2013) (describing the role of the Innocence Project's strategic litigation unit in nationwide eyewitness identification reform).

16 MODEL R. PROF'L CONDUCT 3.8(g)-(h) requires a prosecutor to disclose "new, credible and material evidence creating a reasonable likelihood" that the defendant is innocent to both the court and the defendant. The prosecutor must seek to remedy the conviction if there is "clear and convincing evidence" establishing the defendant's innocence. *Id.* As of November, 2015, two states (Idaho and West Virginia) had adopted the model rule in its entirety; eleven states (Alaska, Arizona, Colorado, Delaware, Hawaii, New York, North Dakota, Tennessee, Washington,

Wisconsin and Wyoming) had adopted a modified version of the rule and six jurisdictions (California, Washington D.C., Nebraska, New Hampshire, Pennsylvania and Vermont) were studying the rule. *See* American Bar Association CPR Policy Implementation Committee, *Variations of the ABA Model Rules of Professional Conduct*, available at www.americanbar.org/content/dam/aba/administrative/professional_responsibility/mrpc_3_8_g_h.authcheckdam.pdf.

17 *See, e.g.*, Brandon L. Garrett, *Innocence, Harmless Error, and Federal Wrongful Conviction Law*, 2005 WIS. L. REV. 35, 111 (2005) (arguing "reform . . . will [not] be accomplished through change in legal doctrine, but rather, through a surprising explosion in public information about the causes of the most egregious errors in our criminal justice system").

18 *See* Mark A. Godsey, *False Justice and the "True" Prosecutor: A Memoir, Tribute and Commentary*, 9 OHIO ST. J. CRIM. L. 789 (2012) (describing Ohio's four-year effort to enact a comprehensive criminal justice reform package); Katherine R. Kruse, *Instituting Innocence Reform: Wisconsin's New Governance Experiment*, 2006 WIS. L. REV. 645 (2006) (discussing Wisconsin's multifaceted approach to achieving reforms in eyewitness identification and false confessions).

19 *See* Christine C. Mumma, *The North Carolina Innocence Inquiry Commission*, in WRONGFUL CONVICTION AND CRIMINAL JUSTICE REFORM, *supra* note 10, at 249–65 (describing the "establishment, operations and challenges" of North Carolina's commission to identify innocence after conviction); Sarah Lucy Cooper, *Innocence Commissions in America: Ten Years After*, in CONTROVERSIES IN INNOCENCE CASES IN AMERICA, *supra* note 8, at 195–217 (discussing commissions in California, Connecticut, Illinois, Oklahoma, New York, North Carolina, Pennsylvania, Texas, Wisconsin, and Virginia); Thomas P. Sullivan, *Repair or Repeal: Repair of Repeal—Report of the Illinois Governor's Commission on Capital Punishment*, 49 SEP. FED LAW. 40 (2002) (summarizing recommendations of the commission convened by the Illinois Governor to address concerns about the administration of Illinois's death penalty, which had led to condemning thirteen innocent prisoners to death).

20 Barry Scheck & Peter Neufeld, *Foreword, supra*, in this volume.

21 *See* Innocence Project, *Homepage*, available at www.innocenceproject.org, for a current list of DNA exonerations. The growth in DNA exonerations is in part due to advances in technology that allow forensic analysts to obtain profiles from minute traces of biological material previously untestable because the sample was too small or degraded. *See* U.S. Dep't of Justice, USING DNA TO SOLVE COLD CASES 1, 5–7 (2002) (current DNA technology can obtain profiles from minuscule samples of saliva, semen, sweat, skin cells, and cellular material found in the root of a hair).

22 National Registry of Exonerations, *Homepage*, available at www.law.umich.edu/special/exoneration/Pages/about.aspx.

23 *Id.*

24 National Registry of Exonerations, *Exonerations Map*, available at www.law.umich.edu/special/exoneration/Pages/Exonerations-in-the-United-States-Map.aspx.

25 Financial expenditures can also include, in addition to the cost of the criminal case, defending and settling lawsuits based on police misconduct. *See, e.g.,* Karen Hawkins, *Chicago Still Paying for Police Torture Claims*, AP ONLINE REG., Aug. 16, 2011 (reporting the city of Chicago has spent at least $63 million defending lawsuits against one former Chicago police commander); Juan Perez, Jr., *Dixmoor 5 Decision Spurs Call Attorneys: Inspect County for "Epidemic" of False Confession*, CHI. TRIB., June 26, 2014 (discussing $40 million and $36 million settlements in Chicago cases involving false confessions).

26 Peter Modaferri, Patricia Robinson & Phyllis McDonald., *When the Guilty Walk Free: The Role of Police in Preventing Wrongful Convictions*, THE POLICE CHIEF, vol. 77, no. 10, at 34, Oct. 2010, available at www.nxtbook.com/nxtbooks/naylor/CPIM1010/#/34 (reporting the Innocence Project's documentation of forty-seven rapes and nineteen murders committed by people who remained at large because an innocent person was wrongly convicted of the crime they committed).

27 Brandon L. Garrett, *Judging Innocence*, 108 COLUM. L. REV. 55, 57 (2008) ("Exoneration cases have altered the ways judges, lawyers, legislators, the public, and scholars perceive the criminal justice system's accuracy.").

28 *See* Pennsylvania v. Finley, 481 U.S. 551, 555 (1987) (the Court has "never held that prisoners have a constitutional right to counsel when mounting collateral attacks upon their convictions" because "the right to appointed counsel extends to the first appeal of right, and no further" (citing Johnson v. Avery, 393 U.S. 483, 488 [1969]). For a proposal advancing legislation to create a right to appointment of post-conviction counsel, see Sandra Guerra Thompson & Robert Wicoff, *Outbreaks of Injustice: Responding to Systemic Irregularities in the Criminal Justice System, infra,* in this volume.

29 Editorial Board, *Pay Up or Go to Jail*, N.Y. TIMES, May 21, 2014, at 28 (reporting that as many as 80 percent of people charged with criminal offenses qualify for indigent defense).

30 *See* National Registry of Exonerations, *Exonerations by Year: DNA and non-DNA*, available at www.law.umich.edu/special/exoneration/Pages/Exoneration-by-Year.aspx.

31 Adele Bernhard, *Justice Still Fails: A Review of Recent Efforts to Compensate Individuals Who Have Been Unjustly Convicted and Later Exonerated*, 52 DRAKE L. REV. 703, 707 (2004).

32 Robert J. Norris, *Exoneree Compensation: Current Policies and Outlook*, in WRONGFUL CONVICTION AND CRIMINAL JUSTICE REFORM, *supra* note 10, at 300 (observing that the "emotional, captivating narratives of human struggle . . . can inspire calls for reform.").

33 Innocence Project, *Today, All 50 States have DNA Access Laws*, available at www.innocenceproject.org/files/imported/dna_innocenceproject_website-4.pdf.

34 For a survey of post-conviction DNA testing statutes, see Justin Brooks & Alexander Simpson, *Blood Sugar Sex Magik: A Review of Postconviction DNA Testing Statutes and Legislative Recommendations*, 59 DRAKE L. REV. 799 (2011).

35 *Id.* at 860–62.

36 Brandon L. Garrett, *Convicting the Innocent Redux, supra,* in this volume.

37 Brooks & Simpson, *supra* note 34, at 862–63.

38 *Id.* at 807–10.

39 *Id.* at 840–45.

40 *Id.* at 858–60.

41 Daniel S. Medwed, *Up the River without a Procedure: Innocent Prisoners and Newly Discovered Non-DNA Evidence in State Courts,* 47 ARIZ. L. REV. 655, 675–86 (2005).

42 *Id.* at 690–95.

43 Stephanie Roberts Hartung, *Post-Conviction Procedure: The Next Frontier in Innocence Reform, infra,* in this volume.

44 SCHECK ET AL., *supra* note 3, at 260.

45 *Id.* at 361.

46 *Id.* at 103–04.

47 Robert J. Norris, Catherine L. Bonventre, Allison D. Redlich, & James R. Acker, *"Than That One Innocent Suffer": Evaluating State Safeguards against Wrongful Convictions,* 74 ALB. L. REV. 1303, 1356 n. 378 (2010–2011) (Connecticut, New York and North Carolina are the three states with permanent criminal justice review commissions).

48 *Id.* at 1349–57.

49 Innocence Project, *Compensation for the Wrongly Convicted,* available at www.innocenceproject.org/free-innocent/improve-the-law/compensation-for-the-wrongly-convicted.

50 Norris, *supra* note 32, at 291–94 (describing the jurisdictional differences between compensation statutes).

51 *Id.*

52 Gould & Leo, *supra* note 10.

53 *Id.* at 841.

54 Norris et al., *supra* note 47.

55 *Id.* at 1304–20 (Georgia, Maryland, New Jersey, North Carolina, Ohio, Rhode Island, Vermont, Virginia, West Virginia and Wisconsin).

56 *Id.* at 1320–29 (Arkansas, Indiana, Maryland, Massachusetts, Minnesota, Missouri, New Mexico, New York, Texas, Virginia, West Virginia and Washington have commissions, while Arizona and Montana have oversight entities).

57 *Id.* at 1329–41 (Alaska, District of Columbia, Illinois, Indiana, Iowa, Maine, Maryland, Massachusetts, Minnesota, Missouri, Montana, Nebraska, New Hampshire, New Jersey, New Mexico, North Carolina, Ohio, Oregon, Wisconsin).

58 *Id.* at 1341–49 (California, Connecticut, Illinois, Montana, Nebraska, Nevada, Ohio).

59 Gould & Leo, *supra* note 10, at 827.

60 Keith A. Findley & Larry Golden, *The Innocence Movement, the Innocence Network, and Policy Reform,* in WRONGFUL CONVICTION AND CRIMINAL JUSTICE REFORM, *supra* note 10, at 104–08.

61 *Id.* at 106.

62 *Id.*

63 *Id.* at 106–07.

64 *Id.*

65 *Id.* at 108.

66 *Id.* at 97.

67 *Id.* at 98–99.

68 Deborah L. Rhode, *Public Interest Law: The Movement at Midlife*, 60 STAN. L. REV. 2027, 2046–47 (2008) (documenting that over the past three decades, the percentage of resources public interest organizations spent on litigation decreased, while the budget for other types of advocacy [such as legislative efforts and community education] increased).

69 Findley & Golden, *supra* note 60, at 93–94.

70 *Id.* at 104–05.

71 Margaret Martin Barry, *A Question of Mission: Catholic Law School's Domestic Violence Clinic*, 38 HOW. L.J. 135, 148 (1994) (observing that "[t]he seeds of the litigation paradigm were planted at the founding of the clinical legal education movement").

72 *Id.*

73 *Id.*

74 *See* Robert MacCrate, *Yesterday, Today and Tomorrow: Building the Continuum of Legal Education and Professional Development*, 10 CLINICAL L. REV. 805, 818–21 (2004) (recounting law school, bar association, and judicial responses to the MacCrate Report).

75 *See Legal Education and Professional Development—An Educational Continuum: Report of the Task Force on Law Schools and the Profession: Narrowing the Gap*, 1992 A.B.A. SEC. LEGAL EDUC. & ADMISSIONS TO THE BAR. vii, 29–103.

76 *Id.*

77 *Report of the Committee on the Future of the In-House Clinic: Report on the Subcommittee on Pedagogical Goals of In-House, Live-Client Clinics*, 42 J. LEGAL EDUC. 511, 512–517 (1992).

78 Jan Stiglitz, Justin Brooks & Tara Shulman, *The Hurricane Meets the Paper Chase: Innocence Projects New Emerging Role in Clinical Legal Education*, 38 CAL. W. L. REV. 413 (2002).

79 *Id.* at 421–30.

80 *Id.* at 422.

81 *Id.*

82 Keith A. Findley, *The Pedagogy of Innocence: Reflections on the Role of Innocence Projects in Clinical Legal Education*, 13 CLINICAL L. REV. 231 (2006); Daniel S. Medwed, *Actual Innocents: Considerations in Selecting Cases for a New Innocence Project*, 81 NEB. L. REV. 1097 (2003).

83 *See, e.g.*, Juliet M. Brodie, *Little Cases on the Middle Ground: Teaching Social Justice Lawyering in Neighborhood-Based Community Lawyering Clinics*, 15 CLINICAL L. REV. 333, 370–84 (2009) (explaining the pedagogical benefits of small-case clinics for law students interested in both public interest and private practice).

84 Medwed, *supra* note 82, at 1127–29.

85 *Id.*

86 *Id.* at 1141–42.

87 Findley, *supra* note 82, at 236.

88 *Id.* at 138.

89 *Id.* at 236–78.

90 *Id.* at 278.

91 *Id.* at 234.

92 Medwed, *supra* note 82, at 1135.

93 *See* Barry, *supra* note 71, at 148 (describing then-existing clinics at Catholic University, Stanford University, Yale University, the State University of New York at Buffalo, and the University of Michigan, which had expanded beyond the client representation model).

94 *Id.* at 135–36.

95 *Id.* at 152.

96 *Id.* at 146–47.

97 Karin & Runge, *supra* note 11, at 568; Shrikantiah & Koh, *supra* note 9, at 453–54.

98 Karin & Runge, *supra* note 11, at 568.

99 Anna E. Carpenter, *The Project Model of Clinical Legal Education: Eight Principles to Maximize Student Learning and Social Justice Impact*, 20 CLINICAL L. REV. 39, 39–41 (2013).

100 *Id.* at 75–76.

101 *Id.* at 75.

102 *Id.* at 76.

103 *See, e.g., id.*; Karin & Runge, *supra* note 11; Srikantiah & Koh, *supra* note 9; Hina Shah, *Notes From the Field: The Role of the Lawyer in Grassroots Policy Advocacy*, 21 CLINICAL L. REV. 393 (2015).

104 Karin & Runge, *supra* note 11, at 570.

105 Carpenter, *supra* note 99, at 41–42.

106 *Id.* at 42.

107 Karin & Runge, *supra* note 11, at 604–05.

108 McMurtrie, *supra* note 8, at 22–23.

109 Jacqueline McMurtrie, *Unconscionable Contracting for Indigent Defense: Using Contract Theory to Invalidate Conflict of Interest Clauses in Fixed-Fee Contracts*, 39 U. MICH. J.L. REFORM 773, 775 n. 8 (2006).

110 *Id.*

111 State v. Slattum, 295 P.3d 788 (Wash. Ct. App. 2013).

112 In re Domingo, 119 P.3d 816 (Wash. 2005).

113 Barker v. Fleming, 423 F.3d 1085 (9th Cir. 2005).

114 *See* Innocence Project Northwest, *Our Client's Stories of Innocence*, available at www.law.washington.edu/Clinics/IPNW/Stories.aspx.

115 Professor Chai Rachel Feldblum, who created a Federal Legislation Clinic, conceived of the term "legislative lawyer" to describe individuals practicing law

within a policy advocacy context and who therefore need to understand how policy and politics influence law. *See* Chai Rachel Feldblum, *The Art of Legislative Lawyering and the Six Circles Theory of Advocacy*, 24 McGeorge L. Rev. 785, 786–87 (2003).

116 RCW 4.100.010.

117 RCW 4.100.060(5)(a)-(b).

118 RCW 4.100.060(5)(c)-(d).

119 RCW 28B.15.395.

120 Levi Pulkkinen, *Seattle Man Left Homeless after Crack Bust by Cop Later Fired for Dishonesty Wants State to Pay Up*, SeattlePI.com, Oct. 3, 2013, available at www.seattlepi.com/local/article/Seattle-man-left-homeless-after-crack-bust-by-cop-4864362.php.

121 RCW 5.70.010 (a).

122 RCW 5.70.010 (c).

123 University of Washington School of Law, *Washington Governor Signs IPNW-Sponsored DNA Bill into Law*, available at www.law.uw.edu/news/2015/ipnw/.

The DNA Era and Changing Views of the Death Penalty

8

How DNA Has Changed Contemporary Death Penalty Debates

MICHAEL L. RADELET

The dramatic increase in the recognition of problems related to erroneous convictions and death sentences over the past three decades has occurred at the same time when we are witnessing a drop in the number of new death sentences, a declining number of executions, and a significant drop in death penalty support. In this chapter, I discuss how the research on erroneous convictions in capital or potentially capital cases since the mid-1980s has fueled this debate. Further, since 1990, DNA has confirmed the earlier arguments that police and other prosecution witnesses occasionally lie, prosecutors suppress evidence, defense attorneys underachieve, witnesses make mistakes, and defendants falsely confess. Indeed, it might be argued that some of the first people to be exonerated by DNA are the researchers who were loudly criticized before the 1990s for making claims about the imperfections of America's criminal justice systems.

I begin by discussing some of the research that predated the use of DNA in uncovering and proving erroneous convictions, focusing primarily (although not solely) on the list of death row inmates released since the *Furman*[1] decision in 1972 because of innocence. This list is now maintained by the Death Penalty Information Center (DPIC).[2] I then turn to the declining support for the death penalty in the United States, and examine several reasons why support is dropping so rapidly. Finally, I look at the relationship between these two trends. In the end I conclude that support for the death penalty is dropping both directly from the impact of the innocence

An earlier version of this paper was presented at a Symposium on Wrongful Convictions, Northeastern University School of Law on September 25, 2015. I am grateful to Professor Daniel Medwed not only for his insightful comments on an earlier draft of this paper, but for his own scholarship and leadership in shedding light on the problems associated with errors in capital cases.

issue, but, more importantly, from what I call its "indirect effects." If the criminal justice system is regularly shown to be so imperfect that it can put totally innocent people on death row, then other arguments about its imperfections, such as racial bias and arbitrariness, become more palatable in the eyes of the public.

BACKGROUND

As Daniel Medwed discussed in the introductory chapter to this volume, the first two exonerations of wrongly convicted criminal defendants in the United States using DNA came in 1989. On January 4 of that year, Virginia Governor Gerald L. Baliles granted a full pardon to David Vasquez, who had falsely confessed to the 1984 murder of Carolyn Jean Hamm. Vasquez, who was developmentally disabled, had given the false confession to escape a threatened death sentence. After his conviction, the authorities identified four additional murders and several rapes that were remarkably similar to the Hamm murder. DNA tied another man, Timothy Spencer, to those crimes. While there was not enough DNA evidence to test in the Hamm case, the authorities were convinced that the circumstantial evidence vindicating Vasquez was strong. Thus, while a bit indirect, Vasquez became the first prisoner (arguably) exonerated by DNA.[3]

Gary Dotson's case was resolved at about the same time. In 1979 he was convicted of a 1977 rape. The victim admitted in 1985 that she had fabricated the rape story, a revelation that resulted in Dotson's release on parole but failed to alter the conviction. In August 1988, DNA tests conclusively eliminated Dotson as the source of the semen. Had this result been promptly acknowledged by the state, Dotson would have been the nation's first defendant to be exonerated by DNA. It was not until a year later, however, that prosecutors finally admitted error and joined the defense in a motion to vacate the conviction.[4] Dotson thus became the second DNA exoneration after David Vasquez.

As of early January 2016, there had been 335 DNA exonerations in the United States added to this tally, for a total of 337 cases.[5] These 337 wrongly convicted prisoners spent an average of fourteen years in prison before their release. DNA has had many consequences, but perhaps the most important is that it has taught everyone that beyond any doubt, every once in a while defendants who are totally innocent are nonetheless convicted of serious criminality.

In addition, there are hundreds and probably thousands of examples of erroneously convicted prisoners in American history who have been vindicated[6] by means other than DNA. The first (and seminal) study of erroneous convictions, *Convicting the Innocent*, was published eighty-five years ago by Yale Law Professor Edwin M. Borchard.[7] Several other twentieth-century scholars followed in his footsteps, including Erle Stanley Gardner,[8] Judge Jerome Frank and his daughter, Barbara,[9] and Tufts University Philosopher Hugo Adam Bedau.[10]

That pre-DNA research was always controversial. As recently as 1988, two Justice Department attorneys who were asked to critique research on errone-ous convictions concluded that the risk of erroneous convictions "is too small to be a significant factor in the debate over the death penalty."[11] Nonetheless, contrary to their assertion, over the past three decades the issue has had a monumental impact on death penalty debates throughout the world.

Furthermore, in those pre-DNA years there were very few places where innocent prisoners could turn for legal assistance in reinvestigating their cases and seeking avenues for vindication and release. Only two organizations existed in the first ninety years of the twentieth century that were devoted almost entirely to rectifying erroneous convictions. The first, the so-called Court of Last Resort, operated for roughly 15 years before 1959,[12] and the second, Centurion Ministries, has (to date) worked to free fifty-three inmates since the organization was founded in 1983.[13] The Court of Last Resort was a group of experts organized by Erle Stanley Gardner, who had gained fame as the author of Perry Mason court dramas. He published frequently in *Argosy Magazine*, and the magazine in turn helped to finance the work of the Court of Last Resort. Centurion Ministries was founded by a theological student named James McCloskey, who had become involved in efforts to free George De Los Santos, who had been wrongly convicted of homicide in New Jersey.[14] His work laid the groundwork for the Innocence Project in New York City, established in 1992 by Barry Scheck and Peter Neufeld, which focuses on possible erroneous convictions in cases in which DNA is available for testing.[15] Their work prompted others to form similar "Innocence Projects," which led ultimately to the 2005 creation of the "Innocence Network," with sixty-nine affiliates in most states and several foreign countries, which typically rely on volunteer law students to investigate cases of alleged wrongful convictions. Some groups work exclusively on DNA cases; others do not.[16]

THE CURRENT PICTURE: DEATH ROW EXONEREES SINCE 1973

Of special concern are cases of erroneous convictions in the so-called modern era of capital punishment that have resulted in death sentences.[17] As of September 1, 2015, the DPIC counted 156 prisoners who had been released from America's death rows since 1973 because of doubts about their guilt.[18] Twenty of these individuals were exonerated by DNA.

This list originated in 1987 in the work of Hugo Adam Bedau and Michael L. Radelet. They included in their catalogue of twentieth-century exonerations fourteen vignettes for cases that involved death row inmates who had been freed since 1972 because of doubts about their guilt.[19] In addition, in a footnote they identified nine additional cases that had surfaced shortly before their Article went to press that they felt might belong on that list, pending additional research. All fourteen cases that had been fully researched at the time, plus six of the nine cases mentioned in the footnote,[20] are on today's list of 156 exonerees identified by the DPIC.

In 1992, Bedau and Radelet, accompanied by Constance Putnam, expanded their list of cases in which defendants on death row had been vindicated since 1972 to thirty-six cases.[21] By that time their total collection of erroneous convictions since 1900 (including all homicides or cases in which people had been sentenced to death for rape) had reached 416 cases.

Building on that base in 1996, Bedau and Radelet, joined by William Lofquist,[22] in a 1996 article in *Cooley Law Review* enlarged that list to sixty-eight relevant cases (including one rape case that resulted in a death sentence),[23] fifty-five of which remain on the current DPIC list.[24] Today's DPIC list also includes eight cases that predate the piece in *Cooley Law Review* that were missed or rejected by Radelet, Lofquist, and Bedau in their 1996 article.[25]

The differences in the original lists compiled by Bedau and his colleagues and the DPIC list stem from efforts made in the mid-1990s by Radelet and Richard Dieter, then-Director of the DPIC, to tighten up the working definition of "innocence." By that time the list of exonerated death row inmates had attracted more attention than we had ever imagined, and our conceptual tightening was in part due to some excellent points made by our critics.[26] At about the same time, Bedau and Radelet turned the list over to the DPIC, thus insuring its status as the sole "official" list. At the same time, the criterion for inclusion on the list became inmates who:

> have been convicted, sentenced to death and subsequently either a. Been acquitted of all charges related to the crime that placed them on death row, or b. Had all charges related to the crime that placed them on death row dismissed by the prosecution, or c. Been granted a complete pardon based on evidence of innocence.[27]

I still prefer the term "possible innocence" or "probable innocence," because in only a few cases – primarily those with DNA evidence – can we say with absolute, total certainty that the defendant was uninvolved in the capital crime. Even in those cases, it remains possible, at least in theory, that there was a blunder in the DNA analysis, leading to incorrect results (although I am unaware of such a case). But it is true that some people who are on the list might fall off after new evidence is discovered. For example, Timothy Hennis was included in the catalogue of cases in the 1992 book, *In Spite of Innocence*,[28] and was on the original DPIC lists after he was acquitted at retrial and released from prison. Hennis had originally been sentenced to death in state court in North Carolina for the murders of two children and their mother, but he was acquitted at retrial in 1989. His inclusion on the list was therefore quite proper given the aforementioned criteria.[29] However, in 2010 he was retried in federal court for the same murders, reconvicted, and is now on death row under federal jurisdiction. Obviously he is no longer on the innocence list, and his case shows that the "Innocence List" is not infallible.

It is also worth noting that since the modern debate about sentencing innocent people to death emerged in the late 1980s, there has been a steady stream of new cases to add to the ever-expanding list. Just recently – in calendar years 2014 and 2015 – there were an additional thirteen cases added, and those thirteen defendants served an average of twenty-five years on death row before being vindicated. The horror stories keep being repeated, with each reinforcing the message of fallibility.[30]

And the problem of erroneous convictions is not confined to capital cases. The National Registry of Exonerations, a project now run by the University of Michigan Law School, was established to document wrongful convictions in criminal cases that have occurred since 1989. As of the end of 2015, they had documented over 1,700 exonerations, 45 percent of which involve erroneous homicide convictions. In 25 percent of the cases the defendant was exonerated by DNA evidence.[31] As originally reported by Bedau and Radelet,[32] they have found that perjury and false accusations are the most frequent cause of error, with a presence in 56 percent of the cases.[33]

When the "modern" era of innocence scholarship began in the 1980s, Bedau and Radelet pointed to twenty-three cases in which they believed that "most people" would today conclude that the executed inmate was "probably" innocent.[34] This claim has been hotly contested by those who support the death penalty, since in none of the cases had there been an "official" acknowledgement of innocence by state authorities.[35] Indeed, at the time no one could point to any case in the twentieth century in which any government acknowledged that a person who had been executed turned out to be innocent. The 1927 hangings of Sacco and Vanzetti come close; on the fiftieth anniversary of their executions in 1977, Massachusetts Governor Michael Dukakis apologized for the massive due process errors in the case, but did not concede their innocence.[36] At the time the twentieth century ended in 1999, the last people to be executed and later exonerated were hanged in the 1880s.[37]

Since 2000, however, six inmates who were executed in the twentieth century have been "officially" exonerated. In Maryland in 2001, Governor Paris Glendening issued a pardon to John Snowden, a black man who was hanged in 1919 for the rape and murder of the wife of a prominent white businessman. Two key trial witnesses had recanted their testimony and before the hanging, eleven of the twelve jurors had pled for mercy.[38]

In 2005, Georgia pardoned Lena Baker, who in 1945 became the only woman to have died in that state's electric chair. Baker, who was black, was convicted of killing a white man for whom she worked as a caretaker. Later authorities who reviewed the case concluded that he was extremely abusive and that he was killed in self-defense, and therefore Baker should have been convicted of involuntary homicide (at most).[39] But even so, it was clear that Baker still killed the man.[40]

In 2009, South Carolina pardoned two African-American brothers, Thomas and Meeks Griffin, who had been electrocuted in 1915 for murdering a white Confederate War veteran. They were convicted on the perjured testimony of the actual murderer, who falsely fingered the men to save himself from the executioner.[41]

On January 11, 2011, seventy-two years after his death, Joe Arridy was issued a "full and unconditional posthumous pardon" by Colorado Governor Bill Ritter.[42] Arridy, who was mentally challenged, was executed in 1939 after a Wyoming sheriff exerted improper influence in extracting a false confession.[43]

On December 17, 2014, a judge in South Carolina, citing "fundamental, constitutional violations of due process," vacated the conviction of George Stinney, who was executed (at age 14) in 1944.[44] Indeed, he was the youngest person to be put to death in the United States in the twentieth century.

None of these six inmates was exonerated because of DNA evidence, and DNA has yet to absolve a single inmate who has been executed in the history of the United States. This may be in part attributable to the fact that only a minority of criminal homicides leave DNA evidence that can be analyzed – and, even if such evidence exists originally, it is presumably long lost or discarded by the time of execution – and also that attorneys who may have thought one of their executed clients was innocent soon move on to other death penalty cases, using their resources to prevent future executions than resolve debates about the guilt of those who are already dead. In addition, inmates may make false claims about their innocence. Roger Keith Coleman, for example, was executed in Virginia in 1992 despite his loud protests of innocence. Fourteen years later, DNA testing conclusively proved his guilt.[45]

In addition to the aforementioned six exonerations, the DPIC lists ten cases in which inmates were executed after 1972 despite "strong" evidence of innocence.[46] Among the best examples on this list is the case of Cameron Todd Willingham, executed in Texas in 2004 for the arson deaths of three of his daughters. A jailhouse snitch who testified against Willingham later admitted that he had lied and that in exchange, he had received a reduced prison term. In March 2015, the prosecutor, John Jackson, was formally accused by the State Bar of Texas of withholding information in the case.[47]

These cases are very likely only the tip of the iceberg. As Professor Sam Gross and his colleagues observed after examining 340 exonerations from 1989 to 2003, "it is certain – this is the clearest implication of our study – that many defendants who are not on this list, no doubt thousands, have been falsely convicted of serious crimes but have not been exonerated."[48] This belief is fueled by the seemingly unending reports of prosecutorial errors in criminal prosecutions. Most recently,

> The Justice Department and FBI have formally acknowledged that nearly every examiner in an elite FBI forensic unit gave flawed testimony in almost all trials in which they offered evidence against criminal defendants over more than a two-decade period before 2000. Of 28 examiners with the FBI Laboratory's microscopic hair comparison unit, 26 overstated forensic matches in ways that favored prosecutors in more than 95 percent of the 268 trials reviewed so far ... *The cases include those of 32 defendants sentenced to death. Of those, 14 have been executed or died in prison.*[49]

And so the reality of erroneous convictions continues to attract regular headlines.[50]

DECLINING SUPPORT FOR THE DEATH PENALTY

At the same time that Americans have become more and more aware of the possibility of wrongful convictions over the past three decades, support for the death penalty has been dropping. Many have argued that this relationship is causal: that is, the awareness of the possibility (inevitability) of error has decreased death penalty support.[51] Below I will argue that the relationship between the two is more nuanced than that, but first we need to look at the declining levels of death penalty support.

Numerous scholars have analyzed the falling support for the death penalty, both internationally and in the United States, over the past quarter century.

Indeed, attitudes toward the death penalty seem to be undergoing a more rapid and significant change than attitudes about any other major social issue, with the exception of attitudes toward same-sex marriage and perhaps recreational marijuana. Very briefly:

- Internationally, Amnesty International reports that in 1977, only sixteen countries from around the world had abolished the death penalty.[52] By the end of 2013, there were 140 countries around the word that had abolished the death penalty in fact or by law.[53] Although most of what we know about erroneous executions comes from the United States, the decline of the death penalty is an international phenomenon and is occurring even in jurisdictions where the issue of error is not as visible as in the United States.
- An April 2015 survey by the Pew Center found that support for the death penalty had dropped to 56 percent, the lowest level in forty years. Pew found that 78 percent of the public supported the death penalty in 1996, and 62 percent supported it in 2011.[54] The same 2015 survey found that 71 percent of the public believed that there is some risk that an innocent person will be put to death, and 61 percent said that the death penalty does not deter people from committing serious crimes.
- Support for the death penalty drops further if respondents are asked if they prefer executions over Life Imprisonment without Parole (LWOP), which (in all thirty-one jurisdictions that use the death penalty) is the automatic sentence for those convicted of capital crimes but not sentenced to death.[55] In October 2014 a Gallup Poll found that 50 percent of Americans supported the death penalty and 45 percent supported LWOP.[56]
- The DPIC reports that in 2014, the number of executions in the United States was at its lowest level in twenty years, and the number of new death sentences was at its lowest level in forty years.[57] In the last ten years, seven states have abolished the death penalty.[58]

WHY IS THE DEATH PENALTY IN THE UNITED STATES IN DECLINE?

Measured in terms of public opinion or new death sentences, there is no question that public support for capital punishment in the United States has been declining over the past two decades. It may very well be that innocence in general and DNA in particular is one explanation for this decline, and below I will discuss how "the discovery of innocence" has had both direct and indirect effects. However, death penalty opinion is complex, and attributing the declining support to one factor, or to say that one factor trumps all others, misses the complexity of the issue. Innocence operates conjointly with several other factors. There are additional factors – not all independent – that are also undoubtedly increasing skepticism about the death penalty. For example, consider the following (in no particular order):

1 Declining homicide rate. Per 100,000 population, the homicide rate in the United States declined from 9.8 in 1991 to 5.7 in 1999. By 2013 it had gone down to 4.5. There were 24,700 homicides in the United States in 1991; in 2013 there were 14,196.[59]

2 The Supreme Court has outlawed the imposition of death sentences on certain categories of offenders, such as those with developmental disabilities[60] and those aged 17 or below at the time of the crime.[61]

3 Today all states that authorize the use of the death penalty also authorize LWOP for those convicted of a capital murder but not sentenced to death.[62] The final state to authorize LWOP was Texas, which did so in 2005.[63]

4 There has been growing recognition of the high fiscal costs of the death penalty, and more thought and discussion about whether these funds can be better used to address high rates of criminal violence and to render assistance to families of homicide victims.[64]

5 The deterrence argument, the leading pro-death penalty justification through the 1980s, has lost support among both scholars and the general public.[65] The 2015 Pew Survey found that 61 percent of the respondents believed that the death penalty did not deter people from committing serious crimes.[66]

6 With few exceptions, the religious community has been more vocal in expressing opposition to the death penalty. This change has at least in part been fueled by what has become the most popular death penalty book in American history, *Dead Man Walking*, a memoir by Sister Helen Prejean, a Catholic nun who works with death row inmates.[67]

7 Undoubtedly prompted in part by recent cases in which African Americans were unjustly killed by police officers, there is a growing concern about racial bias in death sentencing. Numerous studies have found that for similar homicides in the modern era, the odds of a death sentence for those who kill whites are three or four times higher than for those who kill blacks.[68] The 2015 Pew survey revealed that 52 percent of the respondents, and 77 percent of the black respondents, thought that minorities are more likely than whites to receive the death penalty for similar crimes.[69]

This list is not exhaustive, but it is sufficient to underscore the point that whatever role the concern about erroneous convictions has played in the decline in the use of and support for the death penalty in recent years, the "innocence card" is only one card in a much larger deck.

THE CONSERVATIVE CRITIQUE OF THE DEATH PENALTY

A significant source of the skepticism that these developments have fueled has come from more conservative sectors of American society. No doubt conservatives and liberals are equally appalled at erroneous convictions, although (as I see it) liberals tend to define the term more broadly. The movement to reach out to conservatives began in the early 1990s, when Virginia Sloan, then a counsel to the U.S. House Judiciary Committee, formed the Emergency Committee to Save Habeas Corpus, and continued when Sloan created The Constitution Project (TCP) in 1997.[70] TCP works with capital punishment supporters and opponents, conservatives and progressives alike, all of whom believe the system is profoundly broken. The seeds sewn by TCP have only recently begun to bear fruit.

Two prongs of the conservative critique of capital punishment were mentioned earlier. One component of conservative thought is to stand for fiscal austerity, leading to the question of whether the benefits of the death penalty, whatever they may be, are worth the high financial cost (not to mention the emotional costs of forcing the families of the victims to wait nearly twenty years for the anticipated execution). Second, many conservatives are concerned about low levels of religiosity in American society. The growing concern by leaders of major religious denominations about the death penalty feeds into this attitude. In the words of Father Robert Drinan (a Jesuit priest and former member of Congress), "[t]he amazing convergence of opinion on the death penalty among America's religious organizations is probably stronger, deeper, and broader than the consensus on any other topic in the religious community in America."[71]

But the most important component of the conservative critique of the death penalty, as least as I view it, has been to publicize the shortcomings of big government and to sound warnings about the work that government does (or can do) to alleviate social problems, such as health problems, poverty, or even fixing potholes in the pavement or making the post office function properly. Conservative journalist George Will reminds us that "[c]apital punishment, like the rest of the criminal justice system, is a government program, so skepticism is in order."[72] This attitude feeds on publicity about wrongful convictions, reminding us that the death penalty involves making godlike decisions without godlike skills. It is here, as I will elaborate below, where I believe the so-called discovery of innocence has had its strongest impact.

I have one final point about the impact of conservative voices on the contemporary death penalty debate. There is no question that until the past twenty years or so, the voices of the families of homicide victims have been absent from death penalty debates.[73] This has allowed prosecutors to fill this void and become self-appointed champions of victims' rights, lawyers for the individual victim rather than for the state, using the death penalty as a way to honor the deceased and assist the survivors. This has led legal scholar Franklin Zimring to argue that the death penalty has been symbolically transformed into a "victim-service program,"[74] with supporting executions a proxy for showing support for families of the murder victim. Support for harsh punishments transfers retribution from an end-in-itself to a utilitarian goal, necessary to help the surviving families, a goal that fits nicely with the "law-and-order" narratives that are heard more often from the conservative sectors of our communities.

HOW DO ERRONEOUS CONVICTIONS AFFECT DEATH PENALTY OPINION?

Just because more attention has been devoted to the problem of erroneous convictions over the last two decades, and during that time support for and use of the death penalty is dropping, does not mean there is a causal or even a direct relationship between the two factors. There are at least three ways that "The Innocence Card" can affect the death penalty.

1 *Direct Effects*

Undoubtedly there are many Americans who come to oppose the death penalty after hearing about or reading the accounts of erroneous convictions.[75] The death row exonerees formed a group in 2003 called "Witness to Innocence" that functions as a Speakers' Bureau to find audiences to whom the exonerees can tell their stories.[76] Today about thirty former death row inmates are available to speak. At virtually every presentation, audience members tell the exoneree that in some way they have been affected by hearing the stories. If they originally supported the death penalty, their views either temper or change. There is no question that these "direct effects" from hearing the stories of innocence also occur after reading the accounts of wrongful conviction and time on death row in newspapers and magazines, or learning about the cases through television. A powerful book that tells the stories, focusing on the challenges the exoneree faces after vindication and release, has also helped focus attention on the many struggles that exonerees encounter.[77]

It is these impacts of wrongful convictions that I refer to as "Direct Effects." Simply hearing about cases of vindicated death row inmates causes support for the penalty to fall.

2 An Alteration of the Cost–Benefit Equation

One of the nation's top scholarly supporters of the death penalty in the latter part of the twentieth century was Fordham Law Professor Ernest van den Haag.[78] In 1985, when the first draft of Bedau and Radelet's paper (later published in *Stanford Law Review*) was released, van den Haag commented on the twenty-five erroneous executions that (at that time)[79] we included in the paper. He called the twenty-five erroneous executions:

> If true, a very acceptable number. All human activities – building houses, driving a car, playing golf or football – cause innocent people to suffer wrongful death, but we don't give them up because on the whole we feel there's a net gain. Here a net gain in justice is being done.[80]

Van den Haag is using a cost–benefit analysis, much like a balancing scale. He does not deny the drawbacks of erroneous executions, but claims that that this downside is outweighed by the death penalty's benefits in achieving "justice."

Three years later, Stephen Markman and Paul Cassell adopted this same methodological strategy in their important critique of the Bedau/Radelet study.[81] They contended that Bedau and Radelet overstated the slight risk of executing the innocent, and, as the title of their article states, that the *Stanford Law Review* article undervalued the primary benefit of the death penalty –"protecting the innocent" (i.e., its alleged ability to reduce future homicide rates through its deterrent and incapacitative effects).[82] More recently, Ronald Allen and Amy Shavell employed a similar cost–benefit analysis, emphasizing what they see as the deterrent and retributive benefits of executions, leaving them "agnostic" about the death penalty.[83]

While there is no need herein to revisit many thought-provoking points raised by the aforementioned skeptics, on the deterrence point there is substantial new evidence that undermines their claim that the deterrent benefits of the death penalty outweigh its shortcomings. In 2012 a report by the National Research Council of the National Academy of Sciences confirmed that assertion. Their Study Panel was composed of some of the very top criminologists and legal scholars in the United States. The committee found that the research "is not informative about whether capital punishment increases, decreases, or has no effect on homicide rates."[84] This point does not negate the cost–benefit methodology, but it does invite a reexamination of the alleged benefits of executions, particularly in light of (what I would contend) the emerging evidence that the problem of erroneous convictions is bigger than most would have thought. In short, the growing evidence on innocence, coupled with data on other consequences and limitations of the death penalty, invite reanalysis of the cost–benefit ratio.

3 *Indirect Effects: How Innocence Invites Reassessment of Other Death Penalty Drawbacks*

Virtually all the reforms introduced into American death penalty schemes over the past four decades have been directed at the goal of making sure only the "worst of the worst" are sentenced to death. After *Furman*,[85] most states went back and specified aggravating and mitigating circumstances or other narrowing criteria that today result in death sentences for only a small fraction of those convicted of criminal homicides. To the degree that the death penalty fails to get the worst of the worst, letting some of the big fish get away or getting high numbers of tiny guppies along with the big fish, public confidence in capital punishment is undermined.

Arguably the strongest impact of the attention to miscarriages of justice in capital cases is that it opens a window for people to reexamine other flaws in the criminal justice system – flaws that question whether the death penalty is reserved for the worst of the worst. In other words, it opens the eyes of those who might support the death penalty in *theory*, but who might be uncomfortable with the way in which it is *actually applied*.

One prong of this concern deals with arbitrariness, when it becomes difficult or impossible to distinguish between those who are sentenced to death and those who are not. This concern was echoed by Justice Potter Stewart, who argued that the inability to distinguish who is sentenced to death from other murderers made the punishment tantamount to being struck by lightning.[86] This concern thus has a long history, but once people see that the American criminal justice system can still put innocent people on death row, the idea that people are also sent there because of bad luck or by seemingly random selection seems to make more sense.

Or, the recognition that innocent people can be convicted also makes the allegations that death sentencing is influenced by the race of the victim more plausible. If the criminal justice system can put people on death row who are totally innocent, then the idea that death sentences can be influenced by the defendant's and/or victim's racial characteristics becomes more believable.

The issues of geographic disparities in death sentencing, ineffective assistance of defense attorneys, death row inmates with severe intellectual disabilities or mental illness, and vindictive prosecutors also feed into the much broader idea that death sentences are not reserved for the worst of the worst.[87] After all, if prosecutors can put totally innocent defendants on death row, the idea that they can be especially aggressive in cases with poor and marginalized defendants becomes easier to see.

CONCLUSION

With thirteen additions to the DPIC list of prisoners released from death rows because of probable innocence in calendar years 2014 and 2015, the issue of miscarriages of justice in capital cases has grown much larger than many would have predicted a quarter of a century ago, and it is still growing. As I see it, more and more Americans today would disagree with the assertion made in 1988 by Markman and Cassell that "the risk is too small to be a significant factor in the debate over the death penalty."[88] Indeed, the 2015 Pew survey found that 71 percent of the respondents said that there was some risk that an innocent defendant would be put to death.[89] The recognition of these major blunders in death penalty cases has changed public opinion in three ways: 1) by directly changing death penalty opinion, 2) by forcing people to reconsider whether the benefits of the death penalty outweigh its costs and liabilities, and/ or 3) opening eyes to other imperfections in modern death sentencing that render those sentenced to death not necessarily the worst of the worst.

In the end, only one thing is certain: how death penalty attitudes and statutes will change over the next decade, and what will be behind those changes, is impossible to predict.

NOTES

1 Furman v. Georgia, 408 U.S. 238 (1972). In effect, the Furman decision invalidated all existing death penalty statutes in the United States.
2 Death Penalty Information Center, *Innocence: List of Those Freed from Death Row*, available at www.deathpenaltyinfo.org/innocence-list-those-freed-death-row.
3 ROB WARDEN & STEPHEN A. DRIZIN, TRUE STORIES OF FALSE CONFESSIONS 269–77 (2009).
4 For case summary, see Center on Wrongful Convictions, *First DNA Exoneration: Gary Dotson*, available at www.law.northwestern.edu/legalclinic/wrongfulconvictions/exonerations/il/gary-dotson.html.
5 For updates, see Innocence Project, *Homepage*, available at www.innocenceproject.org.
6 By "vindicated" I intend a probability statement, and apply the term to defendants whose innocence has been established by an "overwhelming" probability.
7 EDWIN BORCHARD, CONVICTING THE INNOCENT: SIXTY-FIVE ACTUAL ERRORS OF CRIMINAL JUSTICE (1932).

8 ERLE STANLEY GARDNER, THE COURT OF LAST RESORT (1952).

9 JEROME FRANK & BARBARA FRANK, NOT GUILTY (1957).

10 Bedau's initial work in this area was done in 1962 when he assisted Sara Ehrmann with her seminal paper on erroneous convictions. Sara R. Ehrmann, *For Whom the Chair Waits*, 26 FED. PROB. 14 (1962). *See also* Hugo Adam Bedau, *Murder, Errors of Justice, and Capital Punishment*, in THE DEATH PENALTY IN AMERICA: AN ANTHOLOGY 434 (H. A. Bedau, ed., 1964); Hugo Adam Bedau & Michael L. Radelet, *Miscarriages of Justice in Potentially Capital Cases*, 40 STAN. L. REV. 21 (1987).

11 Stephen J. Markman & Paul G. Cassell, *Protecting the Innocent: A Response to the Bedau-Radelet Study*, 41 STAN. L. REV. 121 (1988).

12 DOROTHY B. HUGHES & ERLE STANLEY GARDNER, THE CASE OF THE REAL PERRY MASON (1978).

13 *See* Centurion Ministries, *Homepage*, available at www.centurionministries.org.

14 *See* Centurion Ministries, *Centurion Ministries, Inc. – How and Why It Was Created*, available at www.centurionministries.org/about/history/1980s.php.

15 *See* Innocence Project, *Homepage*, available at www.innocenceproject.org. According to its website, "The Innocence Project was founded at Benjamin N. Cardozo School of Law at Yeshiva University in 1992, and became an independent nonprofit organization (still closely affiliated with Cardozo) in 2004." *See* Innocence Project, *What Is the Innocence Project? How Did It Get Started?*, available at www.innocenceproject.org/faqs/what-is-the-innocence-project-how-did-it-get-started; BARRY SCHECK, PETER NEUFELD & JIM DWYER, ACTUAL INNOCENCE: FIVE DAYS TO EXECUTION, AND OTHER DISPATCHES FROM THE WRONGLY CONVICTED (2000).

16 *See* Innocence Network, *Homepage*, available at www.innocencenetwork.org.

17 By "modern era," I mean exonerations that occurred after the decision in Furman v. Georgia in June 1972 that (in effect) invalidated all death penalty statutes in the United States. *See* Furman v. Georgia, 408 U.S. 238 (1972).

18 *See* Death Penalty Information Center, *Innocence and the Death Penalty*, available at www.deathpenaltyinfo.org/innocence-and-death-penalty.

19 Bedau & Radelet, *supra* note 10, at 29–31 n. 40 (1987). The authors also included the case of James Adams, executed in Florida despite doubts about guilt. His case is not included on the current DPIC list of death row inmates who were exonerated.

20 Anthony Peek, Perry Cobb, Vernon McManus, Joseph Green Brown, and Juan Ramos.

21 MICHAEL L. RADELET, HUGO ADAM BEDAU & CONSTANCE PUTNAM, IN SPITE OF INNOCENCE (1992).

22 Michael L. Radelet, William S. Lofquist & Hugo Adam Bedau, *Prisoners Released from Death Rows Since 1970 because of Doubts about Their Guilt*, 13 T. M. COOLEY L. REV. 907 (1996).

23 *See id.* at 957 (discussing case of Johnny Ross).

24 The thirteen exceptions are Jerry Bigelow, Mitchell Blazak, Jesse Brown, Patrick Croy, Henry Drake, Timothy Hennis, Sonia Jacobs, William Jent and Ernest Miller,

John Knapp, Andrew Mitchell, Anthony Scire, and Larry Smith. In six cases (Blazak, Jacobs, Jent and Miller, Knapp, and Scire) the defendant pleaded guilty to a homicide, despite strong evidence of innocence, in exchange for immediate release from prison. Henry Drake was released on parole after doubts about his guilt surfaced. In the Croy case, the evidence suggested the homicide was committed in self-defense. Jesse Brown was convicted of several other crimes in connection with the homicide, and in 2000, Andrew Mitchell was convicted of conspiracy in connection with the original homicide. Timothy Hennis fell off both lists after his subsequent conviction (in federal court) for the murder that had originally sent him to death row. Larry Dean Smith, while maintaining his innocence for homicide, admitted that he had been at the scene and participated in a robbery of the victim prior to the murder, and Jerry Bigelow was found guilty of non-homicide charges in connection with the murder that originally sent him to death row.

25 The eight cases are Christopher Spicer, Ernest Graham, Larry Fisher, Clifford Bowen, Vernon McManus, Richard Jones, Jimmy Mathers, and Charles Smith. *See* Radelet et al., *supra* note 22, at 912 (discussing McManus).

26 By far the most useful criticisms were made by Stephen Markman and Paul Cassell. *See* Markman & Cassell, *supra* note 11.

27 *See* Death Penalty Information Center, *Innocence: List of Those Freed from Death Row*, available at www.deathpenaltyinfo.org/innocence-list-those-freed-death-row?scid=6&did=110.

28 RADELET ET AL., *supra* note 21, at 313.

29 *See* Death Penalty Information Center, *Former Death Row Inmate Acquitted in One Court, Now Convicted in Another*, available at www.deathpenaltyinfo.org/former-death-row-inmate-acquitted-one-court-now-convicted-another.

30 It is also amazing to see how much luck is involved in the discovery of many of these errors. For example, Richard Glossip's execution in Oklahoma was delayed by questions surrounding the use of certain drugs for the lethal injection. Ultimately, on a 5–4 vote, his arguments did not prevail, although Justices Sotomayor and Breyer used the case to suggest that it might be time for the Court to reevaluate the overall constitutionality of the death penalty. Glossip v. Gross, 135 S. Ct. 2726 (2015). In the months thereafter, led by celebrities including Richard Branson, Susan Sarandon, Sister Helen Prejean, and television personality Dr. Phil, there were heated arguments about whether Glossip was actually guilty of the offense. *See, e.g.*, Associated Press, *Oklahoma Death Row Inmate Defended by Susan Sarandon Says He Is Innocent*, GUARDIAN, Aug. 16, 2015. As of year-end 2015, Glossip is still alive.

31 *See* National Registry of Exonerations, *The Registry, Exonerations and False Convictions*, available at www.law.umich.edu/special/exoneration/Pages/learnmore.aspx.

32 Bedau & Radelet, *supra* note 10, at 57 Table 6, 61 n. 184.

33 *Id.*

34 *Id.* at 72–75. Indeed, Bedau and Radelet proved to be correct in their assertion that "The evidence for judgment of error in these cases will naturally interest many, but what we can report will satisfy only a few." *Id.* at 74.

35 *See* Markman & Cassell, *supra* note 11, at 121. A response to these criticisms is also available: Hugo Adam Bedau & Michael L. Radelet, *The Myth of Infallibility: A Reply to Markman and Cassell*, 41 STAN. L. REV. 161 (1988).

36 Bedau & Radelet, *supra* note 10, at 74 n. 274.

37 In Illinois in 1893, Governor Peter Altgeld pardoned three of the Haymarket defendants, six years after four of their codefendants had been hanged. An eighth defendant had taken his own life on the eve of his scheduled execution. Altgeld issued the pardons because all eight "had been wrongfully convicted and were innocent of the crime." PAUL AVRICH, THE HAYMARKET TRAGEDY 423 (1984). And in recent years there have been other pardons issued for prisoners executed in the nineteenth century. For example, in 1987, Nebraska Governor Bob Kerry issued a pardon to William Jackson Marion, who had been hanged exactly 100 years earlier in Beatrice for the murder of a man who later turned up alive. ROB WARDEN, WILKIE COLLINS'S THE DEAD ALIVE: THE NOVEL, THE CASE, AND WRONGFUL CONVICTIONS 157–58 (2005).

38 Jay Apperson & Andrea F. Siegel, *Glendening Pardons Black in 1919 Murder: Governor Attempts 'To Correct Inequity'*, BALT. SUN, June 1, 2001.

39 *Briefly: State Officials to Pardon Executed Black Woman*, N.Y. TIMES, Aug. 17, 2005.

40 LELA BOND PHILLIPS, THE LENA BAKER STORY (2001).

41 Christina Sterbenz, *These Are the Only 7 People In the US Pardoned AFTER They Were Executed*, BUSINESS INSIDER, May 19, 2014, available at www.businessinsider.com/people-pardoned-after-their-executions-2014–5; Alex Spillius, *Black Pair's Justice – After 94 Years*, DAILY TELEGRAPH (London), Oct. 19, 2009, at 22.

42 Death Penalty Information Center, *Gov. Ritter Grants Posthumous Pardon in Case Dating Back to 1930s*, available at www.deathpenaltyinfo.org/documents/ArridyPardon.pdf.

43 For details, see ROBERT PERSKE, DEADLY INNOCENCE? (1995). For a later (and shorter) overview of the case, see Alan Prendergast, *Joe Arridy Was the Happiest Man on Death Row*, WESTWORD (Denver), Sept. 20, 2012.

44 DAVID STOUT, CAROLINA SKELETONS (2011); Campbell Robertson, *South Carolina Judge Vacates Conviction of George Stinney in 1944 Execution*, N.Y. TIMES, Dec. 17, 2014; David Zucchino, *'I Never Saw My Brother Alive Again': The Exoneration of George Stinney Jr., Executed in 1944 at Age 14, Eases His Family*, L.A. TIMES, Dec. 19, 2014, at A10. While the judge found that Stinney had not been given a fair trial, to date no formal pardon has been issued.

45 Maria Glod & Michael D. Shear, *DNA Tests Confirm Guilt of Executed Man*, WASH. POST, Jan. 13, 2006.

46 *See* Death Penalty Information Center, *Executed but Possibly Innocent*, available at www.deathpenaltyinfo.org/executed-possibly-innocent.

47 Maurice Possley, *Fresh Doubts over a Texas Execution*, WASH. POST, Aug. 3, 2014; Allan Turner, *State Bar Accuses Prosecutor in Willingham Triple-Murder Case of Improper Conduct*, HOUS. CHRON., Mar. 18, 2015.

48 Samuel R. Gross, Kristen Jacoby, Daniel J. Matheson., Nicholas Montgomery & Sujata Patil, *Exonerations in the United States 1989 through 2003*, 95 J. CRIM. L. & CRIMINOLOGY 523, 527 (2005).

49 Spencer S. Hsu, *FBI Admits Flaws in Hair Analysis over Decades*, WASH. POST, Apr. 18, 2015, at 1 (emphasis added).

50 This issue also attracted renewed attention by the 2014 publication of one of the very best death penalty books published this century: BRYAN STEVENSON, JUST MERCY (2014). The book gives vivid details of the erroneous conviction of Walter McMillian in Alabama in 1988 and his eventual exoneration in 1993.

51 *See, e.g.*, FRANK R. BAUMGARTNER, SUZANNA DE BOEF & AMBER BOYDSTUN, THE DECLINE OF THE DEATH PENALTY AND THE DISCOVERY OF INNOCENCE 9 (2008). While this is an important book, I believe the authors overstate the importance of the issue of innocence in explaining recent declines in the use of and support for the death penalty.

52 *See* Amnesty International, *Death Penalty Trends*, available at www.amnestyusa.org/our-work/issues/death-penalty/us-death-penalty-facts/death-penalty-trends.

53 *See* Amnesty International, *Death Sentences and Executions — 2014*, Mar. 31, 2014, at 64–65, available at www.amnesty.org/en/documents/act50/001/2014/en/. By far the most authoritative book on the international status of the death penalty is ROGER HOOD & CAROLYN HOYLE, THE DEATH PENALTY: A WORLDWIDE PERSPECTIVE (5th ed. 2015).

54 Pew Research Center, *Less Support for the Death Penalty, Particularly among Democrats: Supporters, Opponents See Risk of Executing the Innocent*, Apr. 16, 2015, available at www.people-press.org/2015/04/16/less-support-for-death-penalty-especially-among-democrats.

55 In January 2016, there were thirty-one states that permitted the imposition of new death sentences. The nineteen states without the death penalty include New Mexico, where the 2009 abolition was not retroactive and two people remain on death row, and Nebraska, where the death penalty was abolished by the legislature in 2015, an action that will be reviewed by voters in a 2016 referendum. Death Penalty Information Center, *States with and without the Death Penalty*, available at www.deathpenaltyinfo.org/states-and-without-death-penalty.

56 Jeffrey M. Jones, *Americans' Support for the Death Penalty Stable*, Oct. 23, 2014, available at www.gallup.com/poll/178790/americans-support-death-penalty-stable.aspx.

57 Death Penalty Information Center, *The Death Penalty in 2014: Year-End Report*, available at www.deathpenaltyinfo.org/documents/2014YrEnd.pdf. There were only seventy-two new death sentences in the United States in 2014, compared to 315 in both 1994 and 1996. *See id.*

58 New York (2007), New Jersey (2007), New Mexico (2009), Illinois (2011), Connecticut (2012), Maryland (2013), and Nebraska (2015). *See* Death Penalty Information Center, *States with and without the Death Penalty*, available at www.deathpenaltyinfo.org/states-and-without-death-penalty. The abolition of the death penalty in Nebraska is arguably the most astonishing in this group, given the state's strong

conservative leanings. The original abolition bill was vetoed by the governor, but the legislature, in turn, overrode the veto. However, it now appears that enough signatures have been gathered (in part because of $300,000 in funding from the governor and his family) to put the issue on the 2016 Nebraska ballot. Grant Schulte, *Nebraska Ballot Measure Raises Stakes for Death Penalty Foes*, LINCOLN JOURNAL STAR, Sept. 7, 2015.

59 *See* DisasterCenter.com, *United States Crime Rates, 1960–2013*, available at www .disastercenter.com/crime/uscrime.htm.

60 Atkins v. Virginia, 536 U.S. 304 (2002).

61 Roper v. Simmons, 543 U.S. 551 (2005).

62 A generation ago, few states offered LWOP as an option to death sentences. Julian H. Wright, Jr., *Life-without-Parole: An Alternative to Death of Not Much of a Life At All?*, 43 VAND. L. REV. 529 (1990).

63 *See* Death Penalty Information Center, *Texas Governor Signs Life without Parole Bill Into Law*, available at www.deathpenaltyinfo.org/node/158.

64 For a review of studies on the cost of the death penalty, see Death Penalty Information Center, *Costs of the Death Penalty*, available at www.deathpenaltyinfo.org/ costs-death-penalty. For a discussion of the needs of families of homicide victims and how that relates to the death penalty, see WOUNDS THAT DO NOT BIND: VICTIM-BASED PERSPECTIVES ON THE DEATH PENALTY (J. Acker & D. Karp, eds., 2006).

65 The most recent word from the academic community came in 2012, when a seminal comprehensive report on the deterrent effect of the death penalty was released by the National Research Council, National Academy of Sciences, in 2012. The Study Panel was composed of the top criminologists in the United States. The committee found that the research "is not informative about whether capital punishment increases, decreases, or has no effect on homicide rates." DANIEL S. NAGIN & JOHN V. PEPPER, DETERRENCE AND THE DEATH PENALTY (2012). For a comparison of the views of the general public and the academic community, see Michael L. Radelet & Traci Lacock, *Do Executions Lower Homicide Rates?: The Views of Leading Criminologists*, 99 J. CRIM. L. & CRIMINOLOGY 489, 489–508 (2009).

66 *See* Pew Research Center, *supra* note 54.

67 HELEN PREJEAN, DEAD MAN WALKING (1993).

68 For reviews of this research, see U.S. General Accounting Agency, *Death Penalty Sentencing: Research Indicates Pattern of Racial Disparities* (GGD-90-57) 5 (1990); David C. Baldus & George Woodworth, *Race Discrimination in the Administration of the Death Penalty: An Overview of the Empirical Research with Special Emphasis on the Post-1990 Research*, 39 CRIM. L. BULL. 194 (2003); Catherine M. Grosso, Barbara O'Brien, Abijah Taylor & George Woodworth, *Race Discrimination and the Death Penalty: An Empirical and Legal Overview*, in AMERICA'S EXPERIMENT WITH CAPITAL PUNISHMENT 3d ed. 525 (James R. Acker, Robert M. Bohm & Charles S. Lanier, eds., 2014).

69 Pew Research Center, *supra* note 54.

70 *See* Constitution Project, *Homepage*, available at www.constitutionproject.org. For an earlier discussion of the importance of the conservative critique of the death penalty, see Michael L. Radelet, *The Executioner's Waning Defenses*, in The Road to Abolition? The Future of Capital Punishment in the United States 19, 25–30 (C. Ogletree, Jr. & A. Sarat, eds., 2009).

71 Robert Drinan, The Fractured Dream: America's Divisive Moral Choices 107 (1991).

72 George F. Will, *Innocent on Death Row*, Wash. Post, Apr. 23, 2000, at A23.

73 By far the best collection of essays that examine the death penalty from the eyes of families of homicide victims is Wounds That Do Not Bind: Victim-Based Perspectives on the Death Penalty, *supra* note 64.

74 Franklin E. Zimring, The Contradictions of American Capital Punishment 62–63 (2003).

75 Similarly, there are many who would usually oppose the death penalty, but move to the supporters' ranks when hearing news of a particular brutal homicide.

76 *See* Witness to Innocence, *Homepage*, available at www.witnesstoinnocence.org.

77 Saundra D. Westervelt & Kimberly Cook, Life after Death Row: Exonerees' Search for Community and Identity (2012).

78 Professor van den Haag passed away in 2002. His papers, and those of the late Hugo Adam Bedau (1926–2012), are available in the National Death Penalty Archives, M.E. Grenander Department of Special Collections and Archives, State University of New York at Albany, available at http://library.albany.edu/archive/ndpa.

79 Before publication we decided to focus only on erroneous convictions for homicide, plus rape cases where the death penalty was involved. Thus, after our initial draft we did not include the cases of Julius and Ethel Rosenberg, executed in 1953 for espionage. *See* Bedau & Radelet, *supra* note 10, at 35.

80 David Margolick, *25 Wrongly Executed in U.S., Study Finds*, N.Y. Times, Nov. 14, 1985, at 13.

81 *See* Markman & Cassell, *supra* note 11.

82 *Id.* at 154–56.

83 Ronald J. Allen & Amy Shavell, *Further Reflections on the Guillotine*, 95 J. Crim. L. & Criminology 625 (2005). For a discussion of the limits of the retributive justification of the death penalty, based primarily on the argument that the retributive impact of the death penalty over life imprisonment falls disproportionately on the inmate's family members, none of whom have been convicted of a capital crime, see Michael L. Radelet, *The Incremental Retributive Impact of a Death Sentence over Life Without Parole*, 49 U. Mich. J. L. Reform (forthcoming 2016).

84 *See* Nagin & Pepper, *supra* note 65, at 2.

85 Furman v. Georgia, 408 U.S. 238 (1972).

86 Justice Stewart noted "[t]hese death sentences are cruel and unusual in the same way that being struck by lightning is cruel and unusual." Furman, 408 U.S. at 309–10.
87 Stephen B. Bright, *The Role of Race, Poverty, Intellectual Disability, and Mental Illness in the Decline of the Death Penalty*, 49 U. Rich. L. Rev. 671 (2015).
88 Markman & Cassell, *supra* note 11, at 121.
89 *See* Pew Research Center, *supra* note 54.

9

What Does Innocence Have to Do with Cruel and Unusual Punishment?

ROBERT J. SMITH, G. BEN COHEN AND ZOË ROBINSON

A new body of fact must be accounted for in deciding what, in practical terms, the Eighth Amendment guarantees should tolerate.
—Justice David Souter, dissenting in *Kansas v. Marsh*[1]

INTRODUCTION

As a question of constitutional interpretation, should the risk of executing the innocent matter in evaluating whether the death penalty is a "cruel and unusual punishment" under the Eighth Amendment? Since 1989, there have been one hundred and sixteen individuals exonerated from death row, including twenty-five prisoners freed through post-conviction DNA testing.[2] More than half of these exonerations have occurred in the last fifteen years.[3] A study by the National Academy of Sciences found that since 1973 one in twenty-five sentences involved the conviction of an innocent person.[4] A number of these exonerees spent decades on death row before exoneration, some coming within weeks or even days of execution. Even more worrisome, there is a growing list of individuals who have been executed despite strong claims of innocence: Cameron Todd Willingham, Carlos DeLuna, Troy Davis, and Lester Bower.

In 2004, Texas executed Cameron Todd Willingham for the murder of his three young children based on the testimony of a fire investigator who concluded that someone used an accelerant to start the fire. Two nationally renowned arson experts would later denounce this testimony. One of them

Portions of this chapter are based on the following commentary: Robert J. Smith, *Humane Criminal Justice Is Not Hopeless*, SLATE, Sept. 28, 2015.

concluded that there was "nothing to suggest to any reasonable arson investigator that this was an arson fire," and the other determined that the arson finding was not grounded "in modern fire science" and "could not be sustained."[5] Carlos DeLuna was executed in 1989 for a murder in Corpus Christi, Texas. The *Columbia University Law School Human Rights Law Review* dedicated an entire issue to the case, detailing how DeLuna was executed for a crime committed by Carlos Hernandez. DeLuna's conviction hinged upon a single eyewitness identification that occurred while he was sitting in a police car at the crime scene – despite both a total lack of forensic evidence against him *and* forensic evidence implicating the real killer, Hernandez.[6]

In 2011, Georgia executed Troy Anthony Davis for the murder of a police officer in a case in which seven of the nine trial witnesses recanted their testimony, no physical evidence tied Davis to the crime, and multiple people said that Sylvester "Redd" Coles, one of the two witnesses remaining, confessed to – and even boasted about – killing the officer. The other remaining witness originally told police that he could not identify the shooter, later changed his story after seeing a picture of Troy Davis in a newspaper, and then testified to observing the shooting from an angle and distance (and under lighting conditions) that exceed all limits of reliable human observation.[7]

Texas executed Lester Bower in June 2015. The prosecution alleged that Bower stole an airplane and killed four men at the airport hangar to cover up the crime. But the prosecution did not disclose "a detailed ... tip that the murders were actually connected to drug dealing in the area" or that "allegations existed that one of the victims, Tate, had been involved in cocaine trafficking in the years leading up to the murders."[8] Moreover, a witness came forward after the conviction to reveal that her boyfriend (with whom Bower had no connection) had admitted to killing the men in a drug deal gone wrong. The wife of a friend of this alternative suspect came forward claiming that her husband, too, was involved in the killing. Bower, meanwhile, steadfastly maintained his innocence.[9]

In the face of these alarming statistics and narratives, and despite the Constitution's prohibition against cruel and unusual punishments, the death penalty persists across the United States. Over the past few decades, the U.S. Supreme Court has struggled with the question of the constitutionality of the death penalty in light of the Eighth Amendment jurisprudence, which stipulates "that the penalty of death is qualitatively different from a sentence of imprisonment, however long," and that "[b]ecause of that qualitative difference, there is a corresponding difference in the need for reliability in the determination that death is the appropriate punishment in a specific case."[10]

While the Court's Eighth Amendment jurisprudence is multifaceted, the relationship between the Eighth Amendment and the conception of innocence adds a new prong to the doctrinal matrix that surrounds the constitutionality of the death penalty. As Justice Breyer wrote in his dissent in *Glossip* v. *Gross* in 2015: "In 1976, the Court thought that the constitutional infirmities in the death penalty could be healed, . . . [u]nlike 40 years ago," though "there is significantly more research-based evidence today indicating that courts sentence to death individuals who may well be actually innocent." Moreover, there is "convincing evidence" that "innocent people have been executed."[11] For these reasons, among others, Justice Breyer (joined by Justice Ginsburg) urged the Supreme Court to "ask for full briefing" on the question of whether "the death penalty violates the Constitution."[12]

However, not all of the Justices agree with the line that Justice Breyer drew between the Constitution, the death penalty, and innocence. Other members of the Court have suggested that the possibility of innocence has little, if any, bearing on the question of the constitutionality of the death penalty. For example, in his concurring opinion for the Court in *Glossip*, the late Justice Scalia called Justice Breyer's argument "gobbledy-gook."[13] For Justice Scalia, Justice Breyer's line drawing was flawed; Justice Scalia claimed that Justice Breyer "says that the death penalty is cruel because it is unreliable; but it is *convictions, not punishments*, that are unreliable."[14] Justice Scalia continued:

> [The] 'pressure on police, prosecutors, and jurors' [which Justice Breyer claims is a root cause of unreliable convictions] flows from the nature of the crime, not the punishment that follows its commission . . . That same pressure would exist, and the same risk of wrongful convictions, if horrendous death-penalty cases were converted into equally horrendous life-without-parole cases.[15]

Justice Scalia's derision that it is the convictions that are unreliable rather than the death sentence is somewhat akin to a car manufacturer – in response to multiple deaths from traffic accidents – deriding the demand to recall airbags for failing to deploy by claiming it was the brakes in the cars that caused the accidents.

This chapter takes up this question of whether unreliable convictions (i.e., innocence) implicate the constitutionality of the death penalty, under the Eighth Amendment or otherwise, and explains when, how, and why innocence matters to the constitutionality of capital punishment.

1 *Constitutional Line-Drawing: Convictions versus Punishments*

The demarcation between the conviction and penalty phases in the criminal justice system is constitutionally significant. The reliability of the conviction phase – that is, the veracity of the decision "whether he did it" as opposed to the "now what do we do with him" – is a constitutional consideration governed (at least initially) by the Due Process Clauses of the Fifth and Fourteenth Amendments.

As a matter of constitutional doctrine, once legal guilt has been determined, the governing provision for sentencing falls under the Eighth Amendment. The Eighth Amendment assumes guilt and asks (in a capital case) how the legal system should respond to the guilty murderer. So, for example, while the Supreme Court has held that the death penalty is an excessive punishment for certain offenses (e.g., the rape of a child) or categories of offenders (e.g., juveniles), death remains constitutionally permissible in other circumstances, providing certain elements have been established. Thus, the punishment phase of a capital trial focuses not on guilt, but rather on the factors that aggravate the homicide (e.g., there was more than one victim) or mitigate the culpability of the offender (e.g., the offender has a serious mental illness) in order to determine a legally proportionate punishment in the face of the guilty conviction. The concept of innocence has little, if any, formal legal significance in the punishment phase of the criminal justice system; innocence, then, is a legal concept formally related solely to the conviction phase.

The Court has continued to reinforce the formal irrelevance of innocence to the penalty phase. In *Oregon* v. *Guzek*, a jury convicted Randy Lee Guzek of murdering a husband and wife during a home invasion robbery. Guzek offered an alibi defense at trial, claiming that he was with his mother and/or grandfather when the crime occurred. Obviously, the jury did not buy it. Guzek sought to have his mother testify again during the penalty phase of the trial in the hope that her testimony would establish enough residual doubt to convince the jury not to impose a death sentence. Against the protestations of the prosecution, the Oregon Supreme Court held that the Eighth Amendment requires states to permit a defendant to introduce evidence of *residual doubt* as a mitigating factor that militates against a death sentence.

However, in an opinion authored by Justice Breyer, the U.S. Supreme Court reversed in 2006. According to the Court, the punishment phase of a capital trial "concerns *how*, not *whether*, a defendant committed the crime," Justice Breyer wrote. "But the evidence at issue here – alibi evidence – concerns only *whether*, not *how*, he did so," he continued.[16] Moreover, the Court determined, the negative impact of a rule restricting defendant's ability to introduce *new* alibi evidence is minimized by the fact that "Oregon law gives the defendant the right to present to the sentencing jury *all* the evidence of innocence from the original trial regardless."[17]

Justice Scalia agreed with the result. He also agreed that the punishment phase is about how, not whether, the defendant committed the crime. But Scalia pounced on the rationale that "Oregon law gives the defendant the right to present to the sentencing jury *all* the evidence of innocence from the original trial regardless." He called the argument "an analytical misfit," because while the *whether, not how* rationale suggests "the admission of innocence-related evidence would be improper and unnecessary at a sentencing hearing," the other rationale "suggests that there is no constitutional violation in this case because enough of such evidence may be admitted on remand."[18] As a legal question, innocence is only relevant to the conviction phase of a criminal trial.[19]

2 *The Constitutional Relevance of Residual Doubt*

On the one hand, the idea of residual doubt is tough to take seriously. The legal standard for guilt requires proof beyond a reasonable doubt. So, theoretically, any residual doubt of guilt must be *unreasonable* – otherwise, the jury would have returned a "not guilty" verdict. On the other hand, the "reasonable doubt" standard (even apart from epistemological limitations) operates on questionable tenets: that the relevant evidence is available, the defense discovered and presented it, and the jury assessed it credibly and faithfully applied the standard of proof. Legal fiction aside, then, it is not fanciful to imagine that a jury could find a person guilty and still not sentence him to die out of a lack of certainty as to his guilt. Presumably for these reasons, in 2009, Maryland narrowed its death penalty to cases with "biological or DNA evidence, a videotaped confession or a videotape linking the defendant to a homicide."[20]

The impulse behind the Maryland rule requiring biological or videotaped evidence is to increase the reliability of guilty verdicts in capital cases. For Maryland, amplified standards in the conviction phase increase the reliability of the guilty verdict, consequently decreasing the instance or scope of residual doubt in the penalty phase.

There are lots of reasons to think the goal of heightened reliability is a good idea, particularly in capital cases. Post-conviction DNA testing has resulted in the exoneration of more than twenty condemned prisoners. Of the 116 individuals exonerated from death row, more than half presented a constitutional question of some kind to the Court – which was denied without much review. But even accepting that in the vast number of cases, the question brought before the Court was not one of guilt or innocence, the Court still appears to have gotten it wrong when pushed to answer the question. Consider "the case of the 11-year-old girl raped by four men and then killed by stuffing her panties down her throat" that Justice Scalia wrote about defendants Leon Brown and Henry Lee McCollum, commenting on "[h]ow enviable a quiet death by lethal injection compared with that!" He continued: "If the people conclude that such more brutal deaths may be deterred by capital punishment; indeed, if they merely conclude that justice requires such brutal deaths to be avenged by capital punishment ... the Court's Eighth Amendment jurisprudence should not prevent them."[21] In 2014, DNA evidence exonerated half-brothers Leon Brown and Henry Lee McCollum in that case.

Paul House claimed that the scratches on his body did not demonstrate that he committed murder, but rather that he had obtained the wounds from "tearing down a building, and from a cat."[22] "Scratches from a cat, indeed," Chief Justice Roberts wrote derisively in his dissent in *House v. Bell*.[23] Though the Court concluded that House's "is not a case of conclusive exoneration," it noted that "the central forensic proof connecting House to the crime – the blood and the semen – has been called into question, and House has put forward substantial evidence pointing to a different suspect."[24] Chief Justice Roberts responded: "People facing a murder charge, who are innocent, do not make up a story out of concern that the truth might somehow disturb their parole officer." Moreover, "people do not lie to the police about which jeans they were wearing the night of a murder, if they have no reason to believe the jeans would be stained with the blood shed by the victim in her last desperate struggle to live."[25] In 2009, DNA evidence conclusively exonerated Mr. House.[26]

These exonerations have only served to amplify concerns over residual doubt and the constitutional relevance of innocence to the penalty phase of the criminal process in capital cases. As Justice Souter wrote in his dissent in *Kansas v. Marsh*, the exonerations are "a new body of facts [that] must be accounted for in deciding what, in practical terms, the Eighth Amendment guarantees should tolerate."[27] For Justice Souter, "[w]e are [] in a period of new empirical argument about how "death is different," he continued, "not only would these false verdicts defy correction after the fatal moment, the Illinois experience shows them to be remarkable in number, and they are probably disproportionately high in capital cases."[28]

The idea that "death is different" is a staple of contemporary capital punishment jurisprudence. In this way, innocence could be constitutionally relevant under the Eighth Amendment during the punishment phase in a way that is not tolerated in noncapital cases. In *Woodson v. North Carolina*, the plurality concluded:

> The penalty of death is qualitatively different from a sentence of imprison-
> ment, however long. Death, in its finality, differs more from life

imprisonment than a 100-year prison term difference from one of only a year or two. Because of that qualitative difference there is a corresponding difference in the need for reliability in the determination that death is the appropriate punishment in a specific case.[29]

In *Woodson*, though, the need for heightened reliability appears to refer to the calibration of the punishment and not the accuracy of the guilt determination. Specifically, in that case, the plurality acknowledged that "individualizing sentencing determinations generally [are] enlightened policy rather than a constitutional imperative," but nonetheless held "that in capital cases the fundamental respect for humanity underlying the Eighth Amendment, requires consideration of the character and record of the individual offender and the circumstances of the particular offense as a constitutionally indispensable part of the process of inflicting the penalty of death."[30]

The Court also has invoked this "heightened reliability" standard to prohibit practices – including, for example, forbidding argument that reduced the jury's responsibility, encouraged speculation concerning parole, precluded a lesser included verdict, or provided for mandatory punishment – that tended to make the *punishment* determination unreliable.

In *Ford* v. *Wainwright*,[31] the Court held that a condemned inmate convicted and sentenced to death consistent with the Constitution could not be executed if he or she is insane *at the time of the scheduled execution*. The reason why an insane person cannot be executed despite a constitutionally adequate trial is because the punishment of death serves no legitimate penological purpose when the person being executed has no rational understanding of the punishment being imposed upon him. New evidence that casts doubt on guilt, like new evidence of insanity, is a body of fact that must be accounted for in a system that prizes the accuracy of the death determination. In a previous article, one of us wrote: "innocence does not fluctuate, but, like sanity, the best facts to determine criminal liability might not be available at the trial, through no fault of the prisoner."[32] But this clouds the point, too. Evidence of insanity at the time of the scheduled execution does not undermine the original determination on guilt or innocence in the same way that new evidence that casts doubt directly on the guilty verdict does.

While these examples all evidence circumstances under which the judicial system will treat capital cases differently than noncapital cases, none squarely addresses the question of residual doubt over the initial conviction. This begs the question: why is death different? That is, why should residual doubt over the reliability of the initial conviction be considered in the punishment phase in capital cases? One possibility is that the executioner, an employee of the State, violates the cruel and unusual punishment provision if she performs the execution of a person where there are serious concerns about the reliability of the guilty verdict. This is a framing that is close to the Eighth Amendment doctrine in the context of prison conditions. In *Farmer v. Brennan*,[33] the Court held a prison official violates the Eighth Amendment if she is "subjectively aware of [a substantial] risk of serious harm" and nonetheless fails to intervene to alleviate the risk of harm.[34] An executioner who is aware of serious doubts about the reliability of the conviction would understand that executing a potentially innocent person would serve no legitimate penological purpose.

But the *Farmer* framing necessitates a deeper question – what is guilt? Or, in other words, does the executioner have the right to consider guilt as a fact in the world as opposed to legal guilt? If the reliability of the guilty verdict does not undermine Due Process protections in place in the conviction phase, then what right does the executioner have to interject her own sense of "the Truth" about the defendant's guilt?

This lens forces us to step back and consider the constitutional relevance of innocence not through the lens of the Eighth Amendment but instead the Due Process Clause. Perhaps this is – at least at first cut – a procedural Due Process issue (as opposed to an Eighth Amendment issue). The reasonable doubt standard applies to criminal cases (while the preponderance of evidence standard applies to civil cases) because society realizes the consequences of inaccurate adjudication are greater when life and liberty are on the line. Perhaps, given what we know about the conviction of factually innocent defendants in capital cases, the beyond a reasonable doubt standard is not onerous enough? This seems to be what Maryland was thinking with its law restricting death sentences to cases involving biological or videotaped evidence of guilt. But, as a procedural standard, it is logically difficult to improve upon a standard that requires a not-guilty verdict if any *reasonable* doubt exists. Given human fallibility and the limits of knowledge, what room is there between no reasonable doubts and absolute certainty? Moreover, the problem is often that the evidence was not available (or otherwise was not presented) at the trial. A prospective standard cannot grapple with that structural problem; and thus, even if it were possible to craft an adequate standard of proof, it still could not meaningfully eradicate the problem.

Knowledge and systems of science evolve. Procedures that once were employed with certainty now generate doubt. At its most base, for instance, in 1693 the procedure for determining whether a woman or young girl was a witch included traveling out to sea, dropping the body of the accused into the ocean (with rocks), and determining whether the body could float:

> Witches Teats: A mole or blemish somewhere on the body of the accused Witch is called a Witches Teat. If there is hair on the body, the examiners

will cut it off for a full body exam. If one mole or blemish is found on the body, she is a witch!

Drowning: Rocks are strapped to the accused witch and the accused witch is put into a body of water. If she floats or survives, she is a witch, and if the accused witch truly drowns, she is innocent.

Use the ways above to determine the difference between an innocent person and a witch. The Devil will never stop taking souls from our friends and family, so try to stop him! Always be prepared.[35]

At a bare minimum, execution prevented young women from challenging the quality of this forensic science after it came into disrepute.

In July 2002, in the relatively early days of the innocence revolution – at a time when only twelve defendants had been exonerated from death row based upon DNA (and a potential twenty other defendants exonerated without DNA), Judge Rakoff of the federal district court in the Southern District of New York found the federal death penalty unconstitutional, observing:

> the unacceptably high rate at which innocent persons are convicted of capital crimes, when coupled with the frequently prolonged delays before such errors are detected (and then often only fortuitously or by application of newly-developed techniques), compels the conclusion that execution under the Federal Death Penalty Act, by cutting off the opportunity for exoneration, denies due process and, indeed, is tantamount to foreseeable, state-sponsored murder of innocent human beings.[36]

Judge Rakoff, primarily, cabined his ruling – not on the Eighth Amendment's prohibition against cruel and unusual punishments, but on the basis that executing defendants violated their right to due process. Judge Rakoff observed that just as the Eighth Amendment should "be interpreted in light of 'evolving standards of decency,'" "so too it is settled law that the Fifth Amendment's broad guarantee of 'due process' must be interpreted in light of evolving standards of fairness and ordered liberty. ... To freeze 'due process' in the precise form it took in 1787 would be to freeze it to death."[37]

The Second Circuit reversed, holding any Eighth Amendment claim was foreclosed by *Gregg* v. *Georgia*[38] – and rejecting the claim that the FDPA violated either substantive or procedural due process.[39] The Second Circuit derided Judge Rakoff's concern that there was an "undue risk that a meaningful number of innocent persons, by being put to death before the emergence of the techniques or evidence that will establish their innocence, are thereby effectively deprived of the opportunity to prove their innocence – and thus deprived of the process that is reasonably due them in these circumstances under the Fifth Amendment."[40] All this was before thirteen additional individuals were exonerated from death row based upon DNA, and before almost one hundred additional individuals were exonerated from death row based upon non-DNA evidence. It was before the National Research Council released its report finding "the forensic science system, encompassing both research and practice, has serious problems that can only be addressed by a national commitment to overhaul the current structure that supports the forensic science community in this country."[41]

Cameron Todd Willingham experienced just the type of violation identified by Judge Rakoff, but derided by the Second Circuit. Executed on the basis of arson-expert testimony, Willingham was not able to raise the challenge to the validity of a science that experts now agree is inadequate after his execution.[42] Fire science is not the only forensic science specialty in doubt. A landmark 2009 National Academy of Sciences report found that, aside from DNA, no "forensic method has been rigorously shown to have the capacity to consistently, and with a high degree of certainty, demonstrate a connection between evidence and a specific individual or source."[43] The NAS report found specific flaws in arson investigation, bite mark analysis, and hair analysis. In April 2015, the Justice Department and the FBI acknowledged that their forensic laboratory had overstated forensic matches in hair comparisons "in ways that favored prosecutors" in 268 trials, including thirty-two defendants sentenced to death. News reports noted that fourteen of those had been executed or died in prison.[44] The FBI's press release itself indicated that FBI Hair Analysts have "committed widespread, systematic error," and acknowledged:

> The government identified nearly 3,000 cases in which FBI examiners may have submitted reports or testified in trials using microscopic hair analysis. As of March 2015, the FBI had reviewed approximately 500 cases. The majority of these cases were trials and the transcript of examiner testimony was reviewed. Some of these cases ended in guilty pleas, limiting the review to the original lab report. In the 268 cases where examiners provided testimony used to inculpate a defendant at trial, erroneous statements were made in 257 (96 percent) of the cases. Defendants in at least 35 of these cases received the death penalty and errors were identified in 33 (94 percent) of those cases. **Nine of these defendants have already been executed** and five died of other causes while on death row. The states with capital cases included Arizona, California, Florida, Indiana, Missouri, Ohio, Oklahoma, Pennsylvania, Tennessee, and Texas. It should be noted that this is an ongoing process and that the numbers referenced above will change.[45]

Similarly, investigation into the quality of bite mark evidence has resulted in the exoneration of twenty-four individuals. Reports suggest that despite evidence calling into question the entire field of bite mark analysis, as a junk science, fifteen people remain on death row as a result of that testimony.[46] The National Academy of Sciences report also called into question the validity of some ballistics testimony. In Alabama, in 2015, Ray Hinton was released from death row after it was determined that faulty ballistics testimony resulted in his conviction.[47]

In the face of these scientific revelations – some uncovered after the execution of defendants with no opportunity to litigate the new discovery – the Second Circuit's rejection of due process challenges to capital punishment in *Quinones* is under serious doubt. Hence, Justice Breyer's desire to address the constitutionality of the death penalty writ large. Even if the Eighth Amendment does not prohibit the execution of a factually innocent person, perhaps innocence informs the general question of the constitutionality of the death penalty as a matter of due process?

3 *Innocence and Current Eighth Amendment Doctrine*

Regardless of whether innocence is an overt factor in the assessment of the constitutionality of the death penalty, it is in fact already embedded in Eighth Amendment jurisprudence. Despite Justice Scalia's protestations to the contrary in *Glossip*, the Court's current Eighth Amendment jurisprudence is, at least in part, animated by innocence and residual doubt under three core doctrinal prongs: contemporary standards, penological purpose, and administrative impediments.

3.1 Contemporary Standards

Under current doctrine, when considering a categorical challenge to the death penalty the Court first questions whether there is a consensus for or against the punishment practice. For the first time in recent history, most jurisdictions – including twenty-six states, the District of Columbia, and the Federal Government – have either abolished the death penalty or else have either not performed an execution or not sentenced anyone to death in at least a decade.[48]

Innocence is relevant to this question of consensus because concerns over wrongful executions play a big role in this decline. As Professor Frank Baumgartner explains, support for capital punishment has "declined dramatically" since 1997. This decline corresponds "[w]ith increasing attention to the problem of mistaken judgments" and its result has been that "a thirty year trend toward increasing use of and public support for the death penalty has been reversed."[49]

In addition to the public concern over capital punishment, legislators, too, appear to be disproportionately concerned about the risk of executing a factually innocent person. In Nebraska,[50] Illinois,[51] and elsewhere questions of innocence animated the legislative debate. Gubernatorial moratoriums in Pennsylvania,[52] Oregon,[53] and Washington[54] have been adopted in part because of concern regarding innocence. Outside of sitting governors, there are some powerful conservative voices that have changed their mind on the death penalty because, in significant part, of the possibility of executing an innocent person. Conservative voices like George Will,[55] Rand Paul,[56] and Bob Barr[57] have all expressed deep concern over the government executing innocent defendants.

And so, in contrast to Justice Scalia's suggestion that innocence is irrelevant, innocence appears to drive much of the Eighth Amendment doctrine in capital cases and is relevant to the question of whether the death penalty is a constitutional punishment because concerns over wrongful convictions and executions are primary drivers on the question of whether capital punishment is consistent with contemporary national norms.

3.2 Penological Purpose

In addition to asking whether the death penalty fits with our contemporary standards of decency, the Court also asks whether the punishment serves a meaningful penological purpose. Unless the death penalty meaningfully serves some legitimate end of punishment that cannot be accomplished through a less severe sanction, it is a "penalty with such negligible returns to the State" that it is "patently excessive and cruel and unusual punishment violative of the Eighth Amendment."[58] What penological purposes does capital punishment serve, and how much value does it add? As Justice Breyer explained in *Glossip*, hardly any and not much:

> The rationale for capital punishment, as for any punishment, classically rests upon society's need to secure deterrence, incapacitation, retribution, or rehabilitation. Capital punishment by definition does not rehabilitate. It does, of course, incapacitate the offender. But the major alternative to capital punishment – namely, life in prison without possibility of parole – also incapacitates. Thus, as the Court has recognized, the death penalty's penological rationale in fact rests almost exclusively upon a belief in its tendency to deter and upon its ability to satisfy a community's interest in retribution. Many studies have examined the death penalty's deterrent effect; some have found such an effect, whereas others have found a lack of evidence that it deters crime. ... And, even if that effect is no

more than slight, it makes it difficult to believe (given the studies of deterrence cited earlier) that such a rare event significantly deters horrendous crimes.[59]

This leaves retribution as the only purpose of punishment that the death penalty *arguably* serves. As Justice Kennedy remarked in *Kennedy* v. *Louisiana*, it is retribution that "most often can contradict the law's own ends." He continued: "This is of particular concern when the Court interprets the meaning of the Eighth Amendment in capital cases. When the law punishes by death, it risks its own sudden descent into brutality, transgressing the constitutional commitment to decency and restraint."[60]

Against this caution that retribution is the goal of punishment that must be the most carefully restrained and calibrated, the Justices have registered several concerns: 1) that executions are not limited to those offenders who commit the most serious homicides; 2) that executions are not limited to those offenders with the most extreme culpability; and 3) that the delay between sentence and execution erodes the retributive purpose of the sanction, especially as some condemned inmates transform their lives from the person that they were decades earlier. The relevance of innocence to this penological-purpose determination is that, if we can no longer confidently assume that Due Process guarantees produce reliable verdicts, then the risk of wrongful execution must be weighed against the penological value. As one of us wrote in *Recalibrating Constitutional Innocence Protection*, "as a retributive matter, the harm done to society has not been rectified but amplified ... when it convicts – and especially if it executes – an innocent person, society suffers in terms of both the perceived legitimacy of its power to allocate punishment and the criminal justice system's competence to protect innocent citizens from unjust punishment."[61] How much retributive benefit does the death penalty serve over life without the possibility of parole? It is difficult to say precisely, but surely it is far less than the penological benefits of, say, a sentence of years in prison for rape or homicide. And, perhaps, putting the risk of factual innocence on one side of the scale eliminates any meaningful purpose that capital punishment served.

3.3 Systemic Risk of Wrongful Execution

In *Kennedy* v. *Louisiana*, the Court held that death is an unconstitutional punishment for the rape of a child because, in part:

> There are, moreover, serious systemic concerns in prosecuting the crime of child rape that are relevant to the constitutionality of making it a capital

offense. The problem of unreliable, induced, and even imagined child testimony means there is a "special risk of wrongful execution" in some child rape cases. This undermines, at least to some degree, the meaningful contribution of the death penalty to legitimate goals of punishment. Studies conclude that children are highly susceptible to suggestive questioning techniques like repetition, guided imagery, and selective reinforcement. . . . And the question in a capital case is not just the fact of the crime, including, say, proof of rape as distinct from abuse short of rape, but details bearing upon brutality in its commission. These matters are subject to fabrication or exaggeration, or both. Although capital punishment does bring retribution, and the legislature here has chosen to use it for this end, its judgment must be weighed, in deciding the constitutional question, against the special risks of unreliable testimony with respect to this crime.[62]

It is important to note that Justice Kennedy, writing in *Kennedy* v. *Louisiana*, calculated the risk of wrongful *conviction* in child rape cases as a structural impediment to preventing the risk of wrongful executions; and thus, as a factor that weighs against any purported penological purpose that the death penalty serves.

Similarly, in *Atkins* v. *Virginia*, as a separate basis for holding that the Eighth Amendment prohibited the execution of individuals with intellectual disability, the Court expressed special concern for the possibility of wrongful convictions. The Court noted:

The reduced capacity of mentally retarded offenders provides a second justification for a categorical rule making such offenders ineligible for the death penalty. The risk "that the death penalty will be imposed in spite of factors which may call for a less severe penalty," Lockett v. Ohio, 438 U.S. 586, 605, 57 L. Ed. 2d 973, 98 S. Ct. 2954 (1978), is enhanced, not only by the possibility of false confessions, but also by the lesser ability of mentally retarded defendants to make a persuasive showing of mitigation in the face of prosecutorial evidence of one or more aggravating factors. . . . Mentally retarded defendants in the aggregate face a special risk of wrongful execution.[63]

Justice Scalia mocked the concern for wrongful execution of persons with intellectual disability:

Special risk is pretty flabby language (even flabbier than "less likely") – and I suppose a similar "special risk" could be said to exist for just plain stupid people, inarticulate people, even ugly people. If this unsupported claim has any substance to it (which I doubt) it might support a due process claim in all criminal prosecutions of the mentally retarded; but it is hard to see how it has anything to do with an Eighth Amendment claim that execution of the mentally retarded is cruel and unusual. We have never before held it to be cruel and unusual punishment to impose a sentence in violation of some other constitutional imperative.[64]

Like the case of child rape, wrongful convictions in capital cases are (mostly) not random events in capital cases generally. They instead derive from predictable factors, mainly 1) police misconduct; 2) prosecutorial misconduct; and 3) ineffective defense lawyering. These are factors that plague capital cases, and ones that have not been eliminated through forty years of the Court's regulation and prodding. Moreover, innocence is often not a question of waiting to discover more biological evidence. It is often a messier question. Consider Troy Davis – seven of nine witnesses recant, there is an alternative suspect who appears to have confessed informally on multiple occasions, inconsistent stories and the physical impossibility of remaining eyewitness testimony.[65] Or consider Richard Glossip's case – there was weak evidence at trial, the daughter of the codefendant said that her father admitted that Glossip had no involvement, and Glossip's lawyers never provided the jury with the videotape of the interrogation of Glossip's codefendant where police put pressure on him to implicate Glossip in exchange for taking the death penalty off the table.[66]

While rejected by Justice Scalia, in both *Atkins* and *Kennedy*, the Court weighed the risk of executing the innocent versus the benefit of executions. And while neither *Kennedy* nor *Atkins* reached the broader issue of the constitutionality of the death penalty, these cases demonstrate that – at least when the death penalty is on the table – the line between conviction and punishment is far less clear than formal constitutional principles might suggest. That is, when the possible punishment includes death by the state's hand, the concern of residual doubt appears to drive the Court's categorical exclusion of a number of crimes and offenders. Innocence, then, plays a significant, if not central, role in the penalty phase of capital cases, contrary to the protestations of Justice Scalia and other members of the Court.

NOTES

1 Kansas v. Marsh, 548 U.S. 163, 207 (2006) (Souter J., dissenting).
2 As of September 20, 2015, there have been 1,663 reported exonerations. The National Registry of Exonerations reflects that 116 of these have been from death row since 1989. *See* National Registry of Exonerations, *Homepage*, available at www.law.umich.edu/special/exoneration/Pages/detaillist.aspx?View={FAF6EDDB-5A68-4F8F-8A522C61F5BF9EA7}&FilterField1=Sentence&FilterValue1=Death&FilterField2=DNA&FilterValue2=8_Y.

3 *Id.*

4 *See* Samuel R. Gross, Barbara O'Brien, Chen Hu & Edward H. Kennedy, *Rate of False Conviction of Criminal Defendants Who Are Sentenced to Death*, 111 Proc. Nat'l Acad. Scis. (PNAS) 7230 (2014).

5 A full version of Dr. Gerald Hurst's 2004 report on Willingham's case is available at www.pbs.org/wgbh/pages/frontline/death-by-fire/documents/hursts-2004-report.html. *See also* Steve Mills & Maurice Possley, *Man Executed on Disproved Forensics*, Chic. Trib., Dec. 9, 2004, available at www.chicagotribune.com/news/nation world/chi-0412090169dec09-story.html; David Grann, *Trial By Fire: Did Texas Execute an Innocent Man?*, The New Yorker, Sept. 7, 2009, available at www.new yorker.com/magazine/2009/09/07/trial-by-fire.

6 *See* James S. Liebman, Shawn Crowley, Andrew Markquart, Lauren Rosenberg, Lauren Gallo White & Daniel Zharkovsky, *Los Tocayos Carlos: An Anatomy of a Wrongful Execution*, 43 Colum. Hum. Rts. L. Rev. 711 (2012).

7 For an excellent overview of the issues in Troy Davis's case, see NAACP, *Significant Doubts About Troy Davis' Guilt: A Case for Clemency*, available at www.naacp.org/pages/troy-davis-a-case-for-clemency.

8 Jordan Smith, *Doubts Still Plague the 31-Year Old Lester Bower Case but Texas Is about to Kill Him Anyway*, The Intercept, June 2, 2015, available at theinter cept.com/2015/06/01/lesterbowertodie/.

9 *Id.*

10 Woodson v. North Carolina, 428 U.S. 280, 304–05 (1976).

11 Glossip v. Gross, 135 S. Ct. 2726, 2755–56, 2759 (2015) (Breyer J., dissenting).

12 *Id.* at 2776.

13 *Id.* at 2747 (Scalia J., concurring).

14 *Id.*

15 *Id.* It is possible that Justice Scalia errs when he suggests that the "'pressure on police, prosecutors, and jurors' … flows from the nature of the crime, not the punishment that follows its commission." This conclusion ignores not only the possibility that capital punishment is a trigger for heightened emotion, but Justice Kennedy's observation that "[w]hen the law punishes by death, it risks its own sudden descent into brutality, transgressing the constitutional commitment to decency and restraint." *See* Kennedy v. Louisiana, 554 U.S. 407, 420 (2008). While it is possible that some participants in a capital case (public defenders, prosecutors, judges and jurors) are especially focused by the specter of the death penalty, it is equally possible that in a corollary number of instances emotion, passion and prejudice cloud judgment in the face of a potential death sentence; and that in the place in which restraint is needed most, it is available least.

16 Oregon v. Guzek, 546 U.S. 517, 525–26 (2006).

17 *Id.* at 526–27.

18 *Id.* at 529 (Scalia J., concurring).

19 *See also* Herrera v. Collins, 506 U.S. 390 (1993) (discussing the relevance of actual innocence to habeas corpus review). On the concept of innocence and the criminal

justice system, see generally DANIEL S. MEDWED, PROSECUTION COMPLEX: AMERICA'S RACE TO CONVICT AND ITS IMPACT ON THE INNOCENT (2012).

20 John Wagner, *Maryland General Assembly Expected to Approve New Limits on Death Penalty Case*, WASH. POST, Mar. 26, 2006, available at www.washington post.com/wp-dyn/content/article/2009/03/25/AR2009032501643.html.

21 Callins v. Collins, 510 U.S. 1127, 1128 (1994) (Scalia J., concurring).

22 House v. Bell, 547 U.S. 518, 566–67 (2006) (O'Connor J., concurring).

23 *Id.* at 571 (Roberts J., dissenting).

24 *Id.* at 554.

25 *Id.*

26 *See, e.g.*, Bill Mears, *Man Who Spent 22 Years on Death Row Is Cleared*, CNN, May 12, 2009, available at www.cnn.com/2009/CRIME/05/12/death.row.exoner ation/index.html?iref=topnews.

27 Kansas v. Marsh, 548 U.S. at, 207 (Souter J., dissenting).

28 *Id.* at 180.

29 Woodson v. North Carolina, 428 U.S. 280, 305 (1976).

30 *Id.* at 304.

31 Ford v. Wainwright, 477 U.S. 399 (1986).

32 Robert J. Smith, *Recalibrating Constitutional Innocence Protection*, 87 WASH. L. REV. 139, 166 (2012).

33 Farmer v. Brennan, 511 U.S. 825 (1970).

34 *Id.* at 828.

35 *See Stop the Devil's Assistances How to Tell if Someone Is a Witch*, available at http://people.ucls.uchicago.edu/~snekros/The%20Salem%20Times/The_Salem_ Times_of_1693/Culture_%26_Beliefs.html.

36 U.S. v. Quinones, 205 F. Supp. 2d 256, 268 (S.D.N.Y. 2002).

37 *Id.* at 259–60.

38 428 U.S. 153 (1976).

39 U.S. v. Quinones, 313 F.3d 49 (2d Cir. 2002).

40 *Id.* (citing Judge Rakoff).

41 COMMITTEE ON IDENTIFYING THE NEEDS OF THE FORENSIC SCIENCES COMMUNITY, NATIONAL RESEARCH COUNCIL, STRENGTHENING FORENSIC SCIENCE IN THE UNITED STATES: A PATH FORWARD preface xx (August 2009), available at www.ncjrs.gov/pdffiles1/nij/grants/228091.pdf [hereinafter A PATH FORWARD]. *See also* Michael Shermer, *Can We Trust Crime Forensics?*, SCI. AM., Sept. 1, 2015, available at www.scientificamerican.com/article/can-we-trust-crime-forensics/.

42 Maurice Possley, *Fresh Doubts over a Texas Execution*, WASH. POST, Aug. 3, 2014, available at www.washingtonpost.com/sf/national/2014/08/03/fresh-doubts-over-a-texas-execution/.

43 A PATH FORWARD, *supra* note 41, at 7.

44 Spencer S. Hau, *FBI Admits Flaws in Hair Analysis over Decades*, WASH. POST, Apr. 18, 2015, available at www.washingtonpost.com/local/crime/fbi-overstated-

forensic-hair-matches-in-nearly-all-criminal-trials-for-decades/2015/04/18/39c8d8c6-
e515-11e4-b510-962fcfabc310_story.html.

45 Department of Justice, *FBI Testimony on Microscopic Hair Analysis Contained Errors in at Least 90 Percent of Cases in Ongoing Review, 26 of 28 FBI Analysts Provided Testimony or Reports with Errors*, Press Release, Apr. 20, 2015, available at www.fbi.gov/news/pressrel/press-releases/fbi-testimony-on-microscopic-hair-analysis-contained-errors-in-at-least-90-percent-of-cases-in-ongoing-review.

46 Radley Balko, *How the Flawed Science of Bite Mark Analysis Has Sent Innocent People to Prison*, WASH. POST, Feb. 2, 2015, available at www.washington post.com/news/the-watch/wp/2015/02/13/how-the-flawed-science-of-bite-mark-analy sis-has-sent-innocent-people-to-jail/.

47 Abby Phillip, *Alabama Inmate Free after Three Decades on Death Row. How the Case against Him Unraveled*, WASH. POST, Apr. 3, 2015, available at www.washingtonpost.com/news/morning-mix/wp/2015/04/03/how-the-case-against-anthony-hinton-on-death-row-for-30-years-unraveled/.

48 The following jurisdictions have abolished the death penalty in law: Alaska, Connecticut, Delaware, Hawaii, Illinois, Iowa, Maine, Maryland, Massachusetts, Michigan, Minnesota, New Jersey, New Mexico, New York, North Dakota, Rhode Island, Vermont, West Virginia, Wisconsin, and the District of Columbia. The following jurisdictions have not executed anyone in at least a decade: Colorado, Kansas, Nebraska, New Hampshire, Oregon, Pennsylvania, Wyoming, and the federal government. Montana has not sentenced anyone to death in the past decade. *See* Death Penalty Information Center, *States with and without the Death Penalty*, available at www.deathpenaltyinfo.org/states-and-without-death-penalty.

49 Frank R. Baumgartner, *The Discovery of Innocence: Americans and the Death Penalty*, available at www.unc.edu/~fbaum/Innocence/Baumgartner_Innocence_NCOBPS_2008.pdf. *See also* FRANK R. BAUMGARTNER, SUZANNA DE BOEF & AMBER BOYDSTUN, THE DECLINE OF THE DEATH PENALTY AND THE DIS-COVERY OF INNOCENCE (2008). *Compare* Michael L. Radelet, *How DNA Has Changed Contemporary Death Penalty Debates, supra*, in this volume.

50 For example, Senator Hansen explained that he has "no sympathy" for guilty murderers on death row, but he nonetheless voted to repeal the death penalty because: "We've gotten it wrong in the past. We've seen evidence with the Beatrice Six where the death penalty caused people to give false confessions . . . It does make me worry about the innocence in our society[.]" Also in Nebraska, Senator Davis said: "If you're a pro-life person, I think it really boils down to that life question because to me it is never okay that you would ever risk killing an innocent person for justice and that has no doubt happened." *See* Nebraska Legislature Floor Debate, May 27, 2015, at 98, available at http://nebraskalegislature.gov/FloorDocs/Current/PDF/Transcripts/FloorDebate/r1day87.pdf.

51 In Illinois, Republican Governor George Ryan granted mass clemency to the State's death row inmates because:

We [] had the dubious distinction of exonerating more men than we had executed. 13 men found innocent, 12 executed. As I reported yesterday, there is not a doubt in my mind that the number of innocent men freed from our Death Row stands at 17, with the pardons of Aaron Patterson, Madison Hobley, Stanley Howard and Leroy Orange. That is an absolute embarrassment ... During the time we have had capital punishment in Illinois, there were at least 33 other people wrongly convicted on murder charges and exonerated. Since we reinstated the death penalty there are also 93 people where our criminal justice system imposed the most severe sanction and later rescinded the sentence or even released them from custody because they were innocent. How many more cases of wrongful conviction have to occur before we can all agree that the system is broken?

George Ryan, *I Must Act*, speech delivered at Northwestern University School of Law, published Jan. 11, 2003, available at www.nytimes.com/2003/01/11/national/ 11CND-RTEX.html. Later, when Illinois formally abolished the death penalty, Governor Quinn said as he signed the repeal bill into law: "If the system can't be guaranteed, 100-percent error-free, then we shouldn't have the system ... It cannot stand." Christopher Wills, *Illinois Gov. Pat Quinn Abolishes Death Penalty, Clears Death Row*, WASH. POST, Mar. 9, 2011, available at www.washingtonpost.com/wp- dyn/content/article/2011/03/09/AR2011030900319.html. The *Washington Post* noted how during his post-signing statement, "the governor returned often to the fact that 20 people sent to death row had seen their cases overturned after evidence surfaced that they were innocent or had been convicted improperly." *Id.*

52 In 2015, Pennsylvania Governor Wolf declared a moratorium on executions because, in part:

Since reinstatement of the death penalty, 150 people have been exonerated from death row nationwide, including six men in Pennsylvania. One of these men, Harold Wilson, twice had death warrants signed against him meaning Pennsylvania came within days of executing an innocent man, and might well have done so but for judicial stays. A second man, Nicholas Yarris, was exonerated by newly available DNA evidence after serving twenty-one years on death row. Many more inmates have been resentenced to life in prison after reviewing courts found mitigating circumstances, or flaws in the penalty phases of their trials. If the Commonwealth of Pennsylvania is going to take the irrevocable step of executing a human being, its capital sentencing system must be infallible. Pennsylvania's system is riddled with flaws, making it error prone, expensive, and anything but infallible.

Governor Tom Wolf, *Memorandum*, Feb. 13, 2015, available at www.scribd.com/doc/ 255669059/Governor-Tom-Wolf-Announces-a-Moratorium-on-the-Death-Penalty- in-Pa. *See also* Wallace McKelvey, *Gov. Tom Wolf Declares Moratorium on Death Penalty in Pa.*, PENN LIVE, Feb. 13, 2015, available at www.pennlive.com/politics/ index.ssf/2015/02/gov_tom_wolf_declares_moratori.html#incart_story_package.

53 Governor Kitzhaber expressed a similar sentiment to that espoused by his cohort in Pennsylvania in declaring a still-active moratorium in Oregon:

> And during that time, a growing number of states have reconsidered their approach to capital punishment given public concern, evidence of wrongful convictions, the unequal application of the law, the expense of the process and other issues. Illinois banned it earlier this year, ending a legacy of faulty convictions, forced confessions, unreliable witnesses and incompetent legal representation.

Governor John Kitzhaber, *Governor Kitzhaber Statement on Capital Punishment*, Nov. 22, 2011, available at http://media.oregonlive.com/pacific-northwest-news/other/Microsoft%20Word%20-%20Final%20Final%20JK%20Statement%20on%20the%20Death%20Penalty.pdf. *See also* Helen Jung, *Gov. John Kitzhaber Stops Executions in Oregon, Calls System 'Compromised and Inequitable,'* THE OREGO-NIAN, Nov. 22, 2011, available at www.oregonlive.com/pacific-northwest-news/index.ssf/2011/11/gov_john_kitzhaber_stops_all_e.html.

54 When Governor Inslee in Washington declared the still-active moratorium on executions, he wrote:

> Let me acknowledge that there are many good protections built into Washington State's death penalty law. But there have been too many doubts raised about capital punishment. There are too many flaws in the system. And when the ultimate decision is death there is too much at stake to accept an imperfect system … Since 1981, the year our current capital laws were put in place, 32 defendants have been sentenced to die. Of those, 19, or 60 percent, had their sentences overturned. One man was set free and 18 had their sentences converted to life in prison. When the majority of death penalty sentences lead to reversal, the entire system itself must be called into question.

Governor Jay Inslee, *Governor Inslee's Remarks Announcing a Capital Punishment Moratorium*, Feb. 11, 2014, available at www.governor.wa.gov/sites/default/files/documents/20140211_death_penalty_moratorium.pdf.

55 George Will observed:

> When capital punishment is inflicted, it cannot later be corrected because of new evidence, so a capital punishment regime must be administered with extraordinary competence. It is, however, a government program. Since 1973, more than 140 people sentenced to death have been acquitted of their crimes (sometimes by DNA evidence), had the charges against them dismissed by prosecutors or have been pardoned based on evidence of innocence.

George F. Will, *Capital Punishment's Slow Death*, WASH. POST, May 20, 2015, available at www.washingtonpost.com/opinions/capital-punishments-slow-death/2015/05/20/f3c14d32-fe4f-11e4-8b6c-0dcce21e223d_story.html.

56 2016 Presidential Candidate (and U.S. Senator) Rand Paul has said: "Even in the United States where we have the best due process probably in the world, we have

probably executed people wrongfully for the death penalty, then found out through DNA testing many people on death row are there inaccurately." And talk show host Laura Ingraham has said that she is "troubled by the fact that there are people that have been exonerated through DNA. That's horrific. And we have to do something about that … There could be innocent people probably today on death row." Conservatives Concerned about the Death Penalty, *What Conservatives Are Saying*, available at http://conservativesconcerned.org/what-conservatives-are-saying/.

57 Congressman Bob Barr wrote:

> I've been called a lot of things, but a "bleeding heart liberal" is not one of them. I am a firm believer in the propriety and historic soundness of the death penalty. But, as a proponent of our Constitution and its attendant Bill of Rights, I believe just as strongly in the fundamental fairness that lies at the heart – or should lie at the heart – of our criminal justice system. Because of its obvious finality, the death penalty must be employed with as close to absolute fairness and certainty as humanly possible. Several recent cases, including that of Troy Davis here in Georgia, have raised legitimate questions about just that proposition. True conservatives, as much as the most bleeding heart liberals, should be unafraid to look carefully at such cases.
>
> Cited in Death Penalty Information Center, *Former Conservative Congressman Questions Fairness and Accuracy of Death Penalty*, available at www.deathpenaltyinfo.org/node/235.

58 Furman, v. Georgia 408 U.S. 238, 312 (1972) (White, J., concurring).

59 Glossip v. Gross, 135 S. Ct. 2726, 2767–68 (Breyer J., dissenting).

60 Kennedy v. Louisiana, 554 U.S. 407, 420 (2008).

61 Smith, *supra* note 32, at 140.

62 Kennedy, 554 U.S. at 443.

63 Atkins v. Virginia, 536 U.S. 304, 320–21 (2002).

64 *Id.* at 352 (Scalia, J., dissenting).

65 Smith, *supra* note 32, at 192.

66 Liliana Segura, *Why Is Oklahoma So Eager to Kill Richard Glossip?*, THE INTERCEPT, Sept. 29, 2015, available at https://theintercept.com/2015/09/29/glossip-to-die-tomorrow/.

PART II

A Glance Ahead

What Can Be Done to Avoid Wrongful Convictions in the Future?

Substantive Reforms

10

Flawed Science and the New Wave of Innocents

KEITH A. FINDLEY

INTRODUCTION

DNA launched the "Innocence Movement." Certainly, before forensic DNA technology came along in the late 1980s a few scholars had studied wrongful convictions, and some innocent people in prison found ways to prove their innocence. And at least one organization – Centurion Ministries in Princeton, New Jersey – even dedicated itself to exonerating the innocent, years before the introduction of DNA as a forensic tool. But that scholarship, those exonerations, and that organization all occupied the fringe of the criminal justice landscape. They revealed anomalies, not systemic flaws. Their claims of innocence were often disputed. Their critiques of the system were dismissed by bravado about all the constitutional rights the American system affords the criminally accused that make it the "greatest justice system in the world." As Justice O'Connor put it in 1993 in her concurring opinion in *Herrera v. Collins*: "Our society has a high degree of confidence in its criminal trials, in no small part because the Constitution offers unparalleled protections against convicting the innocent."[1]

DNA changed all that. DNA moved exonerations from the periphery to the front and center. It did so in several ways.

First, DNA exposed wrongful convictions at a rate never before imagined. Starting with just two exonerations in 1989, DNA began to produce a steady and growing stream of exonerations in serious cases, rising to as many as twenty-nine by 2009.[2] By fall 2015, the Innocence Project counted a total of 333 DNA exonerations nationwide.[3]

Second, DNA produced cases in which no one could seriously debate the claim of innocence. For the first time, we had a pool of cases in which we knew with as much certainty as science could generate that we had gotten it wrong. The cases forced innocence skeptics to swallow their certainty (and their pride).

Third, the DNA exonerations created, to some degree at least, new receptivity to the possibility of error in criminal cases, and an impetus to examine cases for error even where there was no DNA. Gradually, the number of exonerations based on non-DNA evidence began to exceed the DNA exonerations, so that the National Registry of Exonerations counted 115 non-DNA exonerations in 2014, compared to twenty-two DNA exonerations that same year.[4] In this sense, "[DNA-based i]nnocence consciousness in turn led to the discovery of more innocents."[5]

Fourth, the confirmed innocence cases also provided the opportunity and the stimulus for intensive scholarly inquiry. With these new pools of exonerations, researchers went to work figuring out what systemic features create the errors, or at least the conditions for error. No longer was this scholarly inquiry a study of anomalies; it became inquiry into the fundamental nature of the truth-seeking mechanisms of the justice system.

Perhaps most fundamentally, DNA launched the Innocence Movement by creating powerful narratives of innocence. The DNA cases provided names, faces, and life stories to go with the arguments about wrongful convictions. They told stories of innocent lives ruined by years – often decades – behind bars, or even on death row. And they told those stories with the clarity, purity, and simplicity that little besides DNA could provide; they were the black-and-white stories of the unambiguously innocent robbed of their lives.

But, as has become clear now, DNA was just the start. While it animated the Movement, it no longer fully defines it. It cannot be the future, at least not the whole or even dominant part of the future.

MOVING BEYOND DNA

Many, including me, long assumed there would be a precipitous decline of DNA exonerations as innocence advocates worked their way through the old cases with untested biological evidence. As DNA became routinely tested before trial, at least in serious crimes, the pool of cases with untested material was bound to shrink. But the DNA cases have not disappeared as quickly as predicted. Their frequency has leveled off, and they now make up a shrinking percentage of annual exonerations, but they remain a significant and persistent part of the innocence landscape, and likely will continue to play an important role for the foreseeable future. Between 2001 and 2014, the annual rate of DNA exonerations has remained flat, averaging over that span just over twenty-one per year, never dropping below thirteen (in 2004) or rising above twenty-nine (in 2009).[6]

DNA appears to have a longer lifespan in the Innocence Movement in part because the technology is continually improving, because the number of innocence organizations and other advocates looking for DNA exonerations continues to expand, and because actors at the trial level will always make mistakes, either by overlooking sources of probative DNA or by mishandling or misinterpreting the DNA. But the numbers will almost certainly diminish eventually, at least in proportion (as is already happening).

Moreover, the DNA exonerations of the future as a group will be less definitive and more contentious than the ones that launched the movement, as DNA is increasingly used at the periphery of cases. While DNA continues to exonerate, increasingly the DNA cases push the envelope of the technology and the evidence. DNA testing on rape kits, looking to see who left the semen recovered from the victim's body, constituted the prototypical DNA exoneration that launched the movement. That form of DNA most clearly proved actual innocence, and even frequently identified the true perpetrator. But it is also the type of case in which the DNA is now being tested routinely before trial. Increasingly, post-conviction DNA is being used where the presence or probative value of the biological evidence is less obvious. Post-conviction DNA testing today is more likely to produce partial profiles from degraded samples, mixed profiles from multiple contributors, and profiles from touch DNA from assorted physical items found at or near the crime scene (which, as the name suggests, might contain miniscule amounts of DNA shed by a person who merely touched the item), all of which will have varying degrees of probative value. No longer is DNA necessarily alone dispositive.

In any event, DNA cannot occupy the field – and never really could – because it always has existed in only a small percentage of cases. Of the more-than 1,700 exonerations listed in the National Registry of Exonerations, three-quarters were cleared without the help of DNA.[7] More than ever, focusing only on DNA cases would mean failure to exonerate the vast majority of innocent prisoners.

All of this means that DNA cannot and need not sustain the movement alone. Indeed, the simple, black-and-white story of innocence represented by the single-perpetrator rape cases can present challenges to the new innocence cases. I have previously argued that,

> [i]n some ways, the DNA exonerations, while clarifying the extent and nature of the problem of wrongful convictions, have simultaneously muddled the picture by creating a category of cases in which there is little, if any doubt that the accused was wrongly convicted and was in fact innocent in a system that generally has no corresponding legal category of clear

innocence. . . . The DNA cases raised the expectation, for some, that 'exoneration' and 'innocence' are findings that can – and must – be established to levels of virtual certainty. But it turns out that even DNA cases come in varying shade of gray. There is no such thing as absolute proof of innocence, just as there is no such thing as absolute proof of guilt.[8]

For all these reasons, the next generation of innocence cases should embrace a broader definition of innocence, one that recognizes innocence where the bases for prosecution have been undermined, but ground truth is fundamentally ambiguous or inaccessible. That claim is, indeed, compatible with most legal standards for relief from a conviction (which generally require a showing of a probability, or a reasonable probability, of a different result, but never a certainty or near certainty of acquittal).[9]

FLAWED SCIENCE AND THE NEW INNOCENTS

Ironically, while scientific evidence (DNA) launched the Innocence Movement by so definitively establishing the truth of numerous innocence claims, the future of the Innocence Movement will be built to a large extent on showing that scientific evidence is frequently wrong. Science-dependent prosecutions – prototypically represented by arson and Shaken Baby Syndrome/Abusive Head Trauma (SBS/AHT) cases – exemplify this new claim of innocence. Similar examples are also found in the recent reliance on flawed identification disciplines, such as Comparative Bullet Lead Analysis (CBLA) and microscopic hair analysis (which, unlike arson and SBS/AHT science, are used primarily to identify the perpetrator). Especially in the SBS and arson cases, the prosecution rests entirely or almost entirely upon scientific or expert opinions not just to establish identity, but to prove the very fact of a crime and the mental state of the perpetrator. But in both types of cases, the science has subsequently been either disproved or undermined in significant ways. Yet the new evidence, unlike DNA, can rarely prove innocence. It undermines the proof of guilt, but not necessarily the possibility of guilt. And it usually does not have the potential to complete the innocence narrative by identifying the true perpetrator; in many such cases it suggests instead that there was no perpetrator at all, because there was no crime. But because the new evidence can negate the evidence of guilt, in our legal system, with its presumption of innocence in the absence of proof of guilt, these are indeed innocence cases.[10] But they are innocence cases that demand that innocence advocates effectively negotiate special challenges posed by "shifted science."[11]

Scholars have long noted that the law's reliance on science creates deep tensions. Science is never definitive, but always tentative, contingent, and evolving.[12] As Dr. Norah Rudin commented in 2015, the law's demand that scientists offer their opinions "to a reasonable degree of scientific (or medical, or whatever the specialty might be) certainty" makes no sense to a scientist. "There is no such thing as scientific certainty," she says. Therefore, any scientist's certainty "can't be reasonable. All science can do is quantify uncertainty."[13] Science is perpetually subject to ongoing research, producing new understandings, revisions of previous theories, and, sometimes, outright rejection of once-dominant views. Yet the law demands certainty, or near certainty, and above all, finality. The court must decide which version of truth is correct in order to reach a judgment.

When those legal judgments rest on scientific or other expert opinions that shift over time, the legal system's fealty to finality becomes problematic. Professor Jennifer Laurin has explained the problem in this way:

> Of course, the potential for changed scientific understanding to undermine the factual basis for criminal convictions is endemic to the justice system's use of scientific evidence in adjudicating guilt. Law's quest for truth must end at some point; we call that point 'justice' and accept, to a degree, the socially constructed nature of its truth function. Science, by contrast, embraces contingent understanding, subject to testability and empirical support. Law cannot, of course, fully bend to science's pace and manner of truth production. But neither can it shut its eyes to scientific change without compromising the integrity of justice.[14]

WHEN THE SCIENCE PROVES THE WHOLE CASE — AND NEW SCIENCE CALLS IT INTO QUESTION

These tensions are evident in prosecutions that depend to any degree upon opinions matching crime scene evidence to evidence related to a particular suspect – that is, the individualization disciplines. Those disciplines include all of the familiar staples of criminal cases, such as fingerprints, firearms and toolmark comparisons (including "ballistics"), bitemarks, hair and fiber analysis, handwriting comparisons, and the like. Until recently, few in the criminal justice system paused to question or examine the reliability of such forensic evidence; the evidence was simply accepted as virtually infallible and precise, whose validity was established by decades of adversary testing through litigation.

But we now know – in no small part due to the game-changing analysis by the National Academy of Sciences (NAS) in 2009[15] – that these disciplines lack a solid scientific foundation, are often highly subjective, and sometimes simply wrong. Indeed, flawed forensic science evidence is the second-leading contributor to wrongful convictions among the DNA exonerations. Of the first 325 DNA exonerations, 154, or 47 percent, included misapplication of forensic science.[16] Only eyewitness misidentification contributed to more false convictions. A detailed analysis of the cases in which a forensics expert testified at trial and DNA later proved innocence found that 60 percent of the experts proffered scientifically inappropriate testimony.[17] In the much larger pool of exonerations counted by the National Registry of Exonerations, misapplied forensic evidence played a smaller but still significant role – flawed science contributed to 23 percent of the more-than 1,700 exonerations in that database.[18]

As problematic as flawed science can be when it is part of any prosecution, it poses the greatest threat to the innocent when the science is the whole case. That can happen when the prosecution uses science to establish not just circumstantial evidence of identity, but all of the legal elements of the offense. Two types of cases often fit that description: arson and SBS/AHT. These are cases in which the science has been used in some cases to establish every element of the charged offense (and they are both case types in which the science has been the subject of extensive and vigorous challenge and revision).

First, in both case types, the science has been used to prove causation. In arson, fire examiners have testified that the fire damage (and often the resulting deaths) stemmed from an intentionally set fire; the experts knew this, they would testify, because the fire "talks to you"[19] – the old arson science taught them that the fire left behind telltale signs of the use of an accelerant or multiple points of origin. In SBS/AHT, the medical experts often testify that the baby's brain injuries (and often death) had to have been the result of violent shaking of the child, or shaking followed by a violent impact; they know this because nothing else (short of a major automobile accident or a fall from a multi-story building) could have caused the pattern of brain and eye injuries found in the child.

Second, in both types of cases, the experts have claimed that the science proved the perpetrator's mental state, or *mens rea*. With arson, the very act of setting a fire with an accelerant inherently meant the perpetrator acted intentionally. In SBS/AHT cases, the medical experts have testified that the forces applied to cause such injuries had to have been so massive (again, likened to the forces from an automobile accident or a fall from a multi-story building), that they could not have been applied accidentally; they had to have been intentional, or at least reckless.

Finally, in both types of cases, the science often has been used to determine the identity of the perpetrator. In SBS/AHT cases, for example, the medical experts often testify that a child so severely brain injured would have been immediately comatose and unresponsive, so the last person with the child prior to collapse had to have been the one who shook or shook and slammed the child. Simply put, the claimed ability of the medical evidence to pinpoint the time of the injuries resolved any question about who did it. Because the medical opinions in SBS/AHT cases thus satisfied every legal element of the offense, Professor Deborah Tuerkheimer has aptly labeled them "medically diagnosed murder."[20]

These cases are deeply worrisome not just because the "science" can be used to satisfy the legal elements of the offenses, but because it is used to establish the most fundamental historical fact in the case: what happened, or put another way, what caused the given fire or the particular child's demise. While dependence on science always poses challenges for the law, "[t]he problems are most salient when scientists are called upon to offer opinions on causation."[21] Douglas Weed, an epidemiologist with the National Cancer Institute, explains why science-based causal claims are more tenuous than other types of either historical or opinion evidence:

> [T]he causal claim itself – that this type of virus caused that sort of cancer – does not have [the] sort of connection back to some unique event that can be documented, verified, and directly observed. The causal claim is a scientific hypothesis and we cannot ever know if it is true in the same sense as the existence of the virus, the cancer, and its author. The hypothesis can be well supported or not by the available evidence. It can be more or less certain, more or less proven, but it cannot ever be true. The reason is remarkably straightforward. Causation cannot be seen. Causation cannot be proven. And the evidence for causation always underdetermines our capacity to choose between the causal hypothesis of interest and its various alternatives.[22]

For this reason, courts in civil cases tend to be skeptical of causal claims made through expert opinions. In medical cases, physicians employ a process known as the differential diagnosis to arrive at a conclusion about medical conditions. The process involves creating a list of all possible conditions that might explain the patient's symptoms or medical findings, and then systematically testing for and eliminating them, until one diagnosis remains. Put another way, a "differential diagnosis" is "the determination of which one of two or more diseases or conditions a patient is suffering from"; it is determined by "systematically comparing and contrasting their clinical findings."[23] But that is different than the kind of causation claim that is made in the law. Causation claims in the law instead address a different question: given the medical findings or the disease or injury, what forces or conditions *external* to the body *caused* those findings or disease or injury?

In civil cases, courts have recognized that when the question is external causation, doctors are not really employing a differential *diagnosis*, but rather a differential *etiology*.[24] The distinction is significant. The differential diagnosis, as a rule, "does not provide an adequate basis for establishing external causation."[25] Rather, the differential diagnosis "focus[es] on diagnosing the disease, not on determining the etiology or cause of the disease."[26] "Differential etiology," by contrast, "describe[s] the investigation and reasoning that leads to the determination of external causation, sometimes more specifically described by the witness or court as a process of identifying external causes by a process of elimination."[27] Civil courts have recognized that "[t]he differential diagnosis method has an inherent reliability; the differential etiology method does not."[28]

To understand why, consider *Bowers* v. *Norfolk S. Corp.*[29] The case was a tort action by a railroad employee against his employer, seeking damages for injuries he claimed he sustained from the vibrations of the train on which he worked. The court held that the differential diagnosis could be relied upon to determine the nature of the plaintiff's medical condition. But determining that the locomotive's vibrations were the cause in fact of those injuries was another matter, beyond the scope of the differential diagnosis and the physician's expertise. The court noted that, when *diagnosing* a patient for *treatment* purposes, the doctor has special incentives that provide assurances of accuracy: misdiagnosis can lead to catastrophic failure, even death, for the patient if the doctor fails to prescribe the correct treatment. And that error can in turn lead to medical malpractice liability.[30] When a physician opines that a train worker's physical injuries were caused specifically by the train's vibrations, or that a child's brain injuries were caused by abuse, however, she is not *diagnosing* the patient for *treatment* purposes. In the SBS/AHT case, the diagnosis is brain injury, and it is that injury that is treated. There is no particular medical *treatment* for abuse. The treatment of a head injury does not change based on how it was sustained. Whether an injury was inflicted or sustained accidentally has no bearing on the way a patient is treated medically.

This reality has other implications that additionally undermine the reliability of the differential etiology. Experience can be a valuable part of any expert's expertise, if it is the sort of experience from which the expert can learn. The true differential diagnosis – diagnosing a patient's medical illness or condition for purposes of prescribing treatment – at least has the potential for enabling the doctor to learn from experience, and hence for improving reliability. If the doctor misdiagnoses an illness or condition, the treatment will likely fail, and the doctor will adjust the diagnosis and the treatment accordingly. But because there is no treatment for abuse, judgments about causation (etiology) do not offer similar opportunities for feedback and learning, and for ensuring experience-based reliability. Asking doctors to draw legal conclusions, like causation, imposes demands on science that it is ill-suited to meet.

Medical professionals have recognized this challenge even in the context of true diagnosis. Eta Berner and Mark Graber, for example, have observed that, where feedback is absent or minimal, overconfidence by the physician can be a significant source of diagnostic error: "[F]eedback that is delayed or absent may not be recognized for what it is, and the perception that 'misdiagnosis is not a big problem' remains unchallenged. That is, in the absence of information that the diagnosis is wrong, it is assumed to be correct ... "[31] And Gordon Schiff has explained how the absence of feedback can undermine reliability, even in the true diagnosis context:

> An open-loop system (also called a 'nonfeedback controlled' system) is one that makes decisions based solely on preprogrammed criteria and the preexisting model of the system. This approach does not use feedback to calibrate its output or determine if the desired goal is achieved. ... [Such a system] cannot engage in learning.[32]

Because opining about the etiology of a child's brain injuries – an opinion that entails legal conclusions about not only what some external actor did, but also what that person's mental state was (abuse typically requires intent or recklessness) – provides no feedback mechanism, the entire enterprise is rendered tenuous. Without the feedback required to "engage in learning," the expert's opinions based on clinical judgment can amount to little more than *ipse dixit*, which the Supreme Court has recognized as problematic under the Federal Rules of Evidence.[33]

As problematic as the causation determination can be in tort cases, that determination, employing a differential etiology methodology, is even more challenging in SBS/AHT cases. The reason is simple. In the typical tort case the question posed to the expert is whether a known historical fact connects causally to a known injury or outcome. But in SBS/AHT cases, the historical fact at issue – whether the accused violently shook or shook and slammed the child – is itself unproven and unknown.[34] In the SBS/AHT context, the expert is not asked to link an observed potential cause to an observed effect, but to relate cause to effect when *only* the effect has been observed; it asks the expert to divine not only the relationship between the precipitating event and the outcome, but to divine even the existence of the alleged precipitating event itself, which has not been observed or otherwise proven.

In the *Bowers* scenario, for example, the train engineer in fact suffered the injuries of which he complained, and he was in fact exposed to the vibrations that he claimed caused those injuries. Similarly, in a toxic tort case, typically there is no dispute that the plaintiff in fact contracted cancer, or was born with birth defects, and that the plaintiff was in fact exposed to the toxins or carcinogens. The question for the expert in either scenario is whether the known exposure *caused* the known outcome. Nonetheless, that is the type of causation claim that Weed observes is so difficult to make, because it "does not have [the] sort of connection back to some unique event that can be documented, verified, and directly observed."[35]

But in SBS/AHT cases (or arson cases), the expert's opinion is needed precisely because the act of shaking or abusing the child (or setting the fire) is otherwise unknown. The children in such cases cannot describe what happened, because they are either preverbal or deceased. And, strikingly, the alleged acts of causing brain injury (or death) by violently shaking a child have never been witnessed. The medical expert must not only infer that shaking *caused* the child's injuries, but that the shaking even occurred in the first instance. As a category of cases, therefore, SBS/AHT (and arson) cases present in stark form the tensions that lie at the interface between law and science.

THE SHIFTING SCIENCE OF SBS/AHT

As complicated as the expert's task is in straddling the science-law divide in SBS/AHT cases, it is made all the more challenging by inherent difficulties in conducting basic scientific research into SBS/AHT, and by shifts in our understandings about infant brain injury that have emerged in the last fifteen years.

The fundamental research challenge is that one cannot, of course, conduct randomized controlled studies by shaking or slamming infants and comparing them to a control group. As a result, most research involves retrospectively sorting brain-injured children into two categories: those believed to have suffered abuse, and those believed to have suffered accidents or natural diseases. The researchers then compare the two groups to try to identify whether certain findings reliably distinguish abuse from nonabuse, so that those findings can be utilized for "diagnosing" abuse.

For years, the result was that doctors believed they could reliably diagnose abuse (primarily shaking) when presented with what became known as the classic "triad" of findings: subdural hematoma (bleeding around the brain), retinal hemorrhages (bleeding at the back of the eyes), and encephalopathy, often marked by cerebral edema (brain swelling). The leading pediatric physicians in the late 1990s and into the early 2000s declared that that triad of findings was, alone, virtually unique to, or pathognomonic of, abuse by shaking.[36]

Eventually, however, physicians began to recognize that the scientific research simply could not support such claims.[37] Physicians began to recognize an inherent circularity problem that confounded any conclusions about the diagnostic significance of the medical findings. The circularity problem arose because, lacking access to ground truth about whether a particular child under study had been abused, researchers categorized the cases for research purposes based on the findings believed to indicate abuse (typically the triad or some variant). When they then compared the "abused" children to the nonabused children, unsurprisingly, they found that the triad was diagnostic of shaking. That is to say, the very findings being examined were the findings used as inclusion criteria in the research. For this reason, today, every serious researcher acknowledges that even the best of the research papers are plagued with circularity. As Shalea Piteau and her colleagues cautioned, in a widely cited meta-analysis of what they concluded were the very best of the research papers: "As there are no standardized criteria for the definition of abuse, most authors developed their own criteria and many of these are fraught with circular reasoning."[38] Likewise, Sabine Ann Maguire and her colleagues, in a similar meta-analysis that also sought to aggregate the findings from the very best of the research, warned that "[d]iagnostic studies in this field are open to criticism of circularity because of their dependence on a constellation of clinical features, as opposed to a single gold-standard diagnostic test, which does not exist."[39]

Researchers have attempted to overcome the circularity challenge by relying on criteria not strictly tied to the diagnostic features being examined, such as legal adjudications, and most prominently, confessions. But these attempts still cannot break free from circularity. The legal adjudications themselves are based upon medical opinions, which in turn are based on the very diagnostic findings being examined. And confessions, while appealing on their face, might also be the product of interrogations or questioning that utilizes the triad or other diagnostic findings as the basis for telling the suspect that the doctors know the child was abused, and so the suspect cannot deny it.[40] Indeed, Judge Richard Posner of the Seventh Circuit Court of Appeals recognized this problem in *Aleman* v. *Village of Hanover Park* when he observed that a parent confronted with supposed medical proof of shaking would have no basis for denying it. His conclusion: "A confession so induced is worthless as evidence."[41] In any event, none of the research papers that rely on confessions makes any attempt to assess the validity of the confessions, the nature of the confessions, or the interrogation tactics used to elicit them; the papers simply assume validity and assert that "[a]n analysis of the investigative techniques involved in eliciting the admissions is beyond the scope of this article."[42] No one has yet examined the interrogations and confessions to determine what weight they can really bear.

But what the research has established in the last fifteen years is that many of the propositions once relied upon by experts to diagnose SBS/AHT, and hence by the legal system to obtain convictions, have unraveled. No longer do knowledgeable physicians claim that the triad is pathognomonic of abuse (although less well-versed physicians continue to rely on their old medical school training to testify that it is).[43] The official position paper of the American Academy of Pediatrics (AAP), revised in 2009, backs off the certainty of the diagnosis that it had expressed in previous iterations; the 2009 paper now asserts that "the mechanisms and resultant injuries of accidental and abusive head injury overlap."[44] As Bob Sege, director of Family and Child Advocacy at Boston Medical Center and a member of the AAP Committee on Child Abuse and Neglect, told NPR in 2015, "The real straw man argument is the idea that diagnosing abusive head trauma relies solely on those three injuries."[45] Carole Jenny, a longtime child abuse pediatrician and SBS-hypothesis advocate and former Brown University Pediatrics professor, now teaches that "the triad is a myth."[46]

Relatedly, all knowledgeable physicians now admit that, contrary to prior beliefs, the findings previously associated exclusively with SBS/AHT can also be caused by a myriad of "mimics" of abuse, ranging from accidents to genetic disorders to a wide range of medical conditions and diseases. The "differential diagnosis" – if one accepts that term in this context – is now widely recognized to include accidental trauma (e.g., short falls), congenital malformations, metabolic disorders, hematological diseases, infectious diseases, autoimmune conditions, birth effects, rebleeds of chronic subdural hematomas, hypoxia (lack of oxygen), childhood stroke, genetic conditions, and much more.[47]

Consistently, biomechanical engineering research has even called into question whether shaking can generate sufficient accelerations to cause serious or fatal brain injuries, at least without causing massive structural damage to the neck and spine. The biomechanical research consistently shows that the most vigorous shaking by an adult generates accelerations far short of the estimated thresholds for brain injury, and that if sufficient accelerations could be achieved, they would inevitably break the neck (not a typical finding in these cases).[48] While proponents of the SBS/AHT hypothesis dismiss these studies, asserting that the modeling must be wrong (without specifying how), or that the true injury thresholds for infant brains are not known, they have not offered any better injury thresholds or any explanations as to how the estimated injury thresholds could be off by so much as to make shaking injury plausible. Moreover, they have not produced any biomechanical research showing that shaking alone *can* produce sufficient accelerations to cause serious brain injury and death.

In sum, the new research challenges the foundational assumption that physicians can reliably diagnose, based on medical findings, the cause or manner of death or serious injury in alleged abuse cases. The new science challenges the proposition that physician opinion testimony can reliably establish the first and most basic element of a criminal case – the historical question of what happened to cause the injuries.

Moreover, the biomechanical research challenges as well the proposition that the science can establish *mens rea* by determining that the forces applied had to have been so great as to have been intentional, or at least reckless. While the biomechanical research suggests that shaking alone probably cannot generate sufficient accelerations to cause serious brain injury and death, impacts – including impacts from accidents like falls from just a few feet onto a carpeted surface – can generate accelerations that meet and surpass estimated injury thresholds.[49] And numerous documented case reports in the literature confirm that accidental short falls have caused fatal brain injuries.[50] While short-fall deaths are rare, they do happen. The research now establishes that what once would have been viewed as relatively trivial trauma can, under the right circumstances, be fatal. No longer can one reliably opine that the forces applied had to be so massive as to evince intent or recklessness.

Likewise, no longer can physicians confidently time the injuries and thereby identify the perpetrator. Contrary to prior beliefs, research now confirms that seriously brain-injured children can and do sometimes experience significant lucid intervals – ranging from a few minutes to hours or even days.[51] During this period between injury and collapse the children typically are not entirely normal – they might be sleepy or clingy and fussy, they might vomit, or they might not sleep or eat normally – but they can be quite alert and responsive.[52] Thus, no longer can the science be relied upon to infer identity.

Professor Deborah Tuerkheimer, herself a former child abuse prosecutor, aptly sums up the new realities of SBS/AHT cases in this way:

> As compared to its predecessor, today's SBS reflects a much greater awareness of the limits of science. No longer can it identify a time frame (and thus, a perpetrator). No longer can it pinpoint a specific causal mechanism – violent shaking – that in the past established not only how a crime was committed, but that the person responsible possessed the requisite mental state. And no longer does it render the triad synonymous with a baby's abuse. Over time,

the meaning of the triad has become less sure as new explanations for it have emerged. No longer a determinate diagnosis, but one steeped in unknowns, modern SBS rests on unstable foundations. When it comes to proving guilt, the new diagnosis simply cannot do the work of the old SBS. Many convictions, however, rest on the old SBS.[53]

THE JUDICIAL RESPONSE TO THE SHIFTED SBS/AHT SCIENCE

Given these shifts, one might think that the legal system would be busy revisiting SBS/AHT convictions that are premised on the old, flawed science. And indeed, some courts are reopening old SBS cases. But the response has been slow and uneven, resulting in what Professor Tuerkheimer has called "fluky justice."[54] The emergent picture is one that again reflects the misfit between the fluidity of scientific knowledge and the static nature of legal judgments. It reflects what Professor Laurin has called a "'science lag': even as scientific understanding evolves, criminal justice outcomes whose epistemic bona fides depend on the reliability of that science remain rooted in discredited knowledge."[55] But it also offers the *potential* for a new systematic examination of a whole category of convictions and the discovery of a new wave of innocents.

The first case to engage this new science in this way involved a Wisconsin mother and in-home childcare provider, Audrey Edmunds.[56] The case was a classic triad-based SBS prosecution, in which physicians at trial opined that nothing short of an auto accident or a fall from a multi-story building could have caused the medical findings except violent shaking, perhaps accompanied by an impact; that the degree of force had to have been massive (showing at least recklessness); and that the child would have become immediately comatose (so the injuries had to have been inflicted when Ms. Edmunds was alone with the child).

At a lengthy post-conviction hearing, the parties presented ten prominent medical experts from both sides of the medical debates (including the original medical examiner in the case who switched his views based on the new science and opined that he could no longer be sure the case involved shaking, or that the injuries had to have been sustained shortly before the child collapsed). On review, the Wisconsin Court of Appeals vacated Edmunds's conviction. The court found that shifts in mainstream medical opinions about SBS constituted newly discovered evidence and required a new trial:

> Edmunds presented evidence that was not discovered until after her conviction, in the form of expert medical testimony, that a significant and legitimate debate in the medical community has developed in the past ten years over

whether infants can be fatally injured through shaking alone, whether an infant may suffer head trauma and yet experience a significant lucid interval prior to death, and whether other causes may mimic the symptoms tradition- ally viewed as indicating shaken baby or shaken impact syndrome.[57]

The court also held that "there has been a shift in mainstream medical opinion since the time of Edmunds's trial as to the cause of the types of injuries Natalie suffered."[58] Significantly, the court concluded that "it is the emergence of a legitimate and significant dispute within the medical community as to the cause of those injuries that constitutes newly discovered evidence."[59]

The *Edmunds* decision was momentous, and held the potential for opening the gate to revisiting countless old-science SBS convictions. It is a gate through which a few cases have passed, but it has not been a floodgate. More than two dozen SBS/AHT convictions have now been vacated, based either on newly discovered evidence (the new science) or ineffective assist- ance of counsel (due to counsel's failure to present the new science). But hundreds, if not thousands, of potentially innocent defendants remain con- victed, and prosecutors continue to obtain new convictions based on the old science, although acquittals also appear to be on the rise. A recent analysis by the *Washington Post* concluded that of approximately 1,800 SBS prosecu- tions initiated since 2001, 200 resulted in acquittal or dismissal.[60] But that, of course, means that 1,600 resulted in convictions. The "science lag" described by Professor Laurin has been a prominent feature of the SBS/ AHT landscape.

Nonetheless, these cases have the potential to be the next wave of inno- cents as the law begins to catch up to the science. Increasingly, courts that hear the experts from both sides of the debates are declaring that the old science is flawed and that the new science requires reconsideration of the cases. In December 2014, a judge in Rochester, New York, reversed an old conviction of another childcare provider, Rene Bailey, who had been con- victed on medical testimony asserting that the classic triad could mean only SBS. Bailey was convicted even though she explained that the deceased child – a two-and-a-half-year-old toddler – had jumped or fallen off of a chair and hit her head, and another toddler in her care repeatedly told others he witnessed the child's fall. After hearing extensive expert testimony at the post- conviction hearing, the court held: "The credible and persuasive evidence presented by the Defense established, by a preponderance of the evidence, a significant change in medical science relating to head injuries in children, generally, and the Shaken Baby Syndrome hypothesis, in particular."[61] More specifically, the court found that "[t]he credible evidence adduced at the hearing established ... the falsity of the existing perception at the time of

Trial, that short falls or low velocity impacts could not cause death."[62] In sum, the court concluded that

> the credible evidence adduced at the Hearing, which was supported by expert testimony from different disciplines and specialties – pediatrics, radiology, pathology, ophthalmology, and biomechanical engineering – established by a preponderance of the evidence that key medical propositions relied upon by the Prosecution at Trial were either demonstrably wrong, or are now subject to new debate.[63]

In 2014, the Supreme Court of Sweden similarly heard expert testimony from both sides and ruled that "[i]t can be concluded that, in general terms, the scientific evidence for the diagnosis of violent shaking has turned out to be uncertain."[64] Accordingly, the Court concluded, a triad-only case could not prove guilt beyond a reasonable doubt, and the Court acquitted the defendant.[65]

Also in 2014, in *Del Prete* v. *Thompson*,[66] a federal district court in Chicago ruled that the new science established that Jennifer Del Prete, who had been convicted of shaking to death a child in her care, had met the standards for proving innocence under the "actual innocence gateway" recognized in *Schlup* v. *Delo*,[67] enabling her to proceed in federal habeas corpus on otherwise procedurally defaulted claims. Judge Matthew Kennelly wrote: "The Court evaluates the new evidence together with the evidence presented at Del Prete's trial and the other evidence presented at the evidentiary hearing to determine whether any reasonable juror who heard all of it could find Del Prete guilty beyond a reasonable doubt. The answer to that question is a rather resounding no."[68] In a remarkable footnote, Judge Kennelly added that "recent developments in this area … arguably suggest[] that a claim of shaken baby syndrome is more an article of faith than a proposition of science."[69]

THE SHIFTING ARSON SCIENCE

An analogous story has developed in arson cases. For years, fire examiners "diagnosed" arson based on telltale signs in the aftermath of a fire: "crazed glass" (windows that cracked in a web-like pattern)[70] and "alligator char" (large, shiny blisters on wood) indicated use of an accelerant;[71] narrow V-shaped smoke patterns on walls indicated "rapid" fires;[72] burn patterns on the floors revealed "pour patterns," also indicating use of an accelerant, because fire burns up, not down, and so only an applied accelerant could burn the floor;[73] and the like.[74]

Like SBS/AHT, however, the dogmas of fire analysis did not fare well when critics began examining the underlying scientific base.[75] Unlike SBS/AHT, however, fire can be studied through controlled experiments. So when scientists began applying scientific methods by, among other things, setting and studying actual fires, they learned that much of the fire "science" that had sent untold numbers of people to prison was simply wrong.[76] Crazed glass is the product of spraying water onto hot glass (think of a fire hose), regardless of the origin of the fire.[77] Alligatoring likewise is not unique to accelerant-initiated fires.[78] The narrowness of V-patterns reveals little about the speed of a fire.[79] And so-called pour patterns are not necessarily the result of poured accelerants, but are typical whenever a closed-room fire becomes so overheated that the entire room reaches "flashover" – when everything combusts, including the floors.[80]

Arson cases share another feature with SBS/AHT cases: the basic methodology has been to start with a conclusion (criminal activity) and reason backwards from that conclusion to see if an innocent cause can provide an adequate alternative explanation. If not, the conclusion of criminality became the "diagnosis." This process – of elimination, or *negative corpus* – has received considerable criticism, because it is nearly impossible to eliminate all accidental or natural causes in a systematic way.[81]

Courts have since revisited a number of arson cases, but as with SBS/AHT, the judicial response has been erratic. The most noted example of the inadequacy of the judicial response is Cameron Todd Willingham, who was convicted in 1992 in Texas of setting fire to his home and killing his three children. The prosecution relied extensively on the arson dogmas of the day, including burn patterns on the floor, broken glass patterns, and melted aluminum believed to be caused by abnormally high temperatures associated with use of an accelerant.[82] In total, fire examiners "identified over twenty indicators of arson that have, since the trial, been highly disputed and subsequently found as not necessarily indicative of arson."[83] One month after Willingham was convicted and sentenced to death, the National Fire Protection Association (NFPA) published new guidelines that undermined or questioned the arson indicators relied upon to secure the conviction.[84] Nonetheless, the Texas and federal courts denied multiple appeals, Governor Rick Perry refused to stay the execution, and the Texas Board of Pardons and Paroles denied clemency. Willingham was executed on February 17, 2004.[85]

Others fared much better. At the same time that the courts were denying Willingham relief based on the new science, sending him to his death, elsewhere in Texas the courts granted relief to Ernest Ray Willis, whose case was "freakishly similar to Willingham's."[86] With the benefit of vigorous post-conviction counsel and a prosecutor willing to consider the new science,

Willis was exonerated and freed on October 5, 2004, eight months after Willingham was executed.

And Willis does not stand alone.[87] As of December 2015, the National Registry of Exonerations lists 35 exonerations in arson cases.[88] Yet hundreds of potentially innocent people, if not more, remain imprisoned in cases that rest upon the old, discredited, arson "science."[89]

SCIENCE-DEPENDENT CASES AND THE FIT WITHIN THE INNOCENCE PARADIGM

Given these numbers and the evolution of the relevant sciences, science-dependent cases such as SBS/AHT and arson convictions promise to be the next wave in the Innocence Movement, even if in most instances they will lack the clarity, simplicity, and certainty of the DNA exonerations. Despite their inherent ambiguity, they represent the future of innocence cases for several reasons.

First, they share an important feature of the DNA cases simply because they are science-based. Therefore, they do not depend on the vagaries of memory or the credibility of dubious witnesses; they instead promise the allure of science. Again, Professor Laurin offers insights on the significance of the science in the new science cases:

> Of course, few scientific changes approximate DNA in terms of the potential for certainty that it provides in criminal cases. Frequently, scientific consensus gives way to controversy rather than new agreement. Nevertheless, there is good reason to open criminal judgments to revision in light of changed scientific understanding without categorical distinction (as the law currently features) between DNA and all other forms of evidence.[90]

And, indeed, legislatures are beginning to notice the parallel, and create procedural and substantive remedies for shifted science cases. Most notably, Texas has now created a statute authorizing habeas relief to prisoners who present new scientific evidence that either "(1) was not available" at the time of trial, or "(2) contradicts scientific evidence relied on by the state at trial."[91]

Second, in part because we seem to be fascinated as a culture with science and scientific evidence, the basis for these innocence claims appears to be translating into compelling narratives, just as the DNA cases have done. Numerous media accounts have now highlighted the scientific nature of the stories and the human aspects of the cases, in both the SBS/AHT and arson cases.[92] Simply put, the narratives of loving parents and caregivers, wrongly convicted by flawed medical or arson science, then exonerated by new science, create powerful stories of innocence that can sustain the movement.

Third, because the cases are science-based, they do not conflict in some ways with the traditional rationales for finality in the law – rationales that make it so difficult to obtain post-conviction relief in many other cases. One of the key justifications for the primacy of finality in criminal cases is that the reliability of the truth-seeking functions is not usually enhanced by the passage of time. Retrial years or decades later can be difficult, as memories fade, witnesses disappear or die, and documents and other physical evidence are lost. But with science-based claims these risks are muted or sometimes nonexistent. When science is the core of a case, the passage of time can indeed enhance truth-seeking, as the passage of time allows fact finders to rely upon new and better scientific knowledge developed in the intervening years. Convictions based upon medical or arson science do not suffer much from faded memories; to the contrary, they can rely on improved science to make better-informed judgments. As Professor Laurin has put it, "[C]hanged understanding within a scientific community is a category of information uniquely outside the control of a defendant, and the passage of time is itself an aspect of the new information's reliability."[93]

Even cases in which the science played a more peripheral role can warrant reversal when the science shifts – as in the microscopic hair comparison and Comparative Bullet Lead Analysis cases. While the scientific evidence in those cases may not have been as central to the conviction as in the SBS/AHT and arson cases, there is good reason to believe that often such evidence, dressed up at trial as scientific proof of identity, was likely important. For "even in cases where scientific evidence might appear on first glance to be cumulative, there is often good reason to think that the original scientific evidence was consequential. Commentators have long posited, and social science research now supports, that jurors attach special weight to the testimony of scientific experts."[94] For that reason, new scientific evidence showing that the crime scene hairs or bullets cannot be linked to the defendant is also likely to be viewed by jurors as especially significant.

Professor Laurin's insightful analysis of shifted science thus perhaps sums it up best:

> To the extent that jurors and other legal actors attach special weight to scientific expertise in part because of the epistemic process to which it lays claim – in particular, the process of continuous experimentation and hypothesis testing – it is only right for law to attempt to take that process on board rather than excluding it in the name of finality.[95]

That, indeed, is a prescription for the future of the Innocence Movement.

NOTES

1 Herrera v. Collins, 506 U.S. 390, 420 (1993) (O'Connor, J., concurring).

2 National Registry of Exonerations, *Exonerations by Year: DNA and Non-DNA*, available at www.law.umich.edu/special/exoneration/Pages/Exoneration-by-Year.aspx.

3 Innocence Project, *Homepage*, available at www.innocenceproject.org.

4 National Registry of Exonerations, *supra* note 2.

5 Keith A. Findley, *Innocence Found: The New Revolution in American Criminal Justice*, in CONTROVERSIES IN INNOCENCE CASES IN AMERICA (Sarah Lucy Cooper, ed., 2014)

6 National Registry of Exonerations, *Exonerations by Year*, *supra* note 2.

7 National Registry of Exonerations, *The First 1,600 Exonerations*, available at www.law.umich.edu/special/exoneration/Documents/1600_Exonerations.pdf.

8 Keith A. Findley, *Defining Innocence*, 74 ALB. L. REV. 1157, 1160–61 (2010–11).

9 *See* Caitlin Plummer & Imran Syed, *"Shifted Science" and Post-Conviction Relief*, 8 STAN. J. CIV. RTS. & CIV. LIB. 259 (2012) (describing the typical standards for post-conviction relief based on new evidence of innocence).

10 *See* Findley, *supra* note 8.

11 Plummer & Syed, *supra* note 9.

12 *See generally* Deborah Tuerkheimer, *Science-Dependent Prosecution and the Problem of Epistemic Contingency: A Study of Shaken Baby Syndrome*, 62 ALA. L. REV. 513, 559 (2011).

13 Norah Rudin, *Forensic DNA Statistics: DON'T PANIC!*, National Association of Criminal Defense Lawyers 8th Annual Forensic Science & the Law Conference, Making Sense of Science VIII, Apr. 18, 2015, Las Vegas, NV.

14 Jennifer E. Laurin, *Criminal Law's Science Lag: How Criminal Justice Meets Changed Scientific Understanding*, 93 TEX. L. REV. 1751, 1753 (2015) (footnotes omitted).

15 NATIONAL ACADEMY OF SCIENCES, COMMITTEE ON IDENTIFYING THE NEEDS OF THE FORENSIC SCIENCES COMMUNITY; COMMITTEE ON SCIENCE, TECHNOLOGY, AND LAW; COMMITTEE ON APPLIED AND THEORETICAL STATISTICS; POLICY AND GLOBAL AFFAIRS; DIVISION ON ENGINEERING AND PHYSICAL SCIENCES; NATIONAL RESEARCH COUNCIL, STRENGTHENING FORENSIC SCIENCE IN THE UNITED STATES: A PATH FORWARD (2009).

16 Innocence Project, *The Causes of Wrongful Conviction*, available at www.innocenceproject.org/causes-wrongful-conviction.

17 Brandon L. Garrett & Peter J. Neufeld, *Invalid Forensic Science Testimony and Wrongful Convictions*, 95 VA. L. REV. 1, 2 (2009).

18 National Registry of Exonerations, *% Exonerations by Contributing Factor*, available at www.law.umich.edu/special/exoneration/Pages/ExonerationsContribFactorsByCrime.aspx#.

19 David Grann, *Trial By Fire: Did Texas Execute an Innocent Man?*, NEW YORKER, Sept. 7, 2009, available at www.newyorker.com/magazine/2009/09/07/trial-by-fire.

20 Tuerkheimer, *supra* note 12, at 552.

21 Margaret A. Berger & Lawrence M. Solan, *The Uneasy Relationship between Science and Law: An Essay and Introduction*, 73 BROOK. L. REV. 847, 849 (2008).

22 Douglas L. Weed, *Truth, Epidemiology, and General Causation*, 73 BROOK. L. REV. 943, 949 (2008).

23 DORLAND'S ILLUSTRATED MEDICAL DICTIONARY 490 (29th ed. 2000).

24 *See, e.g.*, Bowers v. Norfolk S. Corp., 537 F. Supp.2d 1343 (M.D. Ga. 2007), *aff'd*, 300 F. App'x 700 (11th Cir. 2008); DEBORAH TUERKHEIMER, FLAWED CONVICTIONS: "SHAKEN BABY SYNDROME" AND THE INERTIA OF INJUSTICE 75 (2014).

25 TUERKHEIMER, *supra* note 24, at 76.

26 *Id.*

27 McClain v. Metabolife Intern, Inc., 401 F.3d 1233, 1252 (11th Cir. 2005) (citing Mary Sue Henifin et al., *Reference Guide on Medical Testimony*, in REFERENCE MANUAL ON SCIENTIFIC EVIDENCE 439, 481 [Federal Judicial Center, 2d ed. 2000]).

28 Bowers, 537 F. Supp.2d at 1361.

29 *Id.*

30 *Id.*

31 Eta S. Berner & Mark L. Graber, *Overconfidence as a Cause of Diagnostic Error in Medicine*, 121 AM. J. MED. (5 Suppl.) S2 (2008).

32 Gordon D. Schiff, *Minimizing Diagnostic Error: The importance of Follow-Up and Feedback*, 121 AM. J. MED. S38 (2008).

33 *See* General Electric Company v. Joiner, 522 U.S. 136, 146 (1997) ("But nothing in either *Daubert* or the Federal Rules of Evidence requires a district court to admit opinion evidence that is connected to existing data only by the *ipse dixit* of the expert.").

34 I am indebted to my colleague, Kate Judson, for this insight.

35 Weed, *supra* note 22, at 949.

36 *See, e.g.*, David L. Chadwick et al., *Shaken Baby Syndrome: A Forensic Pediatric Response*, 101 PEDIATRICS 321 (1998); Alice W. Newton & Andrea M. Vandeven, *Update on Child Maltreatment with a Special Focus on Shaken Baby Syndrome*, 17 CURRENT OPINION IN PEDIATRICS 246–51 (2005); P.G. Richards et al., *Shaken Baby Syndrome*, 91 ARCH. DIS. CHILD 205–06 (2006).

37 *See generally*, Keith A. Findley, Patrick D. Barnes, David A. Moran & Waney Squier, *Shaken Baby Syndrome, Abusive Head Trauma, and Actual Innocence: Getting It Right*, 12 HOUS. J. HEALTH L. & POL'Y 209, 216 (2012).

38 Shalea J. Piteau et al., *Clinical and Radiographic Characteristics Associated with Abusive and Nonabusive Head Trauma: A Systematic Review*, 130 PEDIATRICS 315 (2012).

39 Sabine A. Maguire et al., *Estimating the Probability of Abusive Head Trauma: A Pooled Analysis*, 128 PEDIATRICS 550 (2011).

40 *See* TUERKHEIMER, *supra* note 24, at 97–126.

41 Aleman v. Village of Hanover Park, 662 F.3d 897, 907 (7th Cir. 2011).

42 Suzanne P. Starling et al., *Analysis of Perpetrator Admissions to Inflicted Traumatic Brain Injury in Children*, 158 ARCH. PEDIATR. ADOLESC. MED. 454, 457 (2004)

43 *See* TUERKHEIMER, *supra* note 24, at 10–11 ("As a categorical matter, the science of SBS can no longer support a finding of proof beyond a reasonable doubt in triad-only cases"); GOUDGE, INQUIRY INTO PEDIATRIC FORENSIC PATHOLOGY IN ONTARIO — REPORT, 528 (2008) ("[T]he predominant view is no longer that the triad on its own is diagnostic of SBS."); Crown Prosecution Service, *Non-Accidental Head Injury Cases (NAHI, formerly referred to as Shaken Baby Syndrome) — Prosecution Approach* (Mar. 24, 2011) (noting that "it is unlikely that a charge for a homicide ... could be justified where the only evidence available is the triad of pathological features").

44 Cindy W. Christian et al., *Abusive Head Trauma in Infants and Children*, 123 PEDIATRICS 1409, 1410 (2009).

45 Tara Haelle, *Doctors Devise a Better Way to Diagnose Shaken Baby Syndrome*, NATIONAL PUBLIC RADIO, July 29, 2015, available at www.npr.org/sections/health-shots/2015/07/29/427449852/doctors-devise-a-better-way-to-diagnose-shaken-baby-syndrome.

46 Carole Jenny, *Presentation on The Mechanics: Distinguishing AHT/SBS from Accidents and Other Medical Conditions*, slide 33, 2011 New York City Abusive Head Trauma/Shaken Baby Syndrome Training Conference, Sept. 23, 2011 (PowerPoint available at www.queensda.org/SBS_Conference/SBC2011.html).

47 Patrick D. Barnes & Michael Krasnokutsky, *Imaging of the Central Nervous System in Suspected or Alleged Nonaccidental Injury, Including the Mimics*, 18 TOP. MAGN. RESON. IMAGING 53, 65–70 (2007); Andrew P. Sirotnak, *Medical Disorders that Mimic Abusive Head Trauma*, in ABUSIVE HEAD TRAUMA IN INFANTS AND CHILDREN: A MEDICAL, LEGAL, AND FORENSIC REFERENCE 191 (Lori Frasier et al., eds., 2006).

48 A.C. Duhaime et al., *The Shaken Baby Syndrome: A Clinical, Pathological and Biomechanical Study*, 66 J. NEUROSURG. 409 (1987); A. Ommaya et al., *Biomechanics and Neuropathology of Adult and Pediatric Head Injury*, 16 BRIT. J. NEUROSURG. 220 (2002); M.T. Prange et al., *Anthropomorphic Simulation of Falls, Shakes and Inflicted Impacts in Infants*, 99 J. OF NEUROSURG. 143 (2003); M.T. Prange et al., *Mechanical Properties and Anthropometry of the Human Infant Head*, 48 STAPP CAR CRASH JOURNAL 279 (2004); N.G. Ibrahim et al., *The Response of Toddler and Infant Heads during Vigorous Shaking*, 22 J. NEUROTRAUMA 1207 (2005).

49 *See supra* note 48 and accompanying text. *See also* N. Ibrahim & S. Margulies, *Biomechanics of Toddler Head during Low-Height Falls: An Anthropomorphic Dummy Analysis*, 6 J. NEUROSURG. & PEDIATR. 57 (2010); M.T. Prange & B.S. Myers, *Pathobiology and Biomechanics of Inflicted Childhood Trauma-Response*, in INFLICTED CHILDHOOD NEUROTRAUMA: AMERICAN ACADEMY OF PEDIATRICS 237 (R.M. Reece & C.E. Nicholson, eds., 2003).

50 John J. Plunkett, *Fatal Pediatric Head Injuries Caused by Short-Distance Falls*, 22 AM. J. OF FORENSIC MED. & PATHOL. 1 (2001); P. Steinbok et al., *Early*

Hypodensity on Computed Tomographic Scan of the Brain in an Accidental Pediatric Head Injury, 60 NEUROSURG. 689 (2007). *See also* Patrick D. Barnes et al., *Traumatic Spinal Cord Injury, Accidental Versus Non-Accidental Injury*, 15 SEMINARS IN PEDIATRIC NEUROLOGY 178 (2008); P.E. Lantz, & D.E. Couture, *Fatal Acute Intracranial Injury, Subdural Hematoma and Retinal Hemorrhages Caused by Stairway Falls*, 56 J. FORENS. SCI. 1648 (2011); Chris Van Ee et al., *Child ATD Reconstruction of a Fatal Pediatric Fall*, ASME INTERNATIONAL MECHANICAL ENGINEERING CONGRESS & EXPOSITION, November 2009.

51 *See* M.G.F. Gilliland, *Interval Duration Between Injury and Severe Symptoms in Nonaccidental Head Trauma in Infants and Young Children*, 43 J. FORENSIC SCI. 723 (1998); Plunkett, *supra* note 50; Kristy Arbogast et al., *Initial Neurologic Presentation in Young Children Sustaining Inflicted and Unintentional Fatal Head Injuries*, 116 PEDIATRICS 180, 181 (2005).

52 *Id.*

53 TUERKHEIMER, *supra* note 24, at 27.

54 Tuerkheimer, *supra* note 12, at 523.

55 Laurin, *supra* note 14, at 1754.

56 Disclosure: I was counsel for Ms. Edmunds in the post-conviction proceedings that led to vacating her conviction.

57 State v. Edmunds, 746 N.W.2d 590, ¶ 15 (Wis. App. 2008).

58 *Id.* at ¶ 23.

59 *Id.*

60 Debbie Cenziper, *Prosecutors Build Murder Cases on Disputed Shaken Baby Syndrome Diagnosis*, WASH. POST, Mar. 20, 2015, available at www.washingtonpost.com/graphics/investigations/shaken-baby-syndrome/.

61 People v. Rene Bailey, 47 Misc.3d 355, 370 (N.Y. Co. Ct. 2014). Disclosure: I was part of the legal team that represented Rene Bailey.

62 *Id.* at 364.

63 *Id.* at 372.

64 M.M. v. Prosecutor-General, Supreme Court of Sweden, Oct. 2014.

65 *Id.*

66 Del Prete v. Thompson, 10 F. Supp.3d 907 (N.D. Ill., Eastern Div. 2014)

67 513 U.S. 298 (1995).

68 Del Prete, 10 F. Supp.3d at 955.

69 *Id.*

70 NATIONAL FIRE PROTECTION ASSOCIATION, NFPA 921 GUIDE FOR FIRE AND EXPLOSION INVESTIGATIONS § 6.13.1.4 (2004) (hereinafter NFPA 921).

71 *Id.* at § 6.5.5.

72 *See* JOHN J. LENTINI, SCIENTIFIC PROTOCOLS FOR FIRE INVESTIGATION (2d ed. 2006).

73 Marc Price Wolf, *Habeas Relief From Bad Science: Does Federal Habeas Corpus Provide Relief for Prisoners Possibly Convicted on Misunderstood Fire Science?* 10 MINN. J.L. SCI. & TECH. 213, 224 (2009).

74 *See id.* at 16–17.

75 *See generally* LENTINI, *supra* note 72.

76 *See* Rachel Dioso-Villa, *Scientific and Legal Developments in Fire and Arson Investigation Expertise in* Texas v. Willingham, 14 MINN. J.L. SCI. & TECH. 817, 823 (2013).

77 NFPA 921, *supra* note 70, at § 6.13.1.4.

78 *Id.* at § 6.5.5.

79 LENTINI, *supra* note 72.

80 NFPA 921, *supra* note 70, at §§ 6.16.2.4.4, 6.17.8.2, & 6.17.8.2.5.

81 Diosa-Villa, *supra* note 76, at 843; JOHN D. DEHAAN & DAVID J. ICOVE, KIRK'S FIRE INVESTIGATION 322 (Pearson, 7th ed. 2012).

82 Dioso-Villa, *supra* note 76, at 829.

83 *Id.* at 830.

84 *Id.* at 838.

85 *Id.* at 840. *See also* Steve Mills & Maurice Possley, *Texas Man Executed on Disproved Forensics: Fire That Killed His 3 Children Could Have Been Accidental,* CHI. TRIB., Dec. 9, 2004, §1, at 1.

86 Grann, *supra* note 19.

87 *See, e.g.,* Han Tak Lee v. Houtzdale Sci, 798 F.3d 159 (3rd Cir. 2015); Souliotes v. Grounds, No. 1:06–cv–00667 2013 WL 875952 (E.D. Cal. Mar. 7, 2013).

88 National Registry of Exonerations, available at www.law.umich.edu/special/exoner ation/Pages/detaillist.aspx?View={FAF6EDDB-5A68-4F8F-8A52-2C61F5BF9EA7} &FilterField1=Group&FilterValue1=A.

89 Wolf, *supra* note 73, at 228.

90 Laurin, *supra* note 14, at 1757 (footnotes omitted).

91 TEX. CODE CRIM. PROC. ART. 11.073 (West Supp. 2013).

92 *See, e.g.,* Emily Bazelon, *Shaken-Baby Syndrome Faces New Questions in Court,* N.Y. TIMES MAGAZINE, Feb. 2, 2011, available at www.nytimes.com/2011/02/06/ magazine/06baby-t.html?_r=0; Debbie Cenziper, *Shaken Science: A Disputed Diagnosis Imprisons Parents,* WASH. POST, available at www.washingtonpost .com/graphics/investigations/shaken-baby-syndrome/; NPR & ProPublica, *The Child Cases: Guilty Until Proven Innocent,* Jan. 26, 2012, available at www.npr .org/2011/06/28/137454415/the-child-cases-guilty-until-proven-innocent; Grann, *supra* note 19; Mills & Possley, *supra* note 85.

93 Laurin, *supra* note 14, at 1758.

94 *Id.*

95 *Id.* at 1759.

11

Prosecutors

The Thin Last Line Protecting the Innocents

GEORGE C. THOMAS III

INTRODUCTION

Read any book or article on wrongful convictions, including research from the past quarter century of DNA exonerations, and you will reach two staggering conclusions: First, there are probably thousands of innocent felony defendants convicted each year, perhaps tens of thousands; and, second, American prosecutors sometimes fail to provide an effective last line of defense to prevent innocent defendants from standing trial. Juries are not very good at discerning innocence, either, but that is not my focus in this chapter. The threat to innocent defendants usually starts with a flawed police investigation that focuses on the wrong suspect and then builds a case based on "evidence" that confirms the preconceived notion of who is the guilty party. Bad as that is, what is worse is that some prosecutors view winning cases as more important than unmasking these fundamental police errors.

Nowhere is this phenomenon more visible than in the breach of the duty to turn over evidence that might be exculpatory, a duty first recognized in *Brady v. Maryland*.[1] We do not know how often prosecutors ignore *Brady*, but we do know that in a recent three and one-half year period, roughly 7,000 state and federal cases in the Westlaw database litigated *Brady* issues. And these cases arise only when the defendant somehow learns of the existence of the nondisclosed evidence. We have no way to know how many thousands or tens of thousands of cases every year involve prosecutors who failed to disclose possibly exculpatory evidence that the defendant never uncovers. We do know, thanks to the National Registry of Exonerations, that failure to

---

I draw my title from James Jones, *The Thin Red Line*, set on Guadalcanal in World War II.
I engage in poetic license because the jury is the thin last line, but prosecutors are the last line of government actors. To add that to the title would have made it ungainly, however.

turn over exculpatory evidence occurs in a significant percentage of the wrongful convictions that have been uncovered. The Registry has catalogued more than 1,700 documented DNA and non-DNA exonerations since 1989.[2] I took a random sample of cases from the Registry, and 13 percent of the sample involved *Brady* violations.

Prosecutorial misconduct in my study goes beyond discovery violations. In one case, the prosecutor lied to the judge in a futile attempt to cover up his violation of the court's order not to unfairly influence witnesses before they testified. The court found that the "prosecutor engaged in a pattern of pervasive misconduct throughout the proceedings [and] ... intentionally acted to prejudice the defendant to the point of the denial of a fair trial."[3] The Pennsylvania court dismissed the charges with prejudice.[4]

Prosecutors are, in theory, the last (thin) line preventing prosecution of innocent defendants because, unlike defense counsel, the prosecutor has a duty to seek justice. One hundred years ago, the Supreme Court recognized this unique role for prosecutors:

> The United States Attorney is the representative not of an ordinary party to a controversy, but of a sovereignty whose obligation to govern impartially is as compelling as its obligation to govern at all; and whose interest, therefore, in a criminal prosecution is not that it shall win a case, but that justice shall be done. As such, he is in a peculiar and very definite sense the servant of the law, the twofold aim of which is that guilt shall not escape or innocence suffer. He may prosecute with earnestness and vigor – indeed, he should do so. But, while he may strike hard blows, he is not at liberty to strike foul ones. It is as much his duty to refrain from improper methods calculated to produce a wrongful conviction as it is to use every legitimate means to bring about a just one.[5]

While the Court's formulation of the prosecutor's duty to avoid wrongful convictions has been quoted roughly 700 times in case law,[6] anecdotal evidence abounds that the "minister of justice" standard has not had the effect the Court intended. In theory, the prosecutor should be happy to discover that the case against a defendant has fallen apart and that he is likely innocent. It is, in theory, better to dismiss charges against a likely innocent defendant than send him to prison. In theory, prosecutors should be eager to turn over any evidence that is even slightly exculpatory because that serves justice. In theory, prosecutors should dismiss weak cases rather than offer plea bargains that are so good an innocent defendant might accept the deal.

But those of us who know how the American system works know that what I just described is not how the real world sometimes operates. Prosecutors, like all human actors, are susceptible to the tunnel vision problem that can lead to the belief that the case is weak because the police didn't do a very good job or the defendant, guilty as sin, just got lucky. While working on this project, I saw an old episode of *Law & Order*. Near the end, McCoy tells the district attorney of a development that strengthened the prosecution, and the DA waves off the news, saying: "Just tell me when we can put this in the win column." I think that tells us much about incentives in prosecutor offices. Indeed, several cases in my sample of exonerations from the Registry involve defendants who almost certainly knew they were innocent but took plea bargains to probation or a few days in jail. I will discuss later the likely reasons for this superficially bizarre behavior.

I should be clear that I am not impugning the integrity of prosecutors. Sure, there are unethical prosecutors, just like there are unethical defense lawyers, judges, and law professors. But the prosecutor who lied to the judge is surely the outlier; indeed, he was fired and eventually disbarred in August 2015.[7] But the problem is not the prosecutor who flouts the rules. It's the prosecutor who seeks to follow the rules but is handicapped by three structural problems. First, the United States has an exceedingly odd system of selecting our "ministers of justice" if we truly expect them to discharge the duty to seek justice. Second, mostly as a function of the selection process, we have built in a series of incentives that are perverse when defendants are innocent (and a surprising number are innocent). Third, we have long exalted "science" that is little more than guesswork. Even fingerprints are not the bulletproof evidence that we have been taught.[8]

Luckily, the "junk" science problem is finally being recognized. As distilled by the *Washington Post*, a 2009 report from the National Research Council of the National Academies

> was highly critical of a wide range of forensic specialties, from fingerprints to hair and fiber analysis to blood spatter analysis. It found that many of the claims forensic analysts have been making in courtrooms for decades lacked any scientific foundation to back them up. Yet judges and juries have taken and continue to take those claims as foolproof science, often because the experts themselves frame them that way.
>
> The report was particularly critical of an area of forensics loosely known as pattern matching. That area encompasses a group of largely subjective specialties in which an analyst looks at two pieces of evidence, such [as] carpet fibers, hair fibers or marks made by tools, and simply declares based on his or her experience and expertise whether the two are a match.[9]

According to the National Research Council of the National Academies, prosecutors have for many years been convicting defendants based on faulty forensic science analyses that have never been subject to rigorous testing.[10]

Unsurprisingly, the American Board of Forensic Odontology rejected this finding and has tried to discredit individual researchers who have rejected bite mark evidence.[11] Prosecutors continue to seek to introduce this dubious science, and at least a few courts continue to allow the jury to hear the testimony.[12] It is a bit of a mystery how bite mark "science" continues to be accepted in the face of the National Research Council conclusion that there are "substantial rates of erroneous results" in the discipline[13] and that the bite mark testimony is "introduced in criminal trials without any meaningful scientific validation, determination of error rates, or reliability testing to explain the limits of the discipline."[14]

A 2015 *Washington Post* series discussed the "science" of bite mark identifications that contributed to the conviction of at least seventeen defendants who were subsequently proven innocent. One case involved Gerard Richardson, convicted of the 1995 murder of a young woman in New Jersey on the basis of an expert who testified that the bite mark on the victim was left by Richardson.[15] No other physical evidence found at the scene (blood, hair, fibers) matched Richardson. And the defense produced an expert witness who said that there was "no way" the bite mark was left by Richardson. Yet the jury convicted. Richardson was released from prison in 2013 when DNA technology had evolved to the point that it could test the small sample of saliva left on the victim. It did not come from Richardson. He had served eighteen years based on phony science. No one knows how many tens of thousands of inmates sit in prison today because of a hair, fiber, toolmark, or bite mark match that falsely implicated the inmate.

A major beachhead in the battle against junk science was David Harris's 2012 book, *Failed Evidence: Why Law Enforcement Resists Science*. Harris collects a mountain of research that calls into question the accuracy of most forensic science.[16] The one gold standard of forensics is, of course, DNA evidence. But some prosecutors are slow to accept even DNA when the risk is losing high-profile cases. DNA evidence in 2008 excluded a man convicted in the rape and battery of a 68-year-old woman, but the prosecutor, Michael Mermel, "suggested the victim had consensual sex with someone else" before she was raped.

> When DNA evidence excluded a man in the rape and murder of an 11-year-old girl, Mermel and another prosecutor suggested that the girl may have been sexually active. The DNA, he said, was a 'red herring.'
>
> And ... when lawyers for the man charged in the killing of his 8-year-old daughter and her 9-year-old friend said in court that DNA evidence from semen excluded him as the perpetrator, the Lake prosecutor had another explanation.

Mermel said DNA may have gotten inside the 8-year-old's body as she played in the woods at what became the crime scene – a place where Mermel said some couples go to have sex. The girl was found fully clothed.[17]

Two years later, Mermel said, "The taxpayers don't pay us for intellectual curiosity. They pay us to get convictions." In 2011, in large part because of these comments, Mermel entered early retirement. The Lake County DA said all the right things in rejecting Mermel's comments: "The sole duty of my office is to seek justice."[18] Yet one wonders if Mermel's views are not widely held if not widely spoken.

Equally troubling, prosecutors often rely heavily, and sometimes exclusively, on eyewitness identifications, which the DNA revolution has shown to be inherently unreliable. There are two problems. First, we now know that memory is not a passive videotape of what happened but, rather, an active recreation in our minds, with gaps filled in as necessary to permit us to see a seamless whole.[19] Second, humans are just not very good at identifying other humans. Dan Simon's book, *In Doubt*, presents many studies that bring home this point. For example, forty-seven bank tellers had to deal with a contentious "customer" who became angry when the teller would not do what he wanted and stormed out of the bank.[20] Later that day, a "police officer" asked the teller if she could pick the suspect from a six-photo array. Only 55 percent picked the actual suspect from the array. "Notably, even when the array did not contain the suspect's photograph, 37 percent of the tellers picked someone. Naturally, those identifications were all wrong."[21]

From here, my chapter seeks to accomplish two quite different goals. First, to bring a bit more rigor to the anecdotal reports of prosecutorial excesses, I drew a random sample of 100 cases from the Registry database and analyzed them for prosecutorial errors that helped lead to a wrongful conviction. I will describe my findings in Part I. In Part II, I offer two sets of ideas about helping prosecutors avoid harm to innocent defendants. The first set is pragmatic and easily achievable. The second set is radical and unlikely ever to pass a legislature. But part of the fun is throwing ideas against a wall to see what sticks.

1 *The National Registry Sample*

I begin by pointing out the methodological limitations of my study. First, obviously, the errors unmasked in wrongful conviction cases are not indicative of cases in which guilty defendants are convicted, and these are surely the vast, vast majority of cases. Second, as my friend Richard Leo pointed out, the convictions in any wrongful conviction database cannot even be understood to represent the universe of wrongful conviction cases. These cases are the ones we have uncovered after someone took the effort to mount a challenge. Thus, they probably overweight the easily provable errors like *Brady* claims and underweight errors like shoddy police investigation, thus showing an overrepresentation of prosecutor errors in the database.

I tried to categorize the summaries into three groups: 1) prosecutorial conduct that is dishonest or unethical (with lying to the judge and failing to turn over exculpatory evidence as prime examples); 2) cases that are so weak that a justice-committed prosecutor would not have brought them; and 3) cases without any obvious prosecutorial overreaching. Granted, these are subjective judgments but since my project is descriptive and not empirical, I present my findings this way. I will happily provide a list of the 100 cases if anyone wants to check my judgments. I should warn that reading these summaries is a depressing project. It's not just, or maybe not especially, the cases of overreaching that are depressing but the kind of routine mistakes that condemn innocent defendants to years in prison.

In one case, the police had two suspects, apparently not acting in concert, who were arrested near the scene of a 2001 robbery and kidnapping.[22] At the scene of the crime there was DNA evidence, which matched Dwayne Jackson. "Faced with the DNA evidence and a potential life prison sentence, Jackson pleaded guilty in 2003 and was released in 2006 after serving nearly three years in prison." Four years later, DNA from the other suspect matched not only a new crime but also the 2001 robbery and kidnapping. Police discovered that they had mixed up the samples in 2001 and sent a provably innocent man to prison.

Consider another equally depressing tale. After ten years in prison, Jerry Lee Jenkins persuaded the courts to do a DNA test on evidence found at the crime scene. But "an extensive search of the Charles County courthouse, the State's Attorney's Office, the Public Defender's Office and the Sheriff's Office failed to turn up the evidence in the case."[23] The inmate served another fifteen years before a search of the sheriff's storage facility "turned up a battered box that contained hairs from the victim's rape kit, hairs from the scene of the crime and fingernail scrapings, along with the victim's purse."[24] The DNA test exonerated the defendant who, by then, had served twenty-six years for a crime he did not commit. Reading 100 cases that involve any kind of justice failure is sobering.

In my 100-case sample, I concluded that 18 cases involved serious prosecutorial misconduct, which I will call type 1 cases; 24 were type 2 cases that I thought should not have been brought; and 58 contained errors other than prosecutorial overreaching. Perhaps unsurprisingly, most of the type 1 cases, 13, involved *Brady* violations. Since there is no way to generalize to all prosecutions, or even all prosecutions that result in a wrongful conviction, there is no inference we can draw from these findings, but I will give examples of the type 1 and type 2 cases.

The first type 1 case featured a prosecution file so weak that it took eighteen months before Joseph Sledge was indicted for the murder of two women and the brutal rape of one.[25] Sledge was black; the victims were white; and the crimes took place in North Carolina in 1976. A critical piece of the State's case was the testimony of a cellmate, Sutton, asserting that Sledge admitted to the killings. Sutton testified that Sledge said that "the black man ... should kill ... everyone ... that really should cross their path." Sutton also testified that he received no favorable treatment or any part of the reward in exchange for his testimony. The first trial produced a hung jury, but the second jury convicted. Thirty-five years later, the North Carolina Center on Actual Innocence learned that the prosecutor had failed to disclose several initial interviews in which Sutton denied that Sledge admitted the crime; also, contrary to his testimony, Sutton received early parole and $2,000 from the reward money for his testimony. That information led the North Carolina Innocence Inquiry Commission to order DNA testing. Joseph Sledge was innocent of the crimes. That the first trial produced a hung jury strongly suggests that had the prosecutor disclosed the exculpatory evidence in his file, Sledge would never have been convicted. If that is right, then Sledge served thirty-six years in prison because a prosecutor failed to seek justice. The current prosecutor apologized to Sledge at the hearing at which he was declared innocent: "There's nothing worse for a prosecutor than convicting an innocent person."

Perhaps the most bizarre type 1 case was that of Dwayne Provience.[26] Rene Hunter was killed in a drive-by shooting in Detroit in 2000. There were seven eyewitnesses. Police made no arrests until Larry Wiley, being questioned about burglary charges, claimed he had also seen the drive-by shooting and identified Dwayne Provience as one of the men in the car from which the shots were fired. His description of the car contradicted six of the seven eyewitnesses that the police had originally interviewed (the seventh could not describe the car). At trial, the prosecution called only Wiley and the eyewitness who could not identify the car. Provience was convicted; the other man in the car, tried separately, was acquitted. In a later case, a prosecutor from the office that had prosecuted Provience told a jury that Hunter was killed, not by Provience, but by local drug lords protecting their business. So, as the famous cross-examination of the witness who has told different stories goes, was the prosecutor lying when he put on a skewed case against

Provience (apparently without disclosing to the defense that six of the eye-witnesses had given a different description of the car) or was the prosecutor lying in the later trial? Either way, this is pretty shoddy conduct for a minister of justice.[27]

For a particularly sad type 2 example, consider Christopher Abernathy's case.[28] A rape/murder of a 15-year-old went unsolved for a year. Abernathy was a learning disabled 18-year-old who was brought in for questioning because an acquaintance said Abernathy had admitted the crime. After forty hours of interrogation (so much for *Miranda*'s protections), he signed a confession because police told him that if he did he could go home to his mother. When that proved a lie, Abernathy immediately recanted the confession. There was no other evidence linking him to the crime – no forensic or physical evidence. But it was enough for a jury to convict. More than fifteen years later, journalism students at Northwestern University began investigating the case, and the acquaintance recanted his trial testimony. His new testimony was that police pressured him to implicate Abernathy who, in fact, had not confessed. Police promised him lenient treatment on some pending minor charges and gave him $300 to buy clothes to come to court – benefits that were not disclosed to Abernathy's defense attorney at trial.

Now, arguably this is a type 1 case because of the failure to disclose information that could have been used to attack the credibility of a key witness. But I rejected it as type 1 because the confession was likely enough to overcome any attack on the acquaintance's credibility. It belongs in the type 2 category, I believe, because the prosecutor went to court with a case centered on a confession made by a learning disabled 18-year-old after forty hours of interrogation that was immediately recanted after the police failed to deliver on their promise to let him go home. I hope we expect more of our prosecutors than that. DNA testing ultimately excluded Abernathy as the perpetrator. When he walked out of prison, he was greeted by his family, including his mother, who had visited him in prison nearly one thousand times during the almost thirty years he was incarcerated.

My second example of a type 2 case involved Mario Vasquez's conviction and twenty-year sentence for sexual assault on a 4-year-old, based solely on the testimony of the child.[29] When tested by a social worker prior to trial, the child was unable to tell the difference between truth and a lie. And there were gaping holes in her story. She identified at least four men as having sexually assaulted her; she called her uncle "Mario" so when she said "Mario" had assaulted her, it was ambiguous; the mother suspected both the uncle and her husband of having sexually assaulted the child – indeed, she had changed her work schedule so that her husband would never be alone with the child;

the victim could not identify the defendant in the courtroom as her assailant. The defense lawyer told the jury he would call an expert to testify about inappropriate interviewing techniques that the police had used but never did so. "After Vasquez was convicted, the lawyer was ultimately disbarred following nearly 100 instances of misconduct in the representation of clients." While it is unfair to charge the prosecution with the defense failure, the prosecutor did know he was going to trial with a case based only on a 4-year-old witness who had told various stories, implicating three men other than Vasquez, and who could not identify him in court. The prosecutor knew that the mother suspected other men. I have never been a prosecutor, and sexual assault of a child is terrible business, but I would like to think this is not a case I would have taken to trial. Vasquez served seventeen of twenty years before he was exonerated; he could have been paroled sooner but he refused to acknowledge guilt.

My last example of a type 2 case is a series of Texas cases. Mostly in the years 2013 and 2014, Houston had a serious problem with field testing of suspected contraband. In forty-three cases in the Registry, the field tests indicated contraband, but the tardy lab tests found no evidence of contraband drugs.[30] Yet forty-three defendants pled guilty before the lab results were available, usually to a few days in jail or probation. But three defendants pled guilty to a two-year sentence and one unfortunate soul accepted a seven-year sentence. What could explain these guilty pleas? One possibility of course is that the defendant believed what he possessed was contraband, that he had been suckered by the seller. A darker possibility is that the defendant thought the police were willing to fabricate the results so he might as well take a few days in jail or probation to avoid the greater harm.

But what in the world could motivate a defendant to accept a seven-year prison sentence for the possession of 200–400 grams of codeine that was not, in fact, contraband? That is the case of Henry Baltrip.[31] The answer, perhaps, is that the seven-year sentence for possession of codeine ran concurrently with a seven-year sentence for possession of 4–200 grams of cocaine. One still wonders why a defendant would willingly accept another felony conviction on his record if he knew the substance was not contraband. So we are thrown back on the explanation that Baltrip was suckered.[32]

This series of cases qualifies as type 2 because almost all occurred in Houston, and one would hope that, after a dozen or two dozen of these cases in 2013 and 2014, the Houston prosecutors would stop taking guilty pleas based on field testing that had been proved false so many times. By the time Amber Roberts pled guilty to possession of Ecstasy that turned out not to be contraband,[33] almost all of the forty-three cases of failed field testing should have been known to the Houston prosecutors. Somebody was eventually paying attention because there are no failed field test cases in the Registry from 2015. One wonders, of course, where defense counsel was in advising their clients. There was a blog posting in March 2014 containing the account of a case I happened to find in my random sample.[34] An article in the *Houston Free Press* in May 2014 detailed several of these false positive cases.[35] To be fair, as the blog post pointed out, in some cases defendants wanted to plead guilty and take probation or a short sentence rather than have the sword of Damocles hang over their head for months or years, and it is easiest to understand if the defendant was in jail awaiting trial.[36]

The type 3 cases have a depressing array of amazingly bad eyewitness identifications, police errors, police coercion, and police misconduct. In a particularly discouraging case, three St. Louis police officers "admitted they had planted evidence, lied about finding drugs and stole money from alleged drug dealers."[37] As a result of the federal investigation of the St. Louis police, "[s]tate and federal prosecutors dropped some pending cases and began reviewing hundreds of convictions that involved the officers' testimony."[38] But these errors do not concern my current project, and I turn now to the issue of how we might be able to get fewer type 1 and type 2 cases.

2 *Reinforcing the Thin Last Line*

When seeking to change the incentives of prosecutors, let us begin with more modest recommendations. Daniel Medwed has written an excellent book filled with examples of prosecutors who seem more committed to winning a case than serving as a "minister of justice."[39] Medwed offers some thoughtful examples of changes that could reduce the incidence of prosecutors contributing to wrongful convictions. One I like very much is an open file discovery process.[40] While prosecutors who want to cheat can beat this system too, by keeping a shadow file or simply not putting exculpatory evidence in any file, there is no system that can end cheating. The goal of an open file discovery process is to remove the temptation the ethical prosecutor might feel to conclude that a piece of evidence is not exculpatory. Why not let the defense lawyer see everything and make up her mind for herself?

Medwed also embraces Angela Davis's idea of a prosecution review board that "would not only review specific complaints brought to its attention by the public, but it would conduct random reviews of routine prosecution decisions."[41] Medwed suggests staffing these boards with retired judges and retired prosecutors who would hopefully have the courage and independence to call out errant prosecutors. A third idea is to control improper coaching of prosecution witnesses by videotaping all witness interviews and making the record available to the defense and the court. Recording interviews would also have the salutary effect of reducing false testimony of jailhouse informants. There is nothing much to be done about the jailhouse informant who comes forward with an airtight, but false, allegation. But having a record of the initial story would make it possible to undermine the credibility of the jailhouse informant who constructs or changes his story during interviews with the prosecutor.

Finally, why not involve judges in plea bargaining?[42] Having an independent party in the room would reduce the prosecutorial bluffing and threats that can occur in our current system. I have written about this case elsewhere,[43] but I cannot get it out of my head that what happened in *Bordenkircher* v. *Hayes*[44] is more like ordeal by fire than a pursuit of justice. Paul Hayes had been convicted of two prior felonies, though neither resulted in even a day's incarceration. When he was indicted for uttering a forged instrument in the amount of $88.30, he faced two to ten years in prison. The prosecutor offered to recommend a sentence of five years if Hayes pleaded guilty. Otherwise, he said, he would seek an indictment under the Kentucky Habitual Offender Act that carried a mandatory life sentence.

Hayes, however, claimed he was innocent of the current charge and insisted on his right to a trial by jury. The prosecutor did exactly what he threatened: He returned to the grand jury and got a new indictment under the Habitual Criminal Act. The jury found Hayes guilty on the uttering charge, and the judge sentenced him to life in prison. A defendant who had never been incarcerated was sentenced to life in prison for uttering a forged instrument in the value of $88.30. And that sentence was passed on him *because he chose to exercise his right to a trial*.

The United States Supreme Court held that the threats did not violate due process because the prosecutor was doing only what he was permitted to do under the law.[45] What difference is there, the Court reasoned, between filing the Habitual Offender charge in the beginning and then negotiating it away in exchange for a guilty plea? There is much to the Court's analysis as a dry, formal matter, though I prefer the view of Justice Powell in dissent: "I agree with much of the Court's opinion, [but] I am not satisfied that the result in this case is just or that the conduct of the plea bargaining met the requirements of due process."[46] Paul Hayes was sentenced to life in prison for uttering a forged instrument for less than $100. Where is the justice in that?

But the point here is not whether the Court was right or wrong. Rather, one assumes (one very much hopes) that a judge who was acting as plea bargaining umpire would rule the prosecutor's actions in *Bordenkircher* out of bounds.

If I were a judge sitting in on that negotiation, I would tell the prosecutor what Justice Blackmun said in his *Bordenkircher* dissent: Had you thought justice required a Habitual Offender charge, you would have filed the case that way in the first place.[47] You may not use the threat of refiling to seek to deter Mr. Hayes from exercising his right to trial by jury.

A simpler case for a judge to "umpire" would be one of the series of forty-three Texas cases where the field contraband tests were erroneous.[48] Presumably, at some point, criminal judges would be aware of the problem with prior field tests and would strongly advise against accepting a guilty plea based on a field test that had yet to be confirmed by a formal lab test; if the defendant was in jail, the judge could order him released on an appearance bond.

To those who draw back in horror at any greater involvement of the judge in settling criminal cases, Professor Jenia Iontcheva Turner has revealed that two American states, Florida and Connecticut, permit at least a partial role for the judge in the plea bargaining process.[49] Moreover, Turner makes a powerful case for the German model, "which entrusts the judge with the duty to ensure the fairness and accuracy of plea bargaining."[50]

With that set of pragmatic recommendations in the books, let us turn to changing incentives from the inside out, rather than as a result of external regulation. In my 2008 book, I recommended a radical solution – that states adopt a version of the old British counsel system where barristers are hired one day to prosecute and the next day to defend.[51] The notion of course is that if a lawyer walks on both sides of the aisle, she will be less adversarial and more willing to cooperate with the other side. But thinking about it since, it occurs to me that we don't want defense lawyers to change much about what they do. They have no duty to achieve justice; they are supposed to "throw pepper in the eyes of the prosecutor" if they can – Jerome Frank's metaphor about our adversary system is that it is akin to throwing pepper in the eyes of the surgeon when she is operating.[52]

Prosecutors, however, must avoid tunnel vision to the extent possible if they are to serve as ministers of justice. Imagine, if you will, two systems for creating a rank of prosecutors. First is a system in which prosecutors are elected or appointed by the governor or president. What life experiences qualify a prosecutor to be a prosecutor in this system? A concern for justice? No. Special training in forensics? No. An even-handed, apolitical view of the world? Not usually. Instead, prosecutors are chosen from the ranks of successful advocates who have either been elected or appointed because of their political ability or connections. Successful advocates who have been elected know how to press the flesh, raise money, and satisfy the electorate. How does a prosecutor satisfy the electorate? By dismissing serious felony cases where she doubts the guilt of the defendant? Of course not. Even if a prosecutor doubts the guilt of, say, a rape defendant or a homicide defendant, if there are no other suspects, the prosecutor will look weak to the electorate if she decides mid-case to drop the prosecution. Better to chance an acquittal; then it's not so obviously the prosecutor's fault.

What about the prosecutor who is appointed because of his political connections and does not have to stand for reelection? While those prosecutors are perhaps more insulated from raw political pressure, their political benefactor surely expects convictions, rather than dismissals, in high-profile cases. And many prosecutors with political benefactors probably want to be political benefactors themselves someday. A good record on convictions, particularly of public corruption, would be helpful in climbing that ladder. When Chris Christie, now governor of New Jersey, assumed the office of United States Attorney, he announced that he "would unleash the full might of his office against corruption."[53] Both the prosecutor who is elected and the one is appointed must always look over his shoulder to make sure that he is satisfying the political actors who put him there and who can replace him.

Now imagine another system in which law graduates have to pass a rigorous entrance exam. Those admitted to the program would take courses in the theory and practice of criminal law, advocacy, case studies, and seminars. After a year or so, graduates of the training process would take apprenticeships in the offices of prosecutors and judges. Finally, they would take a final exam and only those who pass would become prosecutors.

Which system sounds better? Which sounds more likely to produce efficient, capable prosecutors? Which seems more likely to avoid tunnel vision? Which would you choose if you were starting from scratch? If you would choose the first one, the politically driven model, then you might as well stop reading now. That, of course, is the American way. Jack McCoy of *Law & Order* puts another one in the win column.

We do not have to imagine the second system. It exists throughout Europe. In nineteen EU countries, prosecutors are selected through a public competition, "generally through written tests and interviews."[54] In other countries, prosecutors "are selected based on their university grades" or through an application process or interviews.[55] In many countries, one's chances of making it into the program are low; in the Netherlands, for example, 450 candidates are typically whittled down to 50 admitted to the trainee program.[56] The length of training varies from six to thirty-one months in the countries I studied.[57] At the end of the training, candidates would have to pass a final exam before they could be prosecutors. Some would fail. Once qualified as a prosecutor, they would be civil service employees, subject to being fired only for cause.

It is, of course, impossible in the lifetime of anyone reading this chapter for an American jurisdiction to adopt a European-style system with its rigorous entrance examination, its two-to-four-year training program, and a final examination at the end of the training period. Indeed, what I am about to propose is probably also impossible. Assume, for the sake of argument, that my chapter causes a hypothetical legislature to implement a prosecutor training system. What might that approach look like? The legislature could leave in place the selection system currently in use – either election of prosecutors or appointment by the executive. It is difficult to imagine a legislature taking this away from voters or governors and presidents. But if we could require even minimal training for newly minted prosecutors, that would be a large step in the right direction.

How much time could we expect our hypothetical legislature to require for future prosecutors? We could begin with three months of broad-based training that would make them more effective prosecutors in general and would also seek to enhance their awareness of the risks to innocent defendants. They could take specialized courses in forensics, ethical obligations of prosecutors, advocacy, the criminal law of the jurisdiction, advanced evidence law and the law of discovery, examination and cross-examination of witnesses, sociology and criminology, psychology, case studies, seminars, and the relationship between state and federal criminal prosecutions. Part of the ethics training would be exposure to the National Registry of Exonerations, to the large number of books and articles about wrongful convictions, and to the ethics and dangers of plea bargaining. The trainees would see and participate in exercises that show the unreliability of eyewitness identification. Prosecutors who are aware of the inherent unreliability of eyewitness identification and of tests for toolmarks, shoe marks, and bite marks, for example, will be more likely to turn over exculpatory evidence and insist on better proof of guilt. That would strengthen the thin last line of defense for innocent persons caught up in the American criminal justice system.

As for the mechanics, I assume a state legislature could simply mandate that no person could serve as a prosecutor unless he or she has graduated from what we can call advanced prosecutorial training. In states where prosecutors are appointed, the "nominee" would take the training program after the appointment is announced and before the prosecutor begins the job. In states where prosecutors are elected, the elected prosecutor would take the program before assuming the job. I am well aware that such a hybrid system is not as good as the one operating throughout most of Europe. It is difficult to imagine failing a prosecutor who has been appointed by the governor or elected by voters. Perhaps the program could be constructed so that the trainees take an exam after three months; if they pass, they are in the job; if they fail, they have to take another month of training. I realize that even this is an imperfect realization of the European model. But it remains a marked improvement over the system that exists today in all fifty states and the federal system.

So where's my brave legislature that wants to improve the effectiveness of prosecutors and strengthen the thin last line protecting innocent defendants?

NOTES

1 373 U.S. 83 (1963). Westlaw search, Aug. 2, 2015, for Brady & discovery & DA (AFT 01/01/2012), produced 7,102 cases. This is obviously both over- and underinclusive (a defendant can make a discovery claim without citing *Brady* and some cases referring to *Brady* discovery might not actually contain a claim) but it should give us a rough approximation.

2 National Registry of Exonerations, *Homepage*, available at www.law.umich.edu/ special/exoneration/Pages/about.aspx.

3 National Registry of Exonerations, *Case of David Anderson*, available at www.law.umich.edu/special/exoneration/Pages/casedetail.aspx?caseid=4551.

4 Comm. v. Anderson, 38 A.3d 828 (Pa. Super. 2011). Although the court was split 5–4 on the issue of whether double jeopardy should prevent a retrial, it was unanimous that "the prosecutor's actions in this matter amounted to a flagrant disregard for the trial court's October 29, 2007 pretrial order, resulting in inexcusable misconduct, worthy of sanction and even disciplinary proceedings"). *Id.* at 840–41 (Olson, J., dissenting).

5 Berger v. United States, 295 U.S. 78, 88 (1935).

6 Westlaw search, Aug. 2, 2015 for "he may strike hard blows" & Berger produced 705 federal and state cases.

7 *Venango County Assistant District Attorney Fired*, PITT. POST-GAZETTE, Aug. 28, 2013. On February 5, 2015, a disciplinary board hearing committee recommended disbarment, and the Pennsylvania Supreme Court formally disbarred the lawyer on August 12, 2015. *See* Office of Disciplinary Counsel v. Carbone, No. 71 DB 2014, available at www.pacourts.us/assets/opinions/DisciplinaryBoard/out/71DB2014-Car bone.pdf.

8 DAVID A. HARRIS, FAILED EVIDENCE: WHY LAW ENFORCEMENT RESISTS SCIENCE 3–5 (2012) (discussing the Madrid train bombing case where the FBI made a 100 percent conclusive match that proved to be wrong, thanks to the Spanish police who refused to agree that it was a match and ultimately matched the prints to an Algerian suspect).

9 Radley Balko, *How the Flawed "Science" of Bite Mark Analysis Has Sent Innocent People to Prison*, WASH. POST, Feb. 13, 2015. *See* NATIONAL RESEARCH COUNCIL OF THE NATIONAL ACADEMIES, STRENGTHENING FORENSIC SCIENCE IN THE UNITED STATES: A PATH FORWARD (2009), available at www.ncjrs.gov/pdffiles1/nij/grants/228091.pdf [hereinafter A PATH FORWARD].

10 A PATH FORWARD, *supra* note 9, at 4.

11 *Id.*

12 Hill v. Chicago, 2011 WL 2461362 (N.D. E.D. Ill. 2011) (permitting expert bite mark testimony in civil lawsuit brought by inmate); State v. Stipe, 2015 WL 629296 (La. Ct. App. 2015) (testimony of two forensic odontologists admitted after *Daubert* hearing); Chanthakoummane v. State, 2010 WL 1696789 (Tex. Ct. Crim. App. 2010) (bite mark evidence admitted even though expert was not certified as a forensic odontologist by the American Board of Forensic Odontology) (deferring to trial court); Coronado v. State, 384 S.W.3d 919 (Tex. Ct. App. 2012) (bite mark evidence admitted despite challenge based on National Research Council report cited and quoted in text of this chapter) (abuse of discretion standard). *Cf.* Turner v. State, 953 N.E.2d 1039 (Ind. 2011) (affirming conviction based in part on toolmark expert testimony) (abuse of discretion standard).

13 A PATH FORWARD, *supra* note 9, at 47.

14 *Id.* at 107–08.

15 Balko, *supra* note 9.

16 *See* HARRIS, *supra* note 18.

17 Steve Mills, *Prosecutor, DNA at Odds*, CHI. TRIB., Dec. 15, 2008.

18 *Mermel Retiring from Lake County Prosecutor's Office*, DAILY HERALD, Dec. 7, 2011.

19 DAN SIMON, IN DOUBT 95–99 (2012).

20 *Id.* at 50.

21 *Id.*

22 National Registry of Exonerations, *Case of Dwayne Jackson*, available at www.law.umich.edu/special/exoneration/Pages/casedetail.aspx?caseid=3821.

23 National Registry of Exonerations, *Case of Jerry Lee Jenkins*, available at www.law.umich.edu/special/exoneration/Pages/casedetail.aspx?caseid=4191.

24 *Id.*

25 National Registry of Exonerations, *Case of Joseph Sledge*, available at www.law.umich.edu/special/exoneration/Pages/casedetail.aspx?caseid=4627.

26 National Registry of Exonerations, *Case of Dwayne Provience*, www.law.umich.edu/special/exoneration/Pages/casedetail.aspx?caseid=3553.

27 To be sure, there was no DNA exoneration, and Provience might have been guilty. But failing to disclose the six identifications of the car that differed from Wiley's is a violation of *Brady*.

28 National Registry of Exonerations, *Case of Christopher Abernathy*, available at www.law.umich.edu/special/exoneration/Pages/casedetail.aspx?caseid=4640.

29 National Registry of Exonerations, *Case of Mario Vasquez*, available at www.law.umich.edu/special/exoneration/Pages/casedetail.aspx?caseid=4637.

30 *See* series of cases, National Registry of Exonerations, available at www.law.umich.edu/special/exoneration/Pages/detaillist.aspx?View={FAF6EDDB-5A68-4F8F-8A52-2C61F5BF9EA7}&FilterField1=Group&FilterValue1=CIU&FilterField2=Crime&FilterValue2=8_Drug%20Possession%20or%20Sale.

31 *Henry Allen Baltrip*, TEX. TRIB., available at www.texastribune.org/library/data/ texas-prisons/inmates/henry-allen-baltrip/729477/. I am assuming the codeine sentence was concurrent with the cocaine sentence; that is the only possibility that makes any sense.

32 Donald Stiers was sentenced to two years after pleading guilty to possession of 250 Ecstasy pills. National Registry of Exonerations, *Case of Donald Stiers*, available at www.law.umich.edu/special/exoneration/Pages/casedetail.aspx?caseid= 4626. Joe Thurman was sentenced to two years after pleading guilty to possession of cocaine. National Registry of Exonerations, *Case of Joe Thurman*, available at www.law.umich.edu/special/exoneration/Pages/casedetail.aspx?caseid=4580. Both convictions were vacated and charges dismissed.

33 National Registry of Exonerations, *Case of Amber Roberts*, available at www.law.umich.edu/special/exoneration/Pages/casedetail.aspx?caseid=4663.

34 *Williamson County Man Actually Innocent of Drug Possession Where Lab Found No Drugs Existed: Habeas Relief Granted*, GRITS FOR BREAKFAST, Mar. 5, 2014, available at http://gritsforbreakfast.blogspot.com/2014/03/williamson-county-man-actually-innocent.html.

35 Geoff West, *False Positives: An Introduction to Houston's Prosecution Problem*, HOUS. FREE PRESS, May 16, 2014, available at www.freepresshouston.com/false-positive-an-introduction-to-houstons-prosecution-problem/.

36 *Williamson County Man*, *supra* note 34.

37 National Registry of Exonerations, *Case of Stephen Jones*, available at www.law.umich.edu/special/exoneration/Pages/casedetail.aspx?caseid=3849.

38 *Id.*

39 DANIEL S. MEDWED, PROSECUTION COMPLEX: AMERICA'S RACE TO CONVICT AND ITS IMPACT ON THE INNOCENT (2012).

40 *Id.* at 48–50. Though the survey is quite dated, a 1984 ABA survey of U.S. Attorneys reported that of those who responded to the survey, 42 percent had an open file discovery policy, except in cases "in which they felt it would compromise the system – for example, serious drug cases or cases in which there was a considerable risk of witness intimidation." Wm. Bradford Middlekauf, *What Practitioners Say about Broad Criminal Discovery*, 9 CRIM. JUST. 14, 55, Spring 1994.

41 MEDWED, *supra* note 39, at 33 (quoting ANGELA J. DAVIS, ARBITRARY JUSTICE: THE POWER OF THE AMERICAN PROSECUTOR 463–64 (2007)).

42 MEDWED, *supra* note 39, at 64–66.

43 GEORGE C. THOMAS III, THE SUPREME COURT ON TRIAL: HOW THE AMERICAN JUSTICE SYSTEM SACRIFICES INNOCENT DEFENDANTS 205–06 (2008).

44 434 U.S. 357 (1978).

45 *Id.* at 364–65.

46 *Id.* at 368–69 (Powell, J., dissenting).

47 *Id.* at 367 (Blackmun, J., dissenting).

48 *See supra* notes 30–36 and accompanying text.

49 Jenia Iontcheva Turner, *Judicial Participation in Plea Negotiations: A Comparative Perspective*, 54 AM. J. COMP. L. 199 (2006).

50 *Id.* at 201.

51 THOMAS, *supra* note 43, at 190–92.

52 JEROME FRANK, COURTS ON TRIAL 85 (1973 paperback version; originally published in 1949).

53 Alec MacGillis, *The Rise and Fall of Chris Christie*, NEW REPUBLIC, Mar. 3, 2014, at 20.

54 Giovanna Ichino, *Report on EJTN [European Justice Training Network] Question-naires Concerning Initial Training in European Countries* 1, Oct. 13, 2013.

55 *Id.* The generalization omits occasional exceptions. For example, in Portugal, doctors of law do not have to take the test and barristers with at least seven years of experience and a "favourable assessment from the bar" do not have to take the written part of the test. *Id.* at 27.

56 COUNCIL OF EUROPE, THE TRAINING OF JUDGES AND PUBLIC PROSECUTORS IN EUROPE, PROCEEDINGS OF MULTILATERAL MEETING, LISBON 24, Apr. 27–28, 1995.

57 *See, e.g., id.* at 10 (Germany; two years); *id.* at 18 (Spain; six months); *id.* at 27 (Portugal; twenty-eight months); *id.* at 43 (France; thirty-one months). *See* Ichino, *supra* note 54, at 17 (Poland; one year).

12

Ineffective Assistance of Counsel and the Innocence Revolution

A Standards-Based Approach

ADELE BERNHARD

INTRODUCTION

Anyone who studies criminal justice in the United States soon realizes that state governments fail to provide effective and zealous legal counsel to all who are arrested and charged with a crime for which liberty is at stake – despite their legal mandate to do so. In 2004, more than forty years after the Supreme Court decision in *Gideon* v. *Wainwright*,[1] the American Bar Association (ABA) embarked on a comprehensive national listening tour to gauge how well defenders were representing clients in criminal court.[2] The ABA concluded that "thousands of persons are processed through America's courts every year either with no lawyer at all or with a lawyer who does not have the time, resources, or in some cases the inclination to provide effective representation."[3] The ABA heard stories of lawyers discussing plea bargains with clients, negotiating deals with prosecutors, and putting the bargains on the record – all without carrying out the most basic "staples of criminal defense work such as interviewing witnesses, visiting the scene of the crime, or conducting any meaningful, independent, factual investigation."[4]

Although disappointing, the ABA report broke no news.[5] Law reform agencies, defender organizations, and bar association committees are well aware of lawyering deficiencies in the criminal courts and are striving to improve defense services.[6] Studies of the DNA exoneration dataset show that poor defense lawyering is a major factor in the conviction of the innocent.[7] Reform efforts have been stymied by the growth of the criminal justice system[8] and the public's resistance to funding its costs, indifference to the plight of individuals charged with crime, and judicial decisions enshrining deference

Thanks are due to New York Law School for its research support and to research assistants, Carrie Jordan and Stephanie Baehr.

to lawyer decision-making. Now, however, with serious crime diminishing across the country, a reappraisal of mass incarceration, and the Innocence Movement revealing shortcomings in the criminal justice system, the time may be right for change.

Of course, there are many ways to improve the quality of defense services. Law schools should emphasize practical skills training. State legislatures should allocate additional funding for defense organizations to permit staff hiring, training, and caseload reduction. Accrediting organizations should evaluate defender groups and dictate change. This chapter explores one way to improve the quality of services provided to people charged with criminal offenses: through the judicial doctrine of ineffective assistance of counsel.

Courts impact the criminal justice system primarily through judicial decisions.[9] The starting point for any discussion of the judicial doctrine of ineffective assistance of counsel (IAC) is *Strickland* v. *Washington* where, in 1984, the Supreme Court held the "the proper standard for judging attorney performance is that of reasonably effective assistance, considering all the circumstances," and warned that judicial scrutiny of "counsel's performance must be highly deferential."[10] In an effort to leave defenders plenty of independence and discretion in case handling, the Supreme Court articulated a vague standard for assessing the effectiveness of counsel to permit defense counsel maximum strategic flexibility and autonomy.[11] That standard mandated that no conviction would be reversed unless counsel's performance resulted in specific articulable prejudice to the case. Unfortunately, most observers agree that the deferential *"reasonably effective"* standard has proved inadequate to protect the rights of the accused or provide guidance to defense counsel.[12]

I categorized twenty years of successful IAC petitions in federal courts of appeals to investigate whether and how the Innocence Movement, and the lessons learned through dissection of wrongful convictions, might be influencing the courts to manipulate the *Strickland* standard. I found that the courts are changing their approach to resolving IAC claims – but so far only in sentencing. There is no reason why a standards-based approach could not be used to assess performance at the guilt stage of a case as well.

THE POWER OF THE BENCH: EFFECTIVE ASSISTANCE OF COUNSEL AND ITS LINK TO JUSTICE

IAC is a frequently identified cause of wrongful conviction, the most commonly raised legal issue on appeal, and an obstacle to justice that should be amenable to judicial attention and improvement. The Innocence Project's analysis of 330 DNA exonerations demonstrates that a small number of factors disproportionately contribute to wrongful conviction.[13] Those factors include: mistaken eyewitness identification, false confession, bad science, informant testimony, prosecutorial misconduct, and ineffective assistance of counsel.[14]

In every study of wrongful convictions, bad lawyering is identified as a contributing factor. Ken Armstrong and Steve Mills reported, in one section of their *Chicago Tribune* multipart series about miscarriages of justice, that of the twelve men originally sentenced to death in Illinois and exonerated since 1987, "four were represented at trial by an attorney who had been disbarred or suspended."[15] The Innocence Project's internal analysis of the published appeals of individuals wrongly convicted and later exonerated through DNA evidence reveals that 54 of the first 255 DNA exonerees (one in five) raised claims of IAC, which were overwhelmingly rejected (81 percent).[16] James Liebman, Jeffrey Fagan, and Valerie West found that incompetence of defense lawyers is a major cause of reversal of convictions in state capital cases.[17] Observers consistently found, among other failures, that defense lawyers routinely fail to challenge the prosecution witnesses' interpretation of blood evidence, semen, bullets, hair, bite marks, injuries, or burn patterns.

Not only does ineffective lawyering permeate our courts, but convicted inmates routinely raise IAC claims. Ineffective lawyering is the most commonly raised claim in federal habeas petitions. The 2007 National Center for State Courts study of federal habeas petitions found that defendants in 50.4 percent of noncapital cases and 81 percent of capital cases raised ineffective assistance of trial or appellate counsel claims.[18]

IAC claims flood post-conviction criminal litigation for three reasons. First, many defendants are poorly represented and have legitimate claims that their cases were inadequately investigated, analyzed, and tried. Second, almost all convicted defendants, regardless of guilt, can locate error in their record. No lawyer tries a "perfect" case. Third, innocent defendants are sometimes constrained to use ineffective assistance of counsel claims to bring newly discovered evidence of innocence to the attention of reviewing courts.[19] Many jurisdictions lack a procedural mechanism for raising stand-alone claims of "innocence" post-conviction.[20] Defendants are relegated to a back-door approach, arguing that their counsel was ineffective for not finding and introducing exonerating evidence. Thus, not only do courts hesitate to second-guess attorney decision-making, but the sheer number of IAC claims and the difficulty of distinguishing between "legitimate" and "illegitimate" petitions discourage courts from tackling the issue.

Improving counsels' performance improves outcome accuracy. The point was proved by a rigorous 2012 Rand Corporation study. Rand looked at outcomes of 3,173 murder cases in Philadelphia between 1994 and 2005.[21] The overwhelming majority of murder defendants in Philadelphia, roughly 95 percent, are too poor to hire their own counsel and must have lawyers appointed. Philadelphia randomly assigns one of every five indigent murder defendants to its public defender office for representation, and assigns independent private attorneys to the other four. The assignment method created a perfect randomized study for assessing what difference a public defender might make – in a city where the public defender office is well-supported. It compared case outcomes between public defenders and private appointed counsel.

In Philadelphia, the Rand study found significant outcome differences and concluded that the data "strongly suggest[s] that public defender representation is associated with improved case outcomes," and "[i]t appears that public defenders are successful at both reducing the likelihood of the most extreme sanctions and reducing the severity of less extreme sentences."[22] Public defender representation reduces a murder defendant's conviction rate by 19 percent when compared with appointed counsel; the likelihood of receiving a life sentence is reduced by 62 percent; and representation by public defender results in a 24 percent decrease in expected prison terms.[23]

Public defenders can achieve better results than individual assigned lawyers because they are more likely to have manageable caseloads, training, supervision, and resources – such as investigators and experts. Private attorneys must locate their own support, pay for continuing legal education, and often accept too many cases in order to make financial ends meet. Philadelphia has a venerable defender system with a nationally recognized training program. This study showed that when public defenders are better trained, supervised, and supported, and have fewer clients, they provide higher quality services.

Judges have the skill and experience to recognize ineffective assistance of counsel. Most appellate judges were once litigators. Many served as trial judges before joining the appeals bench.[24] Judges know how to represent clients, how to prepare a case for trial, how to conduct discovery and investigation, and how to fashion and argue pretrial motions. They comprehend the essential characteristics of "competent counsel." For that reason, trial judges are frequently asked to review the performance of the litigators who appear before them and have little trouble completing questionnaires asking them to evaluate the competence of counsel.[25] Judges can spot ineffective counsel and understand the difference that quality representation makes to a case.

If innocent people have been wrongly convicted in part due to poor legal representation, if effective lawyers improve case outcomes, and if courts are well-positioned to spot ineffective lawyers, courts should be reversing more convictions on the grounds of ineffective assistance of counsel today than they were twenty-five years ago – assuming that courts care about fairness and accuracy.

WHEN COURTS REVERSE ON THE GROUNDS OF INEFFECTIVENESS: EVIDENCE OF INNOCENCE AND COUNSEL'S FAILURE TO CHALLENGE SCIENCE

I was inspired to look at the evolution of IAC doctrine by two recent court decisions: *Hinton* v. *Alabama*,[26] and *U.S.* v. *Hebshie*.[27] The decisions suggested that lessons taught by the Innocence Movement were encouraging courts to demand more of defense counsel.

The Supreme Court reversed Anthony Ray Hinton's murder convictions on February 24, 2014, finding Hinton's trial counsel ineffective for failing to recognize that he could have hired a competent expert witness in a case where forensic evidence was crucial.[28] According to the state of Alabama, a gun found in Hinton's home fired the bullets used in three separate crimes. The gun was the only physical evidence connecting Hinton to the crimes.

Hinton's counsel asked the trial court to permit expenditure of public funds on a defense expert. The judge authorized spending up to a limit of $1,000, believing that sum was the maximum the court could approve. He was wrong. In fact, Alabama placed no limit on expenditure of funds for expert services and allowed reimbursement for "any expenses reasonably incurred."[29]

Counsel did not research the law and did not spot the judge's error. Unaware that he could have asked for additional funding, counsel searched for an analyst who would agree to review the materials, challenge the state's ballistics conclusions, and testify for $1,000. Counsel found only one analyst, whose credentials were sorely lacking, willing to accept the job. Believing there was no other option, counsel proceeded to trial with an expert who was unable to convincingly explain why the state's ballistics evidence was inaccurate, unscientific, and wrong.

Many years later, Hinton's post-conviction case was taken up by Bryan Stevenson[30] who believed Hinton was wrongly convicted and actually innocent. Stevenson located highly qualified ballistics experts who explained they "could not conclude that any of the six bullets [found at the various crime scenes] had been fired by the Hinton revolver."[31] The State located no experts to counter the new ballistics evidence. The Supreme Court reversed the Alabama courts, finding IAC under the *Strickland* standard because trial counsel failed to discover that he could have obtained additional resources for the expert services at trial.

Four years earlier, a federal district court in Massachusetts granted James Hebshie's request for habeas relief on IAC grounds.[32] Hebshie was convicted of arson in 2006. To establish the fire was intentionally started, the prosecution called fire "experts" – one to explain where the fire started and another who worked with a dog specially trained to alert at the scent of accelerant.

Hebshie's trial counsel declined to request a pretrial hearing on the admissibility of the fire science – much of which was known by that date to be unscientific and false – or the canine evidence. Counsel essentially conceded the arson, dooming his client. Reviewing counsel's omissions in great detail, Judge Nancy Gertner granted Hebshie's federal habeas petition on IAC grounds.[33]

In both *Hinton* and *Hebshie*, federal appeals courts jettisoned the usual and expected deference to trial counsel decision-making. The Supreme Court was under no obligation to take Hinton's case at all, and could have easily determined that counsel conducted a reasonable investigation, calling a ballistics expert. Hebshie's lawyer consulted with an expert and cross-examined the state's witness. It would have been easy for the District Court to deem counsel's work as effective.

Why did the Supreme Court overturn Hinton's case? I see two possible interconnected explanations. First, the Court may have been motivated by evidence of Hinton's innocence. Ostensibly provided to show counsel's ineffectiveness, the new ballistics evidence undercut proof of guilt. Second, apart from innocence concerns, it may be easier for reviewing courts to identify IAC in cases where proof rests on "scientific" evidence. Counsel's failures are clearer where evidence unchallenged at trial can be conclusively refuted as false post-conviction. The same explanations seem relevant to understanding *Hebshie*. Post-conviction evidence showed the fire could have been accidental; the evidence undercut the state's "scientific" proof that a crime occurred. The decisions suggest that lessons from the Innocence Movement – specifically, that innocent people are wrongly convicted as the result of trial counsel error – influenced the courts to reverse. I found the cases encouraging and expected that *Hinton* and *Hebshie* would be representative of forces percolating through the courts, not exceptions to the rule.

IAC JURISPRUDENCE REMAINS IMPERVIOUS TO THE LESSONS OF THE INNOCENCE MOVEMENT – EXCEPT IN SENTENCING

To investigate the impact of the Innocence Movement on judicial IAC doctrine, I could have studied state or federal court decisions since any impact should be visible in both systems. Ineffective assistance of counsel can be raised in three contexts: on direct state appeal from the state conviction, in post-conviction state court collateral attack on conviction and in federal habeas petitions where defendant-petitioners argue the state court incorrectly applied the federal constitutional *Strickland* standard.

Because IAC is so frequently raised, finding and organizing the material in even a single state would be a daunting task. Moreover, federal decisions can be effectively analyzed because of a remarkable resource: The Habeas Report – a compilation of summaries of successful IAC habeas claims in the courts of appeals and in the district courts.[34] And, as federal habeas decisions review state application of federal law, analysis of federal decisions provides broad information about state practice as well as the federal response to state practice.

Issue 27 of the Habeas Report summarizes 285 successful habeas petitions on IAC grounds decided by the federal courts of appeals, starting in 1993 and continuing through the end of August 2013. Since 2003 marked a convenient dividing line in the compilation, I compared the first ten years of the compilation to the second ten. Also, by 2003, post-conviction DNA testing of biological evidence had exonerated 144 individuals,[35] a sufficiently striking number to alert courts and the public to the existence and major causes of wrongful convictions. Finally, in 2003, the American Bar Association issued revised *Guidelines for the Appointment and Performance of Counsel in Death Penalty Cases*,[36] and the United States Supreme Court decided *Wiggins* v. *Smith*,[37] reversing a conviction for IAC at sentencing.

I anticipated seeing a greater number of IAC reversals in the ten years after 2003 than in the ten years prior. But I did not. No matter how I looked at the numbers, there was no evidence of a trend to grant more habeas corpus relief on IAC grounds post-2003. Whatever concerns the federal courts may have about wrongly convicting innocent people, those concerns are not prompting more federal reversals of state convictions for state courts' misapplication of the Sixth Amendment right to effective assistance of counsel – despite the promise of *Hinton* and *Hebshie*.

The total number of successful IAC claims after 2003 was slightly larger than the number of successful claims between 1993 and 2003 and the increase is partly due to my inclusion of the first half of 2013 (an extra six months) in my totals. In the first ten years of the compilation, convicted defendants successfully raised federal IAC claims in the United States Courts of Appeals in 135 cases. In the eleven years following, between 2003 and 2013, inclusive, there were only 150.

During the twenty-year period covered in Volume 27 of the Habeas Report, the number of appeals of habeas petitions docketed in the federal courts of

TABLE 12.1. Successful IAC Claims in the Federal Courts of Appeals, 2003–13

	1st Cir.	2nd Cir.	3rd Cir.	4th Cir.	5th Cir.	6th Cir.	7th Cir.	8th Cir.	9th Cir.	10th Cir.	11th Cir.	Totals
1993–2003	3	9	8	2	10	20	13	18	33	9	10	135
2003 through 2013	0	8	13	5	1	49	18	1	30	6	6	150
Total successful IAC claims in 20 years	3	17	21	7	23	69	31	19	63	15	17	285
	1st Cir.	2nd Cir.	3rd Cir.	4th Cir.	5th Cir.	6th Cir.	7th Cir.	8th Cir.	9th Cir.	10th Cir.	11th Cir.	Totals
Sentencing Pre-2003	0	0	2	0	1	4	2	5	10	2	4	30
Sentencing Post-2003	0	0	4	2	3	16	3	0	14	2	4	48
Sentencing totals	0	0	6	2	4	20	5	5	24	4	8	78
IAC failure to invest. Pre-2003	1	4	3	0	4	6	8	3	20	5	2	56
IAC failure to invest. Post-2003	0	4	7	1	6	20	8	0	12	2	0	60
Total failure to invest.	1	8	10	1	10	26	16	3	32	7	2	116
IAC legal issues Pre-2003	2	5	3	2	5	10	3	10	3	2	4	49
IAC legal issues Post-2003	0	4	2	2	4	13	7	1	4	2	3	42
Total legal issues IAC	2	9	5	4	9	23	10	11	7	4	7	91
Total IAC Over 20 years	3	17	21	7	23	69	31	19	63	15	17	285

appeals remained fairly constant. Between 1993 and 2003, the courts of appeals reviewed a total of 32,067 appeals of habeas corpus petitions – an average of 3,206 per year.[38] Between the end of 2003 and the beginning of 2013, the courts of appeals reviewed 38,065 – an average of 3,806 a year. Averages hide the fact that the numbers fluctuated greatly between years. For example, in 2004 there were 1,276 habeas appeals and in 2005 there were 6,356 – a very large increase, which the Administrative Office of the United States Courts explains as a response to the U.S. Supreme Court decisions in *Blakely* v. *Washington*,[39] declaring the Washington state sentencing system unconstitutional, and *U.S.* v. *Booker*,[40] which held the federal sentencing guidelines to be advisory rather than mandatory.[41] However, despite fluctuations, the number of habeas petitions before the federal courts of appeals increased only very slightly over the twenty-year period, and the percentage of successful IAC petitions to the total number of petitions remained constant.

The Third, Fourth, Fifth, Sixth and Seventh Circuits reversed more convictions for IAC in the ten years following 2003 than in the ten years prior. Of that group, however, only the Sixth Circuit decided a significant total number of IAC cases at all, with twenty reversals in the ten years before 2003 and forty-nine in the ten years after, for a total of sixty-nine IAC reversals. In the Ninth Circuit, which reversed the second most number of convictions for IAC of any Circuit in the country, there were thirty-three successful IAC claims pre-2003 and thirty post-2003 – not a significant change.

Because the Habeas Report summarizes facts and legal issues, it is possible to distinguish between claims raising procedural issues and those raising the sorts of errors more likely to lead to inaccurate guilty verdicts – such as failure to interview witnesses, view the evidence, or engage experts.[42] Petitioners raising errors relating to guilt determinations are more likely to be wrongly convicted. As Brandon Garrett reports after analyzing the Innocence Project's database of wrongful convictions, "[t]he majority of the DNA exonerees who raised ineffective assistance of counsel claims did not raise procedural errors by counsel. Instead they presented claims based on ineffectiveness of counsel relating to important evidence introduced at trial, including failure to use blood evidence, to present alibi witnesses, and to challenge eyewitness identification of informant testimony."[43] Counsels' failure to investigate exculpatory evidence and locate and prepare witnesses to present that exculpatory evidence is the category of malfeasance responsible for many wrongful convictions.[44]

Surprisingly, the number of reversals for failure to investigate, interview, prepare and present witness testimony was essentially the same before and after 2003. Between 1993 and 2003, the courts of appeals found counsel ineffective for failing to investigate – by locating and interviewing witnesses, for example, in fifty-six cases. In the next eleven years, from 2003 through 2013, all the federal courts of appeals in the country found counsel ineffective for failure to investigate in only sixty cases – sixty decisions out of 38,065 petitions.

THOUGHTS ON THE FAILURE OF FEDERAL COURTS TO RESPOND TO THE INNOCENCE MOVEMENT AND HOLD DEFENSE LAWYERS ACCOUNTABLE

There are a number of possible explanations for the federal courts of appeals' reluctance to reverse state court convictions on IAC grounds. First, it is possible that post-2003, trial attorneys are doing a better job of investigating and preparing cases. Contemporary reports do not support that premise. Problems caused by underfunding, lack of training, and high caseloads continue unabated.[45] Although some offices are definitely providing high quality services, excellent providers are not in the majority.

A more likely explanation for the relatively small number of successful IAC claims can be found in the increasingly restrictive rules imposed on the federal judiciary. In the words of Ninth Circuit Judge Stephen Reinhardt, a major limitation in the "Supreme Court's AEDPA jurisprudence came in its needless and highly restrictive view of when a state court adjudication of an individual's federal claim 'resulted in a decision that was contrary to, or involved an unreasonable application of, clearly established Federal law'."[46] Judge Reinhardt explains that the Supreme Court has tied the hands of the federal judiciary through its habeas doctrine and has thus transformed the writ of habeas corpus "from a vital guarantor of liberty into an instrument for ratifying the power of state courts to disregard the protections of the Constitution."[47] Reinhardt points out that federal courts of appeals see the most "serious problems in the criminal justice system when addressing petitions for habeas corpus."[48] But, he would argue, and indeed it seems likely true, that the courts are prohibited from exercising meaningful review of the problems and issues arising in those petitions by *Strickland* doctrine.[49]

As discussed earlier, the *Strickland* test requires reviewing courts to weigh counsel's error deferentially against the proof of guilt at trial: "[t]he benchmark for judging any claim of ineffectiveness must be whether counsel's conduct so undermined the proper functioning of the adversarial process that the trial cannot be relied on as having produced a just result."[50] That is, egregiously negligent work will be excused if the reviewing court is not convinced that a better effort would have produced a different result. If the *Strickland* standard for ineffective assistance of counsel were to be applied to the medical realm, it would forgive a doctor's malpractice in the belief – impossible to validate – that the patient would have died anyway. The standard was designed to assist courts in distinguishing between verdicts where proof of guilt is convincing and those where proof is weak and the jury's decision worrisome, while permitting defense counsel flexibility and autonomy in client representation. But the standard has failed to reliably help courts differentiate between accurate and inaccurate verdicts. It has also proved ill-suited to the task of improving the quality of criminal defense representation because the prosecutor's evidence will always appear unassailable when counsel for the accused neglects to investigate or challenge the prosecution's version of the facts.

SENTENCING AND THE EVOLUTION OF IAC JURISPRUDENCE

Slowly, over the last decade – at least in death penalty cases – some federal courts have started experimenting with another approach to assessing effectiveness of counsel, an approach that was explicitly rejected in *Strickland*. Justice Thurgood Marshall's dissent in *Strickland* advocated using performance standards to assess the quality of counsel. Justice Marshall wrote:

> I agree that counsel must be afforded 'wide latitude' when making 'tactical decisions' regarding trial strategy, ... but many aspects of the job of a criminal defense attorney are more amenable to judicial oversight. For example, much of the work involved in preparing for a trial, applying for bail, conferring with one's client, making timely objections to significant, arguably erroneous rulings of the trial judge, and filing a notice of appeal if there are colorable grounds therefor could profitably be made the subject of uniform standard.[51]

The majority disagreed and declined to adopt Justice Marshall's proposal. That proposal looks more practical and attractive today.

In fact, federal courts are already using performance standards to measure IAC in the sentencing phase of death penalty cases. The success of that approach should diminish reflexive deference to defense counsel in the guilt phase of a capital trial and in other categories of cases – especially in light of the ever-increasing number of exonerations caused in part by defense counsels' mistakes and omissions. Trends in death penalty sentencing prove that the application of performance standards by courts can enhance defense counsels' professionalism and advocacy without impinging on their independence.

Seventy-eight of the 285 successful IAC habeas petitions were reversed by the federal courts of appeals for IAC at sentencing. Courts reversed thirty convictions for errors at sentencing before 2003 and reversed forty-eight after 2003 – a noticeable increase.

There are a number of possible reasons why courts might be more inclined to reverse sentencing determinations than determinations of guilt. The death penalty itself is likely a partial explanation. As Justice Potter Stewart noted, "Death is Different" and "it is unique ... in its absolute renunciation of all that is embodied in our concept of humanity."[52] Any federal court would feel an increased obligation, impossible to quantify, to more carefully review death sentences.

Even in non-death cases, it must be psychologically easier to reverse a sentencing decision than a guilt determination. If a court sets aside a jury verdict finding guilt, the prosecution must retry the entire case, calling witnesses, victims, investigating officers, and experts. Essential evidence may be lost and witnesses reluctant to testify, especially after many years have passed. Further, there is always the worrisome possibility that the convicted defendant might be released pending retrial. If a court reverses a sentence, the convicted defendant remains in jail; no fact witnesses need testify a second time; and no evidence needs to be located. The courts can ensure that the convicted defendant receives due process and effective counsel at sentencing without worrying that a guilty person might go free.

The slight increase in federal reversals of state court sentencing determinations may also reflect the impact of the reissuance of the *ABA Guidelines*. Twenty-three of the forty-eight post-2003 IAC reversals for errors at sentencing cite the *ABA Guidelines for the Appointment and Performance of Defense Counsel in Death Penalty Cases* standards for capital defense work.[53]

The *ABA Guidelines* were promulgated in 1989 and revised in 2003.[54] The 2003 Standards emphasize the importance of investigation in defense work throughout the trial and penalty phases of representation. That year, the Supreme Court directly referred to both the ABA *Performance Standards* and the ABA *Guidelines for the Appointment and Performance of Defense Counsel in Death Penalty Cases* in reversing Kevin Wiggins' death sentence for counsel's failure to investigate possible mitigating evidence.[55] As the Court noted in Wiggins, "[t]he lawyer also has a substantial and important role to perform in raising mitigating factors. ... Investigation is essential to fulfillment of these functions."[56]

We know that the federal courts are finding the *ABA Guidelines* helpful to IAC analysis because at least one federal judge wrote an article to explain just how helpful they are. Federal District Court Judge Mark W. Bennett acknowledged that:

> the ABA Guidelines, especially Guideline 10.11, 'The Defense Case Concerning Penalty,' significantly assisted me in determining whether trial

counsel's alleged failure to investigate and present mitigation evidence of Johnson's mental health at the time of the five murders rose to the level of ineffective assistance of counsel.[57]

Judge Bennett reflected on a particularly difficult death penalty case over which he presided for many years and prolonged litigation. At the very start, aware of how difficult the case would be both legally and emotionally, he appointed what he considered to be an excellent team of experienced death penalty lawyers. After trial and sentencing, the defendant brought a post-conviction motion to reverse for IAC. Judge Bennett applied the ABA *Guidelines* and realized that numerous instances of ineffective assistance of counsel permeated the defense at sentencing. He explained that, "none was more troubling than learned counsels' decision not to pursue psychological mitigation evidence of Johnson's state of mind at the time of the five murders. This alleged 'strategic decision' was so lacking in the type of sound pretrial investigation contemplated by Guideline 10.11(F) that I stripped the decision of the presumption in favor of counsel's strategy, a presumption which generally makes strategic choices virtually unchallengeable."[58]

Because Judge Bennett did not know what investigation the lawyers conducted and how that investigation or lack of it should be reviewed by him, he did not see how the lawyers were failing as they litigated before him. In post-conviction review, looking at the case through the lens of the ABA *Guidelines*, he realized that the lawyers' efforts were constitutionally inadequate.

LESSONS LEARNED

If the *Strickland* standard fails to advance the quality of pretrial criminal defense services, despite the general consensus that those services need enhancement and that poor lawyering contributes to wrongful convictions, what is the solution? As many commentators have urged, courts could abandon the *Strickland* unreasonable performance plus prejudice approach and adopt a standards-based approach. This would require identifying appropriate performance standards or performance guidelines and assessing counsel's efforts at the guilt stage as well as sentencing stage of a criminal case by applying those standards. I agree with Justice Marshall that it is not so very difficult to create and apply standards to all stages of a criminal proceeding.

To think about how standards might be used in post-conviction review of a guilt determination, imagine a criminal case where the state's proof includes a witness identifying the accused as the perpetrator. In such a prosecution, defense counsel should, at a minimum, counsel the client about the way he looked (hair, dress, grooming, and the like) on the day that the crime occurred and on the day of his arrest; visit the scene of the crime to see whether the witness's purported identification is possible; review the police reports to ascertain whether the witness's descriptions match the appearance of the accused and whether they changed over time; learn about the factors that impact the witness's ability to make an identification; consult with experts in identification; and draft a motion to suppress the evidence if there is any reason to believe that the police investigation suggested the accused to the witness or other constitutional infirmities, in addition to developing relevant themes for opening statement, witness examination, and closing argument.

Commentators have already captured these basic tasks for representation in criminal cases. The best description of the various component parts of criminal defense representation can be found in Anthony Amsterdam's classic three-volume treatise, *Trial Manual for the Defense of Criminal Cases*.[59] But Amsterdam's treatise is not the only place to look for guidelines. The ABA Criminal Justice Section has issued comprehensive standards,[60] as has the National Legal Aid and Defender Association,[61] which judges could use to assess counsel's performance.

Although every criminal case is different, the necessary skills required for excellent criminal representation are easily identified. Lawyers conceive of their skill as an art, but it is really closer to a science. Representation can be organized into lists of tasks, which can be prioritized and adapted to each client and every situation. If, for instance, in our imaginary but typical one-witness identification case, counsel failed to visit the scene, failed to obtain and study the police reports, or failed to consult with experts, a reviewing court could find that performance to be ineffective as a matter of law without regard to the proof and without having to attempt to measure prejudice. Anthony Amsterdam's treatise includes a model "interview checklist," which contains numerous questions along these lines for use in a case involving identification.[62] A standards-based approach eliminates the necessity to find "prejudice." The court would assume that if the necessary tasks were accomplished, then the client was represented as well as possible. If the necessary tasks were neglected, the lawyer was ineffective.[63] This is the same kind of checklist approach to complex work that has been so useful in medicine.[64]

Checklists are already used in teaching law. Those of us who teach law students in clinical courses where students represent clients under a professor's supervision routinely assess student performance, growth, and achievement against lists of proficiencies. At the outset, we identify and describe the proficiencies we hope our students will learn and then explicitly teach the skills necessary to achieve proficiency. Students study the skills and ideally achieve mastery through practicing in role.

To identify proficiencies, we are aided by the MacCrate report,[65] which lists and defines fundamental legal skills and values that develop "along a continuum that starts before law school, reaches its most formative and intensive stage during the law school experience, and continues throughout a lawyer's professional career."[66] The MacCrate skills and values are a simple and clear set of performance standards for legal educators – a starting point for best practices. Explicit identification of skills and values intrinsic to legal work assists in the communication and transfer of those skills. At the end of the course, professors evaluate their students with reference to the same list of skills and values introduced at the beginning. Reviewing courts can use the same straightforward, organized and clear approach to assess counsels' performance in criminal cases.

U.S. v. Hebshie[67] is actually an example of what a standards-based review might look like. Although the District Court did not explicitly assess trial counsel's performance with reference to a set of standards or guidelines, the court's analysis models how that might be accomplished. The court reviewed the evidence and outlined exactly what the defense counsel should have done but did not do:

> What counsel *did not do* is to move for a Daubert hearing prior to trial on any expert issue. They *did not* seek exclusion of any of the proposed expert testimony, which was the core of the arson case, or move for its limitation. They *did not* argue that the expert testimony failed to meet the minimal threshold for reliability of scientific evidence in NFPA 921 and should not have been admitted at all.[68]

After summarizing counsel's failures and omissions, the court discussed the significance of the omissions – not just with regard to how those omissions prejudiced Hebshie, but generally how those errors revealed counsel's lack of knowledge about the scientific developments in the field of arson, and general lack of investigation, thoughtful analysis, and preparation. Prejudice flowed naturally and incontestably from the discussion of counsel's deficient performance. The shift in focus from prejudice to performance is similar to what is slowly happening in the federal courts at post-conviction review of sentences where the courts of appeals are using the *ABA Guidelines* to assess effectiveness of counsel. A shift in focus from prejudice to performance at trial, as well as sentencing, would be one way to implement lessons from the Innocence Movement.

NOTES

1 The Supreme Court held in a series of decisions, including the seminal case of Gideon v. Wainwright, 372 U.S. 335 (1963), that everyone charged with a crime for which the loss of liberty is a possible punishment must be represented by effective counsel regardless of ability to pay.

2 The ABA Standing Committee on Legal Aid and Indigent Defendants organized, recorded and distilled testimony from the hearings.

3 STANDING COMM. ON LEGAL AID & INDIGENT DEFENDANTS, AM. BAR ASS'N, GIDEON'S BROKEN PROMISE: AMERICA'S CONTINUING QUEST FOR EQUAL JUSTICE: A REPORT ON THE AMERICAN BAR ASSOCIATION'S HEARINGS ON THE RIGHT TO COUNSEL IN CRIMINAL PROCEEDINGS (2004).

4 Martin Guggenheim, *The People's Right to a Well-Funded Indigent Defender System*, 36 N.Y.U. REV. L. SOC. CHANGE 395, 397 n. 2 (2014) (citing Deborah L. Rhode, ACCESS TO JUSTICE 122–24 (2004), "stating that indigent defense services are grossly underfunded and overextended, particularly in comparison to the resources given to prosecutors and other government entities").

5 Tigran W. Eldred, *Prescriptions for Ethical Blindness: Improving Advocacy for Indigent Defendants in Criminal Cases*, 65 RUTGERS L. REV. 333, 334 (2013) (pointing out that the persistent failure of indigent criminal defendants to receive adequate legal representation is so well documented that it is no longer news).

6 The ACLU has initiated a number of affirmative civil actions designed to improve local jurisdictions' "failing public defense systems." *See, e.g.*, American Civil Liberties Union, Phillips v. California Complaint, available at: www.aclu.org/legal-docu ment/phillips-v-state-california-complaint. The Sixth Amendment Center crafts detailed reports to assist defender systems obtain better funding and resources. Sixth Amendment Center, *Homepage*, available at http://sixthamendment.org.

7 Innocence Project. *Inadequate Defense*, available at www.innocenceproject.org/ causes-wrongful-conviction/inadequate-defense#overview.

8 Our nation increasingly relies upon police arrests and prosecution as a means of social control. *See, e.g.*, Katherine Beckett & Steve Herbert, BANISHED: THE NEW SOCIAL CONTROL IN URBAN AMERICA (2009). As a result, although serious crime has dropped over the last decade, the numbers of arrests for minor crimes, violations, and misdemeanors has remained high. *See, e.g.*, Jenny Roberts, *Why Misdemeanors Matter: Defining Effective Advocacy in the Lower Criminal Courts*, 45 U.C. DAVIS L. REV. 277, 281 n. 11 (2011).

9 Courts make change in ways other than through case decisions. Courts have administrative responsibilities and powers. In some jurisdictions, courts supervise which lawyers are assigned to cases, and can remove ineffective lawyers from case handling responsibilities or ensure that they are not given additional cases. In some jurisdictions, courts have limited the number of cases that can be assigned to defender offices. In response to litigation, courts have ordered widespread change. *See generally* Adele Bernhard, *Take Courage: What the Courts Can Do to Improve the Delivery of Criminal Defense Systems*, 63 U. PITT. L. REV. 293 (2002).

10 Strickland v. Washington, 466 U.S. 668, 685–91 (1984).

11 The first principle in the ABA's *Ten Principles of a Public Defense Delivery System* is the rule that the public defense function be independent from political influence and be subject to judicial supervision only to the same extent as private counsel. *See* AMERICAN BAR ASSOCIATION, TEN PRINCIPLES OF A PUBLIC DEFENSE DELIVERY SYSTEM (Feb. 2002), available at www.americanbar.org/content/dam/aba/administrative/legal_aid_indigent_defendants/ls_sclaid_def_tenprinciplesbooklet.authcheckdam.pdf.

12 *See, e.g.,* William S. Geimer, *A Decade of* Strickland's *Tin Horn: Doctrinal and Practical Undermining of the Right to Counsel,* 4 WM. & MARY BILL RTS. J. 91 (1995).

13 *See* Innocence Project, *The Causes of Wrongful Conviction,* available at www.innocenceproject.org/causes-wrongful-conviction.

14 *Id.*

15 Ken Armstrong & Steve Mills, *Inept Defense Clouds Verdict,* CHI. TRIB., Nov. 15, 1999, available at www.chicagotribune.com/news/chi-110309death-penalty-illinois-gallery-storygallery.html.

16 Emily West, *Court Findings of Ineffective Assistance of Counsel Claims in Post-Conviction Appeals among the First 255 DNA Exonerations,* available at www.innocenceproject.org/files/Innocence_Project_IAC_Report.pdf.

17 James S. Liebman, Jeffrey Fagan & Valerie West, *A Broken System: Error Rates in Capital Cases, 1973–1995,* June 12, 2000, available at www2.law.columbia.edu/instructionalservices/liebman/liebman_final.pdf, *reprinted in* James S. Liebman, Jeffrey Fagan, Valerie West & Jonathan Lloyd, *Capital Attrition: Error Rates in Capital Cases, 1973–1995,* 78 TEX. L. REV. 1839 (2000) (abridged version of the original).

18 NANCY J. KING, FRED L. CHEESMAN II & BRIAN J. OSTROM, FINAL TECHNICAL REPORT: HABEAS LITIGATION IN U.S. DISTRICT COURTS: AN EMPIRICAL STUDY OF HABEAS CORPUS CASES FILED BY STATE PRISONERS UNDER THE ANTITERRORISM AND EFFECTIVE DEATH PENALTY ACT OF 1996 27–31, 45–51 (2007), available at www.ncjrs.gov/pdffiles1/nij/grants/219559.pdf.

19 Ineffective assistance of counsel claims are also the most frequent claims brought by convicted defendants who are not innocent.

20 Daniel S. Medwed, *Up the River without a Procedure: Innocent Prisoners and Newly Discovered Non-DNA Evidence in State Courts,* 47 ARIZ. L. REV. 655 (2005).

21 James M. Anderson & Paul Heaton, *How Much Difference Does the Lawyer Make? The Effect of Defense Counsel on Murder Case Outcomes,* 122 YALE L.J. 154 (2012).

22 *Id.* at 179, 183.

23 *See generally id.*

24 A 2010 Brookings Institute study of federal judges' backgrounds finds most district court judges to be former state court judges, bankruptcy judges, or magistrate judges. Russell Wheeler, *Changing Background of U.S. District Judges,* 93

JUDICATURE (No. 4) 140 (Jan.–Feb. 2010), available at www.brookings.edu/~/media/research/files/articles/2010/2/district-judges-wheeler/o2_district_judges_wheeler.pdf.

25 In New York City, attorneys applying to join the panel of attorneys available for appointment to criminal cases must provide reviews from judges before whom they have tried cases or argued appeals.

26 Hinton v. Alabama, 134 S. Ct. 1081, 1088–89 (2014).

27 U.S. v. Hebshie, 754 F. Supp.2d 89 (D.Mass. 2010).

28 Hinton, 134 S. Ct. at 1081.

29 *Id.* at 1084.

30 Professor Stevenson is the founder and Executive Director of the Equal Justice Initiative and a Professor of Law at New York University School of Law. For more information, see *Bryan Stevenson Biography*, available at www.eji.org/BryanStevenson.

31 Hinton, 134 S. Ct. at 1086.

32 Hebshie, 754 F. Supp.2d at 89.

33 *Id.*

34 The Habeas Assistance and Training Project maintains *The Habeas Report*, available at www.capdefnet.org/hat/pubmenu.aspx?menu_id=114&id=43.

35 *See* Samuel R. Gross, Kristen Jacoby, Daniel J. Matheson, Nicholas Montgomery & Sujata Patil, *Exonerations in the United States 1989 Through 2003*, 95 J. CRIM. L. & CRIMINOLOGY 523 (2005).

36 AMERICAN BAR ASSOCIATION, GUIDELINES FOR THE APPOINTMENT AND PERFORMANCE OF DEFENSE COUNSEL IN DEATH PENALTY CASES (2003), available at www.americanbar.org/content/dam/aba/migrated/2011_build/death_penalty_representation/2003guidelines.authcheckdam.pdf.

37 Wiggins v. Smith, 539 U.S. 510 (2003).

38 I counted all successful IAC habeas appeals except for those filed in the D.C. Circuit.

39 542 U.S. 296 (2004).

40 543 U.S. 220 (2005).

41 United States Courts, *Judicial Business 2005*, available at www.uscourts.gov/statistics-reports/judicial-business-2005.

42 For example, in Lord v. Wood, 184 F.3d 1083 (9th Cir.1999), the Ninth Circuit found counsel was ineffective for failing to present testimony of three witnesses who stated that they had seen the murder victim the day after the petitioner allegedly murdered her. In Horton v. Massie, 2000 WL 107386 (10th Cir. Jan 31, 2000), the Tenth Circuit found counsel ineffective for failing to call petitioner's 3-year-old daughter and a psychologist to corroborate petitioner's claim that she took no part in the crime. I classified those decisions as failures to investigate. If courts granted habeas relief for counsel's failure to object to inadmissible evidence, or to protest an inaccurate charge, or to notice a conflict, I classified those decisions as IAC for legal errors.

43 Brandon L. Garrett, *Judging Innocence*, 108 COLUM. L. REV. 55, 114 (2008)

44 *See, e.g.,* Innocence Project, *Government Misconduct,* available at www.innocence project.org/causes-wrongful-conviction/government-misconduct.

45 *See, e.g.,* Spangenberg Group & Ctr. for Justice, Law & Society at George Mason Univ., *Assessment of the Missouri State Public Defender System* (2009), available at www.nlada.net/sites/default/files/2009%20Assessment%20of%20the% 20Missouri%20State%20Public%20Defender%20System%20(TSG).pdf.

46 Stephen R. Reinhardt, *The Demise of Habeas Corpus and the Rise of Qualified Immunity: The Court's Ever Increasing Limitations on the Development and Enforcement of Constitutional Rights and Some Particularly Unfortunate Conse-quences,* 113 MICH. L. REV. 1219, 1225 (2015)

47 *Id.* at 1219.

48 *Id.* at 1223.

49 *Id.*

50 Strickland, 466 U.S. at 669.

51 *Id.* at 709.

52 Furman v. Georgia, 408 U.S. 238, 306 (1972) (Stewart, J., concurring).

53 Russell Stetler & W. Bradley Wendel, *The ABA Guidelines and the Norms of Capital Defense Representation,* 41 HOFSTRA L. REV. 635, 635 (2013) (noting that the *ABA Guidelines* "as revised in 2003, [are] the single most authoritative summary of the prevailing professional norms in the realm of capital defense practice. Hundreds of court opinions have cited the Guidelines.").

54 AMERICAN BAR ASSOCIATION, *supra* note 36.

55 Wiggins v. Smith, 539 U.S. 510 (2003).

56 *Id.* at 524–25 (quoting the ABA Standards for Criminal Justice).

57 Mark W. Bennett, *Sudden Death: A Federal Trial Judge's Reflections on the ABA Guidelines for the Appointment and Performance of Defense Counsel in Death Penalty Cases,* 42 HOFSTRA L. REV. 391, 409–10 (2013).

58 *Id.* at 411.

59 Anthony G. Amsterdam, reporter, TRIAL MANUAL FOR THE DEFENSE OF CRIM-INAL CASES (1st ed. 1967), a joint project of the American College of Trial Lawyers, the National Defender Project of the National Legal Aid and Defender Association and ALI-ABA Committee on Continuing Professional Education.

60 *See* AMERICAN BAR ASSOCIATION, CRIMINAL JUSTICE SECTION STANDARDS: DEFENSE FUNCTION (3d ed. 1993), available at www.americanbar.org/publica tions/criminal_justice_section_archive/crimjust_standards_dfunc_toc.html.

61 *See* NATIONAL LEGAL AID AND DEFENDER ASSOCIATION, PERFORMANCE GUIDELINES FOR CRIMINAL DEFENSE REPRESENTATION (2010), available at www.nlada.net/library/article/na_performanceguidelines.

62 Amsterdam, *supra* note 59, at § 90.

63 Ideally, every jurisdiction would enact a post-conviction procedure available to bring "newly discovered evidence of innocence" to the trial court's attention so that the doctrine of IAC would not need to be used for that purpose.

64 ATUL GAWANDE, THE CHECKLIST MANIFESTO (2009).

65 The MacCrate report is a shorthand title for the AMERICAN BAR ASSOCIATION SECTION OF LEGAL EDUCATION AND ADMISSIONS TO THE BAR, REPORT OF THE TASK FORCE ON LAW SCHOOLS AND THE PROFESSION: NARROWING THE GAP (Robert MacCrate, ed., 1992).

66 Robert MacCrate, *Preparing Lawyers to Participate Effectively in the Legal Profession*, 44 J. LEGAL EDUC. 89, 89 (1994).

67 U.S. v. Hebshie, 754 F. Supp.2d 89 (D. Mass. 2010).

68 *Id.* at 112.

Procedural Changes

13

Post-Conviction Procedure

The Next Frontier in Innocence Reform

STEPHANIE ROBERTS HARTUNG

INTRODUCTION

The lessons learned from the DNA exonerations over the past quarter century expose a harsh reality in the American criminal justice system: existing appellate and post-conviction procedures fail to identify and remedy viable claims of actual innocence. In fact, in an analysis of the first 250 DNA exonerations, just 13 percent were successful in reversing their convictions through appellate or post-conviction procedures, a figure comparable to the reversal rate in rape and murder cases overall.[1] Furthermore, the work of the Innocence Project in New York City, along with an alliance of similar organizations known as the Innocence Network, has been instrumental in bringing about policy change in the pretrial and trial context, yet very few comparable reforms have occurred in the post-conviction realm. And while existing procedural avenues of relief available to convicted prisoners appear to be vast and exhaustive, they offer little more than a façade of protection.[2]

Over the last twenty-five years, the efforts of groups dedicated to freeing the innocent have had a profound impact on our criminal justice system. It is fair to label these collective efforts, as others have done, as a true "movement." Innocence advocates have achieved more than a thousand exonerations, freeing innocent prisoners proven to be factually innocent of the crimes charged,[3] among them, many whose cases lacked biological evidence for DNA testing. Beyond these individual victories, the Innocence Movement has spearheaded the drive for substantial reform of the criminal justice system as well.[4] It took the infallibility of DNA testing to expose fundamental flaws in our criminal justice system – including many that have been firmly established for centuries.[5] The Innocence Movement's efforts to reform pretrial and trial procedures have been modestly successful, and have begun to help mitigate what are now recognized to be the underlying causes of wrongful convictions.[6] For example, there have been widespread calls for reform relating to police eyewitness identification procedures, police interrogations, and the use of unverified forensic evidence since the dawn of the Innocence Movement.[7] However, success in achieving these reforms has been gradual and fragmented, with some states and local jurisdictions taking action more quickly than others.[8]

Additionally, the innocence reforms that have been implemented to date are primarily prospective, and limited in their scope. Specifically, they seek to prevent *future* wrongful convictions, but offer no remedy for innocent prisoners whose trials occurred long before these reforms took effect. To fully address the wrongful conviction crisis in the American criminal justice system, the proponents of innocence reform must seek retrospective policy change as well. This can be achieved by implementing reforms in post-conviction procedure to facilitate the process of remedying past injustices. Admittedly, lawmakers must balance the competing interests of finality and fairness in constructing post-conviction procedural changes, but in light of the exoneration data available today, a recalibration of this balance is long overdue.

Existing innocence reforms in the pretrial and trial context amount to a step in the right direction, but are insufficient by themselves, to eradicate wrongful convictions. In order to complete the collective mission of the Innocence Network member organizations, innocence reform must look both forward and backward.

1 *Looking Forward: Reforming Pretrial and Investigatory Procedure to Prevent Future Wrongful Convictions*

The Innocence Movement has focused its reform activities on the pretrial and trial context in response to factors identified as playing a significant role in wrongful convictions, that is, eyewitness identifications, coerced confessions, flawed forensics, and prosecutorial misconduct.[9] While many advocates have pressed for reform on these fronts during the last two decades, state courts and legislatures have responded slowly. In fact, policy changes in the realm of pretrial and trial procedure have occurred in somewhat *ad hoc* fashion, and vary greatly from state to state.[10] Further, these reforms have primarily been forward-looking, and have revolved around how to prevent wrongful convictions of the innocent in the future by correcting faulty methods of police procedure and prosecution practice.[11]

1.1 Eyewitness Identification

The exoneration dataset has identified eyewitness misidentification as the primary factor present in wrongful convictions, with one or more such identifications playing a role in roughly 72 percent of the first 300 DNA exonerations.[12] In response to this realization, a few state courts and legislatures have begun to impose – or at least encourage – new police procedures.[13] Specifically, courts have gradually applied more scrutiny to eyewitness identifications, and have imposed new police procedures, such as favoring double-blind administration[14] by police and discouraging oral feedback to witnesses.[15] Additionally, police departments increasingly favor video recording of all identification procedures, and the use of a single sequential photo lineup,[16] rather than the presentation of a simultaneous photo array.[17] However, while reforms of eyewitness identification procedures have begun to take hold in a handful of states, these reforms fall significantly short of a universal change in the law.[18]

Given that eyewitness identification is recognized as the primary factor present in wrongful convictions, one would expect reforms in this realm to be broader reaching.[19] Yet this is not the case. Notably, the National Institute of Justice (NIJ) issued a set of guidelines regarding police identification procedures way back in 1999.[20] These guidelines relied heavily on social science research and sought to mitigate the risk of erroneous identifications. However, as of 2011, fewer than half of the surveyed police departments had instituted any part of the NIJ reform agenda, and those that had, did so in the last year of the study.[21] By 2012, statewide reforms of police lineup procedures had been implemented in just ten states.[22]

The policy work on behalf of the Innocence Network and member organizations on this front has been impressive, and there is undoubtedly cause for optimism regarding future policy change. Even so, the successes in the arena of eyewitness identification policy and procedure fall significantly short of universal reform.

1.2 Police Interrogation Procedures

The prevalence of coerced confessions among the DNA exoneration pool has led to reforms in the realm of police interrogation procedures as well.[23] Of the first 300 DNA exonerations, 30 percent involved false confessions or guilty pleas.[24] In light of the prevalence of false confessions in convictions of the innocent, courts increasingly favor videotaping of all interrogation procedures where possible.[25] However, as with eyewitness identification reforms, discussed in Section 1.1, legislative and judicial reforms in the area of police interrogations vary from state to state, and are far from universal.[26] Indeed, as of 2011, only nineteen states had instituted a statewide mandate that interrogations be recorded.[27]

Additionally, in the wake of extensive social science research on juvenile brain development and behavior, courts have recently applied special scrutiny to juvenile confessions.[28] Given the particular susceptibility of juveniles to coercive police practices, along with the diminished ability to appreciate the long-term consequences of their decisions, courts have gradually begun to impose additional safeguards against coerced and false confessions among juveniles.[29]

Overall, although these reforms are promising, some observers of the criminal justice system have opined that a mandate of videotaping police interrogations, even if widely adopted, will not fully rectify the coerced confessions problem.[30] Instead, some have argued that to fully address the issue, attention must be focused on police training on interrogation tactics. Specifically, greater efforts to educate law enforcement about the dangers of tunnel vision and the coercive impact of existing interrogation techniques are more likely to bring about real change. For example, the Reid interrogation method – still employed in the overwhelming majority of police departments – has been widely criticized for its likelihood to produce false confessions.[31] Overall, while reforms relating to interrogation procedures are beginning to gain favor among state courts and legislatures, these efforts have not had a universal impact on the criminal justice system as a whole.

1.3 Unreliable Forensic Evidence

Finally, certain types of forensic evidence, such as bite mark, ballistics, and hair comparison, have been called into question as a result of the Innocence Movement exoneration data.[32] These data have revealed that faulty forensic evidence – either unreliable methodology, overstatements of the implications of findings or deliberate falsification of results – has played a substantial role in wrongful convictions to date.[33] Unreliable forensic science alone appeared in 52 percent of the first 250 DNA exonerations.[34] Although historically relied upon by prosecutors and courts as unassailable scientific evidence, these types of comparisons often yield unreliable results, given that the techniques have never been subjected to the rigors of scientific analysis.[35]

The clearest manifestation of innocence-related reforms in the realm of forensic science is the *National Academy of Sciences Report*.[36] This report articulated concerns about norms in the forensic science field, and proffered a broad agenda for reform.[37] Specifically, as the flaws in forensic science began to surface, the National Academy of Sciences published a report in 2009 ("NAS *Report*") concluding that an array of forensic methodologies traditionally relied upon to support criminal convictions, such as hair comparison, ballistics, bite mark and arson analysis, are unreliable, and unsupported by nationally recognized scientific standards.[38] The NAS *Report* emphasized the lack of standards implemented in crime labs carrying out forensic testing. These findings are particularly troubling, given the close affiliation that most crime labs have with local law enforcement.

In the wake of the NAS *Report*, there has been a call for state and local crime labs to operate independently from law enforcement.[39] Further, critics of current forensic science policies argue in favor of more robust and uniform accreditation policies for crime labs, and stricter certification requirements for forensic scientists.[40] Indeed, in response to the NAS *Report*, increasing numbers of states have enacted legislation establishing permanent forensic science oversight entities.[41]

Many forensic science disciplines are currently under siege. In response to the NAS *Report*, the FBI has recently undertaken a comprehensive review of all federal prosecutions where hair comparison analysis was relied upon in securing the conviction.[42] In doing so, the FBI and the U.S. Attorney's Office have collectively recognized the fundamental unreliability of – and lack of scientific support for – hair comparison evidence. Convictions supported by expert testimony relating to arson science and Shaken Baby Syndrome have been called into question in recent years as well.[43]

Overall, great strides have been made in recognizing and bringing national attention to how flawed forensic evidence has played a role in the wrongful conviction of the innocent. This public realization has helped create a crisis of confidence in the public's perception of the criminal justice system.[44]

The success of the innocence reform agenda in the pretrial and trial context over the last two decades is undoubtedly significant, particularly in the realm of eyewitness identification, police interrogation procedures, and forensic evidence. While these reforms are far from universal, their impact cannot be denied. However, to fulfill the mission of the Innocence Movement, reforms must not only address the underlying causes of wrongful convictions to prevent future injustices, but must also seek ways to address and remedy wrongful convictions that have already occurred.

2. *Looking Backward: The Need for Post-Conviction Procedural Reform to Remedy Past Wrongful Convictions*

While reform of police and prosecutorial practice is critical to help prevent future wrongful convictions of the innocent, its collective impact offers cold comfort to prisoners already serving time for crimes they did not commit. Granted, the Innocence Network organizations have had fantastic success in exonerating innocent prisoners.[45] Yet for each successful exoneration, countless prisoners with colorable innocence claims remain incarcerated.[46] For example, exonerations are exceedingly difficult to achieve in cases where biological evidence is either nonexistent, or has been lost, destroyed, or sufficiently corroded so as to make testing impossible.[47] Even with DNA evidence, undoing a wrongful conviction is no easy task; without it, the task is Herculean.

2.1 The Existing Post-Conviction Procedural Landscape

Existing state and federal post-conviction procedures erect so many barriers to claims of factual innocence, including strict filing periods and limitations on what constitutes "new" evidence, that courts rarely decide these issues on their merits.[48] And even when they do, the burden of establishing innocence is prohibitively high. Thus, prisoners who successfully uncover new evidence in support of their innocence – but do not have the benefit of "smoking gun" DNA evidence pointing to the true perpetrator – are frequently left without a viable post-conviction procedural avenue for relief.[49] This reality is only exacerbated by the attitudes of many courts and prosecutors, who are resistant to reopening criminal cases once a conviction has been obtained.[50] This institutional bias in favor of preserving convictions at all costs is ubiquitous in red and blue states alike.

As an example, in Massachusetts – an ostensibly liberal and progressive jurisdiction – the Appeals Court in 2014 summarily upheld the denial of a motion for new trial, even in the face of exculpatory DNA evidence.[51] The rape allegations were strongly contested at trial, but the reviewing court deemed post-conviction DNA testing excluding the defendant as the source of the semen in the victim's underwear as insufficient for a new trial.[52] Although it is difficult to imagine what kind of evidence, physical or otherwise, could be more directly supportive of the defendant's innocence, the court dismissed the claim with very little discussion.[53] Although the Supreme Judicial Court has since vacated the conviction and remanded the case for a new trial,[54] this case nonetheless illustrates the uphill battle facing prisoners seeking post-conviction relief based on actual innocence.

Given that state and federal prisoners have an array of appellate and collateral procedures available to them – including direct appeal, state post-conviction review, and federal habeas corpus review – post-conviction innocence reform could target any number of fronts.[55] Indeed, some efforts to enhance state post-conviction review have been moderately successful. For example, District Attorneys' Offices in some jurisdictions have begun to implement Conviction Integrity Units (CIUs) as a means of internally reviewing and correcting wrongful convictions.[56] Some states have even adopted Innocence Commissions with varying roles. Some act as extrajudicial bodies, charged with reviewing post-conviction claims of actual innocence; others study wrongful conviction cases and propose reforms.[57] However, these efforts have occurred in an *ad hoc* manner at the state and local level, and have fallen short of broad national reform.

2.2 The Case for a Federal Post-Conviction Innocence Track

At the federal level, the post-conviction landscape is no friendlier to claims of actual innocence. To the contrary, federal habeas review, as revised in 1996 under the Antiterrorism and Effective Death Penalty Act (AEDPA), has been characterized as an unduly complex procedural labyrinth that is nearly impossible for prisoners or their counsel to navigate.[58] For example, petitioners seeking federal post-conviction relief under AEDPA must contend with rigid statute of limitations requirements, along with onerous rules relating to exhaustion and a high degree of deference afforded to the state courts.[59]

Given the significant procedural barriers imposed at the federal level – and in light of the piecemeal nature of state-level reform efforts – the most effective way to achieve universal reform of post-conviction review of innocence claims in every jurisdiction is to change federal habeas procedures.[60] Any attempt to reform post-conviction procedure at the state level would have to be undertaken state by state in an *ad hoc* fashion, and would fail to provide protection for all innocent prisoners, regardless of the jurisdiction of the underlying conviction. By contrast, the broad application of federal habeas review to all state and federal prisoners provides a more fertile landscape for universal reform of post-conviction procedure.

The original purpose of federal habeas corpus, under the Great Writ, was to provide redress for wrongfully convicted innocent prisoners who remain incarcerated in violation of the Constitution.[61] Yet the enactment of AEDPA operated to essentially foreclose post-conviction claims of innocence in the federal habeas context.[62] Since its passage, AEDPA has been widely criticized by legal scholars on a variety of grounds. In particular, AEDPA's critics have argued that the legislation was passed hastily in response to a national tragedy, with little thought or insight into the preclusive effect it would have on innocent prisoners.[63]

Even in the decades preceding the passage of AEDPA, legal scholars recognized the "primacy of innocence" in federal habeas jurisprudence, emphasizing the need to focus judicial attention on innocence claims in the post-conviction context.[64] However, a dramatic increase in the number of federal habeas petitions in the last several decades – due, in large part, to the impact of the due process revolution brought about by the Warren Court, along with a steady rise in prison populations – set the stage for the radical habeas reform that AEDPA wrought in 1996.[65] Thus, rather than increasing protections for prisoners raising post-conviction innocence claims, AEDPA has had precisely the opposite impact.

Notably, specific provisions of AEDPA have been criticized for erecting insurmountable procedural barriers to raising claims of innocence.[66] For example, AEDPA's bar on successive claims, the one-year statute of limitations, and the high standard of deference to the state courts all operate to weigh particularly heavily against actually innocent petitioners.[67] Essentially, far from striking a balance between competing public policy interests inherent in post-conviction review, AEDPA operated to value finality at the expense of fairness. Thus, the irony of the disparate impact that AEDPA has had on claims of innocence is that the *de facto* victims of its restrictions – innocent prisoners seeking post-conviction review of their convictions – were the original intended beneficiaries of federal habeas corpus review.

A fundamental problem with AEPDA is that it was debated and passed in the mid-1990s, well before the Innocence Movement was in full swing. Thus, as Congress sought to balance the competing interests of finality and fairness, while curbing the perceived "abuse of the writ," it did not have the benefit of the exoneration data available today.[68] In fact, it is not clear that Congress considered wrongful convictions of the innocent to be a significant problem worthy of discussion at all. As of 1996, when AEDPA was passed, just thirty prisoners had been exonerated with DNA – numbers that could be viewed as an anomaly in an otherwise "fair" criminal justice system.[69] Today, those numbers have increased exponentially, and continue to grow with each passing week.[70]

In light of the extensive exoneration data available today – and the depths of the wrongful conviction crisis it has uncovered – a recalibration of the balance between the traditional competing post-conviction policy interests of finality and fairness is warranted. It is undisputed that criminal prosecutions are lengthy and expensive endeavors that warrant eventual closure, for the benefit of the victims, the government, and all other parties involved. However, the knowledge that the conviction rate for the innocent is far more significant than previously believed possible should give pause to participants and observers of our criminal justice system. If nothing else, this realization should manifest itself in a willingness to scrutinize post-conviction claims of innocence more closely.

Given that AEDPA's procedural bars prevent most post-conviction innocence claims from ever being heard on the merits, the most effective way to provide a remedy for innocent prisoners is to adopt a federal post-conviction innocence track.[71] This approach would provide a means of addressing the shift away from the "primacy of innocence" in federal habeas jurisprudence since the passage of AEDPA. It would also revive a proposal raised by Professors Joseph Hoffmann and William Stuntz, more than twenty years ago, before AEDPA was passed.[72] In their influential article, Hoffmann and Stuntz argued that innocence claims should be treated differently than other types of habeas petitions.[73]

The arguments in favor of a federal post-conviction innocence track apply with even greater force today, twenty years after the Hoffman and Stuntz proposal, and in the wake of the havoc wreaked by AEDPA. This approach would operate to restore federal habeas corpus to its original purpose, by focusing judicial resources on petitioners raising viable claims of actual innocence.[74] Further, the establishment of an innocence track in this context would restore the primacy of innocence in federal habeas review,[75] and would strike a more measured balance between the competing interests of finality and fairness than the one achieved by the enactment of AEDPA.[76] Most importantly, this approach would help alleviate the disproportionate impact that AEDPA's provisions have had on prisoners raising claims of actual innocence.

The federal post-conviction innocence track approach contemplates a threshold showing of innocence in order to exempt prisoners from AEDPA's procedural restrictions. Under this proposed track, in order to receive an evidentiary hearing, a prisoner would be required to establish innocence by a "preponderance of the evidence." Restoring the "preponderance of the evidence" standard for demonstrating innocence – the standard historically imposed by common law prior to the passage of AEDPA[77] – would ensure that all viable claims of innocence would be eligible for the new proposed track. While this approach represents a departure from the "clear and convincing evidence" standard imposed under AEDPA, the relaxed standard is warranted given the modern public understanding of the depth of the wrongful conviction crisis. Further, under this proposal, once a petitioner is granted an evidentiary hearing, the burden of establishing innocence would be the more onerous "clear and convincing evidence" standard.

The federal post-conviction innocence track proposed here contemplates either a "naked" claim of innocence, or an innocence claim raised in conjunction with an allegation of a related constitutional violation, such as an ineffective assistance of counsel or *Brady* claim. Thus, the parameters of the federal post-conviction innocence track go beyond the innocence gateway that the Supreme Court established in *Schlup* v. *Delo*,[78] and more recently discussed in *McQuiggin* v. *Perkins*.[79] In both *Schlup* and *McQuiggin*, the Court's reasoning is limited to the context where innocence claims are accompanied by an alleged constitutional violation.[80]

Under this proposal, any prisoner who successfully establishes innocence by a preponderance of the evidence would be entitled to a blanket exemption from procedural bars. This exemption is consistent with the historic purpose of federal habeas corpus and the Supreme Court's jurisprudence. Thus, prisoners eligible for the federal post-conviction innocence track would not be subject to AEDPA's one-year limitations period, its bar against second or successive habeas petitions, or the high degree of deference afforded to the state court. Instead, eligible prisoners would be entitled to *de novo* review of the underlying state conviction.

While admittedly more costly, this approach strikes a more measured balance between the competing post-conviction policy interests of finality and fairness, and more directly reckons with the exoneration data available today. Although this proposal could be criticized as infringing on states' rights by affording less deference to state prosecutions and adjudications, the Supreme Court has long recognized that federal habeas corpus is, at its core, an "equitable remedy."[81] The Court has also repeatedly recognized the need for special treatment of innocence claims to preserve the fundamental purpose of our criminal justice system.[82] Thus, to fully address the depths of the wrongful conviction crisis in the American criminal justice system, the courts must be willing to exhaustively reexamine cases where a threshold showing of innocence has been met. To do otherwise is to turn a blind eye to profound and ongoing injustice.

CONCLUSION

Modern innocence reform in the realm of pretrial and trial procedure has been modestly successful. Judicial and legislative efforts to respond to some of the primary causes of wrongful convictions, including eyewitness identification, police interrogation, and forensic evidence, have indeed been significant in the last twenty-five years since the Innocence Movement has taken hold. However, these avenues of reform are primarily forward-looking, and seek to prevent the occurrence of future wrongful convictions. However, to fully realize the mission of the Innocence Movement, innocence reform efforts must look backward as well. Specifically, they must seek to identify and remedy wrongful convictions that have occurred in the past.

A radical restructuring of federal habeas review procedures presents the best opportunity for universal reform. The adoption of a federal post-conviction innocence track would achieve a more measured balance between finality and fairness and would help bring about the systemic, backward-looking reform of the criminal justice system that is long overdue.

NOTES

1 *See* BRANDON GARRETT, CONVICTING THE INNOCENT: WHERE CRIMINAL PROSECUTIONS GO WRONG 184 (2011) (noting that the 13 percent reversal rate for exonerees was "no different than the reversal rate of other rape and murder trials").

2 Stephanie Roberts Hartung, *Missing the Forest for the Trees: Federal Habeas Corpus and the Piecemeal Problem in Actual Innocence Cases*, 10 STAN. J. CIV. RTS. & CIV. LIBERTIES 55, 64 (2014) (noting that "at the state level, the factually innocent prison is left with the cold comfort of a plethora of review procedures, but no meaningful assessment of guilt or innocence after the trial").

3 *See* Innocence Project, *Homepage*, available at www.innocenceproject.php (as of May 2015, citing 329 DNA exonerations since 1990); National Registry of Exonerations, *Homepage*, available at www.law.umich.edu/special/exoneration/Pages/about.aspx (as of July 2015, citing 1,625 exonerations since 1989).

4 Marvin Zalman & Julia Carrano, *Sustainability of Innocence Reform*, 77 ALB. L. REV. 955, 956–57 (2013–14) ("What distinguishes ... the Innocence Network ... from earlier exoneration-only innocence groups is their realization that systemic policy reform is a necessary component of their work.")

5 *Id.* ("It took a slow-moving catastrophe, catalyzed by the advent of DNA profiling, to change this deep complacency and to begin to move the large and unwieldy adjudication system toward innocence reforms.")

6 *See generally* Robert J. Norris, Catherine L. Bonventre, Allison D. Redlich, & James R. Acker, *"Than That One Innocent Suffer": Evaluating State Safeguards against Wrongful Convictions*, 74 ALB. L. REV. 1301 (2010–11) (discussing the legislative and policy reforms in the criminal justice system in the fifty states in the wake of the Innocence Movement); *see also* Daniel S. Medwed, *Up the River without a Procedure: Innocent Prisoners and Newly Discovered Non-DNA Evidence in State Courts*, 47 ARIZ. L. REV. 655, 656 (2005) (citing the impact of DNA evidence in exposing wrongful convictions and leading to legal reforms in the criminal justice system).

7 *See* Norris et al., *supra* note 6.

8 For example, to date, three state appellate courts – from New Jersey, Oregon, and Massachusetts – have been instrumental in bringing about policy change regarding eyewitness identification procedures in their respective jurisdictions. *See, e.g.,* State v. Henderson, 27 A.3d 872 (N.J. 2011) (applying more expansive scrutiny to police eyewitness identification procedures in response to social science research and Innocence Movement exoneration data); State v. Lawson, 291 P.3d 673 (Or. 2012) (revising admissibility standards for eyewitness identification evidence to reflect new understanding of unreliability in light of social science research trends); Commonwealth v. Gomes, 22 N.E.3d 897 (Mass. 2015) (significantly expanding scope of eyewitness identification jury instructions to take into account new understanding of human memory based on social science research).

9 Tim Bakken, *Models of Justice to Protect Innocent Persons*, 56 N.Y.L. Sch. L. Rev. 837, 838–39 (2011–12) (arguing that Innocence Movement reforms of criminal justice system have primarily focused on pretrial procedural issues relating to police eyewitness identification and interrogation procedures, and prosecutorial misconduct).

10 *See* Innocence Project, *Reforms by State*, available at www.innocenceproject.org/news/LawView5.

11 Zalman & Carrano, *supra* note 4, at 956 ("Within two decades, innocence advocates have advanced an impressive array of criminal justice system changes that are likely to reduce the number of wrongful convictions.").

12 Bakken, *supra* note 9.

13 *See, e.g.,* State v. Henderson, 27 A.3d 872 (N.J. 2011) (applying more expansive scrutiny to police eyewitness identification procedures in response to social science research and Innocence Movement exoneration data); Commonwealth v. Gomes, 22 N.E.3d 897 (Mass. 2015) (relying on findings of state Supreme Judicial Court study on eyewitness identification, court issued new jury instruction template, taking into account social science research about the inherent unreliability of eyewitness identification accounts).

14 Double-blind administration of police eyewitness identification procedures occurs when "neither the witness herself nor the administrator should know which participant is the suspect in advance of the procedure." Nicholas Kahn-Fogel, *Manson And Its Progeny: An Empirical Analysis of American Eyewitness Law*, 3 Ala. C.R & C.L. L. Rev. 175, 187 (2012).

15 *See* Innocence Project, *Eyewitness Misidentification*, available at www.innocence project.org/fix/Eyewitness-Identification.php (recommending reforms to police eyewitness identification procedures including blind administration of live and photo lineup procedures, instruction to witnesses that perpetrator may not be present in lineup, and video recording of all identification procedures).

16 In essence, "[a] sequential procedure presents each photograph or lineup participant individually to a witness, as opposed to a simultaneous procedure where investigators present all the photographs or participants together." Winn S.

Collins, *Improving Eyewitness Collection Procedures in Wisconsin*, 2003 WIS. L. REV. 529, 559 (2003).

17 *See, e.g.*, State v. Henderson, 27 A.3d 872 (N.J. 2011) (applying more expansive scrutiny to police eyewitness identification procedures in response to social science research and Innocence Movement exoneration data).

18 *See* Carla Jones, *A New Age of Eyewitness Identification Evidence in Light of Modern Scientific Research: Why State v. Henderson Does Not Significantly Alter the Management of Eyewitness Identification Evidence*, 44 RUTGERS L.J. 511, 539–40 (2014) (discussing law enforcement resistance to reform of police investigatory procedures); Stanley Z. Fisher, *Eyewitness Identification Reform in Massachusetts*, 91 MASS. L. REV. 55 (2008) (discussing state-level eyewitness identification reforms in Massachusetts).

19 Zalman & Carrano, *supra* note 4, at 962 ("As the acknowledged 'leading cause' of wrongful convictions, eyewitness procedures have often been the first innocence reforms adopted by various jurisdictions.").

20 *Id.* (discussing NIJ guidelines).

21 *Id.* ("Fewer than half of the agencies made any changes in identification procedures after 1999, when the NIJ Guides were published, and the changes that were made were mostly instituted in 2010 and 2011.").

22 *See* Jones, *supra* note 18.

23 *See* Innocence Project, *False Confessions or Admissions*, available at www.innocen ceproject.org/understand/False-Confessions.php (discussing prevalence of coerced confessions in DNA exoneration cases and citing to legislative and judicial reforms).

24 *See id.* ("In about 30% of DNA exoneration cases, defendants made incriminating statements, delivered outright confessions, or pled guilty.").

25 *See, e.g.*, Commonwealth v. DiGiambattista, 813 N.E.2d 516 (Mass. 2004) (articulating judicial preference for audio and/or video recording of police interrogations and entitling defense to a jury instruction explaining that a failure to record can be viewed as evidence of foul play and a potentially involuntary confession).

26 Norris et al., *supra* note 6 (discussing extent of state reforms regarding police interrogation policies).

27 *Id.*

28 *See, e.g.*, Barry C. Feld, *Police Interrogation of Juveniles: An Empirical Study of Policy and Practice*, 97 J. CRIM. L. & CRIMINOLOGY 219 (2006) (examining social science research on juvenile brain development and discussing policy issues including video recording, length of interrogation, and use of false evidence during questioning); Jennifer Walters, *Illinois' Weakened Attempt to Prevent False Confessions and Potential Solutions*, 33 LOY. U. CHI. L.J. 487, 515–21 (2002) (discussing Illinois' law requiring presence of counsel for all juvenile interrogations).

29 *Id.*

30 *See, e.g.*, MARVIN E. ZALMAN & NANCY E. MARION, *The Public Policy Process and Innocence Reform*, in WRONGFUL CONVICTION AND CRIMINAL JUSTICE REFORM: MAKING JUSTICE 31 (Marvin Zalman & Julia Carrano, eds., 2014)

(arguing that videotaping police interrogations "may not be a sufficient resolution of the complex psychological factors that produce false confessions").

31 *See, e.g.,* RICHARD A. LEO, POLICE INTERROGATION AND AMERICAN JUSTICE (2009) (analyzing police interrogation practices in the United States and how they influence judges and juries in determining guilt).

32 *See* Innocence Project, *Unvalidated or Improper Forensic Science,* available at www.innocenceproject.org/causes-wrongful-conviction/unvalidated-or-improper-foren sic-science (identifying forensic techniques such as hair microscopy, bite mark comparisons, firearm tool mark analysis, and shoe print comparison as unreliable and untested by "rigorous scientific evaluation").

33 *Id.*

34 Daniel S. Medwed, *Introduction: Path Forward or Road to Nowhere? Implications of the 2009 National Academy of Sciences Report on the Forensic Sciences,* 2010 UTAH L. REV. 221, 221–22 (2010) (discussing role of faulty forensic evidence in DNA exoneration data).

35 *Id.*

36 *See* NATIONAL RESEARCH COUNCIL OF THE NATIONAL ACADEMIES, STRENGTHENING FORENSIC SCIENCE IN THE UNITED STATES: A PATH FORWARD (2009).

37 Zalman & Carrano, *supra* note 4, at 998 (noting that "for the first time [the NAS] report gave voice to deeper concerns within the forensic science community and proffered the goal of creating a more rigorous, self-critical field in the future").

38 Medwed, *supra* note 34, at 221 (discussing the significance of the 2009 Report of the National Academy of Sciences ["NAS Report"], and noting that the NAS Report supports a conclusion that "there are problems with the manner in which forensic science is (a) initially produced and (b) later presented as evidence in criminal trials").

39 *See, e.g.,* REBECCA MURRAY, LAUREL GEGNER & JUSTIN PELTON, *Policies, Procedures and the Police: An Assessment of Wrongful Conviction Risk in Nebraska,* in WRONGFUL CONVICTION AND CRIMINAL JUSTICE REFORM, *supra* note 30, at 131–32 (discussing findings of National Academy of Sciences Report).

40 *Id.* at 167–81 (discussing scope of forensic science reform in the wake of the Innocence Movement).

41 Norris et al., *supra* note 6, at 303 (noting that, as of 2011, thirteen states had established permanent forensic science oversight bodies).

42 *See Scientists Applaud FBI's Decision to Review Reliability of Forensic Hair Analysis,* MINT PRESS NEWS, July 25, 2013, available at www.mintpressnews.com ("The FBI said in more than 2000 cases from 1985–2000, analysts have exaggerated significance of hair analysis or reported them inaccurately.").

43 For a discussion of developments related to SBS and arson cases, see Keith A. Findley, *Flawed Science and the Next Wave of Innocents, supra,* in this volume.

44 Zalman & Carrano, *supra* note 4, at 997 (noting that the Innocence Movement has "probably generated a greater crisis of confidence in the forensic sciences than in any other adjudication system institution").

45 For the latest statistics on exonerations in the United States, see Innocence Project, *Homepage*, available at www.innocenceproject.php; National Registry of Exonerations, *Homepage*, available at www.law.umich.edu/special/exoneration/Pages/about.aspx.

46 Zalman & Carrano, *supra* note 4, at 956 ("Disquiet deepens when a wealth of scholarship shows that errors of justice are not inevitable results of human fallibility but are produced by systems that are correctible.")

47 *See, e.g.*, Shawn Armbrust, *Reevaluating Recanting Witnesses: Why the Red-Headed Stepchild of New Evidence Deserves Another Look*, 28 B.C. THIRD WORLD L. J. 75, 80 (2008) (noting that "courts are skeptical of newly discovered evidence claims because they are concerned about finality, believe firmly in the jury's ability to make factual determinations and have inherent doubts about the validity of evidence that is discovered after trial").

48 Hartung, *supra* note 2, 75–76 (2014) ("AEDPA has effectively rendered federal habeas corpus procedure a façade that appears to facilitate review of actual innocence claims without actually doing so.").

49 For example, in New York, a motion to vacate a conviction based on newly discovered evidence must be supported by evidence of such character so as to create a probability that had such evidence been received at trial, the verdict would have been more favorable to the defendant. N.Y. CRIM. PROC. LAW sec. 440.10 (2015).

50 *See* Daniel S. Medwed, *The Zeal Deal: Prosecutorial Resistance to Post-Conviction Claims of Innocence*, 84 B.U. L. REV. 125 (2004) (discussing prosecutorial attitudes and general resistance to post-conviction innocence claims).

51 Commonwealth v. Cameron, 17 N.E.3d 1118 (Mass. App. Ct. 2014).

52 *Id.*

53 *Id.*

54 Commonwealth v. Cameron, 39 N.E.3d 723 (Mass. 2015) (vacating rape conviction in light of newly discovered DNA results and remanding case to Superior Court for new trial).

55 *See* Hartung, *supra* note 2, at 59–67 (discussing state and federal direct appellate and post-conviction procedures available to prisoners raising claims of actual innocence).

56 *See* EVELYN L. MALAVE & YOTAM BARKAI, *Conviction Integrity Units: Toward Prosecutorial Self-Regulation?*, in WRONGFUL CONVICTION AND CRIMINAL JUSTICE REFORM, *supra* note 30, at 190–94 (discussing CIUs in Dallas, Manhattan, and Santa Clara County, CA).

57 *See, e.g.*, JON B. GOULD, THE INNOCENCE COMMISSION: PREVENTING WRONGFUL CONVICTIONS AND RESTORING THE CRIMINAL JUSTICE SYSTEM (2009) (discussing the founding and operation of the Virginia Innocence Commission).

58 Hartung, *supra* note 2, at 75–76 ("AEDPA has effectively rendered federal habeas corpus procedure a façade that appears to facilitate review of actual innocence claims without actually doing so.").

59 *See* Stephanie Roberts Hartung, *Habeas Corpus for the Innocent*, 19 U. Pa. J. Law & Soc. Change 1 (2016) (discussing procedural barriers to post-conviction innocence claims created by AEDPA).

60 *See id.* (arguing that "a comprehensive reexamination of federal habeas review and imposition of post-conviction innocence track would help bring about the systemic change absent from the Innocence Movement reforms achieved to date").

61 *See* Joseph C. Hoffmann & William J. Stuntz, *Habeas after the Revolution*, 1993 Sup. Ct. Rev. 65, 85 (1993) (noting that "nowhere is the remedial role of habeas so important as in the case of an innocent person").

62 *Id.* at 76–82.

63 *See, e.g.,* Mark Tushnet & Larry Yackle, *Symbolic Statutes and Real Laws: The Pathologies of the Antiterrorism and Effective Death Penalty Act*, 47 Duke L.J. 1, 2–5 (1997) (identifying AEDPA as an example of a "symbolic statute" where members of Congress seek to "claim credit for doing something about a problem to which they have been calling public attention"); Kenneth Williams, *The Antiterrorism and Effective Death Penalty Act: What's Wrong With It and How to Fix It*, 33 Conn. L. Rev. 919, 923 (2001) (discussing the "alarm" caused by the passage of AEDPA); Nat Hentoff, *Clinton Screws the Bill of Rights: The Worst Civil Liberties President Since Nixon*, Village Voice, Nov. 5, 1996, at 12 (asserting that AEDPA contains "the most draconian restrictions on habeas corpus since Lincoln suspended the Great Writ ... during the Civil War").

64 Hoffmann & Stuntz, *supra* note 61, at 85 (discussing the notion of "the primacy of innocence" in federal habeas corpus jurisprudence); Henry Friendly, *Is Innocence Irrelevant? Collateral Attack in Criminal Judgments*, 38 U. Chi. L. Rev. 142, 142–43 (1970) (arguing that "with few important exceptions, convictions should be subject to collateral attack only when the prisoner supplements his constitutional pleas with a colorable claim of innocence").

65 Nancy King & Suzanna Sherry, *Habeas Corpus and State Sentencing Reform: A Story of Unintended Consequences*, 58 Duke L.J. 1, 12–15 (2008) (discussing changes in state prison populations from 1990–2004).

66 *See, e.g.,* Williams, *supra* note 63, at 920 (discussing AEDPA's negative impact on federal post-conviction innocence claims).

67 *See* Hartung, *supra* note 2, at 76–82 (discussing criticisms of various AEDPA provisions impeding access to federal habeas review for prisoners raising claims of actual innocence).

68 *See* Kyle Reynolds, *"Second or Successive" Habeas Petitions and Late-Ripening Claims after* Panetti v. Quarterman, 74 U. Chi. L. Rev. 1475, 1479 (2007) (discussing the purpose of AEDPA "to restrict the filing of frivolous habeas petitions that are disruptive of judicial finality and parasitic upon official time").

69 *See* Innocence Project, *Know the Cases*, available at www.innocenceproject.org/know (identifying fewer than thirty DNA exonerations as of 1996, when AEDPA was passed).

70 *See* National Registry of Exonerations, *Homepage*, available at www.law.umich.edu/special/exoneration/Pages/about.aspx (as of July 27, 2015, listing seven new exonerations in the previous two months).

71 For a more complete discussion of the federal post-conviction innocence track proposal, *see* Hartung, *supra* note 59.

72 Hoffmann & Stuntz, *supra* note 61, at 85 (proposing a "factually innocent track" in federal habeas corpus procedure).

73 *Id.*

74 *Id.* (discussing the notion of "the primacy of innocence" in federal habeas corpus jurisprudence).

75 *Id.*

76 *See* Joshua Lott, *The End of Innocence? Federal Habeas Corpus Law After In Re Davis*, 27 GA. ST. U.L. REV. 443, 456–57 (2011) (characterizing justice and fairness as "secondary considerations" under AEDPA).

77 *See* Schlup v. Delo, 513 U.S. 298 (1995).

78 513 U.S. 298 (1995).

79 133 S. Ct. 1924 (2013).

80 Schlup, 513 U.S. at 325 (recognizing an innocence gateway to bypass procedural bars when accompanied by constitutional claim); McQuiggin, 133 S. Ct. at 1928 (holding that "actual innocence, if proved, [and when accompanied by a constitutional claim] serves as a gateway through which a petitioner may pass, whether the impediment is a procedural bar ... or ... expiration of the statute of limitations").

81 *See, e.g.*, Schlup, 513 U.S. at 320.

82 *Id.* at 324 (noting that the "individual interest in avoiding injustice is most compelling in the context of actual innocence").

14

Can We Protect the Innocent without Freeing the Guilty?

Thoughts on Innocence Reforms that Avoid Harmful Trade-offs

PAUL G. CASSELL

INTRODUCTION

The other thoughtful chapters in this book call for action to prevent factually innocent defendants from being convicted at trial. These chapters quite rightly draw attention to the fundamental importance of the criminal justice system accurately separating the guilty from the innocent. But the chapters' policy prescriptions, at least in some cases, rest on shakier ground.

In my contribution to the discussion, I address two points. First, protecting against wrongful convictions can create trade-offs. If poorly crafted, a reform measure might not only prevent convicting innocent persons but also guilty persons, allowing dangerous criminals to avoid incarceration and continue to victimize innocent persons. From a public policy perspective, these trade-offs create concern that reform measures may be cures worse than the disease.

With this caution in mind, I offer a second point: that it is possible to craft reforms that help to protect the innocent without allowing the escape of the guilty. A common theme underlying many of these proposals is that they reorient the criminal justice system away from adjudicating procedural issues and toward considering substantive issues – that is, issues of guilt or inno-cence. The truly innocent will benefit in a system that values substance over procedure. We ought to give serious consideration to measures that move the system in that direction.

I appreciate the helpful comments of participants in the Symposium on Wrongful Convictions and the DNA Revolution: Twenty-Five Years of Freeing the Innocent at Northeastern University School of Law and Ron Allen, Patricia Cassell, Sam Gross, Josh Marquis, Daniel Medwed, and Erin Riley. This research was made possible in part through generous support from the Albert and Elaine Borchard Fund for Faculty Excellence.

1 *Comparing and Quantifying the Risk of Wrongful Conviction to the Risk of Victimization*

1.1 Two Kinds of Tragedies

In considering the issue of wrongful convictions, some broader perspective is useful. To be sure, the conviction of even a single factually innocent person is a tragedy. A grave and serious injustice has been done whenever the criminal justice system wrongfully convicts and imprisons someone for a crime he or she has not committed.[1] But, sadly, this is not the only kind of tragedy that the criminal justice system must be concerned about.[2] A properly functioning criminal justice system has to consider not only the suffering of those who have been wrongfully convicted, but also those who have become (or will become) the victims of crimes.

Violent crime victims and their families suffer almost unimaginable emotional and physical pain – suffering that is often aggravated when the victim learns that the crime could have been prevented through a more effective criminal justice system. I will resist the temptation to appeal to the reader's emotions by recounting the specific details of what happened to them. The interested reader can easily find such unhappy details elsewhere.[3] And these kinds of tragedies occur frequently. As Josh Marquis has observed, "[t]he justice system is far from perfect and has made many mistakes, mostly in *favor* of the accused. Hundreds, if not thousands, have died or lost their livelihood through embezzlement or rape because the American justice system failed to incarcerate people who were guilty by any definition."[4]

How to assess these competing risks is exceedingly complex. Fortunately, other thoughtful observers have already done important spadework on this issue. An extremely helpful discussion of the convicting-the-guilty-while-sparing-the-innocent trade-off is found in Professor Ronald Allen and Investigator Larry Laudan's article *Deadly Dilemmas*.[5] They explain that "[w]hile the prospect of convicting or executing a truly innocent person is horrifying, this type of mistake occurs within a highly complicated matrix of relationships where other equally horrifying mistakes go unnoticed in the conventional discourse."[6] Allen and Laudan recognize that some public policy reform measures that reduce the risk of convicting an innocent person may simultaneously increase the risk that a guilty criminal will escape conviction and go on to commit additional violent crimes.

I will join Allen and Laudan in focusing on this possible trade-off – specifically, the risk that putting in place measures to protect against convicting innocent persons will allow guilty criminals to escape conviction. And I will likewise join them in narrowing the focus to a particular risk when the guilty are not convicted – the risk that an unconvicted criminal will go on to commit additional violent crimes (conventionally defined in the FBI's annual crime reports as murder, rape, robbery, and aggravated assault). Allen and Laudan have even attempted a tentative quantification of the precise trade-off that exists in the current structure of our criminal justice system. Rather than try to reinvent the wheel here on quantitative assessments of the trade-off, I want to simply take the Allen and Laudan calculation as accurate. In a separate article, I explore their numbers at greater length.[7]

Allen and Laudan concretely calculated comparative risks of a person being wrongfully convicted of a violent crime and being the victim of a serious crime. They derive an estimated lifetime risk of being wrongfully convicted for a serious crime of about 0.06 percent (6 out of 10,000).[8] They then compare this figure to the lifetime risk of a person being the victim of a violent crime – a risk of about 83 percent (or, for comparison, 8300 out of 10,000). Based on these figures, Allen and Laudan conclude that "we can say with considerable confidence that the [lifetime] risk of being the victim of a serious crime in the United States is significantly more than 300 times greater than the lifetime risk of being falsely convicted of a serious crime."[9]

1.2 How to Think about Trade-offs

What, then, to make of these estimated, and obviously very tentative, risk ratios? Of course, one possible response is to attack the figures that Allen and Laudan derive. Professor D. Michael Risinger, for example, has written a lengthy and interesting critique of the Allen and Laudan calculation[10] – a critique that I discuss at greater length elsewhere.[11] The Allen and Laudan risk ratio does not rest on definitive numbers. Instead, as Professor Marvin Zalman has helpfully suggested, these kinds of calculations are estimates – perhaps akin to a National Intelligence Estimate that is provided in a national security context.[12] But even assuming that the criminal justice system suffers a much higher rate of erroneous conviction than Allen and Laudan suggest, it is clear that the average person stands a vastly higher chance – by many multiples – of being a victim of violence than a casualty of a wrongful conviction. What I want to do here is assume that their calculation is roughly correct and tease out the implications.

Based on their risk ratio, Allen and Laudan contend that "insisting that we spare no efforts to reduce the risk of false conviction – even if the necessary measures significantly increase the risk of being a crime victim – is irrational."[13] In response, Risinger contends that the risk ratio of being a violent crime victim to being wrongfully convicted of a violent crime "does not make much difference" because "some such substantially higher risk must always attach to the risk of being a victim over the risk of being a convicted innocent simply as an inevitability of any likely set of social arrangements in the real world."[14]

If I am reading Risinger correctly, I disagree with his position. The ratio of victims to wrongful convictions will always be (and should always be) greater than one. But surely it makes some difference in assessing proposed reform measures whether the ratio is in the neighborhood of, let's say, 2:1 or 300:1 (as Allen and Laudan suggested) or even more. Where the debate in this country is over what set of "social arrangements" – that is, what sorts of innocence-protecting procedures ought to be in place in the criminal justice system – the size of these potential trade-offs matter. Indeed, Risinger himself does not appear to hold rigidly to his position. In the penultimate sentence of his article, he makes a strong plea for adopting reforms that "help significant numbers of innocent convicted innocents without seriously impacting the rate of true convictions."[15] Of course, making assessments about what are "significant" numbers of innocent persons and whether an impact on the true conviction rate is "serious" requires some consideration of the magnitude of the numbers involved.

Risinger stands on much stronger ground in explaining that reform measures for addressing wrongful convictions can be divided into two categories with different moral implications: Some reforms improve the diagnosticity of the system and thereby reduce the incidence of *both* wrongful convictions and wrongful acquittals or constitute reforms that protect the innocent with no reduction in convictions of the guilty – reforms that should be relatively uncontroversial. Other reforms, however, increase the protections for the innocent at the expense of freeing more guilty persons – reforms that are more controversial precisely because of the trade-off involved.[16]

The possibility that the most significant reforms will produce significant trade-offs cannot be overlooked. One concrete illustration (provided by Allen and Laudan) is reforms regarding eyewitness identification. This appears to be one of the most common causes of wrongful convictions.[17] And yet many of the reform measures to address the problem appear to carry with them not only the prospect of avoiding misidentifications but also the possibility of discouraging accurate identifications.[18] More broadly, as Professor Chris Slobogin has noted, "[m]ost reformist energy has understandably been focused on reducing wrongful convictions, through improved interrogation techniques, and identification procedures, defense involvement in the investigative process, and the like. Most of these reforms, however, could also increase wrongful acquittals . . . ."[19]

Fully assessing the trade-offs involved between what might be called rightful convictions and wrongful acquittals is an issue that dates back at least to Blackstone's suggestion that it is "[b]etter that ten guilty persons escape than that one innocent suffer."[20] A strong argument can be made (and has been made by Risinger, among others in that long tradition) that the State bears a "special responsibility to insure that innocents that it sweeps up in carrying out its crime-control functions are not convicted" – a responsibility that exceeds its obligations to prevent crime that is the "free-will-based choice" of a criminal.[21]

And it also seems likely that the societal costs of a single wrongful felony conviction are higher than the societal costs of a single violent crime (setting aside the special case of homicide). One way to quantify this point would be to compare jury verdicts (or civil settlements) in cases of wrongful conviction with jury verdicts in cases of criminal assaults. A recent study, for example, estimated the total tangible plus intangible pre-offense cost for different crimes (in 2008 dollars). The study concluded that the loss per crime victimization can be quantified as $8,982,907 for a murder, $240,776 for a rape/sexual assault, $107,020 for an aggravated assault, and $42,310 for a robbery.[22] Comparable data could be collected for wrongful conviction cases, where substantial civil judgments (some of them larger than the numbers just cited)[23] have been entered in favor of those wrongfully convicted. A further quantitative refinement of the trade-offs discussed above would then be possible.[24]

But adding to the complexities, there is a good possibility that releasing a guilty criminal produces not a single violent crime, but rather multiple crimes. Criminals have high rates of recidivism and, if not incarcerated, may commit dozens of crimes before caught.[25] Laudan, for example, has estimated that "every false acquittal enables more than thirty-six crimes (including on average seven violent ones) during the time when, but for the false acquittal, the defendant would have been incapacitated."[26]

One other qualitative factor might also need to be entered into the calculation: The general moral culpability of those who have been wrongfully convicted versus those who have been victims of crime. The reader of this book, after seeing numerous accounts of wrongful convictions, may wonder what he or she can do to avoid such a fate. While the other chapters in this book do not discuss the answer to this question in detail, it seems likely that the best single answer is a simple one: Don't commit a serious crime, particularly a crime of violence. While the innocence literature does not highlight the fact, it appears that many of those wrongfully convicted were convicted because they had committed other crimes – either at the time of the crime for which they were wrongfully convicted or earlier. For example, prior arrests can produce police photographs that can end up in a photospread to be misidentified. Or prior crimes may arouse the suspicion of police detectives.

One prominent illustration of how the wrongfully convicted may have some moral culpability is Anthony Porter, who was convicted of committing a drug-related homicide in Illinois. But it was apparently difficult for him to present a defense to that charge, because he may have been committing an armed robbery in the same park at the same time. He ran from the park, gun in hand, in full view of witnesses. Porter then denied not only the murder, but also being in the park – a lie he maintained until after his convictions were affirmed.[27]

The prevalence of criminal activity by those wrongfully convicted is suggested by a case I recently worked on involving an alleged wrongful conviction of Robert Wilcoxson.[28] The North Carolina Innocence Inquiry Commission found Wilcoxson to be innocent of a drug-related murder. But it appears that one reason he fell under suspicion is that (by his own admission) at the time of the murder he was an armed cocaine dealer making tens of thousands of dollars from his crimes.[29] Four other adults also fell under suspicion and were also convicted, wrongfully they have argued. Still, it appears that they may have *all* been involved in doing a series of armed robberies at around the same time.[30] Thus, in this one case, possibly involving multiple wrongful convictions, it appears that all five of the allegedly wrongfully convicted participants were involved in other dangerous crimes apart from the murder for which they were convicted, which made it harder for them to convince authorities of their innocence.

The point here is not to blame those wrongfully convicted for their plight. The more limited point is that, when assessing the priority to be given to competing claims between those wrongfully convicted and those who are past (or prospective) crime victims, in the aggregate the victims may have a far stronger claim. Some support for this position comes from a study reporting that, for homicide and assault cases, the majority of the victims had no prior arrest record, while the majority of the offenders did.[31]

A related point can be made about the wrongfully convicted who have pled guilty. Unless the defendant has entered an *Alford* plea (refusing to plead guilty but preserving his position of innocence), he has almost certainly committed perjury before the Court in entering his plea. Consider, for example, Robert Wilcoxson and Kenneth Kagonyera.[32] At their guilty plea hearings, both swore under oath that they were guilty, that they were satisfied with defense counsel, and that the other requisites for a knowing and voluntary guilty plea existed. So far as the court records reveal, they also made no effort to enter an *Alford* plea. In addition, following Kagonyera's decision to plead guilty, he met with the prosecutor and, in the presence of defense counsel, made a very detailed statement about his involvement in the murder, implicating five other people.[33] Kagonyera made these statements at his own initiative in an effort to convince the District Attorney that he could provide useful information by testifying against his codefendants.[34]

To be clear, if Kagonyera and Wilcoxson were in fact innocent,[35] their guilty pleas were plainly wrongful convictions. And no doubt, their pleas resulted from a plea bargaining process that can be coercive and place considerable pressure on even innocent persons to plead guilty – making the choice of an innocent person to plead guilty in some sense rational.[36] But particularly where defendants (like Kagonyera and Wilcoxson) have made no effort to enter *Alford* pleas,[37] a decision to mislead the Court and enter a guilty plea produces a wrongful conviction that is, at least to some extent, the result of illegal choices on their part and presumably entitled to somewhat less weight in a social harm calculus.[38]

I would like to see more discussion of and data on these questions, and particularly the extent to which those wrongfully convicted had prior criminal records or were participating in crimes at the time of the offense for which they were wrongfully convicted. (Similar data on victims would be interesting too.) But the critical point here is that unraveling such competing claims to priority in reform promises to be very difficult.

In this short chapter, rather than embark on what would be a complicated effort to precisely quantify trade-offs for particular reforms, I would like to search for reforms that help protect the innocent without freeing the guilty[39] – reforms that ought to be relatively uncontroversial, at least for those (including many of the authors in this book) who prioritize innocence issues over other values in the criminal justice system.[40] I agree with those who argue that the risk our criminal justice system poses to the innocent is not trivial.[41] But as the above quantification suggests, neither is the risk to crime victims, who bear the brunt of any failures of the system to apprehend or prosecute dangerous criminals. It is against that backdrop that I turn to possible reforms that try to carefully attend to both sides of the equation.[42]

2 *Protecting the Innocent While Simultaneously Convicting the Guilty*

In light of the risk of potential trade-offs between convicting the guilty while protecting the innocent, the reforms that are most likely to be justified on cost-benefit analysis will be those that do not present any significant risk of increasing crime victimization rates. I have previously offered some thoughts on how this might be done.[43] This short section highlights a few promising possibilities.

2.1 More Research on the Frequency and Causes of Wrongful Convictions

At the top of my list of measures to address the problem of wrongful convictions of the innocent is further research on the extent and causes of the problem.[44] In the previous section, I noted the Allen and Laudan calculations, which rested on very thin data.[45] For public policy purposes, we need more information – information about, for example, wrongful convictions through guilty pleas (a key part of the Allen and Laudan estimate) and solid information about the incidence of wrongful convictions outside the areas of homicide and rape.

The additional research needs to focus on the frequency of false confessions. Professor Samuel Gross has aptly observed that "[t]he most important question about false convictions is also the most basic: How frequently are innocent people convicted of crimes?"[46] To be sure, on the twenty-fifth anniversary of the first DNA exonerations, we now have far more information about wrongful convictions than in the past. But even disregarding the questions about how "innocence" is determined in some of this research,[47] a more fundamental problem is the fact that a collection of alleged miscarriages based on DNA or any other factor may not be representative of the processing of cases in the American criminal justice system.[48]

To avoid this problem, researchers could take a random sample of a large number of felony violent crime cases (1,000 seems like a good number) and then track them through the system to see what happens.[49] While it might not be possible to follow all 1,000 cases carefully, it would seem likely that the cases where a defendant might plausibly be innocent would shrink the numbers down fairly rapidly. Researchers could focus on this subset of cases and try to come up with an initial, plausible number of cases in which a wrongful conviction was even a possibility, and then perhaps press even further to try and get to the bedrock truth in this subset of cases. This methodology has already been employed in other countries in the false confessions area.[50] It should be tried on the broader subject of wrongful convictions. Research of this type might be very valuable for revealing both the scope of the wrongful conviction problem and particular areas where wrongful convictions are prevalent. This would permit a targeted response to the problem, perhaps more narrowly addressing the risk to the innocent without freeing the guilty.[51]

2.2 Refocus Post-Conviction Relief on Claims of Factual Innocence

One of the great problems for the Innocence Movement is trying to find the needles in a large haystack – that is, trying to identify innocent persons in a criminal justice system that processes mostly guilty defendants. Some commentators have made a frontal assault on this problem by proposing that we limit access to some forms of judicial review to those who are making claims of actual innocence. For example, two distinguished legal scholars – Joseph Hoffmann and Nancy King – proposed that federal habeas corpus review of noncapital state court convictions and sentences should, with narrow exceptions, be abolished except for those who couple a constitutional claim with "clear and convincing proof of actual innocence."[52] Relying on a comprehensive study of federal habeas corpus filings,[53] they found that only 7 of the 2,384 noncapital habeas filings in the study (0.29 percent) resulted in a grant of habeas relief, and one of those seven was later reversed on appeal.[54] Hoffmann and King argued that habeas review of such claims "currently squanders resources while failing to remedy defense-attorney deficiencies. Those resources should be redeployed where they have a more meaningful chance of preventing the deficiencies in the first place."[55] They propose moving resources to indigent defense representation instead of largely pointless habeas litigation.

Hoffmann and King's proposal is similar to others that have tried to focus habeas corpus on protecting the innocent. Most famously, Judge Henry Friendly argued that federal habeas relief for most constitutional errors should be conditioned on a showing of innocence.[56] Interestingly, he also proposed that a sufficient demonstration of innocence should itself be a basis for habeas relief,[57] an issue that has bedeviled the Supreme Court in recent years.[58] Similarly, Professors John Jeffries, Jr. and William Stuntz have suggested allowing defaulted federal claims to be raised in federal habeas where those claims present a reasonable probability that the defaulted claims resulted in an erroneous conviction.[59] Professor Samuel Gross has argued for giving a defendant claiming innocence the option for an "investigative trial," in which the defendant would be able to argue his innocence, provided he waived important rights – in exchange, the defendant (if convicted) would be given greater freedom to raise post-conviction claims of innocence.[60] And most recently, in this book, Professor Stephanie Hartung has argued for a post-conviction "innocence track" in federal habeas, under which any prisoner who establishes innocence by a preponderance of the evidence would be entitled to a blanket exemption from procedural bars.[61]

One of the interesting things about post-conviction review is that, by definition, it cannot interfere with the process of convicting the guilty at trial. Accordingly, post-conviction review offers a particularly promising approach for escaping the trade-offs highlighted earlier.[62]

One proposal worth serious exploration combines aspects of the Hoffmann and King proposal, along with Judge Friendly's insight that federal habeas should focus on innocence and Professor Hartung's idea for an innocence track. We could restrict federal habeas to those who have a colorable claim of factual innocence. Those prisoners could then be required to establish factual innocence by a preponderance of the evidence and, if they did so, they would have a blanket exemption from any procedural bars to raising claims for relief in federal court.[63] I would also add to Hartung's innocence track the idea that if a prisoner who had proven he was innocent did not receive federal habeas relief, the federal courts could at least remand the case back to the prisoner's state Supreme Court for further inquiry as to whether state relief might be available.

Professor Hartung (and others) may wonder why the innocence track needs to be coupled with the abolition of federal habeas for those who are raising claims unrelated to innocence. The answer is straightforward: time, energy, and resources are limited. Given Hoffmann and King's finding that federal habeas relief for procedural violations is essentially an impossibility, it make no sense to allow those claims to continue to be pressed before federal courts. Restructuring federal habeas so that it *only* concerns prisoners alleging factual innocence would help federal courts reconceptualize their mission to the benefit of wrongfully convicted prisoners – precisely the sort of change that helps the innocent without freeing the guilty. It seems almost irrefutable that the innocent will benefit from a system concentrating on them – that is, that we can find needles more effectively in smaller haystacks.

2.3 Increasing Resources for Indigent Defense Counsel and Prosecutors to Focus on Issues Relating to Actual Innocence

On the issue of wrongful convictions, the elephant in the room is little discussed but obvious: money. The root cause of wrongful convictions is almost certainly insufficient resources devoted to the criminal justice system. Whatever individual causes might be pinpointed in particular cases, more resources would often have enabled defense counsel (or police and prosecuting agencies) to locate persuasive evidence of innocence.[64] If this diagnosis is correct, then an important part of the true solution to the wrongful conviction problem may be devoting additional resources to the criminal justice system.[65]

Given the fiscal realities of the world we live in, however, it may be an academic proposal to call for significant new funding for defense attorneys, for example.[66] At a macro level, the funds devoted to the criminal justice system are probably roughly fixed and not much is likely to change in the near term.[67] What is needed, then, is to prioritize innocence over other criminal justice expenditures. Fortunately, for those who truly believe in "innocentrism," there are ways to do this – as I discuss in the next several sections.

2.4 Abolishing the Fourth Amendment Exclusionary Rule, and Consequently Shifting Defense Resources Away from Litigating Purely Procedural Claims

If we want the criminal justice system to prioritize the issue of innocence and devote more resources to it, then a good start would be to consider abolishing the Fourth Amendment exclusionary rule. Abolition of the rule and replacing it with a system of civil damage remedies has been advocated by such distinguished legal figures as Chief Justice Warren Burger,[68] Dallin Oaks,[69] Akhil Amar,[70] Bill Pizzi,[71] and Paul Robinson.[72] The classic argument for abolishing the exclusionary rule is that the rule sets criminals free because the constable has blundered.[73] But there is a more subtle, and in many ways more pernicious, defect to the exclusionary rule. Under a regime that allows the "deliberate exclusion of truth from the fact-finding process,"[74] defense efforts will move toward issues involving the validity of evidence collection rather than toward assessing the quality of the evidence itself. Professor William Stuntz perhaps most famously made this point in his writings, explaining how a system with limited resources that emphasizes procedure over substance will give short shrift to factual claims of innocence.[75] Stuntz is cautious in his argument. As he explains, the current system does not simply involve a direct trade-off, but rather "places substantial pressure on [defense] counsel to opt for the procedural claim rather than the (potential) substantive one."[76] But Stuntz's bottom-line conclusion seems unassailable: there is some trade-off in the current regime favoring procedural claims over substantive ones.[77]

In addition to these kinds of trade-offs, the exclusionary rule creates a perverse screening at trial.[78] Jurors deciding cases may believe that a weak prosecution case actually is the result of the exclusion of evidence. Because of facts such as these, it seems difficult to contest that "actually guilty defendants are most likely to benefit from the exclusionary rule."[79]

Given these trade-offs, those with an innocentric view of the world should be the first to jump on the replace-the-exclusionary-rule-with-civil-damages bandwagon. Surely the experience of the rest of the world suggests that the exclusionary rule is not the only way to restrain police abuses.[80] There is good reason to think that we can craft a damages regime for protecting Fourth Amendment rights that will fully preserve them, just as we rely on a damages regime to protect other civil liberties, such as our First Amendment rights.[81]

Once procedural issues regarding the legality of searches are diverted to the civil justice system, the criminal justice system would gain substantial new resources to devote to innocence issues. While the percentage of cases in which the exclusionary rule results in guilty criminals going free is disputed,[82] it does not appear to be disputed that the exclusionary rule results in "tens of thousands of contested suppression motions each year."[83] Instead of filing and litigating these motions that have nothing to do with innocence, defense counsel could turn their attention to substantive issues about who committed the crime. Prioritizing substantive issues of guilt and innocence over procedural issues of the reasonableness of searches is exactly the way the system should be structured – and a way that *both* increases the chance of convicting the guilty while reducing the chance of convicting the innocent.

2.5 Replacing the Miranda Regime with the Videotaping of Custodial Interrogations

The problem of procedure over substance is not confined solely to Fourth Amendment jurisprudence. The same flaw has developed in confession law. Here again, those who are most concerned about innocence should be skeptical of the law's current structure, which relies largely on *Miranda* warnings and waivers to protect against coercive interrogations. As a practical matter, this approach does little to help the innocent and prioritizes litigation about *Miranda* compliance over litigation about the accuracy of confessions. The result has been a regime that is not particularly well-suited to address "false confession" issues[84] – that is, is not well-suited to protecting the innocent. Today *Miranda* "serves mainly to distract lawyers, scholars, and judges from considering the real problem of interrogation, which is how to convict the guilty while protecting the innocent."[85]

The "central problem with *Miranda* is that it was not crafted specifically to prevent false confessions, but rather to regulate interrogations more generally."[86] The problem starts with the probability that innocent defendants are most likely to waive their *Miranda* protections. Innocent persons have nothing to hide from the police, and so they almost invariably waive their *Miranda* rights.[87] Once they waive their rights, the *Miranda* procedures do little (if anything) to restrain police questioning techniques, a point that seems to be generally accepted.[88]

Miranda's procedural requirements, like those of the Fourth Amendment exclusionary rule, also shift defense attorney time and attention away from claims of innocence. The *Miranda* procedures have spawned considerable litigation about whether a suspect was in "custody," whether a suspect "waived" his rights, or whether a suspect "invoked" his right to counsel.[89] These issues generally have little to do with the reliability of any confession that police might obtain through questioning. Thus, like the Fourth Amendment exclusionary rule, these issues tend to draw defense attorney attention toward raising claims about process rather than about substance.[90]

Miranda has also turned the attention of trial judges away from questions of the reliability of confessions and toward questions about police compliance with the *Miranda* rules. As Professor Welsh White has observed, before *Miranda*, reliability "played an important role in our constitutional jurisprudence ... [Since *Miranda*], however, courts and legal commentators have largely ignored issues relating to untrustworthy confessions."[91] To be sure, as a matter of black letter law, the *Miranda* procedural requirements were piled on top of traditional voluntariness requirements. But as a practical matter, judicial attention is a scarce resource. *Miranda* has created a triumph of formalism.[92] Prioritizing one set of claims (*Miranda* compliance) has inevitably reduced scrutiny of the others – to the disadvantage of innocent defendants. As Professor Steven Duke has explained, not only is *Miranda* "virtually useless," but it "replaced a vibrant and developing voluntariness inquiry that took into account the vulnerabilities of the particular suspect as well as the inducement and conditions of the interrogation."[93] The bottom line is that "not only has *Miranda* allowed the police to disregard actual voluntariness, it has enabled the courts to be equally unconcerned with actual innocence."[94]

One last injury to innocent defendants is worth noting. Good reasons exist for believing that *Miranda* has significantly hampered the ability of police officers to obtain confessions from guilty criminals.[95] This has not only harmed law enforcement's ability to convict guilty criminals but also the opportunity of innocent individuals to use those confessions to exonerate themselves.[96] For example, Professor Gross has noted that the number of exonerations when the actual criminal confessed declined sometime between the mid-1950s and the early 1970s.[97] Gross cites among the possible causes the *Miranda* decision, which "may result in some reduction in the number of confessions."[98] Thus, by impairing the system's ability to get to the truth in cases, *Miranda* has caused the innocent to suffer.

A system that respects the constitutional right against self-incrimination, while at the same time providing greater protection for innocent suspects, could be easily designed. There appears to be wide agreement that video recording interrogations would offer far greater protection for innocent suspects than does the current *Miranda* regime.[99] I made a proposal long ago for using video recording of police questioning as a substitute for *Miranda*, based in part in the need to protect the innocent.[100] Other commentators have proposed that recording should supplement *Miranda*.[101] A fair number of jurisdictions are moving forward with requiring video recording of at least some interrogations,[102] although recording is often left to the discretion of police officers or mandated only for very serious crimes. The "Innocence Movement" could speed the adoption of this important reform if they would highlight the extent to which *Miranda* does not offer effective protection to the innocent and suggest that, instead, we should use video recording.

Moving in this direction has the great advantage of not interfering with the conviction of the guilty. It appears that video recording does not greatly interfere with the ability of law enforcement to obtain confessions and, of course, if the *Miranda* rules were relaxed or replaced by video recording, there would be an unambiguous boost to prosecution efforts. As a result, this kind of reform would not only avoid the trade-offs discussed above, but would indeed be a true "win-win": more convictions of the guilty, while fewer convictions of the innocent.

2.6 Requiring All Defense Attorneys to Directly Ask Their Clients, "Did You Commit the Crime?" and Aggressively Investigate Claims of Actual Innocence

A critical resource in the efforts to prevent wrongful convictions is defense attorneys. Yet the great bulk of innocence literature seems to focus attention on prosecutors as the source of the problems.[103] For example, in his chapter in this book, Professor George Thomas calls prosecutors "the thin last line protecting the innocent."[104] And he is surely right that prosecutors have critical steps they can take to reduce wrongful convictions, such as by fully discharging their *Brady* obligations to produce exculpatory evidence (a point I have pressed elsewhere).[105]

But the Innocence Movement has largely overlooked what may be an even more important bulwark against false convictions: defense attorneys. Unfortunately, the mindset of the defense bar toward the question of whether their clients are in fact guilty has been aptly described as one of "staggering indifference."[106] Indeed, it is sometimes even argued that it is inconsistent with ethical obligations for defense counsel to focus on innocence.[107] Defense attorneys simply cannot consider whether their clients are guilty, it is argued, because doing so would impair the quality of the representation they provide.[108] And, more broadly it is argued, focusing on innocence issues may distract society from dealing with mass incarceration and other issues associated with the guilty.[109]

I am unconvinced. Innocent persons ensnared in the criminal justice system have a stronger claim to our attention than do the guilty. If we want to structure an "innocentric" criminal justice system that gives highest priority to preventing the conviction of the innocent,[110] defense attorneys must be involved. In fact, defense attorneys – who (unlike prosecutors) have constant and direct access to defendants – may be uniquely positioned to identify a miscarriage of justice before it happens and take steps to prevent it. They are also well-poised to increase the "diagnosticity" of the system by helping to flag the relatively small percentage of cases genuinely involving factual innocence claims.[111]

Here is one example of how we might think about reorienting defense counsel toward innocence issues. Many defense attorneys do not directly ask their clients whether they are guilty of the crime charged.[112] This ignorance may permit defense attorneys to perhaps raise defenses that might otherwise be barred by rules of legal ethics.[113] But why should we give defense counsel such freedom if we are trying to structure a criminal justice system that focuses on innocence? It is hard to see what larger societal interest is served by allowing counsel to move forward in ignorance of this important fact. It may be true, as some defense advocates have argued, that a defense attorney can never be sure whether her client is telling the truth when a defendant claims to be innocent.[114] But requiring defense attorneys to at least ask that basic question would serve the valuable function of putting this issue squarely out in the open, helping innocent defendants. And the only "cost" is that defense counsel for some guilty defendants might be limited in the kinds of arguments that can be advanced at trial – a cost that society surely ought to be willing to bear to have a system that more accurately sorts the innocent from the guilty.

Simply requiring the defense attorney to ask this straightforward question probably would not make much of a change in the current system. Part of the current criminal justice game seems to be for defendants to deny their involvement in a crime – at least at the start of a case. For example, Professor Robert Mosteller reports that, when he was a defense attorney, virtually all of his clients claimed to be innocent until he recited the advantages of a specific plea offer; at that point, they conceded their guilt.[115] In light of this fact, maybe defense attorneys should be required not only to ask their clients if they committed the crime but also to explore more thoroughly whether a defendant is truly guilty or innocent. This requirement could be enforced by a rule that only if a defendant admits he is guilty would a defense attorney be permitted to explore a standard plea bargain.[116] Such a requirement might promote more frank and open discussion between defense attorneys and their clients about whether they were involved in the crime.

Forcing defense attorneys to truly attempt to learn whether their clients are guilty or innocent would create a real advantage: it would give the criminal justice system one more opportunity to begin sorting innocent defendants from guilty ones through the one person who has the best access to important information – the defendant. Professor Mosteller may properly complain about how defense attorneys have difficulties obtaining access to witnesses and other forms of evidence,[117] but the barriers to information are not all one-sided. Prosecutors are usually precluded from talking to defendants once legal counsel enters the scene. But defendants are obviously in a unique position to provide information that can sort the guilty from the innocent. If defendants can be induced to provide more thorough information to their attorneys about whether they are innocent or guilty, then the system can more effectively protect against wrongful conviction.

With the innocence issue directly on the table for discussion, how should defense counsel proceed when her client reports that he is innocent? Professor Mosteller rightly bristles at the suggestion that there should be some sort of "second-class treatment" of defendants who state clearly that they are guilty.[118] He explains quite nicely that defense counsel have important duties to perform in the criminal justice system, even when performing the far more common duty of defending those who have in fact committed the crimes charged against them. But he interestingly goes on to discuss the idea that perhaps individual defense attorneys – or the criminal justice system more broadly – should try to devote additional resources to cases in which a defendant has a good claim of actual innocence.[119] Of course, defense attorneys – and the system – are not well-positioned to do this if the defendant is not even asked whether he is in fact innocent.

If a defendant claims to be innocent, as a first step defense counsel obviously ought to adequately investigate the claim. Presumably adequate defense investigation happens in many cases,[120] regardless of whether a defendant claims to be innocent or guilty. But if some defense attorneys are not squarely raising the innocence issue because they think ignorance is tactically useful, they may end up missing a chance to discover exculpatory evidence that could set a defendant free.[121]

Following such an investigation, defense counsel should obviously rely on the procedures available in our criminal justice system for presenting a defense. Within our traditional structure, defense attorneys have many tools that they can employ in the defense of innocent clients.

But in reviewing cases of wrongful conviction over the years, one omission from the defense repertoire has always puzzled me. I have always wondered why, in a rare case where a defense attorney believes she is representing a truly innocent client, she almost invariably fails to bring the prosecutor into the discussion. The wrongful conviction literature suggests it is unusual for a defense attorney to communicate her specific concerns directly to a prosecutor.[122] Perhaps this is part of a larger culture of distrust between prosecutors and defense attorneys that appears to afflict at least some jurisdictions.[123] But direct communication on this issue needs to be strongly encouraged.[124]

It would, of course, be naive to think that defense counsel reports to prosecutors could prevent every wrongful conviction of an innocent defendant. But I am surprised to discover that defense counsel so rarely employ this approach. Perhaps an unfortunate reason is that defense attorneys behave in the way that Mosteller suggests: they simply do not view their job as having much to do with guilt or innocence.[125] If defense attorneys proceed in this way, they never learn whether they have an innocent defendant for a client as opposed to a guilty one. This agnostic approach may help to avoid burnout on the job or allow for an increased feeling of self-worth, as some have argued in justification.[126] But this strikes me as a something of a cop-out, leading the Innocence Movement to point fingers first at errant prosecutors and rogue police officers while too often ignoring the role of ignorant defense attorneys. If we wish to leave no stone unturned in our efforts to prevent conviction of the innocent, it is time to broaden our perspective to include defense attorneys as those who have special responsibility – and special abilities – to prevent wrongful convictions.[127]

CONCLUSION

Preventing wrongful conviction of the innocent is a fundamental priority of our criminal justice system. But it is obviously not the system's only goal. Efforts to prevent conviction of the innocent should avoid interfering with other objectives, most prominently the need to convict the guilty and prevent the suffering of future crime victims. Comparing even rough estimates of the risk of a person being wrongfully sent to prison for committing a violent crime with the risk of becoming a violent crime victim suggests that the current trade-offs between the two may incline dramatically toward increasing victimization.

But there are some kinds of reforms that can avoid debate about these trade-offs – true "win-win" measures that simultaneously reduce the number of innocents wrongfully convicted while increasing (or least not decreasing) the number of violent criminals sent to prison. This chapter lays out a few such possibilities, including confining habeas relief to those with claims of factual innocence, replacing the exclusionary rule with a civil damage remedy, moving confession law away from technical *Miranda* procedures, and requiring defense attorneys to explore their clients' guilt or innocence. If we are truly committed to protecting the innocent, we can and should take such specific steps. We can reduce the risk of wrongfully convicting the innocent without setting free the guilty.

NOTES

1 Like other authors in this book, I focus on so-called "wrong man" cases – i.e., cases of the "factually innocent" or "actually innocent" persons being wrongfully convicted. *See* Paul G. Cassell, *The Guilty and the "Innocent:" An Examination of Alleged Cases of Wrongful Conviction from False Confessions*, 22 HARV. J.L. & PUB. POL'Y 523, 535 (1999). *See also* Michael L. Radelet, *How DNA Has Changed Contemporary Death Penalty Debates*, *supra*, in this volume (discussing conceptual issues surrounding innocence); Josh Marquis, *The Myth of Innocence*, 95 J. CRIM. L. & CRIMINOLOGY 500, 508–09 (2005); Keith A. Findley, *Defining Innocence*, 74 ALB. L. REV. 1157 (2010–11).

2 *See* Paul G. Cassell, *Freeing the Guilty without Protecting the Innocent: Some Skeptical Observations on Proposed New "Innocence" Procedures*, 56 N.Y. L. SCH. L. REV. 1063 (2011–12).

3 *See, e.g.,* Paul G. Cassell, *In Defense of Victim Impact Statements*, 6 OHIO ST. J. CRIM. L. 611, 629–30 (2009) (collecting citations to examples of victim impact statements).

4 Marquis, *supra* note 1, at 517–18.

5 Ronald J. Allen & Larry Laudan, *Deadly Dilemmas*, 41 TEXAS TECH. L. REV. 65 (2008). *See also* Larry Laudan & Ronald J. Allen, *Deadly Dilemmas II: Bail and Crime*, 85 CHI.-KENT L. REV. 23 (2010); Ronald J. Allen & Larry Laudan, *Deadly Dilemmas III: Some Kind Words for Preventive Detention*, 101 J. CRIM. L. & CRIMINOLOGY 781 (2011).

6 Allen & Laudan, *Deadly Dilemmas*, *supra* note 5, at 68.

7 *See* Paul G. Cassell, *Comparing the Risk of Wrongful Conviction for a Violent Crime with the Risk of Being the Victim of a Violent Crime* (manuscript on file with author).

8 Their calculation refers to rape specifically, but it appears to be generalizable to other serious crimes as well. *See* Allen & Laudan, *Deadly Dilemmas*, *supra* note 5, at 80 n. 81.

9 *Id.* at 79–80.

10 D. Michael Risinger, *Essay: Tragic Consequences of Deadly Dilemmas: A Response to Allen and Laudan*, 40 SETON HALL L. REV. 991 (2010).

11 *See* Cassell, *supra* note 7.

12 Marvin Zalman, *Qualitatively Estimating the Incidence of Wrongful* Convictions, 48 CRIM. L. BULL. 226, 231 (2012).

13 Allen & Laudan, *Deadly Dilemmas*, *supra* note 5, at 80.

14 Risinger, *supra* note 10, at 1016–17.

15 *Id.* at 1019.

16 *Id.* at 1001.

17 The National Registry of Exonerations listed "mistaken witness ID" as the third leading cause of wrongful convictions, trailing only perjury/false accusation and official misconduct. National Registry of Exonerations, *% Exonerations by Contributing Factor*, available at www.law.umich.edu/special/exoneration/Pages/ExonerationsContribFactorsByCrime.aspx#.

18 *See* Steven E. Clark, *Blackstone and the Balance of Eyewitness Identification Evidence*, 74 ALBANY L. REV. 1105 (2010–11); *see also* Laurie N. Feldman, *The Unreliable Case Against the Reliability of Eyewitness Identifications: A Response to Judge Alex Kozinski*, 34 QUINNIPIAC L. REV. 493 (2016). For a helpful summary of the reform possibilities in this area, *see* BRANDON L. GARRETT, CONVICTION THE INNOCENT: WHERE CRIMINAL PROSECUTIONS GO WRONG 248–52 (2011).

19 Christopher Slobogin, *Lessons from Inquisitorialism*, 87 S. CAL. L. REV. 699, 704 (2014); *see also* D. Michael Risinger & Lesley C. Risinger, *Innocence Is Different: Taking Innocence into Account in Reforming Criminal Procedure*, 56 N.Y.L. SCH. L. REV. 869, 898 (2011–12) (problems with eyewitness misidentification are hard to address because they are "inherent in the phenomenon").

20 4 WILLIAM BLACKSTONE, COMMENTARIES *358; *see also* Alexander Volokh, *N Guilty Men*, 146 U. PA. L. REV. 173 (1997). For a recent and comprehensive effort to lay out a theoretical framework for evaluating such trade-offs, *see* Daniel Epps, *The Consequence of Error in Criminal Justice*, 128 HARV. L. REV. 1065 (2015).

21 Risinger, *supra* note 10, at 1020. *See also* Allen & Laudan, *Deadly Dilemmas*, *supra* note 5, at 81–84 (discussing arguments by Ronald Dworkin and Immanuel Kant); Epps, *supra* note 20, at 1133–35.

22 Kathryn E. McCollister et al., *The Cost of Crime to Society: New Crime-Specific Estimates for Policy and Program Evaluation*, 108 DRUG & ALCOHOL DEPENDENCE 98, 105 tbl. 5 (2010); *see also* Ted R. Miller et al., Nat'l Inst. of Justice, VICTIM COSTS AND CONSEQUENCES: A NEW LOOK 9 tbl. 2 (1996) (using older data to conclude that loss per crime victimization can be quantified as $2,940,000 for a murder, $87,000 for a sexual assault, and $19,000 for a robbery with injury). *Cf.* David A. Anderson, *The Cost of Crime*, 7 FOUNDATIONS & TRENDS IN MICROECONOMICS 209 (2012) (estimating total cost of crime in the U.S. at $3.2 trillion, more than total health care costs). Similar figures from those quoted in the text come from the RAND Center on Quality Policing, which calculates a cost per

murder of $8,649,216, per rape of $217,866, per aggravated assault of $87,238, and per robbery of $67,277. Paul Heaton, *Hidden in Plain Sight: What Cost-of-Crime Research Can Tell Us about Investing in Police*, available at www.rand.org/content/dam/rand/pubs/occasional_papers/2010/RAND_OP279.pdf (2010).

23 *See, e.g.*, Limone et al. v. United States, No. 02-cv-10890-NG (D. Mass. 2007) ($101.7 million judgment).

24 *Cf.* Paul G. Cassell, *Too Severe?: A Defense of the Federal Sentencing Guidelines (and a Critique of the Federal Mandatory Minimums)*, 56 STAN. L. REV. 1017, 1037–41 (2004) (discussing cost-benefit analysis in federal sentencing based on victimization figures).

25 *See* JAMES Q. WILSON, THINKING ABOUT CRIME 145–58 (1983).

26 Larry Laudan, *The Rules of Trial, Political Morality, and the Costs of Error: Or, Is Proof Beyond a Reasonable Doubt Doing More Harm than Good?*, in 1 OXFORD STUDIES IN PHILOSOPHY OF LAW 195, 202 (Leslie Green & Brian Leiter, eds., 2011). *But cf.* Epps, *supra* note 21, at 1090–91 (critiquing this estimate).

27 *See* Marquis, *supra* note 1, at 517. Whether Porter was in fact innocent has been called into doubt by a documentary movie, *A Murder in the Park*. The documentary investigates the fact that Porter was released after a Medill Innocence Project investigation obtained a confession from Alstory Simon to the murder – a confession that led to Porter's exoneration and Simon's incarceration. But later Simon's murder conviction was overturned, in part because of the Innocence Project's coercive investigative tactics had tainted the case against Simon. *See* Jim Stingl, *Duped by Medill Innocence Project, Milwaukee Man Now Free*, MILWAUKEE JOURNAL-SENTINEL, Nov. 6, 2014, available at www.jsonline.com/news/milwaukee/duped-by-innocence-project-milwaukee-man-now-free-b99386015z1-281852841.html.

28 Disclosure: I served as an expert witness for law enforcement officers involved in the civil litigation that resulted from this case.

29 Deposition of Robert Wilcoxson, Wilcoxson v. Buncombe County et al., No. 1:13-cv-00224-MR-DLH (W.D>N.C. 2014).

30 Testimony of Damian Mills to North Carolina Innocence Inquiry Commission, Dec. 18, 2013, at 481–82 (saying that he had been doing a series of breaking-and-enterings with Kagonyera, Williams, Isbell, and Brewton).

31 *See* Amite A. Varnedo, *Characteristics of Offenders Arrested for Aggravated Assault*, A Thesis Submitted to Dep't of Criminal Justice Administration, Atlanta Univ., at 8–9 (May 1987).

32 *See* North Carolina Innocence Inquiry Commission, *State v. Kagonyera/Wilcoxson*, available at www.innocencecommission-nc.gov/kagonyera.html.

33 Memo. from Investigator Raymond to D.A. Moore Regarding Statement of Kenneth Kagonyera, Nov. 30, 2001 (memorializing statements made on Nov. 29, 2001).

34 Kagonyera Dep. 134–35, Jan. 9, 2015 (admitting this fact).

35 The North Carolina Innocence Inquiry Commission has found both men to be factually innocent.

36 *Compare* Josh Bowers, *Punishing the Innocent*, 156 U. Pa. L. Rev. 1117 (2008), *with* Stephanos Bibas, *Exacerbating Injustice*, 157 U. Pa. L. Rev. PENNumbra 53, 54 (2008) (responding to Bowers' article).

37 Currently about forty-seven states, the District of Columbia, and the federal system allow *Alford* pleas. *See* Stephanos Bibas, *Harmonizing Substantive-Criminal-Law Values and Criminal Procedure: The Case of Alford and Nolo Contendere Pleas*, 88 Cornell L. Rev. 1351, 1372–73 n.52 (2003).

38 It is also possible that they choose to plead guilty to the murder because they were guilty of other serious, violent crimes. *See supra* notes 25–26 and accompanying text.

39 I also search for reforms that do not reduce punishment for the guilty. *Cf.* Erik Luna & Paul G. Cassell, *Mandatory Minimalism*, 32 Cardozo L. Rev. 1 (2010) (arguing for reduction in mandatory minimum sentences, a reform that might not only shorten sentences for the guilty but also reduce pressure on innocent defendants to plead).

40 *See, e.g.*, Daniel S. Medwed, *Innocentrism*, 2008 U. Ill. L. Rev. 1549 (2008). *See generally* Daniel S. Medwed, Prosecution Complex: America's Race to Convict and its Impact on the Innocent (2012).

41 Risinger, *supra* note 10, at 999.

42 *See, e.g.*, Keith A. Findley, *Toward a New Paradigm of Criminal Justice: How the Innocence Movement Merges Crime Control and Due Process*, 41 Tex. Tech. L. Rev. 133, 134 (2008) (arguing that the goals of convicting the guilty and protecting the innocent are not mutually exclusive).

43 *See generally* Cassell, *supra* note 2.

44 Others have made similar pleas. *See* Morris B. Hoffman, *The Myth of Factual Innocence*, 82 Chi.-Kent L. Rev. 663, 689 (2007); *see also* Marvin Zalman & Julia Carrano, *Sustainability of Innocence Reform*, 77 Alb. L. Rev. 955, 983–93 (2013–14) (outlining research agenda for innocence issues).

45 *See* Samuel R. Gross, Barbara O'Brien, Chen Hu & Edward H. Kennedy, *Rate of False Conviction of Criminal Defendants Who Are Sentenced to Death*, 111 Proc. Nat'l Acad. Scis. (PNAS) 7230, 7231 (2014) (noting Risinger study, relied upon by Allen and Laudan for error rate, ultimately is based on only eleven cases of wrongful conviction).

46 Samuel Gross, *Convicting the Innocent*, 4 Ann. Rev. L. Soc. Sci. 173, 176 (2008).

47 *Compare* Hugo Adam Bedau & Michael L. Radelet, *Miscarriages of Justice in Potentially Capital Cases*, 40 Stan. L. Rev. 21, 72–75 (1987) (presenting cases of alleged execution of the innocent), *with* Stephen J. Markman & Paul G. Cassell, *Protecting the Innocent: A Response to the Bedau-Radelet Study*, 41 Stan. L. Rev. 121 (1988) (questioning the accuracy of the determinations of "innocence"); *compare also* Richard A. Leo & Richard J. Ofshe, *The Consequences of False Confessions: Deprivations of Liberty and Miscarriages of Justice in the Age of Psychological Interrogation*, 88 J. Crim. L. & Criminology 429 (1998) (presenting cases of alleged wrongful convictions from false confessions), *with* Cassell, *supra* note 1.

48 *See* George C. Thomas III, *Prosecutors: The Thin Last Line Protecting the Innocent,*
    supra, in this volume; Samuel R. Gross & Barbara O'Brien, *Frequency and Predict-*
    ors of False Conviction: Why We Know So Little, and New Data on Capital Cases, 5
    J. EMPIRICAL LEGAL STUD. 927 (2008).

49 Others have proposed creating a commission to study cases of proven wrongful
    convictions. *See, e.g.,* Keith A. Findley, *Learning from Our Mistakes: A Criminal*
    Justice Commission to Study Wrongful Convictions, 38 CAL. W. L. REV. 333 (2002).
    My proposal is slightly different because I propose to conduct research to expand our
    knowledge about a random sample of wrongful convictions, rather than simply study
    the nonrandom sample of wrongful convictions that has already come to light.

50 *See, e.g.,* Gisli H. Gudjonsson & Jon F. Sigurdsson, *How Frequently Do False*
    Confessions Occur?: An Empirical Study Among Prison Inmates, 1 PSYCHOL.
    CRIM. & L. 21, 25 (1994).

51 For example, I have previously proposed that we should pay particular attention to
    issues involving alleged false confessions by the mentally retarded, rather than
    overgeneralizing the problem and proceeding on the assumption that false confes-
    sions are a routine product of police interrogation of those with normal mental
    faculties. *See* Cassell, *supra* note 1, at 580–87.

52 Joseph L. Hoffmann & Nancy J. King, *Rethinking the Federal Role in State*
    Criminal Justice, 84 N.Y.U. L. REV. 791, 820 (2009).

53 NANCY J. KING, FRED L. CHEESMAN II & BRIAN J. OSTROM, FINAL TECH-
    NICAL REPORT: HABEAS LITIGATION IN U.S. DISTRICT COURTS: AN EMPIR-
    ICAL STUDY OF HABEAS CORPUS CASES FILED BY STATE PRISONERS UNDER
    THE ANTITERRORISM AND EFFECTIVE DEATH PENALTY ACT OF 1996 (2007),
    available at www.ncjrs.gov/pdffiles1/nij/grants/219559.pdf.

54 *Id.* at 52, 58, 115–16.

55 Hoffman & King, *supra* note 52, at 823.

56 *See* Henry J. Friendly, *Is Innocence Irrelevant? Collateral Attack on Criminal*
    Judgments, 38 U. CHI L. REV. 143 (1970).

57 *Id.* at 167.

58 *See* Joshua M. Lott, *The End of Innocence? Federal Habeas Corpus Law After* In re
    Davis, 27 GA. ST. U. L. REV. 443 (2011). The Supreme Court has stated that "[t]he
    existence merely of newly discovered evidence relevant to the guilt of a state
    prisoner is not a ground for relief on federal habeas corpus." Herrera v. Collins,
    506 U.S. 390, 398 (1993) (quoting Townsend v. Sain, 372 U.S. 293, 317 (1963)).
    Nonetheless, there has been enough uncertainty about that statement that more
    than one hundred freestanding innocence claims have since been filed in federal
    habeas courts. *See* Nicholas Berg, *Turning a Blind Eye to Innocence: The Legacy of*
    Herrera v. Collins, 42 AM. CRIM. L. REV. 121, 131 (2005).

59 John C. Jeffries, Jr. & William J. Stuntz, *Ineffective Assistance and Procedural*
    Default in Federal Habeas Corpus, 57 U. CHI. L. REV. 679 (1990).

60 Samuel R. Gross, *Pretrial Incentives, Post-Conviction Review, and Sorting Criminal*
    Prosecutions by Guilt or Innocence, 56 N.Y.L. SCH. L. REV. 1009 (2011–12).

61 Stephanie Roberts Hartung, *Post-Conviction Procedure: The Next Frontier in Innocence Reform, supra,* in this volume.

62 A similar point can be made in support of Rob Warden's proposal to give close attention to post-conviction recantations by trial witnesses. *See* Rob Warden, *Reacting to Recantations, supra,* in this volume.

63 For an interesting effort along these lines in the area of direct appeals, see Helen A. Anderson, *Revising Harmless Error: Making Innocence Relevant to Direct Appeals,* 17 TEX. WESLEYAN L. REV. 391 (2011).

64 *See* Robert Gehrke, *If Utah Doesn't Provide Better Legal Defense for the Poor, ACLU May File Lawsuit,* SALT LAKE TRIB., Sept. 20, 2015, available at www.sltrib.com/news/2966774-155/if-utah-doesnt-provide-better-legal (discussing case of wrongful conviction in Utah where overworked public defender was apparently unable to obtain alibi witnesses).

65 *See, e.g.,* Alexandra Natapoff, *Negotiating Accuracy: DNA in the Age of Plea Bargaining, supra,* in this volume.

66 *See* Mary Sue Backus & Paul Marcus, *The Right to Counsel in Criminal Cases, a National Crisis,* 57 HASTINGS L.J. 1031, 1059 (2006); Paul Cassell & Nancy Gertner, *Public Defenders Fall to the Sequester,* WALL ST. J., Aug. 20, 2013 (urging that federal public defender funds not be sequestered).

67 *See* Erik Lillquist, *Improving Accuracy in Criminal Cases,* 41 U. RICH. L. REV. 897 (2007) (noting a common assumption that there are fixed resources devoted to criminal justice).

68 *See* Stone v. Powell, 428 U.S. 465, 500–01 (1976) (Burger, C.J., concurring).

69 *See* Dallin H. Oaks, *Studying the Exclusionary Rule in Search and Seizure,* 37 U. CHI. L. REV. 665, 739–40 (1970).

70 *See* AKHIL REED AMAR, THE CONSTITUTION AND CRIMINAL PROCEDURE 40–45 (1997).

71 *See* WILLIAM T. PIZZI, TRIALS WITHOUT TRUTH: WHY OUR SYSTEM OF CRIMINAL TRIALS HAS BECOME AN EXPENSIVE FAILURE AND WHAT WE NEED TO DO TO REBUILD IT (1999).

72 PAUL H. ROBINSON & MICHAEL T. CAHILL, LAW WITHOUT JUSTICE: WHY CRIMINAL LAW DOESN'T GIVE PEOPLE WHAT THEY DESERVE (2006).

73 People v. Defore, 150 N.E. 585, 587 (N.Y.1926).

74 Stone v. Powell, 428 U.S. 465, 496 (Burger, C.J., concurring).

75 William Stuntz, *The Uneasy Relationship Between Criminal Procedure and Criminal Justice,* 107 YALE L.J. 1, 37–40 (1997).

76 *Id.* at 40.

77 Professor Robert Mosteller responded to Stuntz's argument by reporting his own experience that motions to suppress "posed only a minimal drain on defense resources." Robert P. Mosteller, *Protecting the Innocent: Part of the Solution for Inadequate Funding for Defenders, Not a Panacea for Targeting Justice,* 75 MO. L. REV. 931, 955–56 (2010). But Mosteller concedes that his experience comes from a system in which motions to suppress were set on the eve of trial,

thereby preventing most such motions from being litigated. *Id.* at 956. Such a system seems atypical to me. For example, in both the state and federal systems in Utah, motions to suppress are typically litigated well in advance of trial and thus often produce contested suppression hearings.

78 Tonja Jacobi, *The Law and Economics of the Exclusionary Rule*, 87 NOTRE DAME L. REV. 585, 633 (2015).

79 *Id.* at 636.

80 *See* Roper v. Simmons, 543 U.S. 551, 624 (2005) (Scalia, J., dissenting) (noting that when adopted, the exclusionary rule was "unique to American jurisprudence" and that "a categorical exclusionary rule has been 'universally rejected' by other countries"); *see also* William T. Pizzi, *The Need to Overrule* Mapp v. Ohio, 82 U. COLO. L. REV. 679, 717–29 (2011) (discussing limited use of exclusionary remedies in Canada, New Zealand, England and Ireland).

81 *See* AKHIL AMAR, THE CONSTITUTION AND CRIMINAL PROCEDURE 27–29 (1998) (explaining why the exclusionary rule is a bad way to deter police misconduct compared to a civil damages regime). *Cf.* Yale Kamisar, Mapp v. Ohio 50 *Years Later*, NAT'L L.J., June 13, 2011, at 50 (arguing that critics of the exclusionary rule may not really want an effective alternative remedy because it would be just as burdensome on law enforcement).

82 *Compare* United States v. Leon, 468 U.S. 897, 907 (1984) (arguing that the small percentage researchers deal with masks the large number of felons released from prison based in part on illegal searches and seizures), *with id.* at 950 (Brennan, J., dissenting) (arguing that only a very small percentage of all felony arrests are declined for prosecution on grounds of potential exclusionary rule problems).

83 McDonald v. City of Chicago, 561 U.S. 742, 785 (2010) (quoting William Stuntz, *The Virtues and Vices of the Exclusionary Rule*, 20 HARV. J.L. & PUB. POL'Y 443, 444 (1997)).

84 *See generally* Paul G. Cassell, *Protecting the Innocent from Lost Confessions and False Confessions – And from* Miranda, 88 J. CRIM. L. & CRIMINOLOGY 497 (1998).

85 Steven B. Duke, *Does* Miranda *Protect the Innocent or the Guilty?*, 10 CHAP. L. REV. 551, 566–67 (2007); *see also* Ronald J. Allen, Miranda's *Hollow Core*, 100 NW. U. L. REV. 71 (2006).

86 Tonja Jacobi, *Miranda* 2.0, available at http://papers.ssrn.com/sol3/papers.cfm?abstract_id=2656405.

87 *See* Cassell, *supra* note 84, at 539–40.

88 Christopher Slobogin, *Towards Taping*, 1 OHIO ST. J. CRIM. L. 309 (2003) (arguing that Miranda has had an "immunizing" effect on deceptive interrogation tactics); OFFICE OF LEGAL POLICY, U.S. DEP'T OF JUSTICE, REPORT TO THE ATTORNEY GENERAL ON THE LAW OF PRETRIAL INTERROGATION 97–98 (1986), *reprinted in* 22 U. MICH. J.L. REFORM 437 (1989).

89 *See* 39 GEO. L.J. ANN. REV. CRIM. PRO. 1, 179–99 (2014) (collecting approximately 400 recent federal court of appeals cases on Miranda issues).

90 *See* Stuntz, *supra* note 75, at 44 (advancing the argument that *Miranda* doctrine causes shift of attention away from defendants with factual issues to raise and toward defendants with procedure claims to raise).

91 Welsh S. White, *False Confessions and the Constitution: Safeguards Against Unworthy Confessions*, 17 HARV. C.R.-C.L. L. REV. 105, 156 (1997).

92 JOSEPH D. GRANO, CONFESSIONS, TRUTH AND THE LAW 206–16 (1996).

93 Duke, *supra* note 85, at 564.

94 Jacobi, *supra* note 86, at 12.

95 *See, e.g.*, Paul G. Cassell, Miranda's *Social Costs: An Empirical Reassessment*, 90 NW. U. L. REV. 387 (1996); Paul G. Cassell & Richard Fowles, *Handcuffing the Cops? A Thirty-Year Perspective on* Miranda's *Harmful Effects on Law Enforcement*, 50 STAN. L. REV. 1055 (1998); Paul G. Cassell & Bret S. Hayman, *Police Interrogation in the 1990s: An Empirical Study of the Effects of* Miranda, 43 UCLA L. REV. 839 (1996). These conclusions are not universally accepted. *Compare* John J. Donohue III, *Did* Miranda *Diminish Police Effectiveness?*, 50 STAN. L REV. 1147 (1998) (critiquing the validity of the data used to correlate *Miranda* with diminished clearance), *with* Paul G. Cassell, *Falling Clearance Rates after* Miranda: *Coincidence or Consequence?*, 50 STAN. L. REV. 1181 (1998) (responding to these criticisms).

96 *See* Cassell, *supra* note 84, at 550–52.

97 Samuel R. Gross, *Loss of Innocence: Eyewitness Identification and Proof of Guilt*, 16 J. LEGAL STUD. 395, 430–31 (1987).

98 *See* Cassell, *supra* note 84, at 51. For reasons to think that *Miranda* is the most likely cause of this drop in confessions, *see* Cassell, Miranda's *Social Costs*, *supra* note 95, at 485.

99 *See* Yale Kamisar, *On the Fortieth Anniversary of the* Miranda *Case: Why We Needed It, How We Got It—and What Happened to It*, 5 OHIO. ST. J. CRIM. L. 163, 189–90 (2007).

100 *See* Cassell, Miranda's *Social Costs*, *supra* note 95, at 486–92.

101 *See, e.g.*, Lisa Lewis, *Rethinking* Miranda: *Truth, Lies, and Videotape*, 43 GONZ. L. REV. 199 (2007); Lisa C. Oliver, *Mandatory Recording of Custodial Interrogations Nationwide: Recommending a New Model Code*, 39 SUFFOLK U.L. REV. 263 (2005).

102 *See* Alan M. Gershel, *A Review of the Law in Jurisdictions Requiring Electronic Recording of Custodial Interrogations*, 16 RICH. J.L. & TECH. 9 (2010); Michael Schmidt, *In Policy Change, Justice Dept. to Require Recording of Interrogations*, N.Y. TIMES, May 22, 2014.

103 *See, e.g.*, Dana Carver Boehm, *The New Prosecutor's Dilemma: Prosecutorial Ethics and the Evaluation of Actual Innocence*, 2014 UTAH L. REV. 613 (2014).

104 George Thomas, *Prosecutors: The Thin Last Line Protecting the Innocent*, *supra*, in this volume.

105 *See* Cassell, *supra* note 2, at 1084–86.

106 Barbara Allen Babcock, *Defending the Guilty*, 32 CLEV. ST. L. REV. 175, 180 (1983).

107 Robert Mosteller, *Why Defense Attorneys Cannot, But Do, Care about Innocence*, 50 SANTA CLARA L. REV. 1 (2010).

108 *See id.; see also* Margaret Raymond, *The Problem with Innocence*, 49 CLEV. ST. L. REV. 449 (2001).

109 Abbe Smith, *In Praise of the Guilty Project: A Criminal Defense Lawyer's Growing Anxiety about Innocence Projects*, 13 U. PA. J.L. & SOC. CHANGE 315, 329 (2010).

110 *See* Medwed, *supra* note 40.

111 *Cf.* W. Tucker Carrington, *"A House Divided": A Response to Professor Abbe Smith's in Practice of the Guilty Project: A Criminal Defense Lawyer's Growing Anxiety about Innocence Projects*, 15 U. PA. J.L. & SOC. CHANGE 1, 23 (2011) (providing an illustration of a case in which defense counsel obtained a dismissal from a prosecutor by sharing exculpatory evidence collected by defense investigators).

112 Cassell, *supra* note 2, at 1068–69.

113 *See* MODEL RULES OF PROF'L CONDUCT R. 3.3(a)(3). *But cf.* Harry I. Subin, *The Criminal Lawyer's "Different Mission": Reflections on the "Right" to Present a False Case*, 1 GEO. J. LEGAL ETHICS 125 (1987) (suggesting that there are few limits on the defense and criticizing this view).

114 *See* Mosteller, *supra* note 108, at 41. Most defendants presumably will admit they are guilty. *Cf.* Tony G. Poveda, *Estimating Wrongful Convictions*, 18 JUST. QUART. 689, 701 (2001) (noting that about 15 percent of convicted inmates claimed to have not committed the crime for which they had been imprisoned, implying an 85 percent admission rate).

115 *See* Mosteller, *supra* note 77, at 954.

116 A defense attorney could still explore an *Alford* plea for an "innocent" defendant. *See* North Carolina v. Alford, 400 U.S. 25 (1970). But typically the sort of concessions that prosecutors are willing to offer for such a plea are less than that offered for a full-blown guilty plea.

117 *See* Mosteller, *supra* note 77, at 941–43 (discussing "limited defense access to witnesses and evidence").

118 Mosteller, *supra* note 107, at 7.

119 *Id.* at 68–69.

120 *But cf.* Ion Meyn, *Discovery and Darkness: The Information Deficit in Criminal Disputes*, 79 BROOK. L. REV. 1091 (2014) (arguing that certain structural defects in the criminal justice system mean that defense counsel cannot adequately investigate); Andrew D. Leipold, *How the Pretrial Process Contributes to Wrongful Convictions*, 42 AM. CRIM. L. REV. 1123 (2005) (arguing that current pretrial procedures prevent innocent persons from collecting exculpatory evidence).

121 *See* Abbe Smith, *Defending the Innocent*, 32 CONN. L. REV. 485, 510 (2000) (reporting an example of a seemingly delusional defendant blaming thefts on a

290 *Paul G. Cassell*

"chicken man"; defense investigation discovers that a man in a chicken suit perpetrated the crimes).

122 *See* Carrington, *supra* note 111, at 23 (referring to the "unorthodox" approach of a defense team in a murder case sharing exculpatory evidence with the prosecutor).

123 *See* Lissa Griffin & Stacy Caplow, *Changes to the Culture of Adversarialness: Endorsing Candor, Cooperation and Civility in Relationships Between Prosecutors and Defense Counsel*, 38 HASTINGS CONST. L.Q. 845 (2011).

124 *Id.* at 869.

125 Mosteller, *supra* note 107, at 60–64; *accord* Babcock, *supra* note 106, at 180.

126 *See generally* Barbara Allen Babcock, *How Can You Defend Those People? The Making of a Criminal Lawyer by James S. Kunen*, 53 GEO. WASH. L. REV. 310, 315 (1984).

127 One way to hold defense attorneys accountable for wrongful convictions would be through civil suits against them. Recent cases seem to be broadening defense liability in this area. *See, e.g.*, Dombrowski v. Bulson, 915 N.Y.S.2d 778 (N.Y. App. Div. 2010) (nonpecuniary loss damages are available for criminal defendant's loss of liberty due to attorney malpractice); *cf.* Kevin Bennardo, *A Defense Bar: The "Proof of Innocence" Requirement in Criminal Malpractice Claims*, 5 OHIO ST. J. CRIM. L. 341 (2007) (proposing that defendants should not be required to prove that they are innocent to proceed with criminal malpractice claims).

15

Retrospective Justice in the Age of Innocence
The Hard Case of Rape Executions

MARGARET BURNHAM

INTRODUCTION

The age of innocence presents a perfect moment to revisit the executions of black men convicted of committing rape in the Deep South states. This set of cases constitutes one of the most profound failures of criminal justice in the twentieth century. Studies of exonerations since 1989 reconfirm a well-known reality: a black man charged with the murder and/or rape of a white woman faces a significantly greater risk of wrongful conviction than any other criminal defendant. These recent studies complement the storied work of the criminologist Marvin Wolfgang, who found that 89 percent of persons executed for rape between 1930 and 1974 were black men, all from the former Confederacy and its bordering states.[1] Thus, the double-barreled character of the failure of justice: black men charged with assaults on white women faced a significantly higher risk of false conviction, *and* of receiving the death penalty (before it was declared unconstitutional for a brief period) than blacks charged with other crimes or whites charged with similar crimes. Nor is this increased risk of exposure to false conviction and capital punishment explained by crime rates for black male interracial sexual assault. Race is the beginning and the end of this story.

There are good reasons for exonerating posthumously all the black men who were executed for raping white women from 1900 to 1960. That the factual innocence of these men cannot be established through DNA technology ought not to be the measure of whether a state's most egregious miscarriages of justice require a measure of official correction, even after the appellate process has been completed and the accused executed. If that were the case, Massachusetts's governor would not have made amends for the execution of Sacco and Vanzetti, whose trial, the governor declared, was "permeated by prejudice against foreigners and hostility toward unorthodox political views."[2] Fred Korematsu's conviction for violating federal internment orders imposed on Japanese-Americans would not have been vacated. And George Stinney's conviction would not have been quashed seventy years after his execution because, as a South Carolina judge found, his lawyer's ineffectiveness deprived the 14-year-old of a fair trial.[3] The rape execution cases, like the Salem witch trials (another infamous event redressed, in part, by posthumous exoneration), fell far short of just treatment rules that were extant when the punishment was imposed. Hence, particularly in light of the irrevocable nature of the penalty and the severity of the norm violation, there is a duty to rectify the injustice.

Human rights standards call for rigorous and official examination of systemic miscarriages of justice, even decades after the files are closed. Many other nations have undertaken just such an inquiry. In addition to international practice, there are solid domestic reasons for reexamination. That the history of these particular cases has been erased from official narratives of "evolving standards of justice" – especially those pronounced by the Supreme Court – sharpens the imperative to officially acknowledge and redress the harm to individuals, certainly, but equally to collective national understandings of justice.

This chapter on racially biased rape executions in the Deep South (which pays special attention to a set of Louisiana cases) rehearses the case for official investigations and corrective measures. Because these rape executions constitute a shaping presence in ongoing debates over both capital punishment and the enforcement of rape laws, a remedial initiative would have both normative and informative value. Moreover, while judicial tools are sufficiently flexible to correct some of the most egregious historic errors of our criminal justice system, as with the Korematsu *coram nobis* action,[4] traditional review cannot redress the historic wrongs of the black male rape executions. Alternative remedies are needed.

The chapter engages the lessons learned from a quarter century of the Innocence Movement, and invites reflection on what retrospective justice might look like in the hard case of rape executions. The Innocence Movement has focused public attention on the political and social costs of flawed capital verdicts and on the importance of posthumous relief for the wrongfully executed. Redress in the instance of racially biased rape executions will inform ongoing feminist discourse about rape and criminal justice. Notwithstanding that innocence cannot now be established as forensic fact in these cases, because the targets of these prosecutions were more likely innocent than not the verdicts should be expunged, unless the state can show good grounds to sustain them.

THE INNOCENCE FRAME AND THE NEED TO REMEDY
RACIALLY BIASED RAPE EXECUTIONS

The discovery of innocence since DNA became widely available has provided advocates of progressive reforms in criminal justice an effective and seemingly enduring tie-breaker in debates that previously turned on ethics. Certainly the innocence frame appears to have overshadowed other anti-death penalty arguments, including the claim that because racial bias cannot be wholly extricated from capital case adjudication, there is no "fix" for the system's equal protection problem.[5] But the focus on innocence comes at a price. The ascendancy of the innocence frame is not inconsistent with the entrenched public hostility to the rigorous enforcement of procedural protections that has been a facet of the last half-century's "war on crime." Even those who think we "coddle" criminals in this country agree that the American justice system must protect the innocent, who just might include their friends and family. A bottom-line innocence standard carries the risk of degrading the prevailing test of guilt beyond a reasonable doubt in courtrooms and in policy debates. The innocence frame shifts public attention from a debate over values – that is to say, the question of what constitutes equal, humane, and dignified treatment – to a discourse of efficacy, namely, how can we best protect the innocent.[6]

Indeed, if scientific advances seem to make it possible to protect the innocent without costly, cumbersome, and complicated proceedings, such proceedings may seem redundant. Such a shift concedes enormous ground in a debate that is as old as the Constitution itself, for it suggests that innocence, which of course is not *per se* a constitutional value, is the test against which Fourth, Fifth, Sixth and Eighth Amendment guarantees are to be measured. Miscarriages of justice are generally understood to be cases that fail to meet due process standards, whether because of, for example, prosecutorial misconduct or jury selection bias or inadequate representation. But the innocence frame counts as failures only those cases where the wrong person was convicted of the offense. It is therefore underinclusive in capturing the full measure of unjust results in criminal cases.

It is also true, however, that the focus on innocence has created opportunities to gauge the well-worn fault-lines in criminal justice that contribute to wrongful convictions. It has reaffirmed the ongoing impact of race on outcomes and on decision-making, set a higher bar for the use of scientific evidence, demonstrated that trials free of material error can still result in convictions of the innocent, and illuminated the role of false confessions. In sum, it has generated renewed attention to common systemic problems;

before the Innocence Movement these contentions would typically be characterized as the exaggerated rhetorical grumblings of abolitionists. The Innocence Movement has built a new consensus based on the fragility and error-prone realities of criminal justice adjudication, and readied the public for a searching reexamination of closed cases behind which may lay profound and potentially fatal mistakes.

The ordeal of Kirk Bloodsworth is illustrative. Having spent nearly nine years in prison, including two on death row, in 1993 DNA testing freed Bloodsworth after two trial juries had found him guilty of the rape and murder of a child based on eyewitness testimony. His is one of well over a hundred exonerations in capital cases since 1973;[7] like Bloodsworth's, each case has generated substantial media coverage and concomitant public concern about the integrity of the criminal process and the wisdom of the death penalty. Wrongful convictions of the factually innocent have come to be viewed as an epiphenomenon of a complex system of interrelated decision-making rather than an unfortunate and isolated aberration.

The innocence frame has also spawned a number of posthumous judgments clearing individuals executed decades ago for crimes of which they were either factually innocent or not lawfully convicted. These judgments operate to restore the good name of wrongfully convicted individuals and to reinforce the continuous obligation of penal structures to redress egregious errors. The political officials who granted posthumous relief were primed for the innocence arguments in these decades-old cases. They include cases where there was convincing proof of innocence; where the trial or post-trial proceedings violated constitutional or other legal rules; where the conviction was linked to societal bias; or where the sentence was excessive.[8] In 2001, Maryland Governor Parris Glendening pardoned John Snowden, a black man executed for the rape and murder of a white woman. All but one of the jurors in the 1919 trial of Snowden opposed the death sentence in the case, and two witnesses recanted their testimony. In 2011, Colorado Governor Bill Ritter granted a full pardon to Joe Arridy, who was executed for rape and murder in 1936. The accused had severe intellectual disabilities and the governor concluded he was found guilty based on "false and coerced confessions" and in the face of evidence that he was not likely in the area when the crime took place. In 2005, the Georgia Board of Pardons and Paroles granted a full and unconditional pardon to Lena Baker, a black woman who was convicted and in 1945 executed for murdering her white employer. Baker admitted she killed the man, but claimed he had threatened her life when she sought to leave his farm. The Board found that the failure to pardon her in 1945 was a "grievous error," and that her actions amounted at most to manslaughter, which carried a maximum sentence of fifteen years. In a similar vein, the Texas legislature passed a resolution in 1985 declaring that Josefa "Chipita" Rodriguez did not receive a fair trial when she was convicted of murder and hanged in 1863 at the age of 63. And in 2009, the South Carolina Department of Probation, Parole and Pardon Services pardoned Thomas Griffin and Meeks Griffin, two black men who were executed for murder in 1914 based on the false testimony of an alleged coconspirator.[9]

One could reasonably ask what considerations support singling out the interracial rape executions from the general body of capital executions. Studies of exonerations for all crimes suggest that factors that increase the risk of wrongful conviction are often present in stranger rape prosecutions; before the widespread availability of DNA testing, these cases generally turned on eyewitness identification, victim testimony, confessions, or some combination thereof. In their pioneering study of 340 exonerations between 1989 and 2003, Samuel Gross and his colleagues suggested that the leading causes of wrongful conviction appear to be perjury and false confessions. That study concluded that almost all of the false confessions of exonerated juvenile defendants were African-American.[10] A particularly striking example of the dynamics of false confessions by juveniles is the famous Central Park Jogger rape case of 1989, where five juveniles, four black and the fifth Hispanic, were ultimately cleared of convictions that were based on "confessions and perjured testimony."[11]

A later study put the wrongful conviction rate for all capital crimes from 1973 to 2004 at around 4.1 percent.[12] And a study of convictions in Virginia courts for homicide and rape between 1973 and 1987 found an even higher incidence of wrongful convictions. In those homicide cases that also involved sexual assault, during the period under study, in 5 percent of the cases DNA evidence did not support the conviction, whereas in the rape cases where there was no homicide a highly unsettling 8–15 percent of the defendants were convicted despite the fact that their DNA profiles did not match those found in the rape kit taken from the victim.[13]

One might argue that a 15 percent error rate for rape convictions where there is no homicide is troubling but not cause for alarm. When one zones in on black male/white female sexual assault cases, however, the evidence is even starker. In the first place, the data on noncrime-specific exonerations resulting from post-conviction DNA testing reveal a significantly higher proportion of African-American men in the population of exonerated men than in the prison population. Whereas in 2011 black men were about 40–50 percent of the prison population, they were about 70 percent of the exonerated population.[14] The racial disparity for exonerees wrongfully convicted of rape is higher still. Researchers found that, in a sample of eighty-seven exonerations from 1989 to 2010 where the accused was cleared by DNA evidence of the crime of murder and/or rape, 84 percent of the exonorees were black men charged with the rape and/or murder of a white woman.[15] The study established that African-American men were the alleged perpetrators in just 16 percent of the rape cases where the victim was white,[16] but they constituted 65 percent of exonerations in that interracial crime category. In other words, black men are about *four times* more likely to be exonerated for raping white women than they are to be charged with that specific crime.[17] When the death penalty was in use for rape, for these men it was not like "being struck by lightning," but rather it was like being "the special favorite of the law."[18]

Although the factual innocence of these men likely cannot now be proven, collectively these cases represent a profound miscarriage of justice. As such, they provide an opportunity to consolidate the long debate over the legacy and impact of racialized death sentencing. Nor should the initiatives to correct long-past injustices in the administration of the death penalty be rejected as yesterday's war. As the data on cross-racial rape exonerations reveal, an historical perspective is required to appreciate and adequately address the threats to the rights of suspects today. Posthumous exonerations perform the public function of reinforcing the need for safeguards even if the risks of miscarriages of justice have shifted in character and frequency. Moreover, public confidence in the justice system rests on an understanding that the passage of time will not prevent the correction of its most egregious errors. The rape capital sentences were "wrong the day [they were imposed],"[19] and they should be corrected because they "strike[] at the fundamental value of our judicial system and our society as a whole."[20]

In establishing wrongful convictions as a field of inquiry for policymakers and scholars, the Innocence Movement has created the platform upon which this related initiative regarding wrongful executions could rest.[21] As a strategic matter, the time to reconsider the rape executions is now, for the periods for determining "innocence" – and entitlement to relief, judicial or otherwise – have not yet been rigidly prescribed.[22] Nor should factual innocence necessarily be the criterion against which this subset of cases is judged. Rather, these convictions[23] should be expunged if it is established that the methods used to obtain the conviction were fundamentally flawed.[24]

Indeed, these cases, individually and as a group, present at least as strong a case for judicial redress as the "actual" innocence cases. While avoidable but careless mistakes might lead to the conviction of the factually innocent – bureaucratic incompetence, prosecutorial misfeasance, or judicial error – the rape executions, resulting from mutually reinforcing laws and practices intentionally designed to target a particular racial group, represent a distinctive moral wrong, even in our legal system (*McCleskey* notwithstanding).[25] By this measure, "miscarriages of justice" are those cases where unreliable evidence such as forced confessions were admitted; prosecutors overcharged based on race; juries were racially biased against the defendant or favored the victim; the court allowed the parties to disparage the race of the defendant; unsafe eyewitness testimony was introduced (the single largest contributor to wrongful convictions);[26] the defendant faced a race-based barrier to testifying on the issue of consent;[27] or where public hue and cry influenced the proceedings. If, when all is said and done, these errors were of such a fundamental nature that one could not reliably conclude that had they not occurred, the defendant would nevertheless have been found guilty and sentenced to death, then the conviction should be vacated.

Studies of exonerations make clear that race works against black male defendants charged with interracial rape in two ways. The potential for error based on cross-racial misidentifications or false confessions is heightened,[28] and ingrained racial attitudes of decision-makers, both white and black,[29] from the police to the appellate court judges predispose them to find the accused culpable. If, as researchers have found, these factors are currently at play they were even more devastating in the mid-twentieth century.

RACE, RAPE EXECUTIONS AND THE SUPREME COURT'S CAPITAL PUNISHMENT JURISPRUDENCE

In light of these patterns, it is not surprising that rape executions were the centerpiece of the equal protection and due process arguments advanced in the NAACP Legal Defense Fund's mid-twentieth century campaign challenging capital punishment.[30] However, despite Marvin Wolfgang's evidence of the pernicious and persistent role of race in the administration of capital rape cases,[31] the Supreme Court avoided any substantive reliance on the equal protection problem in *Furman* v. *Georgia*,[32] *Gregg* v. *Georgia*,[33] and even in *Coker* v. *Georgia*.[34] This lapse on the part of the Court was consistent with its pre-*Furman* death penalty jurisprudence, for it was not until nine years after *Brown* that one could find a reference to the rape executions, and even then the concerns did not include the racial discrimination question.[35] Anthony Amsterdam's effort to highlight "the place of race in sentencing" by pointing to Wolfgang's data was unsuccessful in *Maxwell* v. *Bishop*,[36] although Justice Brennan's dissent in *McGautha* v. *California* did discuss race.[37] Nor could the Court have been unaware of the argument from race, inasmuch as it was usually addressed by the accused and always by several of the amici, all to no avail. In *Maxwell*,[38] for example, a group of amici sought to show that the states that had practiced segregation were far more likely than others to impose the death penalty for rape.[39] Even when, in *Kennedy* v. *Louisiana*,[40] the Supreme Court revisited *Coker* v. *Georgia* it was blind to the most constitutionally prominent feature of the rape executions.[41]

The Supreme Court's failure to condemn racially discriminatory enforcement in capital rape cases left black men vulnerable to state and local practices. When it struck down the death penalty for rape in *Coker* on Eighth Amendment grounds, the Court left undisturbed the codes and practices that produced the vast racial disparities which were then the defining feature of rape prosecution. The patchwork of state and local laws governing interracial sexual relations, including rape, meant that what was acceptable in one state could land one in prison in another state.[42]

CAPITAL RAPE IN LOUISIANA

It is well-settled that a symbiotic relationship existed between the anti-miscegenation laws that criminalized interracial sex and rape laws. Much has also been written about the relationship between laws regulating sexual relationships and the actual practices of interracial communities in the mid-twentieth century south.[43] In Louisiana, particularly, beliefs about race and the practices that flowed from them were more contingent, fluid, and complex than the binary world reflected in the statutes. What is perhaps not so clearly understood is how the legal bar against interracial sex operated to restrict the ability of a black man charged with raping a white woman to present a legal defense, even in a community that tolerated a certain degree of interracial sex. Because Louisiana's laws criminalized conduct that was at some level accepted, it created a fundamental tension that in the end penalized only black men whose private behavior across the color line became too obvious to ignore. As one commentator observed, "any abhorrence that whites [in Louisiana] might have felt for interracial sex was balanced by the undeniable fact of its frequent occurrence."[44] A close look at the dual criminal justice system in Louisiana may illuminate the nature of the fatal path from acceptable interracial intimacy to death row.[45]

Once legal segregation replaced the Black Codes at the turn of the twentieth century, as was typical in the Deep South, Louisiana reserved its capital penalty for rape for black defendants charged with sexual assault on whites.[46] Adopted in 1892, Louisiana's aggravated rape statute included the mandatory penalty of death,[47] while rape without aggravating factors was punishable by a term of years.[48] Prosecutors routinely charged blacks with aggravated rape and whites with the simple offense.[49] Since 1900 Louisiana has executed forty-five defendants for aggravated rape; of that number, all but two were black.[50] One of the white defendants, hung in 1906, was convicted of the particularly heinous offense of sexually assaulting a disabled child, and the other, a man from outside the state, was hung in 1907 for raping a white woman. The state never executed a white man for the rape of a black woman, and since 1900 only one black man was executed where the victim was also black.[51]

At bottom, racial discrimination was entrenched in the twentieth century criminal code, which reprised slavery laws and the Black Codes and echoed lynching practices in the state.[52] While charging practices discriminated against black men where the accuser was white, the rape executions also violated other fundamental rights that were well-established at the time the cases were tried.[53] In at least thirty-six of the forty-five cases, the grand and petit jurors were all white.[54] Where trials were conducted, they were public spectacles, attracting large and hostile audiences and inflammatory news coverage. Trial witnesses, the prosecutor, and trial and appellate judges alike could comment upon the defendant's race.[55]

Also, as late as 1948, black rape defendants were doomed by the presence at trial of the hovering mob, Scottsboro-style, reprising the frenzied crowds of the lynching era. About three months after he was arrested on a rape charge in December 1948, Edward Honeycutt was abducted from the parish jail in Opelousas, taken to a nearby river and almost lynched. He escaped but found himself back in the hands of the parish sheriff, whose men had earlier beat a false confession from him. After two trials Honeycutt was convicted and electrocuted.[56] Contested confessions obtained without benefit of counsel were introduced against many of the accused. Typically, the all-white juries deliberated hastily to bring in guilty verdicts and sentence the defendants to death.

Most significantly, racist attitudes made it dangerous to proffer a vigorous defense to a rape accusation.[57] In 1894, two years after it adopted the two-tiered rape statute, Louisiana prohibited intermarriage between blacks and whites.[58] Laws making it a felony to participate in an interracial marriage or habitual cohabitation were not repealed until 1972,[59] and from 1908 to 1942 state law criminalized interracial concubinage.[60] In general, the most effective defense against the charge of rape is that the sex was consensual or that the testimony of the complaining witness is not credible. These defenses were, in effect, foreclosed in cases where the accused was black and the victim white. Whites so feared the disruption of racial hierarchy, and so discounted women's sexual agency, that there could be no hint that white women might be consenting partners in such relationships. Consensual interracial sex was prohibited,[61] and Louisiana prosecutors availed themselves of these laws.[62] Even if a prosecution under the anti-miscegenation statutes was not inevitable, a claim that the sex was consensual flouted both law and social custom; such a defense conceded "criminality" on the part of both the accused and the victim.[63] The laws placed black defendants on the horns of a dilemma faced by no other defendant charged with rape, for the exculpating defense inculpated the defendant *and* the alleged victim of a crime that could result in imprisonment.

Nor were the sentences always lenient for such charges. In a 1959 prosecution, a local prosecutor in a rural parish brought charges against James Brown, a black man, and Lucille Aymond, a white woman, under the anti-miscegenation statute. The two defendants worked together at a dry cleaning store and their boss was distressed because they seemed to be too close. He testified that his concerns were aroused when he saw Aymond "making [Brown] coffee and bringing it to him, drinking coffee with him, she with her cup and he with his, standing together drinking coffee." He reported the two to the sheriff, who brought them in for questioning. After hours of interrogation Brown confessed that he had had intercourse with Aymond once, and Aymond also confessed to the one incident after two hours of questioning. Based on their confessions the two were convicted of miscegenation by a jury and sentenced to a year of hard labor at Angola.[64]

Notable, too, is the commitment to process reflected in the Louisiana rape execution appellate opinions, particularly in the later cases. Given the gravity of the charge, the reasoning and analysis of the earlier opinions is remarkably thin. But the opinions after about 1951 reflect considerable research and fastidious engagement with the procedural challenges raised by the defendants. In *State* v. *Michel*, for example, the Louisiana Supreme Court took care in 1957 to address all of the defendant's claims of error in detail and to make specific findings as to their nonmateriality, rendering Kafkaesque its conclusion that death was the proper sentence for a 19-year old convicted rapist.[65]

RAPE REFORM

Reconceiving rape as a crime of patriarchal power, second-wave feminists were deploying it as a form of social critique at about the same time that Wolfgang was documenting the racial underbelly of capital rape prosecutions.[66] Liberal feminist thinkers and activists rightly overhauled the common meaning of rape by situating women's suffering, objectification, and subordination at the center of the crime; by historicizing the behavior; and by revealing its regularity, familiarity, and pervasiveness. As some feminists explained, rape is more than an act; it is a discourse about sex, crime, and power. At its outer limits, the argument deemed much of heterosexual sex to constitute the imposition on women of male power. It exposed the inadequacy of rules about consent to protect women's bodies and agency in a world of hegemonic male power. "If sex is normally something men do to women," wrote Catherine A. MacKinnon in 1983, "the issue is less whether there was force and more whether consent is a meaningful concept."[67]

In illuminating rape's gender dynamics and ideology, however, feminist thinkers ignored the opportunity to deconstruct its racial origins fully.[68] On the other side of the rape victim's right to justice was the defendant's right to equal justice. In the American context, white racism cannot be extricated from the meaning of rape. If patriarchy rendered the definition of rape contingent, as a legal matter what constituted rape was also defined by who had access to due process and a fair trial. While chastity and corroboration requirements were ignored where the defendant was black, they defined whether the conduct constituted rape where the defendant was white. Just as Louisiana's criminal code was racially bifurcated, so too were there two social meanings for the words rape, rapist, and rape victims.

Hence, rape had always been perceived as the "Negro crime," viz., what "black men do to white women." In reprising the history of the crime, many feminists failed to take on board the differential axes of power in the violence of the act itself and in the accusation of interracial transgression.[69] The rape executions were a convoluted sexualized and racialized space containing multiple versions of legal meaning, including the terms upon which men and women of both races had access to due process and a fair trial. If rape was a fear and a fixture in white women's experience, if it was the emblem of their powerlessness, the same was true for black men over whose bodies the threat of rape constantly loomed. If rape was routine and depersonalizing for women, rape prosecutions functioned in a similar way for black men. And if the law of rape was to be indicted as a source and mainstay of institutionalized patriarchal power, an account of race was the indispensable key to such a reading.

To give but one example: the feminist critique held that the legal construction of rape unduly focused on the male *mens rea* as to whether the woman consented, rather than on whether the woman believed that the sex was unwanted.[70] But the rape executions role-flipped this scenario: black men could never testify to their state of mind, because it was effectively impermissible to suggest that a white woman would consent to sex with a black man. To claim consent would be tantamount to admitting guilt. Everyone knew that interracial sex was practiced and tolerated on a "down-low" level in the South; the transgression was to render it visible.[71] The most effective defense, consent, which on a feminist reading was also the most pernicious, was simply unavailable to the group most likely to be framed on a rape charge.

In sum, the contested space of the rape trial was defined as much by race as by gender, but the feminist project of reforming rape laws never reflected this reality. It is hard to say whether this occurred because of the incendiary nature of interracial rape or because critical analysis often misses the mark in the face of severe, intractable, and enduring violence. This failure of theory matters, because while rape law reform may have dramatically recalibrated the scales for some women,[72] black men remain disproportionately vulnerable to false conviction for rape where the victim is white.

RETROSPECTIVE JUSTICE

Given what we now know, the case for remediating the harms associated with the rape executions is a compelling one. While mechanisms and initiatives to "deal with the past" have proliferated in response to the global consensus that successor states cannot ignore their predecessors' gross human rights violations, judicial institutions thus far largely escaped the kind of scrutiny and pressure for accountability that has led to state apologies, truth commissions, monetary redress, institutional reform, or a combination thereof.[73] Scholars who study the judicial role in transitional processes have observed that judges are by nature and training reluctant to examine their own past practices because they fear compromising their independence and their role as neutral enforcers of good and bad laws alike.[74] But significant, systemic criminal justice failures can only be corrected through rigorous public investigation. In the rape executions the rule of law was all but absent, and in such a case it is not enough for successor public officials to condemn generally the Jim Crow legal order or to acknowledge the role of the judiciary in sustaining the system. Rather, a means must be found to examine the specific mechanics of the miscarriage and remove the taint, rendering the violation of public trust consequential.[75]

Many states across the globe have initiated official investigations into the dynamics of wrongful conviction, particularly in the wake of DNA-based exonerations. In Canada, the Province of Ontario ordered a public inquiry into the erroneous conviction of Guy Paul Morin, who was convicted in 1992 of the murder of a 9-year-old girl, Morin's neighbor. Based on DNA evidence, Morin was later cleared of the murder. But because his conviction raised questions about the administration of justice in Ontario, a commission was directed to examine the proceedings and make recommendations to the lieutenant governor.[76] A Nova Scotia Mi'kmaq man, Donald Marshall, Jr., was convicted of murder in 1971 and later acquitted. A commission convened to look into the case twenty years after the verdict concluded racial bias was a significant factor in the wrongful conviction. The commission's recommendations led to improved standards for prosecutorial disclosure of evidence.[77] And in New Zealand, a 1980 commission investigated the proceedings leading to the wrongful conviction in 1970 of Arthur Allan Thomas for the murder of a farming couple.[78]

Members of the global community have often relied on judges to investigate gross human rights violations on the part of judicial organs. Jurists have served as ombudsmen, organizing and shaping investigations to ensure an impartial outcome. These inquiries are often not rigidly bilateral but focus on broader grievances about past judicial operations. In Northern Ireland, a 1995 law authorized administrative investigations into suspected wrongful convictions and official abuse during the Troubles.[79] Courts in China played a role in redressing the judicial excesses associated with the Cultural Revolution. In 1978, a judicial conference adopted guidelines for such cases.[80] The process lasted until 1983. Over a million cases adjudicated from 1949 to 1978 were reexamined by the courts, and over 300,000 were redressed. About 250,000 Cultural Revolution cases were found to be wrongly, falsely, or incorrectly charged and sentenced.[81] Many were political cases, but a significant number were also common criminal matters. Redress included correcting the judgments, compensating the victims of the judicial violations, and fully reintegrating the wrongly accused into society.

In South Korea, judges have recently participated in "honor-restoration" processes, wherein legal rights have been conferred upon those wrongly convicted. In one case handled by the Seoul District Court, a journalist executed in December 1961 was determined to have been not guilty of the espionage allegation upon which the death sentence was based. Ruling in 2008, the court found that "the deceased did not participate in espionage for the North. And there is no evidence proving that he sided with the communist state."[82]

Truth commissions associated with transitional processes have also devoted attention to the judiciary. In East Timor, for example, the CAVR (Reception, Truth and Reconciliation Commission) concluded, after examining scores of trials, that the

> judges ... failed in their duties to provide an independent and objective adjudication ... allowed obviously fabricated evidence to be admitted ... did not consider allegations of torture ... routinely based their verdicts [on evidence obtained by torture] ... and handed down sentences to persons convicted of political crimes that were disproportionate.[83]

The truth commissions in South Africa and South Korea similarly criticized judicial institutions for gross human rights violations.[84]

And finally some countries have penalized jurists who collaborated with undemocratic regimes. In 1997, the Polish Parliament passed a law sanctioning the judges who supported the former regime from 1944 to 1989. It canceled the pensions of several jurists.

CONCLUSION

Developing norms require states to address grave past injustices and to provide appropriate redress. While every miscarriage of justice cannot be open to review for all time, death is different. When the state takes a life, the process by which it does so should never be foreclosed to official scrutiny. The executions of African-Americans for rape in the southern states in the twentieth century have repeatedly been condemned. Specific cases, such as the Scottsboro matter[85] and the execution of Willie McGee,[86] attracted international attention because they reflected the close relationship between the practice of lynching and that of rape trials.

Recent data, generated by the DNA revolution, makes clear that black men charged with the rape of white women continue to face a markedly heightened risk of wrongful conviction. Any initiative to redress this currently intractable problem must include correcting the historical record. Whether factual innocence should be the standard for posthumous exoneration in these cases is an open question. But what seems indisputable is that all of these men were subjected to flawed justice, and to the death penalty, based in large measure on their race. Remedial action is possible and, developing norms teach, required.

NOTES

1 Marvin E. Wolfgang & Marc Riedel, *Rape, Racial Discrimination and the Death Penalty*, in CAPITAL PUNISHMENT IN THE UNITED STATES 99 (Hugo Adam Bedau & Charles Pierce, eds., 1976).

2 Proclamation by Governor Michael S. Dukakis of Nicola Sacco and Bartolomeo Vanzetti Memorial Day (1977), available at www.saccoandvanzetti.org/sn_display1.php?row_ID=12.

3 Campbell Robertson, *South Carolina Judge Vacates Conviction of George Stinney in 1944 Execution*, N.Y. TIMES, Dec. 18, 2014, at A28.

4 *See* Korematsu v. United States, 584 F. Supp. 1406 (N.D. Cal. 1984).

5 Michael Radelet suggests in this volume that concern about wrongful conviction is only one of several equally significant factors contributing to declining support for the death penalty in the United States. Innocence, he argues, "is only one card in a much larger deck." Michael L. Radelet, *How DNA Has Changed Contemporary Death Penalty Debates, supra*, in this volume.

6 Several commentators have thoughtfully explored the question of whether the focus on innocence poses risks to the constitutional standard of "beyond a reasonable doubt". *See, e.g.,* Abbe Smith, *In Praise of the Guilty Project: A Criminal Defense Lawyer's Growing Anxiety about Innocence Projects,* 13 U. PA. J.L. & SOC. CHANGE 315 (2009); Daniel S. Medwed, *Innocentrism,* 2008 U. ILL. L. REV 1549 (2008).

7 *See* Death Penalty Information Center, *Innocence: List of Those Freed from Death Row,* available at www.deathpenaltyinfo.org/innocence-list-those-freed-death-row.

8 The cases through 2011 are collected in Stephen Greenspan, *Posthumous Pardons Granted in American History,* Death Penalty Information Center, available at www.deathpenaltyinfo.org/documents/PosthumousPardons.pdf.

9 *Id.*

10 Samuel R. Gross, Kristen Jacoby, Daniel J. Matheson, Nicholas Montgomery & Sujata Patil, *Exonerations in the United States, 1989 through 2003,* 95 J. CRIM. L. & CRIMINOLOGY 523 (2005).

11 Susan Saulny, *Convictions and Charges Voided in '89 Central Park Jogger Attack,* N.Y. TIMES, Dec. 20, 2002, at B5.

12 *See* Samuel R. Gross, Barbara O'Brien, Chen Hu & Edward H. Kennedy, *Rate of False Conviction of Criminal Defendants Who Are Sentenced to Death,* 111 PROC. NAT'L ACAD. SCIS. (PNAS) 7230 (2014), available at www.pnas.org/content/111/20/7230.full.pdf.

13 JOHN ROMAN, KELLY WALSH, PAMELA LACHMAN & JENNIFER YAHNER, URBAN INSTITUTE, POST-CONVICTION DNA TESTING AND WRONGFUL CONVICTION 57 (2010), available at www.ncjrs.gov/pdffiles1/nij/grants/238816.pdf.

14 Earl Smith & A.J. Hattery, *Race, Wrongful Conviction and Exoneration,* 15 J. AFR. AM. STUD. 79 (2011). *See also* Brandon L. Garrett, *Judging Innocence,* 55 COLUM. L. REV. 55 (2008).

15 Smith & Hattery, *supra* note 14, at 82. Smith and Hattery draw on Garrett's sample of 200 DNA exonerations from 1989 to 2007, and fifty other cases. It is not clear whether the additional fifty cases are DNA exonerations or what the dates of the exonerations are. In a later book, Brandon Garrett reported that 75 percent of the DNA exonerees (in his study of 250) who were convicted of rape were black or Latino, while only 30–40 percent of all rape convicts are minorities. BRANDON L. GARRETT, CONVICTING THE INNOCENT: WHERE CRIMINAL PROSECUTIONS GO WRONG (2011).

16 Studies show that the crime of rape is largely intraracial, and that there is no statistically significant racial difference in the incidence of rape. *See, e.g.,* Robert M. O'Brien, *The Interracial Nature of Violent Crimes: A Re-Examination,* 92 AM. J. SOC. 817, 817 (1987); Larry W. Koch, *Interracial Rape: Examining the Increasing Frequency Argument,* 26 AM. SOCIOLOGIST 76, 79 (1995).

17 Koch, *supra* note 16, at 83; *see also* GARRETT, *supra* note 15.

18 Between 1908 and 1965, Virginia executed fifty-four men for rape or attempted rape. Every one of them was black. LISA LINDQUIST DORR, WHITE WOMEN, RAPE,

AND THE POWER OF RACE IN VIRGINIA, 1900–1960 32 (2004). A Texas study of 460 capital cases from 1924 to 1968 found that "[t]he Negro convicted of rape is far more likely to get the death sentence than a term sentence, whereas whites and Latins (sic) are far more likely to get a term sentence than the death penalty." Rupert C. Koeninger, *Capital Punishment in Texas, 1924–1968*, 15 CRIME & DELINQ. 132, 141 (1969) (cited in Furman v. Georgia, 408 U.S. 238, 250 (1972)). During World War II, eighteen soldiers stationed in the United Kingdom were executed for murder, rape, and murder-rape. Six of the eighteen men, none of them white, were executed for rape alone. J. Robert Lilly, *Dirty Details: Executing U.S. Soldiers During World War II*, 42 CRIME & DELINQ. (4) 491, 497 (1996).

19 "[W]e think *Plessy* [v. *Ferguson*] was wrong the day it was decided." Planned Parenthood of Se. Penn. v. Casey, 505 U.S. 833, 863 (1992) (O'Connor, J., concurring).

20 Vasquez v. Hillery, 474 U.S. 254, 261 (1986) (quoting Rose v. Mitchell, 443 U.S. 545, 556 (1979), holding that harmless error does not apply where racial discrimination in selection of grand jury is shown).

21 Regarding the debate over risks of an "innocence"-centered anti-death penalty movement, *see* Carol S. Steiker & Jordan M. Steiker, *The Seduction of Innocence: The Attraction and Limitations of the Focus on Innocence in Capital Punishment Law and Advocacy* 95 J. CRIM. L. & CRIMINOLOGY 587 (2005).

22 Regarding the difference between wrongly convicted, actual innocence, and wrongful execution, *see* Daniel Givelber, *Meaningless Acquittals, Meaningful Convictions: Do We Reliably Acquit the Innocent?* 49 RUTGERS L. REV. 1317, 1346 (1997); DANIEL GIVELBER & AMY FARRELL, NOT GUILTY: ARE THE ACQUITTED INNOCENT? (2012); DANIEL S. MEDWED, PROSECUTION COMPLEX: AMERICA'S RACE TO CONVICT AND ITS IMPACT ON THE INNOCENT (2012).

23 While innocence ought not to be the test for posthumous relief, it is possible that the forty-five Louisiana cases examined here could be differentiated. Those cases in which the defendant's guilt is in doubt could be distinguished from those in which guilt is not in doubt but the proceedings were nevertheless unfair.

24 This standard falls between the "neutral observer" standard critiqued by Hugo Adam Bedau and Michael Radelet (whether a majority of "neutral observers" would judge the defendant to be innocent on the available evidence), *see* Hugo Adam Bedau & Michael L. Radelet, *Miscarriages of Justice in Potentially Capital Cases*, 40 STAN. L. REV. 21 (1987), and the strictly "legally innocent" standard (e.g., procedural errors that result in reversal constitute "miscarriages of justice"), *see* Samuel R. Wiseman, *Innocence after Death*, 60 CASE W. RES. L. REV. 687 (2010).

25 Some death penalty proponents have advanced the argument that the cost of a few erroneous convictions of innocent defendants is outweighed by the benefits of capital punishment. *See* Stephen J. Markman & Paul G. Cassell, *Protecting the Innocent: A Response to the Bedau-Radelet Study*, 41 STAN. L. REV. 121 (1988). But this argument falls flat where the errors leading to conviction are not "innocent mistakes" but rather are driven by racial discrimination.

26 *See, e.g.*, Malcolm B. Johnson, *African Americans Wrongfully Convicted of Sexual Assault Against Whites: Eyewitness Error and Other Case Features*, 11 J. ETHNICITY CRIM. JUST. 277 (2013); Jon B. Gould & Richard A. Leo, *One Hundred Years Later: Wrongful Convictions after a Century of Research*, 100 J. CRIM. L. & CRIMINOLOGY 825 (2010); Gross et al., *supra* note 10, at 523–60.

27 In a 1991 case, a black rape defendant who testified that the alleged victim, who was white, consented to sex was excoriated by the prosecutor in his closing argument: "If you're going to believe [the defendant], you have to believe that this [black] man was able to win over the romantic affection of an 18-year-old white girl from Crestview. You saw her ex-husband. This is the kind of man she is attracted to … he is white … it could not be the truth that she was attracted to the defendant." Reynolds v. State, 580 So. 2d 254 (Fla. Dist. Ct. App. 1991).

28 *See* Matthew Johnson, Shakina Griffith & Carlene Y. Barnaby, *African Americans Wrongfully Convicted of Sexual Assault against Whites: Eyewitness Error and Other Case Features*, 11 J. ETHNICITY CRIM. JUST. 4 (2013).

29 *See, e.g.*, Jerry Kang et al., *Implicit Bias in the Courtroom*, 59 UCLA L. REV. 1124, 1141–1142 (2012); Robert J. Smith, Justin D, Levinson & Zoë Robinson, *Implicit White Favoritism in the Criminal Justice System*, 66 ALA. L. REV. 871 (2015).

30 MICHAEL MELTSNER, CRUEL AND UNUSUAL: THE SUPREME COURT AND CAPITAL PUNISHMENT (2011); BARRETT J. FOERSTER, RACE, RAPE & INJUSTICE: DOCUMENTING AND CHALLENGING DEATH PENALTY CASES IN THE CIVIL RIGHTS ERA (2012); Wolfgang & Riedel, *supra* note 1, at 99.

31 Wolfgang found that from 1930 to 1972, 455 males were executed for rape in the United States. Of that number, 443 were executed in the former Confederate states, and of that number 89 percent, or 405, were black. Marvin E. Wolfgang, *Racial Discrimination in the Death Sentence for Rape*, in EXECUTIONS IN AMERICA 109–20 (William J. Bowers, Andrea Carr & Glenn L. Pierce, eds., 1974).

32 408 U.S. 238 (1972) (striking the death penalty as cruel and unusual in three cases where black men were sentenced for crimes against whites, two for rape and one for murder). Justice Douglas did acknowledge evidence that the death penalty disproportionately affected the "poor" and "the Negro," *id.* at 249 (Douglas, J., concurring), and that such discriminatory implementation of the penalty constituted cruel and unusual punishment, *id.* at 257. Justice Marshall mentioned race but only in passing, making careful reference to studies that show the rate of execution of blacks is higher than their rate of participation in crime. *Id.* at 364–65 (Marshall, J., concurring).

33 Gregg v. Georgia, 428 U.S. 153 (1976) (upholding Georgia's "guided discretion" approach to the death penalty).

34 Coker v. Georgia, 433 U.S. 584 (1977) (striking the death penalty for rape as cruel and unusual). Although the defendant in *Coker* was white, in two companion cases the defendants were black. In *Coker*, the American Civil Liberties Union's brief, authored by Ruth Bader Ginsburg, did note that capital punishment was initially "specifically devised as a punishment for the rape of white women by black men." Several of the other *amici* argued similarly.

35 In Rudolf v. Alabama, 375 U.S. 889 (1963), in an opinion dissenting to denial of a
petition of certiorari, Justice Goldberg, joined by Justices Brennan and Douglas,
opined that the Court should consider whether capital punishment for rape was
consistent with "evolving standards of decency." For a careful review of the
Supreme Court's treatment of racial discrimination in the administration of capital
punishment, *see* Carol S. Steiker & Jordan M. Steiker, *The American Death Penalty
and the (In)Visibility of Race*, 82 U. Chi. L. Rev. 243 (2015).

36 Maxwell v. Bishop, 398 U.S. 262 (1970).

37 McGautha v. California, 402 U.S. 183, 248 (1971) (Brennan, J., dissenting).

38 Maxwell, 398 U.S. 262 (reversing the conviction of a black man for rape of a white
woman and remanding to determine if the removal of scrupled jurors violated
Witherspoon v. Illinois, 391 U.S. 510 [1968]).

39 Brief for Synagogue Council of Am. & its Constituents et al. as Amici Curiae
Supporting Petitioner at 26–30, Maxwell v. Bishop, 398 U.S. 262 (1970)
(No. 622–13), 1969 WL 136886.

40 Kennedy v. Louisiana, 554 U.S. 407 (2007) (holding the death penalty for the rape
of a child where no death occurred to be a cruel and unusual punishment).

41 Amici urged otherwise. *See* Brief for ACLU of La. & NAACP Legal Def. Educ.
Fund, Inc., as Amici Curiae Supporting Petitioner, Kennedy v. Louisiana, 554
U.S. 407 (2007) (No. 07–343), 2008 WL 503591. For the history of racialized
punishment in the "death belt," *see* Barry Scheck, Peter Neufeld & Jim
Dwyer, Actual Innocence: When Justice Goes Wrong and How to
Make It Right (2003).

42 *See infra* note 45 and accompanying text.

43 *See* Rachel F. Moran, Interracial Intimacy: The Regulation of Race
and Romance (2003); Randall L. Kennedy, Interracial intimacies:
Sex, marriage, identity and adoption (2003).

44 Charles Robinson, *The Antimiscegenation Conversation: Love's Legislated Limits
1868–1967* 128 (1998) (unpublished Ph.D. dissertation, University of Houston).

45 The case of Louisiana is illustrative, for all the states of the former Confederacy and
many others had laws prohibiting miscegenation. Some states punished intercourse
between a white person and one of another race as a misdemeanor, while in
Alabama, Florida, Georgia, Mississippi, North Carolina, Tennessee, Texas, and
Virginia it was a felony. Some municipalities also criminalized black/white intercourse; a Fort Worth, Texas, ordinance prohibited blacks and whites from having
intercourse within the city limits. For citations to statutes, *see* Charles
S. Mangum, Jr., The Legal Status of the Negro 239–40, 239 n. 7 (1940).

46 An examination of the records from Old Angola Prison by one researcher led him
to conclude that a life sentence was a common penalty for blacks charged with rape
while attempted rape was often punished by a term of years. Civil Rights
Congress, We Charge Genocide: The Historic Petition to the
United Nations for Relief from a Crime of the United States
Government against the Negro People 220 (1970). In 1892, Louisiana

adopted a statute authorizing the death penalty for "aggravated rape." *Id.* at 224. Aggravated rape was a capital offense while simple rape was not.

47 LA. STAT. ANN. § 14:42 (2006) (aggravated rape). After *Furman*, Louisiana adopted a mandatory death sentence for aggravated rape. LA. STAT. ANN. § 14:30. But the Supreme Court struck down the statute in Roberts v. Louisiana, 428 U.S. 325 (1976) (holding the mandatory death sentence unconstitutional and reversing State v. Selman, 300 So. 2d 467 [La. 1974]; state Supreme Court upholding mandatory death for aggravated rape).

48 The prohibitions on rape were recodified in 1942. Article 41 provided the general definition of the offense, while Article 42 defined "aggravated rape," and Article 43 set forth a penalty of from one to twenty years for simple rape.

49 Reporting for the *Pittsburgh Courier* in 1951, civil rights journalist John Rousseau compared two cases involving the rape of 12-year-old girls, one black and the other white. The black man accused of raping the white girl was charged with aggravated rape and sentenced to death, while the white defendant, accused of raping a black girl, was charged with "carnal knowledge of a minor" and sentenced to a year in the Parish prison. John E. Rousseau, PITT. COURIER (La. ed.), Mar. 10, 1951.

50 Burk Foster, *Struck by Lightning: Louisiana's Electrocutions for Rape in the Forties and Fifties*, in LANE NELSON & BURK FOSTER, DEATH WATCH: A DEATH PENALTY ANTHOLOGY 36 (2000). During World War II, three black military men, John Bordenave, Lawrence Mitchell, and Richard Philip Adams, were sentenced to death by military authorities in Louisiana for the rape of a white woman. President Roosevelt commuted their sentences. Adams v. United States, 319 U.S. 312 (1943); NAACP, PAPERS OF THE NAACP, PART 09: DISCRIMINATION IN THE U.S. ARMED FORCES, SERIES B: ARMED FORCES' LEGAL FILES, 1940–1950 (1989).

51 Willie Larkin was executed in 1942 for rape of a black female. Burk Foster, *Convicted Rapists Electrocuted in Louisiana, 1941–1957* (1991) (unpublished manuscript) (on file with author).

52 Of the twelve men lynched in Louisiana between 1932 and 1946, all were black and eight were lynched for alleged sexual contact with white women. Burk Foster, *Lynchings in Louisiana* (1991) (unpublished manuscript) (on file with author).

53 Whether the rights alleged to have been violated were well-established in law is relevant but not dispositive of the question about whether the convictions were unsafe. That question turns on whether, in light of all the circumstances, the judgment of conviction was tainted by racial animus.

54 This pattern in the rape executions would not change until 1950, *see* State v. Honeycutt, 49 So. 2d 610 (La. 1950) (last all-white grand and petit jury), well after Pierre v. Louisiana, 306 U.S. 354 (1939). For an empirical study of juror behavior based on race in capital cases, *see* William J. Bowers, Benjamin D. Steiner & Marla Sandys, *Death Sentencing in Black and White: An Empirical Analysis of the Jurors' Race and Jury Racial Composition*, 3 U. PA. J. CONST. L. 171 (2002).

55 In one case a police witness testified that the alleged victim told him she could identify her assailant by "the odor of him." State v. Wilson, 14 So. 2d 873, 883 (La. 1943). Appellate judges uniformly identified the defendant as a "Negro" and the victim as white in their opinions. *See, e.g.,* State v. Michel, 74 So. 2d 207, 209–10 (La. 1954), where the appellate court identified the parties as "a nineteen year old negro" and "two fifteen year old white girls." By contrast, consider the trial judge's admonition to the lawyers in the Martinsville Seven case: "It must be tried as though both parties were members of the same race." ERIC W. RISE, THE MARTINSVILLE SEVEN: RACE, RAPE AND CAPITAL PUNISHMENT 30 (1995).

56 ADAM FAIRCLOUGH, RACE & DEMOCRACY: THE CIVIL RIGHTS STRUGGLE IN LOUISIANA, 1915–1972 125–27 (1999).

57 In the Honeycutt case, described *supra* note 54, armed guards escorted lawyers to court.

58 *See* 1894 La. Acts 54, revised as LA. STAT. ANN. § 14:79 (1905) (defining the crime of miscegenation and the "marriage or habitual cohabitation" between a white person and a Negro, and setting the maximum penalty at five years).

59 Louisiana law prohibited marriage or cohabitation between a white person and a person of the opposite race, and authorized a sentence of between one to five years with or without hard labor. *See* LA. ANN. STAT. § 14:79 (1950). The act was rendered unconstitutional by Loving v. Virginia, 388 U.S. 1 (1967), and repealed by the state legislature in 1972.

60 LA. CRIM. CODE § 1128 (1932), repealed by 1942 La. Acts 43, § 2.

61 Danger lurked left and right on the question of taking the stand. In one rape case where the defendant's failure to testify was the subject of comment by the prosecutor, the Louisiana Supreme Court found the remark (that the state's evidence was "uncontroverted") nonprejudicial. State v. Bentley, 54 So. 2d 137, 142 (La. 1951).

62 One researcher tracked down nineteen appellate court cases relating to miscegenation between 1868 and 1967. *See* Michelle M. Brattain, *Miscegenation and Competing Definitions of Race in 20th Century Louisiana,* 71 J. SOC. HIST. 621, 634 (2005).

63 In an Alabama case, a trial judge instructed a jury that it could infer that a rape had occurred if the facts established that a black man had engaged in sex with a white female. McQuirter v. State, 63 So. 2d 388, 390 (Ala. Ct. App. 1953) (finding that "in determining the question of intention, the jury may consider social conditions and customs founded upon racial differences, such as that the prosecutrix was a white woman and defendant was a Negro man"). *See* Jennifer B. Wriggins, *Rape, Racism, and the Law,* 6 HARV. WOMEN'S L.J. 103, 111–12 (1983). The defendant's inability to testify to a defense of consent played a peculiar role in Maxwell v. Bishop, 398 U.S. 262 (1970). In one of the lower court cases, Maxwell v. Bishop, 257 F. Supp. 710 (E.D. Ark. 1966), the judge observed that consent was a substantial defense in rape cases, and therefore that Marvin Wolfgang's data on disparities in capital rape convictions in Arkansas was flawed because he had not accounted for the fact that the defense could not be made by black defendants: "from a factual

standpoint [consent was] much less likely to be present in cases in which white women [had] been attacked (sic.) by Negro men." 257 F. Supp. at 720. Since there was rarely a consent defense, the judge reasoned, the disproportionate rate of conviction could be based on the fact that jurors in black/white cases "[had] a firmer and more abiding conviction of the truth of the charges." *Id.* at 720–21.

64 The Louisiana Supreme Court reversed the convictions because the trial judge's charge would have allowed the jury to convict the defendants of habitual cohabitation without a showing of sexual intercourse. Citing Pace v. Alabama, 106 U.S. 583 (1883), the Court upheld the anti-miscegenation statute against a challenge that it violated the federal constitution. State v. Brown, 108 So. 2d 233 (La. 1959). The facts of the case are described in Brattain, *supra* note 62. For other prosecutions under the anti-miscegenation statute, *see* State v. Treadaway, 52 So. 500 (La. 1910); State v. Daniel, 75 So. 836 (1917); State v. Harris, 90 So. 686 (La. 1922).

65 State v. Michel, 74 So. 2d 207 (La. 1954).

66 Wolfgang provided the numbers to support what Ida B. Wells had written about fifty years earlier. IDA B. WELLS, SOUTHERN HORRORS: LYNCH LAW IN ALL ITS PHASES (1892). For studies on rape and discrimination, *see* Jeffrey J. Pokorak, *Rape as a Badge of Slavery: The Legal History of, and Remedies for, Prosecutorial Race-of-Victim Charging Disparities*, 7 NEV. L.J. 1 (2007); Wriggins, *supra* note 63.

67 Catherine A. MacKinnon, *Feminism, Marxism, Method, and the State: Toward Feminist Jurisprudence*, 8 SIGNS 635, 639 (1983). MacKinnon later clarified that the concept of consent was meaningless for women without power: "Politically, I call it rape whenever a woman has sex and feels violated." CATHERINE A. MACKINNON, FEMINISM UNMODIFIED: DISCOURSES ON LIFE AND LAW 82 (1987).

68 Although it does not quite embrace structural patriarchy, Justice Kennedy's opinion in Kennedy v. Louisiana, 554 U.S. 407 (2007), offers a sophisticated reading of rape as an assault on personhood while there is no discussion of the practice of racialized rape prosecutions.

69 *See, e.g.,* SUSAN BROWNMILLER, AGAINST OUR WILL: MEN, WOMEN AND RAPE (1975); SUSAN ESTRICH, REAL RAPE: HOW THE LEGAL SYSTEM VICTIMIZES WOMEN WHO SAY NO (1988). *But see* Angela Y. Davis, *Rape, Racism and the Myth of the Black Rapist,* in WOMEN, RACE & CLASS 172–201 (1981); PATRICIA COLLINS, BLACK SEXUAL POLITICS: AFRICAN AMERICANS, GENDER, AND THE NEW RACISM (2004); Jacquelyn Dowd Hall, *"The Mind that Burns in Each Body": Women, Rape, and Racial Violence,* in POWERS OF DESIRE: THE POLITICS OF SEXUALITY 328–49 (Ann Snitow et al., eds., 1983). *See* Ruth Bader Ginsburg's brief in *Coker,* arguing that the death penalty for rape reinforced understandings of white women as white male property and black men as dangerous. Brief for ACLU et al., as Amici Curiae Supporting Petitioner, Coker v. Georgia, 433 U.S. 584 (No. 75-5444), 1976 WL 181482.

70 Reversing misogynist understandings of consent in rape law has led to the doctrine of "affirmative consent," which holds that sexual engagement with a woman who has not affirmatively consented to the activity violates her rights. Affirmative

consent rules pose their own challenges to rape law given the inherently ambiguous nature of sexual behavior. *See* Janet Halley, *The Move to Affirmative Consent*, Signs: Currents (2015), available at http://signsjournal.org/currents-affirma tive-consent/halley/; Jeannie Suk *"The Look in His Eyes": The Story of* Rusk *and* Rape Reform, in Criminal Law Stories 171–213 (Donna Coker & Robert Weisberg, eds., 2013).

71 Scholars of southern history have observed that the tolerance of interracial relations was higher during slavery – so long as no child came of the union – than in the early twentieth century, when these relationships were seen as an expression of black power. Martha Hodes, White Women, Black Men: Illicit Sex in the Nineteenth-Century South (1997); Diane Miller Sommerville, The Rape Myth in the Old South Reconsidered (1995).

72 *See* Maria Bevaqua, Rape on the Public Agenda: Feminism & the Politics of Sexual Assault (2000).

73 *See* C. Ronald Huff, *Wrongful Convictions, Miscarriages of Justice, and Political Repression: Challenges for Transitional Justice*, in Wrongful Convictions and Miscarriages of Justice: Causes and Remedies in North American and European Criminal Justice Systems (C. Ronald Huff & Martin Killias, eds., 2013).

74 David Dyzenhous, Judging the Judges, Judging Ourselves: Truth, Reconciliation and the Apartheid Legal Order 41 (1997).

75 Some have argued that great care should be taken in examining the role of judges in maintaining an authoritarian state lest the judiciary be drawn into the space of politics. *See, e.g., id.*; David Dyzenhous, *Judicial Independence, Transitional Justice and the Rule of Law*, 10 Otago L.J. 345 (2003).

76 Ministry of the Attorney General, Report of the Kaufman Commission on Proceedings Involving Guy Paul Morin (1998), available at www.attorneygeneral.jus.gov.on.ca/english/about/pubs/morin.

77 Royal Comm'n on the Donald Marshall, Jr., Prosecution, Digest of Findings and Recommendations 19 (1989), available at http://novascotia.ca/ just/marshall_inquiry/ (follow Digest of Findings and Recommendations 1989 link).

78 Royal Commission to Inquire into the Circumstances of the Conviction of Arthur Allan Thomas, Arthur Allan Thomas Royal Commission Report (1980), available at http://netk.net.au/NewZealand/Thomas5.asp.

79 Criminal Appeal Act 1995, c. 35, Part II. *See* Hannah Quirk, *Don't Mention the War: The Court of Appeal, the Criminal Cases Review Commission and Dealing with the Past in Northern Ireland*, 76 Mod. L. Rev. 949 (2013).

80 The policy provided that "if a case was wrongly judged from beginning to end, the judgment of the whole case should be corrected. If part of the judgment is incorrect, only the erroneous part should be corrected and if no mistakes were made in the original instances, no corrections should be made." Sue Travaskes, *People's Justice and Injustice: Courts and the Redressing of Cultural Revolution Cases*, China Info., Oct. 2002, at 1, 5 (2002).

81 *See* Suzannah Linton, *The Role of Judges in Dealing with the Legacies of the Past* 18 (2009), available at http://papers.ssrn.com/sol3/papers.cfm?abstract_id=1423990; Travaskes, *supra* note 80, at 6.

82 *See* Linton, *supra* note 81, at 19; Park Si-soo, *Executed Daily Head Cleared by Court*, KOR. TIMES, Jan. 16, 2008.

83 Linton, *supra* note 81, at 41 (citing Comm'n for Reception, Truth & Reconciliation in East Timor, *Political Trials*, in CHEGA! FINAL REPORT OF THE COMMISSION FOR RECEPTION, TRUTH AND RECONCILIATION c. 7.6 (2005)).

84 In September 2008, the Chief Justice of Korea announced that "I, as the Chief Justice, would like to take this opportunity to apologize to the general public for the disappointment and pain that the Judiciary caused in the past by failing to fully perform its constitutional duties." Linton, *supra* note 81, at 42 n. 141.

85 *See, e.g.*, Michael Klarman, *Scottsboro*, 93 MARQ. L. REV. 379 (2009).

86 ALEX HEARD, THE EYES OF WILLIE McGEE: A TRAGEDY OF RACE, SEX AND SECRETS IN THE JIM CROW SOUTH (2010).

16

Outbreaks of Injustice

Responding to Systemic Irregularities in the Criminal Justice System

SANDRA GUERRA THOMPSON AND ROBERT WICOFF

INTRODUCTION

Wrongful convictions typically result from one or more of the following errors or justice system failures: erroneous eyewitness identifications, false confessions, faulty forensic evidence, prosecutorial misconduct, inadequate defense counsel, false informant testimony, or the presentation of false evidence.[1] Usually, a wrongful conviction is discovered through a reactive process by which attorneys, often through groups like the Innocence Project in New York City, investigate individual cases that have been brought to their attention.[2] An attorney who represents a person raising a claim of innocence typically investigates the discrete facts surrounding only that client's claim. For example, in a case involving faulty eyewitness testimony, the focus would center only upon the mistaken eyewitness testimony in the case under review. Although the investigation might illustrate problems with eyewitness testimony in general, the fact that an individual had provided mistaken eyewitness testimony in one case would not normally suggest that any other convictions would be cast into doubt as a result.

Increasingly, however, something akin to "mass torts" in the civil system has begun to emerge in the criminal system, where the discovery of an error in one criminal case uncovers a unique problem that is common to an entire group of cases. Some of these systemic irregularities may have affected only a few convictions. But other problems, such as situations involving fraud by forensic scientists, may call for the review of hundreds or even thousands of cases in which the same troublesome issue played a role in the convictions. For fiscal 2013 alone, lawmakers in Massachusetts set aside $30 million to handle one such crisis.[3]

In 2013, the Department of Justice and the FBI entered into an agreement with the Innocence Project and the National Association for Criminal

Defense Lawyers (NACDL) to review more than 2,000 criminal cases in which FBI crime laboratory analysts had given microscopic hair analysis testimony.[4] The review has uncovered cases in which FBI analysts gave invalid expert testimony in criminal trials nationwide. However, given that the FBI also trained state and local crime laboratory analysts to testify regarding microscopic hair analysis, it stands to reason that analysts in state and local crime laboratories nationwide may also have given flawed microscopic hair analysis testimony over many years. According to the *Washington Post*, three states have undertaken their own reviews of cases involving microscopic hair analysis, and fifteen other *ad hoc* reviews have begun in other jurisdictions.[5] Many convictions involving microscopic hair analysis remain unexamined, since most jurisdictions have not organized reviews of past cases involving hair microscopy testimony, despite the national publicity surrounding the issue.

Moreover, as will be discussed below, there are other source-specific problems having nothing to do with forensic science that may undermine convictions in groups of cases. These irregularities may stem from the discovery that government officials have engaged in a pattern of misconduct that undermined the integrity of numerous convictions, or simply from a judicial decision invalidating a law or the manner in which a law is applied. Regardless of the source of the systemic irregularity, the system is ill-equipped to respond to such discoveries. Surprisingly, no institutionalized process exists to ensure that persons convicted under statutes or rules of procedure later found to be invalid can be identified, given notification of the problem, and provided with counsel.[6]

The increased discoveries of systemic irregularities pose serious challenges to the criminal justice system. When is a problem significant enough or widespread enough to warrant notification to affected parties? Whose duty is it to notify affected persons of the problem? How are they to be located and notified? Once affected persons are notified, does a system that caused the problem with their conviction bear the responsibility of providing them with counsel?

Further, unless the prosecuting authority agrees to waive procedural barriers, tainted convictions may not be judicially reviewable. In the federal hair microscopy review, the Department of Justice has agreed to waive procedural barriers so that cases raising viable innocence claims can obtain judicial review.[7] Without a similar waiver of procedural barriers, meritorious claims in many jurisdictions will fall victim to serious procedural bars. Only a handful of states currently have post-conviction writ statutes that provide a statutory means of bypassing procedural bars in cases involving new forensic evidence, but as stated earlier, forensic error is only one type of irregularity that may have led to a wrongful conviction.[8]

This chapter attempts to articulate some of the problems that face the criminal justice system when there are such "outbreaks of injustice," that is, where a specific problem or source is common to a body of convictions and may undermine the validity of them all. The challenge facing federal, state, and local jurisdictions is to develop institutionalized ways of responding to these systemic irregularities, rather than the current piecemeal process of reacting to individual cases. Some jurisdictions' responses are discussed in this chapter, primarily from the authors' experience in Texas. That state has experienced its fair share of such systemic irregularities, but has also reacted to such problems by adopting significant legislative reform. The main purpose of the chapter, however, is to articulate the problems facing the criminal justice system when systemic injustices occur, in the hope that it will prompt a discussion of creative responses.

1 Types of Systemic Irregularities

The most common type of systemic irregularity is the discovery of unreliable forensic evidence, caused by problems with a specific laboratory or analyst, or from newfound concerns about the reliability of a scientific discipline itself. A prime example is the recent situation involving a single laboratory analyst, Massachusetts State Crime Laboratory Chemist Annie Dookhan. In 2013, Dookhan was found to have committed wide-scale fraud in the performance of her job by inflating drug weights and falsifying drug tests. She pled guilty to twenty-seven counts of misleading investigators, filing false reports, and tampering with evidence, for which she was sentenced to three to five years in prison. Authorities in Massachusetts have announced an intention to undertake a massive review of the 40,000 cases that Dookhan handled during her time in the laboratory.[9]

In other situations, an entire forensic laboratory's work is called into question, necessitating a review of thousands of cases. The Houston Police Department Crime Laboratory was the subject of an extensive, two-year review by an outside team of investigators, after a wave of adverse publicity raised serious questions about the quality of the forensic science work at the laboratory. The investigation, which concluded in 2007, involved a review of more than 3,500 cases dating as far back as the 1980s.[10]

In addition to such analyst-specific or laboratory-specific problems, another type of forensic problem that may affect large numbers of cases involves situations in which a particular discipline or science used in securing criminal convictions has come under scrutiny. Some entire disciplines have been branded as "junk science," such as dog-scent lineups,[11] while others have evolved to the point that past assumptions in the science are no longer considered scientifically valid, such as composite bullet lead analysis,[12] or have been discovered to lack a statistical foundation to justify traditional statements of their reliability.[13]

In the science of hair microscopy, for example, it is now understood that microscopic comparison of a hair from an unknown source to a hair from a known source should never lead to testimony that they came from the same person, or that they are "a match."[14] Only DNA testing can approach such exacting identification. However, as mentioned earlier, the FBI review of expert testimony regarding microscopic hair analysis has suggested that hair analysts frequently overstated the ability of the science to act as a "unique identifier" of the source of an unknown hair in a high percentage of the cases under review.[15]

Systemic irregularities also include issues other than forensic evidence. A problem may arise from the discovery that a participant in the criminal justice system has engaged in intentional rule violations, or has been shown to be so negligent that all of the person's work thereby warrants review. For instance, a police officer may have engaged in a pattern of misconduct, such as coerced confessions, that calls into question all of the cases where he was the lead investigator.[16] Likewise, a prosecutor's blatant and egregious failure to disclose exculpatory evidence in one case may raise the specter of other instances of misconduct by that prosecutor.

Sometimes the system misfires through no obvious fault of any participant. In Houston, the District Attorney's Office notified defendants and defense attorneys of hundreds of drug convictions in which people pled guilty to charges before completion of drug testing. Subsequent testing showed that no illegal substances were detected, that the weight of the drugs was less than the amount charged, or that a different drug altogether was found through the testing.[17] Although it is unclear at this point whether anyone bears responsibility for the invalid convictions, it is apparent that the system has failed in a way that calls into question hundreds of drug convictions and that a proactive review may be necessary to determine whether other cases may have been affected as well.

A final category of systemic irregularities would be situations in which convictions have been rendered voidable because the criminal statute upon which they are based has been found to be invalid on constitutional grounds, or are otherwise subject to attack because of a court ruling that applies retroactively. For example, the Texas Court of Criminal Appeals in

2014 found the state's "online solicitation of a minor" law invalid on First Amendment grounds, providing a basis for anyone convicted under such statute to challenge his conviction.[18] Judicial decisions invalidating certain procedural or sentencing practices may cast doubt on the convictions or sentences in large numbers of cases.[19] Persons affected may have grounds to challenge their convictions or sentences as a result of such decisions, but only if they are notified of the issue and provided with counsel to investigate their cases.

A court ruling invalidating hundreds of convictions, like a widespread forensic problem or pattern of misconduct by a participant in the criminal justice system, raises serious questions about how the criminal justice system should respond, including the threshold question of who bears the responsibility to determine whether other convictions are similarly affected and to notify those persons that their convictions are now subject to attack.

2 Notification to Parties after Systemic Irregularities Are Uncovered: What, When and How?

Difficult questions arise with regard to the issue of notification to affected persons when systemic problems manifest themselves. A threshold question is whether the problem is serious enough to trigger actual notification to affected persons, should instead be relegated to some form of constructive notification, or even warrants any notification at all. The authors do not presume to answer this question. Prosecutors routinely face the question of whether evidence constitutes exculpatory *Brady* material so as to require disclosure to the defense, but *Brady* does not apply in the post-conviction setting,[20] and only a few states have adopted laws requiring such notice.[21] Thus, it remains to be determined which entity should provide notifications and for what types of systemic irregularities.

At first glance, it might seem that the safest approach to all discovered systemic problems would be to provide actual, personal notification to all affected persons, irrespective of how serious the problem might seem. However, further consideration suggests the need for a more discretionary approach based on the seriousness of the error or malfeasance. Problems that are both widespread and serious (like the forensic fraud by Annie Dookhan in Massachusetts) would seem to call for proactive investigation and actual notice to affected parties. Other situations may involve repeated problems, but the problems may nonetheless be so minor as not to necessitate an institutional response. For example, the FBI database used to calculate the rarity of a Short Tandem Repeat (STR) genetic profile has now been found to have contained discrepancies that may have affected certain DNA test results between 1999 and 2015.[22] According to the author of the report, "these discrepancies require acknowledgement but are unlikely to materially affect any assessment of evidential value."[23] For example, in an assessment performed by one Texas laboratory, after recalculating cases using the amended data, the largest statistical change in any of the cases recalculated went from a 1 in 260,900,000 expression of probability to a 1 in 225,300,000 expression of probability.[24] Thus, the forensic irregularity in these cases, though affecting a large number of cases, may be genuinely inconsequential. Thus, it is arguable whether prosecuting authorities should be required to send notification letters to the large number of people affected when it is currently undisputed that the error could not have been material to any of those convictions.[25]

Defining the point at which affected persons should be notified of a systemic irregularity is a difficult threshold question. The entity in charge of the notification process (whether it be the prosecution or some other governmental body, such as an investigatory commission or public defender's office) could undertake actual notification in every instance, regardless of the frequency of the error and even when its impact was clearly insignificant, on the premise that the court system is best suited to determine whether any error is material to a conviction. However, there are both practical and compelling reasons to avoid blanket notification of systemic irregularities in all instances.

First, a blanket policy of notifying each person affected by a systemic irregularity, even where the possibility that a conviction could be affected by the problem is practically nonexistent, would require tremendous financial resources and manpower. To take the FBI database issue mentioned earlier, the error is likely relevant to many thousands of cases nationwide. As will be discussed below, the process of actual (as opposed to constructive) notification is a daunting one in the best of circumstances, involving locating and communicating with persons who are relatively easy to locate (such as those currently in prison, or on parole or probation), but also involving people who are no longer confined and might be very difficult to contact. Financial resources are not limitless. Although every attempt should be made to undertake actual notification of systemic problems where practical, it is legitimate to ask whether every discovered issue, regardless of its effect, must result in a notification letter to every person affected. Simply, the system may not be able to afford it.

Moreover, there is a human cost worth considering in adopting such a widespread notification policy. People who have been convicted of criminal offenses, and especially those still incarcerated, are especially vulnerable to suggestions that there may be a glimmer of hope in their case. Although persons are certainly entitled to be made aware of problems that may have an effect on their case, the threshold question that must be honestly answered is whether the discovered problem could possibly constitute a real (rather than hypothetical) problem that carries the possibility of undermining a criminal conviction.

To again use the FBI database issue as an example, an inmate receiving an official notice letter from a state commission or a prosecutor's office regarding "database errors" that might have affected the DNA results in his case would likely impute high significance to the letter and might reasonably derive some hope from the fact that the matter was deemed serious enough for the authorities to find him and spell out the problem. That person might also follow up by contacting the convicting court to request the appointment of counsel. Depending on the custom or the legal requirements in the particular jurisdiction, a lawyer may in fact be appointed or a public defender assigned to the case, with predictably pointless litigation to follow. While actual notification of systemic irregularities may be the course to take in most instances, an honest assessment of how serious the problem really is may avoid futile expenditure of limited money and manpower, as well as the generation of false hope.

Another type of situation arises which raises questions about whether a problem warrants notification. Sometimes a single incident may be serious, but it is unclear whether it was isolated, or instead warrants an investigation into whether the problem was widespread and requires notice to affected parties. For example, should the fact that a forensic scientist or a police officer has engaged in misconduct in one case create a presumption about misconduct in all his other cases?[26] Does one act of misconduct, without more, warrant notification to every prosecutor, defense attorney and defendant who has ever been involved in a case involving that scientist or officer on the assumption that every case that person touched is now suspect? Unfortunately, there is no easy way to determine how widespread the notification should be.

Sometimes one act of misconduct is deemed serious enough to trigger widespread investigation and actual notification. For example, in 2012, in numerous counties in the Houston area, a scientist's conclusions in nearly 5,000 drug cases were called into question when it was discovered that he drylabbed[27] results in one case.[28] One instance of drylabbing the results in drug-testing was determined to be such a serious deception that it raised questions about the integrity of all of that scientist's work.

However, what if the problem is not drylabbing, but that the scientist repeatedly misrepresented his credentials when testifying? If the scientist falsely represents that he or she is certified in his or her area of expertise, then the problem would clearly warrant notification to affected persons in other cases in which that expert had testified. For example, Mississippi medical examiner Steven Hayne repeatedly swore under oath in many criminal trials over the years that he was certified by the American Board of Forensic Pathology, which was false testimony (the American Board of Forensic Pathology ceased to exist in 1995).[29] Such false testimony regarding his credentials impacted his credibility as an expert sufficiently to warrant a review of all of the other cases in which he testified.[30] It does not appear that officials in Mississippi conducted an investigation to identify the hundreds of criminal cases in which Hayne had testified over the years so as to provide notification to defendants.[31]

The question of whether to notify becomes muddier if the issue is not that an expert lacked the necessary credentials to testify about the subject matter in question, but that he had testified falsely about the university he attended in obtaining his degree, or about whether he falsely claimed to obtain a degree relevant to his testimony, when he did not. James Bolding, the former director of the Houston Police Department Crime Laboratory, testified repeatedly in criminal trials that he had earned "a Ph.D. in biochemistry from the University of Texas," when in fact he dropped out of the program in 1977 or 1978 because he was having difficulty with the coursework.[32] He obtained only a master's degree from another university.[33] Whatever conclusion one may reach about the need for notification to persons whose convictions were obtained with the help of Bolding's false testimony, it may be a closer question as to whether notification in all of his cases should have been undertaken because of this type of misrepresentation.[34] Although less impressive than a Ph.D., Bolding's master's degree would presumably be sufficient to qualify him to do the job, whereas Hayne's lack of certification may have disqualified him to do the forensic pathology work in question. The point is that one can easily imagine the problem in an expert's testimony becoming increasingly less significant, to the point that no one believes notification should take place for even admittedly false testimony, where it is apparent that it could not possibly have mattered.

It is inherently difficult to devise a test to determine when a systemic irregularity is serious enough to trigger the requirement to notify. There are admitted dangers in an investigative agency or other entity presuming to determine whether an irregularity is serious enough to warrant notification. However, if no preliminary screening is done, and notification is provided for every imaginable irregularity, the investigative body tasked with reviewing the cases would send forth a seemingly endless stream of notifications to prosecutors, defense lawyers, and convicted persons, some of the notifications important, but others no less than silly. It is one thing to get notice that the police officer in one's criminal trial has been found to have extracted false confessions over the years; it is quite another to learn that he routinely testified to having testified "500 times" before when in fact the accurate number was only 425 times. Although he may have testified falsely, it speaks more to an exaggeration than a material error warranting actual notice to affected parties.

Questions surrounding whether to provide actual notice of forensic problems and when to do so are currently the subject of debate in Texas, in the wake of the revelation that perhaps tens of thousands of DNA mixture cases (cases involving two or more contributors to biological evidence) have been improperly calculated and may need recalculation.[35] Although many prosecuting authorities are notifying all affected persons of the DNA mixture recalculation issue, some prosecutors have decided to forestall notice until there has already been recalculation, based on the premise that the new results could produce statistically insignificant changes, or may even provide stronger inculpatory evidence against the defendant.

3 The Duty to Notify and Notification Logistics

Once a systemic irregularity has been discovered and notification is deemed appropriate, it is not always clear whose responsibility it is to provide such notification. When a prosecuting authority discovers a *Brady* violation, even in the post-conviction stage, notification should be the prosecutor's obligation,[36] and Texas law imposes such a duty.[37] But even in a jurisdiction with broad discovery obligations, notification of some systemic irregularities may not be anyone's responsibility as the law currently stands.

For example, when the Texas online solicitation of a minor statute was declared unconstitutional,[38] prosecutors in Houston and neighboring counties took it upon themselves to send notification letters to all persons who had been convicted under the void law. In other jurisdictions, prosecutors did not do so, and many affected parties may still not realize their convictions are subject to attack.[39] Indeed, providing actual notice to affected persons of a court ruling that could overturn their convictions is likely not anyone's legal obligation. Normally, publication of the court's decision is deemed to provide adequate notice, but jurisdictions may want to recognize the structural problem this creates. Some number of people, whether small or large, should be released because the law under which they are convicted is struck down, but realistically they will not have their convictions overturned unless some party takes action. Since the issue arises as a result of a judicial decision, perhaps the courts should bear the responsibility to ensure that affected persons receive actual notice, and, when appropriate, appointment of counsel.

Some states have created investigative bodies that may uncover systemic problems that require notification. For example, the Texas Forensic Science Commission investigates misconduct or other irregularities in forensic science and issues notification to affected parties when allegations of malfeasance have been verified. In order to provide the type of specialized habeas representation needed in cases of forensic irregularities, the Texas legislature in 2015 expanded the Office of Capital Writs (charged with handling many death penalty cases at the habeas stage) and renamed it the "Office of Capital and Forensic Writs."[40] The Forensic Science Commission (FSC) is now authorized to refer cases that are the subject of its investigations to the new office. Although the agency will be empowered to represent defendants whose cases have been referred by the FSC, it is unclear whether the agency will be asked to undertake notification to defendants in the wake of widespread forensic errors.

The question of who shoulders the responsibility to notify affected persons of systemic irregularities merits careful consideration. An independent state agency or other governmental body is one option.[41] In one systemic review in Virginia, *pro bono* attorneys were charged with delivering actual notice to defendants whose case files contained sufficient DNA evidence to allow retesting.[42] One study makes the interesting point that *who* delivers the notification might affect the notification's success, suggesting that "a prosecutor may not be the ideal person to deliver a notification directly to a defendant because a defendant may not choose to associate with the prosecutor's office for a variety of reasons, including fear, the passage of time since conviction, and others."[43] This point proved to be demonstrably true in the notification process following the systemic review of forensic misconduct by laboratory analyst Jonathan Salvador in Texas. When the prosecutor's office in Houston sent notification letters to roughly 400 defendants whose convictions may have been impacted by Salvador's drylabbing misconduct, the letters advised the defendants to contact the public defender's office for further explanation of the problem. A relatively small number of responses were received by the public defender's office as a result of the prosecutor's letter. However, when the public defender's office followed up by sending the same defendants a second letter, which explained the problem in more detail, with available options, a much higher response followed.[44] One can only assume that a defendant, having encountered the criminal justice system before, may be more likely to respond to a public defender's office, a defense attorney, or an independent state agency, than from an entity that he may well view as his nemesis. Moreover, people will be more responsive when provided concrete guidance as the public defender's letter did.

It should also be pointed out that in terms of how notification was delivered by the public defender's office in the Salvador cases, letters were sent by both certified mail and regular mail. Certified mail may generally be viewed as bad news to people who have been in the criminal justice system and may often not only go uncollected but actively avoided, whereas regular mail stands a better chance of making it to its destination and being read.[45]

Finally, for various reasons, the prosecution sometimes discharges its notification obligation rather succinctly or cryptically. For example, a recent three-line notification disclosure by the Harris County District Attorney's Office in Houston informed defendants only that such office had learned that "certain witnesses in your case may have serious credibility issues that possibly affected the outcome of your case."[46] In contrast, a letter from a defense attorney fully explaining the problem that may affect the person's case and offering details about how to pursue relief will increase the chances that its recipient will respond, because it makes clear that the recipient is not in any further trouble and may even benefit by responding.

This discussion concerns perhaps the most difficult aspect of the notification process, namely, how is it to be accomplished? Is actual notification of systemic irregularities required, or will constructive notice suffice? Ideally, every defendant whose case may have been affected by a systemic irregularity would receive actual notice of a problem through personal service of a written communication that explains the problem. Such a goal may certainly be realistic with regard to defendants who are currently in prison, on parole, or on some type of probation. However, for those persons who have discharged their sentence, locating them and providing them with written notification of the problem that may have beset their case is a challenging undertaking.[47]

"Constructive notice" carries its own unique problems. For example, publishing the matter in the "public notices" section of the newspaper or by other indirect means hardly seems adequate when attempting to transmit information as important as notifying a person that his or her criminal conviction may be in question. Although some systemic irregularities are newsworthy and draw much attention (such as the Annie Dookhan situation in Massachusetts), many others (such as the recently revealed discrepancies in the FBI database concerning certain DNA mixtures),[48] are not generally reported in the media.

Thus, to give constructive notice in a meaningful matter, one observer has stressed the importance of repeating the various types of constructive notice that may reach affected individuals, pointing to newspaper announcements, courthouse postings, and the news media as part of a "wider net" in the notification effort.[49] One might add the option to alert prison authorities who can publicize the matter. Another option is to send written notification of the problem to the last attorney who represented the defendant in the case, but such method of constructive notice is less than ideal: unfortunately, many attorneys likely do not view their obligation to past clients as an ongoing one that includes tracking the clients down to explain a letter notifying them of a newfound problem that may have affected their case. Although some attorneys would feel obligated to find their clients and notify them of the problem, there can be little doubt that many would do nothing.

4 Access to Counsel after Notification

As important as it is to notify affected persons of systemic problems that may have affected their case, notification is meaningless unless those persons then have some recourse, in terms of obtaining both counsel and a legal remedy if their conviction was compromised. One can imagine the frustration of a prison inmate, having received a letter notifying him in vague terms that there may be a problem with his conviction, wondering how he is supposed to "take any action deemed necessary in relation to this criminal case."[50] Greater guidance and access to legal assistance are both necessary to give a person a genuine opportunity to investigate the claim and pursue available relief.

As a threshold observation, equity might suggest that when, through no fault of the convicted person, the criminal justice system has failed to operate properly, resulting in that person's wrongful conviction or illegal punishment, that person should not have to hire counsel to correct the system's error, whatever his or her financial resources may be. For an indigent person, the argument in favor of appointing counsel is even more compelling. However, as will be shown below, indigent petitioners have an especially difficult time obtaining legal representation to correct mistakes made by the system.

As is the case in many other jurisdictions, a Texas habeas applicant is not entitled to appointment of counsel in a noncapital case.[51] Thus, there is no constitutional right to assistance of counsel to help investigate the facts related to the habeas application, or to decide what cognizable issues may be available and/or to draft the writ application and supporting memoranda. In the infrequent circumstance where a *pro se* habeas applicant persuades the Court of Criminal Appeals of the need for an evidentiary hearing, the Court will remand the case to the trial court for the appointment of counsel.[52] For most habeas applicants, navigating the important and confusing first phase of the habeas process, a daunting enough task for most attorneys, represents a nearly impossible task for a person who lacks legal training and is confined to a prison unit.

State law sometimes provides a right to appointed counsel. Texas has passed a new statute making appointment of habeas counsel mandatory if the prosecutor's office represents that the applicant is actually innocent, guilty of a lesser offense, or has been convicted under an unconstitutional statute.[53] Of course, laws such as this often run into a "chicken-and-egg" problem; a convicted person simply may not know that he fits within one of the categories entitling him to counsel until he has counsel to assist him. The unfortunate reality is that for those persons finding themselves with a notification letter in hand, unsure of what it means or whether their cases are affected by the problem, obtaining any assistance may be very difficult. If instead an independent agency was tasked with providing notice, the agency might also be authorized by statute to appoint counsel for nontrivial errors.

Additionally, even if the law did provide for the assistance of counsel to all persons receiving notification letters, the sad reality is that quality legal help is difficult to obtain. Few lawyers have experience in criminal habeas corpus law, an area of post-conviction litigation dense with arcane rules and procedural pitfalls. Thus, even for those persons who can afford to hire their own attorney, quality representation may be hard to find.

Harris County, the most populous county in Texas, is illustrative of the uneven approach to providing legal representation for persons affected by systemic errors. Although arguably more proactive than any other county in the state in providing counsel to persons affected by systemic irregularities, Harris County has nonetheless been inconsistent. On the one hand, at least one crisis resulted in the laudable creation of a special task force funded by the district courts,[54] and other situations have resulted in the Harris County Public Defender's Office representing groups of affected persons.[55] However, in most instances, a person whose conviction is cast into doubt by a systemic problem is left with few options in terms of obtaining legal representation.

For example, in 2014, the Harris County District Attorney's Office sent letters notifying approximately two dozen persons whose cases were investigated by a homicide detective who was found to have been neglectful in his investigations. Around the same time, notices were also sent to a larger group of persons whose cases were investigated by a sex crimes investigator later deemed by the district attorney's office to be untruthful.[56] These two situations cast some doubt on the integrity of numerous homicide and sexual assault convictions involving lengthy sentences. Inmates and other convicted persons were again advised by means of letters notifying them to "take any action deemed necessary" in relation to their case. The "necessary action" in these cases would include extensive investigation and the assistance of an attorney before the precise grounds for a habeas application could even be determined. What realistic options are available to persons who receive a notification letter in a situation like this?

One option is for courts to appoint counsel on a case-by-case basis, but this has not proved to be a workable solution. Under this approach, either a prosecutor or the convicted person would request that the convicting court appoint a lawyer and pay for an investigator to handle the case. In Harris County, a court will typically appoint a habeas lawyer for the convicted person if the district attorney's office first approaches the court and suggests that such is necessary. However, though rare exceptions do occur, letters from prison inmates to district courts, asking that habeas counsel be appointed for post-conviction writs, are generally ignored. Courts are undoubtedly aware that if they routinely appoint habeas counsel in response to every *pro se* request, they would open some very expensive floodgates.[57] In the case of the notification letter sent regarding the homicide and sex crimes investigators in Harris County,[58] the district attorney's office has not requested that habeas counsel be appointed and the courts have, almost without exception, ignored *pro se* requests for the appointment of habeas counsel.

In addition to the difficulty that is inherent in even finding experienced habeas attorneys to represent indigent persons whose convictions may have been affected by systemic irregularities, case-by-case appointments are undesirable for yet another reason. If a large number of convictions have been affected by an obscure matter involving forensic science, such as the recently revealed discrepancies found in the FBI database surrounding STR-DNA testing,[59] it does not make fiscal sense to appoint numerous individual habeas attorneys, each of whom must then become familiar with the complicated forensic discipline of DNA testing, in order to represent a single habeas applicant. The better option is to enlist the help of a central organization, like the new Office of Capital and Forensic Writs in Texas, a public defender's office, a criminal defense lawyer's organization, or even a civil law firm willing to work on a *pro bono* basis. Assigning a group of cases to one organization facilitates the centralization of resources and minimizes the duplication of effort in developing the needed expertise to navigate the forensic and habeas issues.[60] Simply put, systemic outbreaks are best addressed through a systemic response.

CONCLUSION

The increasing frequency of systemic irregularities poses a daunting challenge at both the federal and state level. Properly responding to these outbreaks of injustice demands an institutionalized process for investigating the seriousness of a potentially widespread problem and determining the extent to which notification should be provided. This chapter outlines the need for legislatures to tackle this important subject by providing procedures for investigation and relief when systemic irregularities cast numerous convictions or sentences in doubt.

NOTES

1 *See generally* Brandon L. Garrett, Convicting the Innocent: Where Criminal Prosecutions Go Wrong (2011).
2 The Innocence Project, a national litigation and public policy group, has investigated and litigated many individual claims of wrongful conviction. *See* Innocence Project, *Homepage*, available at www.innocenceproject.org. According to data compiled by the Innocence Project, as of September 2015, 330 people had been wrongfully convicted in the United States and later exonerated through post-conviction DNA testing. *Id.*
3 David Abel & John R. Ellement, *Drug Mishandling May Have Tainted 40,000 Cases*, Boston Globe, Aug. 20, 2013, available at www.bostonglobe.com/metro/2013/08/20/annie-dookhan-alleged-rogue-state-chemist-may-have-affected-more-than-people-cases-review-finds/GuEEMIzbAfAssiclatettI/story.html; *see generally* Sandra Guerra Thompson, Cops in Lab Coats: Curbing Wrongful Convictions through Independent Forensic Laboratories 39–46 (2015) (detailing numerous crime laboratory scandals involving fraud, perjury, drug thefts, incompetence, and cheating on proficiency tests); *see also infra* note 9 and accompanying text.
4 *See* Innocence Project, *News and Information: Innocence Project and NACDL Announce Historic Partnership with FBI and Department of Justice on Microscopic Hair Analysis Cases*, available at www.innocenceproject.org/Content/Innocence_Project_and_NACDL_Announce_Historic_Partnership_with_the_FBI_and_Department_of_Justice_on_Microscopic_Hair_Analysis_Cases.php#; Spencer S. Hsu, *FBI Admits Flaws in Hair Analysis over Decades*, Wash. Post, Apr. 18, 2015, available at www.washingtonpost.com/local/crime/fbi-overstated-forensic-hair-matches-in-nearly-all-criminal-trials-for-decades/2015/04/18/39c8d8c6-e515-11e4-b510-962fcfabc310_story.html.
5 *See* Hsu, *supra* note 4.
6 The North Carolina Innocence Inquiry Commission, the first of its kind in the United States, began operation in 2007. While the Commission does create a new avenue for reviewing individual claims of innocence, it does not appear to initiate innocence investigations based on discoveries of systemic irregularities. Rather, individual claims of innocence must be filed with the Commission by a claimant, a claimant's attorney, a state or local agency, or a court. *See* North Carolina

Innocence Inquiry Commission, *Case Progression Flowchart*, available at www.innocencecommission-nc.gov/chart.html. Other states have established innocence commissions, but most of these simply recommend policy changes, rather than conducting investigations. *See* Innocence Project, *State Commissions Seek to Prevent Wrongful Convictions*, available at www.innocenceproject.org/news-events-exonerations/state-commissions-seek-to-prevent-wrongful-convictions.

7 *See* Hsu, *supra* note 4.

8 *See, e.g.,* CAL PEN CODE § 1473(e) (2014); TEX. CODE CRIM. PROC. ANN. art. 11.073 (West Supp. 2014).

9 *See* THOMPSON, *supra* note 3, at 42–43.

10 *See* Michael Bromwich, *Final Report of the Independent Investigator for the Houston Police Department Crime Laboratory and Property Room* 1–3, Jun. 13, 2007, available at www.hpdlabinvestigation.org/reports/070613report.pdf.

11 Winfrey v. State, 323 S.W.3d 875, 884 (Tex. Crim. App. 2010) (holding that "scent-discrimination lineups, when used alone or as primary evidence, are legally insufficient to support a conviction").

12 *See* National Research Council, Committee on Scientific Assessment of Bullet Lead Elemental Composition Comparison, *Forensic Analysis: Weighing Bullet Lead Evidence* (2004), available at: www.nap.edu/catalog.php? record_id=10924.

13 *See* THOMPSON, *supra* note 3, at 97–107 (addressing the lack of statistical foundations for latent print examination and firearms examination).

14 *Id.* at 109–110.

15 *See* Hsu, *supra* note 4.

16 *See, e.g.,* Frances Robles & N.R. Kleinfield, *Review of 50 Brooklyn Murder Cases Ordered*, N.Y. TIMES, May 11, 2013, available at www.nytimes.com/2013/05/12/nyregion/doubts-about-detective-haunt-50-murder-cases.html?_r=0 (discussing how cases involving homicide Detective Louis Scarcella were called into question due to various types of misconduct by the officer, including the procurement of false confessions).

17 *See* Michael Barajas, *Lab Reports Show Hundreds "Convicted in Error" for Drug Offenses*, HOUS. PRESS, Oct. 29, 2014, available at www.houstonpress.com/news/lab-reports-show-hundreds-convicted-in-error-for-drug-offenses-6751687.

18 *See Ex parte* Lo, 424 S.W.3d 10, 27 (Tex. Crim. App. 2013) (online solicitation of a minor statute held unconstitutionally overbroad).

19 In a ruling that could affect the convictions of hundreds of juveniles who were certified to stand trial as adults, some of whom have now been in prison for years, the Texas high court invalidated a widely used procedure for certifying juveniles for felony court and remanded the case that challenged the procedure to the juvenile court to begin anew. *See, e.g.,* Moon v. State, 451 S.W.3d 28, 50–51 (Tex. Crim. App. 2014).

20 *See* Brady v. Maryland, 373 U.S. 83 (1963); District Attorney's Office for Third Judicial Dist. v. Osborne, 557 U.S. 52 (2009); *see generally* Daniel A. Klein,

Construction and Application of Constitutional Rule of Brady v. Maryland, 373 U.S. 83 (1963) – *Supreme Court Cases*, 50 A.L.R. FED. 2d 1 (2015).

21 *See* Douglas H. Ginsburg & Hyland Hunt, *The Prosecutor and Post-Conviction Claims of Innocence: DNA and Beyond?*, 7 OHIO ST. J. CRIM. L. 771, 771 (2010).

22 *See* Tamyra R. Moretti, Bruce Budowle & John S. Buckleton, *Erratum*, 60 J. FORENSIC SCI. 1114, 1114 (2015).

23 *Id.*

24 *See Unintended Catalyst: the Effects of 1999 and 2001 FBI STR Population Data Corrections on an Evaluation of DNA Mixture Interpretation in Texas*, available at www.fsc.texas.gov/sites/default/files/Unintended%20Effects%20of% 20FBI%20Database%20Corrections%20on%20Assessment%20of%20DNA%20Mix ture%20Interpretation%20in%20Texas%20NOTICE.pdf.

25 In Houston, the Harris County District Attorney's Office has begun sending letters to parties in both pending and closed cases regarding this issue.

26 The Texas Court of Criminal Appeals addressed this precise issue as it applied to a forensic scientist, devising a test for courts to employ in evaluating when proven misconduct by a scientist in one case triggers a presumption of misconduct in his remaining cases. *Ex parte Coty*, 418 S.W.3d 597, 605–06 (Tex. Crim. App. 2014).

27 "Drylabbing" is a colloquial term for a form of egregious scientific fraud involving the fabrication and reporting of scientific results for tests that were never conducted. It has been referred to as "the most egregious form of scientific misconduct that can occur in a forensic science laboratory," as well as a "hanging offense" in the scientific community. *See* Bromwich, *supra* note 10, at 5 and 8 n. 10.

28 *See Ex parte* Coty, 418 S.W.3d at 598–99 (addressing laboratory misconduct by Texas Department of Public Safety forensic analyst Jonathan Salvador). To date, although Jonathan Salvador has been shown to have drylabbed results in at most two cases, the nature of the misconduct was serious enough to trigger notification to nearly 5,000 persons whose drug evidence had been tested by Salvador. *See* REPORT OF THE TEXAS FORENSIC SCIENCE COMMISSION: TEXAS DEPART- MENT OF PUBLIC SAFETY, HOUSTON REGIONAL CRIME LABORATORY SELF- DISCLOSURE 9–10, Apr. 5, 2013, available at www.fsc.state.tx.us/documents/ FINAL-DPSHoustonReport041713.pdf.

29 *See* Innocence Project, *More Misconduct in Mississippi: Pathologist Lied about His Credentials*, Apr. 28, 2008, available at www.innocenceproject.org/news-events- exonerations/more-misconduct-in-mississippi-pathologist-lied-about-his-credentials.

30 However, the Supreme Court has held that there is no constitutional requirement to provide petitioners with access to information that might enable them to prove their innocence, such as DNA testing of biological evidence in their cases, even if the tests might be exculpatory. *See* District Attorney's Office for Third Judicial Dist. v. Osborne, 557 U.S. 52, 65–67 (2009). The Court reasoned that after a defendant is convicted at a fair trial, he or she has fewer procedural rights than a defendant who has not been convicted. *Id.* at 68–69. A state law may nevertheless require notifica- tion post-conviction, as it does in Texas. TEX. CODE CR. PROC. Art. 39.14 (k)

(Vernon's 2013). In other cases, political pressure may push prosecutors to provide notification in the post-conviction setting. The federal hair microscopy review only came to pass after intense media pressure. *See* Spencer S. Hsu, *Convicted Defendants Left Uninformed of Forensic Flaws Found by Justice Department*, WASH. POST, Apr. 16, 2012, available at www.washingtonpost.com/local/crime/convicted-defendants-left-uninformed-of-forensic-flaws-found-by-justice-dept/2012/04/16/gIQAWTcgMT_story.html.

31 *See* Campbell Robertson, *Questions Left for Mississippi over Doctor's Autopsies*, N.Y. TIMES, Jan. 7, 2013, available at www.nytimes.com/2013/01/08/us/questions-for-mississippi-doctor-after-thousands-of-autopsies.html.

32 *See* Michael Bromwich, *Fourth Report of the Independent Investigator for the Houston Police Department Crime Laboratory and Property Room*, Jan. 4, 2006, at 26–27, available at www.hpdlabinvestigation.org/reports/060104report.pdf.

33 *Id.*

34 One may take the view that a witness's willingness to lie repeatedly about any matter, regardless of how trivial, discredits him completely, especially when that witness provides critical proof on behalf of the state.

35 Coauthor Wicoff cochairs the Texas Forensic Science Commission DNA Mixture Panel's Subcommittee on Notification and Representation, and is currently charged with the responsibility of coordinating the statewide review of cases affected by the mixture recalculation issue.

36 The Supreme Court has declined to find that prosecutors have a *Brady* obligation to disclose in the post-conviction setting. *See supra* note 20 and accompanying text.

37 *See supra* note 20 and accompanying text. *See also* TEX. CODE CR. PROC., art. 39.14(h) & (k).

38 *See Ex parte* Lo, 424 S.W.3d at 7.

39 One enterprising defense attorney even researched the state's database in order to send notification letters to other affected persons around the state where the district attorneys did not provide such notification. Email correspondence with criminal defense attorney Mark Bennett, May 5, 2015 (on file with author). Thus, the legal system might leverage the fact that private attorneys may have a profit incentive to search public records for affected defendants and provide them with the needed notification.

40 *See* Texas S.B. 1743, available at www.capitol.state.tx.us/BillLookup/History.aspx?LegSess=84R&Bill=SB1743, effective Jun. 1, 2015.

41 The leading example is England's Criminal Cases Review Commission, established in 1995 as a government agency independent of the executive branch that would investigate alleged miscarriages of justice and refer cases to the courts. *See* Stephanie Roberts & Lynne Weathered, *Assisting the Factually Innocent: The Contradictions and Compatibility of Innocence Projects and the Criminal Cases Review Commission*, 29 OXFORD J. LEGAL STUD. 43 (2009). Some have called for the adoption of similar commissions in the United States, although concerns about some aspects of the British model have been raised as well. *See, e.g.*, Robert Carl

Schehr, *The Criminal Cases Review Commission as a State Strategic Selection Mechanism*, 42 AM. CRIM. L. REV. 1289, 1294–95 (2005).

42 *See* Barbara Hervey & Carson Guy, *Brady: Practical Considerations*, 2014, at 10 (citing VIRGINIA STATE CRIME COMMISSION, 2010 ANNUAL REPORT, available at http://leg2.state.va.us/dls/h&sdocs.nsf/By+Year/RD1372011/Sfile/RD137.pdf) (on file with authors).

43 *Id.* at 9.

44 This observation was made by coauthor Wicoff who, as an Assistant Public Defender, participated in the notification process.

45 This observation is made by coauthor Wicoff from his 32 years of experience as a defense attorney.

46 Letter from prosecutor Roe Wilson to a prison inmate, dated April 13, 2015 (on file with authors).

47 For example, it would be impractical to locate the many people who had been deported after they discharged their sentence on the affected conviction and which supplied grounds for deportation – a particularly vexing immigration issue.

48 *See* Hervey & Guy, *supra* note 42, at 11.

49 *See id.* at 9–10 (citing *Defendant Notification after Major Forensic Nonconformance* (2013) (white paper by the FSC and the Texas Criminal Justice Integrity Unit)).

50 *See supra* note 45 and accompanying text.

51 *See* Coleman v. Thompson, 501 U.S. 722, 752 (1991) – citing Pennsylvania v. Finley, 481 U.S. 551 (1987); Murray v. Giarratano, 492 U.S. 1 (1989) (applying the rule to capital cases).

52 When habeas applications reach the Court of Criminal Appeals, and that Court determines that further fact-finding in the trial court is necessary to resolve the issues presented, the Court will remand the case to the trial court for such purpose, and routinely orders, in cases involving indigent habeas applicants, that if that person is not already represented by counsel, counsel must be appointed. *See* TEX. CODE CR. PROC. § 1.051(d)(3) (providing for the appointment of habeas counsel "if the court concludes that the interests of justice require representation").

53 *See, e.g.*, TEX. CODE CR. PROC., art. 11.074 (providing in part that if the prosecuting attorney represents to the convicting court that an indigent person "is not guilty, is guilty of only a lesser offense, or was convicted or sentenced under a law that has been found unconstitutional . . . the court shall appoint an attorney to represent the indigent defendant for purposes of filing an application for a writ of habeas corpus.").

54 In 2007, after an independent investigation of the Houston Police Department Crime Laboratory, the district court judges of Harris County appointed coauthor Wicoff as a "special master" to determine if forensic errors that were found to have affected nearly 200 homicide and sexual assault cases undermined the criminal convictions that resulted.

55 In 2014, in the aftermath of a state criminal statute being held unconstitutional in *Ex parte* Lo, 424 S.W.3d 10 (Tex. Crim. App. 2014), the public defender's office in

Houston represented anyone convicted under such statute who requested representation. That office is also currently representing approximately 400 persons in post-conviction writ proceedings in cases involving drug convictions where it was learned post-conviction that the controlled substance that formed the basis of the charge had either been determined not to be a drug at all, or had been found to fall within a lower punishment range than believed when the case was prosecuted. This information is provided by coauthor Wicoff.

56 Samples of these letters are on file with coauthor Wicoff.

57 In Fiscal Year 2014, a total of 4,161 new habeas corpus cases were filed at the Texas Court of Criminal Appeals, most of them *pro se*. *See* COURT OF CRIMINAL APPEALS ACTIVITY, FY 2014, available at www.txcourts.gov/media/843324/2-cca-activity-report-2014-revised-Feb-2015.pdf.

58 *See supra* note 54 and accompanying text.

59 *See supra* notes 22–23 and accompanying text.

60 Centralizing the appointment of counsel in a group of habeas lawyers offers advantages over relying on innocence projects, which are typically affiliated with law schools. These organizations rely on the work of law students who are supervised by a small number of dedicated attorneys. They normally lack the experience or funding necessary to effectively handle the complex work involved in large-scale case reviews involving forensic irregularities.

17

Exonerating the Innocent
Habeas for Nonhuman Animals

JUSTIN F. MARCEAU AND STEVEN M. WISE

INTRODUCTION

It is hard to conceive of a greater blemish on our justice system than the punishment of innocent persons. The idea of imprisoning or executing an innocent person almost defies the human capacity for empathy; it is nearly impossible to imagine oneself in such circumstances. Advances in science and the work of nonprofits like the Innocence Project have made the exoneration of more than 300 people possible. And while the struggle to liberate unjustly incarcerated persons must continue, and should be accelerated, the cruelty of punishing innocents is not limited to the incarceration of human animals. It is time to consider the need to liberate at least some nonhuman animals from the most horrible confinement. These nonhuman animals are unquestionably innocent, their conditions of confinement, at least in some cases, are uniquely depraved; and their cognitive functioning, much less their ability to suffer, rivals that of humans. It is time to seriously consider habeas-type remedies for nonhuman beings.

We are cognizant that the call for nonhuman habeas may cause some to construe this project as one that dishonors or diminishes the efforts that have led to exonerations and the work that remains to be done in the context of human innocence. Nothing could be further from our purpose. One of us has been involved in death penalty defense and litigating claims of wrongful incarceration since graduating from law school, and the commitment to those issues remains unflappable. Indeed, we hope the salience of the cause of liberating humans will be reinforced by our efforts to cross the species barrier. It does no disservice to the cause of innocent humans to suggest that we pay closer attention to the suffering of nonhuman animals. Just as we look back in disgust at our forefathers who were less careful in their protection of human innocents, we predict that our grandchildren will judge us for the way we collectively treat nonhuman animals.[1]

This chapter proceeds in three parts. First, it analyzes the question of whether exoneration or innocence in the context of nonhuman confinements is illogical. Second, assuming it is a proper question at all, it examines why we would consider exonerating nonhuman animals, that is to say, what are the scientific and social reasons for contemplating relief for humans? Finally, the chapter considers the practical viability of nonhuman habeas at least for a limited class of nonhuman animals subject to particularly harsh conditions. In so doing, the chapter discusses the cutting-edge cases filed in recent years by the Nonhuman Rights Project (NhRP) seeking habeas review for chimpanzees.

INNOCENT ANIMALS – IS IT A NON SEQUITUR?

This is a book about the use of post-conviction DNA testing to exonerate innocent prisoners. At first blush it might seem strange to speak of an exoneration of anything other than a human being. Yet it is not uncommon to speak of corporations, nonprofits, even state or municipal governments as being exonerated.[2] In fact, it is quite common in the white-collar crime literature to speak of wrongly accused corporations and their subsequent "exoneration."[3] There is a debate about whether corporations should suffer more or less of the collateral consequences that typically flow from convictions.[4] It is even possible for these nonhumans to be pardoned or granted clemency.[5] On at least one occasion a federal court has granted a corporation's request for a writ of *coram nobis*.[6] Thus, it is wrong to conclude that exonerations and notions of innocence are the exclusive province of humans.

Notably, the extension of the concept of innocence to inanimate legal fictions such as corporations has not led many to assume, or even consider, that other cognitively complex nonhuman creatures could be innocent. One likely reason for this disconnect is that nonhuman animals cannot be convicted of crimes. They are simply not guilty of any crimes. Legal entities, like corporations, can be prosecuted. But grand juries do not indict dogs, cats, chimps or elephants. But perhaps this critique is too simplistic.

First, although exoneration as the term is typically used in this book implies criminal charges and ultimately the vindication of innocence, the term exoneration supports a broader meaning: "The removal of a burden, charge, responsibility, or duty."[7] The liberation from an unwanted and unpleasant confinement would certainly constitute the removal of a burden, and historically habeas corpus, a primary procedural vehicle for securing an exoneration, has certainly not been limited to correcting unjust convictions.

Moreover, at least in a limited class of cases, society has reflected its tolerance for examining animal behavior under the law in a manner strikingly similar to the way we evaluate human conduct for criminality. For example, leading criminal law theorist Markus Dubber has observed that animal control statutes often function in ways that are very similar to human criminal codes. Not only are the definitions of "offenses familiar from criminal codes," the animal control codes "lay out defenses to an allegation of dangerousness analogous to the defenses recognized in criminal law."[8] Examining the New York animal control code, Dubber noted that an otherwise (criminally) dangerous dog has several available defenses including "defense of others," a "defense of property," "self-defense," and even an "extreme emotional disturbance" or provocation defense.[9] In other words, although nonhuman animals may not be subjected to criminal prosecution in a formal sense, when an animal's actions are subject to review by the state for their propriety, it is taken for granted that some defenses available to humans may also justify the acts of a nonhuman animal. Some nonhuman animals, then, are already exonerated through codified state procedures providing relief from unwanted incarceration or execution. Exoneration is not a concept entirely foreign to the nonhuman realms of law.[10]

Another major hurdle to meaningfully conceiving nonhuman animals as innocent is the law's recognition of them as nothing more than legal things.[11] Illustrative of this trope is a practicing lawyer's recent argument that only true economic damages should be available when one's animal is wrongfully killed:

> Both domesticated pets and domesticated commercial animals were historically deemed to be the personal property of their owners under the law. This makes some sense, as household pets Fifi and Fido and most farm animals cannot file their own lawsuits for damages.[12]

To be sure, if society regards the emotional distress or loss of companionship damages that flow from the tortious killing of one's nonpedigree dog or cat as trivial and measured as "replacement" cost alone,[13] that is, if nonhuman animals are the mere property of people, then it would seem bizarre in the extreme to suggest that one person could seek to exonerate or liberate an animal from the possession of another human. It makes little sense to speak of *things* as innocent.[14] Surely your bed is not guilty or innocent of causing you a bad night of sleep. Nor is your phone that is prone to making unintended calls culpable in any meaningful sense.

But the purity of the property/nonproperty dichotomy as it applies to nonhuman animals has always been a legal fiction.[15] Few serious persons would really contemplate that their dog is an item of personal property, much less an orangutan or chimpanzee. This is not to say that recognizing nonhuman animals as more human than property will be costless.[16] But recognizing that at least some nonhuman animals should have some rights, including a right to be free from grotesque bodily intrusions or cruel confinement, does not fundamentally threaten the human rights this book celebrates.[17] As Laurence Tribe has explained, it is a myth that our legal system "has never accorded rights to entities other than human beings, [and thus] that it is a high wall [that] must be breached or vaulted" if nonhumans are to be afforded rights.[18] Given the scope of rights we afford to nonhumans, including religious liberties[19] and speech rights,[20] recognizing limited animal rights is just a matter of degree; "it is not a matter of breaking through something, like a conceptual sound barrier."[21]

In short, one need not say that the captivity of an innocent chimpanzee is tantamount to the incarceration of an innocent human person. Both have done nothing wrong and can scarcely be expected to understand why they are being punished. But as we collectively celebrate the advances that have made these releases possible and lament the procedural difficulties that impede the vindication of the rights of the innocent, we should also reflect on the possibility that our humanity and pursuit of justice may be improved if we recognize a limited universe of legal personhood that affords the possibility of exonerating some nonhuman animals.

CAPTIVE ANIMALS AS INTELLIGENT AND INNOCENT

Science has brought great victories to the innocent. Advances in DNA evidence have allowed us to exonerate and liberate persons who were previously found under the highest standard of proof known to law – proof beyond a reasonable doubt – to be guilty.[22] Without DNA evidence, most prosecutors and police would not even consider admitting error, much less cooperate in obtaining the release of a prisoner.[23] In short, DNA has had a transformative effect on the criminal justice system. Science of a similarly profound and powerful character is necessary if the societal acceptance of captive animals as property is also going to experience a transformation.

Of course, DNA will not specifically demonstrate the innocence of confined nonhuman animals, because the animal is not charged with any offense. But DNA and scientific advances still have the potential to play an important role in limiting the class of nonhuman animals who would enjoy some sort of legal personhood.[24] For example, it is virtually unchallenged in the scientific community that the DNA of humans and certain nonhuman animals are remarkably similar.[25] A recent article in *Scientific American* explains:

> In 1871 Charles Darwin surmised that humans were evolutionarily closer to the African apes than to any other species alive. The recent sequencing of the gorilla, chimpanzee and bonobo genomes confirms that supposition and provides a clearer view of how we are connected: chimps and bonobos in particular take pride of place as our nearest living relatives, sharing approximately 99 percent of our DNA, with gorillas trailing at 98 percent.[26]

Based on this and other compelling modern findings, the scientific community is finally overcoming its longstanding objection to anthropomorphizing. In the learned circles of the thirteenth century, for example, the possibility of nonhuman animals suffering (or that their suffering would be relevant), was rejected out of hand.[27] By the seventeenth century things were no better for nonhuman animals; the most enlightened persons, including Descartes, reasoned that "the greatest of all the prejudices we have retained from infancy is that of believing that brutes think."[28] And, as Gary Francione has explained:

> Descartes and his followers performed experiments in which they nailed animals by their paws onto boards and cut them open to reveal their beating hearts. They burned, scalded, and mutilated animals in every conceivable manner. When the animals reacted as though they were suffering pain, Descartes dismissed the reaction as no different from the sound of a machine that was functioning improperly. A crying dog, Descartes maintained, is no different from a whining gear that needs oil.[29]

In the face of what appears to be animal suffering, few people retain the view that the animal is not actually suffering pain. In modern times it is odd to suggest that when a dog yowls upon being inadvertently stepped on he is not experiencing pain. Of course we cannot feel his pain any more than we can feel the pain of a child or another fellow human who cries out when they fall or incur injury. This is why advances in the hard sciences are so important for those interested in protecting nonhuman animals from pain. If we see what looks like boredom, pleasure, or suffering in an animal, are we only projecting our own feelings?

Only in the very recent past has the scientific community coalesced around a recognition that nonhuman animals do enjoy consciousness, emotions, and other brain functioning that is similar to that of humans. The research is increasingly conclusive: nonhuman animals can feel, and suffer, and in fact have brains that function very similarly to our own. Just three years ago, in

2013, a group of leading scientists signed the "Cambridge Declaration on Consciousness," which explained that:

> [c]onvergent evidence indicates that human animals have the neuroanatom-ical, neurochemical, and neurophysiological substrates of conscious states along with the capacity to exhibit intentional behaviors. Consequently, the weight of evidence indicates that humans are not unique in possessing the neurological substrates that generate consciousness. Non-Human animals, including all mammals and birds, and many other creatures, includ-ing octopuses, also possess these neurological substrates.[30]

Similarly, leading neuroscientist Gregory Bern is studying the brains of fully awake animals by training dogs to voluntarily enter MRIs and then interacting with the animals to observe brain functioning. Dr. Bern's findings are such a thorough rebuke of the conception that it is folly to anthropomorphize that he titled a newspaper column *Dogs are People, Too*.[31] In his book, summarizing his MRI research, Dr. Bern concludes that existing research finding "strong evidence for theory of mind" only in monkeys and apes or other primates is undoubtedly mistaken.[32] Dogs and other nonhuman animals are able to form complex reciprocal relationships using their brains in ways that are very similar to humans.

Even when it comes to emotions, some scientists have made startling findings linking animals to humans. Dr. Marc Bekoff, for example, has concluded that it is no longer good science to "argue against the existence of animal emotions."[33] Dr. Bekoff had documented complicated language structures and elaborate grieving ceremonies among animals that are not considered to have the most sophisticated brains. For some nonhuman animals the potential for emotion may even exceed the capacities of human emotion. The *New Scientist* reported that:

> It turns out that [many] whales possess spindle cells in the same area of their brains as spindle cells in human brains. This brain region is linked with social organization, empathy, intuition about the feelings of others, as well as rapid gut reactions. Spindle cells once thought to be unique to humans and other great apes, are believed to be important in processing emotions. And whales actually have more of them than humans do.[34]

To be sure, none of this recent scientific evidence regarding the ability of nonhuman animals to think and suffer in ways that are remarkably similar to humans is startling to those familiar with the book *Rattling the Cage*, which admirably attempts to summarize a half-century of scientific research regarding the autonomy, self-determination, and other cognitive abilities of chimpanzees, starting with Jane Goodall's research in the 1960s.[35] But even since 2000, when the book was first published, science in the field has continued to develop and the consensus regarding cognitive ability has grown even stronger. Since its original publication, additional scientists have come forward to augment the already robust record regarding the mental abilities of the human species' closest genetic match, chimpanzees and bonobos.[36] These new accounts are worthy of reading in their entirety, but a recent summary is a helpful crib sheet:

> According to these experts, Chimpanzees possess an autobiographical self, episodic memory (one's long term memory of experience), self-determination, self-consciousness, self-knowingness, self-agency, empathy, a working memory, language, metacognition, numerosity, and a material, social, and symbolic culture. They also have the ability to plan, understand cause-and-effect and the experiences of others, imagine, imitate, engage in deferred imitation, emulate, innovate, use and make tools, and engage in activities such as mental time travel, referential and intentional communication, intentional action, sequential learning, mediational learning, mental-state modeling, visual perspective taking, and cross-modal perception.[37]

NONHUMAN HABEAS

It has been said that as our "sibling species" it "is fitting that [chimpanzees and bonobos] should be the first to acquire rights" or be regarded at least in some instances as legal persons in the eyes of the law.[38] Beginning in 2013, the NhRP began filing habeas corpus cases on behalf of chimpanzees. This litigation followed a trajectory of research and advocacy spearheaded by Steven M. Wise, and seeks the demise of the "Great Wall that has for so long divided humans from every other animal" by recognizing limited legal personhood for chimpanzees and bonobos.[39] This section will briefly summarize the litigation that had occurred up to the time of writing, and more importantly, summarize the legal case for a habeas-type review of the confinement of nonhuman beings.

The NhRP Cases

In the first week of December 2013, lawsuits were filed by the NhRP on behalf of four chimps named Tommy, Hercules, Leo, and Kiko, all of whom had been subjected to lives imprisoned in cages.[40] Each lawsuit asked the court to order that the chimpanzees be moved to the North American Primate Sanctuary, which provides North America's best alternative to living in the wild.[41]

The four chimps all presently reside in difficult to intolerable conditions. Tommy is possessed by a couple that owns a used trailer lot in Gloversville, New York.[42] In addition to using the trailer park to keep pet chimps, Tommy's owners also run a business called "Santa's Hitching Post," which rents out reindeer for Christmas shows.[43] When Tommy was brought to the attention of the NhRP he lived in a tiny, dank, cement cage at the back of a shed with one small TV for entertainment.[44] Kiko also lives his life alone in a cage. He is possessed by Carmen and Christie Presti in Niagara Falls, New York.[45] Kiko is almost completely deaf from being abused on the set of the *Tarzan* movie years ago.[46] As a result, he suffers from chronic motion sickness and has to take frequent medication.[47] Hercules and Leo are 8-year old males, possessed by the New Iberia Research Center in Louisiana, who have lived in cages at Stony Brook University for the last six years.[48] The chimps are forced to participate in studies relating to chimpanzee locomotion, such as stance and swing phase joint mechanics in chimpanzee bipedal walking.[49] Perhaps the most forceful aspects of these lawsuits were the supporting affidavits prepared by many of the leading primatologists around the world, all of whom elaborated on the intelligence, self-awareness, and level of autonomy that chimpanzees possess, and explained how their current living conditions would cause substantial suffering for them.[50]

The lower courts initially denied all three habeas corpus petitions, citing generally a lack of precedent for considering chimpanzees legal persons entitled to habeas corpus relief.[51] Judge Joseph Sise, who presided over Tommy's case, was almost apologetic, stating that "I will be available as the judge for any other lawsuit to rights and wrongs that are done to this chimpanzee because I understand what you're saying. You make a very strong argument."[52] Similarly, Judge Ralph A. Boniello III, who presided over Kiko's case, gave the NhRP encouragement, but stated that he did not want to be the first to "make that leap of faith."[53] The NhRP filed notices of appeal for all three petitions in January of 2014.[54] All three cases raise novel questions about the scope of habeas review for nonhuman animals and, whatever the result in these appeals, it is undoubtedly the first (not the last) word in what will be a new realm of animal law litigation. Actions to liberate some of the world's most intelligent creatures from its most deplorable confinement are likely to become increasingly common in coming years.

The Merits of an Argument for Nonhuman Habeas

In 2015, a federal judge concluded that allegations of torture and inhumane treatment during the state-sanctioned execution of a human being do not provide a cognizable claim under the U.S. Constitution,[55] and the U.S. Supreme Court approved the execution protocols of Oklahoma that carried out the debauched, bloody execution of Clayton Lockett.[56] Likewise, the Supreme Court has held that there is no constitutional right to scientific testing to prove a person's innocence,[57] and there may not even be a right to be released through habeas if a human person is able to prove his or her innocence.[58] These are not isolated examples of the broken criminal justice system; indeed, the list of limits on common law and statutory habeas corpus for the convicted is ever growing.[59] Thus, as someone who has spent much of his legal career involved in legal work for the criminally accused, one of the authors of this chapter acknowledges the disconnect between the justice system's current disregard for human suffering and a call for greater protections for nonhuman animals.[60] And yet as we continue to endeavor for a more just system for reviewing the detention of humans, we should also think creatively about the potential for judicial review of unjust nonhuman detentions. Our understanding of the history of habeas corpus suggests that there is merit to the quest to apply the well-established writ to these unchartered territories.[61]

We acknowledge at the outset the obvious: there is no statutorily granted procedure for nonhuman habeas. Even if a nonstatutory common-law form of the writ survives (and can be extended to nonhumans), there is also no obvious source of codified substantive law that would render the confinement unjust.[62] There are, then, both procedural and substantive hurdles to recognizing the application of the Great Writ as a tool for challenging, for example, the cruel confinement of a chimpanzee. But animal law is in a state of flux; it seems to be on the precipice of a new era. The nonhuman animals need just one major legal victory, a gestalt moment at the hands of a receptive and creative court. Habeas could be a viable platform for this moment, and the history of the writ suggests that this is plausible.

The most important thing to realize about the history of habeas corpus is that it is full of surprises. The writ has endured countless novel uses in order to bring about social change that would seem unlikely based on controlling legal principles at the time. Indeed, without access to alternative judicial avenues, the writ of habeas corpus has served justice (and at times injustice) in so many different forms that it is often scarcely recognizable as the writ of habeas corpus we have come to emphasize in modern times.

One notable example is the use of habeas corpus to resolve family law disputes at common law. As historian Paul Halliday has explained, the family law habeas cases "make up for their small number by their significance since they reveal more about the writ's processes and the writ's possibilities than any other category or cases."[63] The use of habeas corpus by the King's Bench during the seventeenth century, particularly under the leadership of Sir Matthew Hale, allowed for a unique legal forum to protect wives and children from their socially and politically powerful husbands and fathers.[64] At a time when women were deemed the property of their husbands, there was no other legal vehicle that could have been applied, albeit somewhat inconsistently, to protect "wives from abusive husbands."[65] Nor was it conceivable that any other legal procedure would allow children to achieve some measure of self-determination against a parent, particularly a father, and yet Halliday documented instances of the writ being used to protect the self-determination and liberty of the individual child. It is also important to realize that the writ was used by wives and children not just to obtain outright release. As in the case of children and "lunatics," when release would itself be cruel or impractical, the writ was used to "assign custody, not simply to [gain] release from it."[66] Thus, as is relevant for a nonhuman animal seeking habeas in order to be relocated to a sanctuary (and not returned to nature), the history of habeas in the family law context demonstrates that habeas need not simply be understood as a vehicle for complete liberation or freedom. Instead, Halliday has explained that one of the fundamental truths about the writ is its capacity to "resolve conflicts beyond simply declaring someone remanded or released."[67]

The use of habeas in family law is certainly not the only useful analogy for one looking to apply the writ to affect justice for those characterized by the law as nonhumans. Habeas has a venerable history of undermining an unjust status quo and allowing courts to "negotiate solutions to problems" for which there is not a precise legal fix.[68] For example, the "Janus-faced" role of habeas corpus in the fight against slavery provides some novel examples of using the writ to challenge the authority of the prevailing morality and practice of treating human beings as chattel.[69] The story of James Somerset and his 1772 writ of habeas corpus that ultimately led to him becoming a free man is a story that is oft celebrated and that illustrates, if nothing else, the role that habeas can play in bringing moral issues to courts. In 1772, Somerset filed for habeas relief as a slave in an effort to prevent the forcible removal of him from England against his will, and the King's Bench, in a strongly worded decision condemning slavery more generally, granted relief to Somerset despite the lack of a clear procedural or substantive basis in the positive law for such a decision.

To be sure, the *Somerset* case did not have the effect of ending slavery in one fell swoop in England, much less in the American colonies.[70] But the decision did have the effect, if only incrementally, of undermining the long unchallenged claim of authority enjoyed by slaveholders.[71] Habeas for nonhumans could have a similar symbolic, if not functional, effect on the status of nonhuman animals in society.

A final example from very recent U.S. history demonstrates the symbolic and practical effect that habeas corpus can have in challenging social practices that are outdated or unjust. The executive branch of the U.S. Government detained persons believed to be involved in terrorism in Guantánamo Bay, Cuba. The thinking was as transparent as it was cynical: surely noncitizens held outside of the country cannot expect to benefit from the largess of the habeas writ. The result of this policy was the "incarceration of hundreds of individuals, many of whom [were] not ... formally charged with any crime and [who faced] seemingly indefinite extrajudicial detention."[72] In the hopes of winning "either their freedom or an appearance before a judge" many of the detainees – persons who were held in such a way as to deprive them of their personhood for purposes of accessing U.S. courts – sought to challenge their confinement through the Great Writ.[73] Confronted with noncitizens outside the country challenging their confinement, the U.S. Supreme Court reflected on the "core historical functions of the writ"[74] and in so doing held that the Guantánamo detentions fell within the ambit of the federal habeas statute's grant of jurisdiction.[75] When later confronted with a legislative enactment, the Military Commissions Act of 2006, which specifically stripped the federal courts of such statutory power, the Supreme Court held that as a matter of constitutional law – the Suspension Clause – habeas review of the Guantánamo detentions was required.[76] Notably, the constitutional analysis was inexorably linked to the common law – the codified law had unequivocally removed the possibility of habeas review for the detainees. In explaining the scope of the Suspension Clause, the Supreme Court noted that "at the absolute minimum" the Clause protects the writ as it existed at common law when the Constitution was ratified.[77] Thus, the Supreme Court examined the history of habeas corpus and held that the writ was necessarily available to enemy combatants held outside of the United States. Once again, the history of habeas corpus provided for a surprising and radical check on confinement that could not be tested through any other legal procedure.

CONCLUSION

On the one hand, using habeas corpus to bring animal rights issues to the court might be called, in the words of Richard Posner, a "sad poverty of imagination" in simply analogizing to the civil rights movement instead of recognizing the obvious differences in the prior cases. Worse still, the use of the writ to elucidate issues about animal confinement is perhaps an insult to the dignity of human beings who remain incarcerated despite their innocence.[78] On the other hand, John Marshall declared that in order to understand the "meaning of habeas corpus, resort may unquestionably be had to the common law."[79] To be sure, habeas has played many different roles throughout the history of the common law, and if its dynamic historical function retains relevance in our statutory-saturated judicial system, then perhaps nonhuman animals have a viable option for litigating legal person-hood rights – the right of at least some animals to be free from the most egregious liberty deprivations.

At times its help has been ephemeral or nonexistent, but in other instances habeas has served as a unique platform for challenging social structures and detentions for which there was no other available mechanism. Challenging the authority and custody of one's father, one's husband, much less the use of judicial proceedings by slaves, POWs,[80] or noncitizen detainees would have seemed unthinkable until the common law courts permitted it through habeas proceedings. And in applying the writ to new, previously untouched forms of confinement or injustice, it has been noted that "[t]here was no mention of precedents, no analogizing to ostensibly similar cases."[81] Indeed, it is now understood that, contrary to the general historical narrative, "facts rather than law" were generally decisive.[82]

The common law is no panacea and within each of the realms mentioned above there have been ebbs and flows, justices and injustices worked via the writ of habeas corpus. But habeas corpus stands alone in its capacity to provide a vehicle for fact-specific adjudications that run against the grain of contem-porary norms. This is why one leading habeas scholar and historian, Eric Freedman, has said that in examining the common law writ, habeas must be given a "functional rather than a formal definition" such that the focus is always on devising a "pragmatic resolution based on the specific facts at hand."[83] Of course, "access to the 'privilege of the writ' [says] nothing about [one's] entitlement to relief; it merely guarantee[s] that an impartial magistrate would be the one to answer that question."[84] At the end of the day, that is all habeas can provide and that is all the NhRP asks in the cases it is bringing – access to a forum to debate the fact-specific details of certain confinements.

As we commemorate the success of DNA science in forcing the hand of justice to correct an almost unthinkable number of wrongful convictions, we would do well to reflect also on who else deserves greater justice based on advancing scientific understanding. Nonhuman animals are not people and treating them as such, and affording them all the concomitant rights and obligations, would make no sense. But we should consider whether history will look unfavorably upon us if we ignore the mounting scientific evidence about the intelligence of certain nonhuman animals, just as history ought to judge us for our inept handling of wrongful human convictions. Every great legal gestalt has been accompanied by naysayers and those who would prefer to wait for more debate, discussion or legislative action.[85] As Steven M. Wise has said, "[t]he long struggles over the legal status of fetuses, slaves, Native Americans, women, and corporations have never been over whether they are human, but whether justice demands that they should be considered legal persons" that can be valued and considered in the eyes of the law.[86] Habeas corpus is a vehicle for allowing humans to put forward a case in support of their limited legal personhood. Striking a similar tone in the context of gay marriage, the U.S. Supreme Court recently explained, "[i]f rights were defined by who exercised them in the past, then received practices could serve as their own continued justification and new groups could not invoke rights once denied."[87]

NOTES

1 In the context of same-sex marriage litigation, Justice Kennedy recently wrote: "the nature of injustice is that we may not always see it in our own times." Obergefell v. Hodges, 135 S. Ct. 2584, 2598 (2015).

2 *See, e.g.,* Kyle Whitmire, *Alabama Company Is Exonerated in Murders at Columbian Mine,* N.Y. TIMES, July 27, 2007,available at www.nytimes.com/2007/07/27/business/27drummond.html?_r=0.

3 *See, e.g.,* JOEL ANDROPHY, 5 WHITE COLLAR CRIME § 33:16 (2d ed. 2008) ("There have been numerous tales of corporations being charged with outrageous conduct or selling an outrageous product only to find out that allegations are completely false, yet by the time the corporation is exonerated in court, the public's distrust of the company and its product has been established."). There is even a question regarding whether successor corporations are automatically exonerated for the conduct of their predecessor. *See* 3 ANDERSON U.C.C. § 2–314:508 (3d. ed. 2015) ("The fact that the successor corporation is held liable does not, in itself, exonerate the predecessor corporation from liability.").

4 Collateral Consequence Resource Center, *Should Guilty Corporations Avoid Collateral Consequences?,* June 8, 2015, available at http://ccresourcecenter.org/2015/06/08/why-should-guilty-corporations-avoid-collateral-consequences/#more-5104.

5 *Emprise Pardon Rejected,* DAYTONA BEACH MORN. J, Sept. 28, 1977, available at https://news.google.com/newspapers?nid=1873&dat=19770929&id=eXwoAAAAI BAJ&sjid=F8oEAAAAIBAJ&pg=2379,5043820&hl=en (discussing a corporation's request for a formal pardon to President Carter); *White House Rejects Emprise Pardon,* CHI. TRIB. Sept. 29, 1977, http://archives.chicagotribune.com/1977/09/29/page/54/article/white-house-rejects-emprise-pardon; *see also* Ronald Everett &

Deborah Periman, *"The Governor's Court of Last Resort:" An Introduction to Executive Clemency in Alaska*, 28 ALASKA L. REV. 57, 89 (2011) (discussing a governor's grant of a pardon).

6 United States v. Mett, 65 F.3d 1531, 1534 (9th Cir. 1995).

7 BLACK'S LAW DICTIONARY (10th ed. 2014).

8 MARKUS DIRK DUBBER, VICTIMS IN THE WAR ON CRIME 44 (2006).

9 *Id.* at 44–45 (quoting NY AGRIC. & MKTS. § 123(4) (2011)). *See also* COLO. R. STAT. § 18-9-204.5 (applying defenses to "dangerous dogs").

10 DUBBER, *supra* note 8, at 45 ("If anything the canine versions of these defenses are more generous than the human ones.").

11 Richardson v. Fairbanks N. Star Borough, 705 P.2d 454, 456 (Alaska 1985) ("[D]ogs have legal status as items of personal property . . . ."); Fackler v. Genetzky, 595 N.W.2d 884, 891–92 (Neb. 1999) ("In other jurisdictions, the general rule is that an animal, regardless of sentimental attachment, is personal property . . . this court has clearly held that animals are personal property . . . ."); Fowler v. Town of Ticonderoga, 516 N.Y.S.2d 368, 370 (N.Y. App. Div. 1987) ("[A] dog is personal property . . . ."); Casey Chapman, Comment, *Not Your Coffee Table: An Evaluation of Companion Animals as Personal Property*, 38 CAP. U. L. REV. 187, 187 (2009) (stating that many courts and state laws have held that animals are personal property).

12 Amy Lombardo, *Idaho Law Regarding the Measure of Damages for Animals Need Not Be Revisited*, 56 ADVOC. 51, 51 (2013). This conclusion is not nearly so obvious. The fact that nonhuman animals lack one power (the right to sue on their own), does not mean that they are deprived of all other rights or status. Indeed, some prominent legal scholars disagree. Laurence H. Tribe, for example, has explained the idea of owning pets as follows: "[I]t is obscene and evil to treat them as things that anyone can really own. When people ask my wife Carolyn and me whether we own any dogs, we say no. We don't 'own' our dog Annie. I can't really think of myself as owning a dog. We and Annie are a kind of family." Laurence H. Tribe, *Ten Lessons Our Constitutional Experience Can Teach Us about the Puzzle of Animal Rights: The Work of Steven M. Wise*, 7 ANIMAL L. 1, 7 (2001).

13 Lombardo, *supra* note 12 ("The overwhelming majority of states have found that an animal owner cannot recover for emotional distress for harm to one's pet, or for loss of companionship.").

14 Of course, slaves were inexcusably considered property in this country, and yet they could be charged with crimes. This example illustrates that the law's regard for one as a thing does not deprive "it" of the ability to be punished. Even so, truly inanimate property cannot form a culpable mens rea or engage in an actus reus and is thus not punishable under our system of criminal law. *But see* Albert W. Alschuler, *Two Ways to Think about the Punishment of Corporations*, 46 AM. CRIM. L. REV. 1359, 1360 (2009) (surveying the literature and history of deodand, which is the "the punishment of an animal or inanimate object that has killed a person."); OLIVER WENDELL HOLMES, JR., THE COMMON LAW 1–38, 19 (Dover 1991)

(1881) (discussing deodand and providing examples such as a culture that would cut down a tree if it caused the death of a person).

15 Tribe, *supra* note 12 ("[I]t is obscene and evil to treat them as things that anyone can really own. When people ask my wife Carolyn and me whether we own any dogs, we say no. We don't 'own' our dog Annie. I can't really think of myself as owning a dog. We and Annie are a kind of family.").

16 *Id.* at 2–3 ("Guardians would ultimately have to be appointed to speak for these voiceless rights-holders, just as guardians are appointed today for infants, or for the profoundly retarded, or for elderly people with advanced Alzheimer's, or for the comatose. But giving animals this sort of 'virtual voice' would go a long way toward strengthening the protection they receive under existing laws and hopefully improved laws.").

17 It is not just self-interested tort defense lawyers who defend treating animals as pure property. No less than Cass Sunstein and Richard Posner have also worried about the limiting principle problem that will emerge if animals are afforded rights. *See, e.g.*, Cass R. Sunstein, *The Chimps' Day in Court*, N.Y. TIMES, Feb. 20, 2000, available at www.nytimes.com/books/00/02/20/reviews/000220.20sunstet.html (arguing that Wise did not do enough to consider the need for a limiting principle and asking, "Suppose we agree (as I think we should) that nonhuman animals have legal rights; under what circumstances can the interests of human beings, or other animals, override those rights?"); Richard A. Posner, *Animal Rights Rattling the Cage: Toward Legal Rights for Animals*, 110 YALE L. J. 527, 539 (2000) (reviewing STEVEN M. WISE, RATTLING THE CAGE (2000)) (arguing that in the end, arguments for rights undervalue the amount of good that can be done for animals if we candidly acknowledge them as property).

18 Tribe, *supra* note 12, at 2. ("Churches, partnerships, corporations, unions, families, municipalities, even states are rights-holders; indeed, we sometimes classify them as legal persons for a wide range of purposes."). With respect, Professor Tribe mischaracterizes the argument that one of us made in RATTLING THE CAGE: TOWARD LEGAL RIGHTS FOR ANIMALS. The legal wall that requires breaching does not separate humans from nonhumans, but things from persons. *See* Steven Wise, *Chimps Have Feelings and Thoughts. They Should Also Have Rights*, available at www.ted.com/talks/steven_wise_chimps_have_feelings_and_thoughts_they_should_also_have_rights.

19 Burwell v. Hobby Lobby Stores, 134 S. Ct. 2761 (2014) (extending free exercise rights to nonhuman, legal persons).

20 Citizens United v. Fed. Election Comm'n, 558 U.S. 321 (2010) (extending free expression rights to nonhumans).

21 Tribe, *supra* note 12, at 3.

22 According to the Innocence Project, there have been more than 330 post-conviction DNA exonerations in the United States since 1989. *See* Innocence Project, *DNA Exonerations Nationwide*, available at www.innocenceproject.org/free-innocent/improve-the-law/fact-sheets/dna-exonerations-nationwide.

23 Even in the face of DNA evidence, the confirmation bias is so strong that some refuse to accept the innocence of a person they worked to convict. *See* Alafair S. Burke, *Improving Prosecutorial Decision Making: Some Lessons of Cognitive Science*, 47 Wm. & Mary L. Rev. 1587, 1612–13 (2006) (discussing various issues with convincing prosecutors that a defendant is innocent for post-conviction release); Daniel S. Medwed, *The Zeal Deal: Prosecutorial Resistance to Post-Conviction Claims of Innocence*, 84 B.U. L. Rev. 125, 125–32 (2004).

24 Scholars have noted that it is fraught to claim that science can truly distinguish better than our intuition and moral sensibilities in these realms. *See* Tribe, *supra* note 12, at 5 ("[S]earching for a non-intuitive, non-spiritual, wholly objective and supposedly scientifically-based formula for deciding which beings have sufficient autonomy to deserve dignity and hence legal rights is to tilt at windmills."). We appreciate Professor Tribe's point, but think that if the law demands limiting principles, starting with accepted scientific differences between species is a reasonable place to start.

25 American Museum of Natural History, *DNA: Collecting Humans and Chimps*, available at www.amnh.org/exhibitions/permanent-exhibitions/human-origins-and-cultural-halls/anne-and-bernard-spitzer-hall-of-human-origins/understanding-our-past/dna-comparing-humans-and-chimps ("Humans and chimps share a surprising 98.8 percent of their DNA.").

26 Kate Wong, *Tiny Genetic Differences Between Humans and Other Primates Pervade the Genome*, Sci. Am., Aug. 19, 2014, available at www.scientificamerican.com/article/tiny-genetic-differences-between-humans-and-other-primates-pervade-the-genome/.

27 For example, St. Thomas Aquinas believed that animals did not think rationally, rather they acted solely on instinct. *Animal Rights*, BBC, available at www.bbc.co.uk/ethics/animals/rights/rights_1.shtml.

28 Stanley Finger, Minds Behind the Brain 77 (2005).

29 Gary Francione, Introduction to Animal Rights: Your Child or the Dog? 2 (2007).

30 Marc Bekoff, *Scientists Conclude Nonhuman Animals Are Conscious Beings*, Psychol. Today, Aug. 10, 2012, available at www.psychologytoday.com/blog/animal-emotions/201208/scientists-conclude-nonhuman-animals-are-conscious-beings (quoting the Cambridge Declaration).

31 Gregory Berns, *Dogs Are People, Too*, N.Y. Times, Oct. 5, 2013, available at www.nytimes.com/2013/10/06/opinion/sunday/dogs-are-people-too.html?_r=0.

32 Gregory Berns, How Dogs Love Us 226–27 (2013) (suggesting a unique level of intuitiveness and general emotional intelligence in dogs).

33 Marc Bekoff, The Emotional Lives of Animals (2008).

34 Paul Waldau, Animal Rights: What Everyone Needs to Know 16 (2011).

35 Steven M. Wise, Rattling the Cage 131–236 (2000).

36 Affidavit of Christophe Boesch at 6, Nonhuman Rights Project, Inc. v. Lavery, Nov. 19, 2013, available at www.nonhumanrightsproject.org/wp-content/uploads/

2013/11/Ex-5-Boesch-Affidavit-Tommy-Case.pdf ("Chimpanzees clearly possess an autobiographical self, as they are able to prepare for the future and can remember highly specific elements of past events over long periods of time." (internal citations omitted)); Affidavit of Emily Sue Savage-Rumbaugh at 5, *Lavery*, Nov. 22, 2013, available at www.nonhumanrightsproject.org/wp-content/uploads/2013/11/Ex-12-Savage-Rumbaugh-Affidavit-Tommy-Case.pdf ("[W]hen behavioral studies of chimpanzees suggest that they are capable of self-aware conscious action, the capacity to reason and think, the ability to acquire symbolic language, there is reason to take these results seriously."); Affidavit of James R. Anderson at 4, *Lavery*, Nov. 20, 2013, available at www.nonhumanrightsproject.org/wp-content/uploads/2013/11/Ex-4-Anderson-Affidavit-Tommy-Case.pdf ("The close evolutionary relationship between chimpanzees, bonobos and humans is evident not only in terms of physical structure but also behavior and mental processes. No other species comes so close to humans in self-awareness and language abilities, and in diversity of behaviors ... ."); Affidavit of James King at 4, *Lavery*, Nov. 21, 2013, available at www.nonhumanrightsproject.org/wp-content/uploads/2013/11/Ex-8-King-Affidavit-Tommy-Case.pdf ("[T]he simplest explanation for behaviors in chimpanzees that look autonomous is that they are based on similar psychological capacities as in humans .... My research shows the remarkable similarity between chimpanzees and humans in the structure of personality and subjective well-being (or happiness)."); Affidavit of Jennifer M.B. Fugate at 5, *Lavery* (Nov. 22, 2013), www.nonhumanrightsproject.org/wp-content/uploads/2013/11/Ex-6-Fugate-Affidavit-Tommy-Case.pdf ("Many of the expressions in chimpanzees and humans are displayed in similar circumstances, suggesting a common function or meaning."); Affidavit of Mary Lee Jensvold at 4, *Lavery*, Nov. 21, 2013, available at www.nonhumanrightsproject.org/wp-content/uploads/2013/11/Ex-6-Fugate-Affidavit-Tommy-Case.pdf ("There are numerous parallels in the way chimpanzee and human communication skills develop over time, suggesting a similar unfolding cognitive process across the two species and an underlying neurological continuity (internal citations omitted)."); Affidavit of Mathias Osvath at 4, *Lavery*, Nov. 19, 2013, available at www.nonhumanrightsproject.org/wp-content/uploads/2013/11/Ex-11-Osvath-Affidavit-Tommy-Case.pdf ("Chimpanzees are, together with bonobos, our closest living relatives and, as such, we share an abundance of characteristics. We are similar not only in our appearance and physiology but also in our emotions and our cognition." [internal citations omitted]); Affidavit of Tetsuro Matsuzawa at 3–4, *Lavery*, Nov. 23, 2013, available at www.nonhumanrightsproject.org/wp-content/uploads/2013/11/Ex-9-Matsuzawa-Affidavit-Tommy-Case.pdf ("[Chimpanzees and humans have] a number of shared characteristics in the brain that are relevant to such capacities as self-awareness and autonomy as well as general intelligence."); Affidavit of William C. McGrew at 10, *Lavery*, Nov. 21, 2013, available at www.nonhumanrightsproject.org/wp-content/uploads/2013/11/Ex-10-McGrew-Affidavit-Tommy-Case.pdf ("Comparisons between human and chimpanzee cultures demonstrate that the similarities are underwritten by a common set of mental abilities.").

37 WISE, *supra* note 35, at xxii.

38 Jane Goodall, *Foreword* to WISE, *supra* note 35, at xii.

39 WISE, *supra* note 35, at 270.

40 Petition for Writ of Habeas Corpus at 1–2, *Lavery*, Mar. 19, 2015, available at www.nonhumanrightsproject.org/wp-content/uploads/2015/03/2.-Verified-Petition.pdf [hereinafter *Lavery* Petition]; Petition for Writ of Habeas Corpus at 2–3, Nonhuman Rights Project, Inc. v. Stanley, Dec. 2, 2013, available at www.nonhuman rightsproject.org/wp-content/uploads/2013/12/Suffolk-Verified-Petition-of-E.Stein-and-S.Wise_.pdf [hereinafter *Stanley* Petition]; Petition for Writ of Habeas Corpus at 2–3, Nonhuman Rights Project, Inc. v. Presti, Dec. 2, 2013, available at www.nonhumanrightsproject.org/wp-content/uploads/2013/12/Niagara-Veri fied-Petition-E.Stein-and-S.Wise_.pdf [hereinafter *Presti* Petition].

41 *Lavery* Petition, *supra* note 40, at 2–3; *Stanley* Petition, *supra* note 40, at 2–3; *Presti* Petition, *supra* note 40, at 2–3.

42 Michael Mountain, *Bios on the Chimpanzees in New York Lawsuits*, NONHUMAN RIGHTS PROJECT, Nov. 30, 2013, available at www.nonhumanrightsproject.org/2013/11/30/bios-on-the-chimpanzees-in-new-york-lawsuits/.

43 *Id.*

44 *Id.*

45 *Id.*

46 *Id.*

47 *Id.*

48 *Id.*

49 *Id.*

50 Nonhuman Rights Project, *Legal Documents re Tommy the Chimpanzee*, Dec. 2, 2013, available at www.nonhumanrightsproject.org/2013/12/02/legal-documents-re-tommy-kiko-hercules-and-leo-2/; *Lavery* Petition, *supra* note 40, at 2; *Stanley* Petition, *supra* note 40, at 2; *Presti* Petition, *supra* note 40, at 2.

51 Judge's Ruling on Petition for Writ of Habeas Corpus, *Stanley*, No. 13–32098, Dec. 5, 2013, available at www.nonhumanrightsproject.org/wp-content/uploads/2013/12/Suffolk-Decision-Hercules-and-Leo-12-5-13.pdf.

52 *Id.* at 26.

53 Transcript of Oral Argument at 15–16, *Presti*, No. 151725, Dec. 9, 2013, available at www.nonhumanrightsproject.org/wp-content/uploads/2013/12/Transcript_of_Oral_Argument-_Niagara_County_12-9-13.pdf [hereinafter *Presti* Oral Argument].

54 Notice of Appeal, *Lavery*, No. 2013–02051, Jan. 9, 2014, available at www.nonhuman rightsproject.org/wp-content/uploads/2014/01/NoticeofAppeal-Fulton.pdf; Notice of Appeal, *Stanley*, No. 13–32098, Jan. 9, 2014, available at www.nonhumanrightspro ject.org/wp-content/uploads/2014/01/NoticeofAppeal-Stony.pdf; Notice of Appeal, *Presti*, No. 151725, Dec. 9, 2014, available at www.nonhumanrightsproject.org/wp-content/uploads/2014/01/NoticeofAppeal-Niagara.pdf; Nonhuman Rights Project,

Update on Appeals in NY State Chimpanzee Lawsuits, Apr. 22, 2014, available at www.nonhumanrightsproject.org/2014/04/22/update-on-appeals-in-ny-state-chim panzee-lawsuits/ [hereinafter *Update on Appeals*].

55 Estate of Lockett v. Fallin, No. CIV–14–1119–HE, 2015 WL 3874883 (W.D. Okla. July 16, 2015).

56 Glossip v. Gross, 135 S. Ct. 2732 (2015).

57 Dist. Attorney's Office for Third Jud. Dist. v. Osborne, 557 U.S. 52, 74 (2009).

58 *Id.* at 71 ("Whether such a federal right [to be released upon a showing of innocence] exists is an open question."); *In re* Davis, 557 U.S. 952 (2009) (Scalia, J., dissenting) ("This court has *never* held that the Constitution forbids the execution of a convicted defendant who has had a full and fair trial but is later able to convince a habeas court that he is 'actually' innocent.").

59 *See, e.g.*, Justin F. Marceau, *Is Guilt Dispositive? Federal Habeas after* Martinez, 55 WM. & MARY L. REV. 2071, 2152–53 (2014) (examining the erosion of the writ under the federal common law); Justin F. Marceau, *Challenging the Habeas Process Rather Than the Result*, 69 WASH. & LEE L. REV. 85, 117 (2012) (detailing the "Procedural Abyss of Federal Habeas Practice" that prevents prisoners from even introducing facts in support of their federal constitutional claims).

60 Some will no doubt argue that habeas corpus for such nonhumans as chimpanzees is too radical a proposition to take seriously and others argue that it is too banal and uncreative. For example, Judge Posner has said that it is a "sad poverty of imagination in an approach to animal protection that can think of it only on the model of the civil rights movement. It is a poverty that reflects the blinkered approach of the traditional lawyer, afraid to acknowledge novelty and therefore unable to think clearly about the reasons pro or con a departure from the legal status quo." Posner, *supra* note 17, at 539.

61 This is not to suggest a tidy, linear history of habeas corpus. It would be great folly to suggest that the history of habeas corpus can be pithily summarized. Indeed, "conventional histories are useless when it comes to explaining how, if habeas evolved linearly to become the 'great writ of liberty,' it proved so feeble a constraint on the British Parliament in the eighteenth century and on colonial assemblies in the nineteenth." Stephen I. Vladeck, *The New Habeas Revisionism*, 124 HARV. L. REV. 941, 944–45 (2011) (noting that "rather than analogize among cases – follow precedents – [common law judicial] thinking radiated in every direction from this core principle [that unjust detentions could be judicially reviewed]"); PAUL D. HALLIDAY, HABEAS CORPUS: FROM ENGLAND TO EMPIRE 502 (2010).

62 Paradoxically, animal cruelty statutes, which criminalize neglectful or abusive treatment of animals, are often the closest thing to a right that animals have to be free from unjust and cruel detention. But it would be quite novel to argue that a criminal statute (designed to punish humans for their treatment of animals) provides a substantive basis that would allow an animal to challenge his confinement. In its litigation, the NhRP argues that a chimpanzee is entitled to personhood for the purpose of a common law writ of habeas corpus for two reasons. The first reason

is common law liberty; chimpanzees are autonomous and autonomy is a supreme common law value that trumps even the interest of the state in preserving human life. The second reason is common law equality, which prohibits a court from depriving a being of all legal rights based upon a single characteristic, even when that characteristic is that the being is not a human.

63 HALLIDAY, *supra* note 61, at 121.

64 *Id.* at 122–32.

65 *Id.* at 124.

66 *Id.* at 129.

67 *Id.*

68 *Id.* at 133.

69 *Id.* at 175.

70 STEVEN M. WISE, THOUGH THE HEAVENS MAY FALL: THE LANDMARK TRIAL THAT LED TO THE END OF HUMAN SLAVERY xx (2006).

71 There is a history of using both habeas corpus and actions for replevin to litigate issues regarding slaves. But trying to sort out when replevin as opposed to habeas was the more appropriate vehicle is largely "futile because of the informality of colonial legal practice." Eric M. Freedman, *Habeas by Any Other Name*, 38 HOFSTRA L. REV. 275, 277 (2009) (noting that the critical point is that there were frequently "demand[s] for release from unlawful imprisonment ... made in the colonies by invoking many writs or none at all.").

72 *Id.*

73 *Id.*; Todd E. Pettys, *State Habeas Relief for Federal Extrajudicial Detainees*, 92 MINN. L. REV. 265, 266 (2007) (noting that "[t]he Supreme Court forced state judges into the role of idle spectators nearly 150 years ago, in a pair of cases dealing with efforts by the Wisconsin Supreme Court to free an abolitionist and an unhappy teenaged soldier from federal custody. Ableman v. Booth and Tarble's Case together stand for the proposition that state courts cannot grant habeas relief to federal prisoners.").

74 Marc D. Falkoff, *Back to Basics: Habeas Corpus Procedures and Long-Term Executive Detention*, 86 DENV. U. L. REV. 961, 965 (2009) ("Until recently, few have contemplated the core historical functions of the writ, largely because our government has never had a policy of imprisoning persons without providing due process of law.").

75 Rasul v. Bush, 542 U.S. 466, 473 (2004).

76 Boumediene v. Bush, 553 U.S. 723, 771 (2008).

77 *Id.* at 746.

78 *Cf.* Tribe, *supra* note 12, at 8 ("How do we advance the rights of animals who are unjustly confined without diminishing the needs of our fellow humans who are unjustly incarcerated?").

79 *Ex Parte* Bollman, 8 U.S. 75, 93–94 (1807).

80 It has been noted that POWs "could not get writs of habeas corpus," and yet the habeas procedure for evaluating detention still existed. Notably, the attorneys for

prisoners of war could apply for a writ for them, which "would trigger judicial investigation that would give the court an opportunity to conclude the prisoner was actually within the protection and thus not really a prisoner of war, in which instance the court could issue a writ." Eric M. Freedman, *Habeas Corpus in Three Dimensions*, 46 HARV. C.R.-C.L. L. REV. 591, 596 (2011) (quotation omitted).

81 HALLIDAY, *supra* note 61, at 100. By contrast, in denying relief in a state habeas case brought on behalf of a confined chimpanzee, a New York court reasoned, "Petitioner does not cite any precedent – and there appears to be none – in state law, or under English common law, that an animal could be considered a 'person' for the purposes of common-law habeas corpus relief." People ex rel. Nonhuman Rights Project, Inc. v. Lavery, 998 N.Y.S.2d 248, 248 (N.Y. App. Div. 2014).

82 Freedman, *supra* note 80, at 612–13.

83 Freedman, *supra* note 71, at 275. *See also* Freedman, *supra* note 80, at 593 ("The constitutional importance of the writ is in its function, not its name."); *id.* (explaining that the cases challenging custody in colonial America arose through a "variety of writs, including certiorari, supersedes, prohibition, trespass, replevin – or even by a pleading that asked for no particular writ at all.").

84 Vladeck, *supra* note 61, at 969. In modern habeas litigation, it is commonplace for one to have "access" to the writ in the sense that one is permitted to have one's conviction reviewed, but the lack of underlying substantive law favorable to the accused makes the procedural vehicle afforded by habeas an ever futile gesture.

85 *See, e.g.*, Obergefell v. Hodges, 135 S. Ct. 2584, 2605 (2015) (noting a general inclination "to proceed with caution – to await further legislation, litigation, and debate [and] to proceed with caution – . . . before deciding an issue so basic as the definition of marriage").

86 WISE, *supra* note 35, at xix.

87 Obergefell, 135 S. Ct. at 2602.

The International Arena

18

The Global Innocence Movement

MARK GODSEY

INTRODUCTION

The "Innocence Movement," a label that broadly encompasses efforts to rectify wrongful convictions and reform the criminal justice system to improve accuracy, is often thought of as emerging in the United States in the early 1990s with the advent of DNA testing technologies. But this is not necessarily true. As I will explain below, the concept originated in the United Kingdom and can be traced as far back as the 1970s. However, the Innocence Movement only recently began to experience significant global expansion. In the past five years alone it has seen an explosion in interest and activity across the globe. Innocence organizations now exist on every inhabited continent, with a dedicated network of organizations in the United States and Latin America, and one currently forming in Europe. Asia may soon follow suit with a much-needed network of its own.

The Innocence Movement has expanded internationally in an organic fashion. Those of us hoping the Movement will take hold in Germany, for example, cannot set out to convince Germans to take on the issue. Innocence work takes passion and a desire to make the work a focus of one's professional life. Thus, innocence work adheres in a given country *only* when a leading lawyer or scholar or other respected person in a position of influence in that country becomes deeply motivated by the problem and decides to make innocence his or her life work. The Movement expands organically, therefore, when it makes lawyers and scholars around the world aware of the problem, provides opportunities for lawyers and scholars new to the Movement to become involved with others around the world, and then waits for key motivated players to step forward with the necessary passion to tackle the problem in their home country.

There is a significant need for international collaboration in this area. While legal procedures may vary from country to country, all nations use similar types of flawed evidence to obtain convictions. Every criminal justice system relies on eyewitness identification, interrogations, confessions, and forensic sciences to obtain convictions. The flaws in these forms of evidence that have come to light through the Innocence Movement in the United States are relevant everywhere. Indeed, I have discussed elsewhere how the psychological factors that contribute to wrongful conviction, such as memory malleability, confirmation bias, and tunnel vision, are all problems that exist in the human condition, and thus, are applicable regardless of national border.[1] All countries need to collaborate, and learn from the advancements made in other nations, in order to minimize human weaknesses in investigation stemming from these psychological problems. I have highlighted the overlap of these issues across national borders elsewhere, and will not describe them at length here.[2] The purpose of this chapter instead is to illustrate the recent explosion that the Innocence Movement has seen around the globe.

As Co-Chair of the International Committee of the Innocence Network, a lawyer, and a scholar who has been heavily involved in the expansion of the Movement outside the United States, I believe the Movement will continue to expand internationally, eventually becoming a recognized global force – like Amnesty International and similar groups. With this expansion we will see innocence issues – such as the right for all prisoners anywhere in the world to have the benefit of legal procedures to prove their innocence and obtain their freedom – recognized as fundamental human rights. In the sections that follow, I will trace the development of the Innocence Movement from its origins in the UK to its present shape followed by some broad observations about the barriers that the Movement will need to overcome as it expands across the world.

THE ORIGINS OF THE MOVEMENT

Although many credit the United States and the Innocence Project in New York City with developing the Innocence Movement, the idea first emerged in the UK in the 1970s and 1980s after a series of high-profile crimes, Irish Republican Army (IRA) bombings to be exact, resulted in the imprisonment of several individuals who were later determined to be innocent.[3] The convictions often involved false confessions, police misconduct, withheld evidence, and faulty forensic information.[4] The "Guildford Four" and "Birmingham Six" are two very good examples of this occurrence.

In 1975, Paul Michael Hill, Gerry Conlon, Patrick Armstrong, and Carole Richardson were found responsible for the 1974 IRA bombings of Guildford and Woolwich that caused the death of seven people.[5] Each member of the "Guildford Four" was sentenced to life imprisonment.[6] The public began to question the guilt of the Guilford Four when, during the trial of the Balcombe Street Gang in 1977, three members of the IRA admitted responsibility for the Guildford and Woolwich bombings.[7] More than a decade later, in 1989, all four convictions were quashed after an investigation revealed that police lied during the Guildford trial and fabricated the confessions of Armstrong and Hill.[8] Hill, Conlon, Armstrong, and Richardson were released from prison fifteen years after being convicted.[9] Gerry Conlon's story was made into the feature film *In the Name of the Father*, which starred Daniel Day Lewis as Gerry Conlon and Emma Thompson as his attorney, Gareth Pierce.

The "Birmingham Six" spent sixteen years in prison for IRA-attributed bombings before being exonerated in March 1991.[10] On November 24, 1974, two IRA bombs exploded in the Mulberry Bush and Tavern in the Town pubs in Birmingham, England, killing 21 people and injuring 182 others.[11] Six men were arrested for the crime: Hugh Callaghan, Gerard Hunter, Richard McIlkenny, William Power, John Walker, and Patrick Joseph Hill.[12] All six were Catholics from Northern Ireland.[13] The police obtained confessions from four of the men; however, at trial the men maintained their innocence, stating that the confessions were forced.[14] The men remained imprisoned for sixteen years – until a third appeal filed by Solicitor Gareth Pierce succeeded, resulting in their 1991 release.[15] The Crown withdrew its case against the men after the forensic evidence used at trial was discredited and the defense produced proof of police fabrication and the suppression of evidence.[16]

Two innocence organizations developed in direct response to such IRA bombing cases. Following his release from prison, Patrick Joseph Hill of the Birmingham Six cofounded the Miscarriages of Justice Organization (MOJO) as an entity dedicated exclusively to helping innocent people both in prison and after their release.[17] It helps the wrongfully convicted find legal representation and develop media contacts in order to spread awareness about an individual's case.[18] MOJO also provides aftercare to exonerees and their families, helping with acclimation and obtaining benefits.[19] MOJO predates most if not all innocence projects, and is arguably the first organization of its kind, committed to fighting wrongful convictions.

The second organization to develop was the Criminal Cases Review Commission (CCRC). Established by the Criminal Appeal Act of 1995, the CCRC is a public body responsible for investigating alleged miscarriages of justice in the UK.[20] It can send or refer a case back to appeal if it believes that the conviction may be overturned or the sentence reduced.[21] Since it began reviewing cases in March 1997 through July 31, 2015, the CCRC has received a total of 19,773 applications and has completed 18,350 case reviews.[22] During that period, 595 cases have been referred back to court by the CCRC; of the 573 appeals heard after referral, 392 were allowed and 167 were dismissed.[23]

Although the CCRC was the first governmental body established to investigate and correct wrongful convictions, it has received quite a bit of criticism from the innocence community for applying standards that make it too difficult to achieve exoneration.[24] Perhaps the most outspoken of its critics is Dr. Michael Naughton, founder of the Innocence Network UK. Naughton has publically criticized the CCRC for perpetuating what he views as a critical flaw in the UK criminal appeals process.[25] According to Naughton, the CCRC's sole concern is what happened at trial.[26] It focuses exclusively on whether a constitutional violation has occurred, when, in Naughton's opinion, the focus should be on discovering the truth about one's guilt or innocence.[27] As a result, many individuals with legitimate claims of innocence fall through the cracks.[28]

Naughton often cites Neil Hurley's case as a specific example. Hurley was convicted of murder based on witness statements that were later revealed to be coerced.[29] Information learned after trial suggested that the police failed to properly investigate two alternate suspects, one of whom returned home the morning of the murder covered in blood.[30] Hurley also claimed to have an alibi, the owner of a local pub.[31] Yet his case was rejected by the CCRC, because it found no constitutional violations in Hurley's trial; his actual innocence proved to be an inconsequential fact in the matter.[32]

The Innocence Movement emerged in the United States during the 1980s and 1990s. It started with the formation of Centurion Ministries in 1983, a freestanding nonprofit that investigates cases of innocence across the country, and then the Innocence Project in 1992, a student clinic at Cardozo Law School in New York City. The Innocence Project began using newly available DNA testing technologies to prove the innocence of hundreds of inmates across the United States, gaining worldwide attention in the process. Following the Innocence Project's lead, similar organizations soon formed across the United States – most frequently at law schools. As these new projects developed, the trademark "Innocence Project" and its mission became well-known throughout the United States.

Today, these organizations form the Innocence Network, a collaborative effort to combat the issues contributing to wrongful conviction and achieve criminal justice reform. Since 1989, more than 1,600 documented cases of wrongful conviction have occurred in the United States.[33] These cases have been discovered and resolved largely due to the member organizations of the Innocence Network.

Similar organizations began to develop in other English-speaking countries shortly after the Innocence Movement started to flourish in the United States. These organizations include the Association in Defence of the Wrongfully Convicted (AIDWYC) in Canada,[34] the Irish Innocence Project, the Innocence Network United Kingdom (INUK),[35] the Griffith University Innocence Project in Australia,[36] the Sellenger Centre Criminal Review Project at Edith Cowan University in Australia, and the Innocence Project New Zealand.[37] Following the U.S. innocence project model, most of these organizations were based in law schools or other departments in universities, and utilized students to perform investigations. Although the INUK is now defunct as a network, several organizations that had been part of that network are continuing to function.

Among these, for example, the Cardiff Law School Innocence Project in Wales achieved a high-profile exoneration in 2014 with the release of Dwaine George. In 2001, a Manchester teenager was shot dead on the streets of Miles Platting two days before he was due to testify against a man accused of stabbing his friend to death earlier that year.[38] The following year, 18-year-old Dwaine George was tried for the murder.[39] On April 29, 2002, George was found guilty and sentenced to a minimum of twelve years' imprisonment.[40]

George denied involvement in the murder and appealed his conviction but was unsuccessful.[41] In 2005, he applied to the CCRC, requesting review of his case.[42] The CCRC accepted George's case, but in 2007 it informed him that it found no basis for referring the case to the court of appeal.[43] George also contacted the INUK, which referred his case to the Cardiff Law School Innocence Project.[44] Students involved in the project began to investigate George's case and review the evidence used against him at trial.[45]

George was circumstantially linked to the murder through a visual identification by Arron Cunningham, a voice identification by witness Stuart Shaw, and the presence of gunshot residue on a jacket found in his home when he was arrested a month after the murder.[46] The Cardiff students focused their investigation on debunking the gunshot residue evidence and Shaw's voice recognition.[47] The Cardiff Innocence Project reapplied to the CCRC on George's behalf, citing new scientific evidence regarding the significance of gunshot residue and a new court decision involving voice recognition identification.[48]

The CCRC referred the case back to court after it obtained an expert report stating that it was not possible to conclude that the residue found on George's jacket was in any way related to the Dale shooting.[49] According to the report, it was possible that the two particles of gunshot residue present on George's jacket originated from a source other than gunfire, such as fireworks or from the environment.[50] The particles alone could not demonstrate George's involvement in the murder. On appeal it was also pointed out that Stuart Shaw, who identified George by his voice, had also identified another perpetrator by his voice.[51] However, that defendant was acquitted due to the fact that he had a rock-solid alibi.[52] The court agreed that the gunshot residue evidence could not independently support George's conviction.[53] Ruling it unsafe, the appellate court quashed George's murder conviction on December 9, 2014.[54] Thanks to the students at the Cardiff Law School Innocence Project who helped disprove the forensic evidence used to convict George, the 30-year-old was cleared of the murder for which he served twelve years behind bars.

Although the Innocence Movement's expansion throughout the 1990s extended beyond the borders of the United States, it was primarily limited to English-speaking countries. By the 2010s, the Movement started seeing a great influx of interest from scholars and lawyers on every inhabited continent. This was especially apparent to those of us who served on the International Committee of the Innocence Network.

The international expansion of the Innocence Movement was made the primary focus of the 2011 Innocence Network conference held in Cincinnati, Ohio, and sponsored by my organization, the Ohio Innocence Project.[55] More than twenty-five countries were represented at the conference, including Mexico, Japan, China, the Czech Republic, and South Africa. *The University of Cincinnati Law Review* published an edition dedicated entirely to the conference, which had contributions from scholars and lawyers from fifteen countries.[56] This volume remains the most comprehensive review of international innocence issues available. Most notably, the conference ignited an explosion of growth in the Innocence Movement to regions around the globe.

LATIN AMERICA

In 2012, fifty law students, lawyers and academics met in Santiago, Chile to discuss the formation of a network of innocence organizations throughout various countries in Latin America. This network adopted the name Red Inocente.[57] The idea for Red Inocente began to develop at the California Innocence Project (CIP) housed within the California Western School of Law. After being founded in 1999, the CIP started to recognize a need for innocence advocacy in Mexico and other Latin American countries. Red Inocente continues to grow as a network, holding annual conferences in rotating countries. Projects are established or in the process of being established in Argentina, Chile, Colombia, Costa Rica, Mexico, Puerto Rico, and Peru.

Organizations in the Red Inocente network have already achieved a number of exonerations. The Innocence Project Argentina, for example, obtained the exoneration and release of Fernando Carerra in 2012 for a murder he did not commit. The case is the subject of a documentary called *The Raffi Horror Show*.[58] Similarly, the documentary *Presumed Guilty* depicts the exoneration and eventual release of Toño Zúñiga, a wrongful conviction case that received national attention in Mexico.[59]

Red Inocente will likely serve as a model for continental innocence networks as the Movement continues to gain steam.

EUROPE

As mentioned previously, the Innocence Movement has been well-established in the English-speaking parts of Europe, such as Ireland and the UK, for decades. However, the Innocence Movement only recently expanded into many non-English speaking regions of Europe. Norway formed a Criminal Case Review Commission in 2004. Projects were also developed in the Netherlands, France, Italy, and the Czech Republic following the success of the 2011 International Innocence Conference in the United States.

Representatives from many of these projects have come together with lawyers and scholars interested in the movement to discuss the formation of The European Innocence Network. The network would allow projects to coordinate work and help solidify the growth of the Innocence Movement in Europe. This idea developed following the 2015 European Innocence Conference hosted by the Irish Innocence Project in Dublin, Ireland. David Langwallner, Director of the Irish Innocence Project, and Luca Luparia, Director of the Italy Innocence Project, have taken the lead in these discussions, connecting with lawyers and law professors in Spain, Germany, and other countries, to gauge interest in having those countries join the Innocence Movement. Another European Innocence conference was held in Prague in June 2016, at which time a formal European Innocence Network was launched.

The Irish Innocence Project officially launched in March 2010 at Griffith College in Dublin, Ireland.[60] The project is comprised of law and journalism students who are supervised by practicing Barristers.[61] The Irish Innocence Project recently obtained Ireland's first and only posthumous exoneration with the pardoning of Harry Gleeson, a man who was hanged in 1941 for murder.[62] Gleeson was pardoned in January 2015 after the project obtained forensic evidence demonstrating the victim's actual time of death, a period for which Gleeson had an alibi.[63] Later that year, the Irish Innocence Project hosted the 2015 European Innocence Conference. This conference was attended by lawyers and scholars from Europe and around the world.[64]

Norway has been active in the Innocence Movement for several years, forming a Criminal Case Review Commission (CCRC) in 2004 based on the similar organization in the UK.[65] Since its founding, the CCRC there has reopened more than 150 cases of wrongful conviction. This highly successful governmental body has been extensively studied by Ulf Stridbeck, a professor at the University of Oslo. Professor Stridbeck's article in the *University of Cincinnati Law Review* published in conjunction with the 2011 International Innocence Conference provides a thorough overview of Norway's CCRC and some of its high-profile cases.[66]

Knoops' Innocence Project, based at the Knoops law firm in Amsterdam, is highly active and in only a few years has already achieved several exonerations in the Netherlands.[67] One such case involves the wrongful convictions of Wilco Viets and Herman Du Bois. Viets and Du Bois both served seven years and eight months in prison after police pressured the men into falsely confessing.[68]

Du Bois and Viets were apprehended following the January 1994 rape and murder of flight attendant Christel Ambrosius. The men became suspects after a witness reported that the perpetrator was driving a vehicle similar to one Du Bois and Viets happened to be driving the day of the murder. After being subjected to lengthy interrogations, both men confessed to the crime. These confessions, however, were inconsistent and contradicted one another. Furthermore, DNA evidence taken from the crime scene failed to match either of the men.[69]

At trial, Du Bois and Viets both retracted their confessions. The Crown produced two witnesses identifying the men as the perpetrators and presented a forensic expert who theorized that the rape drew out sperm from an earlier, consensual sexual encounter, thus explaining away the presence of the third-party DNA.[70]

Du Bois and Viets were convicted and sentenced to ten years in jail.[71] They remained in prison until after the Dutch Supreme Court overturned their convictions in 2001. The Court's review of the case showed that hairs found at the crimes scene came from the same source as the semen, rendering the Crown's forensic theory even less credible than it was at trial.[72] Following their release, an appeals court acquitted them and awarded Du Bois and Viets 1.8 million euros in damages.[73]

Six years later, in April 2008, the Netherlands' Forensic Institute matched the semen from the Ambrosius murder to Ronald Pieper, a career criminal who once lived in the village where the murder took place.[74] On September 10, 2009, fifteen years after the murder, Pieper was convicted.[75] He was sentenced to eighteen years in prison.[76]

In recent years innocence projects have formed in both France[77] and Italy. Italy has been an active participant in the European expansion of the movement. The Italy Innocence Project, based at the University of Milan and directed by Professor Luca Luparia, hosted the 2014 European Innocence Conference in Milan.[78] The conference was attended by lawyers and innocence scholars from across the continent.[79]

Poland and the Czech Republic are home to established and developing innocence organizations, respectively. An innocence clinic run by Maria Ejchart-Dubois at a law school in Warsaw has been effectively in operation for many years.[80] In the Czech Republic, DNA expert Daniel Vanek and human rights lawyer Jan Voboril formed a project with the intention of basing it at one of the law schools in that country.

Finally, I will include Israel in my discussion of Europe. Although, of course, not located in Europe, lawyers working in the Innocence Movement in Israel have attended European Innocence Conferences and have expressed interest in being included in the emerging European Innocence Network. The Israel project, run by Anat Horovitz and Keren Ablin-Hertz, is based at the Israeli Public Defender's Office and works closely with law students at the Hebrew University of Jerusalem.[81] This office recently achieved success when it won the right to DNA testing of cigarette butts in the high-profile case of Yitzhak Zuziashvilli, a man convicted of murdering a judge. The public defenders in the Re-trial Department (which is in essence the "Innocence Project" arm of the public defenders) argued that even though Israel does not have a DNA testing statute like all states in the United States have now enacted, the High Court should enforce such a right. In response, the High Court urged the prosecution to agree to testing, prompting the prosecution to reverse its position, allowing the testing to take place.[82] The DNA testing in the case is currently ongoing.

ASIA

Asia has seen extensive innocence activity in recent years, with organizations springing up in Singapore,[83] the Philippines,[84] and Taiwan, and discussions regarding projects forming in Japan and China. In fact, the Innocence Project Japan officially launched in 2016 at conferences held in Tokyo and near Kyoto.

The Taiwan Association for Innocence (TAI) was founded in July 2012 by Ping-Cheng Lo, who is known for defending the "Hsichih Trio," one of the most renowned cases of wrongful conviction in Taiwanese judicial history.[85] The TAI has a twelve-member board, comprised of experienced criminal defense lawyers, law professors, forensic experts, and two full-time staff members: Director Shi-Hsiang Lo and office coordinator Chih-Hsien Huang. Much of its work, including case screening, direct representation, and supervising volunteer law students, is performed by volunteer lawyers providing pro bono legal services.

The TAI only accepts post-conviction cases based on innocence, involving either flawed forensic evidence or state misconduct. Since 2012, the TAI has received more than 120 applications, and has accepted only seven. Each case is assigned to one of the twelve Board directors who is responsible for organizing a team of attorneys and law students to work on the case. The students come from clinical programs in the Taiwan University, College of Law and the Chiao Tung University, Institute of Technology Law.

In December 2013, the TAI saw its first victory when the Taiwan High Court granted Chen Long-Qi a retrial for his rape conviction based on new DNA evidence. On March 24, 2009, two female escorts were raped in a warehouse that Chen and his friend rented for business usage. The victims failed to identify the assailants due to alcohol intoxication. Chen maintained his innocence, claiming that he left the warehouse before the crime took place to pick up his wife, Ko, at her workplace. Ko's timesheet corroborated Chen's alibi. An eyewitness also testified that Chen was not at the scene. Despite no testimony linking Chen to the crime, the district court and high court found him guilty of gang rape, along with two other men, based on a 17 Loci Y-STR DNA test that failed to exclude Chen as the contributor of semen found in one of the victims' underwear. In March 2013, Chen was sentenced to serve four years in prison.

Chen sought TAI's help right after his conviction. Refusing to report to prison, he told his lawyers that "Unless they drag me in, I will not voluntarily walk into jail for something I did not do." Chen divorced his wife, worrying that his daughters would be labeled as "daughters of the rapist" in school. He sold his seafood stall and hid in a small apartment that his wife rented. He later told his lawyers, "For many times, I looked down the street from the window of the apartment, thinking that if I should jump to end this nightmare."

To assist in the case, TAI consulted Professor James Lee Chun-I, a forensic specialist, who confirmed that he could only tell from the 17 Loci Y-STR test that there were two or more perpetrators committing the crime. He concluded that, with additional DNA testing, the courts could more accurately determine whether Chen was involved in the rapes. With help from the TAI, Chen filed a motion for retrial in June 2013, seeking to retest the DNA evidence. The court authorized a 23 Loci STR test on the original mixture DNA sample. The tests conclusively excluded Chen from the DNA sample. Based on this new piece of evidence, the court granted his motion for a new trial in December 2013. Chen was exonerated on March 26, 2014. He is now a volunteer for TAI, and is planning to initiate a civil suit against the State.[86]

Singapore and the Philippines, like Taiwan, have active, organized innocence projects, and a project formed in Japan in 2016, but no organization yet exists to fight wrongful convictions in China. China has, however, seen extensive discussion in recent years about the problem of wrongful convictions within its borders. The most famous case of exoneration in China is that of She Xianglin.

In 1994, She Xianglin was found guilty of bludgeoning and drowning his wife, Zhang Zaiyu, who had gone missing earlier that year.[87] Eleven years later, She's alleged victim returned to their village in Hubei Province very much alive.[88] The sudden reappearance of She's wife demonstrated that no crime had actually taken place, proving his innocence. It also revealed a grave miscarriage of justice. She was convicted not once but *twice*, by two different Chinese courts, of murder, a crime that never took place.

She's misfortune began in January 1994 with the unexplained disappearance of his wife.[89] Three months later the badly decomposed body of a female was discovered in a pond near the couple's village in the Hubei Province.[90] The body was identified by a relative as the missing woman.[91] This identification proved sufficient for the local police who chose not to perform DNA tests on the corpse despite its state.[92]

Although She denied involvement, he was arrested and charged with murder.[93] Chinese Authorities interrogated him for ten days and eleven nights, using sleep deprivation and severe beatings to induce a false confession.[94] She eventually confessed, but he quickly recanted the confession and continued to maintain his innocence.[95] He gave four inconsistent accounts of how the murder took place.[96] The murder weapon used in the bludgeoning was never identified.[97]

In late 1994, She was tried by the Jingzhou City Intermediate People's Court.[98] Despite the discrepancies in his confession, the questionable method used to identify the body, and the lack of a murder weapon, he was convicted and sentenced to death.[99] He appealed the conviction to the Hubei Province Higher People's Court.[100] Listing five reasonable doubts the court rescinded the conviction and remanded the case for retrial.[101] In 1998, She was retried by a different tribunal, the Jiangshan County Primary People's Court.[102] He was convicted once again but given the reduced sentence of fifteen years to life.[103] The court feared that if the death penalty were imposed the case would be reversed again on appeal.[104]

She was serving out his term when in 2005, after an unexplained eleven-year absence, his wife returned to their village.[105] She's wife claimed to be unaware of his circumstances, and blamed her absence on mental illness.[106] While away, She's wife remarried and had a child with her new husband.[107] With no crime to justify his conviction, She was released from prison having served eleven years for the murder of his wife.[108] On October 27, 2005, The Jingshan County Public Security Bureau agreed to pay She's family 450,000 renminbi[109] in compensation for his wrongful imprisonment.[110]

Cases like that of She Xianglin have caused serious concern in China. Chinese authorities have vowed to fight wrongful convictions,[111] and in fact have instituted a number of reforms, including the videotaping of interrogations to curb abuse like what occurred in the She Xianglin case.[112] With more than 1,300 wrongful convictions exposed in 2014 alone, China's top judge apologized to the nation in 2015 and vowed to correct the errors that have led to so many miscarriages of justice.[113] Academics in China have hosted a number of conferences aimed at finding cures for the problem, and discussions about creating an organization to fight wrongful convictions are ongoing.[114]

AFRICA

The Wits Justice Project (WJP)[115] at the University of Witwatersrand and the Innocence Project South Africa[116] have had a number of successes. Recently, the WJP helped exonerate Thembekile Molaudzi, who was wrongfully convicted in 2002 of murdering a South African police officer, Johannes Dingaan Makuna.

Makuna was shot and killed in his home during an attempted robbery in August 2002.[117] The only witness to the murder was Makuna's daughter.[118] Eight men were arrested in connection to the crime.[119] Among them was taxi driver Thembekile Molaudzi, a married man in his late twenties who had just had his first child, a son named Mark.[120]

Molaudzi denied involvement in the crime and professed his innocence. During two identity parades, Makuna's daughter identified four men.[121] Molaudzi was not one of them; however, one of the accused men provided a coerced confession in which he implicated Molaudzi and two others who had also not been identified during the identity parades.[122] It was the only piece of evidence tying Molaudzi and the two others to the crime.[123] The admissibility of the confession was challenged at trial because there was suspicion surrounding its veracity.[124] Unfortunately, the judge allowed it to be admitted as evidence.[125] On July 22, 2004, Molaudzi was convicted of murder and sentenced to life imprisonment.[126] At the time of his conviction, Molaudzi's son was only 3 months old.[127]

Molaudzi was taken to a maximum security prison where he was tortured and humiliated by the prison guards.[128] He and the other inmates were stripped and forced to parade around naked in front of women.[129] They were beaten for no reason, sometimes with shock shields.[130] Molaudzi was later transferred to another facility where he endured similar torture.[131] He was regularly beaten by guards and even placed in solitary confinement for four consecutive years.[132]

Molaudzi faced difficulty trying to appeal his case. It took several attempts for him to obtain a copy of his transcripts.[133] Even then, he and his codefendants were forced to pay for the transcripts, which they were constitutionally entitled to receive for free.[134] When the men finally obtained the transcripts they soon discovered that over half of the document was missing, including the parts regarding the admissibility of the confession.[135] Without a full copy of the transcript, Molaudzi could not file an adequate appeal.[136]

Molaudzi contacted several human rights organizations asking for help, but his pleas were ignored.[137] After performing his own investigation, prison guard Levi Maphakane took it upon himself to help Molaudzi.[138] He contacted the WJP and asked them to help Molaudzi obtain his trial transcripts.[139] Within days the WJP obtained a copy of the transcripts but these too were incomplete and missing the most important information.[140] Eventually, with help from the WJP, Molaudzi was able to get a complete copy of the transcripts through a court order.[141] Eight years after he first set out to obtain his trial transcripts, he was finally able to appeal his conviction.[142] The appeal was dismissed.[143]

The WJP continued to investigate Molaudzi's case and try to find a way to prove his innocence. In 2014, the two other men who were implicated in the false confession successfully appealed their convictions.[144] The court found that the statement implicating the men was improperly admitted at trial and should have been corroborated by independent evidence but was not.[145] The men were exonerated and freed.[146] Molaudzi appealed his case again, this time incorporating the new decision.[147] In June 2015, Molaudzi's murder conviction was overturned due to the inadmissibility of the confession that implicated him.[148]

BARRIERS TO OVERCOME

As the Innocence Movement has expanded in recent years, certain obstacles have emerged in some countries to thwart possible successes. Surprisingly, legal barriers are not one of them. In my experience, nearly every country has a mechanism for allowing inmates to challenge their convictions – and seek a new trial – based on new evidence discovered after their conviction. Even China has such a provision in its criminal procedure code, and I have yet to find a country that does not have some sort of provision for reopening a case based on the later discovery of new evidence.

However, outside of the United States, South Africa, and Ireland, I know of no other countries that have established procedures that provide inmates with access to post-conviction DNA testing for the purpose of proving their innocence. This right only recently became recognized in Ireland and South Africa. As access to DNA testing is crucial for many inmates in prison hoping to prove their innocence, these laws must proliferate for the Movement to continue gaining momentum. More countries will need to follow the lead of Ireland and South Africa, and the innocence organizations forming across the globe must be instrumental in helping to pass such laws.

Another major barrier is the lack of access in many countries to police files. In the United States, where the Innocence Movement has a solid footing, the first thing an innocence organization does when it examines a case is file a written public records request under local state laws to obtain the original police files. The United States has a long history with open records, and thus, this is a well-established right in most jurisdictions (although even in the United States law enforcement is often less than enthusiastic to disclose files and delays or obstructions are not uncommon). Having access to police files is essential to developing an understanding of what happened in a case, what evidence was collected, and whether all exculpatory evidence was disclosed to the inmate prior to his trial. Without access to the police files, reinvestigating the case is much more difficult.

I have learned from speaking with innocence leaders and scholars from around the globe that most countries do not enjoy the tradition of open records as does the United States. In the UK, for example, the Innocence Movement has operated in some form for decades, but it has been hampered by the fact that no law exists requiring police departments to disclose their files in cases under post-conviction investigation. While exonerations have been obtained in the UK, the task is made much more difficult when the projects are unable to obtain the police files to provide them with an inside view of how the investigation was conducted and what sort of evidence had been collected initially.

Perhaps the greatest barrier, however, is the arrogance of the criminal justice system, and the belief that innocent men and women are never convicted of crimes they did not commit. This barrier has always proven to be problematic in the United States, but to a lesser degree since the initiation of the Innocence Movement. Indeed, prior to the advent of DNA testing and post-conviction access to DNA, most Americans – including prosecutors and judges – believed that wrongful convictions were a myth. As famous American jurist Judge Learned Hand observed nearly one hundred years ago: "Our procedure has been always haunted by the ghost of the innocent man convicted." But then Hand went on to state that this fear "is an unreal dream."[49] Since that time, however, most Americans have come to realize that wrongful conviction is an actual, widespread, systematic issue that needs to be addressed. Still, in my work in Ohio, I will sometimes run into judges and prosecutors who maintain the antiquated belief that wrongful convictions rarely – if ever – occur.

I find this American arrogance, especially reflected in our international relations, to be an embarrassment. When I first started engaging in innocence work and received pushback from those in the criminal justice system, I far too often heard the following justification, "We have the best criminal justice system in the world. We don't have wrongful convictions here." From these experiences, I came to believe that such arrogance was largely an American phenomenon. But engaging in innocence work around the world has cured me of that belief.

Indeed, I cannot count the number of times I have given a speech about the Innocence Movement in another country, only to be told by lawyers and scholars after my talk something to the effect of, "That's fine for America. You have a problematic criminal justice system that everyone knows is unfair. We don't have that problem here." I typically then ask, "Do you have people in prison who at least *claim* they are innocent?" The answer is always yes. I then ask, "Do you have procedures for these people to have access to DNA testing for them to prove their innocence?" The answer is almost always no. I then ask, "Do you have public records laws that allow inmates, their families, or innocence organizations an opportunity to reinvestigate these cases from top to bottom?" The answer is usually no. I then say, "That is what we thought in America until inmates had such rights. How can you know that your criminal justice system is perfect? It has never been tested."

Indeed, they cannot know whether there criminal justice system is error-proof until cases of alleged wrongful conviction are fully vetted on the back end as they now are in the United States. More importantly, the human errors that lead to wrongful convictions are present in any system run by humans, regardless of the differences in procedure. Eyewitnesses in Germany are as susceptible to the flaws in memory and pressures that result in mistaken identifications as eyewitnesses in the United States. Likewise, lab technicians in Germany are prone to the same wrongful-conviction-causing errors that have been discovered in U.S. labs. There is nothing intrinsic about the German people as a whole that makes it impossible for a German citizen to fabricate a convincing story to frame an innocent person. Indeed, the human factors that cause wrongful convictions are simply not related to the differences in procedure across national borders. They are related to the condition of being human.

Given what we now know about how wrongful convictions are created – through cognitive bias, arrogance, tunnel vision, and a lack of open-mindedness in the pursuit of justice – anyone who asserts that their criminal justice system is flawless exemplifies the mentality that ultimately leads to wrongful convictions. In my opinion, the more arrogant a system is about the infallibility of its procedures, the more likely it is to suffer from wrongful convictions.

CONCLUSION

Although the Innocence Movement began in the UK and the United States, it has become a global phenomenon in the past decade. Indeed, in the past five years the Movement has seen an explosion of interest around the globe. Active organizations dedicated to fighting wrongful conviction can be found on every inhabited continent. A network of collaborating projects is currently taking shape in Europe, with similar networks already existing in Latin America, as Red Inocente, and the United States, as The Innocence Network. Asia already has successful and active projects in several countries, with China openly grappling with the problem of wrongful conviction as well.

As the Innocence Movement continues to expand and take foot around the world, key leaders are now discussing a plan to approach the United Nations about a resolution to recognize innocence issues as international human rights, including the institution of a legal mechanism by which prisoners asserting innocence can introduce new evidence of innocence to obtain their release in all jurisdictions. As the Innocence Movement continues to gain attention across the globe, this idea will someday, hopefully, become a reality.

But as the Movement continues to expand, innocence lawyers and scholars in countries around the world will face many of the same challenges that innocence leaders did at the inception of the Innocence Movement in the United States. They will need to press their leaders for laws allowing access to the police files and biological material for DNA testing. And they will need to make their leaders understand that the arrogant belief that wrongful convictions cannot occur in their jurisdictions is nothing more than proof that innocence work is needed there.

NOTES

1 Mark A. Godsey, *The Human Factor in Wrongful Convictions Across Borders*, in Understanding Wrongful Conviction: The Protection of the Innocent Across Europe and America (Luca Luparia, ed., 2015).
2 *Id.*
3 Criminal Cases Review Commission, *Our History*, available at http://ccrc.wpen gine.com/about-us/our-history/.
4 *Id.*
5 Martin McNamara, *Guildford Four: An Innocent Man's Letters from Jail*, Oct. 4, 2014, BBC News, available at www.bbc.com/news/uk-29429010.
6 *Id.*
7 *Id.*
8 *Id.*
9 *Id.*
10 *Paddy Hill and Birmingham Six*, available at www.irishhistorian.com/People/Paddy Hill.html.
11 *Id.*
12 *Id.*
13 *Id.*
14 *Id.*
15 *Id.*
16 *Id.*
17 Miscarriage of Justice Organization, *Homepage*, available at www.miscarriagesofjus tice.org.
18 *Id.*
19 *Id.*
20 *Id.*
21 *Id.*
22 Criminal Cases Review Commission, *CCRC Case Statistics*, available at www.ccrc.gov.uk/case-statistics/.
23 *Id.*
24 *Id.*
25 *Fighting for Simple Justice*, Bristol Post, Mar. 7, 2012, available at www.bristol post.co.uk/Fighting-simple-justice/story-15419321-detail/story.html.
26 *Id.*
27 *Id.*

28 *Id.*

29 Michael Naughton, *Why Safety in Law May Fail the Innocent-The Case of Neil Hurley*, THE GUARDIAN, Feb. 11, 2010, available at www.theguardian.com/uk/2010/feb/11/neil-hurley.

30 *Id.*

31 *Id.*

32 *Id.*

33 National Registry of Exonerations, *Homepage*, available at www.law.umich.edu/special/exoneration/Pages/about.aspx.

34 Association in Defence of the Wrongfully Convicted, *Homepage*, available at www.aidwyc.org.

35 Although the INUK has recently disbanded as a collaborative network, several projects formerly part of this network continue to remain active in the UK.

36 Griffith University Innocence Project, *Homepage*, available at www.griffith.edu.au/criminology-law/innocence-project.

37 Radio New Zealand National, *Innocence Project New Zealand* (Podcast), Nov. 20, 2013, available at www.radionz.co.nz/national/programmes/ninetonoon/audio/2576990/innocence-project-new-zealand; Rod Vaughan, *New Zealand "Innocence Project" Reignites Debate on Appeals Process*, ADLSI, Feb. 7, 2014, available at www.adls.org.nz/for-the-profession/news-and-opinion/2014/2/7/new-zealand-innocence-project-reignites-debate-on-appeals-process/.

38 Claire Carter, *Former Gang Member, 30, Who Served 12 Years Behind Bars for Fatal Shooting of Teenager Is Cleared on Appeal*, DAILY MAIL, Dec. 9, 2014, available at www.dailymail.co.uk/news/article-2866816/Former-gang-member-30-served-12-years-bars-fatal-shooting-teenager-cleared-appeal.html.

39 *Ex-Gang Member Dwaine George Cleared of 2002 Murder on Appeal*, BBC NEWS, Dec. 9, 2014, available at www.bbc.com/news/uk-england-manchester-30395753.

40 *Id.*

41 *Id.*

42 Dwaine Simeon George v. The Queen, 201305873 BS (Court of Appeal (Criminal Division) On Appeal From the Crown Court at Preston, Nov. 6, 2014.

43 *Id.*

44 *Id.*

45 *Id.*

46 *Id.*

47 *Id.*

48 *Id.*

49 *Id.*

50 *Id.*

51 *Id.*

52 *Id.*

53 *Id.*

54 *Id.*

55 *2011 Innocence Network Conference: An International Exploration of Wrongful Convictions*, available at www.law.uc.edu/institutes-centers/ohio-innocence-pro ject/2011-innocence-network-conference.

56 Mark Godsey, *Introduction*, 80 U. CIN. L. REV. 1067 (2012).

For a discussion of wrongful convictions in England, *see* Carole McCartney & Stephanie Roberts, *Building Institutions to Address Miscarriages of Justice in England and Wales: "Mission Accomplished?"*, 80 U. CIN. L. REV. 1333 (2012); John Weeden, *The Criminal Cases Review Commission (CCRC) of England, Wales, and Northern Ireland*, 80 U. CIN. L. REV. 1415 (2012).

For Ireland, *see* David Langwallner, *The Irish Innocence Project*, 80 U. CIN. L. REV. 1293 (2012).

For the Netherlands, *see* Chrisje Brants, *Wrongful Convictions and Inquisitorial Process: The Case of the Netherlands*, 80 U. CIN. L. REV. 1069 (2012).

For Norway, *see* Ulf Stridbeck & Philos Svein Magnussen, *Prevention of Wrongful Convictions: Norwegian Legal Safeguards and the Criminal Cases Review Commission*, 80 U. CIN. L. REV. 1373 (2012).

For Switzerland, *see* Gwladys Gillieron, *Wrongful Convictions in Switzerland: A Problem of Summary Proceedings*, 80 U. CIN. L. REV. 1145 (2012).

For Poland, *see* Adam Gorski & Maria Ejchart, *Wrongful Conviction in Poland*, 80 U. CIN. L. REV. 1145 (2012).

For China, *see* HE Jiahong & HE Ran, *Empirical Studies of Wrongful Convictions in Mainland China*, 80 U. CIN. L. REV. 1277 (2012); Huang Shiyuan, *Chinese Wrongful Convictions: Causes and Prevention*, 80 U. CIN. L. REV. 1219 (2012); Huang Shiyuan, *Chinese Wrongful Convictions: Discovery and Rectification*, 80 U. CIN. L. REV. 1195 (2012).

For Japan, *see* Kazuko Ito, *Wrongful Convictions and Recent Criminal Justice Reform in Japan*, 80 U. CIN. L. REV. 1245 (2012).

For Singapore, *see* Cheah Wui Ling, *Developing a People Centered Justice in Singapore: In Support of Pro Bono and Innocence Work*, 80 U. CIN. L. REV. 1429 (2012).

For Latin America, *see* Justin Brooks, *Redinocente: The Challenge of Bringing Innocence Work to Latin America*, 80 U. CIN. L. REV. 1115 (2012).

For Chile, *see* Clauio Pavlic Veliz, *Criminal Procedure Reform: A New Form of Criminal Justice for Chile*, 80 U. CIN. L. REV. 1363 (2012).

For Nigeria, *see* Daniel Ehighalua, *Nigerian Issues in Wrongful Convictions*, 80 U. CIN. L. REV. 1131 (2012).

For South Africa, *see* Jeremy Gordin & Ingrid Cloete, *Imprisoned Before Being Found Guilty: Remand Detainees in South Africa*, 80 U. CIN. L. REV. 1167 (2012).

For Canada, *see* Kent Roach, *Wrongful Convictions in Canada*, 80 U. CIN. L. REV. 1465 (2012).

For Australia, *see* Lynne Weathered, *Wrongful Conviction in Australia*, 80 U. CIN. L. REV. 1391 (2012).

Another journal affiliated with the University of Cincinnati – The Freedom Center Journal – published a special edition in 2010 highlighting the creative work of people exonerated from prison. See *Freedom Center Journal Special Edition Highlights Exonerees' Creative Work*, available at http://law.uc.edu/alumni/con nect/freedom-center.

57 See Red Inocente, *Homepage*, available at http://redinocente.org.

58 The trailer for the film is available at www.youtube.com/watch?v=xx538juk1KI. *See also Court Overturn Fernando Carrera Case after Hunger Strike*, ARGENTINA INDEPENDENT, June 5, 2012, available at www.argentinaindependent.com/tag/ fernando-carrera/.

59 Details of the film can be seen here, www.pbs.org/pov/presumedguilty/ and http:// icarusfilms.com/new2010/guilt.html.

60 The Irish Innocence Project, *Homepage*, available at www.innocenceproject.ie/ about/.

61 *Id.*

62 *Man Hanged 70 Years Ago Is to Be Pardoned*, RTE NEWS, Jan. 9, 2015, available at www.rte.ie/news/2015/0109/671543-pardon-harry-gleeson/.

63 Gemma Deery, *Irish Innocence Project, Harry Gleeson Case Facts*, Feb. 8, 2015, available at www.innocenceproject.ie/cases/harry-gleeson/.

64 *Inaugural International Wrongful Conviction Conference & Film Festival*, available at www.griffith.ie/about-griffith/news/inaugural-international-wrongful-conviction-conference-film-festival.

65 The Norwegian Criminal Cases Review Commission, *Homepage*, available at www.gjenopptakelse.no/index.php?id=163.

66 Stridbeck & Magnussen, *supra* note 56.

67 Knoops' Innocence Project, *Homepage*, available at www.knoops.info/en/knoops-innocence-project_en; and http://wrongfulconvictionsblog.org/?s=knoops.

68 Willem A. Wagenaar, *False Confessions after Repeated Interrogation: The Putten Murder Case*, 10 EUR. REV. 519 (2002).

69 *Id.*

70 *Id.*

71 *Murderer Convicted after Two Already Served Time*, Sept. 10, 2009, available at http://vorige.nrc.nl/international/article2382854.ece/Murderer_convicted_after_two_already_served_time.

72 *10 Notorius Dutch Murders*, available at http://netherlandsbynumbers.com/2015/03/23/10-notorious-dutch-murders/.

73 *Murderer Convicted, supra* note 71.

74 *Id.*

75 *Id.*

76 *Decision of the Dutch Supreme Court (in Dutch)*, available at http://uitspraken.rechtspraak.nl/inziendocument?id=ECLI:NL:GHARN:2011:BU3933.

77 *See Project Innocence France*, available at http://wrongfulconvictionsblog.org/2013/01/15/project-innocence-france/.

78 *See* Italy Innocence Project, *Homepage*, available at http://italyinnocenceproject.org.

79 *Id.*

80 *See Innocence in Poland*, available at http://wrongfulconvictionsblog.org/2012/05/11/innocence-in-poland/.

81 *See Launch of Israeli Wrongful Convictions Clinic*, available at http://wrongfulconvictionsblog.org/2013/01/01/launch-of-israel-innocence-project/.

82 *See Citing U.S. Innocence Model, Israel Grants Inmate Right to Post-Conviction DNA Testing in Case of Murdered Judge*, available at http://wrongfulconvictionsblog.org/2015/06/09/citing-u-s-innocence-model-israel-grants-inmate-right-to-post-conviction-dna-testing-in-case-of-murdered-judge/.

83 The Innocence Project of Singapore is based at the National University of Singapore. For details about this organization, *see* Innocence Project of Singapore, *Homepage*, available at http://sginnocenceproject.com/about-us/.

84 For information about this organization, *see* Innocence Project Philippines Network, *Homepage*, available at https://sites.google.com/site/innocenceprojectphilippines/.

85 Rich Chang, *"Hsichih Trio" Are Finally Freed*, TAIPEI TIMES, Sept. 1, 2012, available at www.taipeitimes.com/News/front/archives/2012/09/01/2003541675.

86 The facts relating to the TAI and the Chen case were taken from emails sent to me by the TAI. A short film about the Chen case is available at https://mail.google.com/mail/u/0/#search/joychen723%40gmail.com+video/14bc55c1f7b0acee?projector=.

87 Huang, *Chinese Wrongful Convictions: Causes and Prevention*, *supra* note 56.

88 *Id.*

89 Ching-Ching Ni, *False Conviction Highlights Legal Flaws in China*, SEATTLE TIMES, Apr. 9, 2005, available at www.seattletimes.com/nation-world/false-conviction-highlights-legal-flaws-in-china/.

90 Huang, *Chinese Wrongful Convictions: Causes and Prevention*, *supra* note 56, at 1230.

91 *Id.*

92 *Id.*

93 *Id.*

94 *Id.* at 1224.

95 *Hubei Man Convicted of Wife's Murder Ten Years Ago Exonerated*, CONGRESSIONAL-EXECUTIVE COMMISSION ON CHINA, Apr. 8, 2005, available at www.cecc.gov/publications/commission-analysis/hubei-man-convicted-of-wifes-murder-ten-years-ago-exonerated.

96 *Id.*

97 Ching-Ching Ni, *Chinese Man Freed after His "Murdered" Wife Shows Up*, LOS ANGELES TIMES, Apr. 8, 2005, available at http://articles.latimes.com/2005/apr/08/world/fg-she8.

98 Huang, *Chinese Wrongful Convictions: Causes and Prevention*, *supra* note 56, at 1238.

99 *Id.*

100 *Id.*

101 *Id.*

102 *Id.* at 1239.

103 *Id.*

104 *Id.*

105 Ni, *supra* note 97.

106 *Id.*

107 *Id.*

108 *Id.*

109 At this time, this was the equivalent of about $55,000 USD.

110 *Public Security Bureau Compensates She Xianglin for Wrongful Imprisonment,* CONGRESSIONAL-EXECUTIVE COMMISSION ON CHINA, Nov. 25, 2005, available at www.cecc.gov/publications/commission-analysis/public-security-bureau-compensates-she-xianglin-for-wrongful.

111 *See China's Top Prosecutor Vows to Fight to Prevent Wrongful Convictions,* available at http://wrongfulconvictionsblog.org/2014/09/08/chinas-top-prosecutor-vows-to-fight-to-prevent-wrongful-convictions/.

112 *See China's Innocence Reforms Showing Results,* available at http://wrongfulconvictionsblog.org/2015/01/31/chinas-innocence-reforms-showing-results/.

113 *See China's Top Judge Apologizes to Nation for Wrongful Convictions,* available at http://wrongfulconvictionsblog.org/2015/03/13/chinas-top-judge-apologizes-to-nation-for-wrongful-convictions/.

114 *See Blog Editors Discuss Wrongful Convictions in China,* available at http://wrongfulconvictionsblog.org/2013/10/06/blog-editors-discuss-wrongful-convictions-in-china/; *Wrongful Convictions Conference in Chine Held August 6–8, 2012,* available at http://wrongfulconvictionsblog.org/2012/08/21/wrongful-convictions-conference-in-china-held-august-6–8-2012/.

115 *See* Wits Justice Project, *Homepage,* available at http://witsjusticeproject.com/about/.

116 *See* Innocence Project SA, *Homepage,* available at http://innocenceprojectsa.com.

117 Molaudzi v. State, CCT 42/15 (Constitutional Court of South Africa, June 25, 2015), available at www.saflii.org/za/cases/ZACC/2015/20.html.

118 *Id.*

119 For articles and other coverage, see *Thembekile Molaudzi Update,* available at http://wrongfulconvictionsblog.org/2015/07/22/thembekile-molaudzi-update/.

120 *Id.*

121 *Id.*

122 *Id.*

123 *Id.*

124 *Id.*

125 *Molaudzi v. State,* CCT 42/15 (Constitutional Court of South Africa, June 25, 2015).

126 *Id.*

127 Carolyn Raphaely, *For Thembekile Molaudzi, Justice Delayed Was Justice Denied*, DAILY MAVERICK, June 30, 2015, available at www.dailymaverick.co.za/article/2015-06-30-for-thembekile-molaudzi-justice-delayed-was-justice-denied/#.VcYigPlViko.

128 *Id.*

129 *Id.*

130 *Id.*

131 *Id.*

132 *Id.*

133 *Id.*

134 *See Thembekile Molaudzi Update, supra* note 119.

135 *See* Raphaely, *supra* note 127.

136 *See Thembekile Molaudzi Update, supra* note 119.

137 *Id.*

138 *Id.*

139 *Id.*

140 *Id.*

141 *Id.*

142 *See* Raphaely, *supra* note 127.

143 *Id.*

144 *See Thembekile Molaudzi Update, supra* note 119; *Molaudzi v. State*, CCT 42/15 (Constitutional Court of South Africa, June 25, 2015).

145 *Id.*

146 *Id.*

147 *Id.*

148 *Id.*

149 United States v. Garsson, 291 F. 646, 649 (S.D.N.Y. 1923).

19

Innocence at War

ERIK LUNA

INTRODUCTION

Some years after the Civil War, General William Tecumseh Sherman sought to disabuse military cadets of any sentimental pretense about their future profession: "I've seen cities and homes in ashes. I've seen thousands of men lying on the ground, their dead faces looking up at the skies. I tell you, war is Hell!"[1] Sherman's famous maxim conveyed the essential element of war as violence, with death and destruction as its direct incidents. This unromanticized view is necessary to understand not only the fundamental character of military combat, but also a principal reason for granting a space for law in war. From the codes of chivalry and the just war tradition, to modern treaties such as the Hague and Geneva Conventions, the law of war has sought to diminish the human suffering that inevitably accompanies armed conflict.[2]

The brunt of war is often borne by the "innocent" – defined for present purposes as individuals who are not involved in the hostilities (a.k.a., "civilians" or "non combatants"), as well as supposed participants in combat who, in fact, are free of any wrongdoing.[3] A primary cause of their suffering is the lack of full and reliable information due to the chaos of combat, frontline constraints on time and resources, the use of stratagems by or against the enemy, and so on. As a result, "it may be difficult to discern whether a person is a combatant, a civilian, or a civilian taking a direct part in hostilities."[4] The distinction among these individuals can pose a question of life or death, and it certainly presents the opportunity for justice miscarried. While the civilian may not be intentionally targeted by military operations, as a general rule both the combatant and the civilian taking direct part in hostilities may be killed with impunity.[5] They also may be detained for the war's duration and subjected to trial and punishment for violating the law of war.[6]

This chapter is interested in the parallel between a particular understanding of the practice and law of war, and the developments in domestic criminal justice attributable to the Innocence Movement. As it turns out, many of the issues in domestic wrongful conviction cases are present in aggravated form in the context of war. Though truth and innocence have always taken a beating on the battlefield, the better angels of our nature would seek to prevent miscarriages of justice in wartime, just as they do in times of peace.

1 *Casualties of War*

The impact of warfare on truth-telling and innocence reverberates throughout the ages. If not apocryphal, it is fitting that Aeschylus, the Greek poet known as the father of tragedy, was the one who coined the phrase *truth is the first casualty of war*. Similar sentiments have been uttered in the intervening millennia,[7] sometimes at the outbreak of hostilities but oftentimes much later, when the fog of war begins to lift and the opportunity is provided for reflection.

In his classic critique of lies propagated during World War I, British politician and activist Arthur Ponsonby wrote that the "ignorant and innocent masses in each country are unaware at the time that they are being misled, and when it is all over only here and there are the falsehoods discovered and exposed."[8] Truth's distortion or its outright rejection can be an effective instrument of warfare, intended to deceive the enemy, to gain the support of nonaligned parties, and even to hoodwink a nation's own citizenry. Indeed, people may be prepared to delude themselves to rationalize their own wartime actions. In Ponsonby's words, "there is a sort of national wink, everyone goes forward, and the individual, in his turn, takes up lying as a patriotic duty."[9]

The lies can take many forms, Lord Ponsonby suggested, most of them residing on the level of general political propaganda. But the suspension of truth also has obvious relevance to individual miscarriages of justice, resulting from "false charges made in a prejudiced war atmosphere."[10] Members of the modern Innocence Movement will be familiar with the problematic sources, such as the inherent deficiencies of human testimony:

> No two people can relate the occurrence of a street accident so as to make the two stories tally. When bias and emotion are introduced, human testimony becomes quite valueless. In war-time such testimony is accepted as conclusive. The scrappiest and most unreliable evidence is sufficient – "the friend of the brother of a man who was killed," or, as a German investigator of his own liars puts it, "somebody who had seen it," or, "an extremely respectable old woman."[11]

The ready acceptance of dubious information indicates the success of wartime propaganda principles: the enemy is the face of evil and solely responsible for war; one's nation is defending a noble, if not sacred, cause; the cruelties and injustices of war are always intended by the enemy, but are inadvertent when done by one's own side; and all who doubt the truth of government information are traitors.[12]

If truth is the first fatality in armed conflict, then innocence perishes alongside. Military history serves as a rolling chronicle of civilians killed, injured, or otherwise mistreated during the course of belligerence. Consider the saying, *kill them all and let God sort it out*, which is the modern rendition of a fiery abbot's advice during an early thirteenth-century crusade. Responding to soldiers concerned that they could not distinguish the faithful from the heretics, the abbot purportedly said: "Kill them, for the Lord knows those that are his own" (*Caedite eos, novit enim Dominus qui sunt eius*).[13] And that is precisely what happened in the besieged French town of Béziers, as thousands of men, women, and children were slain without regard to any personal conception of guilt. The massacre occurred, at least formally, under the auspices of Pope Innocent III – perhaps the most ironically named religious leader of all time. The crusader's callous disregard for innocence smacks of hypocrisy, of course, given that Christians historically considered the Romans' mistreatment of Jesus of Nazareth to be the greatest miscarriage of justice. Certainly, it is the best-known wrongful conviction and execution occurring in the throes of a foreign military occupation. As Mark Osler emphasizes in his book, *Jesus on Death Row*: "The Bible takes pains to point out the innocence of Christ in the specific context of his trial, conviction, appeals, and execution. Specifically, two actors in the trial and execution [i.e., Pontius Pilate and an unnamed Roman centurion] seemed stricken with guilt at their actions due to Christ's innocence."[14]

Wartime miscarriages of justice have occurred throughout recorded history, though often the scope of the problem has been unclear. Consider, for instance, the phenomenon of wartime military tribunals. Impromptu trials by court-martial or military commission could dispense "drumhead" justice, purportedly named for the practice of employing a drum as a writing table during the proceedings. The trials were hardly the model of due process, which is unsurprising given that many were held on or near the battlefield. They offered a rough-and-ready means to deal with alleged war crimes by enemy combatants, the wrongdoing or disobedience of one's own soldiers, and even offenses committed by civilians.[15] The improvised procedures of battlefield tribunals were oriented toward maximal efficiency and audience impact, not factual accuracy or the prevention of substantive and procedural injustices. For example, during the Mexican-American War, General Winfield Scott created "councils of war" to try Mexican guerillas for military offenses related to their style of warfare. An alleged enemy guerrilla might be captured, tried, and executed within a few days, so that "as many Mexicans [could] witness the execution as possible" and serve a "blow to guerrillas in that part of the country."[16] Likewise, thousands of trials by military commission were conducted during the U.S. Civil War, often pursuant to informal procedures lacking safeguards against miscarriages of justice. Emblematic of this problem were cases where the accused was tried for the offense of "being a bad and dangerous man."[17]

The twentieth century's global conflagrations witnessed further examples of wartime disregard for truth and innocence, including a particularly grotesque incident at the outset of World War I. In February 1915, the commander of a French infantry division, General Géraud Réveilhac, ordered a series of hopeless assaults on a German redoubt near the town of Souain. Each attack was repelled until the French troops simply refused to leave the trenches, at which point Réveilhac ordered an artillery barrage upon his own soldiers in order to force them into another assault against the German fortifications (thankfully, the artillerymen refused to bomb their comrades). After the final assault failed miserably, Réveilhac ordered the military trial of thirty infantrymen for cowardice, resulting in the conviction and execution of four corporals, all to set an example for other soldiers and to deflect blame for the leadership's disastrous strategy.[18] Not only was the trial a sham, but the arbitrary selection of the condemned men seems reminiscent of the Roman practice of "decimation" – selecting soldiers by lot to be executed for offenses allegedly committed by their military unit (e.g., mutiny or desertion).[19]

Even military trials attracting public attention and reflecting high-level government deliberations have nonetheless adopted approaches lacking the legal safeguards thought to be necessary for accurate fact-finding and the prevention of wrongful convictions. For instance, at the end of World War II, a U.S. military commission in Manila tried and convicted Japanese General Tomoyuki Yamashita for failing to prevent his troops from committing atrocities against civilians and prisoners of war in the Philippines. The tribunal was composed of six U.S. generals, none of whom was a lawyer or had significant experience in combat command. The American military officers appointed to defend Yamashita were given only three weeks to prepare for trial, search for witnesses, and research the 123 charges against their client.[20] Neither the allegations nor any credible evidence directly linked Yamashita to the underlying atrocities.[21] Some offenses were committed under the command of others or in situations where Yamashita could not exercise his authority due to the effectiveness of American forces at disrupting Japanese lines of command and control.[22] Apparently, international correspondents covering the trial believed that the defendant would be acquitted.[23] Nonetheless, the tribunal found Yamashita guilty and sentenced him to death, an outcome upheld a few months later by the U.S. Supreme Court.[24]

In dissent, Justice Frank Murphy said Yamashita had been "rushed to trial under an improper charge, given insufficient time to prepare an adequate defense, deprived of the benefits of some of the most elementary rules of evidence and summarily sentenced to be hanged."[25] Likewise, Justice Wiley Rutledge objected that it was "not in our tradition for anyone to be charged with crime ... in language not sufficient to inform him of the nature of the offense or to enable him to make a defense."[26] Most of all, the dissenters were concerned about the tribunal's disregard for individual culpability as a polestar of justice. In private correspondence, Justice Rutledge wrote that the *Yamashita* decision "will outrank *Dred Scott* in the annals of the Court."[27] But the prevailing attitude was that otherwise legitimate objectives – for example, "to advance the cause of peace and right notions of international law"[28] – could excuse the danger of wrongful convictions. As argued by a former prosecutor in the Tokyo war crimes tribunal:

> Had there been an actual miscarriage of justice with regard to some of the defendants, there would have been no wrong, because it would have been only incidental to the main purpose, namely, the punishment of the guilty.... The situation of the defendants was comparable to that of American soldiers about to take a beachhead; that is, the lives of morally and legally innocent men may be sacrificed in the achievement of the ultimate purpose, but the common good requires the taking of the beachhead.[29]

To be sure, evidence of personal guilt was clear in most post-WWII military trials. Moreover, the tribunals rebuffed most defense attempts to deflect command responsibility, as well as claims by an accused that he was simply following superior orders. The latter argument, now referred to as the "Nuremberg defense," was rejected at the trial of leading Nazi officials before the International Military Tribunal (IMT) in Nuremberg, Germany.[30] The IMT emphasized that "participation in [war crimes] has never been required of any soldier, and he cannot now shield himself behind a mythical requirement of soldierly obedience at all costs as his excuse for commission of these crimes."[31] As for command responsibility, the doctrine is now well-established in international criminal law and requires that a commander knew or had reason to know of his subordinates' crimes but failed to take steps to prevent or punish such wrongdoing.[32]

In the *Yamashita* case, there was no serious dispute as to the extent and savagery of the crimes committed. In fact, General Yamashita may well have known, or at least should have known, of the war crimes being committed by his soldiers. What is troubling to this day, however, is the acceptance of wartime standards that appear to invite guilt by association or perhaps vicarious and strict liability.[33] Alternatively, the *Yamashita* approach to command responsibility may function like a high-end status crime: General Yamashita was guilty simply because he was the *commander* on whose watch various war crimes were committed by his subordinates. Regardless, the broad scope of liability poses a danger to those innocent of any wrongdoing but nonetheless embroiled in the decision-making of belligerents.

2 *Beyond the Fog of War*

To admit that truth and innocence have been victims of war throughout history is not to say, of course, it *ought* to be that way under any decent legal theory. To the contrary, truth and innocence matter greatly both in peace and in wartime. As Harry Frankfurt has argued, even a minimally functional society must maintain a vigorous understanding of the instrumental value of truth:

> After all, how could a society that cared too little for truth make sufficiently well-informed judgments and decisions concerning the most suitable disposition of its public business? How could it possibly flourish, or even survive, without knowing enough about relevant facts to pursue its ambitions successfully and to cope prudently and effectively with its problems? ... [H]igher levels of civilization must depend even more heavily on a conscientious respect for the importance of honesty and clarity in reporting the facts, and on a stubborn concern for accuracy in determining what the facts are.[34]

Decent conceptions of democratic rule and individual liberty seem to demand a level of respect for the truth so as to ensure that government decisions are subject to the political mechanisms of change. The citizenry cannot effectively assess the performance of its elected representatives without knowing what decisions were made, what actions were taken, and the factual basis for both. These concerns are magnified when the decisions concern the military, the most powerful physical institution of humanity. At times, "the only effective restraint on executive policy and power in the areas of national defense and international affairs may lie in an enlightened citizenry," Justice Potter Stewart wrote in his concurrence in the *Pentagon Papers* case.[35] Justice William O. Douglas was even blunter, stating that the flow of truthful information to the public was necessary "to prevent any part of the government from deceiving the people and sending them off to distant lands to die of foreign fevers and foreign shot and shell."[36]

The importance of truth in wartime can also be viewed as a matter of moral precept. "[E]ven God cannot cause that two times two should not make four," wrote Hugo Grotius, the father of international law.[37] For some, the goal is setting the record straight for the sake of justice (however defined). In the words of one prominent international jurist, "there is no peace without justice [and] there is no justice without truth, meaning the entire truth and nothing but the truth."[38] Among other things, the truth-telling function in wartime proceedings can help prevent post-conflict societies from retreating into denial. For Justice Robert Jackson, who served as the chief American prosecutor at Nuremberg, the legacy of the war crimes trials was their documentation of "Nazi aggressions, persecutions, and atrocities with such authenticity and in such detail that there can be no responsible denial of these crimes in the future and no tradition of martyrdom of the Nazi leaders can arise among informed people."[39]

Just as a commitment to truth-seeking is necessary to ensure an accurate historical record of wartime wrongdoing by the guilty, so it is necessary to help safeguard the innocent through the medium of the law of war. As it developed over several millennia, the law of war has taken as a core goal the protection of the *innocent*, understood both as a class of people (civilians or noncombatants) and as an objective truth about certain events (actual innocence). A doctrine of military ethics for violent conflict known as "just war" theory sets out the conditions for resorting to military force (*jus ad bellum*) and the limitations on the use of such force (*jus in bello*).[40] Among the basic principles of *jus in bello* is "distinction" or "discrimination": warfare must be directed toward enemy combatants and not noncombatants (i.e., civilians). The modern, treaty-based law of war – often referred to today as the law of armed conflict (LOAC) or international humanitarian law (IHL) – also codifies the principle of distinction. For instance, one of the protocols added to the 1949 Geneva Conventions requires combatants to distinguish civilians from other combatants at all times, while also prohibiting indiscriminate attacks against civilian populations and the deliberate targeting of individual civilians so long as they do not directly partake in hostilities.[41]

Obviously, military detention and trial in wartime implicate concerns of actual innocence. In his *Yamashita* dissent, Justice Murphy wrote of the "universal and indestructible nature" of certain rights, including the concept of due process protected by the U.S. Constitution:

> No exception is made as to those who are accused of war crimes or as to those who possess the status of an enemy belligerent. Indeed, such an exception

would be contrary to the whole philosophy of human rights .... The immutable rights of the individual ... belong not alone to the members of those nations that excel on the battlefield or that subscribe to the democratic ideology. They belong to every person in the world, victor or vanquished, whatever may be his race, color or beliefs. They rise above any status of belligerency or outlawry. They survive any popular passion or frenzy of the moment. No court or legislature or executive, not even the mightiest army in the world, can ever destroy them.[42]

Justice Murphy may have been on the losing side in *Yamashita*, but his position is more faithful to the modern law of war and its concerns for innocence. With regard to military detention, the fourth Geneva Convention declares that "internment [of civilians] may be ordered only if the security of the Detaining Power makes it absolutely necessary."[43] The provision's objective was "to put an end to an abuse which occurred during the Second World War. All too often the mere fact of being an enemy subject was regarded as justifying internment."[44] The Convention also makes "unlawful confinement" of civilians a war crime, a position later codified by, *inter alia*, the governing statutes of the International Criminal Court (ICC) and the International Criminal Tribunal for the Former Yugoslavia (ICTY).[45] Likewise, a draft code by the International Law Commission would make "arbitrary imprisonment" a crime against humanity.[46] As for prisoners of war, international law makes clear that military detention can last no longer than active hostilities unless the detainees are lawfully being prosecuted or have been tried and sentenced for crimes.[47]

The modern law of war also stresses the importance of personal culpability as the basis for deprivations of liberty. Wartime internment and other methods of confining civilians are "exceptional measures to be taken only after careful consideration of each individual case," opined the ICTY trial chamber. "Such measures are never to be taken on a collective basis."[48] As for trials of civilians and prisoners of war, the Geneva Conventions and additional protocols are adamant that "[n]o one shall be convicted of an offence except on the basis of individual penal responsibility."[49] Nor may anyone be "punished for an offence he or she has not personally committed."[50] Collective penalties are strictly prohibited.[51] As put by the Special Court for Sierra Leone, a hybrid war crimes tribunal:

[T]he prohibition of collective punishments in international humanitarian law is based on one of the most fundamental principles of domestic criminal law that is reflected in national systems around the world: the principle of individual responsibility. The principle of individual responsibility requires that, whether an accused be tried singly or jointly, a determination must be made as to the penal responsibility and appropriate punishment of each individual on trial.[52]

Obviously, the requirement of personal culpability is intended to protect the factually innocent, who are also shielded by a presumption of innocence under the modern law of war. The additional protocols to the Geneva Conventions provide that "[a]nyone charged with an offence is presumed innocent until proved guilty according to the law";[53] other international instruments place upon the prosecution the burden of proving the accused guilty beyond a reasonable doubt.[54] These safeguards of innocence are buttressed by the requisite structure and procedures of wartime tribunals. So-called "Common Article 3" of the Geneva Conventions, which sets out certain non-derogable rules for all parties and armed conflicts, requires that any trial be conducted "by a regularly constituted court, affording all the judicial guarantees which are recognized as indispensable by civilized peoples."[55] Today, the necessary procedures to ensure a fair trial include, *inter alia*: sufficient notice of the charges, adequate time and facilities to prepare a defense, the assistance of legal counsel, the right to be present at trial proceedings, the expectation of a public trial conducted without undue delay, the privilege of the accused not to be compelled to testify against himself, the power to obtain witnesses for the defense and to examine adverse witnesses, and the right of appeal to a higher tribunal.

These requirements for wartime tribunals, like their procedural analogues in ordinary criminal courts, all help to protect the actually innocent. One might argue further that, post-Nuremberg, these procedures have achieved a degree of success in various war crimes trials in The Hague, where international tribunals have often bent over backwards to ensure that only the factually guilty are convicted and punished. As far as I know, the modern hub of international law has not witnessed a viable claim of wrongful conviction.[56]

Other innovations of law and justice include so-called "truth commissions." When a commission tries to live up to its moniker, the process can help decrease the number of lies that go unopposed in a post-conflict society. The outcome is hardly inconsequential, as Michael Ignatieff has observed: "In Argentina, its work has made it impossible to claim, for example, that the military did not throw half-dead victims in the sea from helicopters. In Chile, it is no longer permissible to assert in public that the Pinochet regime did not dispatch thousands of entirely innocent people."[57] The most famous truth-telling body – South Africa's Truth and Reconciliation Commission – through its airing of painful facts and presentation of an unvarnished reality, may have achieved a higher degree of justice *writ large* than any criminal court could have dispensed.

3 *The War on Terror*

Truth and innocence have fared substantially worse in the international and intergenerational wars against terrorism. Some difficulties involve the appropriate definition of terrorism, a problem that I will simply elide here; for present purposes, one could assume that the term "terrorist" refers to an individual or subnational group member who uses violence against civilians for political purposes. Another problem is the lack of agreement on the appropriate legal status of a terrorist – unlawful combatant, civilian participant in hostilities, modern equivalent of a pirate, domestic scofflaw, war criminal, etc. – and as such, confusion reigns as to the applicable rules defining and limiting a nation's responses to terrorism. But for now, let's accept war as the appropriate model for counterterrorism efforts.

Here, I wish to focus on the effect of wartime counterterrorism efforts on truth and innocence. All the problems that war poses for truth-finding and protecting the innocent are present in modern responses to terrorism. In particular, terrorist acts cause panic among a population – indeed, terrorism is intended to do so – which, in turn, prompts government officials to take swift and severe actions which depart from ordinary standards of due process and even the expectations under the law of war. "Societies dealing with terrorism and the fear of terrorism are liable to forget not only that past anti-terrorism laws have not made them safer," wrote legal scholars Kent Roach and Gary Trotter, "but also that they have contributed to miscarriages of justice."[58] Several decades ago, for instance, the United Kingdom suffered a spate of wrongful convictions arising from "the Troubles," the decades-long conflict between Catholic nationalists and Protestant unionists in Northern Ireland, resulting in horrific acts of violence there and across the British Isles. The cases involved actual or threatened bombings and were prosecuted in an environment of public angst over terrorism by the Irish Republican Army and other groups. One prominent British jurist even suggested that it would have been better if the defendants had been hanged in the so-called Birmingham Six case. Although the innocent might be punished, Lord Denning said "the whole community would be satisfied."[59]

Eventually, the Birmingham Six – as well as the Guilford Four and the Maguire Seven – would be released out of concern for what are now know to be common causes of wrongful convictions: false witness statements, unreliable confessions, bogus expert testimony, misconstrued facts, undisclosed evidence, and so on.[60] Still other problems were related to the seemingly martial nature of the conflict in Northern Ireland. Information used against a suspect might involve national security information deemed too sensitive to reveal to the defendant; or it might take the form of raw data from intelligence surveillance, both domestic and military, with the information often arriving in layers of hearsay and perhaps some unsourced judgments. A postmortem report on one of the cases acknowledged that decision-makers were affected by an ethos of fear and belligerence, such that "the context of the prevailing bombing campaign and the atmosphere of the trial made it impossible for them to make a wholly objective and dispassionate appraisal of the admissible evidence alone."[61]

At times, modern counterterrorism efforts have also rejected the ban on collective punishment applicable both in peace and in war. Consider, for instance, house demolitions in the ongoing violent conflict between Israelis and Palestinians. Pursuant to long-standing emergency regulations, the Israel Defense Forces were empowered to demolish a house due to a resident's involvement in terrorism despite the fact that other residents affected by the military order might be entirely innocent. Although "suffering and misery may be caused to persons who did not themselves commit any crime,"[62] the Israeli Supreme Court upheld the house demotions because they served the goal of deterrence based on the belief that "family pressure does discourage terrorists."[63] One dissenting justice wrote that the demolitions violated "a basic principle which our people have always recognized and reiterated: every man must pay for his own crimes."[64] Chief Justice Aharon Barak, the author of the majority opinion, would later express remorse over the ruling and describe house demolitions as "unworthy and of no use."[65]

As discussed earlier, collective punishments are inconsistent with the modern law of war and, in particular, Article 33 of the fourth Geneva Convention, which bans collective penalties as well as "all measures of intimidation or of terrorism."[66] The official commentary on Article 33 notes that in past conflicts some belligerents had resorted "to intimidatory measures to terrorise the population."[67]

> Far from achieving the desired effect, however, such practices, by reason of their excessive severity and cruelty, kept alive and strengthened the spirit of resistance. They strike at guilty and innocent alike. They are opposed to all principles based on humanity and justice[.][68]

The use of the word "terrorism" in Article 33 helps accentuate the irony of the demolition policy, in which the government response to terrorist attacks bears at least some of the hallmarks of terrorism. As Professor Roach has argued, "A democracy that resorts to collective punishment when combating terrorism loses its upper hand by accepting the way of the terrorist by punishing the innocent."[69]

The lessons of prior terrorism-related injustices have not always been heeded in America's post-9/11 counterterrorism efforts, as seen in the U.S. government's wartime approach to apprehension and detention. A month after 9/11, President Bush issued an order authorizing military detention of suspected terrorists and their collaborators, as well as military trials for those who violated the law of war.[70] Beginning in early 2002, individuals captured in Afghanistan and elsewhere were taken to the U.S. Naval Base in Guantánamo Bay, Cuba, with a few people detained at military facilities in the United States. Nearly 800 people, claiming citizenship from forty-eight different nations, would be sent to Guantánamo from places around the world. In the coming years, several Guantánamo detainees would be deemed eligible for trial by military commission.

These practices raise myriad legal questions that are beyond the scope of this short chapter. Here, I wish only to discuss the issues of truth and innocence prompted by such practices. As has been discussed at length elsewhere, the detainees sought to challenge their confinement in federal court, often arguing that they were civilian noncombatants and therefore unamenable to military detention under the law of war. In other words, they claimed to be innocent. The situation for one group of Guantánamo detainees was described as follows:

> They are not nationals of countries at war with the United States, and they deny that they have engaged in or plotted acts of aggression against the United States; they have never been afforded access to any tribunal, much less charged with and convicted of wrongdoing; and for more than two years they have been imprisoned in territory over which the United States exercises exclusive jurisdiction and control.[71]

In a case involving an American citizen held in a naval brig in South Carolina, the Supreme Court wrote that the danger of indefinite detention of suspected enemy combatants was "not farfetched" since "the national security underpinnings of the 'war on terror,' although crucially important, are broad and malleable," and "the current conflict is unlikely to end with a formal cease-fire agreement."[72] If the war on terror is not considered won for several generations, and if a detainee is still regarded as a threat to rejoin the fight against the United States, he could be detained for the rest of his life. Of particular relevance, the Court acknowledged that "the risk of erroneous deprivation of a citizen's liberty in the absence of sufficient process here is very real," referencing an amicus brief that noted the ways in which "[t]he nature of humanitarian relief work and journalism present a significant risk of mistaken military detentions."[73] Similar concerns applied to the Guantánamo detainees, who were being held indefinitely in the absence of legal proceedings to determine their status, an approach that "allows friends and foes alike to remain in detention."[74] Some decent fact-finding process was necessary to ensure "that the errant tourist, embedded journalist, or local aid worker has a chance to prove military error."[75]

Eventually, the few military detainees held within the continental United States were either released or transferred to civil authorities for prosecution in domestic courts. Most of the detainees in Guantánamo were sent before administrative panels known as Combatant Status Review Tribunals (CSRTs), which were established to determine whether a given detainee was an "enemy combatant." This scheme was better than no process, of course, but the protections afforded in CSRT hearings fell "well short of the procedures and adversarial mechanisms"[76] needed to safeguard those detainees who were, in fact, innocent. The most relevant deficiencies concerned a detainee's ability to rebut the factual basis for his designation as an enemy combatant:

> [A]t the CSRT stage the detainee has limited means to find or present evidence to challenge the Government's case against him. He does not have the assistance of counsel and may not be aware of the most critical allegations that the Government relied upon to order his detention. The detainee can confront witnesses that testify during the CSRT proceedings. But given that there are in effect no limits on the admission of hearsay evidence – the only requirement is that the tribunal deem the evidence "relevant and helpful" – the detainee's opportunity to question witnesses is likely to be more theoretical than real.[77]

This process generated a risk of erroneous fact-finding "too significant to ignore," the Supreme Court argued, given that a mistake could result in an individual's detention for the duration of a war that could last multiple generations.[78] The need was particularly acute since, by the time the Court issued its final Guantánamo-related opinion, some of the detainees had been in custody for six years without a definitive judicial determination regarding the legality of their detention. "Within the Constitution's separation-of-powers structure, few exercises of judicial power are as legitimate or as necessary as the responsibility to hear challenges to the authority of the Executive to imprison a person."[79] Among other things, a reviewing court must be able to correct errors that occurred during an executive process like the CSRT, including the authority "to assess the sufficiency of the Government's evidence against the detainee," and "to admit and consider relevant exculpatory evidence that was not introduced during the earlier proceeding."[80]

The Supreme Court's post-9/11 jurisprudence on military detention can be seen as a species of actual innocence law.[81] The Justices provided only the

most basic outlines of an acceptable process, however, and Congress declined
to fill in the details. As a result, the evolving law of wartime detention has been
"written by judges through the common-law process of litigating the habeas
corpus cases of [those] detainees still held at Guantánamo."[82] For instance,
government proof by a preponderance of the evidence was found to be
constitutionally acceptable, although some opinions suggest that detention
might be permitted under a lesser standard of proof.[83] Hearsay has been
deemed fully admissible regardless of any constraints applied in ordinary court
proceedings.[84] In one case, the relevant hearsay concerned travel routes, based
on government claims that "an individual using this travel route to reach
Kandahar may have done so because it was a route used by some individuals
seeking to enter Afghanistan for the purpose of jihad."[85]

In addition, the courts have held that intelligence reports should be given
the presumption that the reporting agent accurately identified the intelligence
source and accurately summarized his statement.[86] In dissent, Judge David
Tatel expressed concern about applying a presumption of regularity to documents produced in wartime:

> [T]he report at issue here was produced in the fog of war by a clandestine
> method that we know almost nothing about. It is not familiar, transparent,
> generally understood as reliable, or accessible; nor is it mundane, quotidian
> data entry akin to state court dockets or tax receipts. Its output [was] prepared
> in stressful and chaotic conditions, filtered through interpreters, subject to
> transcription errors, and heavily redacted for national security purposes.[87]

As a practical matter, Judge Tatel feared that the presumption "comes perilously close to suggesting that whatever the government says must be treated as
true."[88]

In the years since Guantánamo opened, disclosures in court and in the
media have shown that innocent people have been detained for years without
relief. Among the classified documents released by the website WikiLeaks were
U.S. military dossiers revealing that at least 150 of the Guantánamo detainees
were not Al Qaeda operatives or Taliban fighters, but instead innocent people
swept up in a post-9/11 dragnet.[89] They were then held for years due to
mistaken identification, false statements, unreliable interrogation, misconstrued facts, erroneous intelligence, or merely for being in the wrong place at
the wrong time.[90] Allegedly incriminating evidence included wearing a particular type of watch, possessing a calculator, being captured without travel
documents, or simply refusing to cooperate with interrogators. In fact, some
detainees were known to be innocent and yet remained in custody because
they might have some intelligence value. Perhaps the most pitiful example is

that of a 14-year-old boy who had been kidnapped at gunpoint, allegedly raped by a group of men, and forced to work in the compound of a Taliban warlord. Despite being a victim, he was shipped to Guantánamo "because of his possible knowledge of Taliban resistance efforts and local leaders."[91]

Worse yet, there are indications that the executive branch was fully aware of the wrongful detentions in Guantánamo but refused to remedy the situation. A former military officer and high-ranking state department official stated under oath that many of the detainees were "victims of incompetent battlefield vetting" that offered "no meaningful way to determine whether they were terrorists, Taliban, or simply innocent civilians picked up on a very confused battlefield or in the territory of another state such as Pakistan."[92] The continued detention of the innocent rested in part on a cynical calculus that it would be politically impossible to release the detainees. Apparently, "noble cause corruption"[93] infected some high-ranking officials, who were not concerned that many detainees were innocent or that there was no useable evidence warranting detention. "If hundreds of innocent individuals had to suffer in order to detain a handful of hardcore terrorists, so be it . . . Their view was that innocent people languishing in Guantánamo for years was justified by the broader war on terror."[94] In other words, detain them all and let Allah sort them out.

FINAL THOUGHT

This chapter began by referencing General Sherman's declaration that war is hell, which has become a sort of leitmotif of modern writing on armed conflict. In fact, however, war is far worse than hell in the theological sense, as Michael Walzer has pointed out:

> For in hell, presumably, only those people suffer who deserve to suffer, who have chosen activities for which punishment is the appropriate divine response, knowing that this is so. But the greater number by far of those who suffer in war have made no comparable choice.[95]

This reality may be generally tolerated due to the chaotic nature of warfare and the absence of complete and accurate information for military decision-makers. But it is not always the case that innocence must be sacrificed in the midst of armed conflict. While caring for British soldiers in the Crimean War, Florence Nightingale described the "horrors of war" away from the battlefield:

> [T]hey are not wounds and blood and fever, spotted and low, or dysentery, chronic and acute, cold and heat and famine – they are intoxication, brutality, demoralization and disorder on the part of the inferior, jealousies, meanness, indifference, selfish brutality on the part of the superior.[96]

Although we may have no choice but to countenance the death and suffering of innocents in a war's frontline inferno, we should be far less willing to do so away from the battlefield. Halfway around the world, in the safety of a Caribbean naval base, any miscarriages of justice will not occur because of mortar fire overhead and severed lines of communication, but due to the perceived difficulties of accurate decision-making and perhaps a level of apathy toward those who may have been wrongfully captured. The present volume is dedicated to the modern history of exonerations in domestic criminal justice, offering an appreciation of the lessons that have been learned over the past quarter century. Maybe it is time for those lessons to be applied to the burgeoning practice of the law of war.

NOTES

1 ANTHONY KING, THE COMBAT SOLDIER: INFANTRY TACTICS AND COHESION IN THE TWENTIETH AND TWENTY-FIRST CENTURIES 1 (2013) (quoting Sherman).

2 As defined in a recently published U.S. military manual, the law of war is that body of international law, including both treaties and customary international law, "that regulates the resort to armed force; the conduct of hostilities and the protection of war victims in both international and non-international armed conflict; belligerent occupation; and the relationships between belligerent, neutral, and non-belligerent States." U.S. DEP'T OF DEFENSE, LAW OF WAR MANUAL 7 (2015). Also, it should be noted that this chapter uses synonymously the terms "war," "armed conflict," and "hostilities" (as well as words like "combat"), although meaningful distinctions can be drawn among them. In particular, the Geneva Conventions represent a twentieth-century trend toward armed conflict as the operative term. Common Article 2 of the Geneva Conventions states that its provisions "shall apply to all cases of declared war or of *any other armed conflict* ... even if the state of war is not recognized by one of [the belligerent nations]" (emphasis added), while Common Article 3 applies "[i]n the case of armed conflict not of an international character." By contrast, the War Powers Resolution (WPR), Pub. L. No. 93–148, 87 Stat. 555 (1973), uses the word hostilities instead of armed conflict, apparently because the former phrase was thought to be broader in scope, going beyond actual fighting to include "a state of confrontation in which no shots have been fired but where there is a clear and present danger of armed conflict." H.R. REP. No. 93–287, at 7 (1973).

3 For the most part, scholarly discussion has focused on a conception of innocence that distinguishes between combatants and civilians. *See, e.g.,* COLM MCKEOUGH, INNOCENT CIVILIANS (2002). In the context of combat, the term innocent may carry other meanings as well; for instance, it may refer to people ignorant of war's cruelties and whose naiveté is lost in the experience of armed conflict. *See, e.g.,* TOBEY C. HERZOG, VIETNAM WAR STORIES: INNOCENCE LOST (1992). This chapter focuses on understandings of innocence that parallel the term's construction within the Innocence Movement.

4 LAW OF WAR MANUAL, *supra* note 2, at 192.

5 *See infra* text accompanying notes 40–41.

6 *See, e.g.*, Hamdi v. Rumsfeld, 542 U.S. 507, 518 (2004).

7 *See, e.g.*, WAR AND CONFLICT QUOTATIONS: A WORLDWIDE DICTIONARY 115 (Michael C. Thomsett & Jean Freestone Thomsett, eds., 1997).

8 ARTHUR PONSONBY, FALSEHOOD IN WAR-TIME: PROPAGANDA LIES OF THE FIRST WORLD WAR 13 (1942). For a critique arguing that Lord Ponsonby's book was "not an inquiry into propaganda" but rather was "propaganda of the most passionate sort," see ADRIAN GREGORY, THE LAST GREAT WAR: BRITISH SOCIETY AND THE FIRST WORLD WAR 43 (2009).

9 PONSONBY, *supra* note 8, at 16.

10 *Id.* at 24.

11 *Id.* at 22–23.

12 *See* ANNE MORELLI, PRINCIPES ÉLÉMENTAIRES DE PROPAGANDE DE GUERRE 93 (2001) (summarizing and systematizing Ponsonby's principles).

13 EMIL REICH, SELECT DOCUMENTS ILLUSTRATING MEDIAEVAL AND MODERN HISTORY 180–81 (2004).

14 MARK OSLER, JESUS ON DEATH ROW: THE TRIAL OF JESUS AND AMERICAN CAPITAL PUNISHMENT 136 (2009).

15 *Cf.* Hamdan v. Rumsfeld, 548 U.S. 557, 590–91, 595–96 (2006). *But see, e.g.*, *Ex parte* Milligan, 71 U.S. (4 Wall.) 2, 121–22 (1866) (holding that an American civilian is not subject to military trial while U.S. domestic courts remain open and operating).

16 Erika Myers, *Conquering Peace: Military Commissions as a Lawfare Strategy in the Mexican War*, 35 AM. J. CRIM. L. 201, 232 (2008) (quoting Brigadier General Walter Lane).

17 *See, e.g.*, Al Bahlul v. United States, 767 F.3d 1, 27 (D.C. Cir. 2014). *See also* MARK E. NEELY JR., THE FATE OF LIBERTY: ABRAHAM LINCOLN AND CIVIL LIBERTIES 168–77 (1991).

18 The incident provided the basis for Stanley Kubrick's 1957 movie classic, PATHS OF GLORY. *See, e.g.*, Alex von Tunzelmann, *Paths of Glory Clears a Route through World War One's Moral Mudbath*, THE GUARDIAN, Oct. 13, 2013.

19 *See, e.g.*, G. R. WATSON, THE ROMAN SOLDIER 119–20 (1969). Apparently, Réveilhac was later named a Grand Officer of the Legion of Honor. Only after Réveilhac's death were his actions in Souain fully revealed and condemned.

20 *See* Louis Fisher, Cong. Research Service, RL 32458, *Military Tribunals: Historical Patterns and Lessons* 53 (2004) [hereinafter Fisher, *Historical Patterns*].

21 *See id.* at 54.

22 *See, e.g.*, *In re* Yamashita, 327 U.S. 1, 31–35 (1946) (Murphy, J., dissenting); Louis Fisher, *Military Tribunals: A Sorry History*, 33 PRESIDENTIAL STUD. Q. 484, 499 (2003).

23 *See* Fisher, *Historical Patterns*, *supra* note 20, at 54.

24 *See In re* Yamashita, 327 U.S. 1 (1946).

25 *Id.* at 27–28 (Murphy, J., dissenting).

26 *Id.* at 43 (Rutledge, J., dissenting).

27 *See* Fisher, *Historical Patterns, supra* note 20, at 53.

28 JOSEPH B. KEENAN & BRENDAN F. BROWN, CRIMES AGAINST INTER-NATIONAL LAW 155 (1950).

29 *Id.* at 157.

30 *See* The Nuremberg Trial, 6 F.R.D. 69, 110–11 (1947).

31 *Id.* at 177.

32 *See, e.g.,* Allison Marston Danner & Jenny S. Martinez, *Guilty Associations: Joint Criminal Enterprise, Command Responsibility, and the Development of International Criminal Law,* 93 CAL. L. REV. 75, 120–22 (2005).

33 *See, e.g.,* Mirjan Damaška, *The Shadow Side of Command Responsibility,* 49 AM. J. COMP. L. 455, 478–81 (2001).

34 HARRY FRANKFURT, ON TRUTH 15–16 (2006).

35 New York Times Co. v. United States, 403 U.S. 713, 728 (1971) (Stewart, J., concurring).

36 *Id.* at 717 (Douglas, J., concurring).

37 HUGO GROTIUS, ON THE LAW OF WAR AND PEACE 1.10.5.

38 Prosecutor v. Deronjić, Case No. IT-02-61-S, Sentencing Judgment, Dissenting Opinion of Judge Schomburg at ¶ 6 (Mar. 30, 2004).

39 International Conference on Military Trials: London, 1945, *Report to the President by Mr. Justice Jackson,* Oct. 7, 1946, available at http://avalon.law.yale.edu/imt/jack63.asp. Consider also this purported exchange at the Versailles Peace Conference in 1919: When someone suggested that generations of historians would be arguing over who was responsible for starting the Great War, French Prime Minister Georges Clemenceau responded, "Yes, but one thing is certain: They will not say that Belgium invaded Germany."

40 A recent and underdeveloped third area of just war doctrine concerns justice after war (*jus post bellum*). *See generally* JUS POST BELLUM: TOWARDS A LAW OF TRANSITION FROM CONFLICT TO PEACE (Carsten Stahn & Jann Kleffner, eds., 2008).

41 *See* Protocol Additional to the Geneva Conventions of 12 August 1949, and Relating to the Protection of Victims of International Armed Conflicts [AP I], arts. 48, 51(3), 85(3)(b), 41, June 8, 1977, 1125 U.N.T.S. 3. It should be noted that the United States refused to ratify Additional Protocol I out of concern it might legitimize and assist guerilla forces and terrorist organizations. *See* Letter of Transmittal from President Ronald Reagan to the U.S. Senate, Jan. 29, 1987, *reprinted* in 81 AM. J. INT'L L. 910, 911 (1987) (claiming the protocol would "endanger civilians among whom terrorists and other irregulars attempt to conceal themselves"). Regardless, the principle of distinction is firmly entrenched in U.S. military doctrine and its interpretation of the law of war. *See, e.g.,* LAW OF WAR MANUAL, *supra* note 2, at 62–65.

42 *In re* Yamashita, 327 U.S. at 26–27 (Murphy, J., dissenting).

43 Geneva Convention Relative to the Protection of Civilian Persons in Time of War [GC IV], art. 42, Aug. 12, 1949, 6 U.S.T. 3516, 75 U.N.T.S. 287.

44 INT'L COMM. OF THE RED CROSS, COMMENTARY: IV GENEVA CONVENTION RELATIVE TO THE PROTECTION OF CIVILIAN PERSONS IN TIME OF WAR 258 (Jean Pictet, ed., 1958) [hereinafter GC IV COMMENTARY].

45 *See* GC IV, *supra* note 43, art. 147; Statute of the International Criminal Court [Rome Statute], art. 7(1)(e), July 17, 1998, 2187 U.N.T.S. 90; Statute of the International Criminal Tribunal for the Former Yugoslavia [ICTY Statute], art. 2(g), S.C. Res. 827, U.N. Doc. S/RES/827 (May 25, 1993).

46 Draft Code of Crimes Against the Peace and Security of Mankind art. 18(j), Rep. of the Int'l Law Comm'n, 48th Sess., May 6-July 26, 1996, U.N. Doc. A/51/10 (1996).

47 *See, e.g.*, GC IV, *supra* note 43, art. 118. *See also* Jordan Paust, *Judicial Power to Determine the Status and Rights of Persons Detained without Trial*, 44 HARV. INT'L L.J. 503, 510–11 (2003).

48 Prosecutor v. Mucić, Case No. IT-96-21-T, Judgment at ¶ 578 (Int'l Crim. Ct. for the Former Yugoslavia Nov. 16, 1998).

49 GC IV, *supra* note 43, art. 33(1).

50 AP I, *supra* note 41, art. 75(4)(b); Protocol Additional to the Geneva Conventions of Aug. 12, 1949, and relating to the Protection of Victims of Non-International Armed Conflicts [AP II], art. 6(2)(b), June 8, 1977.

51 *See* Convention Relative to the Treatment of Prisoners of War [GC III], arts. 26(6) & 87(3), Aug. 12, 1949; GC IV, *supra* note 43 art. 33(1); AP I, *supra* note 41, art. 75(2) (d); AP II, *supra* note 50, art. 4(2)(b).

52 Prosecutor v. Fofana, Case No. SCSL-04-14-T, Judgment at ¶ 178 & n. 222 (Spec. Ct. for Sierra Leone Aug. 2, 2007).

53 AP I, *supra* note 42, art. 75(4)(d); AP II, *supra* note 51, art. 6(2)(d).

54 Rome Statute, *supra* note 45, art. 66.

55 Geneva Convention for the Amelioration of the Condition of the Wounded and Sick in Armed Forces in the Field [GC I], art. 3, Aug. 12, 1949, 6 U.S.T. 3314, 75 U.N.T.S. 31; Geneva Convention for the Amelioration of the Condition of Wounded, Sick and Shipwrecked Members of Armed Forces at Sea [GC II], art. 3, Aug. 12, 1949, 6 U.S.T. 3217, 75 U.N.T.S. 85; GC III, *supra* note 51, art. 3; GC IV, *supra* note 43, art. 3.

56 To be sure, the norm for domestic exonerations has been painful delays between miscarriages of justice and their revelation, and perhaps one could expect the same delay in the international context.

57 MICHAEL IGNATIEFF, ARTICLES OF FAITH, 5 INDEX ON CENSORSHIP 110, 113 (1996).

58 Kent Roach & Gary Trotter, *Miscarriages of Justice in the War Against Terror*, 109 PENN ST. L. REV. 967, 974 (2005).

59 Clive Walker & Carole McCartney, *Criminal Justice and Miscarriages of Justice in England and Wales*, in WRONGFUL CONVICTION: INTERNATIONAL

Perspectives on Miscarriages of Justice 183, 191 (C. Ronald Huff & Martin Killias, eds., 2008) (quoting Lord Denning).

60 *See* Roach & Trotter, *supra* note 58, at 975–93; Walker & McCartney, *supra* note 59, at 188–93. *See also* Mark Godsey, *The Global Innocence Movement, supra,* in this volume.

61 Roach & Trotter, *supra* note 58, at 979 (quoting public inquiry into the Maguire Seven case).

62 Almarin v. IDF Commander in the Gaza Strip, HCJ No. 2722/92, ¶ 8 (1992) (Isr.).

63 Janimat v. OC Central Command, HCJ No. 2006/97 (1997) (Isr.) (as translated in Judgments of the Israel Supreme Court: Fighting Terrorism Within the Law 61 (2005)).

64 *Id.* at 64 (Cheshin, J., dissenting).

65 Tomer Zarchin, *Former Chief Justice Barak Regrets House Demolitions,* Haaretz, May 27, 2009.

66 GC IV, *supra* note 43, art. 33.

67 GC IV Commentary, *supra* note 44, at 225–26.

68 *Id.* at 226.

69 Kent Roach, The 9/11 Effect: Comparative Counter-Terrorism 106–07 (2011).

70 *See* Military Order of November 13, 2001: Detention, Treatment, and Trial of Certain Non-Citizens in the War Against Terrorism, 66 Fed. Reg. 57,833 (2001).

71 Rasul v. Bush, 542 U.S. 466, 476 (2004).

72 Hamdi v. Rumsfeld, 542 U.S. 507, 520 (2004) (quoting government brief).

73 *Id.* at 530.

74 Rasul, 542 U.S. at 488 (Kennedy, J., concurring).

75 *Id.* at 534.

76 Boumediene v. Bush, 553 U.S. 723, 767 (2008).

77 *Id.* at 783–84.

78 *Id.* at 785.

79 *Id.* at 797.

80 *Id.* at 786.

81 *Cf.* Brandon L. Garrett, *Habeas Corpus and Due Process,* 98 Cornell L. Rev. 47, 121–23 (2012); Gerald L. Neuman, *The Habeas Corpus Suspension after* Boumediene v. Bush, 110 Colum. L. Rev. 537, 561–65 (2010).

82 Benjamin Wittes, Robert M. Chesney, Larkin Reynolds & The Harvard Law School National Security Research Committee, The Emerging Law of Detention 2.0: The Guantánamo Habeas Cases as Lawmaking 1 (2011). *See also* Rabea Benhalim, Robert M. Chesney & Benjamin Wittes, The Emerging Law of Detention: The Guantánamo Habeas Cases as Lawmaking (2010).

83 *See* Almerfedi v. Obama, 654 F.3d 1, 5 n. 4 (D.C. Cir. 2011); Uthman v. Obama, 637 F.3d 400, 404 n. 3 (D.C. Cir. 2011); Al-Adahi v. Obama, 613 F.3d 1102, 1104–05 (D.C. Cir. 2010); Awad v. Obama, 608 F.3d 1, 11 n. 2 (D.C. Cir. 2010).

84 *See* Al-Madhwani v. Obama, 642 F.3d 1071, 1078 (D.C. Cir. 2011); Al-Bihani v. Obama, 590 F.3d 866, 879–80 (D.C. Cir. 2010); Al Odah v. United States, 611 F.3d 8, 14 (D.C. Cir. 2010).

85 Al Odah, 611 F.3d at 14.

86 Latif v. Obama, 677 F.3d 1175, 1185 (D.C. Cir. 2012).

87 *Id.* at 1208 (Tatel, J., dissenting).

88 *Id.* at 1215 (quoting Parhat v. Gates, 532 F.3d 834, 849 (D.C. Cir. 2008)).

89 *See* WikiLeaks, *Gitmo Files*, available at https://wikileaks.org/gitmo/.

90 *See, e.g.*, Amy Davidson, *WikiLeaks: The Uses of Guantánamo*, NEW YORKER, Apr. 25, 2011; David Leigh, James Ball, Ian Cobain & Jason Burke, *Guantanamo Leaks Lift Lid on World's Most Controversial Prison*, THE GUARDIAN, Apr. 24, 2011; Scott Shane & Benjamin Weiser, *Judging Detainees' Risk, Often with Flawed Evidence*, N.Y. TIMES, Apr. 25, 2011, at A1.

91 *See* WikiLeaks, *Gitmo Files: Naqib Ullah*, available at https://wikileaks.org/gitmo/prisoner/913.html; Heidi Blake, Tim Ross & Conrad Quilty Harper, *WikiLeaks: Children among the Innocent Captured and Sent to Guantanamo*, THE TELEGRAPH, Apr. 26, 2011.

92 Declaration of Colonel Lawrence B. Wilkerson (Ret.) at 4 (¶ 9a), Hamad v. Bush, CV 05–1009 JDB, Mar. 24, 2010 [Wilkerson Declaration].

93 *See, e.g.*, MICHAEL A. CALDERO & JOHN P. CRANK, POLICE ETHICS: THE CORRUPTION OF NOBLE CAUSE (3d ed. 2010).

94 Wilkerson Declaration, *supra* note 92, at 6–7 (¶ 11b, d).

95 MICHAEL WALZER, JUST AND UNJUST WARS 30 (5th ed. 2015).

96 1 COLLECTED WORKS OF FLORENCE NIGHTINGALE 141 (Lynn McDonald, ed., 2001).

Index